What I Hope to Leave Behind

EDITED WITH
AN INTRODUCTION
BY ALLIDA M. BLACK

What I Hope to Leave Behind

THE ESSENTIAL

ESSAYS OF

ELEANOR

ROOSEVELT

CARLSON PUBLISHING, INC. BROOKLYN, NEW YORK, 1995

R

A portion of the sales of each copy of *What I Hope to Leave Behind* is donated to the Franklin and Eleanor Roosevelt Institute, Hyde Park, New York.

Eleanor Roosevelt's "Meet the Press" Interview is copyright © National Broadcasting Company, Inc., All Rights Reserved. It is published here courtesy of "Meet the Press." Her Interview with Mike Wallace is published by permission of Mr. Wallace.

Introduction and bibliography copyright © 1995 by Allida M. Black.

Library of Congress Cataloging-in-Publication Data

Roosevelt, Eleanor, 1884–1962.
    What I hope to leave behind : the essential essays of Eleanor
Roosevelt / edited with an introduction by Allida M. Black ; preface
by Blanche Wiesen Cook.
        p. cm.
    "A bibliography of the articles of Eleanor Roosevelt" : p.
    Includes bibliographical references and index.
    ISBN 0-926019-88-0 (hardback : alk. paper)
    1. Roosevelt, Eleanor, 1884–1962—Political and social views.
2. United States—Politics and government—20th century. 3. World
politics—20th Century. 4. Women—United States—Social conditions.
5. Afro-Americans—Civil rights. 6. Youth—United States—Social
conditions. I. Black, Allida M. (Allida Mae), 1952–   .
II. Title.
E807.1.R48A3   1995
973.917'092—dc20   95-38101

Typographic design: C.J. Bartelt

Text typeface: Adobe Janson Text

Composition: Joseph E.L. Fortt

Case and jacket designs: Ann Harakawa

Printed on acid-free, 250-year-life paper.

Manufactured in the United States of America.

First printing, October 1995.

For
Charlene Bangs Bickford
who also practices what she preaches

Contents

C. Civil Rights and the Problems of Black America

D. Women and the World Around Them

E. Education and Problems Confronting Youth

F. Political and Policy Analysis

G. This Troubled World

H. Issues of War and Peace

I. The United Nations and Human Rights

Preface

One day at lunch many years ago, I suggested to my friend Ralph Carlson that he publish every article Eleanor Roosevelt wrote, including each one of her "My Day" columns. Believing then, as I do now, that there was something worthy, something unique, interesting, important about her every effort—I argued that her entire output merited consideration. ER's writings were long overlooked, ignored, trivialized. People failed to appreciate her personal and felicitous style; they underestimated the kernels of bold political truth she occasionally buried in boring fluff. One had to look again, with new expectations. You would be surprised, I assured him, and pleased.

Naturally, paper costs being what they are, the limitations of time and space that regulate our lives being what they are, Ralph was unconvinced by my arguments. But now, he has done the next best thing: In this wonderfully edited volume, he has agreed to publish the very best selections of Eleanor Roosevelt's writings.

Allida Black has done a splendid job selecting the most important issues, the most provocative essays for this anthology. This is a remarkably useful book: All the issues of ER's time remain the most urgent issues of our time, beginning with her own political philosophy of personal responsibility and activism. There is nothing outdated about the role of government in times of crises and human need; the perils and future of democracy; the complexities and contradictions of America's quest for civil liberties and civil rights; the role of women in public and private life; the role of education, libraries, culture, in society; issues of war, peace, and politics; the race between bigotry and human rights worldwide.

Committed to dignity for all people, a life of decency, opportunity and fulfillment, Eleanor Roosevelt was a concerned and earnest writer. She wrote from her heart, with surprising clarity, passion, vigor. There was nothing radical really about her views, but it is amazing how radical they seem in eras of mean-spirited repression. From the 1920s to her death on 7 November 1962, her views were controversial. They are controversial now, and evermore appealing, urgent, needed.

As we enter the twenty-first century, The Declaration of Human Rights, which ER did so much to achieve, remains a beacon of hope for the world. Allida Black's carefully edited anthology enables us to follow ER's public journey through the most gripping challenges and controversies of the twentieth century. They led ER to the United Nations and a commitment to that place of international discourse we would all do well to reconsider. With this book, Allida Black has given all who contemplate a just and democratic future, a very great gift.

Blanche Wiesen Cook

Acknowledgments

Three years ago, my friend and former colleague Charlene Bickford interrupted one my infamous "ER stories" and said "this information needs to be out there." An outstanding editor in her own right, Bickford encouraged me to assemble the articles and to scout for a publisher. When I dawdled, she pushed. This collection would not have happened without her encouragement. I thank her for her support, her expertise, her almost boundless energy, and her commitment to liberal reform.

Helen Veit observed this conversation, endorsed it with typical understatement, and offered to help me with the index. With a unique blend of sarcasm and rigor, she taught me how to use CIndex. It is an experience I will always remember.

Kenneth Bowling and Kenneth Mannings not only helped me track down elusive photographs but also lent their experienced eyes to help select the photographs that are reproduced in this volume.

Blanche Wiesen Cook deserves both my gratitude and my respect. Rather than succumb to territorial disputes, she took time away from her own research on ER to write the preface to this volume, share stories, and offer advice, encouragement, and enthusiasm. In the process of discovering ER, we became colleagues and friends.

Judy Beck prepared the index with grace and precision and did not complain when thousands of pages covered our dining room table.

The entire archival staff of the Franklin Roosevelt Presidential Library and the management staff of the Eleanor Roosevelt Center at Val-Kill deserve special recognition. Frances Seeber, Karen Burtis, Beth Denier, John Ferris, Bob Parks, Mark Renovitch, Nancy Snedeker, and Ray Teichman made each of my forays to ER's papers a homecoming. Patricia Duane Lichtenberg and Angela Stultz introduced me to Val-Kill in a way I will always treasure. Their expertise, patience, and support make them a team that all archival staffs should emulate. In recognition of their professionalism, part of the profit from the sales of this book will go the Franklin and Eleanor Roosevelt Institute and the Eleanor Roosevelt Center at Val-Kill.

Finally, I thank Ralph Carlson, Maud Andrews, and Beth Harrison of Carlson Publishing who efficiently handled all the various crises associated with this anthology and never lost their sense of humor.

Introduction

Eleanor Roosevelt: Activist for Democracy

Allida M. Black

In April 1934, *Pictorial Review* asked Eleanor Roosevelt to tell its readers what she wanted to achieve in her lifetime. She accepted the assignment only to realize that she was more concerned with the present than the future. "I am afraid that I have been too busy living, accepting such opportunities as come my way and using them to the best of my ability," she wrote, that "the thought of what would come after has lain rather lightly in the back of my mind."[1]

Eleanor Roosevelt was not ready to discuss what she wanted to leave behind because her life was full. She was forty-eight years old when she became first lady in 1933. By the time she moved to 1600 Pennsylvania Avenue, she had raised a family, taught school, managed a business, coordinated statewide and national political campaigns, chaired investigative committees and state reform organizations, become a successful journalist as well as a respected lobbyist, and had developed a reputation in her own right as a skilled politician who refused to abandon her commitment to democratic ideals.

ER did not want to check these accomplishments at the White House door. Although she actively supported her husband's campaign for the presidency, she did not want to be first lady. Fearful that she would lose the independence she worked so hard to achieve and that her goals would be subsumed into her husband's agenda, ER wanted a job of her own—a job in which she could be an actor, not just a hostess. Franklin D. Roosevelt declined her offers of help and initially refused to consider her requests for substantive assignments. Although other first ladies had been active behind the scenes, they had concealed their influence from the public. Thus, ER had no precedent to follow for public activism. Ever the realist, she expected criticism for setting her own example, for "moving on to fields unknown." What she did not know was how she would convince the American people to support her own version of "bold experimental action."

"What I Hope to Leave Behind" reflects ER's dilemma. The magazine, ignoring the career she hade made for herself, solicited her article because her husband was president. Yet she wrote the article because she wanted to redefine her own role. Trapped between convention and reform, the ER that emerged from the article seems hesitant, reluctant to declare her own intentions. In the simple, self-effacing style that became her trademark, she refused to discuss her accomplishments, hid her political skills, and refrained from speculating on what her influence on future generations might be. Moreover, while the article rambles through all the issues near and dear to ER's early politics—women's unique responsibilities and political insights, the importance of education, the need to redefine success to include moral conduct as well as economic achievement, and a poignant plea to enjoy life—it concludes with an abrupt abdication to traditional feminine roles. ER the mother suddenly replaced ER the political activist.

What ER chose to make a matter of public record reflects as much what she wanted known of her expertise as what she wanted concealed. Always aware of her traditional obligations as FDR's wife, she nevertheless chafed at the restrictions this identity placed on her. Thus, a quiet tension runs through ER's pronouncements. The documents included here reflect not only her participation in a specific political momentum but also her entanglement in an intricate cultural web in which her identity became "a matter of paragraph and presentation" and her recollections "understated, self-deprecating, monuments to discretion and silence."[2]

However, as the Cold War crises facing the nation increased, ER found this deference more difficult to present. The seeming inability of liberals to implement effective reform angered her. Yet rather than succumb to bitterness or accept lukewarm liberalism, she used her pen to attack the politics of fear and temerity. She survived what Carolyn Heilbrun called "the female moratorium" and placed her "life outside the bounds of society's restraints and ready-made narratives."[3] With a unique mixture of stubbornness, courage, tenacity, idealism, compassion, and pride, ER, to a great degree, transcended cultural stereotypes and political compromise to reinvent her life. And in the process, she helped redirect American politics and redefine American liberalism.

Consequently, twenty-nine years later, ER finally answered the question *Pictorial Review* asked. No longer living in anyone's shadow, a confident, confrontational, but increasingly infirmed ER dedicated a great part of her seventy-eighth year to *Tomorrow Is Now*, her final call to arms. Published posthumously in 1963, the manifesto stands in stark contrast to the self-deprecating naivete that permeated "What I Hope to Leave Behind." Emboldened by her political experiences and convinced that the nation had abandoned its moral and political responsibility, an angry, exhausted ER struggled to call the nation's attention to the problems she believed needed attention and to offer her own solutions to these crises.

In 1962 ER ruefully wondered "what has happened to the American dream?" She worried that the nation had lost its vision and feared that America was in great danger of becoming a nation of complacent hypocrites. "We are facing the greatest challenge our way of life has had to meet without any clear understanding of the facts." That saddened her immensely. "One can fight a danger only when one is armed with solid facts and spurred on by an unwavering faith and determination."[4]

She understood that *Tomorrow Is Now* was her last chance to speak her mind, and she committed herself to the project with passion. She plainly chastised Americans who refused to see how desperate the situation was, bluntly telling her readers that "it is today that we must face the future of the world."

Nor did she spare her own party from her scorn. "Staying aloof is not a solution," she lectured moderates, "but a cowardly evasion."

Clearly, Eleanor Roosevelt's vision of the world had changed. As she aged, she began to view democracy in broader terms. While she still believed in the progressive ideals that characterized her early writings and the legislative programs introduced by the New Deal, by the late forties a new, more realistic assessment of American society appeared in her articles and speeches. Disappointed with the lukewarm commitment to reform displayed by most liberals, she dedicated the last dozen years of her life to explaining complex social issues to a complacent audience. More and more, racial justice, economic security, quality education, affordable housing, civil liberties, and human rights formed the core of her articles and speeches. Even more reluctant to promote someone else's agenda, Eleanor Roosevelt refined and presented her own—one that defined the tenets of liberalism, human rights, and the politics of inclusion.

The more Eleanor Roosevelt saw of the world, the more she reevaluated her politics. Not content to rest upon assumptions, she made the transition from progressive to social feminist to New Dealer to disgruntled liberal. She also perfected her craft as she clarified her politics. By 1940 she also became one of America's most syndicated columnists, with a circulation equal to that of Dorothy Thompson, Walter Lippmann, and Westbrook Pegler. The 50-plus lectures she delivered each summer before packed houses frequently helped her develop points that she later would present more fully in magazine articles, essays, and political monographs. By the time she left the White House, worried that her political influence died along with FDR, she saw herself as more journalist than political leader. However, disturbed by the domestic and international crises the Cold War presented, ER quickly used her publications to challenge American complacency.

Collected from archives, libraries, and manuscript collections across the nation, this collection offers the widest sample of ER's writings and speeches and provides many of the tools necessary to reconstruct her politics. The 126 articles selected here trace ER's development as journalist, politician, activist, diplomat, and educator and clearly demonstrate the ease with which she flowed from one role to another. Organized into nine thematic sections, the articles are arranged chronologically within each topic to reflect ER's changing analysis of the major issues of her day.

Reflections and Personal Testimony introduces the collection. The eleven articles collected here serve as a counterpoint to ER's three-volume autobiography. The woman who emerges from these writings grew from a committed follower of the Social Gospel ("What Religion Means to Me") to assertive political veteran ("In Defense of Curiosity") to nostalgic democratic moralist ("Values to Live By"). Yet ER carefully obscured this development. She succumbed to tradition and presented a conventional depiction of her unconventional life ("The Seven People Who Shaped My Life").

Although ER carefully avoided discussing her power, she did not shy away from either using herself as an example or responding to her critics. Like her progressive foremothers, she turned to religion—"that belief and that faith in the heart of a man which makes him try to live his life according to the highest standard which he is able to visualize"—for justification and inspiration.[5] Yet she understood that such public action would not be painless or popular. When *The New Yorker* parodied her activities in its now-famous cartoon depicting two coal miners responding to her visit "with undisguised horror," ER criticized those who thought "there certainly was something the matter with a woman who wanted to see so much and to know so much." They suffered from a "kind of blindness" that was both selfish and self-defeating.[6] Her strong conviction offset the hurt such criticism inflicted and encouraged her to continue to speak out. If she wanted to "enjoy living," she believed that she must "conquer the fear" these attacks inspired. She had risked too much of herself to turn back. She urged her readers to follow her lead.

The next four parts discuss the issues ER believed central to achieving true democratic reform—informed public participation, protection of civil rights and civil liberties, and recognition of the specific needs and contributions of minorities, women, and youth—and trace ER's development as an activist for democracy. Here ER, as she became more comfortable in the role of first lady, expanded her focus from defending FDR's policies ("The State's Responsibility for Fair Working Conditions" and "Subsistence Farmsteads") to advocating controversial social and political policy central to her political vision ("Insuring Democracy" and "Civil Liberties and the Crisis"). Whether promoting government support of the arts, the National Youth Administration, the Social Security Act, comprehensive public education, national health care, affordable durable housing, or widespread political debate, ER insisted that the four freedoms her husband championed should not be seen merely as goals for the world but must be "translated into the lives of individuals."[7] To do otherwise was to "couple" freedom "with stupidity."[8]

Repeatedly ER asserted that democracy had "a moral basis" that must be applied in the political arena if the nation was to survive the economic and international crises challenging its security. This required the informed, active participation of all citizens. No one should hide behind complacency or apathy. "Democracy cannot be static," she declared in January 1942. "Whatever is static is dead."[9]

For democracy to flourish, each citizen must make the "greatest sacrifice"—reflection and commitment. "We must know what we believe in, how we intend to live, and what we are doing for our neighbors." Reaching this decision was just the first step. Action was the second. "We must fulfill our duties as citizens, see that our nation is truly represented by its government, see that the government is responsive to the will and desires of the people." Americans "must make that will and desire of the people the result of adequate education and adequate material security." The nation "must maintain a standard of living which makes it possible for the people really to want justice for all, rather than to harbor a secret hope for privileges because they cannot hope for justice."[10]

War reinforced her desires to make democracy more effective at home. Worried that a battle-fatigued "civilian morale" might degenerate into attacks on non-native-born Americans, she told readers of *Common Ground* that Americans should "apply [themselves] to the task of drawing our people, in whom there are so many different racial strains, closer together instead of letting them drift apart and be divided by their backgrounds." To do otherwise would not only destroy consensus but would "create 'nations within a nation.' "[11]

After FDR's death in 1945, ER frequently held the nation's attention and tried to prod a reluctant public to action. Released from the constraints that the White House had imposed on her during the war, she became postwar liberalism's most famous champion, declaring to audiences that all Americans had "a social responsibility for individual welfare." As the fear of communism and McCarthyism promoted political intolerance, ER intensified her activities as lay political philosopher and spent the last years of her life explaining complex political issues to a reluctant, suspicious public. "Today our security is in jeopardy and our principles on the defensive."[12] Americans must remember that citizenship required that they act "in the service of truth" or, she concluded, the nation will forget what we are "for" and abandon the American dream.

When she entered the White House, Eleanor Roosevelt did not understand the problems African Americans faced. Yet as she toured the nation during the 1930s, she realized that the Depression effected different groups in different ways. After working with civil rights leaders Walter White, Mary McLeod Bethune, and A. Philip Randolph, ER recognized the pernicious effects of racism and pressured the administration to speak out against racial discrimination and acts of racist violence.

By the early 1940s, she saw civil rights as the litmus test for American democracy. Thus she declared throughout the war that there could be no democracy in the United States that did not include democracy for African Americans. In *The Moral Basis of Democracy* she asserted that people of all races have inviolate rights to "some property." "We have never been willing to face this problem, to line it up with the basic, underlying beliefs in Democracy." Racial prejudice enslaved African Americans and continued to hobble them: "no one can honestly claim that . . . the Negroes of this country are free."[13] She continued this theme in a 1942 article in *The New Republic*, declaring that both the private and the public sector must acknowledge that "one of the main destroyers of freedom is our attitude toward the Negro race."[14] "What Kipling called 'The White Man's Burden,' " she proclaimed in *The American Magazine*, is "one of the things we cannot have any longer."[15] Furthermore, she told those listening to the radio broadcast of the 1945 National Democratic forum, "democracy may grow or fade as we face [this] problem."

ER also realized that such continuous demands for democratic conduct did little to ease the pain African Americans encountered daily, and she tried very hard to understand the depths of their anger. "If I were a Negro today, I think I would have moments of great bitterness," she confessed to readers of

Negro Digest. "It would be hard for me to sustain my faith in democracy and to build up a sense of goodwill toward men of other races." She certainly could appreciate African Americans' rage because she knew that if she were African American, her own anger would surface. Nevertheless, she hoped she could channel her fury constructively, because "there now remains much work to be done to see that freedom becomes a fact and not just a promise for my people."[16]

However, just as African Americans should be wary of promises, ER cautioned all Americans to be suspicious of those who preach tolerance. She believed that "we must . . . take the word 'tolerance' out of our vocabulary and substitute for it the precept live and let live, cooperate in work and play and like our neighbors." "The problem is not to learn tolerance of your neighbors," she lectured to those who promoted such complacency, "but to see that all alike have hope and opportunity and that the community as a whole moves forward." Moreover, America cannot neglect its conscience where race is concerned because to do so would be denying its heritage, tainting its future, and succumbing to the law of the jungle.

Peace did not moderate ER's position on racial justice. Moreover, as she became more familiar with the unique problems African Americans faced, ER abandoned her position as a defender of equal treatment ("The Negro and Social Change") to become a staunch advocate of integration ("Abolish Jim Crow!" and "Segregation") and nonviolent protest ("The Social Revolution"). Thus when Daisy Bates, the organizer of the NAACP's bold campaign to integrate Little Rock's Central High School, decided to write her memoirs, the civil rights activist asked ER to introduce the work ("Foreword to *The Long Shadow of Little Rock*").

She joined the board of directors of the National Association for the Advancement of Colored People in 1945. Indeed, she spent the last seventeen years of her life arguing that the rights to vote, to work, to fair housing and quality education, and to organize in protest of discriminatory practices were crucial to democracy's success. In 1953, she posed for a photograph for the cover of *Ebony* with Mary McLeod Bethune—whom ER described as her "closest friend" among "women of my own age"—and declared "some of my best friends are Negro."[17] When White Citizens Councils formed to oppose *Brown v. Board of Education of Topeka, Kansas,* she declared that such racist activity proved that "there are two sides" to America—"one reaches for the stars, the other descends to the level of the beasts."[18] When the white mobs attacked African Americans and white students on the Freedom Rides, ER found it "intolerably painful to accept the fact" that such violence could occur in the United States. "This was the kind of thing the Nazis had done to Jews of Germany."[19]

Discrimination women faced in the workplace and within the political arena also concerned ER. Influenced by her work with the Women's Trade Union League, the National Consumers League, and the League of Women Voters, she supported working women and lobbied for safer working conditions and minimum wage legislation. Yet once again a tension runs through the image ER had of herself and the image she wanted to present to her husband's constituency. While she blatantly asserted that "women must be the bosses" if politics is to be reformed and a progressive agenda implemented, she simultaneously promoted prescribed gender roles in "Ten Rules for Success in Marriage" and "The Modern Wife's Difficult Job."

"Wives of Great Men" depicts the dilemma in which ER found herself after FDR became governor in 1928. Rather than resign her teaching position at the Todhunter School in New York City and move to the state capital, she worked out a schedule that allowed her to spend four days a week in the city and return to the governor's mansion for weekend functions. When the press gave her commuting schedule prominent coverage, she tried to convince the public that although she had one of America's most complex marriages, she strongly supported conventional relationships.

Using other political couples as examples, ER implied that since she worked in education, not government, her marriage was both traditional and sound. She did not compete with her husband nor did she try to influence his policies. Carefully deflecting critics who assumed she followed a feminist agenda, ER advocated wifely deference. A woman who brought "her own preconceived ideas" to marriage "must keep them to herself." Moreover, a wife "must never make any allusion to her own political opinions when they differ from her husband's." Although she understood that this life would be "exasperating for the woman who has her own gifts," ER nevertheless concluded that the husband's political agenda came first. "The business of governing is one which . . . needs the cooperation of the feminine portion of the household."[20]

ER did not follow her own advice after she became first lady. Indeed, just as she questioned her early positions on segregation, she also questioned progressive assumptions about women's inherent domestic responsibilities ("Should Wives Work?" and "What are the Motives for a Woman Working When She Does Not Have To, for Income"). In 1933 she published her first book, *It's Up to the Women.* "In this present crisis," ER declared, "it is going to be the women who will tip the scales and bring us safely out of it." Their active involvement in fighting the Depression was crucial. "No chain is stronger than its weakest link and it is well for the women . . . to realize that the time has come when drones are no longer tolerated."[21]

The emergencies of war expanded ER's position. When women seemed reticent to assume leadership responsibilities, she asked "What's the matter with women?" "It isn't that women haven't the brains or the ability or the physical strength to dominate." It's just that "they want the world the way it is." Hoping that women's innate patriotism and desire for peace would compel them to act ("American Women in the War"), she nevertheless conceded that "it's man's world now . . . and will be just as long as the women want it to be!" Meanwhile, she acted as an omsbudswoman for women in the military, defense plants, and government service.[22]

Yet despite all the criticism ER received for her activism, she never questioned that women had a unique political responsibility—to shape the values of their families and neighborhoods and the policies of their government. Whether lecturing the National Education Association on "The Place of Women in the Community" or giving advice to Jacqueline Kennedy ("My Advice to the Next First Lady"), ER believed women had a valuable role to play in and out of government. Never doubting that women focused more on results than policy and wanted reform more than recognition, ER pushed American women to speak out, organize, and enter the public arena.

"Women have come a long way," ER wrote in 1950. But, as she told readers of *Good Housekeeping*, before women's influence could "grow," women must realize two things. First, they "must become more conscious of themselves as women and of their ability to function as a group, [while] at the same time they must try to wipe from men's consciousness the need to consider them as a group."[23] Second, women need to recognize "that if a woman wants really to succeed she must do better than a man, for she is under more careful scrutiny."[24]

After the Democrats returned to the White House in 1961, ER pressured John Kennedy to appoint more women to executive positions within the federal government. The president responded by establishing the Presidential Commission on the Status of Women and asking her to serve as its chair. Although her health kept her from taking as active a role as she wished, ER spent part of the last year of her life urging government recognition of the needs and talents of women. She ultimately rescinded her opposition to the Equal Rights Amendment and supported Pauli Murray and Esther Petersen's draft detailing the discrimination American women encountered. Although the commission did not succeed in its immediate goal of changing Kennedy's behavior, it did help give birth to the National Organization for Women and prepared the way for the national campaign in support of the ERA.

ER understood how difficult these attitudinal and policy changes were. The longer Americans looked to past stereotypes as guidelines for political behavior, the longer democracy would be delayed. And as she began to spend more time with young people in and out of the classroom, she became convinced that youth would take the necessary risks to eradicate prejudice and expand democracy. By the late 1920s, she argued in favor of abandoning "the little red schoolhouse" approach to education and replacing it with a demanding public school curriculum.[25]

"School is the beginning of the child's life work," she told readers of *The Woman's Journal* in 1930, because it prepared them for their responsibilities as citizens. If it promoted "curiosity and vision," the "ideal education" could introduce students to "as many as possible of the various types of lives which make up the world" and encourage them to recognize that difference did not threaten society.[26] Once students recognized this diversity, she hoped that schools would no longer "idealize things that are past," recognize that the "world is a hard world for youth," and provide their pupils with the literary and analytical tools they needed to grow as individuals and as citizens of a democracy.[27]

When shortages and racial tensions threatened the American home front during World War II, ER became even more forthright in her pronouncements on education, tersely telling the nation "education is the cornerstone on which we must build liberty." The nation must "make it possible for young people to take the facts of a situation, analyze them, and find solutions."[28]

Never deviating from her commitment to a challenging curriculum, ER urged parents to refrain from censoring their child's reading, supported a twelve-month school year, endorsed public nursery schools and kindergartens, recommended a mandatory foreign language requirement, and defended integrated classrooms. She urged Americans to view teaching as a serious profession worthy of high salaries and the status afforded to other specialized occupations. Moreover, she prodded adults to treat youth with respect and to take their concerns seriously.

As she aged, ER's demands for a strong public education system grew more persistent. Repeatedly she declared that knowledge was the most powerful tool a culture could encourage. Not only could it help redefine success as a measurement "of the amount of satisfaction that people get in living their lives," but it also could help decrease crime and delinquency and provide "tomorrow's citizens" with a "clearer picture" of what "the failures of society are" and "what needs to be changed."[29] Any system that promoted a more traditional, less demanding approach had "as little validity today as the belief that the earth is flat."

The next part, on politics and policies, traces ER's development from New Deal spokesperson to Cold War political leader. A common image runs throughout the articles, speeches, and interviews—ER as liberalism's most outspoken advocate. Whether the subject is social security ("Old Age Pensions"), government support of the arts, or the right of students to question policy ("Why I Still Believe in the Youth Congress"), she pressured her husband's administration to practice what it preached and called for Americans to make their demands known.

As ER's political stature increased, FDR frequently turned to her to help shore up support for policies that did not have widespread support. For example, when the president sought an unprecedented third term in 1940, conservative Democrats ultimately united behind him only to oppose the nomination of Henry Wallace, FDR's choice for vice president. As the convention unraveled, FDR phoned his wife and asked her to fly to Chicago to bring the delegates back in line and thereby assure Wallace's nomination. Speaking without notes, before an unruly throng preoccupied with floor fights, ER took the podium and deftly drew the convention's attention away from individual agendas to the crisis the nation confronted. "This is no ordinary time. No time for weighing anything except what we can best do for the country as a whole." Without mentioning Wallace, she urged the delegates to give the president the assistance he requested, reminding them that "no man who is a candidate or who is President can carry this situation alone."[30] Her plea worked. Indeed, this speech to the convention not only fulfilled her husband's wishes but is considered one of the most important convention speeches of the twentieth century. Recognizing her political acumen, the *Harvard Law Review* and *The New Republic* asked her to review works by leading political scientists and national politicians.

As the nation prepared for war, ER worked to keep the country from abandoning domestic reform. She worried that the United States might win the war only to lose the peace ("Social Gains & Defense" and "You Can't Pauperize Children"). And when business interests criticized labor, she championed those who fought the war by working in the defense industries ("Workers Should Join Trade Unions").

She continued to speak her mind after she left the White House. When Wallace decided to run for president as a third-party candidate, she bluntly reprimanded her friend. Although she did not question his conviction, she did question his vision. "He has never been a good politician, ... he never picked his advisers wisely, . . . [and he has] oversimplified the problems that face us today."[31] She next strove to keep liberals within the Democratic Party, telling them she needed their help to push the party away from the politics of fear and loyalty tests and back in the direction she thought it must take for democracy to flourish ("Liberals in This Year of Decision").

When the Democrats renominated Adlai Stevenson in 1956, ER traveled the country speaking out in his behalf. Her addresses to crowds in Charleston, West Virginia, and Detroit, Michigan—which have never appeared in print—reveal more than just her support of Stevenson. They serve as the perfect prism through which to assess her views of both the Eisenhower administration and Cold War politics.

As Democrats retreated to the "vital center," ER spoke out against the politics of fear the Cold War generated. She defended *The Nation* when its critics tried to suspend is publication ("In the Service of Truth") and praised the United Nations when conservatives wanted to dismantle it ("Address to 1956 Democratic National Convention"). Speaking out against political bosses and the influence they wielded in the early stages of campaigns, she questioned the nomination process, asking "Are Political Conventions Obsolete?" Determined to motivate as many Americans as possible, she refused to limit her appeals to those Americans who only read newspapers or popular magazines. Consequently, when Professor Houston Baker asked her to join with Margaret Mead, Gunnar Myrdal, and other academics interested in public policy who planned to address the major dilemmas facing the nation, she not only agreed to introduce the volume but also adapted her writing style to a more sophisticated audience.

Quickly realizing the political value of television, she made the new medium yet another forum for liberalism. Whether interviewing leading activists and political figures on her own show, "Prospects of Mankind," or appearing on nationally syndicated talk shows to rebut her critics or promote policy, ER addressed this new audience with startling candor. She bemoaned Republican capitulation to strident Cold War politics and challenged recalcitrant Democrats to remain true to democratic principles. Despite pressure from Mike Wallace, she refused to name a Democrat who possessed the "full leadership quality that the present day seems to require."[32] When Eisenhower won reelection, she continued to criticize his foreign and domestic policies and urged the Democrats to stop aping Republican policies and return to their liberal roots. "Our leadership has been [so] poor," she told "Meet the Press," that it seems "lackluster."[33]

As the last three parts reveal, ER's remarks on foreign affairs were just as blunt as her statements regarding domestic policy. Although she refrained from addressing specific international policy while her husband lived, she refused to remain quiet on issues of war and peace.

As the war with Germany neared, Eleanor Roosevelt struggled to reconcile her own antiwar sympathies with the information FDR presented on German conduct. She detested Franco and Hitler, but she had a long-standing commitment to antiwar activism. Throughout the twenties, she campaigned tirelessly for America's entry into the League of Nations and the World Court, passionately endorsed the Women's International League of Peace and Freedom (WILPF), cochaired the Edward Bok Peace Prize Committee, lobbied in support of the Kellogg-Briand Treaty, and circulated memoranda discussing economic reform as a deterrent to war to all her New York State Democratic Women colleagues. In the 1930s, she had supported the efforts of the National Conference on the Cause and Cure of War ("Because the War Idea Is Obsolete"), helped finance the Quaker-run Emergency Peace Committee, joined the advisory board of the American Friends Service Committee, keynoted the 1937 No-Foreign War Crusade, and praised those Loyalists who resisted Franco. She so admired Carrie Chapman Catt's work for WILPF that she told FDR that Catt was the greatest woman she had ever known.

In 1938, she published *This Troubled World*, in which she argued that negotiation and economic boycott, rather than military conflict, were the best ways to curtail aggression and that the nation could "profit" from a careful review of the mistakes made by the League of Nations. Returning to her plea for informed participation, she concluded "we have to want peace, want it enough to pay for it, pay for it in our own behavior and in material ways. We will have to want it enough to overcome our lethargy and go out and find all those in other countries who want it as much as we do."[34]

However, this passionate commitment to peace did not mean an unswerving allegiance to fascism or isolationism. Indeed, as fascist aggression increased, ER became more outspoken in her opposition to isolationist policies. When FDR phoned her at 5 A.M. September 1, 1939, to tell her that Germany had invaded Poland, ER knew that the United States would eventually enter the war and began to assess the role she would have to play. "I . . . could not help feeling that it was the New Deal social objectives that had fostered the spirit that would make it possible for us to fight this war," she later admitted. Well aware of the role she played in fostering these objectives, ER could not easily avoid recognizing that she would have a major part in defining the domestic conduct of the administration's war effort. She recognized that "to win the war" America would "have to fight with our minds, for this is as much a war for the control of ideas as for control of material resources." Her challenge was to highlight the ideas she thought essential to winning both the international war against fascism and the domestic war against intolerance and prejudice. As she wrote for the *Saturday Review*, "If those who say that to win the war we must hate, are really expressing the beliefs of the majority of our people, I am afraid we have already lost the peace, because out main objective is to make a world in which all the people of the world may live with respect and good will for each other in peace."[35]

ER's ability to see the complex relationships between war and peace, propaganda and education, and consensus and dissent placed her in an uncomfortable position politically and personally. The peace movement wanted her to be its voice within the administration and the administration expected her to defend its position with its antiwar critics. But rather than let these expectations confine her, ER worked to find a position she could advocate with conviction ("Defense and Girls" and "What We Are Fighting For").

Just as she refused to believe that the emergencies of wartime justified postponing domestic reform, ER also refused to believe that the war warranted total suspension of political criticism. Consequently, she worked to restrain the zeal with which the administration reprimanded its critics. "We who believe in democracy," she told readers of *The Nation*, "should not so much be concerned with stamping out the activities of those few groups or individuals as with developing among the people in this country a great sense of personal responsibility toward a democratic way of life. . . . We do not move forward by curtailing people's liberty."[36]

Still, the lists of those she defended had important and significant gaps. In fact, there were times when her silence was so notable that she could reasonably be accused of turning her back on her principles. What is clear is that at the beginning of the war, ER and FDR held opposite views of the rights of Japanese Americans. Less than a week after Pearl Harbor was bombed, ER toured the West Coast; praised a plea for racial tolerance by Mayor Harry Cain of Tacoma, Washington; posed with Japanese Americans for photographs that would be distributed over the Associated Press wire service; and editorialized against retribution. FDR, on the other hand, determined to capitalize on the procedures he utilized to monitor his critics throughout the 1930s, immediately summoned aides to discuss the wholesale detention of Japanese and German Americans.

ER opposed internment. She worked closely with Attorney General Francis Biddle to ensure, first, that she understood how the Constitution applied to internment and, second, that the Justice Department presented a strong case against the policy to FDR. However, once FDR signed Executive Order 9066 and internment began, ER fell silent.

ER waited until late 1943 to address internment publicly. By then the vast majority of the Japanese American population had been removed from the West Coast and those interned in the Poston, Arizona, and Manzanar, California, camps had either struck or rioted in protest of their incarceration. Worried that the policy might backfire, FDR asked ER to visit the Gila River camp. She agreed and announced that she would inspect the camps and report her findings to the nation. Yet instead of discussing the psychological and political climate of the camps or the concerns about racism and resettlement the internees raised during their meeting with her, ER wrote columns praising the internees' attempts to beautify their small plots of land.

Despite this lapse into public acquiescence, a decidedly anguished tone resonates through her other depictions of internment life. When ER tried to present the administration's case that loyal Japanese Americans were interned for their own protection, as hard as she tried she could not completely suppress her own doubts about this argument. When she tried to justify the administration's demands for immediate relocation, she introduced as many arguments questioning this statement as she did endorsing it. Finally, she lambasted those West Coast xenophobes who believed that "a Japanese is always a Japanese" by declaring that such "unreasonable" bigotry "leads nowhere and solves nothing."[37]

ER entered the postwar era determined not to repeat this behavior. Just as FDR's death liberated her to speak her mind on Democratic domestic policies, it also allowed her to address international issues with which she disagreed. Yet once again she defied traditional liberal boundaries.

Keenly aware of ER's political stature, Harry Truman appointed her to the first American delegation to the United Nations. ER considered this the most important position of her life and dedicated a great part of her remaining seventeen years to promoting and defending the institution and its policies. As the U.S. representative to the Social, Humanitarian and Cultural Committee of the General Assembly, she guided the drafting and adoption of the Universal Declaration of Human Rights. Modeled after the Declaration of Independence, the Magna Carta, and the Declaration of the Rights of Man, this document—more than any other contained in this volume—reflects ER's vision of the world. From the first sentence of the preamble—"the recognition of the inherent dignity and of the equal and inalienable rights of all members of the human family is the foundation of freedom, justice and peace in the world"—to the last article, the document resonates with ER's commitment to human rights and informed participation. Insisting that citizenship confers rights with responsibility, the document stresses that "everyone has duties to the community in which alone the free and full development of his personality is possible."[38]

Yet as ER revealed in *Foreign Affairs*, drafting the document was politically perilous process. Indeed, it took three years of contentious committee debate before a unanimously supported document could presented to the General Assembly. ER chaired these meetings with a unique blend of discipline and compassion, often challenging grandstanding critics to make their point quickly or be ruled out of order. She then "mapped out our strategy very carefully," reviewing every word of the document with each voting member, diligently marshaling their support. Her diligence prevailed, convincing the Soviets to abstain rather than be the lone voice opposing the declaration.

ER considered the declaration her finest achievement and became its most outspoken champion at home and abroad. Conceding that the declaration carried no sanctions for those nations who violated its provisions and that it could serve only as a model for nations to emulate, ER nevertheless declared it "of outstanding value" because it "put into words some inherent rights" that must be recognized for individual "security and dignity" to prosper. By making rights less intellectual and more "tangible," the declaration not only set "before men's eyes the ideals which they must strive to reach" but also gave them standards that "could be invoked before law."[39]

Those delegates and their staff recognized the historic accomplishment ER's perseverance presented them. When she rose to address the General Assembly before the vote, the Hall of Delegates was filled to capacity. Indeed, when she concluded her remarks presenting the declaration, all members rose and gave her a sustained ovation.

ER received such accolades because the assembly recognized how difficult the adoption process had become and how perilous the implementation process would be. Human rights was a volatile political concept, and the United States and the Soviet diplomatic corps remained extremely leery of supporting documents that mandated its signatories' compliance with economic and political rights. The Soviets insisted that American commitment to human rights was a sanctimonious pronouncement of a racist society, while Americans argued that Soviet support of economic guarantees was merely backdoor communism. When the General Assembly instructed Committee III to present a binding covenant on economic and social rights to the United Nations, the two superpowers continued their entrenched posturings. Once again, ER demanded the hearings move forward while searching for common ground ("Statement on Draft Covenant on Human Rights" and "Reply to Attacks on U.S. Attitude Toward Human Rights Covenant").

Yet ER was not always a patient negotiator. Although she was an instructed delegate to the United Nations and technically had to clear her remarks regarding foreign policy with the State Department, ER often chafed at its reservations. When readers compare her formal remarks with the extemporaneous speeches included in this collection ("Human Rights and Human Freedom" and "The U.N. and the Welfare of the World"), ER's inclination to link social and economic rights with political rights—a position with which the state department disagreed—is very apparent. Americans must realize that they are "responsible not for what we have done in developing our own country but for what we have stood for as a democracy." Urging the nation to live up to its professions, she argued that it was hard to promote democratic values if the nation acted in an undemocratic fashion. As she told the Parent-Teacher Association's national convention, serving in the UN has made her "very conscious of how carefully we are watched by the rest of the world." Make no mistake about it. "It is true that what happens in every one of our own communities is painting the story of what democracy actually is."[40]

ER applied the same independence when it came to defining her view of American foreign policy. Rather than succumb to a zealous Cold Warrior position or support unquestioning collaboration with the Soviet Union, ER carved out her own positions ("Why We Are Cooperating with Tito"). She told readers of *Look* that while "it takes patience and equal firmness and equal conviction to work with the Russians," she "admire[d] the Russians' tenacity." Moreover, she urged Americans "to divorce our fear and dislike of the American communists, as far as possible, from our attitude as regards . . . the Soviet government." Once America insists that Russia not aid American communists, "we can work with Russia as we have with the socialist government in Great Britain."[41]

Grounded in an unyielding commitment to the United Nations, she argued that the world must see itself as a global community that shared certain inalienable rights ("Human Rights and Human Freedom" and "The Promise of Human Rights"). Just as she demanded civil rights at home, she defended the rights of refugees, Jews, and women to a life defined by self-determination and peace ("Arab-Israeli Peace," "The Universal Validity of Man's Right to Self-Determination," and "U.N. Deliberations on Draft Convention on the Political Rights of Women"). Lastly, she urged the world to reject propaganda and shun what she would later call "the politics of fear." "Are we so weak in the United Nations, are we as individual nations so weak that we are going to forbid human beings to say what they think and fear whatever their friends and their particular type of mind happens to believe in?"[42]

Repeatedly ER argued that Americans and the world must learn from the mistakes of the past, from war and discrimination and impoverishment. To focus only on success distorts the record and offers an unrealistic guide for the future. This is "not an easy lesson for any of us to learn, but one that is essential to the preservation of peace."[43]

Clearly, Eleanor Roosevelt, ever aware of democracy's shortcomings, nevertheless envisioned a world in which it might flourish. Whether speaking to students, teachers, reform associations, the general public, members of Congress, political conventions, or career diplomats, ER never wavered from her commitment to participatory democracy, human rights, and the United Nations. The more of the world's injustice she witnessed, the more resolute her belief in democracy became. Yet hers was not a blind faith or a naive abdication of responsibility. ER always understood that democracy could not succeed without hard work, sacrifice, and compassion. As this collection reveals, she urged the world to look beyond national boundaries and political rivalries, to consider other points of view, to read, to think, and to act. Part teacher, diplomat, journalist, and political leader, ER became a very realistic idealist and an extraordinary activist for democracy.

NOTES

1. "What I Hope to Leave Behind," 7.
2. Herbert Leibowitz, *Fabricating Lives: Explorations in American Autobiography* (New York: Knopf, 1990), xix, xxiii.
3. Carolyn Heilbrun, *Writing a Woman's Life*, (New York: Ballantine, 1988), 30.
4. "What Has Happened to the American Dream?" 31.
5. "What Religion Means to Me," 3.

6. "In Defense of Curiosity," 17.
7. "Civil Liberties and the Crisis," 105.
8. "Insuring Democracy," 95.
9. "Let Us Have Faith in Democracy," 98.
10. *The Moral Basis of Democracy*, 88, 89.
11. "The Democratic Effort," 107, 108.
12. "What Are We For?" 121.
13. *The Moral Basis of Democracy*, 80.
14. "The Issue Is Freedom," 514.
15. "What We Are Fighting For," 507.
16. Eleanor Roosevelt, "Freedom: Promise or Fact," *Negro Digest*, October 1943, 8–9.
17. "Some of My Best Friends Are Negro," 171.
18. "Foreword," *The Long Shadow of Little Rock*, 181.
19. "The Social Revolution," 184.
20. "Wives of Great Men," 221, 222.
21. Eleanor Roosevelt, *It's Up to the Women* (New York: Frederick A. Stokes Co., 1933), 256.
22. "What's the Matter with Women?" 267.
23. "Women in Politics," 258.
24. "Women Have Come a Long Way," 278.
25. "On Teachers and Teaching," 310.
26. "The Ideal Education," 297, 298.
27. "Facing the Problems of Youth," 303, 304.
28. "Education is the Cornerstone on Which We Must Build Liberty," 315.
29. "This I Believe about Public Schools," 328.
30. "Address to 1940 Democratic Convention," 373.
31. "Plain Talk about Wallace," 413.
32. "Mike Wallace Interview," 458.
33. " 'Meet the Press' Interview," 453.
34. *This Troubled World*, 490.
35. Eleanor Roosevelt, *The Autobiography of Eleanor Roosevelt* (New York: Harper, 1961), 230; "Must We Hate to Fight?" 511.
36. "Fear Is the Enemy," 499.
37. "A Challenge to American Sportsmanship," 520.
38. "Universal Declaration of Human Rights," 531, 535.
39. "The Promise of Human Rights," 558.
40. "The U.N. and the Welfare of the World," 623.
41. "The Russians Are Tough," 549.
42. "Human Rights and Human Freedom," 541.
43. "The Russians Are Tough," 552.

What
I Hope
to Leave
Behind

Part A

Reflections and Personal Testimony

1

What Religion Means to Me

It is generally conceded that in a world where material values seem to be dropping out of sight further and further day by day, there is a growing realization that something else is needed. Some of us even feel that amidst the many evils and sorrows and injustices which are the fruit of what we call the depression, there may be emerging one thing which will be of permanent value to us all—namely, a new standard which will set above everything else certain spiritual values. In our mad haste for more and more money and more and more luxury we had almost forgotten to count these as part of our heritage in this country.

And yet most of us who are in the forties and fifties today can look back to a childhood where religion and religious instruction were part of our everyday life, but we have come so far away from those days that in writing this article I even feel that I must begin by defining what I mean by religion. To me religion has nothing to do with any specific creed or dogma. It means that belief and that faith in the heart of a man which makes him try to live his life according to the highest standard which he is able to visualize. To those of us who were brought up as Christians that standard is the life of Christ, and it matters very little whether our creed is Catholic or Protestant.

To those of us who happen to have been born and brought up under other skies or in other creeds, the object to be attained goes by some other name, but in all cases the thing which counts is the striving of the human soul to achieve spiritually the best that it is capable of and to care unselfishly not only for personal good but for the good of all those who toil with them upon the earth.

Having established this as the meaning of religion, I can go back and speak for a moment of what most of us with Anglo-Saxon forebears remember as religious training in our youth. Sunday was, indeed, a day set apart from other days and some of the things decreed by my grandmother, who brought me up, I personally very much resented. I could not play games on Sunday; I had to sit on the uncomfortable small seat in my grandmother's large Victoria and drive five miles to and from church; I had special books which I was only allowed to read on Sundays, and I could not read the story in which I might happen to be interested. But I really enjoyed learning the Bible verses and the hymns, which always had to be memorized for Sunday morning, and I have never to this day quite got over the real pleasure of singing hymns on Sunday evening, after supper, as a family. These were very agreeable things and besides your elders had more time to talk to you. They even took little people for

The Forum 88 (December 1932): 322–24.

very pleasant walks on Sunday afternoons and in the winter I can remember open fires and books read aloud, which to this day carry me back to a happy atmosphere. But this religious training was not just an affair of Sundays—there were family prayers every morning and you grew up with the feeling that you had a share in some great spiritual existence beyond the everyday round of happenings.

Many of us have seen changes in religious thought since then, and God and religion may have come to mean many different things to many people, but I doubt if any of us have ever completely lost that feeling of having something outside of one's self and greater than one's self to depend on. There never has been a time when that feeling is more needed than it is today. People in trouble need just what little children need—a sense of security, a sense of something greater than their own powers to turn to and depend on.

The worst thing that has come to us from the depression is fear. Fear of an uncertain future, fear of not being able to meet our problems, fear of not being equipped to cope with life as we live it today. We need some of the old religious spirit which said, "I myself am weak but Thou art strong Oh Lord!" That was the spirit which brought people to this country, which settled it, which carried men and women through untold hardships, and which has given us our heritage of comparative ease and comfort.

After I left home and went to school I came under the influence of a very interesting woman who proclaimed that she had no religion and that the Christians, from her point of view, were rather to be looked down upon because they did right for gain. It might not be gain in this world but it was for gain in the next, and therefore the only people of real virtue were those who believed that there was no future life, but who wished to help those around them to do what was right purely through an interest in their fellow human beings and a desire to see right triumph just because it was right. I was too young to come back then with the obvious retort that making those around you happy makes you happy yourself, and that therefore you are seeking a reward just as much as if you were asking for your reward in a future life, and that perhaps what we know as good in life and what we here think of as praiseworthy will not be counted at all as a spiritual achievement by some more understanding judge. That is why we all of us, whether we are willing to acknowledge it or not, do crave the belief in some power greater than ourselves and beyond our understanding—because we know in our hearts that deeds and outward things mean little and that only someone who can gauge what striving there has been can really judge of what a human soul has achieved.

Today I am an Episcopalian, as I was as a child, but I feel that this makes me neither better nor worse than those who belong to any other church. I believe in the habits of regular churchgoing and regular work for the church because there is help for us all in doing things in common and we care more for things that we give to, of our time, of our material wealth, and of our thought. But these are the outward symbols which should proclaim inner growth, and it is the inner growth which is important. If people can attain it without the help of what might be called religious routine, that is for them to decide. The fundamental, vital thing which must be alive in each human consciousness is the religious teaching that we cannot live for ourselves alone and that as long as we are here on this earth we are all of us brothers, regardless of race, creed, or color.

We must honestly try to put into practice some of the things which have always been considered too visionary to be actually tried in everyday life. We cannot give lip service alone to religion today. We hear constantly that prosperity will soon return, that this or that will bring about better business conditions, but we know of many people who have gone down under the strain of material loss and misfortune. The increasing number of suicides makes us realize that many people are feeling that life is too hard to cope with. That feeling would not exist if out of this depression we could revive again any actual understanding of what it means to be responsible for one's brother. Perhaps the parable of the rich man fits today very admirably, only we are not allowed to voluntarily place ourselves in his position. It is neatly done for us and our part is simply to see that we learn our lesson aright and that we profit by it, and that instead of sinking under the weight of fear we find our souls strengthened by the knowledge that we are part of some great scheme and that our courage springs up from deep wells of tradition, for our forefathers knew that there was a God who gave us strength and who ordered the world in which we live, but that we had to put forth our own strength to the utmost before our spirits could be upheld.

Out of these troublous times perhaps this knowledge will come back to us, and if it does a new day may really dawn for us all. Failure, however, must cease to mean material loss; it is the way we meet adversity, not adversity itself, which counts. If we have life and love and health and hope and a vision to strive for, then we are not failures, but if we are to hold this point of view real religion must be supreme on earth.

It has been true in the past that in all times of great crises there has been a revival of religious feeling. We are going through a time when vast numbers of our people are facing loss of things which they hold dear, some of them are facing actual starvation—though I think we have come to a point where our social conscience has become keen enough for us to make every attempt as a people to prevent, wherever we know of it, actual starvation. It is looked upon today as one of the duties of government to see that no one starves, and that is something which would not have even been thought of two hundred years ago.

But there are many other by-products of the depression which do as much harm as actual starvation. The lack of work, the feeling of helplessness, and the inevitable lowering in many families of the standard of living have a sad effect upon the general morale and habits of life of all the members of the family. Little by little it is being borne in upon us that it is not only life which we have a right to preserve, but that there is something more precious which the need of material things may stamp out of the human soul. Therefore it behooves us so to order our civilization that all can live in the security of having the necessities of life, and that each individual according to his abilities and his vision may at the same time preserve his hope for future growth.

This is Utopia perhaps, and many years distant, but it seems to me that it is the goal of real civilization, and it also seems to me that only through a revival of true religion are we going to achieve this goal. When religion becomes again a part of our daily lives, when we are not content only with so living that our neighbors consider us just men, and when we really strive to put into practice that which in moments of communion with ourselves we know to be the highest standard of which we are capable, then religion will mean in each life what I think it should mean. We will follow the outward observances because they give us help and strength, but we will live day by day with the consciousness of a greater power and of greater understanding than our own to guide us and protect us and spur us on.

2

What I Hope to Leave Behind

I personally have never formulated exactly what I would like to leave behind me. I am afraid I have been too busy living, accepting such opportunities as come my way and using them to the best of my ability, and the thought of what would come after has lain rather lightly in the back of my mind.

However, I suppose we all would like to feel that when we leave we have left the world a little better and brighter as a place to live in.

A man said to me recently, "I would like before I die to live in a community where no individual has an income that could not provide his family with the ordinary comforts and pleasures of life, and where no individual has an income so large that he did not have to think about his expenditures, and where the spread between is not so great but that the essentials of life may lie within the possession of all concerned. There could be no give and take in many ways for pleasure, but there need be no acceptance of charity."

Men have dreamed of Utopia since the world began, and perfect communities and even states have been founded over and over again. One could hardly call the community that this man likes to visualize Utopia, but it would have the germs of a really new deal for the race.

As I see it we can have no new deal until great groups of people, particularly the women, are willing to have a revolution in thought; are willing to look ahead, completely unconscious of losing the house on Fifth Avenue as long as somewhere they have a place to live which they themselves may gradually make into a home; are willing to give up constant competition for a little more material welfare and cooperate in everything which will make all those around them acquire a little more freedom and graciousness in life.

If a sufficient number of women can honestly say that they will willingly accept a reduction in the things which are not really essentials to happiness but which actually consume a good deal of the money spent by the rich, in order that more people may have those things which are essential to happy living, then we may look, I believe, for the dawn of a new day.

When enough women feel that way there may grow up a generation of children with entirely different ambitions, and before we know it, a new deal and a new civilization may be upon us. Perhaps this result is that which technocracy is preaching; but though I have read a little on the subject, I am not yet quite clear just what is the ultimate result that technocrats desire; but I gather that they do expect a revolution of some kind unless we make right use of the information which they have gathered.

Pictorial Review 34 (April 1933): 4, 45.

If these methods of theirs bring about the type of community which I have in mind, the type of education and the ability to appreciate and enjoy, then technocracy has served a good purpose. But if that result does not come to us through technocracy, I still believe it may come to us through the efforts of the men and women of this generation in using their common sense and their dreams.

If I had Aladdin's lamp and could wish for whatever I desired, and see my desires materialize before me, I think the world would be a perfect place to live in, but I doubt if it really would be any more interesting than it is today, for in a way we all of us have wishing rings or something of the kind at hand all of the time. These age-old fairy tales were told simply to remind a generation of people, who happened to learn things more readily by stories, of the realities of life.

We learn things today just as readily by tales, only our tales are a little different. Aladdin's lamp, interpreted, means an individual's will to accomplish, and the wishes are the purposes, the dreams, if you will, the point on which we shape our lives. Of course, we may not be able to make all our dreams come true, but it is an astonishing thing how often, in the words of *Peter Ibbetson*, we can "dream true."

Unconsciously our characters shape themselves to meet the requirements which our dreams put upon our life. A great doctor dreamed in his youth that he would save people, that he would help a suffering humanity. He completed his long training; he steeled himself to see suffering in order that he might alleviate it. Instead of sliding out from under responsibility, he accepted it because he knew that he had to develop all those qualities of mind and heart if he were going to be a great doctor or a great surgeon.

Most women dream first of a happy family. The instinct for reproduction is inborn in most of us. If we have known happy homes, we want to reproduce the same type of thing we have had; and even though we may always be critical of some things in our past, time nearly always puts a halo around even a few of the disagreeable things, and most women dream, as they rock their babies or busy themselves in household tasks, that their daughters will do the same things someday.

In some intangible way it satisfies our hunger for eternity. We may not actually figure it out, but the long line that we see streaming down uncounted years, going back of us and going on beyond us, comes to mean for us immortality.

For a number of years it took so much vitality to keep the home going, and that home represented so many different kinds of activities, that none of us had any urge to go outside of this sphere.

Gradually in every civilization there comes a time when work of the household is done by servants, either human or mechanical.

When the care of the children ceases to be entirely in one person's hands, then in the past, as in the present, women have turned to other things. Some have changed the map of the world, some of them have influenced

8

literature, some have inspired music. Today we are dreaming dreams of individual careers.

I find I have a sense of satisfaction whenever I learn that there is a new field being opened up where women may enter. A woman will rejoice in her freedom to enter on a new career. She will know that she has to make some sacrifice as far as her own life is concerned, and for that reason you will find more and more women analyzing what are the really valuable things in human life, deciding whether a job of some kind will be worthwhile for them from several points of view, whether it will give them sufficient financial return to provide for the doing of certain household things better than they could do themselves, and whether the job they do will give them more satisfaction and make them better-rounded people and, therefore, more companionable and worthwhile in their associations with the human beings that make up their home life.

What is the real value of a home? To me the answer is that the value lies in human contacts and associations—the help which I can be to my children, which my husband and I can be to each other, and what the children can be to us. These are the real values of home life. A sense of physical comfort and security can be produced quite as well by well-trained servants.

I feel that if holding a job will make a woman more of a person, so that her charm, her intelligence, and her experience will be of greater value to the other lives around her, then holding a job is obviously the thing for her to do. Sometimes a woman works not only to make money and to develop her personality, and be more of a person in herself, but also because she is conscious that she wishes to make some kind of contribution in a larger field than that of her home surroundings.

In all the ages there have been people whose hearts have been somehow so touched by the misery of human beings that they wanted to give their lives in some way to alleviate it. We have some examples of women like this today: Lillian Wald and Mary Simkhovitch in New York, Jane Addams in Chicago. They were none of them actuated, when they started out on their careers, by any small personal ambitions. They have achieved great personal success, but that is simply as a by-product; for what they set out to do and have done was to alleviate some of the trials of humanity in the places where they were able to work.

The conditions which are governing the world today are obliging many women to set up a new set of values, and in this country they will, on the whole, be rather a good thing.

We have come to a place where success cannot be measured by the old standard. Just to make money is no gauge anymore of success. A man may not be able to make as much as his wife, may not be able to make enough to support his family, and yet he may be a success. He may have learned to be happy and to give happiness, too, in striving for things which are not material.

A painter may do his best work and yet not be able to sell it, but he is nonetheless a success. You may make your home a success and spend one-tenth of what you spent last year. Bread and cheese cheerfully eaten and shared with other congenial souls may bring a larger return on the investment than do the four- or five-course dinners of a year ago.

There is no doubt that we women must lead the way in setting new standards of what is really valuable in life.

It is a far cry from our pioneer ancestors to a lady who owns a house on Fifth Avenue, and yet if you have to give up your house on Fifth Avenue and you have to change to some other conditions in life, it is not so very difficult to go back and reproduce certain conditions which have faded out of our minds and which, after all, were the essentials of life in, let us say, Governor Winthrop's time.

One of my favorite quotations is:

> To be honest, to be kind—to earn a little and to spend a little less, to make upon the whole a family happier for his presence, to renounce when that shall be necessary and not be embittered, to keep a few friends but these without capitulation—above all, on the same grim condition to keep friends with himself—here is a task for all that a man has of fortitude and delicacy.

I often wish that more people would read Stevenson's "Christmas Sermon." He expresses a philosophy which, if it were carried out and accepted without bitterness, might make of us again a happy nation in spite of the loss of many material things.

As I grow older I realize that the only pleasure I have in anything is to share it with someone else. That is true of memories, and it is true of all you do after you reach a certain age. The real joy in things, or in the doing of things, just for the sake of doing or possessing, is gone; but to me the joy in sharing something that you like with someone else is doubly enhanced.

I could not today start out with any zest to see the most marvelous sight in the world unless I were taking with me someone to whom I knew the journey would be a joy. It may be a drawback which comes with age—you do not crave any new sensations and experiences as much as you did in youth—but it is one of its compensations that you are so much better able to enjoy through other people. You can even sit at home and be happy visualizing others that you love enjoying things which you have prepared them to see and to understand.

One of the things which I hope are coming home to us with a lessening of the abstract desire for money is an appreciation of the fact that some people have an ability to enjoy where others have not, and that one of the things that we must do is to give that ability to enjoy to more and more people.

It is almost entirely a question of education. There is such a thing as going through the world blindfolded. I have known people who were quite unconscious of the play of the sun and shadow on the hills. There was no joy to them in the view from a high hill. A landscape was simply a landscape—nothing else.

As one political dignitary once said to me, "Don't ask me to admire the scenery. I cannot see anything in it." His eyes had never been opened. The waves on the shore and the sweep of the ocean meant little to him. The sound of the wind in the trees, the breath of a crisp October day, all went unnoticed and uncatalogued as a beauty or a pleasure. I doubt if his ear had ever heard music; and the pitiful thing is that so many people can go through the world with the same handicaps either because they will not learn or because they haven't had the opportunity to see things through the eyes and hear things through the ears of a really educated person.

With advancing years I feel I must give this question of what I want to leave behind me greater thought, for before long I shall be moving on to fields unknown, and perhaps it may make a difference if I actually know what I would like to bequeath to a new generation. Perhaps the best I can do is to pray that the youth of today will have the ability to live simply and to get joy out of living, the desire to give of themselves and to make themselves worthy of giving, and the strength to do without anything which does not serve the interests of the brotherhood of man. If I can bequeath these desires to my own children, it seems to me I will not have lived in vain.

3

I Want You to Write to Me

The invitation which forms the title of this page comes from my heart, in the hope that we can establish here a clearing house, a discussion room, for the millions of men, women and young people who read the *Companion* every month.

For years I have been receiving letters from all sorts of persons living in every part of our country. Always I have wished that I could reach these correspondents and many more with messages which perhaps might help them, their families, their neighbors and friends to solve the problems which are forever rising in our personal, family and community lives, not only with my ideas but with the ideas of others.

And now I have a department in this magazine which I can use in this way. The editor of the *Woman's Home Companion* has given me this page to do with exactly as I will; but you must help me. I want you to tell me about the particular problems which puzzle or sadden you, but I also want you to write me about what has brought joy into your life, and how you are adjusting yourself to the new conditions in this amazing changing world.

I want you to write to me freely. Your confidence will not be betrayed. Your name will not be printed unless you give permission. Do not hesitate to write to me even if your views clash with what you believe to be my views.

We are passing through a time which perhaps presents to us more serious difficulties than the days immediately after the war, but my own experience has been that all times have their own problems. Times of great material prosperity bring their own spiritual problems, for our characters are apt to suffer more in such periods than in times when the narrowed circumstances of life bring out our sturdier qualities; so whatever happens to us in our lives, we find questions constantly recurring that we would gladly discuss with some friend. Yet it is hard to find just the friend we should like to talk to. Often it is easier to write to someone whom we do not expect ever to see. We can say things which we cannot say to the average individual we meet in our daily lives.

To illustrate the changing nature of our problems it is interesting to remember that less than twenty years ago the outstanding problem of the American homemaker was food conservation, or how to supply proper nourishment for her family with one hand while helping to feed an army with the other! Ten years ago the same mothers were facing the problem of the postwar extravagance and recklessness; how to control the luxurious tastes of their

Woman's Home Companion 60 (August 1933): 4.

children, the craving for gayety, pleasure, speed which always follows a great war. Today in millions of homes parents are wrestling with the problem of providing the necessities of life for their children and honest work for the boys and girls who are leaving school.

At almost stated intervals the pendulum swings, and so far the American people have each time solved their problems. And solve them we will again, but not without earnest consultation and reasoning together. Which is exactly where this page enters the national picture.

Let us first consider one or two typical problems. You all know that in May the entire nation celebrated Child Health Week. I was among those who spoke on the basic foundations on which the health of a child is built. A few days after I gave this radio talk I received a letter from a mother who wanted to know how she could supply nourishing food and proper clothing for her three children when her husband was earning exactly fifty-four dollars a month!

Again, a couple who had read something I had said about modern methods in education wrote asking what trades or professions would offer the best opportunities for young people in the next few years.

You will note that both of these earnest letters came from parents. This is encouraging, for there never was a time when the sympathy and tolerance of older people were more needed to help the younger people adjust themselves to a very difficult world.

In the hands of the young people lies the future of this country, perhaps the future of the world and our civilization. They need what help they can get from the older generation and yet it must be sympathetically given with a knowledge that in the last analysis the young people themselves must make their own decisions.

You will be reading this page in midsummer when discussion of the summer vacation is paramount in many American homes. I am an enthusiastic believer in vacations. They are, in my opinion, an investment paying high dividends in mental and physical health.

So this month I am going to ask you a question. We all know that we have less money to spend on recreation than we have had for a great many years. How can we make that money cover the needs of a real holiday? I should like to have those of you who have taken holidays inexpensively tell me what you have done.

Perhaps you will be interested in a holiday I myself enjoyed many years ago.

We took four young boys to whom we wanted to show some points of historical interest, at the same time giving them a thoroughly healthful trip. We decided to take our car and strap on the side of it one big tent and one pup tent. The four boys slept in sleeping bags with their heads under the pup tent if it rained. We ran about one hundred and fifty miles a day. We would buy our supplies in some village through which we passed in the late afternoon. Then we would make camp near some river or brook, usually finding a hospitable farmer who would supply us with milk, butter and eggs.

We had to cook our supper and make our camp before it was dark, after which we would have a swim and sit around, talk or read and go to bed in the twilight. We were up again at dawn and during the day we would stop and see whatever historical things might be of interest on the way. Our route ran north through New York State so that we saw Ausable Chasm, the shores of Lake Champlain. We stopped a day in Montreal and two days in Quebec; then we drove down through the White Mountains where we camped two days in order to climb some of them on burros, to the great joy of the children; then east through the beautiful central part of Maine with its lakes and woods, down to the sea to Castine, and home by the road along the shore.

Our actual camping trip lasted ten days and cost us only the wear and tear on the car, the gasoline and oil, and our simple food, with a very little extra for admissions, for donkeys to climb the mountains and the cog railway up Mt. Washington, but these of course could have been eliminated. This was one of the least expensive holidays I have ever taken and it could easily be duplicated with profit and health for all concerned.

A less elaborate trip may prove quite as satisfying. A week or two in a good camp has its advantages if swimming, fishing, and hiking are available, and even weekend picnicking will break the monotony of summer in city or small town.

If you have taken such a trip with family or friends, won't you tell me about your experiences, giving sufficient detail to serve those who wish to duplicate your vacation. Your plan may be just the one I should be glad to pass on to other *Companion* readers.

Please do not imagine that I am planning to give you advice that will eventually solve all your problems. We all know that no human being is infallible, and on this page I am not setting myself up as an oracle. But it may be that in the varied life I have had there have been certain experiences which other people will find useful, and it may be that out of the letters which come to me I shall learn of experiences which will prove helpful to others.

And so I close my first page to and for you, as I opened it, with a cordial invitation—I want you to write to me.

4

In Defense of Curiosity

A short time ago a cartoon appeared depicting two miners looking up in surprise and saying with undisguised horror, "Here comes Mrs. Roosevelt!"

In strange and subtle ways, it was indicated to me that I should feel somewhat ashamed of that cartoon, and there certainly was something the matter with a woman who wanted to see so much and to know so much.

Somehow or other, most of the people who spoke to me, or wrote to me about it, seemed to feel that it was unbecoming in a woman to have a variety of interests. Perhaps that arose from the old inherent theory that woman's interests must lie only in her home. This is a kind of blindness which seems to make people feel that interest in the home stops within the four walls of the house in which you live. Few seem capable of realizing that the real reason that home is important is that it is so closely tied, by a million strings, to the rest of the world. That is what makes it an important factor in the life of every nation.

Whether we recognize it or not, no home is an isolated object. We may not recognize it, and we may try to narrow ourselves so that our interest only extends to our immediate home circle, but if we have any understanding at all of what goes on around us, we soon see how outside influences affect our own existence. Take, for example, the money we have to spend. The economic conditions of the country affect our income whether it is earned or whether it is an income which comes to us from invested capital. What we are able to do in our home depends on the cost of the various things which we buy. All of us buy food, and food costs vary with conditions throughout the country and world.

The Interdependence of Individuals

It took us some time to realize that there was a relationship between the farm situation and the situation of the rest of our country, but eventually wage earners in the East did feel the results of the lack of buying power on the farms in the Middle West. To keep an even balance between the industrial worker and the agricultural worker is an extremely difficult thing. Every housewife in this country should realize that if she lives in a city and has a husband who is either a wage earner or the owner of an industry, her wages or her profits will be dependent, not only on the buying power of people like herself but upon the buying power of the great mass of agricultural people throughout the

The Saturday Evening Post 208 (August 24, 1935): 8–9, 64–66.

country. The farm housewife must realize, too, that her interests are tied up with those of the wage earner and his employer throughout the nation, for her husband's products can only find a ready market when the city dweller is prosperous.

There is ever present, of course, the economic question of how to keep balanced the cost of living and the wages the man receives. The theory of low wages and low living costs has been held by many economists to be sound, for they contend what money one has will provide as much as high wages do in countries where living costs are also high.

We have gone, as a rule, on the theory, in this country, particularly in eras of prosperity, that high wages and high costs make for a higher standard of living, and that we really obtain more for our money, even though our prices are higher.

This question is argued back and forth, and the method by which one or the other theory shall be put into practice is an equally good field for arguments.

It may seem like an academic discussion, but any housewife should know that it is the first way in which her home brings her in touch with the public questions of the day.

The women of the country are discovering their deep concern as to the policies of government and of commercial agencies, largely because these policies are reflected in many ways in their daily lives.

There was a time, for instance, when a telephone was a rare luxury indeed in any farm home, and now electricity is beginning to revolutionize farm work just as the telephone changed farm communication with the outer world. I have heard it said that the more general use of the telephone has decreased insanity on the farm very greatly, and electricity may mean that the farm woman won't look fifty when she is really thirty!

Of one thing I am quite sure, having lived in a house with a party line for some years—namely, that the rural housewife can be just as garrulous as the young debutante who lies in bed to discuss last night's partners with her friends. I have waited sometimes for fifteen minutes for a conversation to come to an end about Mary and Bobby and Johnny's various achievements or ailments and the latest quilting pattern or recipe in the neighborhood. Isn't that better than waiting for days for a letter which may never come?

To the city or suburban dweller, the price of a subway ride is of great importance, for if it costs ten cents a day to come and go from work, he may have enough left at the end of the week to take his wife to a movie, but twenty cents a day may mean that he has nothing left for entertainment. The city dweller could also do much for the price of milk, if he realized the dairy farmer's plight and how important the consumption of milk, and its price, is to general prosperity.

This correlation of interests is something that every woman would understand if she had the curiosity to find out the reason for certain conditions instead of merely accepting them, usually with rather bad grace.

Curiosity Is the Mother of Opinion

To go a bit further afield, trouble with sheep in Australia may mean higher cost on a winter coat, and a low standard of living in a foreign country may affect our own standards. The child whom we cherish within our home may suffer from health conditions quite beyond our control, but well within the control of the community or state. Having grown to manhood, this same child may be taken away from us and die defending his country and its ideals. Unless we have seen our home as part of this great world, it will come to us as somewhat of a shock that the world crowds in upon us so closely and so much.

So many of us resent what we consider the waste of war, but if in each home there is no curiosity to follow the trend of affairs in various nations and our own conduct toward them, how can we expect to understand where our interests clash or to know whether our Government's policies are fair and just or generally selfish?

Out of the homes of our nation comes the public opinion which has to be back of every Government action. How can this public opinion be anything but a reaction to propaganda unless there is curiosity enough in each home to keep constant watch over local, state, national and international affairs?

Therefore, anyone who fully appreciates the value of home life must, of necessity, reach out in many directions in an effort to protect the home, which we know is our most valuable asset. Even the primitive civilizations reached out from the home to the boundaries of their knowledge, and our own pioneer homes reached back into the countries from which they came and out into the new lands which they were discovering and subduing to their needs.

It is man's ceaseless urge to know more and to do more which makes the world move, and so, when people say woman's place is in the home, I say, with enthusiasm, it certainly is, but if she really cares about her home, that caring will take her far and wide.

People seem to think that having many interests or activities must mean restlessness of spirit which can only indicate dissatisfaction and superficiality in an individual. It may be that an interest in the home may lead one to dissatisfaction with certain phases of civilization, but the fact that one is active or busy does not necessarily mean that one is either restless or superficial. Some of the people who are the most occupied remain unhurried in what they do, and have the ability to relax and rest so completely in the time which is free, that they are less weary and give less appearance of hurry than many who fritter away hours of the day in unpurposeful activity.

Repose and a feeling of peace is an absolute necessity to a home. One may find it in a cottage, one may find it in a palace, or one may not find it in either. Repose is not a question of sitting still. It is a kind of spiritual attitude; no superficial human being can have it; real repose requires depth, a rich personality. The person possessing it can create a feeling that life flows smoothly and peacefully. Though they may never sit with folded hands, you may be able to sit with them and experience complete relaxation. It is something that comes from the soul, and no home gives complete satisfaction unless the persons making it can create this atmosphere. Repose, however, does not mean stagnation.

The Gift of Interest in People

I think, at a child's birth, if a mother could ask a fairy godmother to endow it with the most useful gift, that gift would be curiosity.

When I was young, I was taught, as all children were, that curiosity was a fault. Curiosity seemed to mean a kind of ugly prying into other people's affairs, something which "nice, well-brought-up" people refrained from. That is a kind of curiosity which, to this day, I detest. The desire to know the secrets which others may wish to hide seems, to me, cruel. Every human soul has its own secrets and its own right to keep them buried if it wishes. An idle curiosity to furnish later idle gossip is not only cruel but a despicable trait of human nature.

I think, however, that I was born with an interest in people, for I well remember at five years of age being taken by my father to serve Thanksgiving dinner for the Newsboys' Club, which my grandfather had established in New York City. I at once acquired a tremendous interest in some of the little boys who ate so much and seemed so merry in spite of their ragged clothes and their lack of all the things that I looked upon as a part of my daily security.

I was abroad at school and nearly grown up when I identified this interest with curiosity. One evening, Mlle. Souvestre, the head of the school, who was already seventy years old, gathered her pupils in her library, and after reading to us for a while, let us all enter into a discussion. I heard for the first time that night a new definition of curiosity. She turned to us and said, "You must cultivate curiosity, for only through curiosity can you learn, not only what there is in books, but what lies around you in the world of things and people." Then she showed us, one by one, how narrow our backgrounds had been, and gave us little glimpses of what we did not know, and what we might already know if we had had the curiosity, even in our past limited environments. All of us went away from the room with a new idea of what curiosity might do for us.

A Lesson in a Picture

It is perfectly obvious, of course, that intellectual curiosity, which makes you read history and science, will add greatly to your knowledge. Artistic curiosity will open up innumerable new fields in painting and sculpture and music and drama. If you have an opportunity to travel, you can add enormously to what you have already read in books or what you have experienced in art, by seeing with your own eyes some of the artistic masterpieces of the world in architecture and sculpture and in painting, by hearing great musicians and artists perform in their own countries.

You may even reconstruct for yourself, by seeing old cities and old countrysides, civilizations that have gone before us. Egypt or India, the Venice of the Doges, medieval Europe—all can rise before us if we know our history and our art, and have cultivated curiosity sufficiently to have acquired a vivid imagination.

This same teacher that I have spoken of had a theory that Americans were gifted with imagination, and so, when I was sixteen, she took me to spend an Easter in Florence. We did not live in a hotel; we lived with an artist on a hill outside the city. He was painting a great picture of the Last Supper, and every day to his door there came different types of people to pose as the Apostles. Seeing his picture and realizing how he tried, in choosing his models, to pick the type that represented his conception of the character of each Apostle, made me look at every church picture and statue with different eyes, because in each you were seeing not only what the picture meant to you but, at the same time, were getting a glimpse of the artist himself through his interpretation of his subject.

A great soul may go down to the depths, but he can also soar to the heights, and the great Italian masters were never small, and all had the power of rising to heights above the average mind. These things, however, will hardly be understood if, in addition to intellectual curiosity, you do not have what we will call emotional curiosity, because without that, these things will not become alive to us or speak of the human element which has gone into all of them, and which alone makes them speak to us from generation to generation in a language which we can understand.

Every great cathedral in Europe is not merely a building of stone and mortar but the creation of myriads of hearts and hands, giving their work because of their devotion and loyalty to God and their desire to create a fitting temple to honor their belief.

Every beautiful piece of music, every interesting play is the result of human emotions, and people are the most interesting things in the world.

Young people say to me sometimes, "I have tried so hard to talk to So-and-So," and I know at once that they have not, as yet, discovered curiosity. Curiosity will make you take such an interest in finding out what So-and-So has to offer as a human being that you will soon find conversation flowing easily. Curiosity will prevent your being closed behind a barrier, and will add, day by day, to your imagination and make your contacts increasingly easy.

When my children were young, they were occasionally embarrassed because people talked to me wherever we went, but as their own curiosity develops, they do the same thing. A little of the right kind of curiosity will endow you with sympathy, and that will bring you the confidence of your fellow human beings.

For instance, I was traveling on a train once, and I noticed, across the aisle, a woman in tears. Our eyes met, and she came over to sit beside me. I soon found myself listening as the whole pitiful drama of her life unfolded before me. Her husband had been in the Army, but had left it when they married, and they had gone back on the vaudeville stage, where they had worked before. Two children had come to them, whom her mother cared for. As vaudeville actors do, they traveled from place to place, winter and summer, sometimes making fairly good money, sometimes having pretty lean years, always spending everything they had, but, on the whole, it was a gay life, and a happy one, for they loved each other. Then the dread disease of tuberculosis took hold of the man, and the Government took him back and gave him care in a Western hospital. She had to go on the road alone, to feed and house her mother and the children, and give her husband the little extras which meant so much to him. Now and then she would manage to get to see him. Six months before, they had a happy day together, and then came the telegram telling her that he was desperately ill, and, taking all she had, she went, only to see him die and to bring his body home. She was a realist and did not dramatize her situation, so tears were few, and even in her sorrow there was a certain gaiety, for she said, "We had good times, and I hope the children will have them too. Now I must be getting back to work."

Without curiosity, I would never have heard that story and I would have missed the lift which you get when you meet with courage that faces heartache and a future of hard work and anxiety and still can be gay, for this will mean much to you when your own road is rough, as it is sooner or later for every traveler in this most interesting world.

In its simplest form, curiosity will help you to an all-around education. That is why little children are so often living question marks. They naturally desire to know about the world in which they live, and if they lose that curiosity, it is usually because we grown people are so stupid.

I once knew a little boy who found the dictionary fascinating reading, because it gave him information about such a great variety of subjects, and he read it straight through from cover to cover; and to this day he will come out with the most astonishing pieces of information gleaned from that old dictionary!

The thoroughness with which a child will pursue a subject until it has been completely mastered, going over it again and again, until it becomes so thoroughly familiar that you think it must be tiresome, is something which we should all respect, and, instead of trying to curb and stop this type of curiosity, we should always encourage it.

As a wise old horse trainer once said to me about a little boy, "He will sure go far in life, for when he wants to know a thing, he wants to know all there is about it, and he don't give up until he is sure he understands it all." Horses and people have a good deal in common, and a good horse may be terrified by something, but if he is well trained his fears will be conquered and he won't give up until he has mastered those fears and understands how to handle himself in all the situations that he habitually encounters.

A man who trains horses will usually understand people, particularly little folks, who are making their first struggle to understand the world. He will be interested in watching the development of a personality, and, as a rule, he himself will be an interesting personality.

What we talk of as personality is nothing more than the effect of experi- ence and knowledge, filtering through the emotional system of an individual until it becomes part of his inner consciousness and radiates from it in what we recognize as personality. If we feel a person has a negligible personality, it usually means that that person has lacked the curiosity to see life and really understand it. It is quite easy to see a great many things and yet to be so lacking in curiosity and in understanding that one does not know what they mean.

I went to a play once, and in a part which was really tragic, the audience laughed. It was not the playwright's fault, nor yet the actor's, but what was shown upon the stage was so foreign and inexplicable to that particular audi- ence that, instead of seeming tragic, it seemed funny. Laughter and tears are closely allied, but on this particular occasion, it was not nervous laughter, the laughter that verges on tears, but quite patently an inability to believe that a situation such as that play described could exist. On the whole, that particular audience had never been curious about that particular phase of life.

Rubbing Elbows With the Slums

In addressing a fairly rich city audience, I tried to describe certain conditions of life in a distant part of our own country, and thinking if I chose something which all of them possessed, and which was entirely lacking in the homes of the families I was trying to picture, it would mean something to them. I said that until the depression had forced us to set up relief and to find some projects on which women could work, there were innumerable families through- out certain portions of the country that had never known what it was to sleep upon a mattress. I was met with blank faces, and before I said another word, I realized that my audience was thinking, "Well, what did they sleep on?" be- cause it had never occurred to them that it was possible to sleep on anything but a mattress. There might be poor ones or good ones, but that anyone did without a mattress was absolutely impossible for that audience to comprehend.

It is not always our own fault when we lack curiosity, for our environ- ment may have prevented its development. The lack of curiosity in parents will often mean that they will try to eliminate it in their children, and thus keep their homes from stimulating the youthful urge to acquire knowledge.

A few years ago, when I was conducting a class in the study of city government, we took up one of the functions of the government—namely, public health. This is closely allied to housing, so I suggested that our group visit some of the different types of tenements. There was considerable concern among some of the mothers, for fear some illness might be contracted. It apparently never occurred to them that hundreds of young people lived in these tenements all the time, nor that, very likely, there entered into their sheltered homes daily people who served as delivery boys, servants and work- men, who spent much of their time in tenements; so, even if the sheltered children did not visit them, the tenement home radiated out all that was good

23

in it and all that was bad in it and touched the home on Park Avenue. No home is isolated, remember, so why should we not have a curiosity about all the homes that must in one way or another affect our own?

Traveled but Not Broadened

On visiting the various types of tenements, I found again that the lack of curiosity makes a poor background for real understanding. To these children of the rich, I had to explain what it meant to sleep in a room which had no window, what it meant to pant on fire escapes in hot July with people draped on fire escapes all around you, what it meant for a women with her husband and eight children to live in three rooms in a basement, and why a toilet with no outside ventilation could make a home unhealthy and malodorous.

Lack of curiosity in these young people meant lack of imagination and complete inability to visualize any life but their own, and, therefore, they could not recognize their responsibility to their less-fortunate brothers and sisters.

It is a far cry from Marie Antoinette playing at farm life in the Petite Trianon to our comfortable, sheltered young boys and girls, who have always had economic security and at least all the comforts and some of the luxuries of life, but, fundamentally, neither Marie Antoinette nor these children of ease knew real curiosity, so they rarely touched the realities of life. They knew only their own conditions, and they might as well have been blindfolded for all they saw as they walked their particular paths in life.

I traveled in Europe once with some people who could see no beauty in anything because they had so little intellectual curiosity that they had not learned enough out of books to have anything they saw around them arouse in them any picture of the past. All they did was to compare what they had known at home to what they were seeing, usually with a derogatory word for the foreign sight. Their lack of curiosity was such that they never wondered how these new people lived, or what historical background had produced the customs and habits which were theirs today.

This detached and indifferent attitude may give a kind of animal content, but it prevents much enjoyment. If you travel through the world with your knowledge limited to what you have seen or felt or discovered in your experience alone, you might as well stay within the four walls of your home, for you won't get away from your inherited environment. You may be content in doing this, but it will be the way that a dog or a pussycat is content. You will never really feel alive and tingling with new experience and new discovery.

If, on the contrary, you look upon your home as the center of a universe, and allow curiosity to carry you into the various fields of contact around you, you will soon find your life brimming over with interests. Perhaps you will tell me that you live in a small place where nothing ever happens, so you can have but few interests. This is not so.

The great experiences of life are the same wherever you live and whether you are rich or poor. Birth and death, courage and cowardice, kindness and cruelty, love and hate, are no respecters of persons, and they are the occasions and emotions which bring about most of the experiences of life. You cannot prevent unhappiness or sorrow entering into any life—even the fairy god-mother of the legend could not give freedom from these experiences—but curiosity will insure an ever-recurring interest in life and will give you the needed impetus to turn your most baleful experience to some kind of good service.

There was a woman I knew years ago whose three children died of diphtheria, and when antitoxin was discovered and a campaign was put on for the immunization of young children, she was the one who volunteered to go from door to door to talk to the parents about this new discovery.

Her home was in a rural community and there was great opposition to what was commonly thought to be "just a new-fangled notion." In fact, it was usually said that the parents would not put those dangerous bugs into their children "when they did not have nothing the matter with 'em." That woman, however, did the job, and when the day came, she brought 75 percent of the children of that district into the doctor's clinic to be immunized. She had curiosity, and that curiosity led her to do her best to spare other mothers what she had been through. It turned her sorrow into service.

There was an old woman I knew in a poorhouse who always had a new and interesting story to tell me about some of her fellow inmates whenever I went to see her. She was destitute and old, but not yet robbed of curiosity, and so there still remained an interest in life, and a desire to render some slight service, for which, in return, she received the gratitude and affection of those old and weary soldiers of fortune.

It is curiosity which makes scientists willing to risk their lives in finding some new method of alleviating human suffering, often using themselves as the best medium of experimentation. It is curiosity which makes people go down under the water to study the life on the floor of the ocean, or up into the air and out and over new and untried trails to find new ways of drawing this old world closer together.

I often wonder, as I look at the stars at night, if someday we will find a way to communicate and travel from one to the other. I am told that the stars are millions and millions of miles away, though sometimes they look so near, but it seems to me, at times, to be almost as hard for people who have no curiosity to bridge the gap from one human being to another. Perhaps the day will come when our curiosity will not only carry us out of our homes and out of ourselves to a better understanding of material things, but will make us able to understand one another and to know what the Lord meant when He said, "He that hath ears to hear, let him hear." And we might well add: "He that hath eyes to see, let him see."

5

Good Manners

What are good manners? Does anybody know? I can hear many people say excitedly: "Why, everybody who is well brought up must know what good manners are." Well, then, why do we have to have "etiquette experts"? Just to tell the part of the world which isn't "well brought up" what good manners are? Isn't it possible that we might have good manners in New York City and these same manners might seem very bad ones in Shanghai? Then we do need these experts, for we have to find out what the habits and customs are in different places the world over.

But there is one basic rule which does not require much bringing up or much knowledge, and yet which will help us all to meet situations which every one of us, no matter in what particular walk of life we find ourselves, must meet. How about teaching us all in that familiar copybook style not only that "Honesty is the best policy," but that "Kindness is the basis of good manners"?

It seems presumptuous of me to be writing on good manners. Heaven knows I could not pretend to be an Emily Post, and I am afraid I haven't even had the patience to gain a working knowledge of all her good advice and experience.

However, I suppose I have had the opportunity as often as the average person, of being faced with situations which have to be handled quickly. With no manual of good manners at hand, I have found there is one fairly safe rule to follow. The right thing to do is usually the simple, natural thing. The essence of all good manners is a kindly spirit.

We know only too well that as we move around the world we shall find that it is the custom to behave in different ways in different places; but if we are not familiar with these various rules and customs, that does not brand us as having bad manners. That simply means that we haven't had the opportunity to familiarize ourselves with the particular habits of the spot in which we happen to be. If we have fundamental good manners, we shall try to find out what is customary in any group we are with, because we shall be more comfortable if we conform to the customs of the group or country.

Wherever we are, I feel we should find out what are the native customs, and conform to them as far as possible. Of course I imagine that this might put our friends, the explorers, occasionally in a difficult spot. For instance, they may not want to become cannibals even if they are exploring the wilds, but I think our explorer friends will agree that it is wise on occasion, even if they

Ladies' Home Journal 56 (June 1939): 21, 116–117.

disapprove, to keep it to themselves until they have left the place where the people involved would resent their feelings!

If, however, we fail in doing the conventional thing because for some reason we are not aware of the particular point of etiquette involved, we need never feel ashamed or disturbed, so long as we have acted with fundamental courtesy and consideration.

In the particular group in which I grew up, we were taught to get up when an older person came into the room, to let older people walk ahead of us, to say "please" and "thank you" and "good morning" and "good night." Little girls curtsied to their elders and little boys said "yes, sir" to older men when they were spoken to. A boy or a man got up when a woman entered the room, or at meals if a woman got up from table. There were a thousand and one little things which were supposed to be good manners, but they were all rooted in the main idea that you were considerate of other people and did not think of your own comfort and your own concerns first.

I know many people with just as good fundamental manners who were not taught these specific things which we were taught; just as my brother was not taught to kiss every lady's hand, a custom which is second nature to most men brought up in many foreign countries.

I remember once being told by a gentleman from a European country that his father always found it difficult to remember the way in which he should wear the decorations which, from time to time, had been given him by the royal family. One night he found himself a guest in a country house with a member of this family and he wore his decorations. He made a mistake in the way he placed them. When he went to his room that night, the royal guest sent someone to his door requesting his coat and his decorations. They were returned later with the decorations properly placed.

Royalty gives these decorations for some distinguished service, and they must mean something to the recipient, otherwise they have no value and will not inspire other people to try to render similar service to the country.

It was good manners not to say anything to the gentleman in the presence of others. The royal guest was considerate because he recognized this mistake was lack of knowledge. If, on the other hand, however, anyone had been deliberately rude or arrogant, he might have found himself being very sharply reproved. He would have offended against a fundamental rule of good manners, which is the desire to do the thing which will make the person you are with comfortable and at ease.

I never had much contact with royalty, as I had grown up in this republic of ours, so I had to ask what was the accepted manner of behaving in their presence when I met my first royal family. Then I discovered that it mattered very little to most of them whether you forgot some of the details of etiquette. On the other hand, to certain royalties certain things are very important, and good manners require, therefore, that, as far as possible, these wishes be met.

In some parts of the world it is the custom to bow frequently when you meet; to sit on a cushion on the floor, instead of shaking hands and sitting in a chair; and yet in a book which I read lately it was related how a considerate host had imported for his guests a complete set of furniture, so that when they dined with him they should not feel constrained by the habits which prevailed in his household and which he knew were not those of their country.

Naturally, different foods are served in different parts of the world. If we know that a certain guest does not eat a certain kind of food, we do not necessarily eliminate it from our tables, but we do see that there is sufficient variety so that our guest won't go hungry. This is just consideration and therefore good manners.

It is evident, of course, that fundamental good manners will only help to meet emergencies and the conditions of normal living. Education and experience are necessary to make us conversant with all these different habits and customs and conventionalities which we may run up against throughout the world. People who have this experience are often alluded to as men or women of the world. This means only that they have had greater opportunities of coming in contact with situations among various groups in various countries. It is easy for them to move about the world if they are able to conform to situations which they are not accustomed to at home, but which are familiar to them. All of them will occasionally, however, find themselves in new situations and will be forced to fall back on that inward assurance that if they do the simple, kindly thing in any situation, they cannot go very far wrong.

I have seen many Americans in Europe giving grave offense to people of other nationalities, not because they were unaware of certain customs, but because they were evidently so bent on making everybody aware of their ideas and their standards of comfort. This is fundamental bad manners and affects me somewhat in the way I am affected when foreigners visit our country and begin to criticize various things about which they know nothing.

This habit of making critical comparisons about things which we do not understand is rather unfortunate. I remember very well the couple with whom I was traveling once, who could only look at Paris from the point of view of their home city in the United States, and always to the detriment of Paris. Whatever advantages their home city had, it could not have had the age or the historical interest of Paris, but that never seemed to occur to them. Sometimes I think that international good will would be improved by a code of international good manners.

Conventions are akin to customs and have nothing whatsoever to do with fundamental good manners. In themselves they may be good; they probably have their roots in an effort to meet certain difficulties which have come up in organized society from time to time. It is a mistake, however, to look upon conventions as unalterable, for they must change with changing conditions. In my youth it was a convention for young girls and boys to be very much more circumspect in their relationship with one another. My grandmother would have been shocked at the freedom and ease of manner common today, and the lack of many conventions which were prevalent in the society of her day. It means no real change, however, in individuals—just a change in our environment.

Good manners are far more fundamental than conventions, however useful they may be; and if we find ourselves—as I have many times—in that spot where we do not know what on earth to do, just do the kind thing and forget about the critics.

To me it has always seemed strange that so many people think good manners are prescribed only for the relationship with one's friends and acquaintances, and that they are not essential to family life. From my point of view, good manners are more important among people who live together or who see one another frequently than they are in the contacts which are more casual and less frequent. I sometimes think that some of the minor difficulties in married life would be smoothed out if, with the growth of intimacy, we did not forget the importance of good manners.

I know a woman who has a passion for telling her family the truth, whether it is pleasant or unpleasant; and I have sometimes wondered if it were not the part of good manners, as well as wisdom, to refrain even from unpleasant truths when they are not actually forced upon one by a direct question.

Gossip of the critical and harmful kind is nothing more than a lack of good manners and a sign of malicious curiosity and interest in other people's affairs, something which good manners would never allow.

In the last analysis all our training is designed to make living together in small or large groups an easier and happier experience; so cultivate the kindly heart which flowers in good manners.

6

How to Take Criticism

What about criticism? I am always being asked if it troubles me, or makes me angry, or hurts me. Should we be affected by criticism regardless of its source? In private life, of course, criticism is limited to friends and relatives and you live as you choose, and please or displease a limited group.

Curiosity centers, I imagine, about people in the public eye where there is an almost unlimited field for those who wish to criticize. If you listened to them all, would you ever do anything?

Many people feel there is an advantage to doing nothing. It is rather comfortable, you do not have to exert yourself physically or mentally. You can accept all of the privileges that come to you, and have no responsibilities. You are to be envied if your conscience lets you do it!

One of the things which my critics most frequently stress is the fact that I am not elected to any office, therefore, I can have no sense of responsibility, they say, since no one elected or appointed me to any office, so it is clear that I must be seeking publicity.

Let me disabuse them of that idea. People who live in a gold fish bowl cannot escape publicity. It is obvious that the President's wife is not an elected official, but she has certain obligations. First, there is the obligation to run the President's house, his official house, the White House, paying due attention to all the rules and regulations which custom and the law lay down for the running of that House, which belongs to the people of the United States. This is an obligation on which there is little difference of opinion and if I confined myself to giving parties, even in wartime, my critics would be few, I imagine, though one cannot be sure!

The differences arise in regard to other activities. As the President's wife, a great many people throughout the United States think that you can get information for them which they cannot get themselves, or help them to accomplish certain things which they cannot accomplish themselves. In both of these situations, they are quite correct sometimes in appealing to you, and you are able without any impropriety to give them information, and sometimes to impart the information they give you to the proper people. There is one area, however, where criticism of any individual would be entirely valid. A good many people think that because of your husband's position, you can exert influence to obtain favors which they could not obtain on their own merits. If you did this, you would quite rightly be criticized.

All you can do with propriety is to give the facts as you know them to the proper officials and leave them free to investigate and proceed as they see fit.

Ladies' Home Journal 61 (November 1944): 155, 171.

In the natural course of events, however, you get to know a good deal about the country and its people, and conditions and situations as they exist. This gives you an opportunity perhaps to be of service and here is where criticism centers.

Should the President's wife, who is not elected to any office, be interested in working conditions, for instance? She can have rare opportunities for knowing about them if she has eyes, ears and understanding. Should she be blind, deaf and dumb?

There is no question about it—all criticism is entirely permissible. There are no laws as to your conduct, you are a citizen, free like any other, so you live by your own judgment, tastes and conscience. Hence the question is "How much attention should the individual criticized pay to criticism?"

No human being enjoys being disliked so it would be normal to try to avoid actions which bring criticism. When it comes to deciding on whether you will be a Dresden china figure, daintily placed on the mantelpiece, and thus avoid any criticism, or lead a strictly personal life when the world is rocking on its foundations, or of facing criticism and at least trying to live as an independent citizen of the United States, considering it your duty to use such opportunities as come your way for service as you see it, then the decision for certain people will be easy. They will do and be damned, but the others who won't do, what of them? You might expect them to be praised but that is not the way it works. In these situations you're damned if you do and damned if you don't!

In the last analysis you have to be friends with yourself twenty-four hours of the day. If you run counter to others now and then, you have enemies, but life would become unbearable if you thought about it all of the time, so you have to ignore the critics. You know quite well when you face audiences and are among crowds of people, that perhaps everybody present dislikes you cordially. Then you do your best to make others see your point of view, but if you cannot win them over, you still must go on your way because each human being has an obligation to do what seems right according to his own conscience. If you are honest, you will always be your own most severe critic.

There are two kinds of criticism which come to us all in this world. One is constructive criticism. To be really constructive, criticism must come to us from people whom we know and whose judgment we trust and who we feel really care, not only for us as individuals, but for the things which may be affected by the actions or attitudes which we take.

Destructive criticism is always valueless and anyone with common sense soon becomes completely indifferent to it. It may, of course, be cruel at times.

Sometimes it may be unjust and bring the individual a certain amount of bitterness, but I think any sensible person soon learns to recover from the bitterness and to ignore the cruelty.

To do anything constructive or creative in this world, people must have some self-confidence. Therefore people who love them must always be careful even in giving their honest criticism and opinions, not to destroy completely an individual's faith in his own judgment!

It is sometimes better to let people make mistakes and learn from experience. This may be less harmful than being criticized, and told over and over that something you are doing is wrong or inadvisable. Everyone who launches forth on constructive criticism should bear in mind the fact that it is sometimes hard to put oneself in anyone else's shoes. What might be right for you may be quite wrong for someone else, because they approach life from a different angle. In addition, I think that if you care about people you sometimes allow your judgment to become clouded and criticize with a view to preventing them from doing things which you feel will bring them the difficulties of general criticism when as a matter of fact, succumbing to such considerations would perhaps be more painful than all the outside criticism could ever be.

Fear for those we love is one of the reasons that many of us are critical and it is something which we should weigh very carefully before expressing ourselves.

The people who love you may help you greatly, however, with some types of criticism. People whom you have never met but whom you admire, can through their example, give you inspiration, and frequently what they are and what they do and say, will form the basis on which you criticize your own actions.

To spend your life, however, thinking about "what will be said," would result in a completely unprofitable and embittering existence. Since one of the chief things that human beings can do to be helpful in life, is to be cheerful, it would indeed be foolish to dwell upon the criticism of those who can know little about you, who do not take the trouble to verify their facts, and who frequently have ulterior motives for the things which they say or write.

I think it is salutary to read criticisms, even unkind and untrue ones. I do when they happen to come my way in the natural course of events. I do not seek them out, but they certainly tend to keep one from being overconfident or getting what is commonly known as the "swelled head," but all of us must be wary not to have our confidence in ourselves completely destroyed, or we will be unable to do anything. Some criticisms I read and forget. Some remain with me and have been very valuable because I know they were kindly meant and honest and I admired and believed in the integrity of the people who expressed their convictions which were opposed to mine.

I would not want the people I love and who are most often with me to withhold criticism, but since those are the people you must count on for giving you the courage to live with a purpose, they are the ones who have the greatest responsibility to make their criticism constructive, since they know you will pay attention to them.

Sometimes criticisms I have read have seemed unjustified and unkind, and sometimes they have annoyed or hurt me, but I learned long ago that the world is not based on universal justice! One should not expect it, so I think that I have developed a great indifference except where people in whom I believe are involved. I can honestly say that I hate no one, and perhaps the best advice I can give to anyone who suffers from criticism and yet must be in the public eye, would be contained in the words of my aunt, Mrs. William Sheffield Cowles. She was President Theodore Roosevelt's sister and the aunt to whom many of the young people in the family went for advice. I had asked her whether I should do something which at that time would have caused a great deal of criticism, and her answer was: "Do not be bothered by what people say as long as you are sure that you are doing what seems right to you, but be sure that you face yourself honestly."

Friendship with oneself is all important because without it, one cannot be friends with anyone else in the world.

7

Why I Do Not Choose to Run

There has been some curiosity as to why I am not knocking at the door of the members of my political party, who make up the slates for candidates for office, in order to obtain a nomination for some elective office.

At first I was surprised that anyone should think that I would want to run for office, or that I was fitted to hold office. Then I realized that some people felt that I must have learned something from my husband in all the years that he was in public life! They also knew that I had stressed the fact that women should accept responsibility as citizens.

I heard that I was being offered the nomination for governor or for the United States Senate in my own state, and even for Vice President. And some particularly humorous souls wrote in and suggested that I run as the first woman President of the United States!

The simple truth is that I have had my fill of public life of the more or less stereotyped kind. I do believe that every citizen, as long as he is alive and able to work, has an obligation to work on public questions and that he should choose the kind of work he is best fitted to do.

Therefore, when I was offered an opportunity to serve on the United Nations organization, I accepted it. I did this, not because I really wanted to go to London last January, but because it seemed as though I might be able to use the experiences of a lifetime and make them valuable to my nation and to the people of the world at this particular time. I knew, of course, how much my husband hoped that, out of the war, an organization for peace would really develop.

It was not just to further my husband's hopes, however, that I agreed to serve in this particular way. It was rather that I myself had always believed that women might have a better chance to bring about the understanding necessary to prevent future wars if they could serve in sufficient number in these international bodies.

No Woman Has Had Sufficient Backing

The plain truth, I am afraid, is that in declining to consider running for the various public offices which have been suggested to me, I am influenced by the thought that no woman has, as yet, been able to build up and hold sufficient backing to carry through a program. Men and women both are not yet enough accustomed to following a woman and looking to her for leadership. If I were

Look 10 (July 9, 1946): 25.

young enough it might be an interesting challenge, and we have some women in Congress who may carry on this fight.

However, I am already an elderly woman, and I would have to start in whatever office I might run for as a junior with no weight of experience in holding office behind me. It seems to me that fairly young men and women should start holding minor offices and work up to the important ones, developing qualifications for holding these offices as they work.

I have been an onlooker in the field of politics. In some ways I hope I have occasionally been a help, but always by doing things which I was particularly fitted by my own background and experience to do. My husband was skilled in using people and, even though I was his wife, I think he used me in his career as he used other people. I am quite sure that Louis Howe, who was one of the most astute politicians as well as one of the most devoted of friends, trained me and used me for the things which he thought I could do well, but always in connection with my husband's career.

In the last years of his life, Louis Howe used to ask me if I had any ambitions to hold political office myself. I think he finally became convinced that though I understood the worst and the best of politics and statesmanship, I had absolutely no desire to participate in it.

Husband's Work Was More Important

For many years of my life I realized that what my husband was attempting to do was far more important than anything which I could possibly accomplish; and therefore I never said anything, or wrote anything, without first balancing it against the objectives which I thought he was working for at the time. We did not always agree as to methods, but our ultimate objectives were fortunately very much the same.

Never in all the years can I remember his asking me not to say or to write anything, even though we occasionally argued very vehemently and sometimes held diametrically opposite points of view on things of the moment.

I think my husband probably often used me as a sounding board, knowing that my reactions would be the reactions of the average man and woman in the street.

My husband taught me that one cannot follow blindly any line which one lays down in advance, because circumstances will modify one's thinking and one's actions. And in the last year since his death I have felt sure that our objectives would remain very much the same. But I have known that I was free and under compulsion to say and to do the things which I, as an individual, believed on the questions of the day. In a way it has lifted a considerable weight from my shoulders, feeling that now, when I speak, no one will attribute my thoughts to someone holding an important office and whose work may be hurt and not helped thereby. If people do not like what I say nowadays, they can blame me, but it will hurt no one else's plans or policies.

There is a freedom in being responsible only to yourself which I would now find it hard to surrender in taking a party office. I believe that the Democratic Party, at least the progressive part of the Democratic Party, represents the only safe way we have of moving forward in this country. I believe that the liberal-minded Democrats hold to the only international policy which can bring us a peaceful world. I will work for the candidates of my party when I think they offer the best there is in the field of public service, and I will even accept mediocre men now and then if I feel that the rank and file of the Party is strong enough in its beliefs to make those inadequate leaders do better than their own ability gives promise of in the way of achievement.

However, if I do not run for office, I am not beholden to my Party. What I give, I give freely and I am too old to want to be curtailed in any way in the expression of my own thinking.

To be entirely honest I will have to confess that I thought at first one of my reasons might be that I did not want to engage in the rough and tumble of a political campaign. This, of course, would be rank self-indulgence and I should be the last one to allow myself to decline to run for public office because of any such reason, since I have urged on other women the need for developing a less sensitive spirit and for learning to give and take as men do.

She Would Rather Help Others

I do not think that this consideration really enters into my decision. I have lived long in a goldfish bowl, and my husband's death does not seem in any way to have altered the attacks which come upon one from certain quarters. So I do not think that running for office would have brought me any more of the disagreeable things which we must learn to endure. In the long run, the mass of the people are likely to form a fairly truthful estimate of people who are before them in public life.

Had I wanted to run for office, therefore, I imagine in many ways I could have stood up under all types of attack and suffered less than most people. But I would rather help others, younger people, whose careers lie ahead of them and who have years in which to achieve their objectives. What I do may still be important, but it won't last long enough.

In the meantime, I shall be glad to serve wherever my past experiences seem to fit me to do a specific job.

Many people will think that these are all very inadequate answers and that when you are told that you might be useful, you should accept the judgments of others and go to work. All I can say in reply is that during a long life I have always done what, for one reason or another, was the thing which was incumbent upon me to do without any consideration as to whether I wished to do it or not. That no longer seems to be a necessity, and for my few remaining years I hope to be free!

8

The Seven People Who Shaped My Life

What you are in life results in great part from the influence exerted on you over the years by just a few people.

There have been seven people in my life whose influence on me did much to change my inner development as a person.

The first were my mother and father. I suppose it is natural for any person to feel that the most vivid personalities in early youth were those of his parents. This was certainly so in my case.

My mother always remained somewhat awe-inspiring. She was the most dignified and beautiful person. But she had such high standards of morals that it encouraged me to wrongdoing; I felt it was utterly impossible for me ever to live up to her!

My father, on the other hand, was always a very close and warm personality. I think I knew that his standards were nowhere nearly as difficult to achieve and that he would look upon my shortcomings with a much more forgiving eye. He provided me with some badly needed reassurance, for in my earliest days I knew that I could never hope to achieve my mother's beauty and I fell short in so many ways of what was expected of me. I needed my father's warmth and devotion more perhaps than the average child, who would have taken love for granted and not worried about it.

My mother died when I was six. After my father's death when I was eight years old, I did not have that sense of adequacy and of being cherished which he gave me until I met Mlle. Marie Souvestre when I was 15.

The headmistress of the school I went to in England, she exerted perhaps the greatest influence on my girlhood. She was a very good-looking woman with a really massive head. The features were very fine, her white hair soft and wavy, though she was short and rather stout by the time I knew her.

She liked Americans and attributed to them qualities of character and intelligence, which shortly began to give me back some of the confidence that I had not felt since my father's death.

I had lived in a family with some very beautiful aunts and two attractive uncles who looked upon me as a child to whom they were always kind but about whom there was certainly nothing to admire. I was conscious of their pity because my looks fell so far below the family standards and I had no special gifts of any kind to redeem my looks.

Mlle. Souvestre, on the other hand, laid a great deal of stress on intellectual achievements, and there I felt I could hold my own. She took me traveling

Look 15 (June 19, 1951): 54–56, 58.

with her and evidently felt I was an adequate companion. That gave me a great sense of reassurance.

For three years, I basked in her generous presence, and I think those three years did much to form my character and give me the confidence to go through some of the trials that awaited me when I returned to the United States.

Fought Lost Causes

As I look back, I realize that Mlle. Souvestre was rather an extraordinary character. She often fought seemingly lost causes, but they were often won in the long run. The Dreyfus case was one of them. Captain Dreyfus was vindicated in the end, but for the years before he was declared innocent, we who were under Mlle. Souvestre's influence heard every move in his case fought over and over again. I think I came to feel that the underdog was always the one to be championed!

When the Boer War came along, Mlle. Souvestre was pro-Boer. She had a great many friends in government circles; in fact, one of her old pupils was the daughter of an Englishman high in the government at that time. But that did not deter her from being a pro-Boer running a girls' school in England or from her outspoken criticism of British politics. On the other hand, she was scrupulously fair and allowed the British girls to celebrate their victories in South Africa, though she would take the rest of us into her library and talk to us at length on the rights of small nations while the British celebration was going on!

I realize now that it was a unique educational experience I was then given the opportunity to enjoy, and it certainly did me no harm to have my horizons so widened.

Eleanor's Society Aunt

The next important and stimulating person in my life was Mrs. W. Forbes (Hall) Morgan, the young aunt with whom I lived when I first came home from Europe. Aunt Pussie, as she was known in the family, was a good many years older that I was, and a great belle in New York society, which at that time was small enough to mean a great deal to those who had a place in it.

It happened that my family was distinctly a part of what was then called society, not by virtue of having money, but because it had held a place in what might be called the Four Hundred for several generations. People with money were beginning to be important, but the older families, without having to have money, still held their positions.

This young aunt was full of charm and talent. If she had had to earn her living, she probably would have developed this talent into something useful professionally. But since she did not have to, she always remained an amateur.

She was much sought after, and she could see little use in having to look after a very shy and overgrown girl who had to be introduced to the kind of society she herself understood and managed so well. The result was that she was one of the first people who taught me discipline. I admired her inordinately, but I knew that I must not be a nuisance. After a none too happy childhood, I was lonely, friendless, shy and awkward and not a society success. For a Hall, that was not easy to understand, but it hardened me in much the way that steel is tempered. The fires through which I passed were none too gentle, but I gained from them nevertheless and each new ordeal was a step forward in the lessons of living.

The personalities of my husband and my mother-in-law, I am sure, exerted the greatest influence in my development.

My mother-in-law was a lady of great character. She always knew what was right and what was wrong. She was kind and generous and loyal to the family through thick and thin. But it was hard to differ with her. She never gave up an idea she had, whether it was for herself or for you. And her methods of achieving her own ends at times seemed a bit ruthless if you were not in accord. She dominated me for years.

But I finally developed within myself the power to resist. Perhaps it was my husband's teaching me that there was great strength in passive resistance. Perhaps it was that, having two such personalities as my husband and his mother, I had to develop willy-nilly into an individual myself.

Each Sought Kingpin Role

Both wanted to dominate their spheres of life, though they were enough alike to love each other dearly. My husband was just as determined as his mother, but hated to hurt people and never did so unless they really angered him. She won even with him sometimes, but usually he simply ignored any differences in their point of view.

His illness finally made me stand on my own feet in regard to my husband's life, my own life and my children's training. The alternative would have been to become a completely colorless echo of my husband and mother-in-law and be torn between them. I might have stayed a weak character forever if I had not found that out.

In some ways, my husband was a remarkable teacher. His breadth of interests made him always a stimulating person to be with, and you could not live with him and fail to learn many things. This happened not only to me but also to his children and many of his close associates.

For instance, it was he who taught me to observe. Just sitting with him in the observation car at the end of a train, I learned how to watch the tracks and see their condition, how to look at the countryside and note whether there was soil erosion and what condition the forests and fields were in, and as we went through the outskirts of a town or village I soon learned to look at the clothes on the wash line and at the cars and to notice whether houses needed painting. Little by little, I found I was able to answer my husband's questions, after I had taken a trip alone, and give him the information he would have gathered had he taken the trip himself.

Though I had always loved the country, I had had no real knowledge of forestry or flood control. But I could not live with my husband and not learn about those things.

I not only learned what was before my eyes in my own country, but I learned what had happened in other countries of the world centuries ago and through their whole history, and why conditions were as they were in various countries throughout the world.

My husband opened the windows of the world for me. As I think it over, he was perhaps the greatest teacher of the many who contributed to my education.

The last person, probably, to have influenced me much as an individual was Louis Howe, my husband's adviser. He pushed me, not for my own sake but for my husband's, into taking an interest in public affairs.

This was a field I had carefully shunned, feeling that one member of the family with a knowledge of politics was all that one family could stand. But, little by little, I found myself beginning to understand why certain things were done and how they came about. Before I realized it, I was at least interested in the fields of domestic and of foreign affairs.

I can remember no others who exerted enough real influence on me to change me. But I do know that much of what I am today is due to these seven people among the many I have known through the years of my life.

9

Where I Get My Energy

My uncle, Theodore Roosevelt, was known for his remarkable energy. He preached the gospel of the strenuous life and as a child I heard much of his wonderful physical prowess—his hunting, exploring, riding, and polo playing. No matter how busy his life became, he always read prodigiously and still found time to spend with his children.

What was the source of his immense energy and his huge capacity to work and play? Today people ask me the same question. I decided long ago that we must have had some very sturdy ancestors. When I am told that I have extraordinary vitality for a woman of seventy-four, I feel that a good part of the credit must go to my ancient forebears. Although I know little or nothing about them, I am grateful to them for handing down to me good health and a capacity for self-discipline.

From my mother's side of the family—the Halls and Livingstons—as well as the Roosevelts—I also have a heritage of good health and good living. Though both my parents died young, I had many aunts, uncles, and cousins who managed to live to a ripe and vigorous old age. They were surprisingly numerous in an age when diphtheria, typhoid, and many other diseases we no longer fear cut so many lives short. Today, with new safeguards to prolong our lives and much more knowledge about how we stay healthy there seems little reason why the average person cannot remain self-reliant for all his days.

To be able to regulate your life and your habits in a sensible way is perhaps even more important as you grow older than when you are young. I was fortunate in learning self-discipline early. My grandmother who brought me up from the time I was seven was much more severe with me than she had ever been with her own sons and daughters. She had been chiefly concerned with loving them, leaving discipline to my grandfather. Her children were young when he died and she had great trouble controlling them, so she was determined not to make the same mistake with my younger brother and me. We would be taught to obey, and we were brought up on the principle that it is usually safer to say "no" than "yes" to children.

Of course I tried sometimes to escape from her rules and regulations. For instance, my grandmother believed that a daily cold sponge bath kept one from catching cold. If I could manage to get into the bathroom alone, I used to add a little warm water to the basin. But by and large I took a cold sponge bath every day of the year; perhaps this is one reason why today I derive special enjoyment from a warm tub.

Harper's Magazine 218 (January 1959): 45–47.

My grandmother said "no" so often—particularly to anything I wanted to do for pure pleasure—that after a time, I stopped asking her if I might do anything outside of the daily routine. I learned to say I did not want things that I knew in advance would be forbidden, in order to forestall her refusals and keep down my disappointments. I cannot say that I did this with complete cheerfulness, but in retrospect I think it was probably very good for my character.

Common Sense About Health

Social life was very important in my grandmother's world and her social code demanded a great deal of self-discipline—particularly of women. Social obligations were sacred—no matter how you felt, the show must go on. If you were depressed, you certainly did not air your sadness in public. Even in showing appropriate emotions like pleasure or polite regret you were decorous and subdued. If there were social obligations to be met, my grandmother believed it was incumbent on me to see that I felt well. She had no sympathy with a headache, for instance. She simply felt irritated that I had not avoided doing whatever had caused it.

This rather stern code has stood me in good stead on many occasions when more serious responsibilities made it absolutely necessary for me to stay well. I remember one such crisis during the flu epidemic of World War I when my husband was Assistant Secretary of the Navy and we were living in Washington. The city was fearfully crowded because government departments had taken on great numbers of clerical workers. When the epidemic that had been raging throughout the country struck Washington with full force, the Red Cross had to organize temporary hospitals in every available building. Many of these units had no kitchen space, so the junior cabinet wives agreed to supply food to certain buildings every day.

I managed to meet this obligation because my cook and I both contrived to stay well. Otherwise our pleasant house on R Street was an emergency hospital too. Every one of our five children had come down with the flu. Two had developed pneumonia. I had a trained nurse to care for the sicker one; John, who was then a small baby and had only a slight case, was in my room. My husband, who was also down with the flu, was relegated to the dressing-room, with the door left ajar so that I could hear him if he called during the night. Somehow I was able to keep myself in such good condition that I resisted the disease.

Today I still feel that I am largely responsible for keeping myself in good health. My physician, Dr. David Gurewitsch, seems to expect his patients to have a certain amount of common sense. I take the vitamin pills he prescribes and also some chocolate-coated garlic pills which are supposed to have a beneficial effect on my memory which is nothing to brag about. I am still able to work at night when necessary although I try to take a half-hour rest in the middle of the day.

The responsibilities of a family are, I think, excellent training in organizing one's life. Like most women, after my marriage I thought first of my husband and children. Although I had a good nurse and governess, I always breakfasted with the children and saw them off to school. I often had lunch with them and was always there when the came home from school or their afternoon outings. Learning to fit my own activities into the family schedule was good preparation for the demands of work and public life in later years.

Many women who are not married also carry family responsibilities, for an older relative or brothers or sisters. Most women do not feel it is burdensome to adapt their plans to the needs of others. On the contrary, it is what makes life worth living. The things we do just to satisfy our personal desires soon lose their flavor but there is a deep satisfaction in meeting the needs of husband, children, or friends. The self-discipline which these tasks develop is a great treasure for our later years.

Today, of course, there is little reason why I should not organize my life just to suit myself since I live alone. In the city I have a maid who comes in by the day. In my Hyde Park cottage where I spend my weekends, my friends Mr. and Mrs. Lester Entrup, are my housekeepers. The people who know me might, at first, be a little shocked if I suddenly announced that I would no longer be available for my usual activities because from now on I was going to do only the things I really enjoy. Quite soon, I suspect, my friends and family would adjust to this attitude and I would find myself unneeded and forgotten. I think there would be little left that I really enjoyed doing, for I believe that it is giving pleasure to other people that keeps our interest in life alive and makes us look forward to the next day.

On Schedule

I like a regular routine. When I get up at 7:30 I usually take some lemon juice and hot water. I have breakfast at 8:30—orange juice, tea, toast, and jelly. Then I read my paper and start the day's work. My engagement book tells me what is to be done every half-hour, and if I were ever to lose it, I would soon be in a terrible situation.

For instance, this was my schedule on last October 17:

6:45 A.M. Got up a bit earlier than usual; had a quick breakfast and made two urgent phone calls.

7:30 A.M. Took taxi to LaGuardia Airport.

8:10 A.M. Off by plane to Washington; got my paper read en route.

9:30 A.M. My son Franklin met me at National Airport, drove me to his new office to meet his new associates.

10:30 A.M. Back to hotel for conference with Mr. Carl Stover of the Brookings Institution. I agreed to give a talk at the Institution next spring. Mr. Seth

Jackson whom I met on my last trip abroad came to call and to seek advice about his plans.

11:30 A.M. To reception of the Democratic Central Committee of the District of Columbia, at the Mayflower Hotel.

1:15 P.M. Spoke at Committee luncheon.

2:00 P.M. Mrs. Anna S. Miller of the Washington, D.C. Housing Association drove me to the airport and invited me to address her group in May which I will do.

2:30 P.M. Took plane back to New York.

3:45 P.M. Took taxi home.

4:15 P.M. Got to work with my secretary on my correspondence which I usually do right after breakfast. Read my mail and dictated replies; also dictated my column.

5:30 P.M. Guests for tea who left just in time for me to have a very quick tub and change to evening dress.

6:30 P.M. Not quite dressed when a friend arrived to go with me to the Overseas Press Club.

8:30 P.M. Spoke at dinner given in my honor.

10:45 P.M. Home again to work on my correspondence.

1:30 A.M. October 18. To bed.

Sometimes, I must confess, I look with apprehension at a schedule like this one. Yet I know that if my life were not busy, I would feel less alive, even though I might be less tired at night. For me, there are just two remedies for weariness—one is change, the other relaxation. I have never found coffee or tea or any other stimulants helpful. Although I enjoy an occasional glass of wine, I do not take even a sip if I am tired.

Relaxing Through Change

By way of change in the summer, I fill my cottage in Hyde Park—mostly with children. It has a number of bedrooms and a dormitory for young guests so the capacity is considerable. I cannot say that I have less to do than in the city, but my program is completely different. I have a chance to do some really serious housekeeping, to plan interesting meals and go shopping myself. Sometimes it is exhausting to watch over the comings and goings of a household overflowing with lively young people. But this is a different kind of weariness; the mere contact with youth is good for old age, I believe.

One of the most stimulating changes for me is a trip to a new and intriguing part of the world. Of course, travel is tiring too. Some people tell me that after a long plane flight they need a day or so to recuperate, particularly if the hours lost or gained have upset their usual timetable. I do not find this upsets me at all. I just accept the day at whatever hour I arrive; the time lost or gained never seems to make any difference. I have learned to relax and even to take a short nap sitting in a chair almost anywhere. I find the droning of the plane engines soothing and usually manage to sleep an hour or two and sometimes through the whole night. I am perhaps not quite as comfortable as in my own bed at home, but I seldom feel really weary the next day. One of the most delightful sightseeing trips I remember was at dawn in Istanbul where our plane had unexpectedly landed us at five in the morning.

The ability to relax, recuperate, and enjoy is, I suppose, partly an attitude of mind. Like most older people, I am constantly fighting the temptation to slip into self-absorption. If one loses interest in the people who tie one to life, then it is very easy to lose interest in the world as a whole. This, I think, is the beginning of death. For all of us, as we grow older, perhaps the most important thing is to keep alive our love of others and to believe that our love and interest are as vitally necessary to them as to us. This is what makes us keep on growing and refills the fountains of energy.

At present I look like Methuselah but I feel no older than my youngest friends. I am sure that I am no more exhausted at the end of a busy day than many who are half my age. When you know there is so much to be done that is not yet accomplished you are always looking forward instead of backward. This is one of the secrets of having strength and energy. As you grow older too, it becomes easier to think about other people and forget about yourself. Thus you have many interests and these, I think, give you the capacity to do whatever really needs to be done.

10
Values to Live By

I am frequently asked why I engage in the many activities that I do and what motivates me. I have no formal philosophy of life; I simply do the things day by day that come up to be done. Duty has been the motivating force in my life, and I have looked at everything from the point of view of what has to be done.

This goes back to my childhood and early training. It is my firm belief that what we are brought up with as children has a great influence in later life. This includes the attitudes of our homes and the early experiences to which we are exposed which become the basis for our adult activities.

The Role of Religion

I grew up in a family where there was a deep religious feeling. I do not think it was spoken of a great deal. It was more or less taken for granted that everybody held certain beliefs and needed certain reinforcements of their own strength, and those came through their faith in God and their knowledge of prayer. My grandmother insisted that on Sundays I read special books and teach Sunday school to the coachman's little daughter.

Ours was a home where religion was important in shaping character. On Sundays we went to church in a carriage, and in the evenings we gathered around the piano to sing hymns.

I have accepted the way in which I was brought up. This does not mean that I do exactly what I was taught to do with respect to religious forms. But the values taught me in my childhood are a subconscious influence.

My husband too was deeply religious, and this had something to do with his confidence in himself. It was a simple belief in God and His guidance. He felt that human beings were given tasks to perform and with those tasks the ability and strength to put them through. He always insisted on holding church services on Inauguration Day, anniversaries, and whenever a great crisis impended.

I think Franklin actually felt he could ask God for guidance and receive it. Though he never talked about his religion or beliefs, he never seemed to have any intellectual difficulties about what he believed. Once, in talking to him about some spiritualist conversations which had been reported to me, I expressed my own disbelief. He, on the other hand, thought it unwise to say we do not believe in anything when we cannot prove that it is either true or untrue. It is wiser, he felt, to say that there may be spiritual things which we are simply unable to fathom. He said: "I am interested and have respect for

Jewish Heritage 1 (Spring 1958): 44–45, 54.

whatever people believe, even if I can not understand their beliefs or share their experiences."

That seemed to me a very natural attitude for him to take. He was always open-minded about anything that came to his attention, ready to look into it and study it. His feeling was that religion was an anchor and a source of strength and guidance.

The Value of Early Experience

As I look back now I realize in how many ways Franklin had been shaped by his early experiences. Unwittingly his parents had prepared him well, through travel abroad and familiarity with the customs and peoples of many countries, to meet the various situations that he faced during his public life.

I too was shaped by my childhood experiences, and in my case the primary concern was for the welfare of the less fortunate. My grandmother, who had a great sense of the obligation which the well-born had to those less well endowed, raised us to do good deeds for others. I remember how, as a girl of five, I was taken to wait on the tables at the Thanksgiving dinner for the Newsboys' Club (founded by my grandfather Theodore Roosevelt and which later became the Children's Aid Society). My grandmother made me go to the Baby's Hospital one afternoon a week to play with the sick.

Today we have a different concept. When my husband was President, he felt that people had certain rights. What neither my grandmother or his mother could ever understand was his reliance on social legislation rather than on acts of charity.

Concern for Others

Though I had been trained in the old approach of good deeds, I did not find it difficult in later years to accept the human rights approach. Indeed many of my most important adult activities have grown out of the training I received in my youth. At the age of eighteen, when I came back from my schooling in Europe, I taught at the Rivington Street Settlement on New York's lower East Side. I used to take the elevated railway or the Fourth Avenue streetcar and walk across from the Bowery. Needless to say, the foreign-looking people, the crowded and dirty streets filled me with a certain amount of terror.

But this early contact with poverty taught me at a young age not to fear it. While my children were growing up I lost a great deal of my crusading spirit where the poor were concerned because I had been told I had no right to go into the slums or into the hospitals for fear of bringing diseases home to my children. I fell into the easier way of sitting on Boards and giving small sums to this or that charity and thinking that the whole of my duty to my neighbors was done.

But later, when we moved to Washington, I began a series of trips for my husband in which I gathered information and reported to him about conditions in various parts of our country. I made several trips to see the conditions of miners in West Virginia at first hand, which helped my husband to interpret their needs. I tried to interest the wives of cabinet members in remedying the slums of Washington. They went with me on one occasion but I could never get them to go again.

After I left Washington I was happy to accept President Truman's invitation to be a member of the United States delegation to the organizational meeting of the United Nations General Assembly in London. The United Nations seemed and still seems to me to be the one hope for a peaceful world because it provides the machinery for cooperation.

While I try to do the things each day that have to be done, I have come to enjoy being with people of all walks of life and of all races and creeds. I have a curiosity about the peoples and places of the world and have traveled to India, Russia, and many far-flung lands to see as much as I can. I went to Israel, and I was able to look at the people of that land through the Bible.

As long as I live, I hope to continue learning about people and doing what I can do to help work for peace and a better world. I guess I will just go on to the end doing things that happen to come my way and need to be done.

11

What Can I Do About Peace and People?

The question comes to me very frequently as to what I, as one individual, can do about the particular interest I have. What can I do? What can I do about peace and people?

I think all of us get the feeling that we, alone, can do very little and that nobody knows what influence he has. And I am quite sure that some of the people who accomplished so much often wondered if they were doing any good. But, little by little, their influence spread as they did more and more. They may not have had at first a formulated code of personal commitment, but I think they always had an inner feeling that something was so valuable that they must stand for and work for it, and in so doing they influenced others.

Indifference is perhaps the hardest thing that has to be combatted because it is so difficult for people to visualize something they have never seen. I saw just this last year what actually seeing and touching can do for young people. I happened to meet a youngster who had the opportunity to go to East Africa to work in a famine area. He had never seen famine before in his life. The experience broadened and opened and revealed new areas which I thought were invaluable to the development of the human being. And I think such understanding is one of the things that is going to happen as we send more young people out into the rest of the world. They probably at first will not comprehend the values of other cultures. They will probably not quite understand the burdens other people carry, but if they stay here and remain uninvolved, they will probably never understand.

The YWCA with its international services and world fellowship program offers an opportunity to learn about other cultures, their achievements, and their problems. As a part of a world membership Y-Teens have contacts with other nations and a kinship with fellow members there.

The minute the indifference passes into understanding and real participation, then what we are capable of doing as a nation, as individuals of that nation, the strongest in the world, will do so much to make the world a better place in which to live.

And I think that is what commitment really permits you to do, to try to break the indifference: to try to see, understand, and do everything in a personal

The Bookshelf 45 (Summer 1962): 1, 10. Excerpt from speech given at the joint observance of the fiftieth anniversaries of the YWCA and the National Council of Jewish Women, January 1962.

way as well as in your groups to give this opportunity for understanding to as many people as possible.

Part B

Democracy and the General Welfare

12

The State's Responsibility
for Fair Working Conditions

No matter how fair employers wish to be, there are always some who will take advantage of times such as these to lower unnecessarily the standards of labor, thereby subjecting him to unfair competition. It is necessary to stress the regulation by law of these unhealthy conditions in industry. It is quite obvious that one cannot depend upon the worker in such times as these to take care of things in the usual way. Many women, particularly, are not unionized and even unions have temporarily lowered their standards in order to keep their people at work. If you face starvation, it is better to accept almost anything than to feel that you and your children are going to be evicted from the last and the cheapest rooms which you have been able to find and that there will be no food.

Cut after cut has been accepted by workers in their wages, they have shared their work by accepting fewer days a week in order that others might be kept on a few days also, until many of them have fallen far below what I would consider the normal and proper standard for healthful living. If the future of our country is to be safe and the next generation is to grow up to healthy and good citizens, it is absolutely necessary to protect the health of our workers now and at all times.

It has been found, for instance, in Germany, in spite of the depression and the difficulty in making wages cover good food, that sickness and mortality rates have been surprisingly low amongst the workers, probably because of the fact that they have not been obliged to work an unhealthy number of hours.

Limiting the number of working hours by law has a twofold result. It spreads the employment, thereby giving more people work, and it protects the health of the workers. Instead of keeping a few people working a great many hours and even asking them to share their work with others by working fewer days, it limits all work to a reasonable number of hours and makes it necessary to employ the number of people required to cover the work.

Refusing to allow people to be paid less than a living wage preserves to us our own market. There is absolutely no use in producing anything if you gradually reduce the number of people able to buy even the cheapest products. The only way to preserve our markets is to pay an adequate wage.

It seems to me that all fair-minded people will realize that it is self-preservation to treat the industrial worker with consideration and fairness at

Scribner's Magazine 93 (March 1933): 140.

the present time and to uphold the fair employer in his efforts to treat his employees well by preventing unfair competition.

13

Mobilization for Human Needs

The government—state, national and local—has undertaken the responsibility of seeing that people shall not starve. There are, however, things other than food which are necessary to make life worth living. Many agencies have gradually developed in this country because most of us believe we should help each other. Unless we support such agencies now, they will not be able to continue.

The government cannot support all welfare activities. We must try, therefore, to make everybody realize that the help of individuals is needed more now, in spite of the present relief by the government, than it has been for a long time.

For instance, hospitals must have assistance because they must have more free beds than ever before. I know of hospitals that insist on having bills paid or guaranteed before they accept patients even though the applicants are in desperate straits. That to me is perfectly incredible, but it is something that many people have to meet. I have come across the same situation in different parts of the country.

We must drive home to the consciousness of people as one of the reasons why we cannot let our charitable agencies suffer and why we cannot let them go, even though our pocketbooks are slimmer and even though it costs us more to live—the fact that *our country as a whole and each one of us as an individual cannot be secure until we have taken care of our less fortunate brothers and sisters.*

Many people think since they are paying higher taxes they should not be asked again to give charity. They also think they have given all that they can ever give. I cannot help believing, however, that if any of us can bring home to the reluctant contributors what the real needs are in different parts of our country, somehow, everyone will find it possible to give more than before.

The Democratic Digest 8, no. 11 (November 1933): 1.

14

Are We Overlooking the Pursuit of Happiness?

With a committee actually appointed in Congress to consider the efficiency and reorganization of the government's business in Washington, I suppose we may expect a careful survey of all the functions of the federal government departments, and a reclassification to bring into a better grouping such things as are related to each other.

With this in mind, it has long seemed to me that fathers and mothers in this country would be deeply interested in the creation of a department in the Federal Government which dealt directly with the problems touching most closely the homes and the children of the nation.

All government departments touch our homes and our general welfare in one way or another, but certain things very obviously touch more closely than others the daily life of the home. Health, for instance. The Public Health Service does much to cooperate with the various state departments of health and now through the new Social Security Act, we shall be able to do much more than ever before for our handicapped and crippled children, our blind children and for dependent children either living at home with a widowed or deserted mother, or orphaned and living in foster homes or in institutions.

All social welfare measures touch the home very closely. Take the question of old age pensions. This has direct bearing on the employment of youth, for if we take out of the labor market the older people there naturally will be more opportunity for the young. Added to that, many and many a home where young people love their parents has become embittered by the fact that so much had to be given up in order to take care of the old people. I remember a story my mother-in-law used to tell me of an old Scotch farmer who remarked to her that one father and mother could take care of any number of children, but any number of children never could take of one old father and mother!

It is all very well to think that young people are selfish. I have seen them struggle many a time to do what they felt was right for parents, and as their children grew up they wanted to give them opportunities for education or recreation or even provide them with proper food for building healthy bodies for the future, and the drag of the responsibility for the older people became almost more than human nature could stand.

For the old people who have lived so long a life of independence, how bitter it must be to come for everything they need to the youngsters who once turned to them!

The Parents' Magazine 11 (September 1936): 21, 67.

From every point of view, it seems to me that the old age pension for people who so obviously could not lay aside enough during their working years to live on adequately through their old age, is a national responsibility and one that must be faced when we are planning for a better future.

Unemployment insurance in many homes is all that stands between many a family and starvation. Given a breathing spell, a man or woman may be able to get another job or to re-educate himself in some new line of work, but few people live with such a wide margin that they have enough laid aside to face several months of idleness.

Next comes education and we are certainly coming to realize that education is of vital importance. Many of us who have completely accepted the idea that our system of education is perfect in this country have made a mistake in not realizing that nothing in the world is ever perfect and that we should watch and constantly study public education to make it more responsive to the needs of our day.

We must equalize educational opportunities throughout the country. We must see that rural children have as good a general education as city children can acquire, and the advantages of both groups must if possible be made interchangeable. No city child should grow up without knowing the beauty of spring in the country or where milk comes from, how vegetables grow and what it is like to play in a field instead of on a city street. No country child who knows these things should be deprived, however, of museums, books, music and better teachers because it is easier to find them and to pay for them in big cities than it is in rural districts.

With more leisure time, we are discovering that the arts are a necessity in our lives, not only as a method of self-expression, but because of the need for enjoyment and occupation which requires appreciation of many things which we could never hope to understand when we toiled from dawn till dark and had no time for any aspirations.

The arts are no longer a luxury but a necessity to the average human being and they should be included in any department which includes health, social security and education. It seems to me also that crafts and recreation should come under this department.

All these things belong together, they deal with the daily lives of the people.

We are entering a period when there are vast possibilities for the creation of a new way of living. It only requires sufficient imagination and sufficient actual knowledge on the part of all those who are considering this reorganization of government to bring into the government picture today one of the objectives laid down by our forefathers for government, but which seemed in the past too impossible of achievement to receive consideration.

The attainment of life and liberty required most of our energy in the past, so the pursuit of happiness and the consideration of the lives of human beings remained in the background. Now is the time to recognize the possibilities which lie before us in the taking up and developing of this part of our forefathers' vision. Therefore, I hope that the parents in this country will take enough interest in the new reorganization plans to realize that the interests of youth which lie close to their hearts can best be served by a federal department which will include such things as I have suggested and which touch primarily the homes and the youth of America.

15

Keepers of Democracy

Recently a radio broadcast was given, based on a story written by H. G. Wells some years ago, called "War of the Worlds." For the purpose of dramatization it was placed in the United States with the names of regions and people who would naturally be involved if such a thing were to happen today. The basic idea was not changed; these invaders were supernatural beings from another planet who straddled the skyway and dealt in death rays, but it was dramatically done with many realistic touches.

I do not wish to enter into a discussion here as to whether the broadcasting company should do dramatizations of this type, nor do I wish to cast aspersions on people who may not have read the original book. But the results of this broadcast were the best illustration of the state of mind in which we as a nation find ourselves today. A sane people, living in an atmosphere of fearlessness, does not suddenly become hysterical at the threat of invasion, even from more credible sources, let alone by the Martians from another planet, but we have allowed ourselves to be fed on propaganda which has created a fear complex. For the past few years, nearly all of our organizations and many individuals have said something about the necessity for fighting dangerous and subversive elements in our midst.

If you are in the South someone tells you solemnly that all the members of the Committee of Industrial Organization are Communists, or that the Negroes are all Communists. This last statement derives from the fact that, being for the most part unskilled labor, Negroes are more apt to be organized by the Committee for Industrial Organization. In another part of the country someone tells you solemnly that the schools of the country are menaced because they are all under the influence of Jewish teachers and that the Jews, forsooth, are all Communists. And so it goes, until finally you realize that people have reached a point where anything which will save them from Communism is a godsend; and if Fascism or Nazism promises more security than our own democracy we may even turn to them.

It is all as bewildering as our growing hysterical over the invasion of the Martians! Somehow or other I have a feeling that our forefathers, who left their women and children in the wildernesses while they traveled weary miles to buy supplies, and who knew they were leaving them to meet Indians if need be, and to defend themselves as best they could, would expect us to meet present-day dangers with more courage than we seem to have. It is not only physical courage which we need, the kind of physical courage which in the face of danger can at least control the outward evidences of fear. It is moral courage

The Virginia Quarterly Review 15, no. 1 (Winter 1939): 1–5.

as well, the courage which can make up its mind whether it thinks something is right or wrong, make a material or personal sacrifice if necessary, and take the consequences which may come.

I shall always remember someone, it may have been Theodore Roosevelt, saying in my hearing when I was young that when you were afraid to do a thing, that was the time to go and do it. Every time we shirk making up our minds or standing up for a cause in which we believe, we weaken our character and our ability to be fearless. There is a growing wave in this country of fear, and of intolerance which springs from fear. Sometimes it is a religious intolerance, sometimes it is a racial intolerance, but all intolerance grows from the same roots. I can best illustrate this fear by telling you that a short time ago someone told me in all seriousness that the American Youth Congress was a Communist organization and that the World Youth Congress was Communist controlled. This person really believed that the young people who were members of these organizations were attempting to overthrow by force the governments of the countries in which they belonged.

Undoubtedly, in the World Youth Congress there were young Communists, just as there are a group of young Communists and a group of young Socialists in the American Youth Congress, but this does not mean that either of these bodies is Communist controlled. It simply means that they conform to the pattern of society, which at all times has groups thinking over a wide range, from what we call extreme left to extreme right. The general movement of civilization, however, goes on in accordance with the thinking of the majority of the people, and that was exactly what happened in both the American Youth Congress and the World Youth Congress.

The resolutions finally passed by both bodies were rather sane and calm, perhaps a trifle idealistic and certainly very optimistic. There were amendments offered for discussion, and voted down, which many people might have considered radical; but since there is radical thinking among both young and old, it seems to me wiser to discuss and vote down an idea than to ignore it. By so doing we know in which direction the real trend of thought is growing. If we take the attitude that youth, even youth when it belongs to the Communist party, cannot be met on the basis of equal consideration and a willingness to listen, then we are again beginning to allow our fears of this particular group to overwhelm us and we are losing the opportunity to make our experience available and useful to the next generation.

I do not believe that oppression anywhere or injustice which is tolerated by the people of any country toward any group in that country is a healthy influence. I feel that unless we learn to live together as individuals and as groups, and to find ways of settling our difficulties without showing fear of each other and resorting to force, we cannot hope to see our democracy successful. It is an indisputable fact that democracy cannot survive where force and not law is the ultimate court of appeal. Every time we permit force to enter into a situation between employer and employee we have weakened the power of democracy and the confidence which a democratic people must have in their ability to make laws to meet the conditions under which they live, and, when necessary, to change those laws with due political process according to the will of the majority of the people.

When we permit religious prejudice to gain headway in our midst, when we allow one group of people to look down upon another, then we may for a short time bring hardship on some particular group of people, but the real hardship and the real wrong is done to democracy and to our nation as a whole. We are then breeding people who cannot live under a democratic form of government but must be controlled by force. We have but to look out into the world to see how easy it is to become stultified, to accept without protest wrongs done to others, and to shift the burden of decision and of responsibility for any action onto some vague thing called a government or some individual called a leader.

It is true today that democracies are in danger because there are forces opposed to their way of thinking abroad in the world; but more than democracies are at stake. When force becomes so necessary that practically all nations decide that they must engage in a race which will make them able to back up what they have to say with arms and will thus oblige the rest of the world to listen to them, then we face an ultimate Armageddon, unless at the same time an effort to find some other solution is never abandoned.

We in this country may look at it more calmly than the rest of the world, for we can pay for force over a longer period of time; and for a while at least our people will not suffer as much as some of the other nations of the world, but the building up of physical forces is an interminable race. Do you see where it will end unless some strong movement for an ultimate change is afoot?

Someone may say: "But we need only to go on until the men who at present have power in the world and who believe in force are gone." But when in the past has there been a time when such men did not exist? If our civilization is to survive and democracies are to live, then the people of the world as a whole must be stronger than such leaders. That is the way of democracy, that is the only way to a rule of law and order as opposed to a rule of force.

We can read the history of civilization, its ups and its down as they have occurred under the rule of force. Underlying that history is the story of each individual's fears. It seems to me a challenge to women in this period of our civilization to foster democracy and to refuse to fall a prey to fear. Only our young people still seem to have some strength and hope, and apparently we are afraid to give them a helping hand.

Someone said to me the other day that, acknowledging all the weaknesses of human nature, one must still believe in the basic good of humanity or fall into cynicism and the philosophy of old Omar Khayyam. I do still believe that there is within most of us a basic desire to live uprightly and kindly with our neighbors, but I also feel that we are at present in the grip of a wave of fear which threatens to overcome us. I think we need a rude awakening, to make us exert all the strength we have to face facts as they are in our country and in the world, and to make us willing to sacrifice all that we have from the material standpoint in order that freedom and democracy may not perish from this earth.

16

The Moral Basis of Democracy

... I am hoping in this little book to be able to give a clearer definition of the thinking of one citizen in a Democracy. By so doing it may be possible to stimulate the thoughts of many people so that they will force themselves to decide what Democracy means to them—whether they can believe in it as fervently as they can in their personal religion; whether it is worth a sacrifice to them, and what they consider that sacrifice must be.

1

At a time when the whole world is in a turmoil and thousands of people are homeless and hungry, it behooves all of us to reconsider our political and religious beliefs in an effort to clarify in our minds the standards by which we live.

What does Democracy mean to any of us? What do we know of its history? Are there any religious beliefs which are essential to the Democratic way of life?

All of these things have been considered and written about, by many historians. I could not possibly write with as wide a background of historical or philosophical knowledge, but I am hoping in this little book to be able to give a clearer definition of the thinking of one citizen in a Democracy. By so doing it may be possible to stimulate the thoughts of many people so that they will force themselves to decide what Democracy means to them—whether they can believe in it as fervently as they can in their personal religion; whether it is worth a sacrifice to them, and what they consider that sacrifice must be.

Our Democracy in this country has its roots in religious belief, and we had to acknowledge soon after its birth that differences in religious belief are inherent in the spirit of true Democracy. Just because so many beliefs flourished side by side, we were forced to accept the fact that "a belief" was important, but "what belief" was important only to the individual concerned. Later it was accepted that an individual in this land of ours had the right to any religion, or to no religion. The principle, however, of the responsibility of the individual for the well-being of his neighbors which is akin to: "Love thy neighbor as thyself," in the New Testament, seems always to have been a part of the development of the Democratic ideal which has differentiated it from all other forms of government.

Today, as we look at the various philosophies of government under which people live, the totalitarian state makes the individual of little importance.

New York: Howell, Soskin & Co., 1940.

What he means to the state is paramount. Under the Communist ideal the individual again disappears in the group. Under present conditions both theories of government—the Nazi and the Communist—are practically the same. The will of one man, a dictator, seems to become the will of the state, and because people are not considered as individuals, they merge their will into devotion and submission to the force of the state and of the man who is the symbol of power.

This conception of the state emasculates the fundamental idea of self-confidence which arises out of individual liberty and for which men have died. Instead, as in the old days when the serf depended on his master, these new serfs depend on their leaders. They will live well or ill, in proportion to the degree to which they conform to the will of the master. This was equally true of the medieval barons and their serfs.

The Democratic theory of government and of life in a Democracy opposes one-man rule, and holds to the belief that the individual controls his government through active participation in the processes of political Democratic government, but bows to the will of the majority, freely expressed. The motivating force of the theory of a Democratic way of life is still a belief that as individuals we live cooperatively, and, to the best of our ability, serve the community in which we live, and that our own success, to be real, must contribute to the success of others.

I think this belief can be more firmly grounded through a study of the past, and the principles on which we are now charting our future course can be more clearly defined through a better understanding of the development of Democracy in other countries and eventually in our own.

Therefore, very briefly, we will take a look back into the past.

2

Up to the year 1500, there is little or no evidence that anybody gave any thought whatever to the theories of Democracy, but certain basic acts paved the way for the development of practical and theoretical Democracy.

The Magna Carta was the first document drawn up on the theory of Democracy and many of its provisions are now of no more than historical interest. There are, however, many articles which are of continuing importance and current interest. For instance: No taxes shall be imposed except by common counsel. No man shall be imprisoned, exiled or destroyed except by the lawful judgment of his peers or by the law of the land. To no one is right or justice sold or refused. All persons except outlaws or prisoners are free to come and go, free to buy and to sell, except in time of war.

One of the most important provisions in the Magna Carta is that "The English Church shall be free and shall have her rights entire and her liberties inviolate." Many of the articles in it were directed against the abuses of the power of the King and against many grievances which existed because of feudal tenures.

In 1628 a Petition of Rights was signed, and in 1689 a Bill of Rights was signed.

From 1500 to 1700 in Europe, the development was very slow, but the idea of Democracy seemed to be steadily germinating. By 1750 the idea was firmly implanted in the minds of certain radical thinkers—radical, of course, for their period.

The first real growing pains of Democracy might be considered to spring from English oppression, primarily oppression of religious minority groups, which forced certain free-thinkers in England to take refuge first in Holland, which was a tolerant country, but where life was none too easy, and later in the new world across the sea. This land was talked about as the place where one could carve out a future according to new, liberal ideas even though one still owed allegiance to the King of England. These daring and adventurous souls decided to embark upon new careers with no idea of what awaited them.

These Brownists, who later were known as Pilgrims, were only one group of the many people who suffered persecution in Europe in the seventeenth century during the general wave of intolerance that brought about the democratic revolts. In England Catholics had been harassed by Thomas Cromwell, and Protestants by Mary Tudor. From 1629 to 1640 Puritan and Catholic families fled to America, and when the Stuarts were restored in 1660 the exodus was renewed, with such sects as the Quakers joining the emigration.

It is interesting to us, in our study of our *Mayflower* ancestors, to realize what a long way they had to go before they could come to the crystallization of the Democratic theory through the Declaration of Independence and the Bill of Rights.

The first *Mayflower* Contract, signed on the *Mayflower* before the Pilgrims landed in this country, provided: "We, whose names are underwritten, covenant and combine ourselves together into a civil body politic for our better ordering and preservation and furtherance of the ends aforesaid; and to enact, constitute and frame such just and equal laws, ordinances, etc., from time to time as shall be thought most fair and convenient for the general good of the colony to which we promise all due submission and obedience." The interest to me in this first document is the acceptance of self-discipline.

The Fundamental Orders of Connecticut provided that:

> there shall be two yearly general assemblies, one in April and one in September. The first shall be called the Court of Election wherein so many magistrates and other public officers shall be chosen, one to be chosen governor for the ensuing year or until another governor shall be chosen, and always six others beside the governor who shall have the power to administer justice according to the laws here established, and for want thereof, according to the rule of the Word of God. This choice shall be made by all that are admitted freemen and have taken the oath of fidelity and live within this jurisdiction.
>
> Every person present and qualified for choice shall bring in to persons deputed to receive them, one single paper on which is written the name of the

man he desires to have as a governor, and he who has the greatest number of papers shall be governor for that year.

For the others to be elected, the secretary shall read the names and nominate them and everyone shall bring in one single paper with a name written on it, and the one who receives the most written papers, is elected for that year.

No person shall be chosen governor above one in two years, and the governor must be a member of some approved congregation.

The general court in September shall be for making laws and any other public occasion, which concerns the good of the commonwealth.

Each town is impowered to send four freemen as deputies and such deputies shall have power to give their votes to all such laws and orders as may be for the public good and these laws shall bound the towns.

Such deputies shall have the power and liberty to appoint a time and place of meeting together to advise and consult on all such things as may concern the good of the public, to examine their own elections, and if they are found illegal they may be excluded from the meetings. These deputies to have the power to fine any one who was disorderly at the meetings, for not coming in due time.

The General Court to consist of the governor, or someone chosen to moderate the court and four other magistrates at least with the major part of the deputies of the several towns legally chosen. If the governor and the major part of the magistrates refuse or neglect to call a court, it shall consist of the major part of freemen that are present or their deputies with a moderator chosen by them. Said General Court shall have power to make laws, or repeal them, grant levies, admit freemen, dispose of lands, and may deal in any other matter that concerns the good of the commonwealth except election of magistrates which shall be done by the whole body of freemen.

In this court the governor or moderator shall have power to order the court, to give liberty of speech, and silence unreasonable and disorderly speakings, to put all things to vote and in the case of a tie vote, have the casting vote. The courts shall not be adjourned or dissolved without the consent of the major part of the court.

The court may agree on sum or sums of money to be levied on the several towns within its jurisdiction, and a committee chosen to decide what shall be the proportion of every town of the levy, provided the committee be made up of an equal number from each town.

Here we find mentioned for the first time "the rule of the Word of God."

The Fundamental Articles of Rhode Island stated that those who had signed their names, promised to subject themselves in obedience to all orders or agreements which were made for the public good, in an orderly way, by the major consent of the present inhabitants incorporated together into a town fellowship.

This compact in some ways resembles the *Mayflower* Compact, except that in the above, obedience is promised in civil things only, and the term civil is used in contradistinction to ecclesiastical. Obedience is promised in matters pertaining to the state and not to those pertaining to the church.

William Penn's Limited Democratic State was extreme republicanism. He abolished all rules of inheritance, gave all the power to the people to initiate and repeal laws, reserving no veto for himself. All taxes were to be collected by law, the courts were to be open and no oaths required. Penalties were light, capital punishment abolished except for murder (this was remarkable because there were two hundred offenses in the English law which carried the death sentence), prisons were to be workhouses and all children taught a useful trade. All those who professed faith in Jesus Christ were to be eligible to office, and all who confessed an Almighty God were to have free exercise in their worship. In some respects this document was changed, but the one feature to which Penn clung tenaciously was wide religious liberty. The faith in Jesus Christ as here expressed is, I think, the beginning of an idea that this faith would influence the life of the individual and make him better able to meet Penn's standards as a citizen.

Americans led the way in the development of Democracy, and through the first three-quarters of the eighteenth century, certain men developed the thought of the people of this country, and prepared for the Revolutionary War. The Revolutionary War in this country was the first real proof that the theory of Democracy could command the loyalty of a body of citizens and did not require an individual as a ruler to tie the government together.

These "radicals" who prepared for our Revolution were Thomas Paine, Patrick Henry, Samuel Adams and James Otis.

Thomas Paine is, of course, best known for his writings. His pamphlet "Common Sense," arguing for the separation of the American colonies, published in 1776, had a powerful effect. This was the first time the republican doctrines in politics which were inseparable from the individualist trend of the Protestant Reformation in religion had been put down in popular form. He gave practical ideas of representative government, and almost at once the theory upon which our government was to be laid was in every man's mind.

Paine's "The Right of Man," published in parts, the first in 1791, stated the fundamental principles of representative republicanism, in language which everyone could understand, and so cheaply that everyone could read it. The tide of opinion was caught, and "The Rights of Man" made Paine the leader of the republicans in France and the radicals in England.

"The Age of Reason" by Paine contrasts the Bible as absolute truth with the Bible in the light of scientific knowledge and the common sense of the time. It was a break with organized religion, in the train of thought that led to Unitarianism, and to such movements as the Ethical Culture Society. Paine wrote to be read by the people and the people read him. In self-protection the English and American church institutions turned Paine into the Devil himself. This embittered Paine and deprived the Republicans in America of the full use of his great experience and of his talents as a political commentator. Hitler's campaign against the Jews is comparable to the campaign in England against free-thinkers and infidels.

Patrick Henry urged the colonists to go to war on March 20, 1775, at the second convention assembled in Richmond, Virginia, and up to that time no public body or public man had openly spoken of a war with Great Britain. They had admitted that it was highly probable, but not inevitable. He proposed resolutions which were passed.

Samuel Adams was one of the most important men in the work which was done to convince the colonists that they were oppressed. He came into prominence with the passing of the Sugar Act in 1764. From this time almost every state paper in Massachusetts and the initiation of almost every great measure can be traced to him.

James Otis gained public notice by pleading the cause of the Writs of Assistance. His oratory sowed the seeds of the Declaration of Independence and the American Revolution. He was an original political thinker and while he was in imperialist, it was upon natural law as conceived by Otis that the American Revolution was finally defended.

The results of this preparation of American thought flowered in such men as Thomas Jefferson, James Madison, George Mason and the others who helped to write the Declaration of Independence and then to argue for its acceptance as the basis of the establishment of a new type of government.

The Declaration of Independence and the Constitution were documents with completely different purposes. The Declaration of Independence embodies the beliefs in Democracy and the theories of the people of that day. The Constitution grew out of the practical minds of the men who fought the Revolution and who realized that they must consolidate the government of this small group of people, who had decided to be free, into something workable and unified.

The Constitution itself, argued out in the Constitutional Conventions of the day, shows the fears that many men had of Democracy. Many of its provisions tended to safeguard the state from too much power in the hands of the people. This brought about the demand for the Bill of Rights which contains the Amendments to guard the people's idea of Democracy, thus winning the adoption of the Constitution which created a nation.

Jefferson protested loudly against a system of government which gave governors the power to take from the citizens the right to a trial by jury, freedom of religion, freedom of the press, freedom of commerce, the habeas corpus laws. He insisted that the people were entitled to a Bill of Rights against every government on earth.

Patrick Henry said a Bill of Rights "is an indispensable necessity," and a greater necessity in the form of government which was set up in the United States than in any other, if the people wished to keep their inalienable rights.

Purposely the Constitution was left flexible to meet the future needs of the nation. It was recognized by the forward-looking men of that day that these needs would change, and in that they have been proven far-seeing statesmen, for the mere fact that we have been obliged to add amendments to the Constitution from time to time proves that flexibility was necessary.

Benjamin Franklin said about the Constitution:

I confess that there are several parts of this Constitution which I do not at present approve, but I am not sure I shall never approve them; for, having lived long, I have experienced many instances of being obliged by better information or full consideration to change opinions, even on important subjects, which I once thought right but found otherwise.

It is therefore that the older I grow the more apt I am to doubt my own judgment and to pay attention to the judgment of others. Most men, indeed, as well as most sects in religion think themselves in possession of all truth. . . . But though many private persons think almost as highly of their infallibility as of that of their sect, few express it so naturally as a certain French lady who in a dispute with her sister said: "I don't know how it happens sister, but I meet with nobody but myself that's always in the right."

In these sentiments, Sir, I agree to this Constitution with all its faults, if they are such; because I think a general government necessary for us, and there is no form of government but what may be a blessing to the people if well administered; and believe further that this is likely to be well administered for a course of years and can only end in despotism, as other forms have done before it, when the people shall become so corrupt as to need despotic government, being incapable of any other.

I doubt too, whether any other convention we can obtain may be able to make a better Constitution. For when you assemble a number of men to have the advantage of their joint wisdom, you inevitably assemble with those men all their prejudices, their passions, their errors of opinion, their local interests, and their selfish views. From such an assembly can a perfect production be expected? It therefore astonishes me, Sir, to find this system approaching so near to perfection as it does. . . .

Thus I consent, Sir, to this Constitution because I expect no better, and because I am not sure that it is not the best. The opinions I have had of its errors I sacrifice to the public good. I have never whispered a syllable of them abroad. Within these walls they were born, and here they shall die. . . . On the whole, Sir, I can not help expressing a wish that every member of the Convention who may still have objections to it would, with me, on this occasion doubt a little of his infallibility, and, to make manifest our unanimity, put his name to this instrument.

We cannot reread the above often enough, for it holds priceless lessons for us all. Franklin understood human beings, and he knew the extent to which we must all compromise when we come together to formulate plans for the public good.

It was evident, however, that the rights of the individual had to be obtained by continuous vigilance in those days just as the rights can only be maintained today in the same way. So it is interesting to find it stated in James S. Allen's book that Paine, who left for Europe in 1787, before the Constitutional Convention convened and who is considered to be the author of the Declaration of the Rights of Man, issued by the French National Assembly in 1789, succeeded in having incorporated in that document many of the guiding principles of the American Declaration of Independence. Here was a bill of rights such as Jefferson and the American Democrats fought to have included in the American Constitution and which was finally added in the form of the first ten amendments.

Note this "Declaration of the Rights of Man and of Citizen by the National Assembly of France," as given in John Dos Passos' book on Tom Paine.

1. Men are born, and always continue, free and equal in respect to their rights. Civil distinctions, therefore, can be founded only on public utility.
2. The end of all political associations, is, the preservation of the natural and imprescriptible rights of man; and these rights are liberty, property, security and resistance of oppression.
3. The nation is essentially the source of all sovereignty; nor can any individual, or any body of men, be entitled to any authority which is not expressly derived from it.
4. Political liberty consists in the power of doing whatever does not injure another. The exercise of the natural rights of every man has no other limits than those which are necessary to secure to every other man the free exercise of the same rights; and these limits are determinable only by law.
5. The law ought to prohibit only actions hurtful to society. What is not prohibited by the law, should not be hindered; nor should any one be compelled to that which the law does not require.
6. The law is an expression of the will of the community. All citizens have a right to concur, either personally, or by their representatives, in its formation. It should be the same to all, whether it protects or punishes; and all being equal in its sight, are equally eligible to all honors, places and employments, according to their different abilities, without any other distinction than that created by their virtues and talents.
7. No man should be accused, arrested, or held in confinement, except in cases determined by the law, and according to the forms which it has prescribed. All who promote, solicit, execute, or cause to be executed, arbitrary orders, ought to be punished; and every citizen called upon or apprehended by virtue of the law, ought immediately to obey, and renders himself culpable by resistance.

8. The law ought to impose no other penalties but such as are absolutely and evidently necessary; and no one ought to be punished but in virtue of a law promulgated before the offense, and legally applied.

9. Every man being presumed innocent till he has been convicted, whenever this detention becomes indispensable, all rigour to him, more than is necessary to secure his person, ought to be provided against by the law.

10. No man ought to be molested on account of his opinions, not even on account of his religious opinions, provided his avowal of them does not disturb the public order established by the law.

11. The unrestrained communication of thoughts and opinions being one of the most precious rights of man, every citizen may speak, write, and publish freely, provided he is responsible for the abuse of this liberty in cases determined by law.

12. A public force being necessary to give security to the rights of men and citizens, that force is instituted for the benefit of the community, and not for the particular benefit of the persons with whom it is entrusted.

13. A common contribution being necessary for the support of the public force, and for defraying the other expenses of government, it ought to be divided equally among the members of the community, according to their abilities.

14. Every citizen has a right, either by himself or his representative, to a free voice in determining the necessity of public contributions, the appropriation of them, and their amount, mode of assessment and duration.

15. Every community has a right to demand of all its agents, an account of their conduct.

16. Every community in which a separation of powers and a security of rights is not provided for, wants a constitution.

17. The rights of property being inviolable and sacred, no one ought to be deprived of it, except in cases of evident public necessity, legally ascertained, and on condition of a previous just indemnity.

An Englishman, Francis W. Hirst, in his "Life and Letters of Thomas Jefferson," quotes a passage which shows Jefferson's appreciation of the part Tom Paine played in preparing our people for Democracy. Jefferson wrote:

> The soil for the seed of independence ... was sown broadcast by Tom Paine's "Common Sense," one of the most powerful and influential pamphlets ever published in the English language. It appeared on January 10, 1776 ... "Common Sense" ran like wildfire through the Colonies. It shattered the King's cause by setting forth in simple language the virtues of Democracy, the utility of independence, and the absurdity of submitting to the arbitrary rule of an hereditary tyrant. To the conservative and slow-moving mind of Washington its doctrine seemed "sound" and its reasoning "unanswerable." Within three months 120,000 copies had passed into circulation, and the lingering doubts of many plain peaceable folk reluctant to break with Britain were dispelled.

France sent men over to participate in our Revolution primarily, of course, because of her antagonism to England, but among those who came were men who, like Lafayette, were fighting for the theory of Democracy. The French Revolution which followed ours may have gained impetus because of our example. After the French Revolution in 1789, the calling of the Estates General in France is the first instance of universal manhood suffrage.

3

Under our Constitution, the union established was really a republic with a representative form of government and a series of checks and balances to control the various arms of government as well as the people of the country.

While the Revolution was produced by the agitation of Paine, Otis, Adams, and others, the first individuals who came to power under our republican form of government were Washington, Hamilton, John Adams, John Jay—all of them conservatives, well rooted in English traditions.

With the arrival in power of the radicals, the reform group headed by Jefferson, Madison, Duane, and others, we find a change in the theory of our republican form of government and the crystallization and stabilization of some of the beliefs of what political Democracy must eventually recognize.

Jefferson believed in the honesty and ability of the average man, regardless of his social position, education, wealth and other opportunities. Jefferson's position is explicitly stated in the second paragraph of the Declaration of Independence:

> We hold these truths to be self-evident, that all men are created equal; that they are endowed by their Creator with certain inalienable rights; that among these are life, liberty and the pursuit of happiness.

Jefferson believed in the education of all classes, and a government with a minimum of power that would not infringe too much on the independence and liberty of a free and active individual. He was for the freeing of the slaves.

In Jefferson's beliefs we get the clearest statements for his day of a true understanding of human beings. He wanted no slaves because he realized that slavery was the denial of the equality of man. It meant that if we denied equality to any man we lost the basis of Democracy. If we are honest with ourselves today, we will acknowledge that the ideal of Democracy has never failed, but that we haven't carried it out, and in our lack of faith we have debased the human being who must have a chance to live if Democracy is to be successful.

The slave is still with us, but his color is not always black, and I think we will also have to acknowledge that most of our difficulties arise today from the fact that in the rush of material development we have neglected to keep close enough to the Revolutionary idea, guided by religious feeling, which is the basis of Democracy. We have undertaken, under our form of government, to carry out the ideal which can exist only if we accept the brotherhood of man as a basic truth in human society.

We may belong to any religion or to none, but we must acknowledge that the life of Christ was based on principles which are necessary to the development of a Democratic state. We accept that fact and measure every undertaking by that rule. But, it is easy to understand where our difficulties lie today. Even Thomas Paine said: "The rights of property being inviolate and sacred, no one ought to be deprived of it, except in cases of evident public necessity, legally ascertained, and on condition of a previous just indemnity."

Our present situation, our present difficulties arise from the fact that in the development of civilization we have neglected to remember that the rights of all people to some property are inviolate. We have allowed a situation to arise where many people are debased by poverty or the accident of race, in our own country, and therefore have no stake in Democracy; while others appeal to this old rule of the sacredness of property rights to retain in the hands of a limited number the fruits of the labor of many.

We have never been willing to face this problem, to line it up with the basic, underlying beliefs in Democracy and to set our actions side by side with the actual example of the Christ-like way of living.

Thus, within our nation there are many who do not understand the values of Democracy, and we have been unable to spread these values throughout the world, because as a people we have been led by the gods of Mammon from the spiritual concepts and from the practical carrying-out of those concepts conceived for our nation as a truly free and democratic people.

4

What are our problems today?

I have reviewed the past and pointed out the association of a Christ-like life to the Democratic ideal of government, inaugurated to produce a Democratic way of life.

Now, let us look at our country as it is today and see if, from this examination, we can get a better understanding of some of our problems, and some of the decisions which we have got to make in the near future.

First of all we are a great nation of 130,000,000 people. We cover about three million, seven hundred thousand square miles, including our outlying dependencies such as the Philippines, Puerto Rico, the Virgin Islands, etc. Our people stem from every nation in the world. We include Orientals, Negroes, Europeans, Latin Americans. We are in truth the melting pot of the world. Our solidarity and unity can never be a geographical unity or a racial unity. It must be a unity growing out of a common idea and a devotion to that idea.

Our national income last year, 1939, was $69,378,000,000. It went down as low as $40,074,000,000 in 1932 in contrast with the peak in 1929, which was $82,885,000,000.

We are slowly climbing out of the economic morass we fell into, but so long as we have the number of unemployed on our hands which we have today, we can be sure that our economic troubles are not over and that we have not found the permanent solution to our problem.

There is going to be almost an entire continent of vast natural resources under the direction of an opposing philosophy to ours, and an opposing economic system. Either we must make our economic system work to the satisfaction of all of our people, or we are going to find it extremely difficult to compete against the one which will be set upon on the Continent of Europe.

We hear a good deal of loose talk about going to war. As a matter of fact we are already in a war—an economic war and a war of philosophies. We are opposing a force which, under the rule of one man, completely organizes all business and all individuals and takes no chances except with such uncontrollable phenomena as weather, fire, flood or earthquake. This one man in Europe has no limit on what he can spend for the things he desires to bring about. If he wants quantities of armament, he simply goes ahead and has quantities of armament. His nation has functioned on an internal currency. When he has need for things from outside, he has obtained them by barter of his manufactured goods or by simply taking the gold which he needed to buy goods from other nations, from those who happen to have it in his own country or from some other country that he decided to take over.

His people receive the wages *he* decrees, they work the hours *he* decrees, they wear the clothes *he* allows them to wear, they eat the food *he* allows them to have. They go away or do not go away for vacations according to his caprice, and they take no vacations outside of their own country without his permission, and even when a visit outside their own country is permitted, they can take only a specified sum of money with them.

An effort to set up similar conditions is quite evidently being made in Japan in the Far East. Our entire continent must be aroused to what it will mean if these ideas are successful. Our Democracies must realize that from the point of view of the individual and his liberty, there is no hope in the future if the totalitarian philosophy becomes dominant in the world.

Here, in this country, it seems to me that as the strongest nation in the battle today, we have to take an account of just what our condition is; how much Democracy we have and how much we want to have.

It is often said that we are free, and then sneeringly it is added: "free to starve if we wish." In some parts of our country that is not idle jest. Moreover, no one can honestly claim that either the Indians or the Negroes of this country are free. These are obvious examples of conditions which are not compatible with the theory of Democracy. We have poverty which enslaves, and racial prejudice which does the same. There are other racial and religious groups among us who labor under certain discriminations, not quite so difficult as those we impose on the Negroes and the Indians, but still sufficient to show we do not completely practice the Democratic way of life.

It is quite obvious that we do not practice a Christ-like way of living in our relationship to submerged people, and here again we see that a kind of religion which gives us a sense of obligation about living with a deeper interest in the welfare of our neighbors is an essential to the success of Democracy.

5

We are, of course, going through a type of revolution and we are succeeding in bringing about a greater sense of social responsibility in the people as a whole. Through the recognition by our government of a responsibility for social conditions much has been accomplished; but there is still much to be done before we are even prepared to accept some of the fundamental facts which will make it possible to fight as a unified nation against the new philosophies arrayed in opposition to Democracy.

It would seem clear that in a Democracy a minimum standard of security must at least be possible for every child in order to achieve the equality of opportunity which is one of the basic principles set forth as a fundamental of Democracy. This means achieving an economic level below which no one is permitted to fall, and keeping a fairly stable balance between that level and the cost of living. No one as yet seems to know just how to do this without an amount of planning which will be considered too restrictive for freedom. The line between domination and voluntary acquiescence in certain controls is a very difficult one to establish. Yet it is essential in a Democracy.

For a number of years we seemed to be progressing toward a condition in which war as a method of settling international difficulties might be eliminated, but with the rise of an opposing philosophy of force, this has become one of our main problems today. It brings before us the question of whether under the Democratic theory we can be efficient enough to meet the growing force of totalitarianism with its efficient organization for aggression.

This question is of special interest to youth, and added to the question of unemployment, it creates for them the main problem of existence.

The youth which is coming of age in our country today is living under a government which is attempting to meet a great many internal problems in new ways, and with methods never before tried. These ways are questioned by a great many people; but few people question the fact that the problems are with us and must be faced.

Youth seems to be more conscious than anyone else of the restrictions of opportunity which have come with our form of civilization. Some of these restrictions may be due to the development of the nation to a degree which leaves few physical frontiers to master; some of them may be due to a lack of social development, to a system which hasn't kept pace with the machine and made it possible to use advantageously more leisure time. Such malfunctioning makes it impossible to lessen the burden of labor without curtailing the volume of work, so that many people are left with nothing to do, and therefore without the wherewithal for living.

Nowhere in the world today has government solved these questions. Therefore, as their elders leave the stage, it remains for youth to find a way to face the domestic situation, to meet the conditions which confront their country in this relationship with the other countries of the world.

It is not enough to adopt the philosophies and methods which have appeared in other countries. These difficulties have been met elsewhere by deciding that one man who orders the lives of great numbers of people can best arrange for the equable distribution of the necessities of life. From the point of view of our Democratic philosophy and our belief in the welfare of the individual this has fatal drawbacks.

Youth must make a decision. It will have to decide whether religion, the spirit of social cooperation, is necessary to the development of a Democratic form of government and to the relationship which human beings must develop if they are to live happily together. If it is, youth will have to devise some means of bringing it more closely to the hearts and to the daily lives of everyone.

It is not entirely the fault of any of the churches, or of any of the various religious denominations that so many people, who call themselves Catholic, Protestant or Jew, behave as though religion were something shut up in one compartment of their lives. It seems to have no effect on their actions or their growth or on their relationship to their surroundings and activities.

Leaders of religious thought have tried for generations to make us understand that religion is a way of life which develops the spirit. Perhaps, because of the circumstances which face us today, the youth of this generation may make this type of religion a reality. I think they might thus develop for the future of this country and of the world a conception of success which will change our whole attitude toward life and civilization.

6

Youth wishes to do away with war. But youth and the men and women of Democracy will have to set their own house in order first, and show that they have something to offer under a Democratic form of government which is not offered by any other philosophy or any other theory of government.

It will be an exciting new world if it is created on these principles. It will not mean that great changes take place overnight, because people have been born for generations under conditions which it will take generations to change; but a new concept held by the youth of today as a basic meaning of Democracy, and its foundations in a religion, which shows itself in actual ways of life, will, I think, change the future generations.

We cannot expect, of course, that any development will go on without some setbacks, and we are at present in one of the most serious of retrogressions. If any of the young people of 1917 and 1918 could return to us today they would undoubtedly feel that the sacrifice of their lives had been valueless. Yet, I have a feeling that perhaps in the long run that sacrifice will be the one thing that will drive the young generation of today into doing something which will permanently change the future. They know that a gesture of self-sacrifice is not enough; that they cannot in one war change the basic things which have produced wars. They know that they must begin with human beings and keep on, each in his or her own particular sphere of influence, building up a social conscience and a sense of responsibility for their neighbors. They have begun to build bridges between the youth of their own nation and the youth of other nations. These bridges may be stronger because of the fiery trials so many young people are going through today. The value of human liberty may have a more tangible meaning to the next generation than it has in the present because for so many human beings it has temporarily disappeared.

The challenge of today is, I think, the greatest challenge that youth has faced in many generations. The future of Democracy in this country lies with them, and the future of Democracy in the world lies with them as well. The development of a dynamic Democracy which is alive and actively working for the benefit of all individuals, and not just a few, depends, I think, on the realization that this form of government is not a method devised to keep some particular group that is stronger than other groups in power. It is a method of government conceived for the development of human beings as a whole.

The citizens of a Democracy must model themselves on the best and most unselfish life we have known in history. They may not all believe in Christ's divinity, though many will; but His life is important simply because it becomes a shining beacon of what success means. If we once establish this human standard as a measure of success, the future of Democracy is secure.

7

The war-ridden, poverty-stricken world of today seems to be struggling essentially with problems of economics and its ills seem to be primarily materialistic. Yet, I believe that we do not begin to approach a solution of our problems until we acknowledge the fact that they are spiritual and that they necessitate a change in the attitude of human beings to one another.

War is the result of spiritual poverty. People say that war is the cause of a great many of our troubles; but in the first analysis it is the fact that human beings have not developed the ability to rise above purely selfish interest which brings about war. Then war intensifies all of our social problems and leaves us groping for the answers.

As we look at France today we realize that her plight is partly due to the fact that some of her people actually believed that the Communists were more of a menace than the Fascists. Both were an equal menace, for their hold on the people comes from the same sources—discontent and insecurity. The people who were comfortably off never looked below the surface in France to find out why the Communists could get such a hold on the imagination of people in a country which has supposedly so much liberty and equality.

Some people say salvation can come only through a form of selfish interest which brings about the realization by those who have their share of the good things of life, that nothing which they have in a material sense will be preserved unless they share it with those less fortunate; that some charitable way will be found to distribute more equably the things which the people as a whole lack. This would be a reaction to fear, of course, and it does not seem to me a final answer.

Somehow or other, human beings must get a feeling that there is in life a spring, a spring which flows for all humanity, perhaps like the old legendary spring from which men drew eternal youth. This spring must fortify the soul and give people a vital reason for wanting to meet the problems of the world today, and to meet them in a way which will make life more worth living for everyone. It must be a source of social inspiration and faith.

It is quite true, perhaps, that "Whom the Lord loveth, He chasteneth"; but nowhere is it said that individual human beings shall chasten each other, and it seems to me that all of us are sufficiently chastened by the things which are beyond our power to change. We can do nothing about death, or physical disabilities which science does not understand and cannot therefore remedy; nor can we help the maladjustments of various kinds which lie in the personality and not in the physical surroundings of the individual.

So the chastening will come to us all, rich and poor alike. But hunger and thirst, lack of decent shelter, lack of certain minimum decencies of life, can be eliminated if the spirit of good will is awakened in every human being.

8

I am not writing a political thesis, otherwise I might explain how we have been groping for a way during the past few years, to achieve some of these ends through government. In this little book, however, I am trying to go a little bit deeper and point out that court decisions, and laws and government administration are only the results of the way people progress inwardly, and that the basis of success in a Democracy is really laid down by the people. It will progress only as their own personal development goes forward.

When I have occasionally said to people that perhaps some of us had too much of this world's goods, and that we are thereby separated too widely from each other and unable to understand the daily problems of people in more limited circumstances, I have often been met by the argument that these more privileged people are the ones who open up possibilities and new vistas for others. They are the people, I am told, who because of greater leisure have developed an appreciation of art; they build art galleries and museums, and give to other people an opportunity to enjoy them. They are the people who could envision the possibilities of scientific research, thereby building up great research laboratories where students make discoveries which increase our knowledge along so many lines. They are the people who create foundations which help the unfortunates of the world. All this is true, and we must be grateful for it, but perhaps it is time to take a new step in the progress of humanity.

I wonder if part of our education does not still lie before us and if we should not think of educating every individual to the need of making a contribution for these purposes which have been recognized only by a small group in the past as their contribution to society. The development of art, science, and literature for the benefit of our country as a whole is a concern of the whole country, not of a privileged few. I wonder if the support for these things should not come through an infinite number of small gifts rather than through a few great ones.

I recognize the fact that this development is slow and in some ways may be a question of years of evolution, particularly until we approach the better understanding of people of different races and different creeds. This country is perhaps the best example, however, of the fact that all people can learn to live side by side. We have here representatives of almost every nation and almost every religious belief.

There have been times when waves of bigotry and intolerance have swept over us. There is still a lack of true appreciation of the contributions made by some of these nations to the development of our culture, but the fact remains that, by and large, we live happily and understandingly together and gradually amalgamate until it is hard to distinguish what was once a separate nationality and what is today entirely a product of the United States of America.

This should give us courage to realize that there can be a real development of understanding among human beings, though it may take a great many years before there is sufficient change throughout the world to eliminate some of the dangers which we now face daily. There must be a beginning to all things and it seems to me the beginning for a better world understanding might well be made right here. Our natural resources are very great, and are still far from being fully developed. Our population is mixed and we are still young enough to be responsive to new ideas and to make changes fairly easily.

Some people feel that human nature cannot be changed, but I think when we look at what has been achieved by the Nazi and Fascist dictators we have to acknowledge the fact that we do not live in a static condition, but that the influences of education, of moral and physical training have an effect upon our whole beings. If human beings can be changed to fit a Nazi or Fascist pattern or a Communist pattern, certainly we should not lose heart at the thought of changing human nature to fit a Democratic way of life.

9

People say that the churches have lost their hold and that therein is found one of our greatest difficulties. Perhaps they have, but if that is true, it is because the churches have thought about the churches and not about religion as a need for men to live by. Each man may have his own religion; the church is merely the outward and visible symbol of the longing of the human soul for something to which he can aspire and which he desires beyond his own strength to achieve.

85

If human beings can be trained for cruelty and greed and a belief in power which comes through hate and fear and force, certainly we can train equally well for gentleness and mercy and the power of love which comes because of the strength of the good qualities to be found in the soul of every individual human being.

While force is abroad in the world we may have to use that weapon of force, but if we develop the fundamental beliefs and desires which make us considerate of the weak and truly anxious to see a Christ-like spirit on earth, we will have educated ourselves for Democracy in much the same way that others have gone about educating people for other purposes. We will have established something permanent because it has as its foundation a desire to sacrifice for the good of others, a trait which has survived in some human beings in one form or another since the world began.

We live under a Democracy, under a form of government which above all other forms should make us conscious of the need we all have for this spiritual, moral awakening. It is not something which must necessarily come through any one religious belief, or through people who go regularly to church and proclaim themselves as members of this or that denomination. We may belong to any denomination, we may be strict observers of certain church customs or we may be neglectful of forms, but the fundamental thing which we must all have is the spiritual force which the life of Christ exemplifies. We might well find it in the life of Buddha, but as long as it translates itself into something tangible in aspirations for ourselves and love for our neighbors, we should be content; for then we know that human nature is struggling toward an ideal.

Real Democracy cannot be stable and it cannot go forward to its fullest development and growth if this type of individual responsibility does not exist, not only in the leaders but in the people as a whole.

It is vitally important in the leaders because they are articulate. They should translate their aspirations and the means by which they wish to reach them, into clear words for other people to understand. In the past I think they have never dared to voice all their dreams, they have never dared to tell all the people their hopes because of the fear that the people would not be able to see the same vision. Unless there is understanding behind a leader, and a compelling desire on the part of the people to go on, he must fail.

This Democratic experiment of ours is in its infancy; in fact, real Democracy has never been realized, because it involves too much individual responsibility, and we have been slow to accept it.

Democracy does not imply, of course, that each and every individual shall achieve the same status in life, either materially or spiritually; that is not reasonable because we are limited by the gifts with which we enter this world. It does mean, however, that each individual should have the chance, because of the standards we have set, for good health, equal education and equal opportunity to achieve success according to his powers; and this opportunity should exist in whatever line of work, either of hand or head, he may choose to engage in. It also means that through self-government each individual should carry his full responsibility; otherwise the Democracy cannot be well balanced and represent the whole people.

I think that our estimate of success is going to change somewhat and that the man or woman who achieves a place in the community through service to the community will be considered a more successful individual than anyone who gains wealth or power which benefits himself alone. Changing the standards of success is going to mean more to the future of youth than anything else we can do, so perhaps this is the time for us to consider what is the future of youth.

10

There are two questions which young people in our country have to face. What are we prepared to sacrifice in order to retain the Democratic form of government?

What do we gain if we retain this form of government?

Let us consider first the sacrifices that we make in a real Democracy. Our basic sacrifice is the privilege of thinking and working for ourselves alone. From time immemorial the attitude of the individual has been one of selfishness. As civilization has advanced people have thought of their families, and finally of a group of people like themselves; but down in our hearts it has always been the interest which you and I had in ourselves primarily which has motivated us.

If we are able to have genuine Democracy we are going to think primarily of the rights and privileges and the good that may come to the people of a great nation. This does not mean, of course, that we are going to find everyone in agreement with us in what we think is for the good of the majority of the people; but it does mean that we will be willing to submit our ideas to the test of what the majority wishes.

That is a big sacrifice for Democracy. It means that we no longer hold the fruits of our labors as our own, but consider them in the light of a trusteeship. Just as the labor itself must be put into avenues which may no longer be bringing us what at one time we considered as satisfactory returns, but which are serving some socially useful purpose in the community in which we live.

This does not mean that we will work any less hard. It does not mean that we will use less initiative or put less preparation into the field of work in which we are entering. It does mean, however, that we will execute to the best of our ability every piece of work which we undertake and give our efforts to such things as seem to us to serve the purposes of the greatest number of people.

The second sacrifice which we make for Democracy is to give to our government an interested and intelligent participation. For instance, if a city, town or county meeting is called, we will not find something more interesting or attractive to do that evening. We will go to the meeting, take part in it and try to understand what the questions and issues are. Thus we start the machinery of Democracy working from the lowest rung upward.

We often make the mistake of believing that what happens at the bottom makes no difference. As a matter of fact, it is what we do at the bottom which decides what eventually happens at the top. If all the way down the line every able-bodied citizen attended to his duties, went to the community meetings, tried to find out about the people who were going to hold office, knew the questions that came before them, there would be a radical change in the quality of people who take active part in political work.

We must have party machinery because there must be people who attend to such things as calling meetings, sending out notices, going from door to door to distribute literature or bring the issues to the voters before Election Day. These issues can be presented in many different ways, according to the understanding and the feeling of the people who present them. It would not be so difficult to find people to run for office if we knew that the citizens as a whole were going to know something about them and their ideas, and were going to vote not on a traditional basis, but according to their actual knowledge of the questions at stake and the personalities of the candidates. There would be less opportunity for calumny, for unfairness, and for the acceptance of untrue statements if, every step of the way, each individual took his responsibility seriously and actually did his job as a citizen in a Democracy.

There is no reward for this kind of citizenship except the reward of feeling that we really have a government which in every way represents the best thought of all the citizens involved. In such a Democracy a man will hold office not because it brings certain honors and considerations from his constituents, but because he has an obligation to perform a service to Democracy.

Perhaps the greatest sacrifice of all is the necessity which Democracy imposes on every individual to make himself decide in what he believes. If we believe in Democracy and that it is based on the possibility of a Christ-like way of life, then everybody must force himself to think through his own basic philosophy, his own willingness to live up to it and to help carry it out in everyday living.

The great majority of people accept religious dogmas handed to them by their parents without very much feeling of having a personal obligation to clarify their creed for themselves. But, if from our religion, whatever it may be, we are impelled to work out a way of life which leads to the support of a Democratic form of government, then we have a problem we cannot escape: we must know what we believe in, how we intend to live, and what we are doing for our neighbors.

Our neighbors, of course, do not include only the people whom we know; they include, also, all those who live anywhere within the range of our knowledge. That means an obligation to the coal miners and share-croppers, the migratory workers, to the tenement-house dwellers and the farmers who cannot make a living. It opens endless vistas of work to acquire knowledge and, when we have acquired it in our own country, there is still the rest of the world to study before we know what our course of action should be.

Again a sacrifice in time and thought, but a factor in a truly Democratic way of life.

Few members of the older generations have even attempted to make themselves the kind of people who are really worthy of the power which is vested in the individual in a Democracy. We must fulfill our duties as citizens, see that our nation is truly represented by its government, see that the government is responsive to the will and desires of the people. We must make that will and desire of the people the result of adequate education and adequate material security. We must maintain a standard of living which makes it possible for the people really to want justice for all, rather than to harbor a secret hope for privileges because they cannot hope for justice.

If we accomplish this, we have paved the way for the first hope for real peace the world has ever known. All people desire peace, but they are led to war because what is offered them in this world seems to be unjust, and they are constantly seeking a way to right that injustice.

These are the sacrifices future generations will be called upon to make for a permanent Democracy which has a background of spiritual belief.

11

And now, what do we gain from Democracy?

The greatest gain, perhaps, is a sense of brotherhood, a sense that we strive together toward a common objective.

I have sat with groups of people who for a few short minutes were united by the ideas and aspirations that had been presented to them by leaders able to express their vision or their dreams.

Those few minutes have made clear to me the possibility of strength that someday might lie in a moral feeling of unity brought about by a true sense of brotherhood.

By achieving improvement in our own small sphere, we would gain, too, a tremendous satisfaction in realizing that we were actively participating in whatever happens in the world as a whole. The decisions at the top would be ours, because, in the first place, we had started choosing our men at the bottom and had thus brought about a real representation at the top. The new world which we conceived could become a reality, for these men, the leaders, would share the vision of the people.

It would be no Utopia, for the gains made by Democracy, which are the gains made by human beings over themselves, are never static. We fight for them and have to keep on fighting. The gains are slow and won in day by day effort. There is no chance for boredom or indifference because of a lack of further heights to climb. In such a society the heights are always before one, and the dread of slipping backward ever present.

One of the gains of Democracy would be that constant sense of vigilance and alertness which makes of life an adventure and gives it a continuous appeal. We cannot remove sorrow and disappointment from the lives of human beings, but we can give them an opportunity to free themselves from mass restrictions made by man.

There is nothing more exciting in the world than to be conscious of inwardly achieving something new; and anyone who puts into practice the life of Christ on earth, cannot fail to feel the growth in his own mastery over self. Under the Democracy based on such a religious impulse, there would still, of course, be leaders, and there would still be people of initiative interested and prodding other people to attempt the development of new ideas, or to participate in new enjoyments which they had not before understood or experienced.

Under such a Democracy the living standard of all the people would be gradually rising. That is what the youth of the next generation will be primarily interested in achieving, because that is the vital gain in Democracy for the future, if we base it on the Christian way of life as lived by the Christ.

17

Insuring Democracy

I do not think that I am a natural-born mother. I had dolls as a little girl, but I cannot remember being concerned about them, and even though I was some years older than my little brothers, and of necessity had to take a certain amount of responsibility about them, I do not think I ever did it with the maternal affection which is seen in some small girls.

I did have a sense of duty and of obligation and that was fostered in me by my mother and then by my grandmother. If I ever wanted to mother anyone, it was my father and not my baby brothers. That sense of obligation to smaller and weaker children remained with me through my school years and gained great impetus through my first year of teaching some classes of small girls in a New York City settlement house. There I saw with my own eyes some of the disadvantages of conditions brought about by economic insecurity.

I think I approached my own motherhood with a keen sense of responsibility but very little sense of the joy which should come with having babies. It was a long time before I gained enough confidence in my own judgment really to enjoy a child. I do not know that even today I have it, but the old sense of responsibility is still with me. I never felt, even as a young woman when I did nothing outside and put all my energies into having children and keeping house, that I was right about my plans for bringing up my children. I often wonder today why I have been so fortunate to have some of the children develop a sense of respect and friendship for me, because I administered discipline not because I wanted to, but because of the convictions of others, and my love was always overshadowed by my duty. I enforced certain rules, I lived up to certain habits in the family and only rarely departed from the strict supervision and suggestion of others.

I remember that it took all of my courage, and the fact that everybody else in the house had the flu, to trust myself to move the youngest of our five children into my own bedroom and take complete responsibility for him when he had an attack of bronchial pneumonia. I could get only one trained nurse and she had complete care of one of the other children who had double pneumonia. Practically everybody in the city and in the house was laid low, and so I had to rise to the occasion, otherwise I doubt if I would have felt like trusting myself to carrying that amount of responsibility without direction from others close at hand all the time!

But all children, it seems to me, have a right to food, shelter, and equal opportunity for education and an equal chance to come into the world healthy

Collier's 105 (June 15, 1940): 70, 87–88.

and get the care they need through their early years to keep them well and happy. And though one may not trust oneself to direct their lives, every mother should encourage them to self-confidence and should give them the feeling that whatever happens in life, there is a place where they can turn for understanding and help.

If you have this feeling about your own children, you should have it about all children, and for that reason I have always been interested in the problems of the children in our communities. Under the standards which we have set to guide us in the upbringing of our children, we used to be very individualistic, with, however, certain strongly marked influences such as those of the church, and group traditions in which we had grown up. For instance, in New England the customs of the Pilgrims shaped the child's education, just as later the Quakers had a great deal to do with the character and upbringing of the young Philadelphians.

To Make Better Citizens

Thirty years ago the President of the United States felt that we needed to bring together, to formulate standards for our guidance, the people who had some influence on the general thought of what should be done for the children of the nation. This became the first White House Conference on Children under President Theodore Roosevelt. Since then there have been three others—1919, 1930 and 1940.

As Miss Katharine Lenroot, of the Children's Bureau in the Department of Labor, says:

> The 1909 conference called by President Theodore Roosevelt stated a principle that is now recognized in all parts of the country: that the home is the place for children and that no child should be deprived of his home for reasons of poverty alone. The stimulus of this conference led to the creation of the Federal Children's Bureau in 1912, a national center of research to serve the growing child-welfare movement.
>
> The 1919 conference called under President Woodrow Wilson's auspices formulated a set of child-welfare standards that have guided and still guide the programs of public and private children's agencies and state and federal legislation affecting children.
>
> The 1930 White House Conference on Child Health and Protection called by President Herbert Hoover brought together an outstanding series of reports describing the content and character of care and protection needed for children and revealed the limited extent to which such services were available for many children. The findings on medical care raised to a new level the recognition of the care needed for the health of mothers and children in the United States. The committee reports on hazardous occupations for minors laid the groundwork for the later regulation of the employment of minors in hazardous occupations under the Fair Labor Standard Act of 1938. The discussion throughout the country of the Children's Charter and other conference

recommendations helped to pave the way for the inclusion in the Social Security Act of 1935 of the federal-state programs for aid to dependent children, for maternal and child-health services, for services for crippled children and for child-welfare services, and for the subsequent development of these programs in our states and territories.

The standards set up in these conferences are very much the same standards that any able and intelligent parent will set for himself in contemplating the upbringing of his own family. First we consider the health program, which brings us to the question of maternity and infancy care. As a result of the conference in 1919, the Sheppard-Towner Act was passed in August, 1921. It brought before the people statistics on the shocking loss of mothers and of infants during the first year after birth. The right of children to normal family life received recognition, and today mothers' pensions keep families together even in the face of economic disaster through the loss of fathers or the impairment of their earning capacity. In turn, we came to consider education and recreation. Today we are considering the more difficult question of the right of youth to work, and last and most difficult of all, though most important, we are considering the moral values which our children must acquire if they are to feel a sense of responsibility for themselves and their neighbors, and so develop the type of democracy which they have inherited into a more perfect instrument of self-government.

Again in Miss Lenroot's words: "The 1940 conference has counted the gains made for children even during the years of economic depression and has planned, for the coming ten years, that we seek to provide for children in every community in the United States the essential services and benefits for the preparation of responsible citizens of a democracy. The conference emphasized the fact that the family has the primary opportunity and responsibility for the care of children and for introducing them to the experiences that lead to a full personal life and to successful community life. The report recognized the economic and social factors that condition family and community life. It points out the gains that can be made for children through joint planning and effort on the part of individuals and groups in each community, through the leadership of state agencies, and through federal action that provides for nationwide programs."

Making the Most of Their Dollars

The people who attended the conference and who listened to the President's speech can go back to their own communities, influence public opinion and demand:

1. Some kind of medical program.
2. That all our citizens take an active part in shaping the policies in the public schools; that all of us know our public-school teachers and give them any help and assistance that they desire.

3. That all of us take an interest in recreation programs designed not only to be of value to children in school, but to help our young people who are unfortunate enough not to find suitable jobs immediately.
4. That in every community we set up, in conjunction with the nearest employment service, an auxiliary to help young people to obtain the most suitable jobs.

This last year we have come to realize that instead of thinking only of what should be done for the mother in pregnancy and at the birth of her child, we should find out what economic situation forced the mother and child at these crucial moments to be a burden on the community. Instead of being concerned with obtaining proper diets for small children through charitable agencies, we should be concerned with the education of the average girl and boy so they will make the most of their dollars, to learn through practical experience how to make use of food in order to keep well.

If we relate the immediate problems of the child to the problems of the family as a whole, we will find ourselves concerned with housing, medical and dental care, education and recreation. We will be interested in wages and hours for labor, and we will try to figure out an adequate family income.

We are beginning to realize that what the family can do must be supplemented by what the community can do for its children. Population and income studies show that in many cases the ability of a community to supplement the family income and to contribute to a child's well-being is particularly low in the areas where we have the greatest number of children.

Where the local income falls short I think the state or even the nation should be called upon to make this equality of basic rights applicable to every child.

A Menace to All Workers

We are learning that rural slums may be quite as bad as city slums. We are learning that it is not because of the adult members of the family alone that we must do away with these slums. The children born and brought up in them are apt to be conditioned for the future by their earliest environment. What happens to our children is the concern of the whole nation because a democracy requires a standard of citizenship which no other form of government finds necessary. To be a citizen in a democracy a human being must be given a healthy start. He must have adequate food for physical growth and proper surroundings for mental and spiritual development. Under a dictatorship it may be sufficient to learn to read and write and to do certain things by rote, but in a democracy we must learn to reason and to think for ourselves. We must make our decisions on the basis of knowledge and reasoning power. In a democracy we must be able to visualize the life of the whole nation. When we vote for candidates for public office to be our representatives, we must decide on the qualities to be required of the men and women who are to hold public offices.

These men will not only decide what shall be done for us in the present day, but they will be laying the foundations on which our children will have to build.

Poor schools in our communities today mean poor citizens in these communities in a few years—men and women ill-prepared to earn a living, or to participate in government. A three-months school year in certain communities certainly does not give a child the same advantage he would have with a nine-months school year in another community.

One minority group of American children that I feel deserves particular attention are about five million Negroes, Indians, Mexicans and Orientals under sixteen years of age. They have all the handicaps of other children with the addition of a number of special handicaps of their own. Their families are usually in the lowest income groups and the restrictions put upon the opportunities offered them for health, for education, for recreation and later for employment, are very great because of prejudice and lack of understanding or appreciation of their needs and capabilities. This conference should set the example and perhaps start our thinking in a new way—in America good standards apply to all children regardless of race or creed or color.

Child labor has frequently flourished in underprivileged groups. Child labor, of course, is a menace not only to other young people but to all workers. We have been handicapped by the fact that many people have thought that the regulation of child labor would mean interference in the home and prevention of ordinary home training in work habits. This, of course, is not child labor, and there is much child labor in this country which we should make every effort to control. We are concerned about the children before they are born, but we should follow them through every step of their development until the children are firmly on their feet and started in life as citizens of a democracy.

Our particular task in this conference has been to emphasize the fact that children in a democracy are all-important and that in leaving unsolved many economic and social problems, which touch the lives of children, we have jeopardized the future of democracy. We feel we are more advanced than many other nations in this respect, but after looking at some pictures of the health work in schools for German children I think we are not as intelligent in this field as the German people have been for years past. Long before the present regime, scientists in Germany paid special attention not only to the physical health of the child but to a completely rounded-out development which took into account all the new knowledge to be obtained in the field of medicine and psychology.

I have often heard people say they would rather have a democracy, even if it had to be inefficient, than regimented efficiency. We love our freedom, but must we of necessity have freedom coupled with stupidity? Is it not possible to face our situation and recognize the inequalities in the economic background of America's children, inequalities in educational opportunities, in health protection, in recreation and leisure-time activities and in opportunities for employment?

I began by telling you how inadequate I felt when I was bringing up my children. I feel the mistakes I made serve to give me a little more wisdom and understanding in helping people who are trying today to preserve our democracy. We cannot direct youth altogether but we can give courage to the next generation and stand back of them so that they will feel our protection and good will.

I think we may find in 1950 that we have made strides far beyond our expectations.

18

Let Us Have Faith in Democracy

One day as I entered the village postoffice at Hyde Park, I noticed that a representative of the Forest Service had an office there. I wondered what work the Forest Service was doing in Dutchess County; and for the first time, I asked about it.

It occurred to me that perhaps this work was too concentrated on one particular thing; that many more things needed to be done. Then I inquired whether other representatives of the Department of Agriculture were doing some of the tasks that suddenly seemed to me to be so important; and I discovered a great number of worthwhile things being done in my own county which I had never known before.

This experience made me realize that we Americans have not yet scratched the surface in understanding what activities are being carried on and what services are available in our communities. And unless we do know what is being done in our own communities, either by Government services or by other organizations, it is impossible for us to function at our best as active citizens in a democracy.

Out of all the organizations and services available in our home communities, most of us have a clear impression of only the one or two with which we have the most direct and frequent contact.

In every locality, citizens should get together and talk over the life of their community and all the governmental functions that touch it—the needs and the ideas behind each program. Of course, no one can spread himself so much that he takes part in every community activity, and still make an effective contribution, but very often he can make a better contribution to one activity if he sees the overall picture.

A democratic form of government, a democratic way of life, presupposes free public education over a long period; it presupposes also an education for personal responsibility that too often is neglected.

The most important task in the development of a workable philosophy to insure the success of democracy is the awakening of every citizen to a real awareness of his own community. Through that awakening will come the sense of responsibility that is essential to make democracy function all the time. It functions now in spurts. Often it is totally unconscious of events in government or even of trends in thinking, as the people define the way of life they wish to lead.

Time and again a man or woman will say, "My representatives in Congress or the State Legislature are such poor representatives; they never seem to understand what I really think they should do."

Land Policy Review 5 (January 1942): 20–23.

And then, instead of feeling a personal responsibility for those representatives, the same people will vote for them again at the election, or fail to vote at all. The reason a certain number of people have been willing to accept dictatorship is that they were unwilling to think for themselves and to take the responsibility that is ours if we accept the philosophy of a democratic form of government.

Freedom to Think

Our greatest safeguard is the constant exercise of the right of the people to express their changing opinion at the polls and the acceptance by all people of the majority decision so expressed—until it is again altered at the polls. The only alternative is a constant use of force, with the physically strongest group gaining the upper hand.

An individual may not like the decision of the majority, but if he overthrows it he has destroyed his own right to change his mind. The thing that really preserves freedom is the liberty of every individual to express his thinking of the moment; and, since thinking can change, individuals in the minority need never feel they are not being fairly treated. They have every opportunity through education to change that minority into a majority.

Democracy cannot be static. Whatever is static is dead. Democracy cannot be frozen into words that will remain the same today, tomorrow, and forever. Our conception of the government we want and the way of life we want must be set by what we think today. However, if we think of democracy as a method by which people can express their changing opinions at regular intervals, then it is a workable philosophy of human relations in a complex world. The fact that each individual lives under the decision of a majority is fundamental in the democratic functioning of any government.

Sometimes people become too impatient. They want to see effected the things they believe should happen even before they have gone through the democratic process of convincing people through persuasion and education. To those who think certain ideas should hold sway, it often seems that the democratic process is pretty slow. But we must be willing to recognize the fact that the democratic process depends upon the ability of the people to understand and accept certain beliefs, and to make themselves conform to those beliefs.

It is one thing to believe in a theory and quite another to be willing actually to put that theory into practice. That is one of the things that make people wonder sometimes whether democracy can actually work in the world as it is today. It requires a people who can read—who can inform themselves; a people really able to listen to arguments and sufficiently open-minded to weigh those arguments.

Only in a democracy do individuals actually have the opportunity to help decide the policies of their State and Nation. Nowhere else does the individual have to shoulder so great a responsibility as under democratic government.

We in the United States have the greatest opportunity in the world today for developing in our citizens a realization of what democracy can mean. If it means what it should to this Country, it will mean something to the rest of the world.

Of course, no one can say that everyone in this Country has a feeling of responsibility for the government and of understanding for its many functions. Nor would everyone be able to participate in the real functions of government, if he or she had that feeling. But our citizens come closer to this ideal than those of any other nation.

Recently a friend remarked, "I would not dream of undertaking this job if it wasn't that the emergency is so great, but I think by working in all the hours I have used for leisure, I'll be able to do the two jobs."

That is the sort of thing a person does only under the pressure of the feeling that his convictions are at stake and the he owes it to his future stability to work hard for the things he believes in.

If we all share that feeling, if we do our best to develop our responsibility as citizens and as individuals, we will come through this difficult period with a better Nation, and a valuable contribution to the rest of the world.

We can be certain there will be enormous material demands upon us because of all the material things now being destroyed. We will have just as great demands on our spiritual and mental capacities. We will be asked to draw on all our imagination, all our knowledge of history, to understand the plight of the people in devastated countries. We will be asked to have faith, and to transmit it to people who have lost faith.

Only if we ourselves have faith in the fundamental decency and unselfishness of mankind, can we restore it to the rest of the world. And only if the world regains that faith, can it hope to avoid future conflagration, and hope to make it possible for democracy to flourish in all lands.

19

Civil Liberties and the Crisis

In saying how much I appreciate the proclamation which linked me with this day, I think it's a very wonderful thing to be able to come to Chicago and talk about our civil liberties on the birthday of the Statue of Liberty, because that statue, I think, has probably given more courage to people coming to this country from other countries where they have suffered from oppression than any other thing which they saw as they entered the country of hope.

And, of course, this day has another significance (which I did not realize until I was reminded of it): it is also the day dear to the hearts of the Czechoslovakian people, for this is the birthday of their freedom also.

In these days when we are living through a great emergency, it is quite natural, I think, that we should be troubled about the preservation of our civil liberties, fearful lest some of the other necessities of the moment should curtail these liberties which in the long view mean the preservation of our freedoms. I don't think any of us, however, who are here tonight need worry as yet about the real loss of any of our civil liberties. There are very few people in this country who are really afraid of speaking their minds today. There are very few people who hesitate to do whatever they may feel like doing in this country to express their point of view; and as long as that is the case, I think we may feel fairly safe.

If you lived in the White House, you would know one thing which I think is one of the best things that can happen to a nation, and that is that in this country nobody hesitates to write to the President of the United States and his wife and say exactly what they think.

I was at a play in New York the other night, a very amusing play in spots, a very moving play in many ways; but the amusing part of it was the fact that Mr. Wookey, who is a gentleman who owns a tug and lives in the East End and on the docks of London, is not in accord with the way the country has entered this war with Germany and its carrying on of the war. But Mr. Wookey, when he finds that a member of his family is caught at Dunkirk, puts his boat in with all the other boats to help the people get away from Dunkirk. And he does a good job, evidently, but he's asked to pay and he doesn't think he should pay for his gasoline. So when he returns he sets himself down and he writes a letter to Mr. Winston Churchill, and the letter is respectful but not in any way restrained. He tells him just what he thinks; and as he was dictating the letter in the play, I couldn't help thinking of some of the letters which come to my desk—and which are not restrained, either.

Address at Orchestra Hall, Chicago, Illinois, October 28, 1941, fifty-fifth anniversary of the Statue of Liberty.

But quite seriously, of course, this is a time when we must think very seriously of how we preserve our liberties, of how we defend them, and of how we do not abuse them, because there is a danger sometimes of forgetting that those liberties carry with them grave responsibility, that if you have liberty you must also be aware of the danger sometimes of doing unwise things in the name of liberty. Justice Holmes said (I don't think I can quote it exactly, but I can give you the gist of it) that freedom of speech was perfectly all right, but it didn't give man the right to cry "Fire!" in a theater and cause a panic. And I think that we should all remember, in times like these, that the best defense of our civil liberties is the exercise of responsible citizenship—the exercise of the kind of citizenship which thinks of the obligations of the citizen to the good of the whole community.

We're coming very soon to the date when we celebrate the anniversary of the Bill of Rights. And I think that one of the valuable things that we should all do, when we come to this anniversary, is to reread the Bill of Rights. We can't reread it too often. And as we reread it, I think we will be conscious of the fact that many of us give lip service to many of the principles laid down in the document and do not really see to it that all over this country that document is actually a reality to all the people of the United States.

For instance, it says: "No person shall be deprived of life, liberty, or property without due process of law; nor shall private property be taken for public use without just compensation. In all criminal prosecutions, the accused shall enjoy the right to a speedy and public trial by an impartial jury and be confronted with the witnesses against him, to have compulsory process for obtaining witnesses in his favor, and to have the assistance of counsel for his defense." Now some of those things, in some places, are not always done. And at the present time in our country, I think it very important that if we wish to preserve and affirm before the world that democracy does believe in civil liberties, does believe in the four freedoms which the President enunciated, that if that is so, we shall examine ourselves and make sure that we do all we possibly can do to make the Bill of Rights a reality for all of our people.

You may be rather weary of going over those four freedoms, and yet I think we can never go over them too often. We have spoken of the freedom of speech and of expression which the President said "was to be free for everyone everywhere in the world." And it's that "everywhere in the world" which I think is so important because if we could once obtain freedom of speech and expression everywhere in the world, I think it would be very much easier to obtain real peace in the world.

Then, the freedom of every person to worship God in his own way everywhere in the world. That seems almost an impossible thing at the present time to believe that we can hope for a long time to come. We certainly cannot hope for it until what we know as fascism has departed from amongst us; and I think we want to remember that that is one of the freedoms on which democracy is based, that we must have the right to freedom of worship in our own way, that no one must be questioned in their right to their own religion. And as far as possible in this country, we should not even bring up the question of what religion any person may belong to.

The third freedom, the freedom from want, "which, translated into world terms, means economic understandings which will secure to every nation a healthy, peace-time life for its inhabitants, everywhere in the world." That, of course, is a simplification of something which is going to require from our people and from all the other people in the world a great deal of intelligence, a great realization of the new world in which we live. Twenty-odd years ago we were not ready to accept responsibility in the world where this kind of freedom was to exist; because with that kind of freedom comes a responsibility of all the rest of the world, for all the other peoples living in the world, a responsibility to see that the raw materials, the things which people require to make a living, shall be accessible to all nations.

Twenty-odd years ago we decided that that didn't concern us, that we were concerned primarily with what happened within our own nation; and we thought that if we minded our own business and didn't want any part of anybody else, but also didn't concern ourselves particularly about any good that was to come to anyone else, just simply stayed within our own shores and our own interests, then we would be able to keep on regardless of what happened to the rest of the world.

I want to point out that with the best will in the world on our part, we woke up to find ourselves in the midst of a world that was on fire; and once the world is on fire, the little unit that stays calm and cool and collected in the middle gets very hot.

I had a visit from a lady the other day. She's a very fine woman, and she came to see me because she wanted to know if the President, in person, would receive a petition which a small group of people wanted to present to him. The petition would pray that he would suggest that the time had come for peace to come to the world. And I asked her whether she thought the President's suggestion would have much effect on the people who were actually at war, particularly on Mr. Hitler, and how Mr. Hitler was to get the message. And she said she thought it was such a rich, powerful, and wonderful nation that everybody knew we had no self-interests, we were not doing anything which was in our own interest, we were entirely altruistic and therefore we would have a spiritual strength which would make Mr. Hitler think about a "just peace." Well, a "just peace" for one person might not be quite what the other person considered a just peace. I asked her if she had in mind just what she would ask for as a just peace for all the nations that would be involved. She seemed a little vague about that, and I was reminded of the time when my husband, visited by a number of groups who were interested in peace, were at his side, and said, "I'm quite in accord with all their wishes, but I wish they'd go and talk to the people who really want war."

Well, it seems to me today that if we want that third freedom, which really is the basis for having peace in the world, the best thing we can do is to take a very practical attitude and face realities; face the fact that to get that kind of freedom from want is going to cost all the people who have had a good deal, and then we are going to have to want peace enough to pay for it materially and in personal effort.

I don't think that even when peace comes we're going to be without serious problems, that we are going to be without emergency situations to meet; and I think we might, as the strongest nation in the world and the one that is the great democracy and therefore has to prove to the rest of the world that democracy, a government by the people, where people really *take* responsibility, is able to face problems and meet them as well as any other type of government, face the problems now, realize that the world we're going to live in in the next few years is not going to be the kind of world we've lived in before.

We're not going back. The thing which has made the dictators successful—Nazi, Fascist, Communist—has been that they promised the people a new order, and the people wanted a new order because they were not satisfied with the world as it was.

Now, we might as well face the fact that democracy is building today a new order, and it has to be a new order that does give hope to all the people of the world. I can be realistic enough, and you are, too, to know that freedom from want is not going to come overnight to all the people of the world. It's going to be hope that many people live on, just as they've been living on it in this country for some time—many people. Well, many people will live on hope, but we will have to give them something tangible to show that their hope has a foundation in fact. And that means that we will have to be building through this period something really better in the way of machinery, in the way of functioning in our communities, which will be proof that there is a hope for all the people to have a better order.

I believe that our civilian defense in this country is based very largely on our being very able to have a vision now of service in the way of the civilian defense, of really coming together in our communities and seeing that we as a unit function better for the good of the whole community. I believe that is basic civilian defense. That's why I think that every woman who in this emergency learns how to feed her family better, learns how to buy better, learns how to use the government agencies and educate herself to do these things better—every woman who does that is doing her part in civilian defense and should be entitled to recognition for doing it. That is basic civilian defense, and it is building towards the reality of this third freedom, freedom from want.

And I hope we're going to look at most of the voluntary services in civilian defense from the point of view of making it serve the needs of the present but improve the possibilities of tomorrow, because we're going to need as much thinking into the future as we can possibly do, and that is one of the ways of preserving our freedoms.

Now, the fourth freedom is freedom from fear, "which, translated into world terms, means a world-wide reduction of armaments to such a point and in such a thorough fashion that no nation will be in a position to commit an act of physical aggression against any neighbor, anywhere." Well, that's one way, but only one, I think, of freeing us from fear. It's a very important one in the world as a whole, that physical reduction of armaments which puts temptation out of our way to a certain extent. But there are other fears which we will have to allay before we are sure of that freedom.

The fear of want—by that I mean not the fear of want translated into world terms, but the fear of want translated into the lives of individuals. We've been facing that fear all through the past few years in trying to find ways to allay it.

I think that many of the things which have been done under the Social Security Act have helped to free us from one kind of fear. We need more things done. We need things done in the way of health and in the way of recreation, in the way of education, and in the way of learning to be good neighbors and to really have brotherly feeling about each other regardless of any difference of race or creed that may exist. Those are all part of the fear which I think we must be free of before we are sure of our freedom.

Now, I've tied these freedoms up with the preservation of our civil liberties because I think they go hand-in-hand. I think that a nation which has a consciousness of the importance of the civil liberties of the people will eventually win through to these four freedoms. And if we do, I believe that we will be able, perhaps, to bring to the world an example, an example which the day peace comes is going to be all-important. For none of us know as yet exactly what we will be dealing with on that day when peace comes. But one thing we may be sure of is that the people that have the strongest sense of security in their own way of life and in their own government are going to give a sense of security to other people who may be floundering in insecurity and certainly will be down in the depths of need and want and even of starvation, and may have to face the pulling of themselves up from those depths under very difficult circumstances.

That being the case, I think all of us can look into the future with a sense of grave responsibility. I believe that a nation, to carry great responsibility, must also have, however, a gay heart. You must be able to meet life with the feeling that life is worth the struggle; and you can't do that unless you can keep some measure of gaiety about that struggle. Serious it may be; but in the end, there must be something there which gives you a lift as you go out of it. And that's the way I hope that every one of us is going to face the defense of our civil liberties, the defense of our freedoms, the responsibility of being the strong nation in the world, the nation that can prove the right of the individual to take part in their government, because as individuals we carry our responsibility.

Only by doing that and by feeling that as each individual takes their share they become strong with the strength of all the others who join with them, that individual responsibility which grows into unity, grows into the great unity of an ultimate purpose, an ultimate determination that here in this nation there shall be freedom, civil liberties, and, above all, brotherly love.

20

The Democratic Effort

It is important to that little-understood and intangible thing called civilian morale that we should apply ourselves to the task of drawing our people, in whom there are so many different racial strains, closer together instead of letting them drift apart and be divided by their backgrounds because of the war. We have prided ourselves for years on our ability as a country to live and work together peacefully, regardless of where our forebears came from, or when they came; and we have felt our success in this an example to the world.

There is one large group in the United States which now can help us greatly on morale—the people who have lived through some years of the war in other countries, or the years preliminary to the actual war. Their experiences can be of great value to us, and we should not fail to make use of them.

Most of these people, of course, come in the category of aliens under the law; yet they are here in our country with us, and their morale is therefore just as important as that of citizens. It does not help this morale for us to be thinking of them as aliens and treating them as such. As citizens we must keep reminding ourselves that at one time our ancestors were also newcomers to this country and "aliens" too, that most of the people to whom the term now applies came to the United States many years ago to make their homes here. The more recent comers are with us because they were considered the enemies of their undemocratic governments and were therefore persecuted. Here they are eager to join in the fight for democracy.

Yet in spite of their eagerness to help and be part of us as a united nation defending ourselves against aggression and oppression, we read in the Help Wanted advertisements that "Aliens need not apply." We hear of employers who are discharging admittedly loyal and efficient workers merely because they are not citizens or because they have foreign-sounding names. We hear of communities where those who are not citizens under the law are not permitted to take part in local civilian defense activities. In addition to this, now come the rigid wartime regulations and restrictions upon the conduct and freedoms of those who came here from nations with which we are now at war.

We know—and so do they—that the greatest care must be taken in these perilous days. But I am concerned with the possible consequences if we do not make every effort to differentiate between the many loyal American non-citizens and the comparatively few who may be truly alien to our way of life.

A similar problem of morale concerns us and our citizens who stem from German, Italian, and Japanese backgrounds. The war situation is very difficult for them and for us. A small minority in these groups have not been loyal; and

Common Ground 2, no. 3 (Spring 1942): 9–10.

this, of course, puts the loyal ones on the defensive, and the suspicion with which they are regarded alienates them from the democratic effort. As citizens of a democracy we must not set ourselves up as judges of other individuals. Being bitter against an American because of the actions of the country of his predecessors does not make for unity and the winning of the war. We must learn to think of the people in these groups as individuals, not as groups; we must treat them as individuals. They, on their part, have an obligation to refuse to listen to arguments and false statements made by agents of our enemies who will try to trade on any unfairness or bitterness. They have an obligation equal with the rest of us of making sure of the sources of their information.

The same Bill of Rights covers all our citizens, regardless of the country of origin. For basic civilian morale we need to stress, through every medium of expression that we have, understanding and consideration and acceptance of people as individuals. We cannot afford to have any number of our citizens in a position where it is hard for them wholeheartedly to accept and endorse democracy as a form of government and a way of life. The Government has agencies which can be trusted to guard against the few who will be disloyal. We must remember that we cannot tell the difference between a loyal and a disloyal citizen or between a citizen and a non-citizen just by looking at him or his name, by seeing the color of his skin, or by hearing him talk.

We have a great task ahead—the winning of this war. We have the even greater task of proving to the world that democracy does work—can work for all the world—in order that we may hold out hope for the future to oppressed people everywhere. Walt Whitman wrote years ago that America is "a nation of nations." Therein lies our strength. If we do not want to create "nations within a nation," if we wish a united spirit and a united defense so essential to ultimate victory, we must judge and act only on the true tests of loyalty, usefulness, and love of America.

21

Restlessness of Youth:
An Asset of Free Societies

Youth is never satisfied with things as they are. Young people in all countries wish to protest against the injustices they see about them. They are not easily fooled by facades of high-sounding words thrown up to conceal bad deeds. They tend to cut through words to the heart of an issue.

When they hear the phrase "free world" they want to know what is meant. They are not satisfied with the way things are going in any part of the world. They see great tasks and hard struggles ahead of them to make a better life. The "free world" cannot be used as a pious phrase to suggest that the people in one part of the world have achieved the full freedom they seek. It is rather a phrase which points the direction toward which the peoples can move and are moving.

In the "free world" the dissatisfaction with things as they are, the striving for ideals and hopes, can find peaceful expression through free institutions. The restlessness of youth is a precious asset of free societies because it always promises regeneration of new vitality from decade to decade.

But where fundamental freedoms and human rights have been suppressed by ruling oligarchies, the youth has no outlet for its struggles against the status quo. Its dynamic urges are channeled through marching clubs, military machines, and propaganda organizations in support of a ruling class which is self-perpetuating.

While such a dictatorship is in the first bloom of its own youth, it can attract the youth by revolutionary words, by pageantry, and by vigorous activities. But tyrants grow old and become increasingly corrupted by arbitrary power.

Their high-sounding words soon stand in bleak contrast to their evil deeds. Their promises are in contrast to their performances. It is my deep conviction that any society which does not provide freedom for the upcoming generations to work openly and honestly for their aspirations contains within it the seeds of its own destruction.

Youth's Obligation

Youth which is free to work for a better life in the open with the tools of human rights has first of all the obligation to strengthen this freedom and preserve it against all attacks. Young people who are still free to read, to

Department of State Bulletin 26 (January 21, 1952): 94–96. Address made before Les Jeunes Amis de la Liberté, Paris, on December 18, 1951, and released to the press by the U.S. Mission to the U.N.

discuss, to question and to seek the truth can find out for themselves how freedom has been bludgeoned in Eastern Europe and in the Soviet Union. They can see for themselves the growing gaps between words and deeds behind the Iron Curtain. They can take direct testimony from those who are fleeing from these slave societies.

They can read for themselves the new laws in the so-called people's democracies which state plainly that anything which is not published as a government hand-out is to be regarded as a state secret, and whoever inquires about such things is guilty of espionage or spying. They can see that these laws make it impossible for the people to find out from the public press or radio anything which the government doesn't want them to know.

Of course, these laws are in themselves proofs of the weakness and fear of the ruling minorities who try to impose them. You and I know that they cannot work for long, because people, and especially young people, have ways of satisfying their hunger for news and truth.

Yet, it is a sad thing to have to suffer long years of darkness, and to have to struggle for a new light of freedom.

You have precious freedoms which you do not have to lose if you will use them in your struggles for a better life and defend them against both the wiles of propagandists and the threats of aggressors.

You know from bitter experience what it is like to live under a dictatorship imposed by an aggressor. You know how precious freedom is by recalling your own experience of the Nazi occupation. And you know, as we have learned in the United States, that freedom can be preserved or rewon only by the collective effort of free men.

The United Nations is the greatest agency we have through which free men may cooperate to preserve their freedom by collective actions. In the United Nations they can work together for social and economic improvements, and thus strengthen their free societies. In the United Nations they can unite their moral, political, economic, and military strength for collective defense.

The forces against freedom understand that their only hope of imposing dictatorial regimes on new areas of the world lies in the disunity of the free world. Hence, they use every propaganda trick to sow confusion and dissention in the ranks of free peoples. They exploit every feeling of fear and antagonism to divide the free nations, and break the spirit for collective resistance to aggression.

If we are determined not to lose our freedoms, we must use our heads in an active campaign to expose the propaganda designed to divide us, and to promote the unity and cooperation of free people.

At this General Assembly, we are engaged in a great effort to keep the issues clear on the questions of peace and security, in the hope that the Soviet Union will recognize the determined will and clarity of thought of the people of the free world and abandon its policy of substituting propaganda for honest negotiation on real disarmament.

Truth vs. Slogans

We should realize that the truth about complex problems is harder to understand than slogans and emotional appeals that do not meet the issue. Therefore, those who wish to defend their freedoms have a difficult task of education to perform constantly in order to prevent the sloganized propaganda from misleading people.

One of the main issues on which we must all be clear is the question of peace and disarmament. As you know, France, the United Kingdom, and the United States joined in putting before the General Assembly a proposal for the limitation, control, and balanced reduction of all arms and armed forces. This proposal has been ridiculed by Mr. Vyshinsky, who has put forward old Soviet proposals which are simple and beguiling. His main purpose is to confuse the issues of peace and to slow up or stop our actions to build collective security.

The people of this world want peace itself, not mere words in new pacts of peace. They got pacts of nonaggression from Hitler as his favorite prelude to his blitzkriegs. Now they want deeds, not words.

Let us remember that the making of war itself is an international crime. This was firmly established at the Nuremberg trials. This was accepted by every government which ratified the United Nations Charter. This means that the use of any weapon from a gun to an atomic bomb to attack or to threaten another state is prohibited. Regardless of what weapons may be used, aggression is a crime and is strictly prohibited. We have all signed the paper containing this promise.

But this is not enough. The people want us to translate our promise into performance.

Knowing as they do the terrible destruction that armies, planes, and tanks and guns can cause, they will not accept a mere paper prohibition of one weapon. They want all weapons and all armies put under international control so that war itself is effectively prohibited.

When a nation only wants to prohibit the one weapon that happens to offset its mass armies, its hypocritical purpose is easy to expose. The real test for a nation is its willingness to submit to international control its whole military machine so that it becomes impossible for any nation to launch an aggression.

On the problem of the control and prohibition of the use of atomic energy for weapons, there is a perfect illustration of the need for clarity of thought on the part of free people in order not to be deluded by Soviet tricks of propaganda. Let me try to put the issue in the simplest way.

Suppose I held in my right hand a small block of Uranium 235. It is often called "fissionable material." I am going to call it "the stuff that explodes." This stuff is what people the world over want to have put under international control so it cannot be used in weapons.

Suppose I held in my left hand a piece of paper on which I have written these words: "Cross my heart, I promise never to use the explosive stuff in a bomb if you will agree to let me keep it and use it as I please."

This, in my right hand, is the stuff that threatens destruction. This, in my left hand, is the paper pledge to prohibit the use of it in a bomb.

Now I ask you: Do you want signatures of foreign ministers on this piece of paper, or do you want to have the United Nations control this stuff? Which will be effective in prohibiting its use for destructive purposes?

Would you trust any signature on the paper if the signer refused to give up his possession of the stuff to an international authority?

Only Soviets Say "No"

The United Nations plan calls upon all nations to put this explosive stuff in the hands of an international guard. So far only the Soviets have said "no." They have insisted on having and controlling the explosive stuff to use for purposes they say are "peaceful."

They just want a new piece of paper which says none of us shall use this explosive stuff in bombs. After we sign such a piece of paper, they say we can probably work out some sort of inspection to find out whether anybody actually has any containers of this stuff labeled "bombs." However, the inspectors will not be allowed to find out how much of this stuff anyone may have in containers labeled "peacetime use."

There is only one simple fact that people have to understand to see that this affords no protection at all. The simple fact is that the stuff that explodes is exactly the same for bombs as for peacetime use.

We say, "Let's have international control of the stuff that goes bang."

They say, "Let's just sign a paper promising not to let the stuff explode."

They ask the people of the world to take their word. We ask that the United Nations take control of the stuff itself so nobody can break his word.

Ah, but we are told that this would prevent countries from doing what they please with this explosive stuff. It certainly would.

The people aren't afraid of words and labels; they are afraid of the stuff that explodes. They aren't so simple as to feel safe if this explosive stuff is nicely labeled "peacetime use only," when they know it can become bombs by just putting it in special boxes marked "A-bombs."

The United Nations plan says each country can have as much of the stuff as it can use up in peaceful projects week by week, month by month. We must have an international authority to guarantee that atomic stuff is being used as each country claims it is being used.

But if each nation has a big warehouse of the atomic stuff, and it is even a secret how much they have, the labels can be changed overnight from "peacetime use" to "bombs." What kind of prohibition is that? Who would feel safe under that kind of control?

Why do the Soviet spokesmen reject the idea of getting what they need as they need it from the United Nations authority? Oh, they claim they couldn't trust the international authority to let them have what they need.

You see, we come back to the question of trust. They want us to trust them on their own word not to change the labels on this explosive stuff and use it in bombs. But they won't trust the authority composed of all nations to allot to them what they need for peacetime use.

In other words, they simply refuse to put this stuff under international control.

The United Nations plan is the best way advocated so far to control the explosive stuff and thus prohibit its use in weapons. We are ready to consider any other plan that will control the explosive stuff as effectively. But we demand real control of the stuff that explodes.

This is only one illustration of why clear and realistic thinking is required if free men are not to lose their freedom in a fog of confusion and sophistry.

It goes without saying that no man would knowingly give up his freedom for mere promises of food or shelter or employment. Most people realize that these things have to be produced and cannot be promised or merely voted by politicians. The basic question is: Will they be produced by free men or by slaves?

Free men have never deliberately chosen the path of dictatorship. They have never in a free election voted for parties advocating totalitarian doctrines. In a clear contest between the principles of freedom and the doctrine of dictatorship, there is no doubt where the overwhelming majority will stand.

The danger comes from the confusions and dissensions which the skilled propagandists of totalitarian parties disseminate—not primarily to win supporters but to divide and weaken their adversaries.

You have the great opportunity of helping this generation to face its problems with responsibility and realism. You can help unite freedom-loving people to prevent aggression and promote peace.

22

Social Responsibility
for Individual Welfare

I am happy that in this remarkable conference that has been called to celebrate and to deepen the thinking and knowledge of our people throughout the country on these subjects, we should have the stress laid on this particular subject: "Social Responsibility for Individual Welfare."

Every woman is proud that the first woman to be in the Cabinet to head a Department of Social Welfare is Mrs. Oveta Culp Hobby, and we know that she will have the backing of the women of this country in every struggle to really bring to the people of the country a greater sense of welfare and opportunity and justice in the life of our land.

Now, it has come about that when you talk about the welfare state, as a rule people think that that is a rather derogatory term—that a welfare state is somehow not a good thing. But if we could just change it around a little and say that we believed that society included the government, the individuals themselves as individuals, and all other groups—universities, the people who form the policies, the industrialists, the people who guide commerce, industry, and agriculture—if we thought of them altogether as working together to increase the welfare of the individual, then we would cease, I think, to have fear of just the mere words "a welfare state." We would have a truer conception of what the words really mean.

It is basic in a democracy that leadership for the welfare of the people as a whole must come from government. It is true that we pride ourselves on holding the reins of government, but we need leadership. We need a voice to define our aims, to put into words the things we want to achieve; and so we look to government to do just that—so that we do not stand still but move forward. Just as Alice in Wonderland had to run very fast to stay in the same place, we must run even faster to stay in the same place, and we have to do even more in order to go forward. We will go backward unless we go forward.

My husband used to say that we progressed by crises, that when the crisis was so bad that we wondered how we were going to meet it, then we were ready to try something new, to try something that perhaps we would otherwise have hesitated to undertake.

When sometimes I hear it said that in my husband's time we started something dreadful, something which they called "creeping socialism," I wonder

National Policies for Educational, Health and Social Services, edited by James Earl Russell, Columbia University Bicentennial Conference Series (Garden City, N.Y.: Doubleday, 1955) pp. xxxv–xxxviii.

whether instead we didn't really face the fact that a democracy must meet the needs of its people, and whether what we did was not actually to save democracy, to save free enterprise, to keep for ourselves as much freedom as we possibly could. Had we not met the needs of the people, we might have waked up and found ourselves not just in creeping socialism, but perhaps going actually to the far extremes of either fascism or communism, because we could not find a way to meet the needs of the people.

As I have been around the world it has seemed to me that we in this country, when we talk of capitalism or free enterprise, should explain what we mean, because there are many areas of the world in which it is not at all understood what we actually mean when we talk of our own capitalism, of our own development in the past thirty years or forty years, let us say.

We have had great changes, but they have been the changes which had to come if our people were to have a chance for full development. To be sure, some of the things were very new; now they seem very old. I can remember when we started old-age pensions. Now the idea is not very shocking to us—a mutual contribution towards this security in old age. We started care for the blind and the crippled. Many said that it was simply a humanitarian gesture, but it was more than that. It is real insurance so that they will not remain a burden on society. That is why we continue to develop the employment of the crippled and the blind. We continue to find useful ways of using people, even handicapped people.

Old-age pensions, as now accepted, are contributed to throughout the working life of every individual. Care for the blind and the crippled may sound completely humanitarian, but on the contrary it is really an insurance so that society will not have an obligation to carry handicapped people as a complete burden. In the underdeveloped areas of the world the only thing open to the handicapped individual is to beg. We not only try to extend the best medical care but we try to train these individuals to earn a living, and we are constantly working with industries to open occupations to trained handicapped people, while many industries also have undertaken training programs of their own. This whole program eliminates a burden from society, just the same as pensions do which are paid for during the working life of an individual.

We believe in unemployment insurance. We know that it is not perfect in operation. We know that a number of things that are done for general welfare are not perfect in the way they work out, but that it would be unwise to wipe out the whole of something because there needed to be certain reforms and changes. It was felt that as we went along we would realize that unemployment insurance was not just for the benefit of the individual; it was for the benefit of our economy. It was to try to keep us from having debacles, from actually having buying power so reduced as to hurt the economy of the nation as a whole. It is part of our economic insurance.

There are many things that, just like freedom, we must constantly be studying and watching when we do things for the welfare of people, because we do not want to remove from people their sense of responsibility and initiative. We want them to feel that they are partners in each thing that we do, that if they function in a democracy, then what their government does comes from them. They acquiesce, they work it out, and they must not lose initiative.

We have not completely solved the unemployment problem because it is still open to abuses. It is safeguarded to some extent by the fact that government offices try to find jobs for people within their range of employment, which they are expected to accept. But many people have had the experience of knowing individuals who took advantage of unemployment insurance when they really could have obtained work. The law was not written to encourage such people, and so ways should be sought to eliminate existing loopholes so that it would be impossible to get unemployment insurance unless one is unable to find work in a field where one is competent.

All these social measures were designed to protect society from sudden fluctuations in the economy and to protect the individual from situations beyond his control which he could not completely handle by himself. They were designed as cooperative measures between the individual and his government, which, I think, is a step forward. They should not tend to remove initiative from people nor keep them from feeling a sense of individual responsibility and ambition.

The advantage of a democracy over the socialist state would seem to be a greater freedom, which provides for the development of the individual for free choice of a way of life and for a sense on the part of the individual of participation in the decisions made which affect his life and his future. His government tries to remove from the individual a fear of want so that he may be freer to fully develop, but it does not countenance a stepping in of government to take over the major part of the responsibility for man's existence.

I was struck in France by the difference between our philosophy and theirs, which are still miles apart. They do not think that it is important that a man earn a living wage. We do. I think it is the basis of the welfare of the individual.

Under the social-security system of France nearly every employer pays his employees less than a living wage. He pays from 35 to 50 per cent of the wage, not to the employee, but into a *caisse* or fund managed by the government and distributed under government auspices to families according to their size. Under this system a man with five or six children receives a considerable sum more from the government than he earns. In a democracy like ours we think it important for industry to be so organized that a man receives wages commensurate with his work and on which he can support his family. In other words, what we hope to ensure to every individual is an ability to earn a living, and the benefits of a welfare state are simply auxiliary to meet emergencies and to help a human being to meet situations that may arise in his life which he ordinarily could not meet alone.

There I was told very calmly, "Oh, but you do not understand our system. We know we don't insist upon a living wage, but the government gives to families, according to the number of children, an allowance. If you have five or six children you might almost as well not work because the government pays you so much more than you can possibly earn."

We have to recognize that our type of capitalism in this country is different from what the same word connotes in some other countries. From the time of the last depression we have taken great strides in the recognition of the responsibility of government and industry to cooperate to prevent any disasters to the normal economy of the country. We have to be prepared to meet disasters caused by nature. These we expect the government to cooperate in meeting, but we recognize the responsibility of industry today as well as of the individual. We believe that together we should strive to give every individual a chance for a decent and secure existence, and in evolving our social patterns we are trying to give both hope for better things in the future and security from want in the present.

Basically, all of us believe that where the people feel they have justice, opportunity, and freedom and can actually rely on the interest of their government and on the attitudes of society to help them achieve stabilization and as much security as one can ever count on in human life, there will be belief in the government and the security that no other isms will really undermine the faith in the ideas on which this country was founded.

We believe that together we should strive to give every individual a chance for a decent and secure existence; and in evolving our social patterns we are trying to give both hope for better things in the future and security from want as far as possible in the present.

These aims should not affect either the initiative of the individual or his sense of responsibility, but should give him a feeling of partnership in his government and with the economy of his country as a whole, which we hope will be a pattern that far transcends the economic pattern and the ideological promises that are made in parts of the world by Communism.

If we live and work for the basic ideals that our country was founded on and have justice and freedom, I think we need not have loyalty boards. We need not have inquisitions. We can trust that what we believe in and stand for will be strong enough so that we can trust each other and other people as a whole.

23

In the Service of Truth

I was talking to some young people the other night, and someone asked me if I ever found that I had to change my mind. I looked at him for a minute and said, "Yes, sometimes the very next day." It is surely a terrible thing when young people think that what you think at eighteen means that you can never think any differently, or that you are going to be held to account for what you thought at eighteen. It seems to me that means a loss of freedom.

It is refreshing to pay tribute to a journal that has lasted ninety years and has managed to remain free. I am quite sure that it is going to remain free. It will state the truth as the individuals who write for it see the truth. And that is something we cannot always be sure of finding today.

I think all writers should make up their minds that they must write as freely and as truthfully as they possibly can, because we are living in an age when people must feel sure that they are given the truth as nearly as one can find it. The atomic age is a difficult time for a democracy. If people do not understand what problems they face, it leads to apathy, to indifference, to shifting the responsibility that each individual ought to feel. That must be avoided if a democracy is really going to be a democracy.

We know, all of us, that if we use atomic energy for making war it is quite possible to destroy our civilization, but most of us do not know, as yet, what can happen in a world where the same energy is used for peaceful purposes. I obtained just an inkling when I was in Oak Ridge this spring. It gave me a sense of how important it was for the peoples of the world to know what good atomic energy could bring them. I hope that gradually the peoples of the world will know, but that will require patience and restraint and great confidence that the democracies will do something for them which no totalitarian government can possibly accomplish.

It will take *The Nation* and all that it can do, and many other courageous newspapers and journals and writers and speakers, to help us have faith that what we believe can win out in a world at peace.

The Nation 181 (July 9, 1955): 37.

24

What Are We For?

Eleanor Roosevelt and Huston Smith

Less than fifteen years ago the United States stood on top of the world, its reputation as unrivaled as its power. As C. L. Sulzberger has observed, we were almost in a position to dictate a *pax americana*.

Today our security is in jeopardy and our principles on the defensive. In the years since World War II the initiative has slipped from our grasp to the point where, as Walter Lippmann has concluded, the North Atlantic community is "no longer the political center of the world." George Kennan is not an alarmist, but even he has reported the United States to be the object of world obloquy, disapproval, and "in some cases of outright hatred," to a degree unprecedented in our history. A decade of anti-American demonstrations in Paris, bombs in the American library in Athens, outrages against Vice-President Nixon in South America, and a world-circling trail of broken plate glass in front of offices of the United States Information Service form a sobering backdrop to his observation.

Why this severe decline in our world stature and prestige? Many factors have contributed, of course. Some of them may have been unavoidable. American G.I.'s have belted the world, and soldiers are never a nation's best ambassadors. Our superior wealth and power may have provoked envy regardless of how we behaved. Perhaps the world simply expected more of us than any nation can provide and we are feeling the backwash of its disenchantment.

But in the end, such explanations are excuses. The major responsibility for the decline in our world position lies with the way we have conducted our foreign affairs. And back of this lies the question of what we have wanted our foreign policy to accomplish.

I

During the first hundred years of our national life we wanted little more from the world than that it leave us alone. So adequate was our continent for our needs, so engrossed were we in building it up, that our prime request of the world was that it not distract us from our indigenous tasks. During the next fifty years, the years that led up to World War II, we passed from being a debtor to a creditor nation. This transition led us to want more from the world. We now wanted it to provide us with a field in which we could expand

The Search for America, edited by Huston Smith (Englewood Cliffs, N.J.: Prentice Hall, 1959), pp. 3–12.

economically, for raw materials and markets, and safe foreign investments had become important to our economic life. Since World War II our basic objective has again shifted. In this period we have wanted above all else to keep the world from falling into Communist hands. Each of these periods has had its slogans: "no entangling alliances" and "isolationism" for the first; "Open Door," "Manifest Destiny," and "dollar diplomacy" for the second; and "Communist containment" for the third.

Each of these objectives continues to have some relevance for today. We still want a world which will permit us to work out our national life in our own way, which will be conducive to our economic development, and which will stand up to Communism. But none of these former objectives provides an adequate keystone for our present foreign policy.

We need to see this clearly. So, having noted the continuing truth in these former objectives, let us note their deficiencies.

Isolationism, which advocates an essentially "live and let live" approach to the world, may have sufficed in our past. But quite apart from the question of whether it is even logically feasible in a world as interrelated as ours, two things should be obvious: one, that for such an approach to succeed, all nations possessing any power at all must subscribe to it; and two, that the contemporary world contains at least one such nation that hasn't the slightest interest in doing so. From the beginning of the Communist epoch, the Soviet Union has geared itself for world outreach. In part this thrust roots from historic centrifugal forces that have been pressing outward for a hundred years, to the Pacific, the Balkans, and the Middle East. But this is not the whole story; we deceive ourselves if we miss the extent to which the Soviet outreach springs from a sense of mission. The Communist is convinced that the whole human race is destined to become one Communist brotherhood. Consequently there seems to be no corner of the earth's surface he considers too insignificant for his attention. A Communist isolationist is a contradiction in terms. While Soviet missions are busy in Latin America trading machinery and oil for wool and coffee, Arab and Asian students are being trained in Moscow, Russian teachers are touring West Africa, and technical advisers are dispatched to India, Burma, and Indonesia.

Faced with such a rival who is out to remake the world in its image, it is obvious that if we want a world different from that of the Communists, we shall have to work for it. To put the matter paradoxically, even if we should want nothing more than a "live and let live" world, we would now have to exert our influence in every land to insure its continuance or evolution. And we would have to exert this influence with as much force and ingenuity as the Soviets.

It may be supposed that our commitments around the world and the regularity with which we now vote a substantial portion of our annual budget to programs of foreign aid is evidence that we have put isolationism behind us. But this is only partially correct. Certainly raw, crude, "Fortress America" isolationism is dead. Two and a half world wars and the continuing cold one have taught us that we must take the world seriously and work with it intimately. But isolationism is not completely routed by involvement. There remains the question of what engagement is for. In its subtle form isolationism admits that we have no alternative to being deeply involved with the world, but it holds that the purpose of this involvement is to preserve a world in which we can still substantially go our own way. This sophisticated variety of isolationism still characterizes our outlook. We go forth to the ends of the earth, but not to remake the world toward goals we believe are relevant to all human living. We go to hold back our antagonists.

Woodrow Wilson's thesis of the self-determination of nations may inadvertently contribute to this subtle form of isolationism, for whereas in dealing with people it is easy to see that indifference is not the only alternative to domination, in the dealings between nations this point is less obvious. Here every contact, every influence, tends to be regarded with suspicion, as if it were a feeler or feeder for imperialism. Actually there is no reason why this should be the direction of its intent. If a mayor has goals for his city, it does not follow that he intends to undercut the autonomy of its residents. The relevant questions are not whether nations do influence one another, or even how much, but rather what the influence is for and how it is exerted.

There is, then, nothing inherently undemocratic in the concept of world objectives. Our goals should differ from those of the Communists, but they should embrace the world as wholeheartedly. They should be as clear as the Communists' goals, and we should work as hard in their behalf, using, of course, means that are consonant with them. The ease with which such words can be written belies the wrench from our past that will be required if we take them seriously. For if we accept the fact that we not only have world goals, but that they must henceforth take precedence over national ones because we can no longer have the kind of nation we want unless we have the kind of world we want, our foreign policy ceases to be primarily defensive—a shield for our security. It becomes instead a channel through which we pour our resources and energies to remake the world. For too many years already, while the Soviet Union has pegged its goal at international proportions we have conceived our goal parochially—to build here, in this sweet land, the good society. To lift our sights to world proportions is a staggering assignment. It will take money, resolution, and a shift in our total national attitude toward the world. But there is no reason to regard the shift with dread. As a people we have always been at our best when engrossed with large problems, and there is danger that if world objectives do not arise to direct our energies outward, our local factional disputes, between management and labor, Negro and white, North and South, will begin to bore us and bog us down.

If isolationism has ceased to be an adequate guide for our foreign policy, so has economic expansion. Obviously we should continue to work for a world that will provide us with raw materials, markets, and secure investments, but we cannot permit mercantile interests to dictate or even dominate our foreign policy. The Biblical dictum to "seek first the kingdom and all these things will be added unto you" is relevant here. Insofar as we succeed in building a world that is stable and prosperous, we shall prosper too. But if we let our actions be

123

guided by our private economic advantage, our prosperity is likely to topple by having the world's entire industrial economy pulled out from under it. So what begins by sounding like moralism turns out to be stark realism, for it is one of the undernoticed phenomena of our times that we are at one of those unusual junctures in history where, internationally speaking, what is good for us and what is good for others very nearly coincide. Unless the world prospers, it will not be able to buy from us as we wish. And unless justice is effected, passions will erupt into a war which is likely to destroy everything.

The greatest need of our foreign policy, however, is to transcend the "Communist containment" objective that has obsessed us for the last decade.* Communism needs to be contained. But to make its containment our top and direct objective is a mistake.

There are at least two reasons for this. One is that "containment" is a negative objective, and these can never match the appeal of positive ones. People live by affirmations, not negations. The late Alfred North Whitehead put this succinctly when, in another context, he pointed out that "if man cannot live by bread alone, still less can he live by disinfectants." Most of the world's population wants change, and if we knew their lot we would not blame them. If, then, we put ourselves in the position of resisting change while our opponents advocate it, we proceed under a hopeless handicap. Logic, too, works against a defensive position. When a positive position wins, its position is enlarged; when a defensive position wins, it merely holds the line. And as nobody can win all the time, the best a negative position can hope for is to hang on a little longer.

The second defect of our "containment" policy really concerns the means by which we have sought to effect it. These means have been preponderantly military; the ratio of our military to our economic aid to foreign countries shows this quite clearly. But since Korea, the Communist offensive has not relied on military advances. It has switched to economic maneuvers and internal subversion against which our airstrips and missile ramps have stood starkly impotent. In some cases our preoccupation with answering Communism with might may inadvertently have encouraged its spread, for military bastions tend to increase local burdens rather than alleviate them, contributing thereby in impoverished countries to the desperation on which Communism feeds. Is not this in part the story of the Baghdad Pact and the Eisenhower Doctrine that now lie virtually in ruins amidst Communist advances in the strategic Middle East? Military power must play a part in our international dealings, but we

---

*Since these words were written, Senator William Fulbright, chairman of the Senate Foreign Relations Committee, has released a survey of the opinions of retired high-ranking diplomats who were asked to express their views on American foreign policy as they saw it in practice. The dominant conclusion that emerges from this survey is concern over the predominantly "defensive posture" of our foreign affairs—our propensity, in Senator Fulbright's summarizing words, "merely to react to Soviet challenges rather than to put into effect our own comprehensive and positive policies and, especially in recent years, an inability to come forth with any creative and dramatic programs."

have banked on it in recent years for more than it can deliver, at the same time underrating what can be achieved through wise diplomacy and imaginative nonmilitary use of our economic resources especially through the joint agencies of the United Nations.

II

The argument up to this point can be summarized in three propositions:

1. United States foreign policy should shed the remnants of its isolationism and direct itself to achieving world goals.
2. The world goals toward which our policy is directed should not be weighted to our advantage at the expense of other nations and peoples.
3. The goals must be positive rather than negative ones. We must break the present image in which we give the world the impression that whereas the Chinese and Russians have something to believe in, Communism, we have something to *dis*-believe in, also Communism.

It might help us break out of this predominantly negative approach if we ask: Suppose Communism were to evaporate overnight. What would we do? What would be our policy?

It ought not to be difficult for us to formulate constructive goals. America was born dedicated to a proposition whose ingredients—equality, inalienable rights, life, liberty, and the pursuit of happiness—brought response from the entire world. Our greatest leaders, our Jeffersons, our Lincolns, our Wilsons were great because they spoke to humanity at large and extended their vision to the entire family of man. The greatest need in our international life is to recapture the affirmative, world-relevant vision of these leaders and discern its implications for our present situation.

There seem to be no slogans today to take the place of those of yesteryears—"the war to end all wars," "the war to make the world safe for democracy," "the four freedoms," "the century of the common man." But in prose if not in poetry we can specify the ends toward which our foreign policy should be directed. The aim of the United States should be to build a *peaceful* world of *autonomous, prospering democracies*. As all the peoples of the world would benefit from the realization of these goals, perhaps the phrase "world welfare" can serve to summarize them here.

Obviously we are not going to get such a world at once, and in the give and take of international negotiations, one or more of the objectives listed in the preceding paragraph must often yield for the time being to others. In such cases, it would seem wise as a rule to give priority to the objective appearing earlier in the sentence.

Peace must come first because the prospect of the world being reduced to radioactive dust is so awful that we must be patient about other objectives if pressing for them would throw the world into total war. Even peace cannot be

125

absolutized, for if the Soviets were to demand our capitulation, we would fight. But peace comes first in the sense that our pressures for the autonomy, prosperity, and democratization of other lands must not be impetuous to the point of bringing the world to war.

Autonomy will in certain cases have to wait. This is true both for nations like Hungary or Tibet which are under Communist hegemony, and for the few remaining nations in which political consciousness has not matured to a point where independence is feasible. Somaliland is an example here, with a population of one and a half million, of which perhaps fifty are literate. In cases like these, we should make clear that we favor not only independence when political maturity has developed but also steps which will hasten such maturity.

Tibet illustrates why, even in poverty-stricken regions of the world, autonomy should generally take precedence over increased prosperity. The Chinese went to Tibet offering industrialization and a higher material standard of life. It was assumed that to people as poor and illiterate as these simple peasants who live on the roof of the world and have nothing to lose but their yaks this "argument of the stomach" would prove conclusive. But their brief, sad revolt, fought with such great courage and so little hope, has proved how limited is the doctrine of "economic man."

Democracy in our list of objectives means the presumption of freedom for individuals within their nations. Such freedom has three components: personal, political, and economic. Personal freedom involves the individual's right to think for himself, to express his opinions vocally and in print, to live under the authority of law rather than personal whim, to have a fair trial if he violates this law, and to be educated. Political freedom involves the individual's right to affect his government's actions and procedures by electing those who will rule over him and voting directly on measures of special import. It is the application of the concept that as protection against the abuse toward which power inclines, this power should be distributed broadly among the populace. Economic freedom involves the citizen's right to choose his field of employment, to improve his income by merit and exertion, and to initiate enterprises of his own and realize profits therefrom.

The urge for this freedom which democracy seeks to safeguard appears to be innate in the human makeup. Hold the arms and legs of an infant and he will struggle to be released. Similarly peoples, though subjugated for years or generations, will reach out for freedoms if they become possible. The young Hungarians had known nothing but tyranny. They had received the full measure of Soviet indoctrination. Yet when the restraining pressures slackened, they fought for freedom as if they had known nothing else. When post-Stalin Russia and Mao's "let a hundred flowers bloom" China gave hints that freedom of opinion might be tolerated, political commentaries in the form of articles and wall newspapers blossomed overnight as if to prove that freedom's flower, though dormant through a long winter, was far from dead.

By defining democracy as the presumption of freedom we guard against the notion that freedom can be absolutized. When absolutized it jams and becomes nonfreedom: political freedom founders in anarchy (France before the return of DeGaulle was almost an example of this); civil liberties slip into license, and economic freedom moves toward monopoly, exploitation, and unemployment. In this respect freedom, as Gide has remarked, is like a kite that cannot rise on the wind unless restrained. When freedom is presumed rather than absolutized it carries no implication that governments are best which govern least. On the contrary, it accepts Lincoln's principle that government must do for the people what needs to be done but what they cannot do at all for themselves or cannot do as well. Specifically in our own case this involves accepting social security and a host of governmental policing and regulating measures as supports of freedom. In doing so, however, it remains aware on the one hand of freedom's worth and on the other of the way in which concentrations of power, both political and economic, can choke this freedom. Consequently it prefers that things be done nongovernmentally where they can be done as well this way; it leans toward letting its citizens follow, alone or in groups, where their minds and spirits will lead them until evidence arises that their freedom is interfering with the freedom of other citizens. We have the most dramatic evidence we could desire for the validity of this "presumption of freedom" principle in the fact that even the Soviet bloc has begun to veer toward it by decentralizing industry, returning farming toward its private basis, introducing incentive measures to both, and permitting greater freedom of expression.

Even qualified as "the presumption of freedom," democracy must take last place on our list of world objectives. There are places in the world where, if political power were distributed among citizens, they would be too inexperienced to run their nations effectively: the reversion of Indonesia, Burma, and Pakistan to dictatorships within the last year is evidence of this general point. Similarly with respect to economic freedom where capital is nonexistent and centralized planning and government operation is needed to get the process of industrialization off the ground, to hold out for economic freedom in any sense that resembles capitalism in our own country may thwart development intolerably. Yet democracy with its three ingredient freedoms remains an important part of our creed, for though we admit that there are situations in which it is currently inapplicable, we profoundly believe that it is the noblest form of political life man has yet devised. Where conditions such as poverty and illiteracy make it inappropriate, therefore, these stand as calls to us to do what we can to alleviate such conditions.

III

No statement of objectives provides a simple criterion by which decisions can be made. This is especially true in international relations where ambiguities, paradoxes, and compromises must inevitably abound. The clearest present example of such ambiguity is to be found in our alliances. Our military pacts often strengthen governments that work against our democratic and humanitarian principles. Few would argue that Jeffersonian principles are furthered by

127

buttressing Franco's despotism, the dictatorships of Chiang Kai-shek and Syngman Rhee, or King Saud's slaveholding absolute monarchy. Yet to say we ought therefore not to have entered into these alliances would be to forget that autonomy precedes both prosperity and democracy among our objectives. For all their odious aspects, these pacts have helped to retain the independence of nations that would otherwise have fallen before the Communist advances.

When security is threatened, our differences must usually take a back seat. But this does not mean that they need have no seat at all. Our fault lies not in allying ourselves with governments with which we ideologically differ. Our fault lies in becoming so preoccupied, even obsessed, with matters of immediate military security that we let our other objectives go by the board completely. There is a text for this point too if we want it: "these ought ye to have done, and not to leave the other undone." Concern for the autonomy of western Europe may require that we include Spain in our military alliances, but it does not require the we do nothing to induce General Franco to use our support to increase freedom and prosperity of his people, especially in view of their complaint that the actual effect of our dollars and tanks is just the reverse: to shore up a regime which would otherwise have to reform or be overthrown. Sometimes we give the impression that we are willing to accept any terms such countries dictate as long as they stay on our side, as though, as Mr. Kennan has remarked, "it was we, rather than they, who had the most to lose if they went too far in the relations with Moscow."

A quick swing around the world through the eyes of notable political analysts will indicate a striking convergence of opinion, not that military alliances are unnecessary, but that we have developed them to the neglect of the direct needs of the people.

Regarding the Far East, Helen Mears writes: "The major weakness of our policy-making for the Far East is the fact that our government quite openly puts the assumed military and strategic needs of the United States ahead of the human needs of the people who live in the region."

Regarding Asia as a whole, the Indian Christian statesman M. M. Thomas writes: "Forces of national health, self-government and self-development have been weakened [by the] present system of military alliances in Asia. . . . Although in one or two cases these alliances were made necessary by the immediate situation, there was no such compulsion in other cases, and the tragedy imposed was not the inevitable resolution of the problem."

Regarding Africa, Hans Morganthau writes: "The United States . . . has subordinated its long-range interest in the autonomous development of the native population to short-range considerations of strategy and expediency."

Regarding Latin America, Carlton Beals writes: "Peacetime Western Hemisphere defense as it is now constituted . . . has no significance in the balance of world power [and] has turned back the clock of democratic evolution and freedom in many countries by a generation. It is a prime cause of instability, disorder, rioting, and revolution—for the reverse side of this false coin is military dictatorship, actual or nascent."

Where mutual security is not at stake there is even less excuse for supporting oppressive dictatorships and stagnant feudalisms. Cuba, Venezuela, the Dominican Republic, and Haiti are cases in point. In Haiti every leading newspaperman if not already killed is in jail, yet we continue to supply the country with military aid which has no effect on the balance of world power but serves only to bolster a vicious dictatorship. No wonder we are developing a "lover of dictators" reputation in South America. Our relations with these countries are not even dominated by "containment" considerations but rather by short-range economic advantage as seen by powerful American industries. Japan provides another example in the category of economic shortsightedness. All four of the world welfare goals we have proposed require freer trade to help her out of her truly appalling straits, but we bow to narrow sectional interests in our country and keep our barriers high.

The only conclusion possible is that our foreign policy has, in fact, as we have suggested, been dominated by objectives of communist containment, economic advantage, or indifference—a dimension of isolationism; objectives which are proving themselves increasingly inadequate to the needs of our time. The people of the United States are beginning to recognize this and throughout the nation there is a groundswell of restiveness with our present approach. What remains lacking is a leader with imagination great enough to see the convergence of our national interest with *world* welfare defined in terms of peace, autonomy, prosperity, and democracy, and who possesses the leadership ability to translate his vision into concrete policies that will carry the support of the people.

Never has our nation stood in greater need of such a man.

25

What Has Happened to the American Dream?

On January 4, 1961, the New York *Herald Tribune* carried on page 9, subordinated in space to a story of a castle for sale for $12 million, a news item from Russia. It described the new propaganda drive which is in line with the world Communist manifesto recently published. This manifesto declared "the United States is the bulwark of world reaction and the enemy of all the peoples of the globe."

Writers, lecturers, and agitators are being trained in special schools to spread this propaganda wherever they can. How many Americans read that news item? How many of them glanced at it and shrugged or laughed and dismissed it from their minds? How many of them were aware of the slow and relentless effect of Soviet propaganda among the uncommitted nations of the world and its effect on our standing among many peoples? I don't know, but I am sure that there were not enough. Not nearly enough. We are facing the greatest challenge our way of life has ever had to meet without any clear understanding of the facts.

There is in most people, at most times, a proneness to give more credence to pleasant news than to unpleasant, to hope that, somehow or other, things "will come out all right." But this was not the frame of mind that created the United States and made it not only a great nation but a symbol of the way of life that became the hope of the world. One can fight a danger only when one is armed with solid facts and spurred on by an unwavering faith and determination.

On my first visit to Russia I had watched the training of small babies. On my second trip, I studied the older children, their conditioning, their discipline, their docility, their complete absorption in the Communist system. Every child learns his Marxism backwards and forwards. By the time he leaves school, he is prepared to take not only his skills but his political ideas with him, wherever he may be sent, to whatever part of the world.

Wherever I went in Russia I found no personal hostility. But there was an unshaken conviction that the United States not only threatens but actually desires and seeks war. Here we are, equipped with the best communications in the world, and yet we have not learned how to use them in a way that can reach people.

Today, we are one of the oldest governments in existence; ours has been the position for leadership, for setting the pattern for behavior. And yet we are

The Atlantic Monthly 207 (April 1961): 46–50.

supinely putting ourselves in the position of leaving the leadership to the Russians, of following their ideas rather than our own. For instance, when the Russians set up a restriction on what visitors to the country may be allowed to see, we promptly do the same thing here, in retaliation. Whenever we behave in this manner, we are copying the methods of dictatorships and making a hollow boast of our claim that this country loves freedom for all. We owe it to ourselves and to the world, to our own dignity and self-respect, to set our own standards of behavior, regardless of what other nations do.

By practicing what we preach, putting democracy to work up to the very hilt, showing the world that our way of life has the most to offer the men and women and children of all countries, we may regain our lost leadership. Against those mindless millions we can oppose the unleashed strength of free men, for only in freedom can a man function completely.

When I visited Morocco in 1958 I had my first opportunity to see for myself the difficulties that arise in the transition stage between colonialism and independence. The troubles that Morocco was encountering were, it seemed to me, fairly typical of the basic difficulties of all young nations in transition.

As the French withdrew from Morocco, taking their nationals along, the villages found themselves stripped of teachers and doctors. Countless villages were without a single person trained to give medical assistance. The Moroccans themselves were not yet prepared to replace the doctors, the teachers, the civil service employees with their own men. It may be decades before they are ready to do so. Where, then, are the necessary people to come from? I feel that in that answer lies the key, or one of the major keys, to the future.

The great problems seem to be that, while people may be able to fight successfully for freedom, they may not yet be prepared to set up a stable and functioning independent government. The French pulled out, but the Moroccans had no one to replace them. They were totally unprepared for self-government. They were, in fact, much worse off than they had been a year before.

Today, this is happening again, in the Congo with the withdrawal of the Belgians. The time for colonization has gone forever, but some intermediate transition system is essential if chaos is not to follow.

A recent Afro-Asian resolution in the United Nations reveals the difficulty of the position by these words: "Inadequacy of political, economic, social or cultural preparedness" shall not serve as a pretext for denying independence. Now, it is certainly true that such a pretext has often been used in denying the right of self-determination. But it is equally true that without some basic qualifications, self-determination will lead to self-destruction.

In the Near East one finds the fluctuating and uncertain position of young countries which are in transition from the ways of the past to those of the future, with no certain path to tread and with the ultimate goal still obscure. That is becoming the situation of an increasing number of infant nations as they shake off the fetters of colonialism, of the ancient laws and customs, and grope for their own place in the sun. And what that goal is to be, what kind of place they are to occupy, what political philosophy they will choose in the long run will depend in great part on how we, in this country, prepare to meet the challenge.

Is what we are doing good enough? Have the changes that have revealed themselves in recent years, particularly in Africa and the Near East and the Latin American countries, shown overwhelming evidence that we are doing an intelligent job, an adequate job? I am afraid not. Genuinely afraid.

To me, the democratic system represents man's best and brightest hope of self-fulfillment, of a life rich in promise and free from fear; the one hope, perhaps, for the complete development of the whole man. But I know, and learn more clearly every day, that we cannot keep our system strong and free by neglect, by taking it for granted, by giving it our second-best attention. We must be prepared, like the suitor in *The Merchant of Venice*—and, I might point out, the successful suitor—to give and hazard all we have.

Man cannot live without hope. If it is not engendered by his own convictions and desires, it can easily be fired from without, and by the most meretricious and empty of promises.

What I learned on these trips around the world has been much on my mind. Why, I wondered, were we not more successful in helping the young nations and those in transition to become established along democratic lines? Why was it that the Russians were doing so much better? The answer can be oversimplified, and an oversimplification is false and misleading. But part of the answer, and I think a major part, is that Russia has trained its young people to go out into the world, to carry their services and skills to backward and underdeveloped countries, to replace the missing doctors and teachers, the scientists and technicians; above all, to fill the vacant civil service jobs, prepared not only by training for the job itself, but by learning the language, by a complete briefing in the customs, habits, traditions and trend of thought of the people, to understand them and deal with them. Where the young Russians go, of course, they take with them their Marxist training, thinking, and system.

And our young Americans? Are they being prepared to take their faith in democracy to the world along with their skills? Are they learning the language and the customs and the history of these new peoples? Do they understand how to deal with them, not according to their own ideas but according to the ideas of the people they must learn to know if they are to reach them at all? Have they acquired an ability to live and work among peoples of different religion and race and color, without arrogance and without prejudice?

Here, I believe, we have fallen down badly. In the last few years I have grasped at every opportunity to meet with the young, to talk with college students, to bring home as strongly as I can to even young children in the lower grades our responsibility for each other, our need to understand and respect each other. The future will be determined by the young, and there is no more essential task today, it seems to me, than to bring before them once more, in all its brightness, in all its splendor and beauty, the American dream, lest we let it fade, too concerned with the ways of earning a living or impressing our neighbors or getting ahead or finding bigger and more potent ways of destroying the world and all that is in it.

No single individual, of course, and no single group has an exclusive claim to the American dream. But we have all, I think, a single vision of what it is, not merely as a hope and an aspiration, but as a way of life, which we can come ever closer to attaining in its ideal form if we keep shining and unsullied our purpose and our belief in its essential value.

That we have sometimes given our friends and our enemies abroad a shoddy impression of the dream cannot be denied, much as we would like to deny it. *The Ugly American*, impressive as it was, struck me as being exaggerated. True, one of the first American ambassadors I ever met in an Eastern country was appallingly like a character in the novel. There are doubtless many others, too many others; men who accept—and seek—the position of representative of their government abroad, with no real interest or respect for the country they go to, and no real interest or respect for the image of their own country which they present to other people.

Such men buy their positions by gifts of money to their party or seek them because of the glamorous social life they may lead in exotic places.

"Oh, you must go there. You'll have a wonderful time. And the polo is topnotch."

They often do not know the language of the country; they are not familiar with its government or its officials; they are not interested in its customs, or its point of view.

The Russians, and I say it with shame, do much better. They are trained in the language, history, customs, and ways of life of a country before they go to it. They do not confine themselves to official entertaining but make a point of meeting and knowing and establishing friendly relations with people of all sorts, in every class of society, in every part of the country.

When we look at the picture of Russian greed in swallowing one satellite nation after another and contrast it with the picture of American generosity in giving food, clothing, supplies, technical and financial assistance, without the ulterior motive of acquiring new territory, it is stupid and tragic waste that the use of incompetent representatives should undo so much useful work, so great an expense, so much in the way of materials of every kind.

Of course, what the Russians have accomplished in training their young people for important posts in the underdeveloped countries—which, I must repeat, may affect the future course of these countries—has been done by compulsion. That's the rub. For what we must do is to achieve the same results on a voluntary basis. We do not say to our young people: "You must go here and take such a job." But we can show them that where we fail, the Russians will win, by default. We can show them the importance of acquiring the kind of training that will make them useful and honorable representatives of their country wherever they may go abroad.

Perhaps the new frontier today is something more than the new revolution in textiles and methods and speed and goods. It is the frontier of men's minds. But we cannot cast an enduring light on other men's minds unless the light in our own minds burns with a hard, unquenchable flame.

One form of communication we have failed in abjectly: that is in the teaching of languages. Most school children have several years of inadequate teaching in one language or another. I say inadequate because the study of a language, after all, is inadequate if one cannot learn to read and write it, to speak and to understand it. During the last war, the government found a simplified and most effective method of teaching such difficult languages as Japanese and Chinese to American GIs. In a matter of weeks they had mastered more of the language than formerly they would have acquired in the same number of years. And yet in our schools the old cumbersome, unproductive methods are still used.

It seems to me so obvious that it should not need to be said that we must increase and improve the teaching of languages to our young people, who will otherwise find themselves crippled and sorely handicapped in dealing with people of foreign races and different cultures.

These are things our children should be told. These are the conditions they are going to have to meet. They ought to be made to understand exactly what competition they will encounter, why they must meet it, how they can meet it best. Yet I rarely find, in talking with them, that they have been given the slightest inkling of the meaning of the Soviet infiltration of other countries, or that the future the Soviets are helping to build is the one with which they will have to contend. I rarely find that anyone has suggested that our own young people should have any preparation whatsoever to cope with the problems that are impending.

That is why, in the course of the past several years, I have fitted into my schedule, whenever I could, occasions to talk with the young. Sometimes they come up to Hyde Park by the busload to ask questions or to discuss problems. Sometimes I talk at their schools or colleges.

The other night, three boys from Harvard, one of them my grandson, came to see me. The head of the temporary government of Tanganyika had requested that some American students be sent there to teach English to their students, so that when the latter came to America to study they would be able to understand and communicate without difficulty. The young American students were also to participate in work projects and live in the native villages, where they could study conditions.

Thirty Americans, as a pilot project, were needed, and the cost for each was estimated at $1500. There was, I am happy to say, no problem in getting recruits. The difficulty came in raising money. The big foundations turned them down, whether because the project seemed unimportant, whether because of the youth of the people involved, or whether because they had failed to draw up a sufficiently complete, telling, and comprehensive prospectus of their plans, I do not know.

135

I was greatly interested, for it is out of such undertakings that bridges of understanding are built. I urged them to draw up the clearest possible statement of their plan and then to ask for scholarships. Certainly there must be thirty people willing to finance one scholarship each, in order to establish bonds of friendship and cooperation with a young nation.

Of course, there are great numbers of American college students with little information about and even less interest in the world in which they live. They are absorbed in their own concerns, in the social activities and the sports of their colleges, or in planning for their future careers. All this is natural enough. The trouble is that, on the whole, college students in some other countries start much earlier to relate themselves to their world and to become informed about the conditions which they must learn to meet in life.

What can we do to prepare young people to carry the American dream to the world in the best possible way? What I would like to say is this:

Today, our government and the governments of most of the world are primarily concerned—obsessed—by one idea: defense. But what is real defense, and how is it obtained? A certain amount of military defense is necessary. But there comes a point where you must consider what can be done on an academic and cultural basis.

It seems to me that, in terms of atomic warfare, we should henceforth have a small professional army of men who have voluntarily chosen this profession as an obligation to their country. But what then? What about the hundreds of thousands of young people who leave school every year, either from high school or college? Are they, from now on, to have no participation in contributing to the welfare of their country?

Far from it. As matters stand now, we draft young men into service, train them until they are useful, and then let them go. This seems to me monstrous waste.

It is my own personal conviction that every young person should be given some basic military training that might, eventually, be useful to his country. This could easily be handled either in school or at college. Instead of calling up all young men for compulsory military service, why should it not be possible to offer a counterproposal along these lines:

If you do not want to spend two years of compulsory military training, here is an alternative which is open to you. Whether you finish college or high school, you may decide what country you would like to spend two years in. You will be given two years of basic training, either during school hours or in the evenings. If you want to go, say, to Africa or one of the underdeveloped countries, you will, from the age of fifteen or seventeen, be taught the language, the history, the geography, the economic background of the country. You will be prepared to take with you a skill, or be trained for the most crying need in many transition nations—to fill the civil service jobs that Russia is now so rapidly filling. Or, if you are preparing for a profession, you may make use of that. New industries are needed in these countries; there are technical needs in almost all areas. The economy has to be bolstered in countless ways. New techniques are required in agriculture. And nearly all of these countries need teachers badly.

For people in young nations, which are still in a transition stage and setting up governments, such a course of action on our part could be more valuable than a large standing army or economic aid, particularly when in the new country there is no one capable of administering the aid effectively. Obviously, like anything else, this new concept cannot be carried out well without preparation and the clear thinking out of economic problems, based on comprehensive knowledge of the conditions of the country.

If we achieve—and why not?—a cooperation between universities and government, we might be able to equip some of our young people to take up the slack in underdeveloped countries and to bring our skills and our attitudes and our principles to them as free men.

These two-year volunteers could be doctors, engineers, teachers, scientists, mechanics, and administrators. It is possible that a system of scholarships might be worked out, which would enable us to use some of our young talent and ability in helping young countries get established. In such cases, there should be some sort of guarantee, some sort of facilities put at the use of these people when they return to their own country, to enable them to get jobs at home. This service, of course, could be in lieu of military service, but, it seems to me, it would be far more valuable.

The present long period of basic military training, which removes our young men from civilian life for two years and then returns them to it, seems to me a wasteful and pointless procedure. Certainly it could be made possible for them to have much of this basic military training that is required while they are in school. But military service, in an atomic, specialized age, should, like other professions, be on a voluntary basis and become a chosen career.

I have said that the Russians have accomplished by compulsion what we must accomplish voluntarily. But there is one element of this Russian training that is of paramount importance. They have taught their young to feel that they are needed, that they are important to the welfare of their country. I think that one of the strongest qualities in every human being is a need to feel needed, to feel important. Too often, our own youngsters do not feel that they are really essential to their country, or to the scheme of things. We have not had enough imagination to show them how very much we need every one of them to make us the kind of country that we can be.

If many of our young people have lost the excitement of the early settlers, who had a country to explore and develop, it is because no one remembers to tell them that the world has never been so challenging, so exciting; the fields of adventure and new fields to conquer have never been so limitless. There is still unfinished business at home, but there is the most tremendous adventure in bringing the peoples of the world to an understanding of the American dream. In this attempt to understand and to give a new concept of the relationships of mankind, there is open to our youngsters an infinite field of exciting adventure, where the heart and the mind and the spirit can all be engaged.

Perhaps the older generation is often to blame with its cautious warning: "Take a job that will give you security, not adventure." But I say to the young: "You have no security unless you can live bravely, excitingly, and imaginatively; unless you can choose a challenge instead of a competence."

Part C
Civil Rights and the Problems of Black America

26

The National Conference on the Education of Negroes

Mr. Chairman, Dr. Zook, Ladies and Gentlemen: It is a great pleasure for me to be with you this morning because I am following with interest all that you are doing in this conference. I noticed in the papers this morning the figures given of the cost of certain states per capita for the education of a colored child and of a white child, and I could not help but think as I read that item how stupid we are in some ways, for of course in any democracy the one important thing is to see as far as possible that *every* child receives at least the best education that that child is able to assimilate.

Now, that does not mean that education should not vary in different communities, because we all know that the needs of some communities are different from the needs of others, just as we know that some individuals (and this is not confined to any race) need a different type of education from others, and we should really bend our energies now, with our better knowledge of education, to giving to children the opportunity to develop their gifts, whatever they may be, to the best that is in them. We cannot all become geniuses, we cannot all reach the same level, but we can at least have the opportunity to do the best we can with what the Lord has given us.

I feel that while we have been fortunate in this country in having many fine men and women interested in the education of the Negro race, we have also been slow, many of us who are of the white race, in realizing how important not only to your race it is, but how important to our race that you should have the best educational advantages. The menace today to a democracy is unthinking action, action which comes from people who are illiterate, who are unable to understand what is happening in the world at large, what is happening in their own country, and who therefore act without really having any knowledge of the meaning of their actions, and that is the thing that we, whatever our race is, should be guarding against today.

There are many people in this country, many white people, who have not had the opportunity that they should have, and there are also many Negro people who have not had the opportunity that they should have. Both these conditions should be remedied and the same opportunities should be accorded to every child regardless of race or creed.

The Journal of Negro Education 3 (October 1934): 573–575. Address delivered at the National Conference on Fundamental Problems in the Education of Negroes, Washington, D.C., May 11, 1934.

Of course I feel this should be done because of our intelligent interest in children, but if we have to put it on a self-interest basis, then it should be done for the preservation of the best that is in the ideals of this country, because you can have no part of your population beaten down and expect the rest of the country not to feel the effects from the big groups that are underprivileged. That is so of our groups of white people and it is so of our underprivileged groups of Negro people. It lowers the standard of living. Wherever the standard of education is low, the standard of living is low, and it is for our own preservation in order that our whole country may live up to the ideals and to the intentions which brought our forefathers to this country, that we are interested today in seeing that education is really universal throughout the country.

Now I know what the facts are today, and I know that you know them. I know that in many communities people have been so badly off that they have not been able to keep up schools and pay teachers and do the things that should be done for the children of this generation. I think the Federal Government is trying to help in every way that it can in the crisis; but I think we have to go further back than the present crisis and realize, that even before we had the depression, there were people in the country who did not understand that not giving equal opportunity to all children for education was really a menace. It was felt that possibly it was better not to educate people to want more than they were at that time getting, and the thought which goes a little beyond this was dormant in a great many places. This thought which had not yet been accepted will make us realize that to deny to any part of a population the opportunities for more enjoyment in life, for higher aspirations is a menace to the nation as a whole. There has been too much concentrating wealth, and even if it means that some of us have got to learn to be a little more unselfish about sharing what we have than we have been in the past, we must realize that it will profit us all in the long run. We have got to think it through and realize that in the end all of us, the country over, will gain if we have a uniformly educated people; that is to say, if everywhere every child has the opportunity to gain as much knowledge as his ability will allow him to gain. We know that there are in every race certain gifts, and therefore the people of the different races will naturally want to develop those gifts. If they are denied the opportunity to do so they will always feel a frustration in their lives and a certain resentment against the people who have denied them this opportunity for self-expression.

I believe that the Negro race has tremendous gifts to bring to this country in the way of artistic development. I think things come by nature to many of them that we have to acquire, such as an appreciation of art and of music and of rhythm, which we really have to gain very often through education. I think that those things should be utilized for the good of the whole nation, that you should be allowed and helped to make your greatest contribution along the lines that you want and that give you joy. And therefore I am very happy to see this conference, and I have the hope that out of it will come a realization not only to you who are here but to all the people throughout the country who may be listening in today and who may later come in contact with those of you who are here, that we as a democracy in these times must be able to grasp our problems, must have sufficient general education to know not only what our difficulties are, but what the Government is trying to do to help us meet those difficulties. Without that ability in our people and without the willingness to sacrifice on the part of the people as a whole, in order that the younger generation may develop this ability, I think we have harder times ahead of us than we have had in the past. I think the day of selfishness is over; the day of really working together has come, and we must learn to work together, all of us, regardless of race or creed or color; we must wipe out, wherever we find it, any feeling that grows up, of intolerance, of belief that any one group can go ahead alone. We go ahead together or we go down together, and so may you profit now and for the future by all that you do in this conference.

27

The Negro and Social Change

Governor Nice, Mayor Jackson, members of the Urban League, and friends: It is a pleasure to be with you tonight to celebrate this twenty-fifth anniversary of the Urban League, because of the purpose for which the League was founded—better understanding and cooperation of both the white and Negro races in order that they may live better together and make this country a better place to live in.

Much that I am going to say tonight would apply with equal force to any of us living in this country. But our particular concern tonight is with one of the largest race groups in the country—the Negro race.

We have a great responsibility here in the United States because we offer the best example that exists perhaps today throughout the world, of the fact that if different races know each other they may live peacefully together. On the whole, we in this country live peacefully together though we have many different races making up the citizenry of the United States. The fact that we have achieved as much as we have in understanding of each other, is no reason for feeling that our situation and our relationship are so perfect that we need not concern ourselves about making them better. In fact we know that many grave injustices are done throughout our land to people who are citizens and who have an equal right under the laws of our country, but who are handicapped because of their race. I feel strongly that in order to wipe out these inequalities and injustices, we must all of us work together; but naturally those who suffer the injustices are most sensitive of them, and are therefore bearing the brunt of carrying through whatever plans are made to wipe out undesirable conditions.

Therefore in talking to you tonight, I would like to urge first of all that you concentrate your effort on obtaining better opportunities for education for the Negro people throughout the country. You *must* be able to understand the economic condition and the changes which are coming, not only in our own country, but throughout the world, and this, without better education than the great majority of Negro people have an *opportunity* to obtain today, is not possible. And without an improvement which will allow better work and better understanding, it will be difficult to remove the handicaps under which some of you suffer.

I marvel frequently at the patience with which those who work for the removal of bad conditions face their many disappointments. And I would like

Opportunity 41, no.1 (January 1936): 22–23. Address delivered at the celebration of the 25th anniversary of the founding of the National Urban League, Baltimore, December 12, 1935.

to pay tribute tonight to the many leaders amongst the colored people, whom I know and admire and respect. If they are apt at times to be discouraged and downhearted, I can only offer them as consolation, the knowledge that all of us who have worked in the past, and are still working for economic and social betterment, have been through and will continue to go through many periods of disappointment. But as we look back over the years, I have come to realize that what seemed to be slow and halting advances, in the aggregate make quite a rapid march forward.

I believe, of course, that for our own good in this country, the Negro race as a whole must improve its standards of living, and become both economically and intellectually of higher calibre. The fact that the colored people, not only in the South, but in the North as well, have been economically at a low level, has meant that they have also been physically and intellectually at a low level. Economic conditions are responsible for poor health in children. And the fact that tuberculosis and pneumonia and many other diseases have taken a heavier toll amongst our colored groups, can be attributed primarily to economic conditions. It is undoubtedly true that with an improvement in economic condition it will still be necessary not only to improve our educational conditions for children, but to pay special attention to adult education along the line of better living. For you cannot expect people to change overnight, when they have had poor conditions, and adjust themselves to all that we expect of people living as they *should* live today throughout our country.

This holds good for *all* underprivileged people in our country and in other countries. For instance, not long ago I was talking to a woman from England, a social worker, who told me that she had found it was not sufficient to give people better housing, to give them better wages; that you also had to have some leadership and education in how to live in those houses and how to use the better wages. And I have seen that proved in the last few years in some of the mining sections of our country. The stock is good American stock, but they have had long years of hard times, and some of the communities that I happen to know have been given good houses and a little economic security, but no leadership. And another community that I know has had both education from nursery school up, and leadership, and adult education. And someone said to me the other day in comparing a number of communities, that the particular community where this leadership has been given, was Paradise compared to all the others.

So that I think I am right when I say that it is not just enough to give people who have suffered a better house and better wages. You must give them education and understanding and training before you can expect them to take up their full responsibility.

I think that we realize the desirability today of many social changes; but we also must realize that in making these changes and bridging the gap between the old life and the new, we have to accept the responsibility and assume the necessary burden of giving assistance to the people who have not had their fair opportunity in the past.

One thing I want to speak about tonight because I have had a number of people tell me that they felt the Government in its new efforts and programs was not always fair to the Negro race. And I want to say quite often, it is not the intention of those at the top, and as far as possible I hope that we may work together to eliminate any real injustice.

No right-thinking person in this country today who picks up a paper and reads that in some part of the country the people have not been willing to wait for the due processes of law, but have gone back to the rule of force, blind and unjust as force and fear usually are, can help but be ashamed that we have shown such a lack of faith in our own institutions. It is a horrible thing which grows out of weakness and fear, and not out of strength and courage; and the sooner we as a nation unite to stamp out any such action, the sooner and the better will we be able to face the other nations of the world and to uphold our real ideals here and abroad.

We have long held in this country that ability should be the criterion on which all people are judged. It seems to me that we must come to recognize this criterion in dealing with all human beings, and not place any limitations upon their achievements except such as may be imposed by their own character and intelligence.

This is what we work for as an ideal for the relationship that must exist between all the citizens of our country. There is no reason why all of the races in this country should not live together each of them giving from their particular gift something to the other, and contributing an example to the world of "peace on earth, good will toward men."

28

Civil Liberties—
The Individual and the Community

Ladies and gentlemen: I am glad you gave an award to the press tonight, because that gave them the opportunity to tell us just what they could do. Now we have come here tonight because of civil liberties. I imagine a great many of you could give my talk far better than I could, because you have had first-hand knowledge in the things you have had to do in Chicago over the years to preserve civil liberties. Perhaps, however, I am more conscious of the importance of civil liberties in the particular moment of our history than anyone else, because as I travel through the country and meet people and see things that have happened to little people, I realize what it means to democracy to preserve our civil liberties. All through the years we have had to fight for civil liberty, and we know that there are times when the light grows rather dim, and every time that happens democracy is in danger. Now largely because of the troubled state of the world as a whole civil liberties have disappeared in many other countries. It is impossible, of course, to be at war and to keep freedom of the press and freedom of speech and freedom of assembly. They disappear automatically. And so in many countries where ordinarily they were safe, today they have gone and in other countries, even before war came, not only freedom of the press and freedom of assembly and freedom of speech disappeared, but freedom of religion disappeared and so we know that here in this country we have a grave responsibility. We are at peace. We have no reason for the fears which govern so many other peoples throughout the world, and, therefore, we have to guard the freedoms of democracy. Civil liberties emphasizes the liberty of the individual. In many other forms of government the importance of the individual has disappeared. The individual lives for the state. Here in a democracy the government still exists for the individual, but that does not mean that we do not have to watch and that we do not have to examine ourselves to be sure that we preserve the civil liberties for all our people, which are the basis of our democracy. Now you know if we are honest with ourselves, in spite of all we have said, in spite of our Constitution, many of us in this country do not enjoy real liberty. For that reason we know that everywhere in this country every person who believes in democracy has come to feel a real responsibility to work in his community and to know the people of his community, and to take the trouble to try to bring about the full observance for all our people of their civil liberties.

Reference Shelf 14 (1940). Address to the Chicago Civil Liberties Committee, March 14, 1940.

I think I will tell you a little story that brought home to me how important it was that in every community there should be someone to whom people could turn, who were in doubt as to what were their rights under the law, when they couldn't understand what was happening to them. I happen to go every now and then to a certain mining community and in that mining community there are a number of people who came to this country many years ago. They have been here so many years that they have no other country. This is their country. Their children have been born here. They work here. They have created great wealth for this country, but they came over at a time when there was not very much feeling of social responsibility about giving them the opportunity to learn the language of the country to which they had come, or telling them how to become citizens, or teaching about the government of this country. I had contact with a family where the man had been here over thirty-five years, and the first time I went to see him in his house it came about this way. I was standing with a group of people, and a young girl with arms full of packages came along the road. She stopped to look at me and said, "Why, you are Mrs. Roosevelt. My mama say, 'She is happy if you come to her house.' " I said, "Where is her house!" "Up the run." So I walked with her and when I got to the house a Polish woman was sitting at the table. The girl walked in and said, "Mama, this is Mrs. Roosevelt," and the woman got up and threw both arms around me, and I was kissed on both cheeks. She told me she had been expecting me to come for a long time. She wanted me to come because she wanted me to see how really nice her house was, and we went through the four rooms and it was nice. She had made crochet pieces which decorated every table. The bedspreads were things of real beauty. We admired everything together. We came back to the kitchen and she said, "You eat with us?" and I said, "No, I just had breakfast." She wouldn't let me leave without eating something, so we had a piece of bread there together.

Six months later I came back and I went again to visit my friend. The minute I crossed the threshold I knew something had happened in that house. It was quite dark. In a few minutes the old man came through from the back room and said, "Mrs. Roosevelt, you have come. I have wanted to ask you something for a long time. The mine, it close down, no more work. I work on W.P.A. for a time and then they tell me I no citizen. Mrs. Roosevelt, I vote. I vote often. Why I no citizen?" There was nobody that stood out in the community that he dared trust, that he felt he could go to find out what his rights were, or what he should do. Well, of course, it was true that he had never become a citizen. His children were born in this country; they were citizens, but he was not. And they had lived, those two people by being allowed by the county to take in four old men who would have gone otherwise to the county poor house. Six people were living on the allowance of those four old men. The allowance was pitifully small. As I looked at the stove at what they were going to have for supper, I realized the woman wouldn't again say, "Sit down and eat." There wasn't enough for a stranger, and that was the breakdown of her morale. It hurt you. Something was wrong with the spirit of America that an injustice like that could happen to a man who, after all, worked hard and contributed to the wealth of the country. It should have been somebody's business, first of all, to see that he learned the English language well enough to find things out for himself. Secondly, when he was in trouble, to fight for his rights and to tell him how to go about to remedy what was wrong. I felt there was something wrong with any community where you had to wait many months for a stranger to come to listen to your story and help you straighten out what was a manifest injustice. He couldn't be on W.P.A. He could start out to become a citizen, and he could get relief and, at least, have the feeling that there was an interest on the part of someone in justice. I think that is, perhaps, one of the greatest things that the civil liberties committees do, and I wish we had one in every place throughout the country—one group of people who really care when things go wrong and do something when there is an infringement of the individual's rights.

There are many times when even with freedom of the press and freedom of speech, it is hard to get a hearing for certain causes. I often think that we, all of us, should think very much more carefully than we do about what we mean by freedom of speech, by freedom of the press, by freedom of assembly. I sometimes am much worried by the tendency that you find today in our country only to think that these are rights for the people who think as we do. Some people seem to think these rights are not for people who disagree with them. I believe that you must apply to all groups the right to all forms of thought, to all forms of expression. Otherwise, you practically refuse to trust people to choose for themselves what is wise and what is right, and in doing that you deny the possibility of a democratic form of government. You have to be willing to listen or to allow people to state any point of view they may have, to say anything they may believe, and trust that when everyone has had his say, when there has been free discussion and really free expression in the press, in the end the majority of the people will have the wisdom to decide what is right. We have to have faith that even when the majority seems to decide as we think wrongly, we still believe the fundamental principles that we have laid down, and we wait for the day to come when the thing that we believe is right becomes the majority decision of the people.

Well, of course that means that we have to have a real belief that people have sufficient intelligence to live in a democracy, and that is something which we are really testing out in this country today, because we are the only great democracy and we are the only democracy that is at peace and that can go on and live in what we consider a normal and free way of living. It is only here that people don't have to tremble when they say what they think. I don't know how many of you have read a book that I have been reading, but I think it is a most vivid picture of the kind of fear that has gradually come to all the people of Europe. It is *Stricken Field* by Martha Gellhorn, a young woman who was a war correspondent. The story was put in novel form and is about the taking over of Czechoslovakia. Certain people in Czechoslovakia were considered dangerous to the new regime—and the whole description is horrible of what they called "going under-ground," living in hiding, afraid to speak to each other, afraid to recognize each other on the streets, for fear they would be tortured to death. Only great fear could bring people to treat other people like that, and I can only say that it seems to me that we should read as vivid a story as this now, just to make us realize how important it is that for no reason whatsoever we allow ourselves to be dominated by fears so that we curtail civil liberties. Let us see that everybody who is really in danger in our community has, at least, his or her day in court. Constituted authority has to work under the law. When the law becomes something below the surface, hidden from the people, something which is underground, so to speak, and over which the people no longer hold control, then all of us are in danger.

Never before was it so important that every individual should carry his share of responsibility and see that we do obey the laws, live up to the Constitution, and preserve every one of those precious liberties which leave us free as individuals. One of the things that we have to be particularly live to today is the growth of religious prejudice and race prejudice. Those are two things which are a great menace because we find that in countries where civil liberties have been lost, both religious and race prejudice have been rampant. I think it would be well for us, if we could define what we mean when we say that we believe in religious freedom. I sat at a desk in a political campaign once. I was running the office dealing with women for the National Democratic Committee. Over my desk came literature and material which I did not suppose anyone would print in the United States, and much of it was written and published by people who belong to various religious denominations. It seems to me that the thing we must fix in our minds is that from the beginning this country was founded on the right of all people to worship God as they saw fit, and if they do not wish to worship they are not forced to worship. That is a fundamental liberty. When religion begins to take part in politics, we violate something which we have set up, which is a division between church and state.

As far as having respect for the religion of other people and leaving them to live their lives the way they wish, we should teach that to every child. Every child should know that his religion is his own and nobody else has the right to question it. In addition to that I think we should begin much earlier to teach all the children of our nation what a wonderful heritage they have for freedom. For freedom from prejudice, because they live in a nation which is made up of a great variety of other nations. They have before them and around them every day the proof that people can understand each other and can live together amicably, and that races can live on an equal basis, even though they may be very different in background, very different in culture. We have an opportunity to teach our children how much we have gained from the coming to this land of all kinds of races, how much it has served in the development of the land, and somehow I think we have failed in many ways in bringing it early enough to children how great is their obligation to the various strains that make up the people of the United States. Above all, there should never be race prejudice here, there should never be a feeling that one strain is better than another. Indians are the only real inhabitants of the country who have a right to say that they own this country! I think this is the reason that we should preserve freedom of mind on the things which are basic to civil liberties. And it should be easy for us to live up to our Constitution.

I am very much interested to find that in our younger generation, however, there is a greater consciousness of what civil liberties really mean, and I think that is one of the hopeful things in the world today, that youth is really taking a tremendous interest in the preservation of civil liberties. It is a very hard period in the world for youth because they are faced with new kinds of problems. We don't know the answers to many of the problems that face us today and neither do the young people, and the problems are very much more important to the young because they must start living. We have had our lives. The young people want to begin and they can't find a way to get started. Perhaps that has made them more conscious of civil liberties. Perhaps that is why when you get a group of them together you find them fighting against the prejudices which have grown up in our country, against the prejudices which have made it hard for the minority groups in our country. The other night someone sent up a question to me: "What do you think should be done about the social standing of the Negro race in this country?" Well now, of course, I think the social situation is one that has to be dealt with by individuals. The real question that we have to face in this country is what are we doing about the rights of a big minority group as citizens in our democracy. That we have to face. Any citizen in this country is entitled to equality before the law; to equality of education; to equality at earning a living, as far as his abilities have made it possible for him to do; to equality of participation in government so that he or she may register their opinion in just the way that any other citizens do. Now those things are basic rights, belonging to every citizen in every minority group, and we have an obligation, I think, to stand up and be counted when it comes to the question of whether any minority group does not have those rights as citizens in this country. The minute we deny any rights of this kind to any citizen we are preparing the way for the denial of those rights to someone else. We have to make up our minds what we really believe. We have to decide whether we believe in the Bill of Rights, in the Constitution of the United States, or whether we are going to modify it because of the fears that we may have at the moment.

Now I listened to the broadcast this afternoon with a great deal of interest. I almost forgot what a fight had been made to assure the rights of the working man. I know there was a time when hours were longer and wages lower, but I had forgotten just how long that fight for freedom, to bargain collectively, and to have freedom of assembly, had taken. Sometimes, until some particular thing comes to your notice, you think something has been won for every working man, and then you come across as I did the other day a case where someone had taken the law into his own hands and beaten up a labor organizer. I didn't think we did those things anymore in this country, but it appears we do. Therefore, someone must be always on the lookout to see that someone is ready to take up the cudgels to defend those who can't defend themselves. That is the only way we are going to keep this country a law-abiding country, where law is looked upon with respect and where it is not considered necessary for anybody to take the law into his own hands. The minute you allow that, then you have acknowledged that you are no longer able to trust in your courts and in your law-enforcing machinery, and civil liberties are not very well off when anything like that happens; so I think that after listening to the broadcast today, I would like to remind you that behind all those who fight for the Constitution as it was written, for the rights of the weak and for the preservation of civil liberties, we have a long line of courageous people, which is something to be proud of and something to hold on to. Its only value lies, however, in the fact that we profit by example and continue the tradition in the future. We must not let those people back of us down; we must have courage; we must not succumb to fear of any kind; and we must live up to the things that we believe in and see that justice is done to the people under the Constitution, whether they belong to minority groups or not. This country is a united country in which all people have the same rights as citizens. We are grateful that we can trust in the youth of the nation that they are going on to uphold the real principles of democracy and put them into action in this country. They are going to make us an even more truly democratic nation.

29

Intolerance

People keep asking: "Is a wave of intolerance sweeping over our country? Are we getting away from our traditional attitude that all races and religions are equal in the eyes of the law?"

The answer is obviously "Yes." A wave of intolerance most certainly is sweeping over us. But we need not behave as though it were a phenomenon which we had never before experienced, and we should not magnify it. On the whole, we are a tolerant people.

War anywhere develops intolerance everywhere. Notice how in this country today, because of the activities of a noisy minority, we see Germans who have lived here most of their lives, and who came to us because they believed in what the United States represented, suspected of disloyalty. The same is true for other refugees. War breeds fear and intolerance.

Intolerance has its roots in fear. Many of the people who have testified before the Dies Committee—White Camellias, Silver Shirts, Brown Shirts, or what have you—are examples of this fear. They are afraid that we cannot solve our problems in accordance with our own traditions, and so they turn to the solutions found in other countries and hide foreign ideologies under the names of American patriotism. They typify the very traits which true Americans have sought to eradicate ever since the Declaration of Independence and the Constitution were written.

Perhaps the wave of anti-Semitism is our greatest manifestation of intolerance today, though in some places anti-Catholicism runs a close second, and in others fear of the Negro's aspirations is paramount.

Persecution and confiscation of property, largely for the Jewish race, but also for Catholics and Protestants who do not agree entirely with the "powers that be," have swept parts of the world because of economic conditions and *fear*.

The ideas which crop up anywhere are bound to affect the rest of the world. Especially is this true when selfish foreign interests take advantage of our traditional freedom and put their ideas before us with little regard for truth. I want to tell you a story which illustrates the foolishness of such fears. A friend of mine told me of finding himself at a dinner given by the Chamber of Commerce in a small town at a time when the Ku Klux Klan was active in that section. On his right sat the treasurer of the organization, and to his surprise the man was a Jew. Beside the chairman sat the secretary, a Catholic.

"Is the Klan strong in this vicinity?" my friend asked the chairman.

Cosmopolitan (February 1940): 24, 102–103.

"Yes; oh yes," was the reply.

"Then how is it that two of the officers of your organization are respectively a Jew and a Catholic?"

The answer came unhesitatingly: "But we know *them*. They are good fellows and important in our community."

I was in a western state some years ago when a general strike occurred, and I made the discovery that when people are made uncomfortable, the spirit of tolerance disappears. No longer are they interested in what is right or wrong; they want action and a return to comfortable living conditions. Every time we succumb to this degree of selfishness, we fail to live up to the citizenship of which our forefathers thought we would be capable.

All of us in this country give lip service to the ideals set forth in the Bill of Rights and emphasized by every additional amendment, and yet when war is stirring in the world, many of us are ready to curtail our civil liberties. We do not stop to think that curtailing these liberties may in the end bring us a greater danger than the danger we are trying avert. I do not believe that people like Mr. Kuhn or Mr. Browder can have great success in injuring us as a nation. They may well be undesirable citizens of the United States, however, because, as has been made evident, their first loyalty belongs to some other country. They may be good citizens of the other nation; they are not good citizens of the United States.

Under our present laws we can deal fairly with our own people and still safeguard ourselves against those who would destroy democracy. We should constantly guard our civil liberties, to be sure that all get equally fair treatment, and try to teach greater tolerance. Actually, complete tolerance has not been realized as yet. My husband's ancestress, Anne Hutchinson, could have testified that the early New Englanders were not very tolerant. In 1637 she was expelled from the Boston Church because "she broke from a covenant of works in favor of a covenant of grace."

These New Englanders had left their native land out of a desire to be free from such prejudices as existed there, yet they persisted in their own type of intolerance. They were a good example of the sort of people who believe in tolerance so long as the opposition agrees with them. We always have that kind of tolerance with us.

Then again, we had a long fight to establish the fact that the right of man to govern himself does not depend upon his material possessions. We believe that in a democracy a man should participate in government even if he owns very little of this world's goods.

Strange to say—though we rarely think about it—that fight isn't yet won. We disenfranchise many people every year.

In a minor degree, our present intolerances have existed for a long time.

We not only accepted immigrants from the Old World; we welcomed them with open arms. Some of them came as political refugees and were the cream of the countries which they left, but a great many were sought primarily for their ability to do a heavy day's work with their hands and to live on a submarginal standard, and we assumed a rather superior attitude toward them. We called foreigners "wops," "hunkies" and other names, and thought it beneath us to study foreign languages. It was up to the people who came here to learn our language, or at least learn enough to understand the orders issued to them in the day's work.

By our very attitude we strengthened these people and weakened ourselves. Our children learned no new language, while theirs did. Our children had no special difficulty to overcome. Their children did, and in the end they gained thereby.

We would not see that the newcomers frequently had a heritage of culture and skill to give us. For instance, even today the great majority of our expert cabinetmakers are of foreign extraction, and one of our greatest experts on early American furniture is a Russian Jew.

No, we did not profit by the foreigners' skills as much as we might have done. In this attitude toward the many foreigners who now make up our nation lie the roots of some of our present-day intolerance.

I sometimes meet people in drawing rooms who talk about the unemployed as though the latter were a different race, and occasionally remark: "Well, if they cannot support themselves, they are probably better off out of the way. They are not doing the country any good."

I leave with the feeling that these people were not my people, yet often we had much the same background.

Some persons I talk to remind me of a social worker who once refused assistance to a woman who had three starving children. When I inquired the reason for her hardness of heart, she responded: "My dear lady, the children are illegitimate!" Unfortunately, starvation does not take this item of morals into account!

Real tolerance does not attempt to make other people conform to any particular religious or racial pattern. We are within our rights, of course, in refusing to go to church with another man if we do not like his church, but we are certainly not within our rights in condemning him because he attends that church.

I should say that our open manifestations of intolerance today are still of minor importance. The great majority of our people stand behind the leaders who insist on freedom of speech, freedom of assembly, freedom of the press, and equality before the law. We do not attain these freedoms everywhere, but we like to think we do. The Ku Klux Klan is pretty well discredited. Similar organizations are probably going the same way.

The best recent example of real tolerance that I can think of was the protection given the meeting of the German-American Bund in New York by Mayor LaGuardia, even when the speakers denounced the mayor and his actions.

This is the kind of tolerance that recalls the statement attributed to Voltaire: "I disapprove of what you say, but I will defend to the death your right to say it."

On the whole, we back the authorities when they try to clean up conditions in business and politics which are irreconcilable with our traditions. With better education, some of our other prejudices will pass, but one factor we *must* face: the economic situation. As yet we haven't done so.

As I have said, the economic situation is the reason for much of our intolerance today. People who are having a hard time will complain about certain races, or certain groups, because they fear the economic competition of certain individuals who, either because of racial background or because of former experiences, may succeed better than they have succeeded.

Every individual who sees himself sinking below the economic surface fears his neighbor who can survive.

Because of the economic situation there is not enough work for men, so it is suggested that women be barred from economic independence. First it will be married women who should be supported by men, then it will be all other women, "Because woman was created to be the slave of man and should be dependent whether she likes it or not."

In 1939, twenty bills were introduced in as many legislatures in the United States to prevent married women from holding some kinds of positions. This was the direct result of economic intolerance. We *fear* that we cannot solve our economic difficulties. If we act in accordance with these fears, the results will be retrogression in civilization, as we may discover by looking back in history.

We must solve our economic problems from the point of view of re-employment, or we can never hope to wipe out intolerance.

Businessmen say our failure to solve the problem of giving men work is the fault of certain policies of the government. They have asked for certain changes which it is to be hoped Congress will make, insofar as these changes tend to increase employment.

We might as well face the fact, however, that for many people a revival of business is not regarded primarily from the point of view of the re-employment of men, but is though of as an opportunity to make more money. Re-employment is spoken of as a thing which will naturally follow business revival.

I confess to some trepidation where re-employment is not the first consideration; where it is not fully realized that earned wages for more people is our best way to create better markets, and thus to establish our economic system on a firm basis. If we put the making of money first, I am afraid we shall have the cart before the horse.

In my opinion, the solution of this problem of giving men a chance to earn a decent living is the most important consideration before us at the present time, because ending unemployment will, to a very great extent, end intolerance.

30

Race, Religion and Prejudice

Madame Chiang Kai-shek's recent articles force us all to realize that one of the phases of this war that we have to face is the question of race discrimination.

We have had a definite policy toward the Chinese and Japanese who wished to enter our country for many years, and I doubt very much if after this war is over we can differentiate between the peoples of Europe, the Near East and the Far East.

Perhaps the simplest way of facing the problem in the future is to say that we are fighting for freedom, and one of the freedoms we must establish is freedom from discrimination among the peoples of the world, either because of race, or of color, or of religion.

The people of the world have suddenly begun to stir and they seem to feel that in the future we should look upon each other as fellow human beings, judged by our acts, by our abilities, by our development, and not by any less fundamental differences.

Here in our own country we have any number of attitudes which have become habits and which constitute our approach to the Jewish people, the Japanese and Chinese people, the Italian people, and above all, to the Negro people in our midst.

Perhaps because the Negroes are our largest minority, our attitude towards them will have to be faced first of all. I keep on repeating that the way to face this situation is by being completely realistic. We cannot force people to accept friends for whom they have no liking, but living in a democracy it is entirely reasonable to demand that every citizen of that democracy enjoy the fundamental rights of a citizen.

Over and over again, I have stressed the rights of every citizen:

Equality before the law.
Equality of education.
Equality to hold a job according to his ability.
Equality of participation through the ballot in the government.

These are inherent rights in a democracy, and I do not see how we can fight this war and deny these rights to any citizen in our own land.

The other relationships will gradually settle themselves once these major things are part of our accepted philosophy.

It seems trite to say to the Negro, you must have patience, when he has had patience so long; you must not expect miracles overnight, when he can look back to the years of slavery and say—how many nights! he has waited for

New Republic 106 (May 11, 1942): 630.

justice. Nevertheless, it is what we must continue to say in the interests of our government as a whole and of the Negro people; but that does not mean that we must sit idle and do nothing. We must keep moving forward steadily, removing restrictions which have no sense, and fighting prejudice. If we are wise we will do this where it is easiest to do it first, and watch it spread gradually to places where the old prejudices are slow to disappear.

There is now a great group of educated Negroes who can become leaders among their people, who can teach them the value of things of the mind and who qualify as the best in any field of endeavor. With these men and women it is impossible to think of any barriers of inferiority, but differences there are and always will be, and that is why on both sides there must be tact and patience and an effort at real understanding. Above everything else, no action must be taken which can cause so much bitterness that the whole liberalizing effort may be set back over a period of many years.

31
Abolish Jim Crow!

A senator stood up in the Congress the other day after listening to a lengthy discourse on the poll tax, and spoke his mind on the discussion which was going on. Later he asked: "Are we fighting the Civil War all over again?"

Sometimes when I look at the Lincoln statue and read the things which he said, I think that we fought a bitter war which brought suffering to many people and yet achieved no answer to the question—are the colored people free in fact or only in word?

In that war we succeeded in establishing our unity. We would be one nation and not two and we said that all the people in our nation should enjoy equal rights and privileges, but in our hearts we never really believed what we said.

That is why we have to set to work to persuade our citizens not only to give lip-service to the results of the Civil War, but actually to put those results into practice, even though we are engaged in fighting a war to assure these same rights and privileges of freedom throughout the world.

A great many people believe that there should be no intermingling of races. Hitler has proved with bloody massacres that he holds this belief. Nevertheless, down through the ages, it has been proved over and over again that this is one of the questions which people settle for themselves, and no amount of legislation will keep them from doing so. We would not have so many different shades of color in this country today if this were not so. This is a question, therefore, that I think we have to leave to individuals, not only all over the United States, but all over the world, to handle.

There is no more reason to expect that there will be more intermarriage if the four fundamental basic rights of citizens are granted to all people in this country than there will be if they are withheld. In fact, I think it probable that there would be less.

An equal opportunity for education may raise economic standards as a whole—may make it possible for colored people to get equal pay, because they will have training equal to that of white people. There will be more self-respect; the dignity and pride of race will be enhanced and the bitterness of inferiority removed.

I am not writing from the point of view of the scientists, as their point of view is amply covered in many scientific books. I am trying to state the case clearly because we need firm ground to stand on as we fight this war.

Many a boy, when asked, still says he does not know what he is fighting for. While he knows we have to beat Hitler and the Japs, he will be glad when

New Threshold 1 (August 1943): 4, 34.

it is done and he is back home again. That would be all right if winning the war would settle all the racial questions, but it is after the war when we live together that they will become really important. In addition, if every boy was sure that he would be going back home again, he could decide later for what objectives he had fought and work for them, but if he is to die, he must be sure that what he died for is worthwhile to his parents, his brothers, his sisters, his wife or his sweetheart.

We are fighting a war today so that individuals all over the world may have freedom. This means an equal chance for every man to have food and shelter and a minimum of such things as spell happiness to that particular human personality. If we believe firmly that peace cannot come to the world unless this is true for men all over the world, then we must know in our nation that every man, regardless of race or religion, has this chance. Otherwise we fight for nothing of real value.

So here at home I think we have to fight for these four simple freedoms.

Equality before the law, which assures us of justice without prejudice, for Jew or Gentile, for any race or any color, as far as human beings can obtain justice.

Equality of education for everyone, because of the need for an equal opportunity in life.

Equality in the economic field, which means we are so organized in our communities and in our system of economics that all men who want to work will have work and that work will be suited to their capacity and will be rewarded without prejudice.

Finally, because we believe in the democratic and republican form of government, by which we are governed through the consent of the governed, we must give to all the citizens of a democracy a chance for equality of expression. We believe that there should be no impediment which prevents any man from expressing his will through the ballot.

The acceptance of these fundamental rights seem to me the only basis on which the men who fight this war can look forward into the future with real hope to a world organization which may gradually bring about a betterment of human conditions the world over.

If we have no hope that this is going to be the case, and that this is the real objective for which we fight, then I think there are many people who will feel that they cannot bear the sacrifice and the cruelty and the horror which those they love have to go through. If the future only holds a repetition of the past, if in each nation there are to be real slaves, even though they do not exist in name, then the boys who say they do not know why they fight have a right to say so. There would be no world worth fighting for and the only men who would have any reason for fighting would be the professional soldiers who fight for the love of fighting. No man would be fighting for a cause or a country because they provided a fulfillment of his hopes and desires, or at least the right to struggle for them. Our men are not professional soldiers, they fight because they believe that the cause involved is worth fighting for—the freedom of people the world over to strive for greater happiness.

There will be ups and downs in the future, because progress is never made on an even course. If we can keep steadily marching forward so that each generation can count some gains in human progress, if we can eliminate war and feel that we are again devoting all of our energies to constructive instead of destructive ends, I believe that youth will have enough hope to keep on with the struggle. With hope and faith they can solve the economic questions, the racial questions, the spiritual questions, which are bound to arise from time to time and bring the world nearer to Tennyson's vision of The Brotherhood of Man.

32

Freedom: Promise or Fact

If I were a Negro today, I think I would have moments of great bitterness. It would be hard for me to sustain my faith in democracy and to build up a sense of goodwill toward men of other races.

I think, however, that I would realize that if my ancestors had never left Africa, we would be worse off as "natives" today under the rule of any other country than I am in this country where my people were brought as slaves.

In a comparatively short period of time the slaves have become free men—free men, that is, as far as a proclamation can make them so. There now remains much work to be done to see that freedom becomes a fact and not just a promise for my people.

I know, however, that I am not the only group that has to make a similar fight. Even women of the white race still suffer inequalities and injustices, and many groups of white people in my country are slaves of economic conditions. All the world is suffering under a great war brought about because of the lag in our social development against the progress in our economic development.

I would know that I had to work hard and to go on accomplishing the best that was possible under present conditions. Even though I was held back by generations of economic inequality, I would be proud of those of my race who are gradually fighting to the top in whatever occupation they are engaged in.

I would still feel that I ought to participate to the full in the war. When the United Nations win, certain things will be accepted as a result of principles which have been enunciated by the leaders of the United Nations, which never before have been part of the beliefs and practices of the greater part of the world.

I would certainly go on working for complete economic equality and my full rights under a democratic government. I would decide which were the steps that I felt represented my real rights as a citizen and I would work for those first, feeling that other things such as social relationships might well wait until certain people were given time to think them through and decide as individuals what they wished to do.

I would not do too much demanding. I would take every chance that came my way to prove my quality and my ability and if recognition was slow, I would continue to prove myself, knowing that in the end good performance has to be acknowledged.

I would accept every advance that was made in the Army and Navy, though I would not try to bring those advances about any more quickly than they were offered. I would certainly affiliate with the labor movement because

Negro Digest 1(October 1943): 8–9.

there is the greatest opportunity for men to work side by side and find out that it is possible to have similar interests and to stand by each other, regardless of race or color.

I would try to remember that unfair and unkind treatment will not harm me if I do not let it touch my spirit. Evil emotions injure the man or woman who harbors them so I would try to fight down resentment, the desire for revenge and bitterness. I would try to sustain my own faith in myself by counting over my friends and among them there would undoubtedly be some white people.

33

The Minorities Question

I was brought up in a home where learning Bible verses, Collects and Hymns was a daily and Sunday practice. As children we were often asked if we had read our portion of the Scriptures every morning and every night as we were expected to do, and though I am afraid that those good habits have slid away from me in this busy world of today, when decisive moments come in life, it is curious how often the Bible verses that fit the occasion come into my mind.

The Second Commandment, "Love Thy Neighbor as Thyself," has often been before me when I have heard people generalize about groups of their neighbors who, like them, are citizens of the United States.

There is no use in shutting our eyes to the fact that racial and religious tensions in this country are becoming more acute. They arise partly from experiences back in the past, experiences very often in other countries where wars were carried on between people of various nationalities. I think they persist in this country largely because of the insecurity of some of our people under our economic system. If times are hard, jobs scarce and food hard to get, we always prefer that someone else be the victim of these difficult situations and we fight to keep ourselves on top. We come to attribute certain characteristics to different races and nationalities. We differentiate too little and even where religions are concerned, if they are not our own, we are apt to lump people all together as doing certain things because they are Jew or Gentile, Catholic or Protestant.

I have come to think, therefore, that the basic thing we must do is to stop generalizing about people. If we no longer thought of them as groups but as individuals, we would soon find that they varied in their different groups as much as we do in our own. It seems to me quite natural to say: "I do not like John Jones." The reasons may be many. But to say: "I do not like Catholics or Jews" is complete nonsense. Sometimes people go further and say "All the Irish here are Catholics and all Irish Catholics are politicians, therefore they are corrupt," or, "All Jews engage in sharp business practice." More nonsense and futile generalities. Because the Jews have been oppressed through the ages and have learned in a hard school, since their opportunities are restricted, to work harder when opportunities open up for them, is not strange. All disadvantaged people do the same and when opportunities are open to them the Negroes will work hard too.

The Irish Catholic can be as scrupulously honest in public office as anyone else. I have known Jews who lived according to the highest ethical

Essay written for the Joint Commission on Social Reconstruction, October 1945.

standards and were generous not only to people but to causes. It is individuals we must know, not groups!

The Negroes perhaps suffer more from this lumping together of people than any other race. Because the south has created a picture, a charming one of mammys, old-fashioned butlers and gardeners and day laborers, we must not believe that that is the whole picture. They have rarely shown us the picture of the intellectual or of the soldier or of the inventor. Because of circumstances there are relatively fewer of them in the colored group, but they do exist. I think many people, if they closed their eyes, and talked to a mixed racial group would find it hard to tell the difference either from the voice or sentiments expressed between the cultivated white man and the cultivated Negro.

Many people will tell you they object to breaking down the barriers between the races or to allowing them to associate together without self-consciousness from the time they are children because of their disapproval of intermarriage between races. They feel that races should stay pure blooded as far as possible. When people say that to me, I sometimes wonder if they have taken a good look at our population. If there ever was a nation where people have mixed blood, it is right here in the United States, and yet we seem to have remained a strong and virile nation. Besides, this particular objection which people advance is somewhat irrelevant since when people want to marry, they are usually past reasoning with! Reason is swallowed up by emotion and the people involved usually say to all objections: "This is my life and I shall live it as I see fit." It is such a particularly personal thing to decide as to whom you will marry that I have a feeling it is a very bad basis on which to decide how people shall live in the year 1945 in a free country under a democratic form of government.

If we really believe in Democracy we must face the fact that equality of opportunity is basic to any kind of Democracy. Equality of opportunity means that all of our people, not just white people, not just people descended from English or Scandinavian ancestors, but all our people must have decent homes, a decent standard of health and educational opportunities to develop their abilities as far as they are able. Thus they may be equipped with the tools for the work which they wish to do and there must be equality of opportunity to obtain that work regardless of race or religion or color.

Where the Negro is concerned, I think they have a legitimate complaint. We have expected them to be good citizens and yet in a large part of our country we haven't given them an opportunity to take part in our government. We have, however, made them subject to our laws and we have drafted them into our army and navy. We have done better than ever before, I think, in really integrating some of them with their white brothers in the various services. It has been an uphill fight, however, and the tendency has been to keep them in the menial positions performing the kind of services which are needed but which do not give an opportunity for glory or for compensation to the same extent that other services might do.

It is true that because of lack of opportunity for education, many of our colored people are not capable of rising to great heights, but we should have differentiated between those who were capable and those who were not. We would not then find so many men with such a deep sense of injustice who when they return to civilian status, find themselves confronted with discrimination and segregation, may easily become a real menace in our communities.

I am prepared to believe that it will take us sometime as a nation to accept the Commandment: "Love Thy Neighbor as Thyself," but I am a little nervous lest the time allowed for readjustment is not as long as it seemed to be before the war. The day we dropped our atomic bomb, we closed an era. Our only real defense in a very insecure world is friendship among peoples. We are the strongest and richest nation today. We are richer in manpower and in national resources than most of the other nations. Our manpower has gained self-confidence as it has rolled up a victory in two distant parts of the world. Our manpower will not lack initiative, they haven't been starved, they haven't been under the heel of a conqueror, neither has our whole civilian population, therefore the rest of the world looks to us for leadership.

How much can we give them? If we cannot solve our economic questions who else in the world has the strength and resources to do so? If we cannot and will not learn to live side by side in peace and unity, how can we expect that the people of the world are going to learn this most difficult lesson? It is much easier to fight about things than to settle them by law. We have come to a rule of law within our borders for most of our citizens. We are ashamed when we hear of a lynching. Most of us hope the day will come when injustice is even handed and the laws operate for all people alike within our borders. The responsibility, therefore, is great. As far as we are concerned we must find a way to live with our neighbors in peace in order that we may help the rest of the world with the job of peaceful understanding which must be done if we are all of us to remain on this globe and continue to develop our civilization.

What is needed is really not a self-conscious virtue which makes us treat our neighbors as we want to be treated, but an acceptance of the fact that all human beings have dignity and the potentiality of development into the same kind of people we are ourselves. When we look at each individual without thinking of him as a Jew or as a Negro, but only as a person, then we may get to like him or we may dislike him, but he stands on his own feet as an individual and we stand with him on an equal basis. Together we are citizens of a great country. I may have had greater opportunity and greater happiness than he has had and fewer obstacles to overcome, but basically we build our lives together and what we build today sets the pattern for the future of the world.

34

Some of My Best Friends Are Negro

As I look back over the years that have given me so many opportunities for personal growth and understanding of peoples, I find that I count among my closest and oldest friends many Negro Americans.

It is neither unusual nor new for me to have Negro friends, nor is it unusual for me to have found my friends among all races and religions of people.

It is a bit odd, perhaps, that I came to know Negroes and find among them many good friends, after I had first had contacts with foreigners. From my earliest childhood I had literary contacts with Negroes, but no personal contacts with them.

Reading about Negroes came about this way: On Saturdays we visited my great aunt Mrs. James King Gracie, who had been born and brought up on a Georgia plantation. She would read to us from the Brer Rabbit books and tell us about life on the plantation. This was my very first introduction to Negroes in any way.

It was rather a happy way to meet the people with whom I was later to make many friends because all the stories our aunt told us were about delightful people. Our aunt had conducted a school for little Negro children and taught many of them when no other facilities for education were available to them.

But it was not until I was more than 15 and in Europe that I actually met a Negro. It was even after I had worked at a Rivington Street settlement in New York that I met and knew Negroes. That was after I returned from Europe and I was very shocked to hear some of our little American youngsters calling the children of immigrants by opprobrious names. I felt it was dreadful. After all, I had been a guest in those children's parents' countries.

While in Paris I very likely met Negroes, but they made no special impression, very likely because they were English-speaking Americans just as I was. I never dreamed they had a special problem of any kind.

I think I really began to understand their problem when I went to Washington, D.C., for the first time. Millie and Frances came to work for us and I learned a great deal from them. I think Millie and Frances were the first Negroes I ever shook hands with. But that is just customary. I always shake hands with older people.

Perhaps my first really close friendship with a Negro of about my own age started with a woman who is now a dear friend: Mrs. Mary McLeod Bethune. When I first met her I did not realize that the years would bring us

Ebony 9 (February 1953): 16–20, 22, 24–26.

so close together, but I was from the first meeting deeply impressed with her Christianity and intelligence.

I do not recall whether we first met in Daytona Beach or in Washington. Perhaps she can recall our first meeting. She might have asked me down to her school or I may have first met her after her appointment in Washington. But it was in Washington that we really got to know each other very, very well. I have always marveled at her and thought it was wonderful that she could go through so many hardships and emerge so free of bitterness.

I remember clearly the first time we lunched together because of something shocking that happened before the lunch. The lunch was with a white lady who was deeply interested in Bethune-Cookman College. Mrs. Bethune told me there had been considerable question as to whether she could lunch with us in Florida. It was quite a shock to me because it seemed so perfectly dreadful that there should be any question about it.

But in Florida she did come to lunch and perhaps that was an advance. Some of my friends tell me that was the first "victory" we were able to achieve by working together.

Later she often came to the White House. I can't tell about any particular meal because there were so many—she came to many things. And the National Council of Negro Women came. And a great many other colored women were in the other organizations which came.

Entertaining in Washington

In Washington, I think, we managed to break down the notion that we were doing anything out of the ordinary in entertaining Negro Americans as social equals. Gradually it became pretty well accepted.

This was so much so that in later years newspaper people did not even notice when there were colored people present at various functions. I remember at the last inauguration I was so tired I could not see the faces in front of me. They all merged, and I did not know whom they were, even my best friends. Finally one of the women reporters came up to me and said, "You have not been around all the rooms and you have not seen all the people who are here. But I want to tell you if this were the first inauguration, I would write a story that would be headlined all over the country 'Negroes Invade White House.' I have just walked through the rooms. There are many colored people here. All have come because of their jobs or invitations. Some are friends of yours, but all are here because they have the right to be, and it is not news any more."

I thought that was very good because once you get to take a thing for granted, you lose self-consciousness about it. For myself, I take it for granted and I now have colored friends of all ages. I have a habit of making friends with young people and I have a great many young colored friends. Some I don't see very often, but when we do meet we have wonderful times.

One of my finest young friends is a charming woman lawyer—Pauli Murray, who has been quite a firebrand at times but of whom I am very fond.

She is a lovely person who has struggled and come through very well. I think there were times when she might have done foolish things. But now I think she is well ready to be of real use.

My relationship with Pauli is very satisfying. I notice I call her by her first name. I was brought up in another generation. It is not easy for me to call people by their first names. It is not easy for me to have people call me by my first name. Now I notice that all the younger people who are really close friends of mine call me "Mrs. R." When they are younger it is quite easy for me to call them by their first names. That is why I call Pauli by her given name.

But with people of my own age I address them as Mr. or Mrs. It does not change the way I feel about them. It is just the way I was brought up. But those are not set rules of conduct. I simply call Walter White "Walter." And, by the way, he calls me "Eleanor" which is very rare. I think he just started calling me by my first name shortly after we met. It was the thing he wanted to do. I accepted it because most people don't dare. It is rather difficult for most people to address me by my given name.

First name or last, he is one of my friends. Of course I don't see much of him because we are both very busy.

Another person whom I see often is Channing Tobias. I remember a very stirring incident in connection with Dr. Tobias.

It was at the Paris General Assembly in 1951. Dr. Tobias had to deliver an important statement. I wanted to sit behind him, but they told me I was not supposed to because I was the leader of the delegation at the time. To have sat behind could be interpreted by some to mean I was advising him or telling him what to say. No one ever has to tell Dr. Tobias what to say. But the next day he had to answer a Russian charge.

I sneaked out and came back in to sit behind Dr. Tobias. The Russian delegate said, "Mr. Tobias, you should not be here telling us about our treatment of spies. You should be telling us about how your people are treated in the United States." He named every state in the Union, telling of its laws. Then he mentioned Georgia.

Dr. Tobias in his calm, learned way said: "I was born in the state of Georgia which has such bad laws. But today I represent my entire country in the United Nations. I have never said that we do not have states with bad laws, nor that we do not have states with good laws which are not enforced. I do say that we have the opportunity to move forward and so I am proud to represent my country—all 48 states."

Then Dr. Tobias went back to his original point, but there was dead silence from the Russians. It was a most eloquent handling of what could have been an embarrassing situation. If I had argued the point it would not have had half the effect it had coming from him.

For years my work has brought me in contact with Negroes and that is why I have made friends with them. Through my work at the UN I met one of the grandest people I know. His name is Ralph Bunche. He is always the senior adviser on colonial problems. I also know his wife.

I now take all these friendships for granted. I have asked him to meet my best friends—and I felt grateful when he came to see them.

The Bunches came to tea with me to see the Sarah Lee dolls and I got him and some other friends to choose the best dolls.

Dr. Bunche told me he would not take the position offered him in Washington because he said it was harder on his children to live in Washington than in New York. Of course I quite understand that.

I should like him to reconsider someday because I should like to see him in any post we had to give. I particularly would like to see him as an ambassador to a country which required the special qualities he has. He has such special qualities that I should like to choose rather carefully the country to which he should be sent to represent us.

On a more casual level I know A. Philip Randolph. I think he is serene, charming and nice looking. I only have had the pleasure of seeing him at various labor dinners and on committees with labor people.

I know him about as well as I knew the late Dr. Louis T. Wright. I felt that Dr. Wright had done wonderful things in the medical field and I always wanted to become better acquainted. I regret that it is now too late. There are so many grand people to meet—you cannot really get to know them all.

Edith Sampson is a great friend of mine. I am very fond of her because she is a warm person. I like her very much but I realize that because she is so warm and so outgoing, she sometimes irritates people. A few people object to her manner, but I understand it and like it.

I always kiss her when we meet but I don't think I call her by her first name. My grandchildren in Paris loved her. She was wonderful to them—she went shopping with them and they thought she was marvelous. I agree with them and I recall an amusing little story about her.

She was in one of the Scandinavian countries and discovered that a re-issue of *Uncle Tom's Cabin* had been published there. She wrote to me to ask me how she could possibly tell the people and make them understand that Uncle Tom is dead.

Her letter was such a cry from the wilderness that I had to smile and be amused. I wrote back and said that Uncle Tom is dead, but we will have to live with the book the rest of our mortal lives.

She did well, I think, on those trips. I have a high regard for her. I recognize the things that people might find in her that rub them the wrong way. But I think they come from such a warm heart and a desire to be friends that I like them. In friendship it is necessary to understand your friend's good and bad qualities. It must be a mutual examination of each other and it must be forgiving and understanding. Sometimes, in my friendship with Edith Sampson I have found that she will do almost more than is necessary. As a result she may make people a little uncomfortable by her over-friendliness. I, of course, am never made uncomfortable.

Two personalities have made a significant but different contribution to our United Nations delegation—Channing Tobias and Edith Sampson. He is a different kind of person. He is friendly and warm, but quiet and an intellectual. He has a very different contribution to make. You cannot compare these two people professionally or as friends because they are so different. I not only think Mrs. Sampson did well on all her trips but she made friends for us in the U.N. Because I know her so well and like her so much I would like everyone to appreciate her contribution.

Negro Friends Never Self-Seeking

Among women of my own age, as I said, Mrs. Bethune is my closest friend, but I always have young friends too. Old, young or middle-aged, all my Negro friends are quite interesting people, and they are never self-seeking. Rarely do they ask personal favors, and if they do, it is with great embarrassment. I appreciate that. Often they ask for favors, or help, for other people however. That is a different kind of request, and one that is often easier to grant.

A man who often has asked for my intervention or advice is Walter White. It is always, however, for someone else. I think Walter is a sensitive man and a friendly man and I like to list him among my personal friends. He has suffered often I fear and I remember one story which shows the kind of loyalty he has to his race. One time he said he was washing his hands in the Senate washroom, I think. One of the senators came in and asked him: "Why do you insist on being a Negro?"

Walter's response was so simple and so all-embracing. He said, "Because I am a Negro." He is as fair as any Nordic and I can see how it is difficult to consider him a Negro, but he told me his father was unmistakably colored.

One of my younger friends is Josh White. I met Josh at a concert at which he was singing, and asked him if he would come to Hyde Park to sing at a Christmas party for the children from Wiltwyck School. I, also, invited his son, little Josh, because he sings too. They both came and we became friends.

Two of my best friends are Mrs. Alice Freeman and William White. They run my home at Hyde Park and I would be lost without them. Alice has been with me for fourteen years and of course I rely on her completely.

My son told Josh that I was looking for a man to stay in the house as I did not think it a good idea for women to stay in the country without a man around the house. Josh surprised him by his answer. He said, "I think my brother William would like to see your mother." At first, I did not think William would like it too well. He had been in the entertainment world a long time with Josh, I knew. One day without announcement, William appeared. We shook hands and he sat down and I interviewed him.

I said to him: "It will be very difficult for you to do housework, to drive a car." William said, "No, Mrs. Roosevelt, since the war, I don't feel like singing anymore." That was three years ago, and he has been with me ever since. I have an affectionate feeling for William, and I hope he has an affectionate feeling for me.

Some of my Negro friends thought that I was creating what they call a social problem by having one brother as a rather frequent guest and another brother as a servant, more or less. I never saw that as a problem. Each has a dignified, necessary contribution to make.

Sometimes, when Josh comes, William will come in and sing with his brother, but I always have to persuade him. Sometimes, I cannot persuade him, so Josh sings alone, unless Elliott or one of the other boys joins in.

There are many times when Josh comes, and I don't know anything about it. He simply drops in to see his brother. Then he and William eat together. Sometimes, when Josh comes as a guest, he says, "I'd rather eat with William." And he does. Other times he eats with us, and William serves us. It seems most reasonable to me, and I have never had the slightest difficulty from the arrangement and never expect any. Perhaps, that is because I never saw anything unusual in it.

I don't think I have ever lost a Negro friend. One that I could have lost had we been friends would have been Paul Robeson, but I never really knew him. I had a great admiration for him as an artist. I was once told the story of his youth and I held him in high regard. I deeply regret that because of his gratitude to the Russian people for giving him what he thought he wanted, he has allowed himself to be fooled by the kind of life he was able to lead there. I think he has done his people and my good friends a disservice. In a way, he has misused his great talent to do this. It is too bad, because he should be using his talents to help rather than to destroy his country.

Despite his intelligence, I feel that he has not demonstrated any analytical qualities. Surely he has not examined the Soviet system, because it does not permit real democratic freedom. The kindest thing I can say about him is, perhaps, that he believes that communism will give all people equality. This everyone should have. But Mr. Robeson and all of us have a greater chance of getting it here in the U.S. than anywhere else in the world.

One of the odd things about my Negro friends is their consistent failure to invite me to their social gatherings. I am rarely invited to their weddings, musicals or teas. I invariably invite them to my house, but the invitation is not returned. I suppose this is because they have an understanding of my busy schedule and are a little shy.

The Walter Whites have invited me, however. The most enjoyable dinner I have had this year was at their house. There were several other agreeable guests present and we had a most relaxing evening.

In friendships and in inviting different people to your home, hostesses often worry about mixing—will the different kinds of personalities clash?

That is my only concern in inviting guests in. Some of my white neighbors around Hyde Park were alarmed when Father Divine bought across the river from us, but they were never alarmed at seeing Negro guests at my table.

Once some of my neighbors and I were serving at a big buffet party. One of my neighbors found she was serving a Negro guest. Afterwards she told me she had never thought that she would serve and talk with a Negro. She said it did not bother her at all and she was glad that it did not.

I have never had any white person object. I value and enjoy my Negro friends equally with my white friends.

I remember once dancing the Virginia Reel and having a colored partner because he knew how to dance it. I do not recall who he was.

Now that I recall that small incident, I am reminded of another, much bigger one. At a political meeting in Georgia during one of my husband's campaigns they placed on each seat in the auditorium a crude drawing showing me dancing with a Negro. Under the picture it said "Nigger Lover—Eleanor." At that time I had never danced with a colored person and the drawing was a fabrication and an insult to me and to Negroes because of the nasty word they used.

During that period there were many strange and unreal rumors circulated against my husband and me in the South. I remember they had something they called "Eleanor Clubs." Negro members of these clubs were supposed to push white people on Thursdays or something really strange.

I asked my close Negro friends if they had ever heard of such a club. Of course they had not because they did not exist. Then Franklin had the Secret Service and FBI investigate. We found not one single "Eleanor Club" and we never found out who started the rumors. I do not personally mind being criticized because of my friends. But that was at a time when criticism of me could have hurt my husband and because of that I was worried.

The American people knew that the "Eleanor Club" was a pure fabrication and most of them did not believe they existed. Shortly after that, while we were in the White House, we began to hear another kind of story from some of my Negro friends. The story was that I had advised and encouraged the President in his awareness of the needs of Negroes in America. One of the versions of the story was that I was responsible for FEPC and other things the President believed in. This is not true.

Franklin always had an awareness of the most important things he had to do. If he had to get the southern vote in order to get something essential to the whole country, he could not take a stand that would upset the South. But he never said that I could not take a stand. Sometimes, after talks with my Negro friends and with their white friends too, I used to ask Franklin, "Do you mind if I do so and so." And he would answer: "I shall stand or fall on what I have been able to accomplish. You have a right to do what you think is right."

He did not know Negroes as individuals and as friends as well as I did. He was not able to get about easily. But I had the opportunity to do so and I made friends. I was never asked by him not to do anything I wanted to do with them or for them. Franklin had such a deep sense of justice and an over-riding wish to see all Americans treated as equals that he never prevented me from taking any stand even though I sometimes worried if my actions in regards to my friends would harm his campaigns.

I also think that we were privileged to start something in Washington that will be continued: the acceptance of Negroes as social equals and as friends.

In a way I feel that it is harder for a Negro to become friends with a white person than for a white person to accept a Negro friend. In the past the

Negro has been hurt much more and sometimes he has become bitter and hesitant.

Mrs. Bethune is not bitter however, or is Mrs. Sampson hesitant. There is great fear among some people about the development of social equality but I believe it can be achieved. Friendships can be lasting and valuable.

Sometimes my Negro friends praise me because they think I have sacrificed too much for them. There have been no great sacrifices because all friendships are rewarding.

When more whites and Negroes become friends and lose whatever self-consciousness they started out with, we shall have a much happier world.

35

Segregation

Segregation has existed in the U.S. for a long time. It has been less pronounced in certain parts of the country than in others. Owing to the fact that slavery was not really needed in the North, slaves never really became a part of the social fabric of the Northern states, but in the South they were needed to cultivate the crops so that the pattern of slavery persisted until the war between the States and Lincoln's Emancipation Proclamation. This freed the slaves legally, but there is more to freedom than a mere legal pronouncement. Real equality can only be obtained by a change in the minds and hearts of men and that change comes about very slowly. There is not yet real equality in the North, though there are not as many restrictions as exist to this day in the South.

Democracy is a form of government which tries to actually give equal opportunity to all its citizens and to give equal justice to all people. This is impossible as long as segregation exists. The mere fact of segregation means discrimination and there can be no equality where there is discrimination.

In the world as a whole there has been a tendency for the white race to look upon itself as the superior race because through early development in certain areas it was able to conquer and to hold in subjection many of the colored peoples of the world. As a result the colored peoples developed more slowly because of lack of opportunity. In the past few years, however, a wave has swept over the world and country after country in one way or another has managed to gain its freedom.

Segregation has not always been based on color. Sometimes it has been based on religion or sex. It can take on many forms and one finds it between people of the same color, simply based on nationality or caste. But segregation in all its strange patterns is on its way out because of the wave of freedom which is passing over the world. Every nation which has newly gained its freedom is particularly sensitive to the attitude of other peoples. There is a desire for the recognition of the dignity of the new nation and its place of equality among the nations. At the beginning many of the new nations will have great difficulty because there are only a comparatively few people in them who have a sufficient amount of training and education to set up and operate their new government. Sometimes only one section of a nation is prepared to really understand the experiment in democracy which is being undertaken. No matter how difficult this is going to make the first years of freedom, we cannot doubt but that freedom is going to come to more and more countries in the

The Educational Forum 24, no. 1 (November 1959): 5–6.

colored areas of the world. Therefore, segregation must slowly vanish in the relations between human beings.

The overall struggle in the world today is one between Communism and Democracy. If Communism understands the problems brought about by segregation, accepts wiping out of segregation, and is more helpful to the new nations than those among us who profess Democracy, then I think Communism will have won a distinct advantage over the Democratic nations of the world. It behooves us, therefore, to realize that the significance of the segregation of races is the effect that our approach, as members of Democratic nations, can have in the final decisions arrived at by these new nations. These new nations actually hold the balance of power for the future in their hands. They hold this balance because they cover such large areas of land and such great numbers of people.

We in the U.S. have a two-fold problem because what we do is watched everywhere and therefore our actions have international significance. It we cannot solve our difficulties and remove segregation from our country, why should it be possible to attract the colored peoples of the world to our philosophy, to our form of government, to our way of life when we are unwilling to give our own colored people an opportunity for equality and justice? This is the underlying significance for us in the U.S. in the whole question of segregation and it is to be hoped that it will be recognized by our people throughout the nation and that serious thought and changes in attitudes will result.

Some people hold that the black race cannot develop to the same heights mentally as the white race but that notion is disproved by the exceptions among them who have already done so in spite of all the handicaps placed in their way.

Changes, particularly in the mores which have endured for several generations, are always painful and very difficult but it may well be that these are a part of the problem of survival and therefore worthy of study by the best objective minds in the country and in the world.

36

Foreword to *The Long Shadow of Little Rock*

This is a book which I hope will be read by every American. It is simply told and easy to read, but not pleasant. Gathered together here is a chronicle day by day of what happened in what would ordinarily be considered a rather progressive, pleasant, medium-sized city in the U.S. It happened because of the actions of a highly prejudiced, unthinking governor. He called out all the worst side of other prejudiced individuals throughout his area of the States.

Within all of us there are two sides. One reaches for the stars, the other descends to the level of the beasts. The picture of mobs in Little Rock, and later in other areas of the South, shows clearly that the beast in us was predominant. The record of burning crosses, bombings, shootings, etc., is a record of the beast on the march. No one in authority in this city of Little Rock tried to control and draw out the best in people instead of the worst. This is the sad thing about it. Not even the few courageous ministers could kindle even a spark of courage which would have turned the tide. We do not yet seem to have learned the lesson that where there is prejudice and oppression in one area it invariably spreads in many other areas. It may not happen today or tomorrow but surely at some point it will erupt and there will be a new reason for the beast to march. This is seen in history.

As you read this story where all the incidents are drawn together, you marvel at the courage of the Colored community, but you marvel even more at the courage of the few white people who fought down the beast and remained human beings. There were even a few white children who had this courage. Of course it seems to me nothing short of a miracle that the nine Negro children had the stamina to live through this period and their parents must have suffered even more than they did. To give your child for a cause is even harder than to give yourself.

The hardest part of the story is the change brought about in young people by the influence of their elders. The story shows how at the beginning a Colored girl who was attractive and could sing, was asked to join the Glee Club, and some of the other children were asked to join some of the white children at lunch. Gradually, however, the atmosphere changed. The parents had been at work. The children could have found a way to live together but the parents would not let them. Then the beast took over in the children, and children can be cruel. They can devise all kinds of tortures and enjoy them,

By Daisy Bates (New York: David McKay, 1962), pp. xiii–xv.

and here the beast within them was being praised and they were looked upon as heroes at home.

I wish that Mrs. Bates who suffered so much and had such courage throughout all her difficulties, who could bear to see with her husband their life's work destroyed and still go on and work for the cause she believed in, had been able to keep from giving us some of the sense of her bitterness and her fear in the end of her book. Given the circumstances, this was almost too much to expect even from such a fine person. I have paid her homage in my thoughts many times and I want to tell her again how remarkable I think she was through these horrible years. I only hope that before too long the people of my race in my country will wake up to the fact that they are endangering the peace of the world. The world is made up of people of many races and many colors. They must be accepted as people and treated with the same dignity and respect wherever they are. Until we do this with our own citizens at home we will be suspect to the world, our leadership will have little value and we will endanger the peace of the world because we have the responsibility to give an example of how nations can live together in peace and unity.

This book should shock the conscience of America and bring a realization of where we stand in the year 1962 in these United States.

37
The Social Revolution

Be an opener of doors for such as come after thee, and do not try to make the universe a blind alley.

Ralph Waldo Emerson

The economic revolution is bringing with it social changes that are being felt everywhere. As the life of human beings is lifted above the animal level, they become aware of new aspirations, beyond the immediate and pressing need for food to eat, and develop a passionate longing for independence. What is stirring like yeast everywhere is the revolution of equality, the assertion by men and women of their human dignity, and their demand for its recognition and acceptance by others.

Certainly it is this particular revolution which the United States should be able to win, hands down, because this is the concept upon which our life is based.

"We know," Barbara Ward wrote recently, "that the passionate desire of men to see themselves as the equals of other human beings without distinctions of class or sex or race or nationhood is one of the driving forces of our day."

We know—yes. But what are we doing about it? We are dealing today with millions upon millions of people of diverse religions. That should be easy for us. This country, after all, was founded upon the principle of religious freedom. But how is it working out in actual practice?

Many of us still remember, with shame, the burning crosses, the revival of the Ku Klux Klan that accompanied Al Smith's campaign for the Presidency. All of us remember, more recently, during John Kennedy's campaign, the fantastic claims that, if a Catholic were elected to the Presidency, the Pope would take over the direction of the policies of the nation. Even now when this nonsense has been shown to be without foundation, I know of no one who has withdrawn his original cry of alarm or admitted that he was mistaken.

In a very real sense, the United States is the world's show window of the democratic processes in action. We know, too well, what people see when they look in that window. They see Little Rock and Baton Rouge and New Orleans. They see Albany, Georgia. They see the deep-rooted prejudice, the stubborn ignorance of large groups of our citizens, which have led to injustice, inequality, and, sometimes, even brutality.

I think what most of us remember most vividly about the riots and the cruelty of Little Rock, Baton Rouge, and New Orleans is the pictures we saw

Tomorrow Is Now (New York: Harper & Row, 1963), pp. 49–65.

in our newspapers, pictures which gave us a tremendous shock when we realized what ugliness and degradation mass fear could bring out in human beings.

Grown women wanted to kill one poor little nine-year-old girl, one of the children going into the Little Rock school. The cold fact is hard to believe that anywhere in our country women would be screaming for the death of a child because she was going into a white school. Yet this is what happened. This was the result of mass fear and mass psychology.

The beast in us is something we have to learn to control. It would be wise if we came to realize how it functions on many different levels. Habit is one of the controlling factors. If we can learn to subdue the emotions arising from prejudice, if we can learn that the social revolution in which we are engaged should, among other things, provide all our people with an equal opportunity to enjoy the benefits that have been the privileges of a few, we are going to be astonished to discover that many whom we considered incapable of development were only underprivileged; that given the opportunity for education there are latent endowments which will be valuable not only to these people in themselves but to their country and the world as well.

It is this minority of strident and prejudiced people, with their unwillingness to accept race equality—at whatever cost—who provide the Communists with most of their ammunition against the democratic system, who are loudest in their expression of hatred for Communism.

One of the most difficult experiences I have ever been through was that of serving as Chairman for the Commission of Inquiry into the Administration of Justice in the Freedom Struggle, held in Washington in May of 1962. I found it difficult—and intolerably painful—to accept the fact that things such as I have described could happen here in these United States. This was the kind of thing the Nazis had done to the Jews of Germany—and there, also, as a misguided effort to demonstrate their race superiority.

Only by focusing the attention of the nation as a whole upon this situation can we find a remedy for it. The overwhelming pressure of public opinion would accomplish more than any other single factor to rectify the condition and to help eliminate it.

What emerged, of course, was that, as had been true since before the Civil War, it was largely whites whose economic condition was little better than that of the Negroes who represented the most virulent element, concentrating the chief hatred, prejudice, and—yes, downright brutality. It was, perhaps, the only way in which they could proclaim their superiority. They appeared to be terrified for fear the Negroes would be permitted to stand on their own merits, and might, in many cases, leave them far behind.

And here, too, emerged another and unmistakable similarity to the Nazism we had believed destroyed—at least in Germany. Most of the dictators of the West—Franco, Mussolini, Hitler—claimed that they were "saving" their lands from the threat of Communism. Today, as I have learned over and over to my cost, one needs only to be outspoken about the unfair treatment of the Negro to be labeled "Communist." I had regarded such expression to be the only honorable and civilized course for a citizen of the United States.

To digress for a moment, this recurring matter of labeling "Communist" anyone who does not agree with you is essentially an act of dishonesty and it should be nailed every time for what it is. Few of the Southern politicians who resented my stand on integration ever troubled to examine it. Instead they said "Communist." The Nazis excelled at this sort of thing. It has no place in America.

To return to the Commission of Inquiry, there appeared before us a succession of people who had set out to test the operation of the laws in regard to civil rights. The methods they used were peaceful enough. Some of them indulged in public prayer; some of them rode on buses to see whether segregation was still practiced on buses and in terminal facilities; some of them sat in at lunch counters for the same purposes; some of them picketed a segregated lunchroom for *one minute and a half!* And one young man was teaching Negroes, who had been driven from their farms for attempting to register to vote, how to make a kind of leather tote bag so that they could earn enough money to hold back starvation.

These were the people who suffered indignity, danger, arrest on preposterous charges; people who are even now facing incredibly long prison sentences; people who, in some cases, were treated with a brutality that sickens one to think of.

I would like to quote from the words of Carl Rachlin, one of the counsels for the Commission, who opened that horrifying hearing, because it seems to me vital that these facts should be clearly known to all the American people:

> . . . patterns of official conduct interfering with the rights of Negroes to pursue activities in every way lawful . . .
>
> Mass arrests and jailing on criminal charge upon criminal charge, some dreadfully serious, is the pattern in Baton Rouge. . . .
>
> In Mississippi, it is impossible to obtain a bail bond for any arrest in a civil rights case. As a result cash bail has had to be raised in these cases in that state. . . .
>
> Much of the testimony will show brutality, official indignity and failure of police protection. At the same time it will show, we believe, the good faith, the good spirits, the peaceful intentions of the people who participated in such activities in behalf of equality. . . .
>
> The normal appeal of American citizens to petition their state government and representatives for redress of wrongs is . . . closed to the participants in these activities.

I'd like to look for a moment at a few of these cases, at conditions that could only have existed because, as a people, we are paying only lip service to our democratic principles; we have, at least in this area, been tending to lose our social revolution.

Ronnie Moore was one of those who sat in at a lunch counter; one of those who participated in the picketing which lasted just one minute and a half. He was arrested and had to raise a cash bond of $1,500. Rearrested, the charge became "conspiracy to commit criminal mischief." There was an additional $2,000 bond. After serving twenty-one days in jail, he was released, and this time arrested for "criminal trespassing and disturbing the peace." (He was taking shelter from the rain.) By now the bond was up to $6,500.

For fifty-eight days, Ronnie and another young man were kept in a seven-by-seven-foot cell, without a window; and taken out only twice a week for a shower. After his release there was a new charge, "criminal anarchy," and the bond had now reached a total of $16,500.

Let's take another case, that of a young Negro minister with a group of students who intended to pray and sing in protesting the arrest of the picketers. They sustained a barrage of forty-seven tear gas bombs; police dogs attacked them. Later, three hundred young students had to be treated for dog bites and tear gas, and for having been trampled upon.

A white boy named John Robert Zellner, the young son of a Methodist minister in south Alabama, was arrested for protesting the expulsion of a colored girl from a high school. The charge, ironically enough, was "disturbing the peace and contributing to the delinquency of a minor."

While he was a prisoner in the white section of the jail, the other white prisoners, furious because he was attempting to help Negroes, "threatened me with castration . . . said if I went to sleep I'd wake up with a knife in my back."

"I thought," Robert commented during his testimony, "it was quite ironic that the United States was able to launch a man into space and let him go around the world three times and yet they weren't able to take care of a small human relations problem."

Frank Nelson, another white man, who had been a student in engineering at Cooper Union and then served with the United States Coast Guard as a civil engineer, was asked: "Why are you, as a white person, participating in these activities?"

"Actually," he answered, "it was just a matter of getting down to finally doing what just about everybody thinks is correct and I . . . got tired of sitting around in the living room and discussing how bad things were . . . and finally decided to see if I could perhaps do something to change things."

How much must be changed was made clear in the repeated pictures of brutality: of policemen directing some of the vandalism, of the police dogs and the tear gas, of the young man who was blackjacked and had to have fifty-seven stitches taken in his head; of the white boy on whose hand they put what they called a "wrist breaker," a metal clamp which they tightened until the victim fainted several times from pain.

Then—unspeakable ugliness in this our own country—"An electric stock probe, used in stockyards to shock cattle and make them move along, was used around the private parts. It was very painful stuff. I was picked up and held in the air by the private parts." This was the young man who had attempted peacefully to teach the dispossessed Negroes to earn a living by making tote bags.

It was because of such people as this that Gerald Johnson, a Negro student, answered as he did when he was asked, "What made you get in all this trouble?"

186

"I have grown up under segregationist rule . . . and I didn't like the way things worked. . . . When I heard people like Bob Zellner . . . the things that they have been through for people like me . . . I couldn't face sitting back doing nothing, and I don't want my children to grow up under something like that."

"In other words," he was asked, "you wanted to fight on the home front for some of the liberties and privileges of American citizenship that the Negro soldiers fought overseas to guarantee to the rest of the world?"

"Right," he said.

When I first introduced this painful and shameful subject, I said that its solution rests with public opinion. So it does. The President of the United States can lead only if he has followers. It is the voice of America that he must hear clearly.

Realizing at the inquiry that many of the young victims of race prejudice and savagery were bitter about the kind of judges before whom their cases were heard, I tried to make the following point:

> I think you have to realize that under our political system, judges have to be endorsed by the senators and congressmen of their district.
>
> Now, unless you can awaken public opinion to have some effect in the South, you are asking the President to risk very often a vote on his Administration's policy bills and perhaps not get them passed because he has refused to follow recommendations of the elected representatives of the district.
>
> This points up, I think, the need for the individual citizen to be awakened and held responsible, because it is the people in these areas who are really responsible.
>
> They elect their representatives. They are the ones who feel this way and I think they will respond to the real feeling of the rest of the country, if it is brought out and crystallized and made clear what they are doing to their country in the eyes of the world and in the eyes of their own nation and of their own people.

The great Russian pianist Anton Rubinstein once said hotly, "Despots never think the people ripe enough for freedom." We still have too many people in this country who feel that the Negro is not ripe for equality, in education, in the economy, in housing, in opportunity.

If this is our lesson to the nations who are trying to bridge the gap between primitive living and the age of nuclear fission, and to those other nations whose culture was already old while ours was primitive, they can only reject it entirely. In making their great transition to the modern world, these people need all the help we can give them; they need our respect; they need our recognition of their essential dignity as human beings. But while we fail in such recognition to those of our own people whose skins are colored—as are the skins of two out of three of all the peoples of the world—they will never believe in our sincerity, never believe that we pay more than lip service to the ideals of democracy which we claim to defend.

One of our blind spots comes with the persistent and fondly cherished idea that, because some peoples have lagged behind in civilization and in cultural development, they are congenitally incapable of that development. This has been disproved over and over by such anthropologists as Margaret Mead. It can be disproved almost daily if we look about at some of the magnificent achievements of Negroes.

"You can't," say the people who take comfort in speaking in clichés, "change human nature."

Now the only way we can judge human nature is by human behavior, and behavior is modified and changed and developed and transformed by training and surroundings, by social customs and economic pressures. When we wince, sickened, at some of the grosser violence of an Elizabethan play, we are simply indicating that our "human nature" has undergone some drastic alterations in the past three hundred years.

Some years ago, I studied a snapshot which I have never forgotten. It was a picture showing two men standing outside a primitive grass hut in the Philippines. One of the men was naked except for a loincloth. He had wild bushy hair. In either hand he held a skull. He was a headhunter from the bush.

The young man beside him wore a white suit and glasses. In his hand he carried a small professional bag. He was a trained physician, working in the field of public health. He was the headhunter's son!

That transition, from headhunter to scientist, was not even the work of one generation; it was the work of perhaps fifteen years at the outside. What had been required to "change human nature" and make the leap from the Stone Age to the present? Opportunity, education, recognition of his human potentialities and a chance to be trained for a job in the field for which he was best suited.

But we must not overlook the operative factor. The young scientist had been trained. Too often, we tend to expect too much of people to whom we have given no training.

As far back as I can remember every attempt at improvement in the standard of living for Negroes was met by complaints that they were not ripe for equality. Because I was interested in housing, I was involved many years ago in one of the first slum clearance projects. People said, "It is ridiculous to give a bathroom to these people. They don't know how to use it. Some of them are keeping coal in the bathtub."

Our answer to that was to put a director in charge who helped people to learn about their new surroundings and to adapt to them. As soon as they became familiar with the various conveniences they used them properly.

Of course, difficulties are apt to develop if people are provided with modern conveniences without being given any guidance or instruction in their use. Certainly it is unfair to expect people without training to use properly what they have never encountered before.

And here, I think, there is a responsibility both for the whites and the Negroes. Too often, it is true, Negroes from underprivileged areas move into apartments or neighborhoods and, because they have been taught no better, clutter the hallways with filth and arouse reasonable resentment and alarm in the white tenants, who naturally do not want to see their way of life deteriorate. The function of democratic living is not to lower standards but to raise those that have been too low.

It seems to me that men like Martin Luther King might well perform a great service to the cause of equality for which they fight so gallantly, if they were to help some of the underprivileged Negroes to prepare themselves to fit in to better surroundings.

If we are going to belong to our world we must take into account the fact that the majority of the peoples of the world are non-whites. We must learn to surmount this deepseated prejudice about color. Certainly we must face the evidence that the color of the skin does not regulate the superiority or inferiority of the individual.

Now and then, when I have pointed out example after example of non-whites whose superiority in their fields cannot be challenged, I am told, "Oh, but those are exceptions." The same thing may be said of superior people among the white population. They, too, are exceptions. Most of us fall far below them in ability and in achievement.

It is interesting to study our own racial problems and to compare them with the problems that exist in Africa. The basic issues are quite different. I have had African nationals tell me that the struggle for the liberation of the Africans from colonial powers was initiated by the efforts of the Africans themselves. Here in America, they said, it has nearly always been the whites and not the Negroes who saw the injustices and tried to correct them. Indeed, it is the success of the Africans in attaining their liberty, and the dignity that has grown out of their new status, that has lent a new spirit to our own Negroes.

Of course, one of the stumbling blocks in creating this equality in our own social revolution is another cliché like the one "You can't change human nature." This is used as a final stopper to any discussion of the subject. "Would you," these people ask, "like to see your daughter marry a Negro?"

Now this is a red herring if I ever saw one. Racial intermarriage is not involved in job equality, in educational equality, in housing equality. In fact, I strenuously doubt that any father who ever asked that challenging question had the slightest fear that his daughter wanted to marry a Negro. Nonetheless, the inference from his question is that his daughter is quite likely to do so unless she is prevented by the enforced segregation of Negroes.

All this is really preposterous. No one knows it as well as the person who clings to his question as though it were actually an answer to the problem. The immense majority of people instinctively seek their own kind. France, for instance, has long had race equality but comparatively little intermarriage has resulted. The issue of intermarriage is used as a stumbling block in the path of human justice; it is used to hold back opportunity for millions of our citizens to develop their full potentialities in an ambience of mutual respect.

True, there are occasional—but very rare—cases of great attraction between different races. There are some successful marriages; for instance, those of Walter White with a white woman and Marian Anderson with a white man. And I know of others. But these, of course, are exceptional people, strong enough to escape the aura of martyrdom that so often hamstrings such a marriage.

But I still contend that the use of this fatuous question to prevent the development of the Negro race is essentially an act of dishonesty. It is used, like sleight of hand, to distract our attention from inequalities in wages, in living quarters, in education, that are an ineffaceable disgrace to us as a people.

It often seems to me that prejudice so blinds us that we see only what we expect to see, what we want to see. An example of this comes to mind.

At Wiltwick, a school for problem children across the river from Hyde Park, a school in which I have long had a deep interest, there was a small boy named Tommy. One weekend he was allowed to go home to visit his mother. When he returned, he went to see his social worker, a gentle and understanding woman.

"I hates white people," he told her.

"Oh, no, Tommy!"

"Yes, I does. They makes my Mommy cry. They're mean to her."

"I don't blame you for not liking the ones who are mean to your mother, but not *all* white people, Tommy!"

"Yes, I does!"

"Do you hate me?"

"Oh, no, I loves you."

"But I'm white." In fact, she was a Norwegian with blond hair, big blue eyes, and a milky complexion.

"You is?" He looked at her in surprise. Then he patted her cheek consolingly. "You sure don't look it."

While it is essential for us to cope at once with the social revolution in this country we must, at the same time, learn to adjust to the social revolutions in other parts of the world. This is not only a matter of common decency, it is a matter of common sense. If there were no desire on the part of the African peoples to enter the modern world we would not be able to develop new markets for ourselves.

These people are looking for guidance on that long and difficult climb, a climb that they must make swiftly. We took our guidance in building a nation from the patterns of England and Western Europe, using what we needed, what served our purpose; developing new lines where we felt them to be an improvement.

Where are the Africans to turn for guidance? To the Eastern world or to the Western world? One thing is sure. We cannot convince them of the value of our ideas, our principles, and our ideals unless we know clearly what they are, unless we are able to express them, unless we are prepared to implement

ER watches Jim Farley, postmaster general and chair of the Democratic National Committee, congratulate Molly Dewson on her appointment as head of the DNC's Women's Division. In early 1933, Dewson and ER presented FDR with a list of 60 women who should receive a top government position. By April 1935, FDR had appointed 50. [*The Bettmann Archive*]

ER poses with the Woman's Advisory Committee of the NRA Coat and Suit Code, who inform her of the progress made by New Deal wage and hour policies. Although the NRA would be declared unconstitutional six months later, the Wagner Act and the Fair Labor Standards Act protected NRA labor policy. (10/10/34). [*The Bettmann Archive*]

ER joined the New York Women's Trade Union League in 1922. This photograph was taken on May 5, 1936, when she addressed the 12th annual National Convention of the League. She is flanked by Rose Schneiderman (right), President of the League and Elizabeth Christman (left) the Secretary and Treasurer. [*The Bettmann Archive*]

Mary McLeod Bethune, Director of Negro Activities for the National Youth Administration, became one of ER's closest friends. Together, they served on numerous boards, investigated race riots, and acted as ombudswomen for civil rights. They are pictured here at the opening session of the National Conference on Problems of the Negro and Negro Youth. (1/7/37). [*The Bettmann Archive*]

ER confers with CIO president John L. Lewis at the National Youth Advisory Committee of Business, Labor and Education Leaders in February 1938. Ten years later, the two would become political adversaries. [*The Bettmann Archive*]

Throughout her life, ER remained a strong supporter of black educational institutions, serving on the board of directors for both Howard University and Bethune-Cookman College. Here she buys the first ticket for a musical benefit for Bethune-Cookman from guest conductors Fred Norman, Bunny Berrigan, Tommy Dorsey and Lionel Hampton and guest maestro, Frank Sinatra. (8/7/40) [*The Bettmann Archive*]

ER presents the NAACP's coveted Spingarn Medal to contralto Marian Anderson on July 2, 1939. The preceding April the DAR has refused to allow Anderson to perform in Constitution Hall in Washington. ER resigned from the DAR and was instrumental in arranging a performance for Anderson at the Lincoln Memorial on Easter Sunday, which was attended by over 75,000 people. [*The Bettmann Archive*]

When FDR decided to run for a third term in 1940, he wanted the convention to nominate him unanimously and to second his choice of Henry Wallace for vice-president. The Democrats united behind FDR, only to splinter over Wallace. FDR sent ER to secure Wallace's victory. Speaking without notes (see pages 373–74), ER so swayed the delegates that Wallace won on the first ballot, leading one Senator to call her "the Sherman of the convention." (7/18/40) [*The Bettmann Archive*]

ER addresses the members of the AFL-CIO during her visit to the Hudson Shore Labor School on July 11, 1942. [*FDR Library*]

ER and A. Philip Randolph are photographed here attending a rally on February 28, 1946 to save the Fair Employment Practices Committee from extinction. The Committee was set up by FDR [Executive order 8802] when Randolph, frustrated with government promises to African Americans scheduled a "March on Washington" for July 1, 1941 with the motto: "We Loyal Negro American Citizens Demand the Right to Work and Fight for our Country."[*FDR Library*]

ER meets with Harry Truman in the Oval Office. Although Truman had appointed her to the American delegation to the United Nations, ER remained suspicious of Truman's commitment to liberal reform. [*FDR Library*]

ER is pictured here receiving the first American Award in Human Relations. The citation recognized "Her outstanding contribution to the cause of harmony among all men." With ER (left to right): William H. Kilpatrick; Bernard Baruch; and John Foster Dulles, the principal speaker at the testimonial dinner. (4/5/49) [*The Bettmann Archive*]

Abba Eban, Israel's permanent representative to the United Nations, confers with ER before the opening session of the UN Security Council October 25, 1949. ER so strongly supported recognizing Israel that she told Truman she would resign her position if he declined to acknowledge the new nation. [*The Bettmann Archive*]

ER displays a Spanish edition of the *Universal Declaration of Human Rights*. Her crowning achievement at the United Nations, she called the *Declaration* a "magna carta for mankind." This photograph was taken in Lake Success, New York, in November 1949. [*FDR Library*]

them. And we cannot address any people successfully unless we know and understand—and respect—that people.

We can no longer oversimplify. We can no longer build lazy and false stereotypes: Americans are like this, Russians are like that, a Jew behaves in such a way, a Negro thinks in a different way. The lazy generalities—"You know how women are. . . . Isn't that just like a man?"

The world cannot be understood from a single point of view.

If we cannot understand the people who make up our own country, how are we going to understand the people we are trying to lead in the world as a whole? The Soviets tell them that they are better suited to be of assistance to them because they are closer to their problems than we are. Our simple assertion that this is not true is meaningless. We must prove that it is not true.

How? Well, the Soviets invite people to their country and show them what they want them to see. But our country is open to all who wish to move around. They can judge for themselves. Both the good and the bad are open for inspection.

And, on the whole, even our bad spots are not as bad as most visitors have been led to believe. Often the reality of a situation will seem much better than the fantastic tales that have grown up about what actually goes on in our country. For instance, a few years ago, the idea of most Africans about what happened to the colored people in this country was so completely erroneous and exaggerated that the stories were unrecognizable. Whatever visitors from these countries saw here was a vast improvement on what they had been told. Nonetheless, our obligation to improve our own conditions is not diminished.

One thing is certain: in this modern world of ours we cannot afford to forget that what we do at home is important in relation to the rest of the world. The sooner we learn this, the sooner we will understand the meaning of our social revolution.

It is not too much to say that our adjustment to our own social revolution will affect almost every country in the world. Nor is it too much to say that we should be able to make our adjustment with comparative ease. What is required of us is infinitesimal compared to the adjustments that are to be made in the backward nations—in prejudice, in superstition, in ignorance, in habits and customs. They are coming out of the bush; we have only to come out of the darkness of our own blind prejudice and fear into the steady light of reason and humanity.

You will tell me, perhaps, that to cope successfully with our social revolution we must bring about a revolution in the mentality of the American people. While there is much truth in this, it is well to remember that, in many respects and in many areas of the United States, that revolution has been fought—and won. In his first inaugural my husband said, "We do not distrust the future of essential democracy."

The ensuing years, up to the Second World War, revealed that, when they had taken a wrong turning, the American people were willing to shift their position, to look freshly at conditions, and to find new methods of tackling them. And they were able to do this within the framework of the American system; they were able to find a middle course that upheld the capitalistic system at a time when most of the world seemed to have adopted the policy of extremes—either the extreme right of Nazism or the extreme left of Communism.

What we have failed too often to do is to appeal to this capacity for flexibility in the people.

The revolution in our social thinking appears, in capsule form, to my eyes, in one family I know well—my own. My mother-in-law belonged to the established world of the last century. She accepted its shibboleths without questioning. To her these things were true.

When she died, in September, 1941, my husband felt strongly this ending of an unshakable world behind him. And yet, he told me, it was probably as well for his mother to leave us at that time. She was immersed in her old world and the new one was alien to her. The adjustment for her would have been impossible.

In using the term, I do not mean adjustment merely to the dramatic and obvious physical changes: to modern transportation and electrical gadgets and all the scientific inventions that have transformed our world. Within an incredibly short time, no matter how drastic is such change, one adjusts to it. It simply becomes one more convenience.

No, the basic change in the social revolution has been the change in values. To my mother-in-law, for instance, there were certain obligations that she, as a privileged person, must fulfill. She fed the poor, assisted them with money, helped them with medical expenses. This was a form of charity required of her.

The point of view that she simply could not accept was my husband's. He believed—as I trust most civilized people believe now—that human beings have rights as human beings: a right to a job, a right to education, a right to health protection, a right to human dignity, a right to a chance of fulfillment.

This is the inevitable growth in our thinking as a nation—the practical application of democratic principles. No one today would dare refer to the mass of the people, as Alexander Hamilton once did, as "that great beast." And that, perhaps, is a minor victory in the long battle for human rights.

Part D
Women and the World Around Them

38

Women Must Learn to Play the Game as Men Do

Women have been voting for ten years. But have they achieved actual political equality with men? No. They go through the gesture of going to the polls; their votes are solicited by politicians; and they possess the external aspect of equal rights. But it is mostly a gesture without real power. With some outstanding exceptions, women who have gone into politics are refused serious consideration by the men leaders. Generally they are treated most courteously, to be sure, but what they want, what they have to say, is regarded as of little weight. In fact, they have no actual influence or say at all in the consequential councils of their parties.

In small things they are listened to; but when it comes to asking for important things they generally find they are up against a blank wall. This is true of local committees, State committees, and the national organizations of both major political parties.

From all over the United States, women of both camps have come to me, and their experiences are practically the same. When meetings are to be held at which momentous matters are to be decided, the women members often are not asked. When they are notified of formal meetings where important matters are to be ratified, they generally find all these things have been planned and prepared, without consultation with them, in secret confabs of the men beforehand. If they have objections to proposed policies or candidates, they are adroitly overruled. They are not allowed to run for office to any appreciable extent and if they propose candidates of their own sex, reasons are usually found for their elimination which, while diplomatic and polite, are just pretexts nevertheless.

In those circles which decide the affairs of national politics, women have no voice or power whatever. On the national committee of each party there is a woman representative from every State, and a woman appears as vice-chairman. Before national elections they will be told to organize the women throughout the United States, and asked to help in minor ways in raising funds. But when it comes to those grave councils at which possible candidates are discussed, as well as party policies, they are rarely invited in. At the national conventions no woman has ever been asked to serve on the platform committee.

Politically, as a sex, women are generally "frozen out" from any intrinsic share of influence in their parties.

The Red Book Magazine 50, no. 6 (April 1928): 78–79, 141–142.

The machinery of party politics has always been in the hands of men, and still is. Our statesmen and legislators are still keeping in form as the successors of the early warriors gathering around the campfire plotting the next day's attack. Yes, they have made feints indicating they are willing to take women into the high councils of the parties. But, in fact, the women who have gone into the political game will tell you they are excluded from any actual kind of important participation. They are called upon to produce votes, but they are kept in ignorance of noteworthy plans and affairs. Their requests are seldom refused outright, but they are put off with a technique that is an art in itself. The fact is that generally women are not taken seriously. With certain exceptions, men still as a class dismiss their consequence and value in politics, cherishing the old-fashioned concept that their place is in the home. While women's votes are a factor to be counted upon, and figure largely in any impending campaign, the individual women who figure in party councils are regarded by their male confrères as having no real power back of them. And they haven't.

Men who work hard in party politics are always recognized, or taken care of in one way or another. Women, most of whom are voluntary workers and not at all self-seeking, are generally expected to find in their labor its own reward. When it comes to giving the offices or dealing out favors, men are always given precedence.

They will ask women to run for office now and then, sometimes because they think it politic and wise to show women how generous they are, but more often because they realize in advance their ticket cannot win in the district selected. Therefore they will put up a woman, knowing it will injure the party less to have a woman defeated, and then they can always say it was her sex that defeated her. Where victory is certain, very rarely can you get a woman nominated on the party ticket.

Of course there are women all over the United States who have been elected to high and important offices. There are three women in Congress; there have been two woman governors; and women sit in various State legislatures and hold State offices. In New York City one could cite several who have not only been elected but who have conducted themselves in office with ability and distinction. But does that indicate any equal recognition of share in political power? Infinitely more examples come to mind of women who were either denied a nomination or who were offered it only when inevitable defeat stared the party leaders in the face.

When, some years ago, it came to putting women on the Democratic State Committee in New York, only two outstanding men openly approved of the move. A number were willing, but a great many more were indifferent. Governor Smith wanted women on the committee, believing they had something to contribute, and that they should have recognition for what they could do. Quite unlike Governor Smith, many other men come to mind who hold important positions of power in New York State. They deal with the women in a spirit of most deferential courtesy; but as many of us know, they heartily dislike the idea of women mixing in politics, are antagonistic to those who are active, and can be depended upon to do all in their power to render the women's influence negative.

Beneath the veneer of courtesy and outward show of consideration universally accorded women, there is a widespread male hostility—age-old, perhaps—against sharing with them any actual control.

How many excuses haven't I heard for not giving nominations to women! "Oh, she wouldn't like the kind of work she'd have to do!" Or, "You know she wouldn't like the people she'd have to associate with—that's not a job for a nice, refined women." Or more usually: "You see, there is so little patronage nowadays. We must give every appointment the most careful consideration. We've got to consider the good of the party." "The good of the party" eliminates women!

When no women are present at the meetings, the leaders are more outspoken. "No, we're not going to have any woman on the ticket," declared one leader according to a report once made to me. "Those fool women are always making trouble, anyway. We won't have any we don't have to have, and if we have none, let's get one we understand."

It is a strong and liberal man, indeed, who speaks on behalf of the women at those secret conclaves, and endeavors to have them fairly treated.

To many women who fought so long and so valiantly for suffrage, what has happened has been most discouraging. For one reason or another, most of the leaders who carried the early fight to success have dropped out of politics. This has been in many ways unfortunate. Among them were women with gifts of real leadership. They were exceptional and high types of women, idealists concerned in carrying a cause to victory, with no idea of personal advancement or gain. In fact, attaining the vote was only part of a program for equal rights—an external gesture toward economic independence, and social and spiritual equality with men.

When the franchise was finally achieved, their interest was not held by any ambition for political preferment or honors. To learn the intricate machinery of politics and play the men's game left them cold. The routine of political office held no appeal. One of the most prominent of those early crusaders today gives her energies to campaigning for world peace. By nature a propagandist, it would be impossible to interest her in either of the major parties. Another woman, who donated hundreds of thousands of dollars to the cause, frankly admits she has never even cast a vote. She considers the situation, with women coping with men in the leading parties, utterly hopeless. Like many others, she regards suffrage as an empty victory, equal rights a travesty, and the vote a gesture without power.

An extreme point of view, in my opinion. There is a method—and not the one advocated by certain militants who hold aloof from party politics—by which, I believe, the end of a fair representation and share in control may be attained.

Personally, I do not believe in a Woman's Party. A woman's ticket could never possibly succeed. And to crystallize the issues on the basis of sex-opposition would only further antagonize men, congeal their age-old prejudices, and widen the chasm of existing differences.

How, then, can we bring the men leaders to concede participation in party affairs, adequate representation and real political equality?

Our means is to elect, accept and back women political bosses.

To organize as women, but within the parties, in districts, counties and States just as men organize, and to pick efficient leaders—say two or three in each State—whom we will support and by whose decisions we will abide. With the power of unified women voters behind them, such women bosses would be in a position to talk in terms of "business" with the men leaders; their voices would be heard, because their authority and the elective power they could command would have to be recognized.

Women are today ignored largely because they have no banded unity under representative leaders and spokesmen capable of dealing with the bosses controlling groups of men whose votes they can "deliver." These men bosses have the power of coordinated voters behind them. Our helplessness is that of an incoherent anarchy.

Perhaps the word "boss" may shock sensitive ears. To many it will conjure all that is unhealthy and corrupt in our political machinery. Yet when I speak of women bosses, I mean bosses actually in the sense that men are bosses. The term *boss* does not necessarily infer what it once did. Politics have been purged of many of the corruptions prevalent a quarter of a century ago. In neither of the political parties are there many, if any, such bosses, great or small, as were such common types in the heyday of Quay and Tweed. As things are today, the boss is a leader, often an enlightened, high-minded leader, who retains little of the qualities imputed by the old use of this obnoxious word, but who still exercises authority over his district. I therefore use the word, as it is the word men understand.

If women believe they have a right and duty in political life today, they must learn to talk the language of men. They must not only master the phraseology, but also understand the machinery which men have built up through years of practical experience. Against the men bosses there must be women bosses who can talk as equals, with the backing of a coherent organization of women voters behind them.

Voters who are only voters, whether men or women, are only the followers of leaders. The important thing is the choosing of leaders.

We must be fair, and admit the blame for our present ineffectuality in politics does not lie wholly with the men. If we are still a negligible factor, ignored and neglected, we must be prepared to admit in what we have ourselves failed.

The trouble with many women is that they won't work. They won't take up their jobs as men do and put in seven or eight real working hours a day.

They lack knowledge, and at that many won't take the pains to study history, economics, political methods or get out among human beings. If they take a volunteer political job, it is a thing of constant interruptions, with no sense of application, concentration, business efficiency or order. One of the reasons why men leaders so often do not consider as important what a woman says is that they do not feel sure she has been active among the mass of women voters and has learned what they want. In fact, many women do make the mistake of "talking out of a blue sky" instead of going about, mixing with women, and getting their point of view from close personal contact and practical experience. When a man leader says his following want certain things, the men higher up realize that he knows what he is talking about, and that he has gone through his district.

There are two classes of men in politics—those for whom it is a game or relaxation, and those for whom it is bread and butter. These latter are usually small office-holding politicians, bosses of small groups of men. At their head are men who are deeply interested for the good of their country as they see it, and who often for patriotic reasons hold government offices for a time. But you will find as a rule that their first interest is in some other career in which they have made a name, worked their best and hardest, and gained the wherewithal to live and support their families. Politics—public service—is something apart.

Women are different. Many of them have no professional careers. If they go into politics it is usually because of some interest which they realize is dependent on government action. I know women who are interested in education, in health conditions, in the improvement of rural life, in social problems, in housing, and all active in politics because they have come to realize by that way they may further their particular cause. Politics is less of a game to them because they haven't had the same training for games as men, and their first contact with great groups of people is an exciting and disturbing experience, not to be taken lightly but almost prayerfully.

In this I am not speaking of the small army of women who are trained in some profession, some of whom hold minor political offices, and a few of whom hold minor positions of importance in the parties. Some of these have attained the attitude of men, and meet them on the same ground. Then there are women, as there are men, who frankly are in politics for what they can get out of it. I remember well one woman who had worked hard in an organization and was denied recognition in the tangible way she desired—namely, a paid job. Whereupon she announced she was going over to the opposing political party, where, when they wished to reward a worker, they created a job if one was not available at the time!

This attitude is comparatively rare, however, because most women working in all political organizations are volunteers. Their motives for being volunteers may be mixed. I am far from claiming that as a sex we have a monopoly of disinterested desire to serve our country. Human nature is much the same in men and women. But the fact remains that the great mass of women working in political organizations all over this country are unpaid, and they are so far allowed to do the detail work which bores the men.

In the average home a woman's job is full of interruptions; and so, unless she sets out to methodize her life, she is apt to go through many wasted motions. Now many volunteer political workers come out of such unorganized homes. When the children are small, if they have little help in their homes, the mothers cannot do outside work. But as the children grow up—or in rare cases before they are married—they may turn to politics as an outside interest. If they are women of means and have more help at home, they may still have led disorganized lives, for of necessity a home and children make unexpected demands.

I should not want the average woman, or the exceptional woman for that matter, who for one reason or another could not do a public job well, to take one at present. For just now a woman must do better than a man, for whatever she does in the public eye reflects on the whole cause of women. There are women in the United States I would gladly see run for any office. But if we cannot have the best I should prefer to wait and prepare a little longer until women are more ready to make a fine contribution to public life in any office they might hold.

An old politician once objected, "Don't you think these women lose their allure, that the bloom is just a little gone? Men are no longer interested?"

Frankly, I don't know. I imagine the answer is individual. It was once said that men did not marry women who showed too much intelligence. In my youth I knew women who hid their college degrees as if they were one of the seven deadly sins. But all that is passing, and so will pass many other prejudices that have their origin in the ancient tradition that women are a by-product of creation.

Remember, women have voted just ten years. They have held responsible positions in big business enterprises only since the war, to any great extent. The men at the head of big business or controlling politics are for the most part middle-aged men. Their wives grew up in an era when no public question was discussed in a popular manner, when men talked politics over their wine or cigars, and pulled their waistcoats down, on joining the ladies, to talk music, or the play or the latest scandal. Can you blame them if the adjustment to modern conditions is somewhat difficult?

Certain women profess to be horrified at the thought of women bosses bartering and dickering in the hard game of politics with men. But many more women realize that we are living in a material world, and that politics cannot be played from the clouds. To sum up, women must learn to play the game as men do. If they go into politics, they must stick to their jobs, respect the time and work of others, master a knowledge of history and human nature, learn diplomacy, subordinate their likes and dislikes of the moment and choose leaders to act for them and to whom they will be loyal. They can keep their ideals; but they must face facts and deal with them practically.

39

The Modern Wife's Difficult Job

What is the master key to success in the modern wife's job?

Of the three fundamentals of her task—being a partner, being a mother, and being a homemaker—which is the most vital to success in married life?

A generation ago we should probably have answered, "Being a mother, of course," with the housekeeping next, and the partnership last. But now, according to Mrs. Franklin D. Roosevelt, wife of New York's Governor, if we are up to date we realize that the most important part of a wife's job is to be a good companion—that everything else depends upon the success of the wife and the husband in their personal relation.

"Just what is a wife's job today?"

"In what respect does it differ from the job as it used to be?"

"How is it managed by women who manage it in the modern way?"

These three questions were put to Mrs. Roosevelt, in her home at Albany, by M. K. Wisehart, who humbly confessed that he was one of several millions of men who could not answer them, and who tells in the August *Good Housekeeping* how the first lady of New York State enlightened his ignorance. He applied to her for this knowledge, he says, because he remembered that in war times her Washington home was regarded as a model for large households.

"Celebrated as a hostess," he adds, "a partner in a furniture-manufacturing enterprise, a teacher in a New York day school for girls, mother of five children, four boys and a girl, this ideal type of the modern wife happens herself to be a grandmother."

Mrs. Roosevelt believes that modern conditions compel the wise wife to change her ways or adopt new ones. The wife's is an old, old problem, but it has many new aspects, and to cope with them, she says, requires as many changes of method as a man has to make in his business or profession. Remarking that the most successful marriage she has ever known was the most complete in its partnership, she continues:

"Partnership! Companionship! And fitness for it! It is the major requirement for modern marriage.

"I am not saying that the wives of today can hope to be better companions than were some wives of the past. The great change is that, far more

The Literary Digest 106 (August 30, 1930): 18–19. Condensed from M. K. Wisehart, "Mrs. Franklin D. Roosevelt Answers the Big Question—What Is a Wife's Job Today?," *Good Housekeeping* 91 (August 1930): 34–35, 166, 169–173.

generally we recognize the importance of such companionship. Today, I think, there are far more wives who are good companions than there used to be.

"How well we realize today that it is essential for a woman to develop her own interests—in music, literature, club life, church, community activities, and hobbies, for instance—so as not to lose the possibility of being a stimulating personality!

"I have in mind the case of a woman who is sensitive, delicate, and a little timid. She married a man of very strong and dominating character. From the very beginning of their marriage their conversations were almost exclusively about his affairs, seldom hers. He completely dominated her. She had really great artistic gifts, but, owing to the situation in their home, she did not continue developing them after her marriage. In the end, their relationship came to mean nothing to him, mainly because she was afraid of him. Having taken out of her everything that was good, he lost all interest in her. Eventually they were divorced, and he married again.

"In his relations with his first wife this man represents what might be called the 'vampire husband,' dominating ruthlessly and discarding what he ruined.

"With the second wife it was different. She did not fear him. Seeing that she had an extraordinarily quick mind and a tremendous personality to deal with, she promptly adjusted herself to the circumstances in what I should say was the modern way, neither subordinating nor effacing herself. She, too, had talents and abilities, and she maintained her right to develop them. Tho deeply interested in all her husband's affairs, she never sacrificed her own interests. The difference in the result has been remarkable. The relationship apparently has been perfectly satisfying, and the marriage a complete success."

We also have the vampire wife—the woman who looks upon her husband as merely a source of supply, and who seems to think that he should sacrifice everything for her, while she gives him little or nothing. In neither case can the marriage be a success, says Mrs. Roosevelt, adding:

"More than ever before a wife must be able to take an intelligent interest in her husband's interests. Notice that I say in his 'interests,' not merely in his 'job.' Her interest must not cease with his job. Women have found it a terrible thing to be just a heavy partner, sharing business and home cares only, and not a light partner, sharing in the diversion of pleasure hours.

"The modern way means that she must fit herself, and keep herself fit to share not only responsibilities and burdens but intellectual pursuits, recreation, diversion, and pleasures of all kinds.

"On the other hand, each should, I think, have the opportunity for some experiences and interests that are not entirely shared by the other. As one sociologist puts it, 'Each must have a separate foothold, personal activities which are entered upon alone, and which are not immediately rehashed in lieu of other conversation. These detached and personal activities maintain that sense of "illusiveness" characteristic of courtship days. So that their companionship may not pall, there must always be some distinct territory in the life of each that has never thoroughly been explored by the other.' "

Mrs. Roosevelt, we are told, goes from Albany to New York to teach in a girls' school three days of each week, because she loves to teach. That is her "separate foothold" at present.

When the interviewer asked her to name "the particularly modern aspects of the mother phase of the wife's job," she replied.

"How much more we know today about the care and rearing of children than women formerly knew!

"The difference between the methods of today and those of yesteryear consists mainly of this: We do not have the old-fashioned idea of making a child do a thing simply because he is told to do it. From his earliest days we teach him the reason back of what is asked of him. As much as possible, we let him learn by experience. Nevertheless, we still tell him what to do, and require his obedience.

"If he does not quite understand the reason for what is asked of him, he must, nevertheless, obey, if for no other reason than because he has learned that mother is trustworthy. In the future, of course, he may demand an explanation, and this the wise mother will do her best to give."

Children need two parents, and many of the things that should be done for their proper development cannot be done by the mother without the father's aid, Mrs. Roosevelt points out:

"Take the religious side, for instance. A woman may feel that to make religion a reality to youth, a certain amount of formal observance is necessary. If she does feel this way about it, and the husband himself does not practice such observance, a time will come when disturbing questions will arise in the minds of their children. They will realize that one of the people they admire does not think such observance necessary. They may question the wisdom of what the mother has asked. In the end this may prevent the life of the family from being a unified thing."

There are still too many "smothering mothers"—mothers who work havoc on their children's lives by doing too much for them, thus keeping them from developing their own personalities and initiative—mothers who actually take their grown daughters' beaux away by assuming the center of the stage themselves, says this observer, concluding:

"The essential thing for a mother to realize is that smothering should and can be avoided. The great safeguard lies in this. As her children grow older, and do not require physical care, a mother must take pains to develop new interests of her own in church, community, or welfare activities, say. She must not let herself be completely dependent for her interest in life on the lives that her children live."

The homemaker part of the wife's job has changed utterly since the days when most of the necessities of life were produced in the home, says Mrs. Roosevelt; now most homes have the necessities, and the wife has to "plan on what are the next greatest values for the family after the necessities are taken care of—in itself an important and momentous new task." She exclaims:

"Think of the things a woman must know today! So much more reliable information is available as to what are the proper things to eat, and how they should be cooked.

"If it is a home where she does most of her own work, she has the problem of systematizing that work, and of using as many labor-saving devices as she can afford. She must learn to do it in the easiest and quickest possible way so that all goes as smoothly as possible, and so that it may not seem a burden to her.

"If it is a home in which there are servants, she must inform herself as to reasonable and satisfactory rates of compensation. She then has the same problems to meet that an employer in business has. Definite agreements must be made and lived up to, with time off, and compensation for loss of free time. That is to say, this must be the case if we regard servants as people like ourselves who happen to be engaged in the business of modern housekeeping."

To succeed as a wife in this age requires a tremendous fund of energy, the Governor's wife has discovered, and it is important "to budget not only expenditures, but time and energy." In order to do this, she says, one must learn to choose the things that are most important, and eliminate the rest:

"Many women, floored by the rapidity of movement in the world today, have said to me: 'I cannot keep up with my children! Motor cars carried them so fast! Now they want to fly! There are so many things I should, but cannot do. I cannot read or hear or see enough to keep up to date.' To these women I say: 'The first thing to do is to sit down and become immovable. Get possession of yourself! Let the world go by altogether until you have decided for yourself just exactly what you want."

40

Ten Rules for Success in Marriage

In a city of some forty thousand population in upstate New York, Dr. F., by years of patient, earnest application, had established himself as the leading physician. His earnings were modest, his prestige tremendous, due to his inspiring character. He had never married.

The girl he loved had grown up side by side with him in the same community. She had married, and was most unhappy. It was one of those cases in which the man takes all that the woman has to give, offering little or nothing in return.

Dominated by her husband's selfishness, she lost her natural gaiety and wit, her self-confidence, and her intellectual interests. The marriage ended in divorce.

Dr. F. and his boyhood sweetheart married late. They were mature, past the middle thirties, seasoned in experience and judgment. They had had many long talks about the kind of home they would have and the purpose of their life together. With perfectly clear ideas as to the significance of marriage, they established their partnership with the hope that, as they gained happiness, their power for usefulness and service would increase.

They had three children. A happy home. It seemed that life was to give this couple all that one could ask. Then, at a time when their oldest boy was only five, and when Dr. F. had become a power in the community and his wife a great influence, the blow fell. Dr. F. learned that he was afflicted with an incurable malady and apparently had a very short time to live.

They met the situation in the most wonderful way, undertaking together a new project—the education of the wife in preparation for the many large responsibilities which her husband presently would no longer be able to share.

He schooled her in business principles. As far as possible she acquired from him a man's point of view about the education of their two boys and the baby girl. In every way he sought to build up in her a tremendous readiness and self-confidence. "Your judgment will always be good, Margaret," he would say. "No one will know better than you how to meet every situation."

When Dr. F. died he left very little in the way of material possessions. But Margaret had a great practical experience and a splendid spiritual heritage. She was, indeed, equal to everything, and was able to carry through, until they were grown, all the ideas that she and her husband had had for their children.

Long after Dr. F. was gone, for years and years, and until this day, all that happened to his widow and the children was evidence of his sanity, vision, and imagination, the three essential factors that are required for success in

Pictorial Review 33 (December 1931): 4, 36, 44.

marriage. Marriage! If only more of us would see that it is a partnership in which neither can succeed without the other and that the success of both depends upon the success of each!

Sanity! Vision! Imagination! These are three great essentials for success in marriage. Marriage is not only a responsibility, but an opportunity, a never-ending source of growth and education. In this school one never graduates. It takes time, trouble, patience to make a marriage go. You must *grow* along with it. It is a relationship that must always be looked after.

One of the world's great writers begins a famous novel, *Anna Karenina*, with this statement: "All happy families are more or less like one another; every unhappy family is unhappy in its own particular way." This observation has caused me to reflect upon what the common denominator of married happiness might be. Fundamentally, I believe, the things that make for happiness in marriage are mainly matters of character.

You cannot expect to be happy unless you have acquired a certain amount of self-control, the ability to see yourself honestly, to meet things squarely, to put yourself through any really difficult situation without self-pity and without weakening in the main purpose of your life. Hence I would say that the common denominator of married happiness is unselfishness, thoughtfulness, consideration for others. These are among the first essentials that must be looked after.

The marriage of one woman I know has failed because she has never really tried to make the most of her own possibilities. Well-to-do, lacking imagination, she has never sought pursuits that would keep her mind occupied, and has no stimulating interests of her own. Her home is an exceedingly dull place. Gradually her husband and children had drifted away, leaving her a very lonely person.

Divorce? No! They have not left her in that way. But there has ceased to be a community of interests in this home, largely because she thinks so much about herself that she has no inclination to think of others. Always, she has expected them to bring something into her life, while she has brought nothing into theirs. Husband and wife and the children, each has drifted into a different channel. They still live in the same house. They might as well be living in different cities. There is no real home.

All the successful marriages that I know have one factor in common, a more or less definite understanding between the partners as to the real purpose of the partnership. Sometimes this understanding comes with the years; sometimes it is arrived at in advance of marriage by deliberate analysis and definition. In general, I believe that marriage should be more definitely planned than is usually the case.

It holds true for all young couples that in a large, general way their ideals should be set for the same goal. They must have some conception as to what they want to make of their lives. They must decide what they will consider is success for each individually and for their partnership. Then they can do the things which will contribute to that success.

There are three things upon which I think every young couple should be sure that they agree before they marry; first, to live well within their income so as to allow a margin for savings and insurance; second, to choose their friends from among those whose values of life coincide with their own; third, difficult though it is when young, they must look ahead and plan mental and spiritual satisfactions which will not depend upon their material progress.

In many respects marriage will always remain a gamble. If we could take the gamble out of it, it would be far less interesting. On no phase of the question dare one be hard and fast. However, as I think over the marriages I have known and the experiences that have been confided to me, I am tempted to say that there are ten rules, not hard and fast, but safe and sane, the observance of which makes for success in marriage.

1. Have a plan, some central idea, as definite a pattern for your life as possible, and a clearly understood object for the joint project.
2. Remember that sooner or later money is apt to be a cause of friction. Keeping a budget is a practical way of eliminating the irritations and dissatisfactions that come to married people over the outlay of money.
3. Apportion your time and energy, allowing each his share for the joint homemaking duties, as well as for individual responsibilities.
4. Let neither husband nor wife strive to be the dominating person in the household. A victory for either in this respect means failure for the partnership.
5. Expect to disagree. Two people may hold entirely different views on many subjects and yet respect and care for each other just the same.
6. Be honest. Each must be honest with himself and with the other, not trying to think and be things he is not.
7. Be loyal. Keep your differences to yourselves. The less said about your married troubles, except between yourselves, the better. The feeling that many young married people have, that they can complain to their parents when things do not go just right, is bad for them and brings more serious trouble later on.
8. Talk things over. When hurt do not keep it to yourself, brooding over it. Meet every situation in the open. Troubles that seem momentous quickly vanish when frankly dealt with.
9. Avoid trivial criticisms. Grumbling and complaints use up the vital forces of man or woman.
10. Keep alive the spirit of courtship, the thoughtfulness which existed before marriage. Look for traits in the other that can be admired and praised. You can accomplish much by stimulating self-confidence in your partner. For one who reacts to encouragement with "But, I'm afraid I can't," there are ten who feel, "I'm really quite a fellow after all! I mustn't let her (or him) down in what she (or he) expects of me!"

As a result of my experience and observation there are two things which I would counsel fathers and mothers and all "in-laws" to bear in mind. First, I would say: "Offer as little advice to the newly married as possible, preferably none. Once the young people have begun their life together, their elders can be of great service simply by standing by, ready to help if called upon in real crises. Volunteering advice is not the privilege of the older generation; it is a serious infringement of the rights of the younger."

Second, "I have known many promising marriages to be wrecked because the young people began their life together in the home of their parents or had parents come to live with them. Even though father and mother are lonely it is better for the young people to start out alone. It is exceedingly difficult for several generations to live under the same roof. Only the most exceptional people can work it out successfully."

Perhaps I have more definite views as to the function of the engagement than many seem to. As I see it, it should be nothing less than a period of almost daily contact. Do not misunderstand me! I am not advocating trial marriage! I mean that, short of trial marriage itself, the engaged couple should have almost constant association with the object of discovering whether they can really stand the jars and jolts and routine of life together and whether they have similar conceptions as to what they want to make of their lives.

Always the hasty marriage is undesirable. In most cases, I should say, the engagement should last at least six months, long enough for serious disagreements to arise. That engagement during which the young people see so little of each other that disagreements, quarrels, or tiffs do not occur, I would consider a failure.

The greatest crosses in married life concern little things. Almost anyone can rise to great occasions and meet real crises well. The things most likely to drive people crazy with their life partners are small peculiarities—the way one's hair is brushed, for instance. He (or she) may repeat the same joke or the same commonplace phrase times without number. Perhaps one lays down the law, passes judgment, solves problems in a too literal, sober, and positive way. Or may eat rapidly and finish the whole meal in a minute, while the other eats slowly and methodically. The real difficulty is not that your husband beats you, so much as it is that he reads his newspaper while you sip your morning coffee!

So I would encourage an engaged couple to see so much of each other that they know each other extremely well. I would give them every chance to break their engagement if they find that this familiarity brings to light irksome, unbearable little peculiarities of the sort I have mentioned. Let him be invited to breakfast every day in the week for three months! Truly, fond hearts only may be expected to survive such a test!

Our young people should have no illusions in this respect. Married people are bound to disagree. They should have every chance to disagree before they marry, and experience in adjusting their differences. It is a valuable thing for them to learn that they can disagree and still care for each other. If they find that they care less because they disagree, they may then go a step further and conclude that they are not suited as life partners.

I have in mind a girl who was much in love and engaged to a man considerably older than herself. She had been brought up in an atmosphere of extreme free thought. Her mother was not a member of any religious denomination. The conversation in this house had always been very open, without thought as to whether or not it was in accord with the conventional ideas of the people around them.

One day, when talking with her fiancé, Charlotte expressed herself frankly on a certain religious topic. Shocked, he told her that when he took her home to his own people she must never say anything of that kind because they would resent it.

"I cannot live with anyone with whom I have to be careful as to what I say!" returned Charlotte angrily.

"Perhaps you cannot live with me then?" returned her fiancé.

"I have never lived with people who did not say exactly what they thought," returned Charlotte. "Everybody ought to respect what everybody else thinks."

Thus the quarrel began. Charlotte went to her mother, who was of great help to her in the crisis. "I'm going to break my engagement!" Charlotte declared. "It isn't that I don't care for Howard, but I just can't live in an atmosphere where I cannot be myself and say what I think! I will be shocking him to death!"

"But my dear," returned her mother, "the question is not one of your right to be yourself. It is a question of ordinary thoughtfulness and courtesy toward people. You have a perfect right to think what you please and to express any opinions you wish in intercourse with your friends. That does not justify you in deliberately expressing ideas which will hurt other people who hold very strong opinions, contrary to yours."

Eventually all ended well. The disagreement was an invaluable experience for both Charlotte and Howard. Charlotte was prompted to consider more seriously than ever before what it was going to mean to her to live with Howard. Howard came to respect her for the stand she had taken. An older man, he had been expecting to mold her whole thought on any question that came up.

Realizing, as a result of this quarrel, that she felt strongly about being allowed to hold opinions of her own, he came to look upon her, not as a child whom he was going to develop and make into his own creature, but as another being with whom he was going to live as an equal.

One of the very real shortcomings in the education of our young people today is due to our failure as fathers and mothers to require them to assume definite responsibilities at a sufficiently early age. Duties about the home early in youth are a splendid means of stimulating responsibility and initiative on the part of our children.

I have in mind a young man of twenty-four who is the father of a boy two and a half years old. Only the other day he said to me, "I never realized what it would mean to have a son and to feel responsible for him. It's something awful! If I had realized it I never would have married!"

Now, the responsibility which weighs upon this young man is not of a financial nature. He is not concerned about expenses for medical care, clothes, and the education of his child. These he is perfectly well able to meet. The truth is that having a son has interfered with his comfort. He was out of patience because he has had to walk the floor with the baby.

His whole attitude is one which I think would be quite different had he had the right kind of training in boyhood, acquiring habits of unselfishness and the understanding that in this world no great good can come to one without some inconvenience, *giving* as well as taking.

It has always been accepted as a truism that boys should be encouraged to be independent and to take the initiative. I think it is equally important in the education of the girl; and this means, for one thing, that she should not be kept under the control of her mother too long.

By the time a girl is fifteen, if she has been properly brought up, it should be possible to trust her to meet many of the usual occurrences of life. Nowadays, at fifteen, many girls are at work earning their living. Just because a girl does not have to go to work as early as fifteen is no reason why she should be allowed to be a helpless human being. At this age she should know how to walk in the street and not be too noticeable; how to conduct herself in street-cars and in trains.

If she has been brought up in a family in which there are other children, she should have learned a great deal from helping care for the younger ones. She should know how to get a doctor, how to turn in a fire alarm, what to do in case of accident or injury, where to turn for help. She should know enough about the world to be able to meet anyone on an equal basis and to look after herself under all ordinary circumstances.

Before a girl marries it is important, I think, that she have considerable experience in spending money and in actually running a house. I recall how a friend of mine, a well-to-do woman who occupies an important social position, trained her daughter in this respect. When the daughter was seventeen the mother gave her an allowance to cover all personal expenditures. At eighteen the girl was put in charge of her mother's house and ran it for a period of six months. She managed six servants and bought everything used in this large household except the house furnishings.

Of course, the mother stood back of her. If the girl found herself in difficulties she could ask her mother for help after trying to settle the matter herself, but she could not go to her mother before first attempting to solve the difficulty herself. Once the girl has had an experience of this sort she is really trained and capable of managing a home. This girl is now married and happy in her home and in her dealings with those about her.

In another respect, quite different from anything I have yet mentioned, the wisdom and experience of older people can be made to serve the younger generation. Great tact and delicacy are necessary to accomplish what I have in mind now. Perhaps two illustrations from real life will best illustrate exactly what I mean.

Consider the case of a certain high-school girl, sixteen and a half years old, the daughter of a private banker in an upstate city of New York. For two years she had been going to parties and other entertainments with a boy who was in her class in high school. She imagined that she was in love with him. Suddenly, one day, perceiving the course events were taking, her parents, without explanation, took her away for a two weeks' visit to an aunt in another part of the State. Upon their return this girl's mother forbade her to see the youth with whom she had previously been on such friendly terms.

Three days later the girl slipped out of the house and eloped with her boyfriend! Falsifying their ages and other details required for obtaining a marriage license, they married. The father and mother were, of course, heart-broken. They stipulated that the young people should not live together until after graduating from high school. Then the father furnished an apartment for them, and the young people were permitted to begin their married life. Within six months the girl was completely disillusioned, and in the course of a year she was as eager as her parents to have the marriage annulled.

As I see it, there were two fundamental mistakes in the way the parents handled this matter. First, a girl of sixteen and a half should never have been allowed to entertain the idea that she was old enough to marry; second, if we wish to prevent our children from falling in love with those we consider undesirable we must remember that our guidance is most apt to have weight before the acquaintanceship has ripened.

Furthermore, it seems to me that it is obviously absurd to believe that because two young people have been separated for such a brief interval as two weeks they will cease to imagine themselves in love. In all probability such a separation would have to be for a year, possibly two, with opportunities for work and diversion in an interesting environment.

Two years ago this incident happened in a very fine family that I know well: An eighteen-year-old daughter confided in her mother that she was certain that she was in love with a youth she had met at college. The family of the young man was known to the girl's parents only by reputation. They were people of wealth. It appeared that the values which counted most with them could be weighed only in money. The girl's parents were very well-to-do too, but highly cultivated. Her whole background was one of refinement. Fortunately, her mother was a wise woman.

"Surely, Doris," said her mother, "if you are fond of C. bring him home. Have him spend a week with us!"

So C. came to visit. From the first he was obviously not at home and did not feel comfortable. He became self-assertive and a little arrogant. His voice was too loud, his laughter too boisterous, and his mind was rather limited, whereas Doris had been accustomed to a variety and range of ideas.

He was bored and Doris was bored, and the realization came to her that there was no real communion of feeling and interest between them which might form the basis of friendship and even a deeper feeling. Instead there was a mere physical attraction which at the best could last but a short time. In a week the youth departed and he was never heard of again.

211

Often our children meet some friend outside the family circle with whom they are carried away for the time being. If he is invited into the home, then it will appear whether or not he has the qualities that can let him shine in the eyes of the father and mother. If he does shine—all right! If not, a great mistake may have been avoided.

One of the greatest safeguards boys or girls can have in the selection of life partners, as in the selection of friends, is the unconscious standards which grow in the proper kind of atmosphere. There is something which no real fellow can do without, whether the fellow be boy or girl, namely, the feeling which we call good taste, which makes us know instinctively when we meet people, no matter what their outer shells may be, whether they are real people, with that kernel of gold which is the one requisite for a deep and true relationship.

A man and a woman may come from different backgrounds, they may not have had the same opportunities, and therefore they may lack certain knowledge and education in social customs and habits, but if, at bottom, they are the right kind of people, if the kernel of gold is there, then good taste will recognize and claim unswervingly its mate for friendship and for love with very little chance of future disappointment.

We all know that when two people are in love they are easily carried away by their emotions. Some psychologists go so far as to say that love is a kind of sickness owing to the abnormal mental and psychological reactions it produces.

The time to teach young people what happens to them when they are in love is *before* they are in love. Thus they may be better able to use judgment and critical ability in deciding whether the object of their affection is suitable as a life partner. There is, of course, no sure way by which one can distinguish between the emotion of a passing attraction and that affection which can be elevated into a lasting human relationship. One thing we can do—encourage our young people to go slow, and try to make them realize that they must not rely entirely upon their feelings.

Perhaps the very thing I am suggesting here is now being brought about through the new freedom between the sexes which is characteristic of our time. I am familiar with the pessimistically critical views which many express with regard to this freedom. But, for my part, I am convinced that the greater freedom of our young people today, together with proper training for developing qualities of character which we all need, will eventually lead to happier lives.

Between the freedom of youth today and the restraints which surrounded older generations the difference is indeed vast. Our young people "play around," as we say, a good deal more than did the young people of an earlier generation. They talk about all sorts of topics which older people did not discuss when they were young. Together, our boys and girls now argue about questions which deal with life and reveal their outlook upon it. They talk about a million things—morality from different aspects, differences in the economic standards of different classes of people, the freedom of the man and the woman, and the development of individuals.

Through these discussions our young people come to know each other's viewpoints very well, discovering likes and dislikes and similar and dissimilar points of view. On the whole it is a splendid thing.

Success in marriage means compromise. Each must find a way out for himself. When a man finds that the woman he has married has certain ideas he does not like, or disapproves, the easy thing is to say, "She is not exactly what I thought she was! I'll get a divorce and try somebody else!"

The right thing is to seek the compromise by which they can get on. By patience, serenity, sanity, tact, a little more honesty in viewing oneself, a little more imagination in viewing the other, a relationship which at times may seem hopelessly impossible can be converted into one that is not only possible but precious and ennobling.

Unquestionably there are many unnecessary divorces. As a people, I think we are softer than we used to be. Many of us lack the stamina to face and see uncomfortable situations through. Today many seem to think that marriage is like a position in employment, which one can leave when everything does not go well. We *should* think of it as a permanent, lifetime job.

Statistics seem to show that one in seven marriages in the United States ends in divorce. A large proportion, but I do not think it so discouraging as some alarmists do. It means that out of fourteen persons two fail to make a go of this difficult and delicate relationship.

It is far better for two people who cannot get along to separate than to lead a quarrelsome life. If there are no children, I would say that divorce is justifiable when either husband or wife, or both, find that life together has ceased to have any real spiritual value. If there *are* children, I still think it is better that a home should be broken than that the children should live where the father and mother are continually pulling against each other.

In connection with the question of divorce the main problem must always be the rights of the children rather than those of the parents. A child has a right, if possible, to its own father and mother, not several fathers and mothers, all pulling in different directions and with different ideas as to what life really means.

Every young couple should remember that when they marry and have children they can no longer say, "I am entitled to lead my own life in the way which gives me the most happiness." Once we have children there should be no such thing as putting our own happiness or our own lives ahead of theirs.

41

Wives of Great Men

In my youth there we no political arguments to enliven the dinner table. The minds of most women were empty of such speculation. I was no exception to this rule. Politically I was totally ignorant as a young girl and as a young woman. It might be thought that, as a niece of President Roosevelt, I must have lived in an atmosphere of political excitement and grown up with a profound political penetration.

This was far from being the case. While I always cherished a great admiration for this distinguished uncle, I learned nothing whatsoever of the science of government from him. Although I stayed occasionally at Oyster Bay and knew my little cousins, they were more interested in badgers and pigs and snakes than in politics. Their father's influence was primarily exerted in outdoor life and in character-building. He would never permit any child to shirk or be afraid of anything. They learned that courage was a cardinal virtue and the lack of it intolerable. Aunt Edith also, through her quiet strength, taught us much. For all his outdoor enthusiasms Uncle Ted could also send us to the realm of books. He often read poetry and excerpts from other books aloud to us, and developed in all his children a real love of reading.

I went to his inauguration as President, and after I was eighteen went sometimes to Washington to stay with my aunt, Mrs. Cowles, or at the White House. But still politics meant nothing to me.

I have thought often of my own youth when I have seen Mary keeping a sharp eye on the school board, or met her on her way to the library for a background book on the Manchurian situation. I was the typical old-fashioned girl of my period, brought up from the time I was nine by my grandmother, Mrs. Valentine Hall, who had strict ideas as to the sphere of women. I learned early that a women should keep house with care. As a child I was allowed to bother the cook and the laundress, that I might learn these household tasks. I was even given a playhouse in the woods equipped as a kitchen. My grandmother and a strict Alsatian nurse spent hours teaching me to sew. Consequently my ideas of a wife were strictly concerned with the household. No kindly relatives worried over my civic convictions. I was trained to be useful in my home and to recognize an obligation to engage in some kind of philanthropic work.

How different from the modern young girl, who, if she does not hear politics discussed in her home, is exposed to it in the newspapers, in the motion pictures, on the radio. Her education includes courses in municipal, state, and national government, and some foundation in the social sciences. No wonder today's maiden has opinions and is inclined to stand by them.

Liberty 9 (October 1, 1932): 12–16.

My own education included nothing of the sort. My first glimpse into public affairs came more or less by accident, and then as a blurred, bird's-eye view, from the heights. I peered into the world of politics from the rarefied regions of foreign affairs. Nor, as a matter of fact, could my first acquaintance with this interesting phenomenon rightly be called a view of politics. It was more a perception of the idea that there might be such a thing as international ethics. It was a very advanced idea!

I was in England in school during the Boer War. The cultivated, far-sighted woman who conducted the school was vigorously opposed to the war. She could not, of course, discuss her views with her English students, whose parents might have considered them heretical, if not traitorous. But with the American girl, within the privacy of her own library, she had no such obligatory reservations. She could, and did, speak freely. Her discourse, however, was no mere diatribe against the stupidity or injustice of the government, but contained analyses of international ethics.

However, it took me a long time to apply them to my own country. I had no opinions, as the result of such an education, to trouble my friends or my family. I was no trial to my husband in the early days of our marriage. Well do I remember the first time I was asked a direct question concerning our government, the first time I was confronted with the fact that I should know something about it. For I was covered with confusion because I was not only unable to express any opinion, but I was not even able to explain briefly an important part of the Constitution.

When I was twenty I was abroad with my husband. We were visiting friends of the family at their home near Edinburgh. Our hostess was a lovely and a brilliant woman, typical of the alert Englishwoman who knows the politics of the hour to the last detail. We were having tea one day on the lawn. I was basking in contentment until suddenly Lady Helen turned to me and said: "Do tell me how your country is run. I should particularly like to know the relationship of the federal government to the states. Both seem to have so many separate functions that I do not understand the ways they work together."

I was terrified. I could not say one word. I looked frantically at my husband and he came to my rescue. While he explained the manner in which the Constitution defines the powers of the central government, and how they have been applied in cooperation with the states, I pondered over my predicament. Obviously it was wrong to know so little about such matters.

I thereupon registered a solemn vow that I would learn about politics. Alas, I did not do a great deal to keep it! I began to study a little when I returned to my home. When my husband went to Albany, as a state senator in 1911 he did not, however, have a wife with whom he could debate an issue. I was still far from being an expert observer in the world of politics.

In Albany I did go frequently to the galleries and listen carefully to all the discussions, although I was as interested in the truly remarkable characters in the legislature at that time as in the subjects they argued.

Finally the organization and working of parties filtered through my brain. Talking over Mary's future with her father I recalled these years.

"I shouldn't be concerned about her," I reassured him. "For, though they may disagree, Mary and Jonathan are mutually tolerant. This essential tolerance is of not greater quality or degree than that necessary if they were of different religions. The laissez-faire attitude is always requisite where husband and wife hold varying opinions. As a rule they enjoy presenting their own points of view. But the only result I can see from Mary's ardent endorsement of the League of Nations, for example, and Jonathan's thorough dislike of it is that she has more to talk about than what small Jonathan said before he went to bed, or the bad no-trump bid of her partner.

"Rarely do men and women whose conviction is sincere convert each other. Where there is a lack of emphasis on the part of either, then the more enthusiastic member of the family may be able to change his partner's attitude. Not otherwise.

"Even if a woman has the most definite ideas, she must never try to persuade her husband to do anything he does not consider right. She might not concede that he has the right to change her convictions, but neither must she attempt to change his."

It is imperative that a wife should not interfere with her husband while he is in office. She must fulfill her obligations, perform her duties, and then, *though she may keep her own convictions—she must keep them to herself.*

Decidedly she should not attempt to meddle with her husband's plans, his procedure, or his principles. Nothing is worse, more futile when a man is strong, or politically more ruinous if he is weak. The first duty of the wife of an officeholder is to help him in her own domain; never to control him.

There is no place for conflict where a husband's political career is concerned. The wife's opinions must be subordinated.

It has been my experience that if my husband and I differed upon any important matter, we would talk it out. Then, as with any other person, if we still differed, he would go his way and I mine. We could only have such independence when he was neither holding office nor was candidate for office. When he is actively engaged in public or party business, and I disagree with the stand he takes, I do not discuss it with him or in any way attempt to place my reaction to his action before him.

A wife, I have always held, has a perfect right to her own opinion, but she should *never* nag her husband. She has a right to state her opinion, but she should not go on, in the privacy of their home, emphasizing their differences; nor need she make them public.

I say what I believe, but I will not stump against my party, regardless of its program. I will not sit on the platform where the subject of the speeches is one upon which I differ with my husband and his party; nor will I issue statements about it.

Family differences are always the subject of great public interest. Many other members of the Roosevelt family are Republicans. Yet unless my husband is running for office they do not make a point of discussing their differences. Families are families in spite of political opinions. If, however, my husband's interests clashed with theirs politically, I should support my husband to the best of my ability.

It is natural that I, like most other wives, should have interests of importance to me, and with which my husband disagreed. Yet if a campaign were in progress I should set such an interest aside and give it no further attention until a more expedient moment. Never would I make a household issue of it!

There are few avenues of life where men and women agree on everything. In politics they differ along very definite lines.

Men tend to look at things from a legalistic point of view; women from a practical one.

Women will ask, "What result will this bring?"

Men will question, rather, "How can this be done?"

Women are not interested in laws, and often come into politics because of certain ills they see must be remedied. Somehow it is brought to them that they must achieve this result through politics. Therefore this is the avenue they take to accomplish their aims. Between a man and his wife there is frequently the difference of opinion which comes from the types of things which interest them and the emphasis they lay upon different matters. This sort of difference is often hardest for them to understand. The women in this state, for instance, are supporting legislation for the old-age pension because of their sympathy with its human aspect. They have given little thought to it in terms of taxation and ultimate cost to the state. Such details they have brushed aside.

Women generally are more interested in reforms than in tax laws. Consequently, if a bill dealing with maternal and infant welfare is before the legislature a wife is quite likely to consider it the most important measure before the body. Her husband might disagree, insisting that income-tax revision should take priority. Here there is no adjustment of opinion. Each must keep his own. The approach is fundamentally different.

It is necessary to realize that my generation of women were trained to think along certain lines: the charitable work which meant going to a neighbor's house and staying with the baby while its mother had an hour's recreation at the meeting of the sewing society; or church work; or finding food and fuel for the needy.

My own experience has been that of many women of my generation, namely, an approach to social and economic problems via the route of a personal interest in the miseries of humanity. Women have thought more in the trend of homes, and of charity to alleviate hardship in homes, in illness, and growing children. When participation in politics was thrust upon them they seized upon the side of life they knew. Only lately have they become accustomed to other sides of the government and recognized their relations to the things in which they are interested. They are just beginning to realize that questions of tariff, of organization, of running town and state, keeping down civic expenses, are nothing but group housekeeping; and that foreign relations are nothing but relations between neighbors.

The young woman of today is better able to see the broader aspects of the problems with which state and nation are dealing. Nevertheless she still has the practical personal sense which is the tradition of her sex. This unquestionably gives rise to differences of opinion so inherent that she has them, whether she may have a right to them or not! Like measles or blue eyes, they exist.

Since 1920 the intrafamily divergence of political opinion has occasionally taken a virulent form, demanding drastic measures. The dangerous phase of this disturbance comes when both members of the marriage have embarked upon political careers. When they belong to the same party and subscribe to the same policies, it is possible. When they differ, it is a catastrophe.

IT IS IMPOSSIBLE FOR HUSBAND AND WIFE BOTH TO HAVE POLITICAL CAREERS. It requires all the energy and united effort of an entire household to support one.

This situation was laid before me in the most interesting fashion a few years ago by a woman I shall call Mrs. John Ames. She was a Democrat, a member of the State Committee. A former schoolteacher, she was intelligent, persevering, reliable, but not brilliant. Her husband, however, was an unusually promising young lawyer, a Republican whose practice had led him into politics, where he apparently had a glowing future.

They were a happy pair despite their burning differences anent the tariff or our foreign relations. He had been a member of the Republican County Committee, and their partisan opposition had always been amusing rather than bitter.

Now he was candidate for state attorney. There was no doubt that he would be a competent prosecutor, and might easily follow his victory with others. In addition to being capable, he was a member of the organization of the majority party in his district.

"It is so hard to know what to do in this dilemma, Mrs. Roosevelt," Mrs. Ames worried. "I thought perhaps you might help me. John's work heretofore has been chiefly of the organization type, and so our campaigning against each other has been a party and not a personal matter.

"Everyone thinks John is slated for big things, and I'm very proud to be his wife. Still, I'm in politics myself. I too think I have a future. We have no children, and I have planned to devote my time to politics. It has never before interfered in our home life.

"But now I shall either have to campaign against John, which will hurt him politically because everyone will say that if a woman fights against her husband there must be something strange about it, or else I shall have to give up my own position and my own principles and support him. I am so distressed by this situation. I wonder if you will advise me?"

It *was* a difficult problem and I did not advise her. Advice as to the relations of husband and wife, even when their problems touch the skirts of politics, should always be taboo.

I did try to explain to her my belief that no member of a marriage should try to influence the other. I waited with interest the decision she would make.

After careful deliberation of a few weeks longer, she resigned from the Democratic State Committee. While she changed neither her politics nor her party for the sake of her husband, neither did she intrude her own convictions, or campaign against him. She remained merely a graceful wife.

He is well up the ladder today, and she is still enrolled in the Democratic Party.

When both husband and wife want political careers, like John Ames and his rational wife, the question naturally arises, which one should withdraw? While it still seems abnormal for the husband to leave the political reins in his wife's hands, it sometimes happens.

I believe that under such circumstances the one who cares the less for public life, or is the less fitted to meet its exigencies, should withdraw.

In England, Nancy Astor had such an intense interest and love of politics, and such an obvious flair for it, that her husband withdrew from any family competition. He helps her, instead. When this is the case it is equally or perhaps even more important that the husband should not trespass on his wife's domain, attempt to direct her policies or mold her opinions. His advice should be available whenever it is requested, but he should never try to remake her convictions or offer unsolicited suggestions.

Emily Newell Blair and her husband, Harry Blair, are a happy example of the way in which such principles contribute to a satisfactory career and a successful marriage. Although Mr. Blair had entered upon interesting political activities in his home city of Joplin, Missouri, he encouraged his wife in the public activity in which she became interested during the suffrage fight. In those exciting times Mrs. Blair used to bring luncheons of sandwiches and coffee into her tiny hot office, and her husband would come to share them, his experience, and his information.

When her work had led her farther afield, and she had become vice chairman of the Democratic National Committee, Mr. Blair had given up all participation in politics himself.

Mrs. Blair today says with pleasure and gratitude that she could never have had a political career without her husband's generous sacrifices, without his occasional suggestions, his willingness to talk over knotty problems, or his support and help during two trying national Presidential conventions. But never did he force his ideas upon her.

However, it is still exceptional for a husband to relinquish his ambitions and leave all civic responsibility upon the shoulders of the distaff member of the partnership. There are more Mrs. Ameses than there are Nancy Astors. And a politician always has need of a conscientious, competent wife.

Matrimony in official life is no small job. When her husband came into office, Mrs. Ames found that the duties of a politician's wife are sometimes interesting, sometimes irksome, always demanding good temper, discretion, discrimination, and—by far the greater part of her time.

The wife of any politician must step into her own office, expecting to find her work hard, and complicated by tasks which must be discharged with energy and tact, sometimes with endurance, and usually with infinite patience.

She must be absolutely impervious to personal reactions, whether of praise or blame, in the attitude of the public toward her husband. She must treat everyone she encounters equally well, regardless of what one or another may have said about her husband the night before. She must never be carried away by a desire to seem intelligent or seem to know a great deal. As a wife she must never make any allusion to her own political opinions when they differ from her husband's. She must never agree to try to convince him on any point, whether regarding some stand already taken or upon some matter upon which he has not yet passed judgment.

She must conduct a home which meets all of his needs, whatever they may be, without any friction. It must be elastic as regards hours and guests, and likewise afford him perfect comfort and quiet. She must do her official entertaining heartily and graciously. Her work is practically a career in itself.

I myself have endeavored to construct a routine which will accommodate my required duties and yet permit me to preserve my own interests. My first object in the morning, whether in Albany or at home, is to start the household moving. I make a memorandum for the steward or the cook containing the menus, the hours of the meals, and the number of people expected for each. Then I give any necessary household orders, go through my mail, and am free until luncheon.

In the afternoons I occasionally make speeches, especially when I am in Albany, to women's clubs or to similar gatherings. Also, I see people. At Albany I am at home every Wednesday during the legislative session from 4:30 to 6 o'clock to anyone who wishes to come. Sometimes I entertain two guests; sometimes a hundred. Mrs. Herbert Lehman, wife of the Lieutenant Governor, or one of the other official women, comes to pour tea. As I teach three mornings a week in New York, I leave Albany after dinner on Sunday nights, and return in time to be home on Wednesday afternoons.

Sometimes such a life is exasperating for the woman who has her own gifts, particularly if she would like to employ in a more congenial fashion the time taken up by the infinitude of small demands made upon the wife of a politician. The business of governing is one which, like the homekeeping of the pioneers of old, needs the cooperation of the feminine portion of the household.

The younger servants of the public naturally have wives reared in the new trend toward individual independence of thought and action. The urgent need for peace and agreement between the politician and his wife is consequently often difficult for a young and eager woman to fill. It is hard for her to refrain from discussing the other side of the issues with her equally alert friends.

I learned with my husband the ideas as well as the technique of public service.

I learned from him principles and policies, as well as procedure, organization, and the conditions which prompt them.

Thus, with no struggle at all we found ourselves agreed, for example, on the tariff issue. We are unanimous in feeling that customs should be reduced. We agree heartily in our liberal views on foreign relations, although I tend to be somewhat more radical than he. This is a common phenomenon in this realm, where women have no heritage of national inhibitions, no obsolete credos taught in youth to obstruct their views.

We both believe that our country is showing a hopeful tendency in some ways. Yet we do feel that we have been too completely absorbed in our own materialistic gains—certainly not an attitude or a policy designed to bring about a real and lasting solution of international affairs, or national ones. A state ruled wholly by the self-interest of a few cannot be just.

Governor Roosevelt and I both have great confidence in the judgment of the average man. We believe in wide distribution of civic work and hold that as many people as possible should be interested in public service. The more power resides in the people as a whole, the better we think it is for each of them and for the nation.

Naturally labor conditions and their improvement have always attracted our mutual attention, and we have always been agreed in our interest in prisoners and wards of the state, and what should be done for them; and, indeed, for the administration upon the most liberal lines of all state institutions.

However, whether the political wife grows up with the family opinions as her own, or whether she brings her own preconceived ideas together with the wedding presents and heirlooms into her husband's home, she may keep them, but she must keep them to herself.

42

Today's Girl and Tomorrow's Job

Three mornings a week I teach at a private school which takes girls up to the point of college entrance. I have a family of my own, a daughter and four sons. I have also taken a fairly active part in politics. I present these facts for the reason that they have a special bearing on the subject of youth and its place in the community. My observations, in some respects, cover a greater variety of experiences than usually falls to the lot of the average person. I am especially interested in the girl of today because she fits into my job as a teacher, a mother, a civic worker. I have occasion to see her as a child, as a growing girl and as a young woman. Judging from my experience with her I am bold enough to say that she is meeting life exactly as she has been prepared to meet it.

To fit the girl of today for her experience of tomorrow is a large order, in many respects a larger order than our parents and grandparents had to fill for us. The world grows increasingly larger in the number of things there are to do and to think about, but increasingly smaller in respect to distance. A young person today is caught in a flux of changing vibrating life and what to choose, what to discard, what to concentrate upon, becomes increasingly difficult to decide. Without help or direction of some sort she is lost. Yet fundamentally the problem of parents today is no different from the problem of parents of all time. The purpose of education and child-training has not changed. First and foremost is the building of character. Second in importance is the stimulation of curiosity about the world we all live in.

In my own life some of the things I look back upon with the greatest happiness are the hours I spent with my father at an early age. He died when I was very young but the memories of his sympathy and understanding patience in dealing with the growing mind of a child I shall never forget. His brother was Theodore Roosevelt; their father, my grandfather, was the type of man who felt keenly his duty toward the community and this duty included giving time and thought to his children. You can also put it the other way round. He felt that his duty toward his family and children included a duty toward the community. My father passed on this atmosphere to me, young as I was, and it never quite left me; for later I found myself receptive to certain ideas because they recalled stories and emotions of my childhood.

My grandmother, under whose care I came directly from the time I was seven, was an extremely lovable but an extremely old-fashioned woman. Her idea of education was equipping a girl with the things that would make her agreeable

Woman's Home Companion 59 (June 1932): 11–12.

in a drawing-room. She had a responsibility toward the community but for her that responsibility could be expressed only in charitable activities, never in civic or community affairs. I learned and followed all the rules and taboos laid down by her; I neither rebelled nor revolted. My life, in other words, was not unusual in its preparation for maturity other than in the vitally important fact that together with the background of old-fashioned upbringing, there was the inspiration of a man, my father, who had felt it important to acquaint a child with a world in which all the people were living.

The next great influence in my life was a remarkable woman, Mademoiselle Souvestre, the daughter of the French writer, Emil Souvestre. Under her care I lived for three years in Europe. She was the head of the school I attended and she took me traveling with her during many vacations. To her I owe more than I can ever repay for she gave me an intellectual curiosity and a standard of living which have never left me.

For a long time I did nothing constructive with this curiosity which had been aroused in me. At eighteen, together with a friend of mine, I took a class in a settlement on Rivington Street. Shortly afterward I married and the next ten years were spent in having children and caring for them. It was not until the war came that I began taking a really active interest in things beyond the immediate boundaries of the home. But those years of apparent inactivity in the social or community sense were not lost years. The interest, the curiosity, fostered and nurtured in childhood were there waiting for the proper moment of expression.

I have gone into these personal details not because I think of my life as exceptional but because I know that the things which have brought me the greatest happiness and satisfaction never fail to lead me back to the influences of my childhood, the things that so many children of today are missing. Over and over again it is impressed upon my mind that this is the place where parents make their greatest mistake. If it were possible I should like the adult generation of today which decries youth's irresponsibility, to hear its children tell them the things that home life means to them. Parents might then be able to get some notion of the inevitable connection between cause and effect, might get some idea why the lives of their children are spent within a narrow vitiating circle of pleasure that either does not know or refuses to recognize its relationship to mankind in general and its obligation to do something in a world beyond the one bounded by social pleasures.

No school can do its job alone without the aid of parents. No child can take its school education seriously if its parents do not. No child will assimilate and respect the fundamental laws of character-building taught at school if it sees them disregarded and broken in the home.

In many respects public schools are doing a much better job with their children than are the private schools. Their pupils have a very much better idea of the world we live in than do children in private schools, are much more ably fitted to cope with conditions of living. To a great extent this is due to the fact that they come from the homes of the great mass of our population; that familiarity with particular and individual needs, in the home and outside it, means familiarity with the framework of American society. They are members of the machinery that makes the wheels of American community life, politics, industry and commerce go round. From early infancy they are part and parcel of it. Education, school, mean something definite to them: the tools that will give them their place in life.

But there is more to it than this. Apart from the material advantages that a good education will give their children, these parents are interested in education in the abstract, education as a cultural and social asset. In many instances fathers and mothers are seeing their children getting the education which life for one reason or another withheld from them and the progress of their children becomes for them a vicarious fulfillment of their own frustrated desires. Especially is this true in cities and towns that have a considerable sprinkling of foreign populations, although it is not peculiar to them.

To parents of this type parent-teacher associations are not a burden but a happy expression of community importance. They want to know the principal of the school and the teachers; they are interested in the progress of their children; they are extremely anxious to cooperate in the work of building character and directing tendencies. These are the people who are really America's ablest citizens. American ideals and standards still mean something alive and real to these parents and no sacrifice is too great to achieve them.

If I were asked what is my ideal of American citizenship, I should be tempted to say it is that of the first or second generation American who still sees this country as a land of freedom and opportunity and who is proud to serve it in any way he can. Generally speaking, Americans of older vintage have unfortunately gone beyond this point. Since they have no background of frustrations against which to make comparisons, the turning of the wheels of American government means nothing to them, the vote is not a privilege but an obligation, community service a trial and not an opportunity. This feeling is transmitted to the growing generation and again, often in the very homes where we should have the greatest understanding of American life and American institutions, we have the least.

Our public schools recognize their problems and face them squarely. Having a heterogeneous group to work with, children coming from all ranks of American life, from many nations and many backgrounds, they assume at the start the pupils' total ignorance of the fundamentals of government in all its aspects and take upon themselves the responsibility of dispelling it. Judging from the examples of men and women that come from the ranks of our public schools, I should say they succeed extraordinarily well.

The purpose of education is not the accumulation of facts. Certain fundamentals must of course be absorbed. A well-educated woman must know, when Dickens is mentioned for instance, who he is and what he stands for. She must know similar things in other basic subjects. But that alone is not education. No human being can learn all the facts and information that have been piled up with the years but every human being who has within his reach the advantages of an education can forge the tools which will make his life in all its stages of growth and development a fuller and richer one. Apart from character, the greatest thing that education can give is curiosity about the changing life about us.

In my work with the girls in school I have two current events classes. One of them consists of older girls, some of whom are graduates of the school; the second is made up of girls of about sixteen. The older class this year elected to study the government of the City of New York. It seemed to me a good way to do this was to see the various departments of the city in action. We visited City Hall and sat in on some of the meetings, we visited schools, the department of labor, police headquarters. I also took my class last year down to the children's court and the things they heard there shocked them into a realization of what the streets of New York and poverty and poor heredity and no chance at the start of life can do to young human beings.

With the younger class of current events students, I start with a background of the explanation of government and the reading of the daily newspapers. It is important that they know the relationship between state and city government, the difference between state and federal government. Very few, I find, can at the start tell me what departments there are in the national government and what in the state.

Awakening curiosity in minds that prefer to slumber is no small task. Often when I ask a girl what she has read of importance in the morning newspaper, she tells me that she hasn't read her newspaper. One actually informed me that she didn't like newspapers and wasn't interested in "such things;" "such things" being matters of civic importance. I laughed and asked whether she would feel comfortable riding in her car without traffic policemen; whether she'd be happy knowing that the water she drank was not inspected against pollution. I shall not say that I succeeded in reforming her but I can say that for once in her life she realized how she fitted into a scheme of government she hitherto had considered completely divorced from herself.

We cannot know life unless we live it. If the function of a school is to prepare young people for life, then let them see it, feel it, know it, during their formative years. Often when I speak of the work of my classes in civics and current events, I am told that a very small percentage of the girls in them will take an active interest in politics and that therefore such studies are wasted on them. That sort of criticism leaves me speechless. Are people ignorant enough to believe that the girl who marries has no place in the life of her community, that as a wife, as a mother, as a member of society, she can do nothing, influence nothing or nobody in making her community a better place for herself and family to live in, a finer place for her children and other people's children to grow up in?

When I speak of schools preparing a girl for life, I am speaking of the average girl, the girl in every kind of school, public and private, whose life will follow the normal pattern. I am old-fashioned enough to believe that every girl ought to marry and have a family. I am also modern enough and progressive enough to believe that it is as much the function of the school to prepare her for that job as it is to prepare her for the expression of other phases of her life. There are no jobs in the world so important as marriage and motherhood and I am inclined to believe that if girls were taught to consider them as jobs there would be fewer failures and more successes. I would not place an interest in community affairs as the first essential for a successful marriage but certainly I would give it second place.

First of course comes character. What I mean by that is difficult to explain in a few words. It means discipline, it means restraint, it means good nature, it means thinking of other people as well as of yourself, it means an appreciation of the fact that the goal of life is not happiness and amusement. Youth doesn't like to swallow all that, especially the last, and I am not entirely unsympathetic there. Very few among us older people achieve this knowledge except at the cost of trying experience.

I said character comes first and an interest in the community second. "An interest in the community" sounds very forbidding and formal. I intend nothing like that.

The first ten years of a girl's marriage, broadly speaking, should be devoted to the home. As the children grow older, however, other horizons should open to her. Curiosity about life, about people, about how the various members of her community live and work and play, should begin to bestir itself more actively. She should know who are the men in office in the government of her community; she should know whether or not they are doing their jobs honestly and efficiently. This interest is in no way divorced from her interest in the home; it is part of it, essential to it. Her children are growing up, their minds are being formed and molded by the thought of the community and by the conversation about community affairs, government affairs, they are hearing at home. What is right, what is wrong, what is acceptable, what is not, these are things that growing children make judgments upon according to the light of their experience and their experience depends largely on the life their parents lead, on the attitude toward social and ethical problems taken by their parents.

There are other girls who do not marry or, if they do, postpone it until they have had greater experience with the world outside school and their social activities. In increasing numbers the girls in my school tell me they are going to take jobs when they finish their formal education. If getting a job means getting contact with life, it is a fine thing. But there are other factors to be taken into account in this subject of job-getting by girls who are economically outside the pale of need.

Two generations ago, when the girl who came from a family of means took a job, it was usually with an organization engaged in social welfare or philanthropic work of some kind. In other words, it was volunteer service. Today when the girl of means goes out looking for work she has in view a job with a salary. In order to feel her importance in the job she is doing she demands money for it; it gives her a feeling of really belonging to the scheme of economic life she is entering. No one can justly blame her for this. But let her taking a job presuppose the idea that in time she will be in a position to create jobs for those who actually need them.

The question may be asked, suppose the girl after establishing herself in business decides to marry, what will happen then? Nothing disastrous should happen. The girl of brains and ability will find the way to build up a business in a manner that will enable her to marry and carry on at the same time. I hope eventually some of them will take the initiative in this direction.

The girl of today who will be the woman of tomorrow, no matter what her economic status, has still another field of activity open to her. I mean politics. I do not mean political office. While I am extremely keen on seeing women in political office, I do not want them to run for it until they know the job thoroughly.

That there is a place for women in politics I am absolutely convinced. But politics is a comparatively new field for women and for their own good as well as for the women who will come after them, to say nothing of the community at large, they should keep out of office until they are confident they can hold it with ability and personal integrity. And when I say personal integrity I mean more than dollars-and-cents honesty. I mean the consistent loyalty to an intelligent idea of service which does not allow itself to be swayed by what older people in office might call politic or expedient.

Paradoxically the world expects a better job from a woman in office than from a man and although it seems unfair, and is unfair, I am glad that it is so. In a manner of speaking it is a safeguard for women. It will put into office and keep in office only those who are preeminently fitted for the job and that, as I see it, is the only reason they should have it. Perhaps this sounds discouraging to many women. It shouldn't. I want to see women taking an interest in politics, taking active part in campaigns, organizing their strength for proper legislation and proper legislators. But I cannot say too often that taking an interest in politics is not synonymous with holding political office. It is more important for a million women to know whom to vote for than it is for one to hold office. It is a matter, again, of intelligent public opinion, of breadth of interest, of training and education. All this brings me back to the beginning. The place to start for every job is in the home and in the school.

43

What Ten Million Women Want

What do ten million women want in public life? That question could be answered in ten million different ways. For every woman, like every man, has some aspirations or desires exclusively her own.

We women are callow fledglings as compared with the wise old birds who manipulate the political machinery, and we still hesitate to believe that a woman can fill certain positions in public life as competently and adequately as a man.

For instance, it is certain that women do not want a woman for President. Nor would they have the slightest confidence in her ability to fulfill the functions of that office.

Every woman who fails in a public position confirms this, but every woman who succeeds creates confidence.

Judge Florence Allen on the Supreme Court Bench in Ohio, Frances Perkins as Labor Commissioner in New York, have done much to make women feel that a really fine woman, well trained in her work, can give as good an account of her stewardship as any man, and eventually women, and perhaps even men, may come to feel that sex should not enter into the question of fitness for office.

When it comes to the matter of having a woman as a member of the President's Cabinet, there are I think, many women who feel that the time has come to recognize the fact that women have practically just as many votes as men and deserve at least a certain amount of recognition.

Take the Department of Labor for instance. Why should not the Secretary of Labor be a woman, and would not a woman's point of view be valuable in the President's Council? There are many other places to which women may aspire, and the time will come when there will be new departments, some of which will undoubtedly need women at their heads.

When we come to finances we realize that after all, all government, whether it is that of village, city, state or nation, is simply glorified housekeeping.

Little by little we are getting budget systems into our public housekeeping and budgets are something all women understand.

Every woman knows that dire results happen when she exceeds her own budget, and it is only a short step from this to understanding what happens in the city, the state or the nation when finances are not carefully administered and watched. Every woman demands that her government be economically managed, but she knows, far better perhaps than the average man, that there are two kinds of economy. There is such a thing as parsimonious spending

The Home Magazine 5, no. 3 (March 1932): 19–21, 86.

which in the end costs more than a wise study of the needs of the future, and the spending which takes into account the social side of life.

For instance, it may be wise to spend fifty thousand dollars this year in buying space for parks, first because the land will increase in value, secondly because we are beginning to recognize that for the youth growing up in the cities, play space in the city and play space in the country beyond, is most important for healthful development. Perhaps we could save this sum today, but it would cost us far more in physical and spiritual value twenty years from now, as well as in actual cash.

Women are detail minded, they have had to be for generations, therefore, they are much more apt to watch in detail what is done by their public officials in the case of finances than does the average man.

Ten million women may not at the moment be quite awake to their opportunities along this line, still I think we can safely say that this is one of the wants that lies back in the mind of every woman.

Do women want to take an active part in framing our laws? I think the answer to that is decidedly yes. There are more and more women elected to Legislative Bodies every year. This session of Congress has six Congresswomen on its roll, three Democrats and three Republicans.

The names of Ruth Bryan Owen and Mrs. McCormick are far better known than those of many male Congressmen. We have in this new Congress for a time at least, the first active woman United States Senator in Mrs. Caraway. She was elected this January for the full term and she will be, from all indications, a real power in the Upper House, and very far from a rubber stamp.

Welfare legislation touches very closely the home life of every woman, and therefore demands her interest and careful criticism both in the provisions of the laws, and in the administration of those laws when they actually become effective. Because these laws are interpreted and enforced by our courts, I think women feel they are entitled to places on the bench.

Women judges are no longer a novelty, and in some classes of courts, particularly those dealing with juvenile offenders, the women have proven themselves decidedly superior to the men.

I do not think women would approve of having women heads of police departments. I do think they feel policewomen and matrons a necessity for the proper care of girl and women offenders. As for a national police commissioner, male or female, I think women are decidedly opposed to it.

It is our conviction that crime to be dealt with successfully, must be dealt with locally with a thorough understanding of local conditions. Every woman is, of course, deeply interested in the crime situation.

But I think because of her education and knowledge of the home, she realizes that it is through better education and better living conditions in our crowded cities that the prevention of crime, which is the ultimate aim of all criminology, must be achieved.

While I do not believe in a national police commissioner, or a national police commission, I think women approve the recommendation that there should be available at Washington a national department where data relating to criminals, and statistics relating to crime should be available for the use of all the state and local police departments of the country.

I think that those women who have given this question of crime most serious consideration are generally in agreement that the first and most practical step to its eradication would be in the wiping out of certain tenement house localities in our big cities and the raising of educational standards generally.

Women to whom, after all, the education of the child is largely entrusted by the men, understand far better than the average man the need of education and improvement in teaching.

Too often, the father's actual knowledge of how his child is being educated is gleaned from a hasty scanning of the report card once a month, but the mother knows all the virtues of the successful teacher and the faults of the poor one. She understands the defects of our system which produces, I am sorry to say, so many who have not the heaven-sent gift of instructing the young successfully.

There is much research work that a Department of Education might be doing. What actual education possibilities does each state offer? Are all children furnished with standard textbooks? Are libraries accessible for all children? Do we need, for a great majority of children more specialized and vocational training?

All these questions should be made the subject of research on a national scale, but there is a great division of opinion as to what authority should be vested in a national department of education.

The women who travel over this country realize that standards of education are woefully low in certain places, and there is no doubt it would be most useful for the public at large to know that the actual standards vary greatly in different parts of the United States. But this is a very different thing from placing absolute control over the various state departments of education in a "Department of National Education," such as has been proposed by some.

What do women want to do about prohibition? Women generally consider prohibition as social legislation, not from the economic standpoint as the men do as a rule, but when you ask "what do women want to do about prohibition?," the answer is the same as it would be if we asked "what do men want to do about prohibition?"

Not only are political parties split, but there is no uniform answer to this in the case of either sex. No one can say what the women want to do about prohibition.

We can say this, however, that few women are completely satisfied with the present-day conditions, and many are not satisfied with any of the remedies which have been as yet set forth. Only a few fortunate people feel they have found the answer to this problem and not enough people agree with them as yet to settle it.

The matter of proper laws dealing with marriage has been one much considered by all women in every state in the union interested in social conditions. Everyone feels it should be harder to get married and more solemnity and sense of permanence should accompany the ceremony. Uniform divorce laws might help to this end.

My fourth point is the woman's desire to see government lighten her burdens. The first of these burdens is the taxes. On the whole when women see that taxes which they pay bring direct returns in benefits to the community, I do not think that they are averse to paying them, but I do think that our ten million women want much more careful accounting for how their taxes are expended in the local, state or national government. They want to see the actual good which comes to them from these expenditures.

They feel very strongly that governments should not add to their burdens but should lighten them. They are gradually coming to grasp the relation of legislation to the lightening of these burdens, for instance, in such questions as the regulation of public utilities and the development of the water power of our nation. They realize now that cheaper electricity means less work in the home, more time to give to their children, more time for recreation and greater educational opportunities.

In Canada, across the border from Buffalo, where so much power is generated, there are proportionately many more electric washing machines and ironers and electric stoves and vacuum cleaners and hot water heaters in use because of the cheaper cost of electricity, than we have on this side of the line, although we have the same possibilities before us, and the women are beginning to ask why they are not within our grasp. Hence their interest is growing daily in the aspects of the whole public utilities question.

Then we come to the fifth point, which after all while it is entirely in the hands of the national government, still comes back to the home of every individual woman. She may wake up someday to find that her nation is at war and her boys and even her girls in one war or another, are drafted into service, a service from which they may not return, or they may return with mangled bodies, but if they do return to her with physical bodies unchanged, there may be some kind of mental and spiritual change which will alter their characters and their outlook on life.

It may do them good, but the reading of history does not lead us to hope for great benefits for the younger generation from any war. Therefore, every woman's interest in the amicable relations of her country is very great and she has come to realize that this is not merely a question of polite phrases between diplomats.

The only danger that women will not get what they want lies in the fact that there are still a goodly number who do not know how to use their influence and how to make known their ideas.

I heard a teacher not long ago discussing a referendum with her class; she suggested that in New York State such a referendum had been taken in the last election when the people voted on certain amendments. One of the children looked up brightly and said, "Oh, yes, my mother knew nothing about any of those so she voted 'no' on all of them!" This is a dangerous attitude for any woman to allow herself if she hopes to get what she wants from her government.

If ten million women really want security, real representation, honesty, wise and just legislation, happier and more comfortable conditions of living, and a future with the horrors of war removed from the horizon, then these ten million women must bestir themselves.

They can be active factors in the life of their communities and shape the future, or they can drift along and hide behind the men. Today is a challenge to women. Tomorrow will see how they answer the challenge!

44

Women and the Vote

There is one new activity which entered the life of women with the passage of the Nineteenth Amendment in 1918. With the right to vote, a whole new field of responsibility and direct power came into the hands of the women of the country. A few of our states had already given women the right to vote and in some communities they were allowed to vote in school elections, but they did not enjoy the full privileges of citizenship as the equals of men throughout the whole country until 1918.

Many fine men and women had worked for this change for many years and the stories of Elizabeth Cady Stanton, Dr. Anna Shaw, Susan B. Anthony and Carrie Chapman Catt are inspiring reading, because of the unselfish devotion they brought to this cause, which they felt meant a just recognition of the rights of a big group of people. Looking even beyond the justice of the cause they felt this power given to women would herald great changes for the good of mankind.

Fourteen years have now gone by and everywhere people are asking, "What have the women done with the vote?" I often wonder why they don't ask the men the same question, but I realize that it is a high compliment to women that evidently they were expected to bring about some marked change in political conditions and so I would like to look into the question of women as citizens and see just what we have done and are doing and then perhaps dream a little about what we may do in the future.

The vast majority of women, like the vast majority of men, have little time to give to anything but the earning of their daily bread either by actually working themselves or by caring for home and children and making other people's earnings go as far as possible. Their good citizenship consists in leading their lives so as to make them as productive of good for all around them as they can be, and their public duty is expressed by using their vote as intelligently as possible.

A vote is never an intelligent vote when it is cast without knowledge. Just doing what someone else tells you to do without any effort to find out what the facts are for yourself is being a poor citizen. When women first had the vote, many of them did not know how to get information on questions of government. Others had seen the men for years go and vote, had heard them talk a little during the weeks just before election about this or that candidate or this or that party, but had never gathered that there was much concern for the things the parties stood for. You were a democrat or a republican because your family belonged to one or to the other party, because your people had been in

It's Up to the Women (New York: Frederick A. Stokes Company, 1933), pp. 189–204.

the north or in the south at the time of the war between the states, or because it was easier to get advancement in business in your locality if you belonged to one or the other party. These reasons and some others like them did not greatly stir the patriotism of the women. A few women formed the League of Women Voters, a non-partisan organization which tries, as far as human agencies can do so, to control the prejudices of its members and have them look at both sides of political questions and to furnish unbiased information to any women asking to know about candidates or measures proposed by any political party. Other organizations sprang up for political study and long-established women's clubs added departments of citizenship where their politically minded members could study such questions as interested them. The vast majority of women, however, remain as indifferent to the vote and how they use it as are the vast majority of men.

If we look about us in the world today or read past history, we will find that benevolent monarchs and good dictators have as a rule had contented, well-governed people. The reason, I fear, is that we are all glad to let someone do our thinking for us as long as we go on fairly comfortably and happily. It is only when bad rulers oppress their people for a long time that those people begin to think for themselves and eventually overthrow their rulers.

Those of us who live in democracies have known of such occurrences in the past but if our leaders have led us through fairly still waters we are as content as other peoples under other forms of government to let some people do our thinking for us, and it takes stern times to shake us out of our apathy.

Women are no different from men in this and though certain subjects may be of greater interest to them, they have been slow as a group to act because political thought and action were new and following women leaders was new. How many times have I heard older women say, "Well, I really feel safer with a man doctor and I take a man's advice on certain questions because he's been at it so much longer than we women!" The sex is still the basis of judgment; they don't just say, "I like Henry as a doctor better than Susie," or "I think James' opinion on that question is more sensible than Jenny's." That day is just beginning to arrive and, strange coincidence, it is arriving just when stern necessity is driving many people in our country to think about questions which for years they have been willing to leave to their leaders.

For a number of years I, with many other women, have traveled our various states trying to arouse women to an interest in government, pointing out how it affected their homes, building and working conditions, the water they drank, the food they ate, their children, the schools, the public health, the recreations. We have used the World War to show how much, as women, we are concerned with governments in other lands and our relations with them. We have showed the necessity for women of different lands, whose fundamental interests are the same, to know and understand each other. We have tried to dramatize some of the lessons learned between 1914 and 1920 as to the waste and futility of war and frequently found a polite response, a temporary burst of interest and then the old apathy creeping back as the sense of present security and comfort spread around our women.

236

Now, there is for many people no sense of security and no comfort and no ease and no luxury, and even the right to work, not always looked upon as a blessing, has become a precious and sought-after right. Now you do not, either in men or women, have to arouse interest in their government; it is the one hope they have and they look to it for salvation. Political news in papers has become interesting; books on economics and on government are eagerly read; there is a revolution in thinking and that always presages a revolution in action. One can have a bloodless revolution if one can count on leaders of sufficient vision to grasp the goal for which the mass of people is often unconsciously striving, and courage enough in the nation as a whole to accept the necessary changes to achieve the desired ends.

Some women have been educating themselves in the past fourteen years; the mass of their sisters is now awake. Are there women ready to lead in these new paths? Will other women follow them? We do not know, but one thing is sure, the attitude of women towards changes in society is going to determine to a great extent our future in this country. Women in the past have never realized their political strength. Will they wake up to it now? Will they realize that politics in the old sense, a game played for selfish ends by a few politicians, is of no concern any longer to anyone and that recognition in the sense of receiving a political job is perhaps necessary but only important because of the opportunity it affords a woman or a man to show what they conceive to be the duty of a government servant? If our government offices are not held in the next few years by men and women with new conceptions of public service, then our revolution may not continue to be bloodless and changes may not come gradually as they are coming now, but violently and suddenly as they have come in the past in France and in Russia and we will go back before we gather up the pieces and move forward again.

So in reviewing the past fourteen years let us acknowledge that women have made a few changes in politics. It is quite safe for them to be at polling places on election day and very gradually the men are accepting them as part of the party machinery and today if a woman wants to work and can prove her ability and is not too anxious and insistent upon recognition and tangible reward, she can be part of almost any party activity except the inner circle where the really important decisions in city, county and state politics are made! She can get into this inner circle in national politics more easily than in state, county and city and I wonder if the reason might be that men in Washington are a little more formal with each other and therefore the presence of a woman does not "cramp their style" to the same degree that it would in the other conferences? Women have made no great changes in politics or government and that is all that can be said of the past and now for the present.

Women are thinking and that is the first step toward an increased and more intelligent use of the ballot. Then they will demand of their political parties clear statements of principles and they will scrutinize their party's candidates, watch their records, listen to their promises and expect them to live up to them and to have their party's backing, and occasionally when the need arises, women will reject their party and its candidates. This will not be disloyalty but will show that as members of a party they are loyal first to the fine things for which the party stands and when it rejects those things or forgets the legitimate objects for which political parties exist, then as a party it cannot command the honest loyalty of its members.

Next, I believe women will run for office and accept victory or defeat in a sporting spirit. The proportion of women holding elective office is small. There are two reasons for this: one is that many women have dreaded the give and take of a campaign, they have dreaded the public criticism, they have not learned to discount the attacks of the opposition; but business and professional life is paving the way and this reason will not deter them much longer.

The second reason is that as a rule nominations which are given women by any of the political parties are in districts where it is almost impossible for one holding their political beliefs to win; in other words, a woman who is willing to make a well-nigh hopeless fight is welcomed by a local leader trying to fill out his ticket. The changing attitude towards women in general may bring a change in this. We have good women in political office today and much depends on their success. They are blazing the new paths and what is far more important they are exemplifying what we mean by the new type of public servant. When Frances Perkins says, "I can't go away because under the new industrial bill we have a chance to achieve for the workers of this country better conditions for which I have worked all my life," she is not staying because she will gain anything materially, for herself or her friends, but because she sees an opportunity for government to render a permanent service to the general happiness of the working man and woman and their families. This is what we mean as I see it by the "new deal." Look carefully, O people, at the record of some of your public servants in the past few years! Does this attitude strike you as new? If so, the women are in part responsible for it, and I think at present we can count on a more active interest from them and a constantly increasing willingness to bear their proper share of the burdens of government.

Now for the dreams of the future:

If women are really going to awake to their civic duties, if they are going to accept changes in social living and try to make of this country a real democracy, in which the best of opportunity is available to every child and where the compensations of life are not purely material ones, then we may indeed be seeing the realization of a really new deal for the people. If this is to come true, it seems to me that the women have got to learn to work together even before they work with men, and they have got to be realistic in facing the social problems that have to be solved. They cannot accept certain doctrines simply because they sound well. I have often thought that it sounded so well to talk about women being on an equal footing with men and sometimes when I have listened to the arguments of the National Woman's Party and they have complained that they could not compete in the labor market because restrictions were laid upon women's work which were not laid upon men's, I have been almost inclined to agree with them that such restrictions were unjust, until I came to realize that when all is said and done, women *are* different from men. They are equals in many ways, but they cannot refuse to acknowledge their differences. Not to acknowledge them weakens the case. Their physical functions in life are different and perhaps in the same way the contributions which they are to bring to the spiritual side of life are different. It may be that certain questions are waiting to be solved until women can bring their views to bear upon those questions.

I have a friend who wrote me the other day saying that because she and her husband lost all of their money, they have been obliged to go and live in a rural community in a small farmhouse. She and her daughters are doing all their own work and they have chosen the community in which they are living not because they found a house which they liked, but because they found a school for the children that they felt would give a real education. After the school was found, they found the house. She adds, "I do not regret the money— it has been a marvelous experience, giving my children a true sense of values, and I have learned what real people my country neighbors are. Because we have struggled together we know each other far better than do the average people who live in far easier circumstances."

There are many people who may make this same discovery and it is not always necessary to lose everything in order to make it, but it is necessary to attain the vision of a new and different life.

I was reading lately a book which Ramsay MacDonald wrote about his wife who died in 1911 and who seems today to be alive as one reads the pages of the book. She was far ahead of her time in many ways, but her most striking characteristic, from youth up, was the feeling of not being able to live in comfort when so many others suffered. She felt that all human beings were her brothers and sisters and her work has lived after her. Many women in this country have been carrying on similar work and perhaps we are going to see evolved in the next few years not only a social order built by the ability and brains of our men, but a social order which also represents the understanding heart of the women.

45

Should Wives Work?

Is it possible for a woman to marry and still have a career? This question has been asked of me so many times that I am glad at last to sit down and write some of the things which always come to my mind.

To begin with, the question is foolishly worded, for there are very few women who have careers. Those with real careers are a little group by themselves needing separate consideration. Most women marry and work, and the work will not be a "career." The question put this way also seems to imply that marriage in itself is not a career. Anyone who believes that has no real understanding of marriage.

There is no general answer which any one individual can give to this question, no matter how it is worded, for it is one of those questions that depend for their answer largely upon the individuals involved, both men and women.

The question should really be phrased in this way: Are you able to carry on two full-time jobs? Have you the physical strength and the mental vigor to do this day in and day out—particularly when you are young, first married, adjusting yourself to a stranger's personality, and perhaps bearing children, which is an added physical strain?

I can hear you ask, "Why do you say, 'adjusting yourself to a stranger's personality'?" The answer is quite simple: no two people really know each other until they have been married for some time, and one of the most exacting duties of family life is the adjustment of the various personalities that make up the family circle. The mother adjusts herself not only to her husband, but to each of her children and to the other near relatives, and she tries to explain and to adjust them to one another. It is not always an easy task.

More and more households are being managed by the housewife alone, particularly among the young people. That means pretty nearly constant attention to household tasks, if a good job is to be done, in the same way that it would be done in an office or wherever the woman might be employed for pay. This housekeeping job can be as scientific and as engrossing as any office job, or it may be a slipshod, haphazard affair with everything at sixes and sevens. It all depends upon the woman whether she makes this side of marriage a career or not.

There is another important aspect to this career. Any woman who means to make marriage a successful career will study her husband, his capabilities, his interests, even his peculiarities. She should know about his business and about his pleasures. It is possible for her to be a great factor in his success, not

Good Housekeeping 105 (December 1937): 28–29, 211–212.

by thrusting herself forward as an advisor, but by understanding so well his character and his career that she can supplement his shortcomings, bring out the best that is in him, and expand his interests by adding her own. Thus she can have a vicarious career by virtue of what she has put into her husband's.

Perhaps the woman who does this is the happiest and most successful woman, but she has to have the kind of temperament that can do it and do it well, and in addition the circumstances of married life have to make it possible. We might as well face the fact that today circumstances are making it more and more difficult for a woman to lead what two generations ago was considered the normal and natural life for any woman. In those days even a woman who did not marry tried to find a niche that she could fill in somebody's home. A maiden aunt or cousin often took the place of a nurse or governess or even a hired servant and was looked upon with pity, and expected to work early and late for her room and board, and to be as devoted to the children of the family as though they were her own.

Women today would not accept this situation calmly, and the fact that they can be and are largely self-supporting changes their economic condition. It also changes their relationship to men and marriage.

The economic situation is such today that few young people can marry at the age when their grandparents did. Many people, rather than put off their marriage indefinitely, get married with the realization that both of them will have to continue working and that children are out of the question until they have laid enough money aside or the man has had enough increase in salary to take care of all the family expenses.

This is not a case of whether you prefer marriage or a career. It is a case of marriage and work together, or no marriage and work alone. Work must go on in either case. For most women there is something so satisfying in creating a home that they do it frequently by themselves. It seems to fulfill a deep inner need to do the little homely things of everyday living, and I think that is one reason why so many young people get married and set up homes of their own long before their financial resources warrant it.

If they want to have children as soon as they are financially established, they usually do so, but a craving for a home of her own is the first stirring of maturity in a woman. To many women, however, a home is not wholly satisfying unless she is making it for someone else, and nature has made most women yearn for a man to mother.

I know one young couple who were married when the boy was getting twenty-five dollars a week and the girl was getting the same as a stenographer. Both of them went on working. Everything seemed to be going very well, and she managed her two jobs quite successfully. The most successful part of it was the fact that she induced her husband to feel an equal responsibility for the house. I remember that when I dined with them, he put on an apron after dinner and helped wash the dishes as naturally as if that were the normal occupation for a man. When a marriage works out this way, it is very successful, especially if the man has a knack for doing things about the house, because it keeps him busy when his wife is busy.

Children can be postponed if two young people have a home and a mate. If a woman has to work to have a home and husband, she will do it happily, but I do not think that always means that she longs to work. It is unfortunate that so often she is forced to for material security.

Where circumstances verge on poverty, marriage is even more of a career, for then more depends on the woman's ability to manage. Of course, when it comes to the mothers of families who work in mills, factories, and stores, we know quite well that there is no question of choice—poverty drives them, and they work because they have to, and only a few would hesitate if they were offered an opportunity to stay at home, and look after their home and their children.

I remember visiting a mill town once, and as the women came off the night shift—for there were no laws at that time in that particular state against women's working on night shifts—they met their husbands going to work on the day shift. We followed one woman home. Tired from the hours in the mill, she nevertheless had to set to work immediately to get the children fed and off to school. Then she had her house to set to rights, washing and ironing to do, and dinner to get for the children and supper to be left for the man when he came back from work and she went on. In the afternoon she snatched a few hours of sleep, and the children who were not in school played unwatched and uncared for. She knew that her home life was not satisfactory, and she did not work long hours in the mill because she wanted to, but simply because there was not enough food to go around unless her earnings supplemented those of her husband.

There are women, however, who work for the love of working. They may love their homes and their children and still crave the satisfaction of doing a job themselves. Sometimes it is just because they love the kind of work they do; sometimes it is because they must have the independence which being able to earn money gives them.

I know one young woman who has managed to develop for herself work which she can do in her own home. She feels that her children need her at home, and yet she was very unhappy without some outside interests. She had a musical talent which she shared with her husband, and together they developed a unique project which involved research and execution, giving them a joint interest and allowing her to earn a little extra money.

Very occasionally it is possible for a man and a woman to work together and to have an even closer tie than they would have if the woman remained the man's helpmate in the home.

The happiness of husband and wife is often wrecked by too little dependence on each other, for to be happy two people must need each other in everything they do. I could tell you many stories of young people who have drifted apart partly because the man was too absorbed by his business and the woman did not have enough to do. One story I remember, however, is a little different, because it was a case in which both the man and his wife had interests which were so divergent that neither of them took any pleasure in being

243

with the other or in hearing about what the other was doing. The man wanted to lead a rather quiet life, and the woman was young and pretty, active-minded, physically energetic. She wanted to do something which would bring in money and make it possible for her to have some of the luxuries and pleasures which she coveted and to which her husband was completely indifferent. They stuck to their own interests, and while they lived in the same house and while they had children and while they were never separated in a formal way, they could not have been further apart if they had lived at the two poles. I question if the children ever knew what it was to feel a community of interests in that home.

It would be well if men realized the need that some women have for a little financial independence. Occasionally marriage is wrecked because the woman feels that her work at home is as much a financial contribution as the man's work out in the world. She sees no recognition of this in their relationship or in their environment and becomes more and more restless and dissatisfied.

I remember one woman saying rather bitterly to me once that she made more money by saving and good management than her husband did, but that he seemed to think the generosity of giving was all on his side, forgetting that she gave her strength and her time. The work which she did she might have paid someone else to do; and her careful buying actually put in the bank money which her husband could use in his business.

As a rule, the woman spends the major part of the family income, but if it is given her for the house and she has to resort to subterfuge to get any personal pocket money out of it, it is not a happy arrangement. Of course, when two people are planning together every penny of expenditure, the case is different; but when a man has any money which he calls his own, a woman should have some also in recognition of the services she performs for the home. She is more apt to make her housekeeping a good job and to be happy in her family relations.

In many cases a woman who holds a job feels that she is a better companion for her husband because she has more individuality and comes to him more full of different interests when they meet. She may not have the kind of temperament which makes it possible for her to bring up her children herself. She may find that even with less time to give them, she can really do more for them. All these things are subjects for the individuals to consider and decide together.

"Why do you work?" I once asked a friend of mine who seemed very weary.

She smiled and said: "I work because I found that when Stephen came home at night, I had nothing to talk to him about. He is out in the world and meets people and does things. I was in a little backwater and lost the habit of thinking about the same things that are on his mind. I had to go back to work to regain the same atmosphere and to be a companion."

"But," I said, "you have to pay someone to take care of the children. Wouldn't it be cheaper to do it yourself?"

"Far cheaper," she said, "but even the children are better off. Now, when I come home, I am full of interests I can share with them, and I am nowhere nearly so impatient as I used to be when I answered their questions all day long and directed every minute of their lives. I do not mind now saying, 'Johnny, wash your hands,' or, 'Sara, don't bite when you fight.' I have to do it only between 6 and 8 P.M. But if I do it from 6 A.M. until 8 P.M., many a harsh word is spoken, and many a hasty gesture passes between us, much to my regret afterward."

One thing is certain: Any woman who decides to work after she is married must have good health and be a fairly well disciplined person, and her life must be systematized so that one part does not interfere with the other, and the man must understand and sympathize with her interests and desires.

The man's temperament is as important as the woman's, for there are men who deeply resent their wives' doing any work and who want to feel that their home is entirely dependent on their own efforts. There are other men who go even beyond that and want to feel that the woman whom they have married is dependent upon them for all she has in a material way, forgetting often that their mental and spiritual contacts count also in any relationship. Then again there are men who, if their wives are self-sufficient and capable, will do exactly what so many woman are accused of doing—become parasites and willingly allow themselves to be taken care of in every way, even in a material way.

I knew one man whose wife mothered him until he completely lost his initiative. He was sweet to her, but he really felt that life was made by her and he had to make no effort. Suddenly he met a woman who was weaker and more clinging than he was, and she awakened in him all his dormant chivalrous instincts. He asked his wife for a divorce. He married the weaker woman and became a strong man. The first wife remade her life, which was not astonishing; but he remade his, which seemed unbelievable.

All the things I have mentioned and one more enter into this question of whether a woman who has the ability to do a job outside the home should do it or not. In the last few years I have been getting many letters from women whose husbands have fallen ill or died and left them alone or with dependents. Those who have had no training are the most pathetic, but those who once worked and then gave up altogether are in almost as difficult a position.

I doubt that it is ever wise for a woman who has once had a skill to allow herself to lose it entirely, for, granting that she makes a marriage a career, there may come a time when she will need work, and there will certainly come a time when her children are grown. If the demands on her time are fewer and she is well, she may feel the necessity of taking up some kind of regular work again, particularly if in her youth she was trained to keep busy. This may not be a financial necessity, but merely something to take the place of the duties which were hers when marriage was her only job.

In my own experience I have found there is one other thing that may happen to a woman. For some reason she may have to interest herself in things that have seemed to be more directly her husband's interests and in which she never expected to take any personal part. She may find she becomes interested for a variety of reasons. This necessity of developing interests of her own which take her out of her home will find her better equipped if she has once done a job for pay and kept on doing it now and then throughout her life so that she is able to maintain a professional attitude toward all work, both in her home and out of it.

There are just a few women who have special gifts, who have established careers before they meet the men they wish to marry. If they give up these careers, they may find much of the savor of life is removed when they are not doing something which requires independent thought and initiative. These are the women who go to work because they are conscious of a capacity within themselves which cannot be denied, and they should marry only men who understand this and are willing to make some compromises. It can be done very happily, but it depends on both the man and the woman in each case. These "career" women do a job for the love of it. They may be so gifted that they can cope successfully with household affairs from the administrative point of view. They may not be interested in doing any of the homely things of life. They may be quite helpless at home and need someone else to cope with household measures. For them it is probably impossible to settle down to a homemaker's career and watch over somebody else's career and development and achievement. They are fortunate if they marry the right men!

The women who I feel should undoubtedly have outside occupation, however, are the women whose homes are taken care of by competent hands and feet other than their own, who with ordinary capacity for management can give the necessary orders in fifteen minutes every morning and have the rest of the day in which to do nothing. These women might as well do something even if they have no special gifts, for as idlers they encumber the earth. They are not doing things at home that keep women busy and happy.

I think any young couple is fortunate when the woman has to do everything about the house and does it happily, but in view of all the different angles that this problem presents, I would give no advice, only urge young people to think over what they want out of life very carefully when they are making the decision of how they will start their life together.

46
Divorce

I have watched with interest, as no doubt other people have, the results of the poll taken on divorce by the *Ladies' Home Journal* among the women of the country, and their verdict as to the contributing factors to unhappy marital relations.

There seems to be, among all those who acknowledge that divorce is possible, a feeling that it should continue to be possible, but that the different states should have uniform divorce laws.

I was interested to find that the women of the country feel that differences about money cause the vast majority of divorces. I think that is probably true, and yet there is one thing which was not mentioned at all and which seems to me the fundamental factor in the success or failure of any marriage.

I am one of those who believe that in almost everything we do in life, prevention is preferable to cure. I feel that a better understanding of the things which make marriage successful, and a few more difficulties and safeguards thrown around this very serious step in the lives of young people, might be helpful and sometimes prevent the necessity for divorce.

For that reason I want to point out this factor which I think so important.

If you and your partner in this marital contract do not share the same interests and the same enjoyments, you are not going to find life together very agreeable. If you do not have the same standards of conduct, if you do not believe in the same principles and your codes of ethics are at variance, you are going to lose respect; and love flies quickly in the wake of respect. In addition, if your taste is daily offended by a succession of little acts which keep you in a state of constant irritation, your life will be intolerable.

I believe that where children are involved a divorce should be avoided if possible, because a child has a right to both of its parents. A child should have a real home, and a real home means a home without friction and where an atmosphere of affection and graciousness prevails.

Where two people love each other this may be accomplished even though each of the parents has had to forgive faults in the other. Where there is constant irritation about little things, however, and an atmosphere of visible self-control and repression, then life in the home is apt to become so ungracious that children cannot grow up normally and happily.

I have known both men and women in marriages to care enough for each other to forgive very serious offenses. I knew a woman once who stood by her husband, though he had committed murder, because she knew that his sudden burst of rage which resulted in his victim's death had been the result of a great

Ladies' Home Journal 55 (April 1938): 16.

temporary temptation, and that fundamentally her husband suffered as much as a result of his crime as she did. I knew a man who stood by his wife through a sentence in prison for stealing, because he knew that she had yielded to a temptation which she regretted afterward as much as he did.

I have known two people who reached a point where they could no longer live together because one of them felt that the other had fallen below certain fundamental standards of honesty, and in consequence every little act and every little self-indulgence became a cause for irritation.

Divorce is necessary and right, I believe, when two people find it impossible to live happily together, after every effort has honestly been made to come to an understanding, if their religious beliefs do not forbid it under any circumstances whatsoever. The conditions necessitating a divorce frequently do not mean that either the man or the woman has been in any way sinful, however, and it does not seem to me quite fair to insist, as we do in so many places, that divorce shall be granted only for reasons which leave a stigma on the moral character of the individual, and therefore reflect on the inheritance of the children.

Incompatibility of temper sounds like a trivial cause for divorce, and yet I am not sure that it is not the most frequent cause. It is responsible for quarrels over money, and it drives husbands and wives away from each other to other interests and other people, and brings about the more serious acts for which divorce is usually granted. It seems to me that these results only add to the bitterness of a situation which at best is tragic.

People who face divorce without having gone through a great deal of suffering are rare indeed. When there is no necessity, why must we add to this suffering and insist on ignoring the first and most usual cause of disagreements? Thus we drive them to some kind of desperate action in order to obtain divorce and freedom from a bond which no longer means anything.

When love does not exist in marriage, there is no real marriage. Too many people marry without realizing this fact. Sometimes they are too young, and no one tells them what loves means. Sometimes the circumstances of their lives have made them think that they can do without love if they can have material compensations. Sometimes they think that love needs no tending, whereas in truth it is like a very delicate flower requiring care and attention. Love may be killed by neglect and forgetfulness, though it starts out a hardy, healthy plant.

I doubt if we elders remember often enough to point these things out before marriage to the young people of our acquaintance. They should understand that they are undertaking a full-time job which is going to be part of their everyday existence from the time the marriage ceremony is read until "death do them part," a job which they cannot neglect for a day without being confronted with failure.

47

Women in Politics

We are about to have a collective coming of age! The women in the United States have been participants in government for nearly twenty years. I think it behooves us to look back on this period in which we have been serving our apprenticeship and decide what our accomplishments have been, how much good our education has done us, and whether we really are able to consider ourselves full-fledged citizens.

Where did we start and how far have we come?

Twenty years ago, when we were granted the right of suffrage, some people thought that women were going to revolutionize the conduct of government. Yet all we were given was the right to vote. Men had had the vote on a fairly universal basis ever since the country was established—without achieving Utopia. Everyone knew that corruption still existed, and that the gentlemen did not always devote themselves to their civic duties in the unselfish and ardent manner that might be expected in a democracy. In 1919, however, this fact did not seem to prevent the belief that all desirable reforms would come about by the granting of suffrage to women. Alas and alas, the reforms just did not happen!

Perhaps it would be as well to mention also that some of the dire results prophesied if women were given the vote haven't come about, either.

Let us see what women have actually done in public life thus far.

It is fair, I think, to speak first of some of the women who were leaders in the fight for suffrage because of their influence on the thought of the men and women of the period, even though they may not actually have held public office. By studying them, I think we can get a very good idea of the qualities women must bring to public life. Dr. Anna Howard Shaw is dead; but Mrs. Carrie Chapman Catt is still alive, and I have had the privilege of knowing her for many years. Both seem to have certain qualities in common: a deep belief in the justice of a cause; the power to organize and inspire other women; the ability to speak fluently, and to be both humorous and dramatic. Add good physical health—not a quality, perhaps, but an essential—and you have a picture of these two suffrage leaders.

Certain other suffrage leaders I know only from hearsay. Inez Milholland, for instance, was probably very able, and she certainly used her personal attractions to drive home her point! There is no question about it, both charm and good looks are useful weapons, which ladies can always use to good advantage when they have them, no matter what offices they hold.

Good Housekeeping 110 (January 1940): 8–9, 150; (March 1940): 45, 68; (April 1940): 201–203.

Available facts about women who have actually occupied political office during the past twenty years are incomplete, and it is extremely difficult to get accurate information. We can get figures for certain years and nothing for other years. Fortunately, the League of Women Voters will shortly publish its 1939 compilation on women in public office, which will supplement our information.

There are certain trends, however, that even incomplete figures seem to show. In the past ten years fewer women have been elected to Congress and to state legislatures. The peak was reached in 1929, when thirty-eight states could boast of one hundred and forty-nine women in state legislatures. In 1939 there were only twenty-eight states having women representatives, and the total was only one hundred and twenty-nine women.

However, the change is so very slight that I think we may consider it a temporary fluctuation, indicating nothing more than that women haven't yet gained real confidence in themselves in that type of competition. Besides, as we shall see, the number of women in appointive positions is steadily increasing.

In the United States Senate, Gladys Pyle, Republican of South Dakota, was elected in November 1938 for an unexpired term, which ended January 3, 1939. And three other women Senators were appointed to finish out unexpired terms and then retired. Mrs. Hattie Caraway, Democrat of Arkansas, is the one woman who has really served as a United States Senator. She was first appointed to succeed her husband in 1931, and then elected in 1932 and reelected in 1938. She has, I think, gained confidence in her ability and is respected by men in political life. At first one heard that she was under this or that influence; that she was a rubber stamp; that she did little thinking for herself; but of late one hears a great deal more about her being a useful member of the Senate and having a mind of her own. There is no doubt that she has grown and that her record can bear comparison with that of any of her colleagues.

In the House of Representatives, we have had twenty-one women members. Jeannette Rankin served before the adoption of the federal suffrage amendment. Her state of Montana had passed a suffrage act of its own. She will always be remembered for her inability to vote for war. One of the dramatic incidents reported in the newspapers of the day was how she burst into tears and refused to cast her vote in favor of war. I was not present, but I have always had a certain sympathy with the gesture even though it was futile.

Of these twenty-one members, eleven have been Republicans and ten Democrats. In the short session of the 71st Congress, nine women's names were carried on the rolls of the House of Representatives. This is the largest number carried at any one time. Since then the number has been steadily decreasing, till today there are only four women members of the House: Mary Norton of New Jersey, Caroline O'Day of New York, Edith Nourse Rogers of Massachusetts, and Jessie Sumner of Illinois. Three of these women I know well; all are good, hard-working members and on a par with the men who have served with them.

I always think of Mary Norton as being primarily interested in welfare work, though she has grown far beyond those first interests. Caroline O'Day has fixed ideas on the subject of war, which nothing could change. Anyone who has seen her signature would know that she can wield the artist's brush, so it is no surprise to find that she was for many years a painter and illustrator, working here and in Paris. Edith Nourse Rogers still has her interest in World War soldiers, and she still looks charming in her old Red Cross uniform.

I remember also Ruth Hanna McCormick Simms, who, as a member of the House of Representatives, did credit to a family that has often served the public. And Mrs. Florence Kahn of California was an able and witty member, who would be welcomed back by the House with open arms. The picture is much the same in state legislatures.

We have had only two women state governors, both Democrats—Mrs. Nellie Tayloe Ross of Wyoming and Mrs. Miriam A. Ferguson of Texas. I met Mrs. Ferguson once and then only for a few minutes; but it is generally conceded that her job was that of being her husband's mouthpiece. This is pardonable in private life, but extremely unwise in public life, where every individual should stand on his or her own feet.

Mrs. Ross went into politics through the urging of her husband's friends, notably the present Senator, Joseph O'Mahoney of Wyoming. As far as I know, she filled her office creditably, had good advisors, knew her own limitations, and was on the whole an average good governor, though not a great one. She was elected for one term only, and that does not permit a man or a woman to accomplish much.

We will find on the rolls of both the elective and appointive officials, according to the laws of their respective states, a number of women as secretaries of state, state treasurers, state auditors—which looks as though women are better mathematicians than they are credited with being!

In the appointive positions, the trend shows an upward curve in both state and federal governments. This would seem to prove me correct in my surmise that women are not yet prepared to go out and stand up under the average political campaign. In addition men rarely are inclined to give them nominations for elective positions if there is a chance to elect a man; so, frequently, a woman is beaten for an elective office before she starts to run.

In the old days men always said that politics was too rough-and-tumble a business for women; but that idea is gradually wearing away. There is more truth in the statement that men have a different attitude toward politics than women. They play politics a little more like a game. With the men, it becomes a serious occupation for a few weeks before election; whereas women look upon it as a serious matter year in and year out. It is associated with their patriotism and their duty to their country.

There are moments when I think that women's fervor to work continuously does not make them very popular with the gentlemen!

Mrs. Mabel Walker Willebrandt won my admiration long before I actually met her, while she was making a name for herself in President Hoover's administration. She helped to attain a model federal prison for women. This

251

institution, headed by Dr. Mary Harris, does great credit to the vision of the women who fought so hard to obtain a new type of prison for women offenders. The head of the Department of Home Economics in the Department of Agriculture is Dr. Louise Stanley. She has been working there for a great many years, just as has Mary Anderson, the head of the Women's Bureau in the Department of Labor. Both of them have built up able staffs and are considered to be very useful government employes.

Katharine Lenroot, for instance, now chief of the Children's Bureau in the Department of Labor, followed Grace Abbott, with whom she had worked for many years. Both women have done a social-service job; but at the same time they have had to be good politicians, for their job could be carried on only if the men in Congress were convinced that it was being well done and that the people at home were receiving a service which they desired and in which they believed.

In 1933 about thirty-five women came into important positions in Washington, and in the last six or seven years there has been an increase in the number of women appointed to more important offices. Strange as it may seem, I think this is due to the work of a woman who never held any office, except that of Vice-Chairman of the Democratic National Committee in charge of the Women's Division—Miss Molly Dewson.

Miss Dewson was interested in politics because of what she thought women could achieve through political organizations. She began her career in Boston, at the age of twenty-three, as a supervisor of the Girls' Parole Department of Massachusetts. She made her contact with state legislatures while she worked for the Consumers' League. She came into partisan political work during a national campaign. When that was over, she stayed on in the National Democratic Committee, and I think virtually all the men, from the President and Postmaster General Farley to most of the other heads of Departments, will concede that there has rarely been a woman more active in getting women into political positions! She was almost uncomfortably honest, at times somewhat brusque; but she had a sense of humor and a loyalty and devotion that made many people admire her and grieve when she was transferred from political work to the Social Security Board and when, finally, because of illness, she had to retire from active work.

Many women in Washington today hold positions because of ability and preparation that has little or no connection with political work. They have been distinguished along some special line, and frequently they came in long before the present administration. But those who came in during this administration owe a great deal to Molly Dewson, and women as a whole should be grateful for the fact that she never backed a woman whom she did not think capable of holding the job she was trying to get. The record of women in office during the past few years shows that her judgment was, on the whole, good.

We have, for instance, the first woman member of a President's Cabinet—the Secretary of Labor, Miss Frances Perkins. Most of us find it difficult to recall the names of former Secretaries of Labor. I happen to remember one or two; but I find, when I ask my friends about them, that the only Secretary of Labor whom they know much about is Frances Perkins, the present encumbent. They do not always sing her praises; but they do know that she exists—first, because she had a career before she held her present office; next, because she has held an extremely difficult position in a most trying period and, on the whole, has acquitted herself well. She has never really learned to handle the press, so her newspaper contacts are bad. This is partly because she is suspicious of reporters, and those around her, trying to protect her, accentuate this suspicion. I cannot say that this attitude is never justified; but with her keen intuition and her wide experience and contact with human nature, she should be able to distinguish between the fine and trustworthy correspondents and those who cannot be trusted. Newspaper correspondents are no different from other human beings—they are good and bad. Years ago Louis Howe told me that no group of people has a higher standard of ethics, and I still believe that to be true.

This inability to deal with the press is, I think, Frances Perkins' greatest weakness. I think she has been the best Secretary of Labor this country has had. Mrs. Nellie Tayloe Ross, whom I have already mentioned as a former Governor of Wyoming, was Vice-Chairman of the Democratic National Committee in 1928 and was appointed Director of the Mint in the Treasury Department in 1933. There is nothing spectacular about her job; but it requires steady work. I think she has always performed her duties conscientiously.

The first woman Assistant Secretary of the Treasury was appointed in 1934: Miss Josephine Roche of Colorado. She has long been interested in social questions, and she transformed her coal mines in Colorado, when she inherited them from her father, to meet the standards she felt should exist in that industry. She came to Washington a proved executive. She retired of her own volition, feeling that her business required her attention; but she has retained the position of Chairman of the Committee to study medical service in this country. This Committee is doing an excellent piece of work.

In one other important branch of the government, the diplomatic service, we have had our first woman minister to a foreign country—Ruth Bryan Rohde, who was appointed our Minister to Denmark in 1933. She identified herself to such an extent with the interests of the country to which she was accredited that she returned to us married to a Dane. She resigned in 1936. Mrs. J. Borden Harriman was appointed Minister to Norway in 1937. From all accounts, she has taken a great interest in the conditions of the people there and has been able to give to our country a very much better understanding of the Norwegian people.

Two women held major judicial posts in 1930. Florence Allen, a judge on the Supreme Court Bench in Ohio, and Genevieve R. Cline, who had been appointed to the United States Customs Court in New York City, which is a life commission. In 1939 Florence Allen was appointed by President Roosevelt

253

to the United States Circuit Court of Appeals, 5th District. Miss Cline remained on the bench in New York. Miss Garrick H. Buck was made judge of the 5th District of the Supreme Court in Hawaii.

In the Labor Department we find Miss Mary La Dame, special assistant to the Secretary of Labor. Everyone knows the name of Mrs. Lucille Foster McMillin, on the Civil Service Commission. She, like Mrs. Ellen Woodward, formerly head of the women's and professional projects under the Works Progress Administration, and now on the Social Security Board, would impress you first as a very feminine woman with charm and social distinction; but both of them know how to be good executives and work hard. They may carry their sympathetic understanding of human problems with them in their working hours, but they also carry level heads and a keen intelligence, which makes them acceptable members of any men's conference. Mrs. Florence Kerr, who is now in the Works Progress Administration, is proving herself to be a good executive, also.

Miss Katherine Blackburn is head of one of the most interesting bureaus in Washington, the Bureau of Press Intelligence, which will get for any member of the government information on any subject! To be sure, the Library of Congress will do this, too, but not quite in the up-to-date, last-minute manner that Katherine Blackburn has evolved.

Over in the Printing Office is a woman who won her knowledge in the printing rooms of a number of newspapers. Miss Jo Coffin comes from the ranks of labor, just as does Miss Rose Schneiderman, who was a valuable member of the Advisory Committee of the National Recovery Administration while it functioned, and who today is in the New York State Department of Labor as Secretary to the Commissioner. Both of them are interesting women, capable of firing the imagination of young people, resourceful, tactful, patient, and therefore valuable in their contacts with their superiors and their fellow workers.

Marian Bannister, the sister of Senator Carter Glass of Virginia, reminds me of the old French nobility. I am sure she could walk to the guillotine with absolute dignity and calm! She signs the President's paycheck and all the mail that goes out of the office of the Treasurer.

Mrs. Jewell W. Swofford is chairman of the United States Employment Compensation Commission. And Laura S. Brown and Lucy Howorth are doing good work in the Veterans Administration, For the first time there is a woman, Marion J. Harron, on the Board of Tax Appeals.

In 1939 there were approximately fifty-five women in major positions throughout the federal government. The number of women in clerical, fiscal, and professional positions has grown to 162,518.

Many other women I have not mentioned are competently filling important positions; but my list is already too long. I do not wish to close, however, without mentioning three women. Mrs. Mary Harriman Rumsey, who headed the Consumers' Division in the old NRA days, had a thankless job. She devoted herself to it nevertheless, and had she lived, would, I think, have helped in a field not as yet sufficiently developed in this country.

Two other women, while not actually holding public office, have done so much to affect the thinking of both men and women on political questions that I feel they should not be forgotten. One is Anne O'Hare McCormick, who was chosen last year as the woman of distinction for 1939. She has established a record in her interviews with important people who make world policies today; Her fairness, her ability to understand varying points of view and to report the essence of a conversation have won her distinction and a following among thinking people everywhere. Her analysis and presentation of world situations has helped clarify many difficult and universally interesting points.

The other woman is Dorothy Thompson, also a political writer of distinction, swayed perhaps by her own emotions, personal interests, and past experience, but still with such a gift of expression that she has a great following.

All these women are blazing trails for women in the future, and by the success or failure of their work they will either increase the possibility of women's participation in government or make the public less anxious to place women in positions of responsibility.

To me it seems that those who have borne the brunt of the fight thus far are rather shining examples of what women can do in the political arena if they really work, and I think it will be interesting to watch not individual women, but the accomplishment of women as a whole in the field of public affairs.

Now that we have considered what has happened to women in the political arena since they were granted the right of suffrage, I think it is only fair to deal with that perennial question: "What have women accomplished for human betterment with the vote?"

Of course, I never felt that there was any particular reason why we should expect miracles to occur as a result of giving women the right to vote. It was denied them for so long that men acquired great interest in public questions and women felt these questions were not their responsibility. Therefore, women for many years have been accustomed to centering their interests in the home or in allied activities. They have left the administration of government almost exclusively in the hands of men.

Changing the habits of thought of any group of people, men or women, is not a rapid process, so I am not in the least surprised, at the end of twenty-one years of suffrage, that the answer to: "What have women accomplished by their vote?" is frequently a shrug of the shoulders.

Women have used this suffrage, as far as I can tell, approximately as much as men have. There is a great percentage of people, eligible to vote, who do not vote on election day, and there is no proof that they are predominately either men or women. And, strange though it may seem, women apparently make up their minds on public questions in much the same way that men do.

I think it is fairly obvious that women have voted on most questions as individuals and not as a group, in much the same way that men do, and that they are influenced by their environment and their experience and background, just as men are.

There are women, however, who, either because they have no confidence in themselves, or because of the age-old tradition that men are superior for some reason or other, will say: "Oh, Mrs. Roosevelt, it is all right for you to urge women to think independently and clearly on all these social questions, but I still like to take my guidance from the men and do as they tell me." Well, perhaps there are some men who, for the sake of peace in the family, accept a woman's point of view even on political questions.

You will find, I think, women divided in the same groupings that have divided men, and they approach any question before the electorate in much the same way. There are liberals and conservatives among the women as well as among the men. As far as I can judge, only one thing stands out—namely, that on the whole, during the last twenty years, government has been taking increasing cognizance of humanitarian questions, things that deal with the happiness of human beings, such as health, education, security. There is nothing, of course, to prove that this is entirely because of the women's interest, and yet I think it is significant that this change has come about during the period when women have been exercising their franchise. It makes me surmise that women who do take an interest in public questions have thrust these interests to the fore, and obliged their fellow citizens to consider them. Whereas in the past these human problems have remained more or less in the background, today they are discussed by every governing body.

No revolution has come about because women have been given the vote, and it is perfectly true that many women are not thrilled by their opportunity to take part in political-party work. They probably do not like it so well as the men do, for we do not find them competing for places on party committees or for actual recognition in the political positions.

The women, however, are gradually increasing their activities. There are more women in civil-service positions and there are more women in rather inconspicuous, but important positions in city, state, and federal governments where technical knowledge is required.

When I went to Washington, I was so much impressed by the work they were doing that I started to have parties for women executives in various departments, and I discovered an astonishing number of women doing very important work, but getting comparatively little recognition because government is still a man's world.

As a result of all this, however, I find the influence of women emerging into a more important sphere. There was a time when no one asked: "What will the women think about this?" Now that question comes up often. It is true that we had more women in elective positions a few years ago; but I think the change is so slight that it is just a temporary fluctuation, and due to the fact that women haven't yet gained real confidence in themselves in that type of competition. Women are quite willing to compete in an examination that tests their knowledge even though there is still a prejudice against appointing them to certain positions because of their sex. To come out and fight a political campaign, however, is still difficult for most women. That is one reason why a woman who does hold an office, either elective or appointive, so often obtains it at her husband's death or as a result of his interests. She is continuing work she might never have taken up on her own initiative.

We have had, of course, a few failures among women who have taken office either because men have urged them to do so, or because they have followed in their husbands' footsteps. When a woman fails, it is much more serious than when a man fails, because the average person attributes the failure not to the individual, but to the fact that she is a woman.

Let us acknowledge that there has been no really great change in government and that there is no sign that when moral questions come up, women rise in a body to bring about certain reforms.

Their achievements certainly do not justify their having the suffrage; but then there are people who question whether men's achievements justify their having the suffrage. I think Mr. Hitler and Mr. Mussolini quite openly question this and are perhaps rather successfully curtailing the independence of both men and women, for the good of the human race and the state, so they say! We do not agree with that point of view; but the dictators have persuaded a good many people to accept it. I think we in this country feel that suffrage is not a question of achievement, but merely a right granted to individuals, and women, because they are individuals, have this right in exactly the same measure as men.

Let us acknowledge, too, the fact that women frequently try to stay out of fights which have to be made to get rid of corruption in politics. As far as I know, it was very largely a group of young men, perhaps assisted by a few women, who cleaned up the Kansas City, Missouri, situation and finally proved that the political-boss system under Mr. Pendergast—or anybody else, for that matter—rarely brought about an honestly run government. The same thing might be said about the Hines case in New York City. These political bosses, who used their political power for personal gain, were the result of a system. Probably Mr. Pendergast and Mr. Hines are kind and good in many ways according to their own lights. They happened to fall on times which were evil for them because the public conscience has changed as to what is right and wrong in positions of public responsibility. These men may feel that they were unjustly singled out, for many other men have done much the same things they have done, but the conscience of the public was not yet aroused against them. I fear, however, that we cannot claim that women have any greater part in this change than have men.

Looking for concrete achievements, I feel we can really credit to the women only one over this period of years, and that is the one already mentioned—the government's attitude of concern for the welfare of human beings. On the whole, more interest is now taken in social questions. The government is concerned about housing, about the care of citizens who temporarily are unable to take care of themselves, about the care of handicapped children, whether handicapped by poor homes or by straitened circumstances.

This is a general change, which I attribute to the fact that men had to appeal for the vote of the women and have therefore taken a greater interest in subjects they feel may draw women to their support.

There are, of course, many men who have been conscious of the need for some changes; but a big majority of them have of late been moved to action in certain situations to which they had given little thought in the past. Women have become better educated, and women have taken more active part in helping to educate men connected with government to think in terms of human betterment. Therefore, I should say that, while one could claim no particular accomplishment, there has been a tremendous change in the outlook of government, which can be attributed to the fact that women have the ballot.

When people ask: "Have women in politics advanced temperance or other moral reforms?" I always point out that they have been as divided on moral questions as on political questions. They did not have the vote when the prohibition amendment was originally passed. The Women's Christian Temperance Union group undoubtedly worked for the passage of this amendment and against its repeal; but other groups of women were undoubtedly a factor in its ultimate repeal. Many of the best workers in the women's organizations for repeal worked because they felt a moral obligation to something greater than prohibition. They sensed the fact that we were developing a group of law-breakers in this country, and, sad to say, many of the leaders of public thought were offenders in this respect. These leaders said that breaking a law was justified if you felt that a law did not represent the will of the majority. I always felt that anyone had a right to work to have the law changed, but that we should live up to it as long as it remained on the statute books. However, I think that my stand was distinctly a minority stand, and as far as women are concerned, they were divided on this as on many other moral questions.

What the future holds, none of us knows; but in this country we now hold that women have the same rights as men have. They do not have to justify their achievements as a group. I think we might legitimately ask whether as a democracy we have gone forward in the past twenty-one years, and take it for granted that if we have, it means that the majority of the women, as well as the majority of the men, have justified their right to suffrage.

Where are we going as women? Do we know where we are going? Do we know where we want to go?

I have a suggestion to make that will probably seem to you entirely paradoxical. Yet at the present juncture of civilization, it seems to me the only way for women to grow.

Women must become more conscious of themselves as women and of their ability to function as a group. At the same time they must try to wipe from men's consciousness the need to consider them as a group or as women in their everyday activities, especially as workers in industry or the professions.

Let us consider first what women can do united in a cause.

It is perfectly obvious that women are not all alike. They do not think alike, nor do the feel alike on many subjects. Therefore, you can no more unite all women on a great variety of subjects than you can unite all men.

If I am right that, as I stated above, women have caused a basic change in the attitude of government toward human beings, then there are certain fundamental things that mean more to the great majority of women than to the great majority of men. These things are undoubtedly tied up with women's biological functions. The women bear the children, and love them even before they come into the world. Some of you will say that the maternal instinct is not universal in women, and that now and then you will find a man whose paternal instinct is very strong—even stronger than his wife's maternal instinct. These are the exceptions which prove the rule, however. The pride most men feel in the little new bundle of humanity must grow gradually into love and devotion. I will not deny that this love develops fast with everything a man does for the new small and helpless human being which belongs to him; but a man can nearly always be more objective about his children than a woman can be.

This ability to be objective about children is one thing women have to fight to acquire; never, no matter what a child may do or how old he may be, is a woman quite divorced from the baby who once lay so helpless in her arms. This is the first fundamental truth for us to recognize, and we find it in greater or less degree in women who have never had a child. From it springs that concern about the home, the shelter for the children. And here is the great point of unity for the majority of women.

It is easy to make women realize that a force which threatens any home may threaten theirs. For that reason, I think that, as women realize what their political power might mean if they were united, they may decide now and then to unite on something which to them seems fundamental. It is quite possible, in the present state of world turmoil, that we may find women rising up to save civilization if they realize how great the menace is. I grant you that things will have to be pretty bad before they will do it, for most women are accustomed to managing men only in the minor details of life and to accepting the traditional yoke where the big things are concerned.

I have heard people say that the United States is a matriarchy—that the women rule. This is true only in nonessentials. Yes, the husbands spoil their wives; they let them travel and spend more money than foreign women do, but that is because money has come to us more easily in the past and therefore we have spent it more easily. The Frenchwoman who is her husband's business partner has more real hold on him than the American woman who travels abroad alone has on her husband. She buys all the clothes she wants without knowing whether her husband will be able to pay the bills, because she is completely shut out of the part of his life that holds most of his ambition and consumes the greater part of his time.

This country is no matriarchy, nor are we in any danger of being governed by women. I repeat here what I have so often said in answer to the question: "Can a women be President of the United States?" At present the answer is emphatically "No." It will be a long time before a woman will have any chance of nomination or election. As things stand today, even if an emotional wave swept a woman into this office, her election would be valueless, as she could never hold her following long enough to put over her program. It is hard enough for a man to do that, with all the traditional schooling men have had; for a woman, it would be impossible because of the age-old prejudice. In government, in business, and in the professions there may be a day when women will be looked upon as persons. We are, however, far from that day as yet.

But, as I said before, if we women ever feel that something serious is threatening our homes and our children's lives, then we may awaken to the political and economic power that is ours. Not to work to elect a woman, but to work for a cause.

There may be a women's crusade against war, which will spread to other countries. I have a feeling that the women of the United States may lead this crusade, because the events of the last few months have left us the one great nation at peace in the world. Some of our South American neighbors have as much potential greatness as we have, but are not yet so far developed. We women may find ourselves in the forefront of a very great struggle some day. I think it will take the form of a determination to put an end to war for all time.

It is obvious that American women cannot do this alone; but throughout the world this might prove a unifying interest for women. When they get to the point of feeling that men's domination is ruining their homes, then they will use whatever weapons lie at hand.

I think we in this country should be prepared for something of this kind. That is why I said that we must become more conscious of ourselves as women and of the force we might wield if we were ever to have a women's cause. We must be careful, however, not to try to wield this force for unimportant things. If we do, it will split up, for we are as individualistic as men in everyday affairs.

The consideration of future possibilities for peace seem to me of paramount importance; but other things of worth enter into our present considerations. Great changes in our civilization have to be considered, and the women are going to weigh the effect of these changes on the home. I believe women can be educated to think about all homes and not so much about their own individual homes. If certain changes have to be made in industry, in our economic life, and in our relationship to one another, the women will probably be more ready to make them if they can see that the changes have a bearing on home life as a whole. That is the only thing that will ever make women come together as a political force.

Women should be able to weigh from this point of view all questions that arise in their local communities. They should vote with that in mind. But when it comes to standing for office or accepting administrative positions, they should realize that their particular interests are not the only ones that will come up, and that, while they may keep their personal interests, they must prove that as persons they can qualify in understanding and in evaluating the interests of the men, too.

Now let us consider women in the other phases of activity where they wish to be persons and wipe out the sex consideration.

Opposition to women who work is usually based on the theory that men have to support families. This, of course, is only saying something that sounds well, for we know that almost all working women are supporting someone besides themselves. And women themselves are partly to blame for the fact that equal pay for equal work has not become an actuality. They have accepted lower pay very often and taken advantage of it occasionally, too, as an excuse for not doing their share of their particular job.

If women want equal consideration, they must prepare themselves to adjust to other people and make no appeals on the ground of sex. Whether women take part in the business or in the political world, this is equally true.

A woman who cannot engage in an occupation and hold it because of her own ability had much better get out of that particular occupation, and do something else, where her ability will count. Otherwise, she is hanging on by her eyebrows, trying to exploit one person after another, and in the end she is going to be unsuccessful and drag down with her other women who are trying to do honest work.

In the business and professional world women have made great advances. In many fields there is opportunity for them to work with men on an equal footing. To be sure, sometimes prejudice on the score of sex will be unfair and a woman will have to prove her ability and do better work than a man to gain the same recognition. If you will look at the picture of Mrs. Bloomer, made a hundred years ago, and think of the women today in factories, offices, executive positions, and professions, that picture alone will symbolize for you the distance women have traveled in less than a century.

In the political field they haven't gone so far. This field has long been exclusively the prerogative of men; but women are on the march. I do not think that it would be possible or desirable to form them into a separate women's political unit. Too many questions arise in government which are not fundamentals that stir women as women. Women will belong to political parties; they will work in them and leave them in much the way that men have done. It will take some great cause that touches their particular interests to unite them as women politically, and they will not remain united once their cause is either won or lost.

I do not look, therefore, for a sudden awakening on their part to a desire for greater participation in the government of the nation, unless circumstances arise that arouse all the citizens of our democracy to a feeling of their individual responsibility for the preservation of this form of government. Otherwise, I think it will be a gradual growth, an evolution.

There is a tendency for women not to support other women when they are either elected or appointed to office. There is no reason, of course, why we should expect any woman to have the support of all women just because of her sex; but neither should women be prejudiced against women as such. We must learn to judge other women's work just as we would judge men's work, to evaluate it and to be sure that we understand and know the facts before we pass judgment.

Considering women as persons must begin with women themselves. They must guard against the temptation to be jealous. That little disparaging phrase one sometimes hears, which suggests that a woman has failed because she is a woman! A woman may fail; but women must begin to impress it upon everyone that a woman's failure to do a job cannot be attributed to her sex, but is due to certain incapacities that might as easily be found in a man.

A good example of the way women tend to follow and play up to a man's opinion came out in a conversation I once overheard. In a hotel corridor a man was loudly proclaiming: "No woman should be Secretary of Labor; she isn't strong enough. These labor guys need someone to knock their heads together." The little woman next to him murmured gentle acquiescence and added, "Miss Perkins has never seemed to me to be a very womanly woman." Of course, she did not know Miss Perkins, and, of course, she was only saying what she thought would please her man; but it was a perfect example of our inability as women to think objectively of other women in business or politics. Her comment had nothing whatsoever to do with the gentleman's assertion that a strong man was needed as Secretary of Labor; but the little woman could think of nothing more disparaging to say at the moment, and she knew it would be an entirely acceptable remark!

There is one place, however, where sex must be a cleavage in daily activity. Women run their homes as women. They live their social lives as women, and they have a right to call upon man's chivalry and to use their wiles to make men do the things that make life's contacts pleasanter in these two spheres. Sex is a weapon and one that women have a right to use, because this is a part of life in which men and women live as men and women and complement, but do not compete with each other. They are both needed in the world of business and politics to bring their different points of view and different methods of doing things to the service of civilization as individuals, with no consideration of sex involved; but in the home and in social life they must emphasize the difference between the sexes because it adds to the flavor of life together.

Some people feel that the entry of women into industry has brought about the fact that there are not enough jobs. But we don't need to eliminate workers, we need to create jobs. We certainly haven't reached a point of satiety when all around us we can see that work needs to be done. Let us, therefore, as women unite for great fundamental causes; but let us insist on doing the work of the world as individuals when we wish to be modern versions of Mrs. Bloomer, and let us function only as women in our homes. We need not feel humiliated if we elect to do only this, for this was our first field of activity, and it will always remain our most important one.

We must be careful, however, to remain in the home not as parasites, but because our abilities lie along the lines of domestic life. Remember that a home requires all the tact and all the executive ability required in any business. The farmer's wife, for instance, must get into her day more work than does the average businessman. Many a woman runs the family home on a slender pay envelope by planning her budget and doing her buying along lines that would make many a failing business succeed.

It will always take all kinds of women to make up a world, and only now and then will they unite their interests. When they do, I think it is safe to say that something historically important will happen.

48

What's the Matter with Women?

A man's world! Is it, or isn't it? Some people say that we American women really rule the United States of America—make our men do what we want—run our houses as we want—lead our lives as we want—run away for vacations when we want—work when we want!

The assertions are so numerous and so positive that I sometimes wonder if it is true that I belong to a group that is really holding the reins of power in our country. I feel quite important and begin to puff myself up like the frog in the fable which you doubtless remember, and then some little thing makes me pause.

Why do I change the menu for dinner because Mr. "Smith" is coming? I never change the menu for Mrs. "Smith." Why do I have good plain chops or steak, baked potatoes and vegetables when my sons come to a meal? I never think about what food my daughter likes. Why do I give away a hat because some gentleman makes a derogatory remark about it? I never do if I am told by Mrs. "Jones" that she does not like my hat.

While I am afraid I shall have to admit that we women may be selfish, and we may do what we want in some things, and we may like our apparent independence, in the long run, I think, way down deep inside of us, there is one thing that cannot be eradicated—we like to please the gentlemen.

This is the basic reason why this is still a man's world. The men like to run the world and only very few women care whether they run it or not. What we women really care about is that our homes shall run smoothly, and our men be well cared for and happy. When we have any energy and ability left over after these two things are accomplished, we use it a number of ways, but somehow or other they always tie up with that basic quality that was planted in us by Mother Nature. We produce and protect the human race, and that fact does certain things to us. We will fight for a law which we can see affects the people we care about, but we leave the great field of lawmaking and its interpretation and administration very largely to the men.

People complain bitterly that the American home is being destroyed. It is perfectly true that many of the industries which kept women busy in the home have been removed from it. A visit to Mount Vernon, where Martha Washington ruled while her husband freed the United States from Great Britain, will soon show you that Martha Washington was needed every day to manage a number of industries, but she did this because it served the needs of her people. Without those industries, the happiness and comfort and safety of

Liberty 18 (May 3, 1941): 12–13.

those she loved and who lived around her would have disappeared. She was preserving life and love.

Today many of those home industries are run by men in factories, and some of the women who used to work on these industries at home go out to work in the factories, but the reasons for doing so are just the same as they used to be. These women need what they make for the same reasons, namely, security in the home, health and happiness.

Religion, from which so many people derive the courage which keeps them strong in the face of disaster, and gives them strength enough to go on in a world which seems difficult to cope with—religion is left almost entirely to the direction of men. Few of the denominations allow women to lead the people in a spiritual way, because this is still a man's world and men must control the important factors in the lives of the human race.

And who can doubt that the moral laws were framed by men? They have been accepted, until very recently, without any question by women, and always, I think, they have been more liberal and the penalties have been lighter for transgression where the man is concerned than where the woman is concerned. In the very nature of things, men have wanted to set the women on a moral pedestal because it is so very useful to the men to have it that way. The women must hold the family together. The men can be forgiven because it is not really necessary for them to hold family life intact. The race and its preservation belong to the women; therefore put them on a pedestal and they will have to carry the burden.

Lately some rifts have come in this old theory; but, on the whole, man-made codes of morals and conventions, built up to preserve society, are all to the advantage of the men. Because woman's instinct to preserve the race is so strong, they recognize that many of these rules are fundamentally good, and again they let the gentlemen have their way.

Most governments, no matter what type or in what place, are in the hands of men. I am generalizing, of course, because there are examples of women rulers in history, and we have known of some women who were preachers, legislators, and government officials. On the whole, however, government is in the hands of the men.

Through government, our relationships with each other are defined and carried out, not only in our own country but between nations. Sometimes it is said that if women got together and took a determined stand we could do away with war. They tell us we could stop having children, we could refuse to allow the production of armaments, etc., etc.

War is something, however, that has its roots far back. Nothing happens suddenly and without cause, and when war comes, it is too late to stop it. The children are born and there are always enough people to produce armaments.

War is something which has to be done away with by first changing the course of the relationships between individuals, building up an entirely new method of approach which shall be achieved first within groups and then perhaps later between nations.

The reason why women do not come together in an effort to do this is that they really have very little ability to control the factors which lead to war. They can be an influence, but that is as far as they can go for the present, because they prefer still to leave in the hands of the men and in the minds of the men the avenues which control economic situations, spiritual development, and education.

There are great women scientists, and there have been great women doctors, writers, poets, artists, and yet over and over again I have heard women say that a man doctor could inspire them with more confidence than a woman doctor, which is part of the fundamental attitude of women toward men. They accept, with hardly an effort to combat it, the doctrine that most creative ability springs from a man's forehead!

A woman always feels that she must build up a man's confidence in himself as long as he is "her man." No sacrifice of herself is too great to prove her love for her menfolk, and she assumes quite naturally that he is the leader and controls the world.

A good example of this is the attitude taken when the depression hit us about "working wives." Suddenly their place was in the kitchen! Some said we would have no unemployment if all women stayed in the home, where they belonged. These statements were made quite without reference to the fact of whether there would be a home to stay in or a male to assume responsibility for support!

Many women realized that there was a basic fallacy in all the arguments and fought the dismissal of women from gainful occupations on the broad grounds of the need for their work and the right of all individuals who want to work to do so. They believed that work generates work and that women able and willing to work should not be barred or wasted.

It was never suggested, however, at any point that men without dependents or having an income to live on should be removed from the labor market. A fact which I felt proved the basic argument that work produces work and also that the movement was just a part of the old "the men rule the world" idea!

It isn't that women haven't the brains or the ability or the physical strength to dominate. It is that they want the world the way it is and for the most part are content. What will happen when they really want something different, I hesitate to say, because I have a firm belief in the ability and power of women to achieve the things they want to achieve. It is a man's world now, however, and will be just as long as the women want it to be!

49

American Women in the War

Our women are serving actively in many ways in this war, and they are doing a grand job on both the fighting front and the home front.

Some 12,000 of our Army and Navy nurses are now overseas, taking care of our sick and wounded fighting men. I have seen some of these nurses in Great Britain, in many of the islands of the Pacific, in New Zealand and Australia, and I have the greatest respect and admiration for them. They take everything in the spirit of soldiers, keeping their troubles to themselves. They suffer from homesickness, they experience the hardships of severe climates and the actual perils of war, yet they remain ever cheerful. Their smiles are wonderful medicine for the men they care for.

I recall vividly some of the nurses' barracks I visited on my recent Pacific trip. Roofs constructed of native matting or of woven palms made good nesting places for rats and insects. In many places the climate was so damp that I doubt if the women ever put on a garment which was entirely dry. Some of the nurses lived for months at a time up near the combat zone, where it was impossible ever to get a hot bath. Add to all this the hazards of air raids and you have a stern test of hardihood. Yet I never heard a single nurse complain.

At home, many women have become nurses in civilian hospitals. With so many of our regular nurses at the far corners of the earth, these women have a heavy load to carry: they are just as much a part of the war effort as though they were actually at the front. Their spirit is illustrated by an 18-year-old student nurse whom I met on a train not long ago. She looked so young that I wondered if she realized what hard work she was embarking on. She assured me she knew quite well it would be very difficult; but she was determined to have a profession and be a useful member of her community.

Then there are the many women in our military services. Commanding officers feel that, in many cases, they have performed their duties more efficiently than the men whom they have freed for active service.

So far the Wacs have been the only ones allowed overseas. This seems to me ridiculous. The restriction on the activities of our other women's military services is not due to any feeling of Congress or the military authorities that women cannot do the job. It is due, rather, to a false chivalry, which insists that women be protected from war hazards and hardships, even against their own wishes. Some women accept this point of view, but I believe most of us would rather share more fully in the experiences of our men.

I think this idea of sheltering women is a shortsighted policy, since one of the great postwar difficulties will be the readjustment of men and women

The Reader's Digest 44 (January 1944): 42–44.

who have been long separated. That readjustment will be easier if both have experienced a similar discipline and acquired a similar attitude toward life.

Besides those in uniform, over 2,300,000 of our women have gone into war industries; 1,900,000 of them are doing regular factory work. Many of these workers feel they are not being allowed to produce as much as they could. I think their dissatisfaction would be remedied if we had labor-management committees in all war industries throughout the country, so that their ideas and grievances could obtain a hearing.

Some of the married women workers are not doing their best because we haven't taken into consideration their personal problems. Their homes must still go on. Their children must be cared for. Day nurseries are now being established, but they are not always properly organized. Sometimes they are not located conveniently for the mothers—I was told of one nursery which was five blocks from a bus stop, which meant that a woman had to walk 20 blocks every day. To a tired woman carrying a child, those blocks seem very long.

Working mothers also have difficult shopping problems. There are two workable solutions. One is an organized shopping service in every block, so that a woman may leave her entire order for the day with one person, and pick the packages up in the evening near her home. The other is to have certain shops in every neighborhood reserve a supply of staple foods from sale until the women return from work.

The task of buying food and cooking it for the family would be made far lighter if we adopted the British restaurant idea. In England the municipality and the Ministry of Food cooperate to set up restaurants which provide one good three-course meal a day at a reasonable price and without ration points.

These matters require detailed community organization. But while we have carefully organized our civilian defense services—many of which we may never need these—things which we *do* need have too often been completely neglected.

The many thousands of women who are not doing any unusual work, but are simply running their houses quietly and efficiently, are contributing more to the war effort than they themselves realize. The woman who meets war difficulties with a smile, who does her best with rationing and other curtailments, who writes her man overseas the kind of letters he must have to carry him through successfully, is making a great contribution to this difficult period. If, in addition to this work at home, a woman is giving her services to any of the volunteer organizations, our hats must be off to her.

Undoubtedly there are some women who are leading the same sort of life today that they have always led; but I think they must be having a difficult time finding companionship. For the vast majority of women in this country, life has changed. Their thoughts and their hearts are concerned with what is happening in North Africa, Italy, the Southwest Pacific and countless other places in the world. They are only content as they feel they are contributing something toward the speedier ending of the war and a better chance for their particular men in the world of the future.

50

Woman's Place After the War

"Will women want to keep their jobs after the war is over?" When I asked Miss Mary Anderson of the Bureau of Women in Industry, she told me it all boils down to economic necessity. Married women usually keep their jobs only when they have real need for money at home. This, of course, does not mean that women who take up some kind of work as a career will not stay in that work if they like it, whether they are married or single.

Let us analyze this whole question of women who work. Our attitude in this country has always been that any individual is more worthwhile if he pays his way in the world. We even have a little contempt for a woman who is nothing but an ornament.

Of late years since we have counted success so largely in the amount of money that people earned, it has become more and more natural for women to feel that if they actually were working to their full capacity, they must have recognition in the same coin as the male members of their families, or they would not be considered successful. An ever-growing number of young women in every walk of life are taking jobs as they finish school or college, but *the main job of the average woman in our country still is to marry and have a home and children.*

I surmise that the major occupation of a married woman in this country at the close of the war will be what it has always been—the care of the family as long as the family requires her care. There will always be exceptions, of course, as when a woman must take on the burden of work outside the home to supplement what the man earns, or, if the man cannot work, even must assume the place of the head of the family and earn a living for the household.

Many women, because of the urge to help their country and their own men during the war, will have acquired skills—skills which they will be able to use in the future. But I do not think they will use them if they have families and homes calling them back to a different kind of existence.

Recently, I saw women who drove long distances and worked long hours in a shipyard in New England. Most of them had made temporary arrangements for the care of their homes and children, and were working with their husbands if their husbands had not gone to war, so as to pay the mortgage on the farm, buy certain things long coveted which would make life easier in the future, or lay aside some money which would give the children some special advantages. They knew the work was temporary and feared they would never have the opportunity to achieve certain desires if they did not take advantage of the present need for workers.

Click 7 (August 1944): 17, 19.

Women's Work Prospects Depend Upon Job Availability

The first question that will be faced in the postwar period is simply to what extent jobs are available. *The first obligation of government and business is to see that every man who is employable has a job, and that every woman who needs work has it.* A woman does not need a job if she has a home and a family requiring her care and a member of the household is earning an adequate amount of money to maintain a decent standard of living. If, however, there is a margin of energy left in men or women and they want to put it into bettering their standard of living, it seems to me that they should have the opportunity. We should struggle to gear our economy to a place where we can give all people who desire to work, whether full-time or part-time, a chance to work on something which gives them creative satisfaction.

From my point of view, there is no justification whatsoever for labor leaders to oppose the employment of women at the present time wherever they are needed. Foresight is valuable, but foresight that dreads to meet a present situation because there may be some difficulty in the future shows a lack of confidence in the intelligence and ability of human beings to cope with new situations.

There is one point, however, upon which I think labor leaders have a right to insist: *women should not come into any labor group and allow themselves to be used at present or in the future as a body for keeping down the wages of men, either because they can live on less or because they, being unorganized, have never understood the need to stand together with any group in order to help the group.*

A girl living at home and having few expenses may be able to accept, let us say, $10 a week for her work, using that money only for her own personal needs. Her employer will say to a man, "We can use girls in this job, therefore we do not need you; but if you want the job, you can have it at $10 a week." If the man can find no other job, he may be forced to take the one for $10 a week, which means that his family will live at a very low standard. And this will be the fault of the girl who did not understand that she was part of a big labor group and that she had to consider the good of the whole body.

So, I think labor leaders have a right to insist that women, as long as they are in the labor market, should be part of the organized labor movement and should not permit themselves to be used as competition for men to the advantage of unscrupulous employers.

Children of Working Mothers Must Have Adequate Care

A certain number of women, both in the professions and in skilled and unskilled trades, may not marry. But if they do, they must either subordinate their desires for work outside the home, or make arrangements which will be adequate for proper care of the home and children.

Rarely can anyone replace a mother, but there are some women who are not gifted with children and resent having to do the work of the home. In that case, it may sometimes be better to find someone who loves to do that job, and release the mother for a different kind of work. She will probably be a better mother and a better companion for her husband when she is home is she does work she enjoys. However, such cases are rare.

As I said in the beginning, whether women remain in the labor market or not will be, as it always has been, mainly a question of economic necessity.

51

Women Have Come a Long Way

As I look back over a rather long life I am impressed with the great changes that I have witnessed in the status of women. I was brought up by my grandmother from the time I was eight years old, so perhaps I see the differences in a somewhat more exaggerated form than some of my contemporaries who were never under the direct influence of a member of that earlier generation. To my grandmother it was unthinkable that a girl should go to work unless she was destitute or at least really impoverished; and that she should wish to go to college seemed preposterous. But I imagine that most women who were brought up at the time I was, and in roughly the same sort of surroundings, will share my sense of the contrasts that have come about.

I learned to ride horseback, but I rode side-saddle. I can remember the excitement there was over girls who rode bicycles wearing bloomers, and how outrageous many people thought them. We went bathing in bathing suits with skirts, and long black stockings; propriety demanded that we be completely covered. And some girls even wore hats in bathing to shield them from the sun, for it was considered important to preserve the whiteness of one's skin; young ladies would have been dismayed at getting the healthy look of tan that today they deliberately acquire in the South in the winter, and wherever they are in the summer.

At eighteen I was introduced to New York Society. I was a frightened young girl who had spent three years at a finishing school in Europe and had practically no friends, either male or female, in this country. There was still a Four Hundred in New York Society. If you belonged you were asked to the "right parties" and if you didn't belong you were not asked. In those days it took not only money but a really concentrated campaign to get recognition if you came as an unknown in New York. I remember a few lovely girls who took the city by storm, arriving from other parts of the country, but either they were great beauties or had a reputation for having brains and knew some of the "right" people to introduce them. People were just beginning to accept the fact that a Miss Livingston could marry a Mr. Mills from California; but on the whole New York Society was compact and chary of outsiders.

It was conceded that girls of Society families had an obligation to do some kind of charitable work, but very, very few of them took money-earning jobs; and if they "had to work," as the phrase of the day went, they were largely limited to becoming teachers, trained nurses, social workers, or librarians. Miss Elizabeth Marbury once told me how horrified the New York Society of her young days was when she had to go to work and began to

Harper's Magazine 201 (October 1950): 74–76.

represent artists and build a talent office. A girl whose family was on a lower income level could be a clerk in a store or work in an office, but generally speaking she did this only so long as it was an absolute economic necessity; male pride and general public opinion frowned on any woman who worked outside the home if she could manage to avoid it. Not many executive positions were held by women and they had hardly begun to be recognized in the professions. That has come only after a long, hard fight; and few young things today have any idea of what they owe to the women who pioneered in higher education and in working in the professional fields.

We still heard with amusement and horror in the early nineteen-hundreds of the early fighters for suffrage who had worn trousers and walked around the streets of New York in them. Women were doing a great many things for the first time, but most of them were content to be housekeepers and mothers who stayed in the home—where they often worked very hard indeed—and many became pretty Society butterflies, spoiled and ruled by their husbands.

A change came with World War I. For large numbers of women who had to go to work when their husbands were in the service found that they liked the new freedom and continued in their jobs after the war was over; the percentage of women working for wages outside the home jumped upward.

My mother had been well educated for a girl of her generation and she took a great interest in my education, but in those days a solid foundation of learning and training in the ability to think were less highly regarded then the social graces which made you attractive and charming in Society. I learned to speak French fluently before I learned to speak English, but my arithmetic was learned by rote without the slightest understanding of why certain things produced certain answers. I learned the whole of the first four books of Euclid by heart, and I have never understood what use that was in preparation for the life that I was expected to live in the future. Of course, I have had quite a different life from the one that my mother and grandmother envisioned for me; I was certainly not consciously prepared for it.

I was fifteen when I came in contact, in Europe, with the first women I had ever known who were really intellectually emancipated, and I found this experience extremely stimulating. The Boer War was being fought out and the Dreyfus case was still being argued. I heard the rights and wrongs of such public issues discussed at length and heatedly, in fact with passion—something I had never heard at home. In my grandmother's home politics were never mentioned and I think she was rather ashamed to acknowledge that even by marriage anything so contaminating as a government official was related to the family.

But if I was not brought up to be useful or to think of the obligations to society that must be recognized by a conscientious citizen of a democracy, I was nevertheless given a very free rein in my intellectual development along many lines. The library in our country house, as in the city house we lived in, was filled with books gathered by my grandfather, who had had a special bent toward theology, though apparently he never had any inclination to become a minister. I never wanted to read the books on theology (though I remember shedding tears over the illustrations in the Doré Bible); but other books on those shelves—the classics, biographies, travel, novels, stories about life anywhere of any kind—fed the interests of my childhood and helped to show me, eventually, why so many women were beginning to fight for equality in the political and social world which up to that time had seemed of very little importance to me.

I had my first contact with the suffrage movement rather late, and consider myself lucky to have heard Anna Howard Shaw speak and to have known Carrie Chapman Catt before she was widely recognized as the great leader of women in the struggle for equal political rights.

As a result of the shift of public opinion which these women helped to bring about, there have been far-reaching amendments during the past fifty years to the laws which touch on the rights of women. These vary in different parts of the world and, for that matter, in different states in our own country. The old Blue Laws which were accepted throughout New England at one time may still be on the statute books, but even where such antiquated legislation remains it is completely ignored, and by and large women seem to be considered as equals before the law in the United States. Of late there has been a great agitation to pass an equal rights amendment; but I think that if one looks over the reforms of the past generation one must decide that it would be easier in our particular situation to change such state laws as seem to discriminate against women than to pass a federal amendment.

Women have now become an integral part of nearly all the trade unions, and it is interesting to note that some of the unions in the industries which employ largely women are as good as any there are.

In family life, too, the change has been great. Fifty years ago women had to resort to subtlety if they wished to exert influence; now their influence is exerted openly and accepted by husband and children. Fifty years ago no young girl had an apartment of her own while she was single; "Mrs. Grundy" frowned on that. Today no one questions the right of an adult woman to have her own home.

In my lifetime I have seen women accepted as doctors, surgeons, psychiatrists, lawyers, architects, and even, during the war, as mechanics on the assembly line. I remember the day when John Golden said in the White House that women lacked the power to be creative and that there had never been any great creative women artists. I took that up seriously with him later, and contended that this might seem to be true in our time, but had not always been true in the past; and that if it was true now, this was not because women lacked ability but because they lacked opportunity. I think that today we must realize that in the past generation we have developed many very able writers and painters and some very able sculptors among the women of this country and other countries. Modern life moves very quickly and the distractions and multitudinous occupations that are thrust upon women tend to make the development of an artist's creative talents more difficult than in the past; but in spite of these outward circumstances the urge to create is so strong that I think we are going to find more and more women expressing themselves not only through the bearing and rearing of children but through the creative arts.

One thing that strikes me particularly today is the way in which women are accepting responsibility in creating the pattern for the new states. Take India, for example. I have seen in the United Nations a women delegate, Madame Pandit, the sister of the Prime Minister, lead her delegation—the only woman to occupy such a position.

I have been impressed, too, with the number of women of charm and ability who have come to the United Nations with good backgrounds of work in various fields that fit them for their duties in that body. I think at once of Madame Lefoucheaux of France, who was chairman of the last meeting of the Commission on the Status of Women; Miss Bowie, who represented the United Kingdom on the Human Rights Commission; Madame Hansa Mehta of India, also on this commission; and many women who have acted as advisers to the harried delegates and brought us the information without which some of us would have found it very difficult to carry on the work confronting us in fields in which we had had little or no experience. Even ten years ago, if there had been such a body as the United Nations, it would hardly have been possible to find women sitting as delegates, and certainly it would have been considered doubtful whether the United States would ever send a woman as a delegate. Now it sends a woman alternate as well!

Perhaps the position of women in the United Nations is the best example of the fact that they have graduated from exclusion from business and the professions to almost complete acceptance and equality; and that they are now generally treated as virtually on a par with men in the political world at home and abroad. Some nations are slower in granting this recognition than others, but the trend is unmistakable. It is toward complete equality.

I think it might still be said that if a woman wants really to succeed she must do better than a man, for she is under more careful scrutiny; but this is practically the only handicap under which women now labor in almost any field of endeavor.

52

What Are the Motives for a Woman Working When She Does Not Have To, for Income?

What makes a woman work when she doesn't have to earn a living? The simple answer that you have to earn so many dollars to buy food and clothing and shelter, I think is not really very important for obviously if the money for these necessities has to be earned in one way or another it must be done, but as a matter of fact every human being has to earn his living or life has no savor. You may be fortunate to have the dollars you need for existence, but to earn a living means a great deal more than that.

To earn a living a human being must have a sense that he is making a creative contribution to the world around him. And I believe that the standards and the values which women have, probably have a great deal to do with the actual level of civilization attained by different countries in different areas of the world. The woman who is satisfied to earn her living by being man's plaything—spending her time making sure that she is beautiful and physically appealing—is certainly earning her living, but she is putting a rather low standard of value on her achievement. In the areas of the world where, because of custom or religion, women have been more or less the slaves of men, many women earn their living just this way. But I have always felt that the poorer the situation was, the more real self-respect the women could have because there was work to be done in the household and they could feel that they were a working part of the life of their small world. Women in rich homes where the men have all the power, often create, in spite of the handicaps surrounding them, real and important roles within their restrictions so that they can feel they have earned their living on a high level, but it is a little simpler and more direct in the areas of the world where women are freer and where they really use all of their faculties, for them to make a greater contribution and gain satisfaction in more ways than one.

A woman earns her living when she has children, when she uses all her feminine wiles to attract and manage the menfolk of her family. But in our own world she can earn a living in so many direct ways too. And she can perhaps get even more satisfaction from competition which is not limited to the age old competition for the attention and consideration of a man. Many a woman with no need to earn the wherewithal for an existence and with no need to justify her existence by bearing children, still has children because they

Unpublished article, August, 1945.

fulfill an instinct held within her heart, which was implanted there for the preservation of the human race.

But some women never have children. Are they not to have the satisfaction that comes with earning a living? Women, as well as men, were given minds to use and the ability to develop skills in various ways. I believe this is so primarily because, in the scheme of the universe, for real satisfaction every human being must earn his living. If you have gifts, natural gifts, and you never develop them, you are as guilty as the man in the Bible who wrapped his talent in a napkin and buried it so he could return to his Master what his Master had given him.

The fact that in our particular civilization the contribution of a human being is often gauged by the money which he can earn is probably one of the reasons why both men and women who do not have to earn a living still want to prove that what they do is worthy of receiving the reward by which success ordinarily is judged. In my young years I lived among people who felt that it was largely a man's business to provide the wherewithal of existence and the woman's business was circumscribed by making a home and by helping the man in any way required to make his life a success. And yet though these standards were set before me and I lived a good many years by them, I remember with great satisfaction the first time someone offered me money to do a job. It was a teaching job. I had earned a little by writing articles before and each time I was actually paid I think I gained in self-confidence, in the belief that since my contribution was being recognized in the way that was ordinarily accepted, then I must be doing something of value. Later I came to think that if you did things which ordinarily were paid for, you must ask for what you had earned and ask for the full price, since it was not fair to enter into competition in a way which might lower the price standard for other people who had to earn a living.

There is no question in my mind that many people who never earn a dollar still earn their living, but I believe that it is really valuable to every human being to know that he can earn the wherewithal on which to exist and even to cover the existence of others, if necessary. It gives confidence and a sense of achievement in the market place which, in our particular civilization, is almost essential to self respect.

This is the answer, I think, to the question with which we started this article. There are many more things one can say but the important thing is that each one of us must justify our existence, and we do that which we feel really contributes to our self-confidence and self respect, and in doing it probably achieve more than we would otherwise.

53

My Advice to the Next First Lady

Whichever party wins this month's election, the next First Lady will be a young woman. And she will find herself in a position that is often extremely difficult as well as extremely interesting. Her official role, the only role required of her as the President's wife, is that of official hostess for the United States Government. But, of course, she does have to confront a wide range of unofficial responsibilities. What actually is expected of the First Lady? What will she find on entering the White House? Her first task, of course, must be undertaken before the inauguration: She will visit the White House, acquaint herself with the second and third floors, which are set aside as the private apartments of the President and his family, and decide how to allot the rooms to meet the demands of her own family and what changes she wants to make in the rearrangement of furniture.

She does not have to bring with her any furniture, china, glass, silverware or linen. All these are provided in abundance. But she is free to use her own fancy and her own taste in the arrangement of the family rooms. There are, however, certain traditions which every First Lady has been hesitant about breaking. For instance, one treats the Lincoln bedroom with respect and is reluctant to move the furniture. The Oval Room, which is used by the President as his study, reflects the interests of the incumbent in its books and pictures, but the general arrangement will be much the same.

There is a storehouse of White House furniture and an allowance for buying what is needed by the new First Lady, so there is no need to bring personal belongings. All of us, however, have special things we like to live with and any family will move these into their new surroundings.

It is also important that the President's wife know the kind of wardrobe, at least in its basic essentials, required in this new and exacting position.

Inaugural day is full of activity and is tiring. The inauguration itself is followed by an official parade, a luncheon at the White House, a reception in the late afternoon and the inaugural balls in the evening. The fairly warm dress and coat—for it is cold in Washington in January—may be worn right through the day until time to dress for dinner. But—and I am reminded of one horrible occasion—it is wise to arrange to have a complete replacement of wardrobe waiting for you at the White House.

One unforgettable inauguration day my husband and I drove in an open car through a downpour and arrived at the White House with our clothes sodden. To make it worse for me, the dye in my hat had run down my face in a

Redbook 116 (November 1960): 18–21, 95–96.

startling fashion. My only relief was that the dye did not touch my hair and have any effect on it!

The President and his wife go out rarely in the evenings. Most of their formal social life is confined to the White House. A basic minimum wardrobe would comprise three or four formal evening dresses, half a dozen afternoon dresses, a couple of suits and a few silk dresses with lightweight coats for the early spring.

One of the most exhausting duties of the First Lady is to stand in reception lines, often for two hours at a time. In order to survive this it is most helpful to abandon fashion for the occasion and wear low-heeled shoes. I still suffer from what I call my "White House" feet.

It is important to be more conscious than ever before in your life that your accessories must all match, that they belong with the dress or suit that you are wearing. For though you may theoretically be prepared for the fact, you will still discover with a shock of dismay that henceforth you are not a private person. Every move you make will be photographed, every piece of clothing will be watched with a critical eye and there will be someone to write immediately and caustically if the handbag did not match the shoes or the necklace was wrong for the dress. You will feel that you are no longer clothing yourself; you are dressing a public monument.

It is assumed that the apartments on the second and third floors of the White House are a place where the family can live its private life. But even with the most strenuous efforts it is almost impossible to achieve a truly private life. You must be prepared for the fact that you will rarely during your occupancy of the White House sit down to a family meal, whether breakfast, luncheon or dinner. There are always people with whom the President needs to talk, people for whom the brief appointment time during the day is not sufficient.

My Aunt Edith, who was First Lady while Theodore Roosevelt was President, told me that it was a terrible job to bring up small children in the White House. People made too much fuss over them and spoiled them and it was a losing battle to try to keep them disciplined and without self-consciousness. When my daughter, Anna, left the White House she said she knew it would be much better for her small children. Only the day before, her son had said, "Why do people stare at us through the fence? Are we different in some way?"

The children risk something more grave than the danger of too much publicity and too much attention. That is having too little of their father's time and attention. There are simply not enough hours in the day. The President must make grave personal sacrifices when he becomes a public servant, and one is that there is little leisure for his children and their problems.

Along with the publicity attending the First Lady's movements and the discovery that even mealtimes are no longer an occasion for the family to be together in a simple way and the problem of coping with the excessive attention paid the children, she will discover two other real losses in her personal life. The first is the fact that it is not judicious for her to carry on her old friendships. From now on each person she sees acquires a fictitious prominence, meaning is read into a simple walk or a luncheon or a chat over a tea table. "Is this woman trying to make it easy for her husband to meet the President through the First Lady?"

This applies with even greater force to one's foreign friends. A White House wife must observe protocol, and it is impossible for her to call on people in diplomatic circles, even though they may be old and warm friends, more than a limited number of times. The moment it is noticed that one group or one individual has an advantage over another, there is jealousy and there may even be serious international repercussions. You must remember that from now on anything you do, however innocent, however trivial, is blown up to huge proportions by publicity and speculation. Whether you know it or not someone, somewhere, is watching you.

The most serious loss, however, is the fact that the President is the most occupied man in the world. His attention is claimed by every quarter hour of the day. So many appointments crowd his time that much of his serious work must be done at night. And with momentous issues at stake, with his thoughts necessarily claimed by basic and far-reaching decisions, he inevitably has less time for personal relationships. This is the biggest sacrifice which the First Lady has to make but she must be prepared to do it, and cheerfully.

No two First Ladies have ever coped with their problems in the same way. It would be absurd to try, for they are all different people, living under different circumstances.

My own personal activities outside the White House, which caused some comment while I was First Lady, were an effort to bring my husband firsthand accounts of conditions and places that he could not observe personally. If he could have made these trips himself, mine, of course, would not have been required. But those were exceptional days and his were exceptional circumstances.

While he and I always discussed my impressions, the result was merely the addition of more data for his consideration and not an attempt to shape his opinion. That was not the job of a President's wife.

Varied as the tastes and interests of each First Lady are bound to be, the general routine of running the White House remains fairly static through all changes in administration. Usually the first duty in the morning is to see the housekeeper and go over the menus; then see the head usher to tell him what people are coming or going, what transportation must be arranged for the family and for visitors; and finally discuss with her social secretary those interminable seating charts for any kind of party which is to be given.

All this seems formidable, particularly for a person who has had no experience with protocol, but here the First Lady will find able and trained assistance at hand. The State Department's official in charge of protocol is prepared with advice on the seating charts and he also informs the First Lady of what indispensable official entertaining must be done.

My suggestion to the next First Lady would be to get in touch with this State Department official before moving to the White House to get the whole situation clear.

In fact, if the head usher and the major-domo can take over all the arrangements for inauguration day, it will make life much easier for the new incumbent and his wife, for whom the day will be full enough without being cluttered by perplexing details of protocol.

The White House belongs to the people of the United States. This point must never be forgotten. Before long the new official hostess will feel that she is being bombarded with requests to receive large groups of women. Practically every feminine group meeting in Washington asks to be received, and usually the women who attend men's conventions. This is a constant swallower of one's time and a drain on energy, but it seems to me that whenever possible such a request should be granted.

To give two or even three afternoons a week to receiving large numbers of strangers is extremely difficult at first. In the past, anyone leaving a card at the White House expected to be invited to a reception. Two things I learned from these functions. One was to stop the receiving line for five minutes at the end of an hour and sit down quietly, even though people were waiting restively in the East Room and on the staircase. At least when they passed me I would be able to see them and greet them with some spark of intelligence instead of becoming entirely glassy-eyed. There were times when I did not stop the line, and greeted some of my closest friends without even being aware that they were there and that I had gone through the motions of shaking hands with them.

The other thing I learned was that the people whom one receives in this way are only too aware that the White House is theirs and they keep a stern eye on detail. Mrs. Hoover told me that she had received a sharp letter of complaint because of a darn in a curtain, and people reproached me because they got dust on their white gloves from the stair railing. If I stayed at home, these people implied, I could keep an eye on the housekeeping. I explained—but rather helplessly—that the railing is dusted every half hour.

The degree of formality or informality of what may possibly be termed family life is determined by the wishes of the incumbent. My husband disliked dressing for dinner when we were not entertaining formally, and we used the small dining room, as a rule. In fact, we never used the big state dining room except for formal parties.

Perhaps I carried informality too far, and I know that I often shocked the head usher. I was told gently that the President's wife was not supposed to run the elevator for herself, but this I obstinately insisted on doing. I am inclined to believe that the young woman who becomes the White House hostess will not bother much, either, about restrictive rules of this kind.

Another thing that would be helpful for the First Lady would be to meet as soon as possible the young military and naval aides who are at her disposal in filling out dinner parties. She has ten—or used to have—on whom she can call at any time. Nothing, I imagine, short of death or sudden emergency excuses an aide from accepting a White House invitation.

And while she is becoming acquainted with the people who are available for social occasions, it would be wise to meet and know, as far as possible, all the individuals who make up the complicated staff of the White House. If they feel that they can speak to her, it will relieve a great deal of friction, which is bound to arise from time to time no matter how expert the housekeeper may be.

Sooner or later the First Lady is going to have to contend with the problem of gifts, masses of them, and of the strangest variety, which come from people whom she will rarely know or even have heard of. Sometimes these are bona fide, sometimes not. Occasionally a gift will be followed after a couple of weeks or months by a demand for payment. I found that the best way to cope with the situation was to have bins built in a large closet. Here we placed everything that came in as a gift, arranged by months, which we kept for a year as a safeguard against a demand for payment.

But there is no safeguard, alas, against gossip, personal criticism and, more painful, the criticism of one's husband and children. There is no way to clear the record, to straighten out the facts, to stop the flood of rumor and conjecture and malice that breaks like a wave over anyone in public life. If you cannot stop it or alter it, then it seems to me wisest, and least painful, to try to remain as ignorant of it as possible. Of course, injustice to one's children and one's husband is much harder to bear than criticism of oneself, but none of it is pleasant to bear.

The job of the President's wife is in many ways quite an onerous one, restricting her private life and turning her slightest act, her most trivial word, into a public action.

It is also tremendously interesting. One is living at the very heart of great events. One constantly meets some of the most fascinating and valuable people in the world. The next First Lady can never be sure what excitement or what unforeseen problems each day will bring. The only thing, in fact, that she can be sure of is that her job will never be an easy one.

Part E
Education and Problems Confronting Youth

54

Good Citizenship:
The Purpose of Education

What is the purpose of education? This question agitates scholars, teachers, statesmen, every group, in fact, of thoughtful men and women. The conventional answer is the acquisition of knowledge, the reading of books, and the learning of facts. Perhaps because there are so many books and the branches of knowledge in which we can learn facts are so multitudinous today, we begin to hear more frequently that the function of education is to give children a desire to learn and to teach them how to use their minds and where to go to acquire facts when their curiosity is aroused. Even more all-embracing than this is the statement made not long ago, before a group of English headmasters, by the Archbishop of York, that "the true purpose of education is to produce citizens."

If this is the goal—and in a democracy it would seem at least an important part of the ultimate achievement—then we must examine our educational system from a new point of view.

I am going to ask you to go back with me for a minute some thirty years or more and think of the changes wrought by the last few years.

At that time Theodore Roosevelt's example was for the first time awakening in many young men of America the feeling that their citizenship meant a little more than the privilege of living under the Stars and Stripes, criticizing the conditions of government and the men responsible for its policies and activities, enjoying such advantages as there might be under it, and, if necessary, dying for it in a war which they had had no share in bringing on or in trying to avert.

Theodore Roosevelt was teaching by precept and example that men owed something at all times, whether in peace or in war, for the privilege of citizenship and that the burden rested equally on rich and poor. He was saying that, no matter what conditions existed, the blame lay no more heavily on the politician and his machine controlling city, State, or nation, than on the shoulders of the average citizen who concerned himself so little with his government that he allowed men to stay in power in spite of his dissatisfaction because he was too indifferent to exert himself to get better men in office.

So young men of all kinds were hearing of a "service" which did not mean being a sailor or a soldier, a doctor or a minister, the only professions in which the word "service" had heretofore had a meaning! Thus began to be spread abroad the idea that "a service" was owed to the country in peace, and

Pictorial Review, April 1930: 4, 94, 97

that this could only be rendered satisfactorily when every citizen took an interest in good government.

As girls went in those days, I suppose my own education was fairly typical, and I confess with some shame that at the age of twenty, when asked by an Englishwoman how our government functioned, I was as completely floored as if she had asked me to describe the political events on the moon! I had heard the men in the family mention political happenings, but it was not a subject of general or frequent conversation in our presence.

Women did not vote and were not expected to be interested. Besides there was something dark and sinister about politics, and it was more respectable not to know politicians or political methods too well. Business might necessitate some dealings with these rather inferior and nefarious beings, but the general attitude of the righteous was like that of a high-minded and upright citizen of New York City who once remarked to me that a certain political organization was undoubtedly corrupt, but he preferred (tho belonging to an opposite political party) to keep this wicked organization in power as "you paid for what you wanted and were sure to get it, whereas reform administrations were not so reliable in this ability to 'deliver the goods'!"

I do not think I am unfair in saying that in most secondary schools, at least, the teachers of American history in those days laid more emphasis on the battle of Bunker Hill than they did on the obligations of citizenship which the children before them would soon be assuming. And this was largely because they could not teach what they did not understand, and few of them knew or cared what these obligations might be.

Gradually a change has come about. More young men and more young women (since the latter have had the vote) are doing political work. And even if they do not hold political office they have felt the need to understand their own government. In our schools are now given courses in civics, government, economics, current events. Very few children are as ignorant as I was. But there still remains a vast amount to be done before we accomplish our first objective—informed and intelligent citizens, and, secondly, bring about the realization that we are all responsible for the trend of thought and the action of our times.

How shall we arrive at these objectives? We think of course of history as a first means of information. Not the history which is a mere recital of facts, dates, wars, and kings, but a study of the life and growth of other nations, in which we follow the general moral, intellectual, and economic development through the ages, noting what brought about the rise and fall of nations and what were the lasting contributions of peoples now passed away to the development of the human family and the world as a whole.

Then we come down to our own history, observing the characteristics and the backgrounds of the people who founded our nation and those who have come to us since; the circumstances of pioneer life and the rapid industrial development. We trace the reasons for present-day attitudes of mind and for the establishment of customs and points of view which make up the rather elusive and yet unmistakable thing known as the "American spirit." We study the men in our history who have really made a constructive contribution, and those who have held us back, in order that we may know what qualities of mind and heart formed the characters which have left a mark on their time.

Gradually from this study certain facts emerge. A nation must have leaders, men who have the power to see a little farther, to imagine a little better life than the present. But if this vision is to be fulfilled, it must also have a vast army of men and women capable of understanding and following these leaders intelligently. These citizens must understand their government from the smallest election district to the highest administrative office. It must be no closed book to them, and each one must carry his own particular responsibility or the whole army will lag.

I would have our children visit national shrines, know why we love and respect certain men of the past. I would have them see how government departments are run and what are their duties, how courts function, what juries are, what a legislative body is and what it does. I would have them learn how we conduct our relationships with the rest of the world and what are our contacts with other nations. The child seeing and understanding these things will begin to envisage the varied pattern of the life of a great nation such as ours and how his own life and environment fit into the pattern and where his own usefulness may lie.

It is not, however, only in the courses bearing directly on history and government that citizenship can be taught. The child taking Latin and mathematics is also learning invaluable lessons in citizenship. The power of concentration and accuracy which these studies develop will later mean a man or woman able to understand and analyze a difficult situation. For example, arithmetic is necessary to a later understanding of economic questions. As citizens economic problems will often claim our attention, and the power to understand them is essential to wise solutions.

There are many questions today between capital and labor in our own country, and for that matter in the other countries of the world, which are drawing us closer and affecting our home conditions more and more each year. Mathematics and humanity are strangely intertwined, and an ability to understand both is essential to well-balanced decisions in questions of this kind. From the point of view of character-building, the harder these subjects are to master the greater will be the sense of self-mastery and perseverance developed.

The other school contacts—social activities and athletics—develop team play, cooperation, and thought and consideration for others. These are all essentials in good citizenship.

The practical side of good citizenship is developed most successfully in school because in miniature one is living in a society, and the conditions and problems of the larger society are more easily reproduced and met and solved. To accomplish this, however, presupposes a high grade of teaching, a teacher who not only teaches a subject but is always conscious of the relation of the subject to the larger purpose of learning to live.

Learning to be a good citizen is learning to live to the maximum of one's abilities and opportunities, and every subject should be taught every child with this in view. The teacher's personality and character are of the greatest importance. I have known many erudite and scholarly men and women who were dismal failures as teachers. I have known some less learned teachers who had the gift of inspiring youth and sending them on to heights where perhaps they themselves were unable to follow.

Knowledge is essential and much to be admired, but no one can know all there is to know in the world, and to inspire a spirit of humbleness toward those who have a real knowledge in any subject and to add to that the "insatiable curiosity" so well described in Kipling's "Just So Stories" is a greater achievement than to establish the idea that the teacher's knowledge is infallible and all-embracing.

You will be thinking that few teachers of this type exist and you will be right. The blame lies with the attitude toward teachers and the teaching of our present generation. We have set up a money value, a material gauge by which we measure success, but we have frequently given more time and more material compensation to our cooks and chauffeurs and day-laborers, bricklayers, carpenters, and painters than we have to our nurses, governesses, and tutors and teachers in schools and colleges.

We entrust the building of our children's characters and the development of their minds to people whom we, as a rule, compensate less liberally than we do the men and women who build our houses and make our day-by-day existence more comfortable and luxurious. These men and women teachers, paid from $1,200 to $5,000, and in extraordinary cases $10,000 a year, mold the future citizens of our country, and we do not treat them with the respect or consideration which their high calling deserves, nor do we reward them with the only reward which spells success according to our present standards.

One of our hard-worked businessmen said to me not long ago, "Why, these teacher fellows have a snap. Look at their long summer holidays, and you can't tell me it's as hard to tell a lot of youngsters about logarithms or Scott's novels as it is to handle my board of directors at one end and my shop committee at the other." My thought was that if he and his fellow members on the board of directors and the men on the shop committee had had the right kind of teaching his job would be easier because at both ends he would have men better able to understand the whole problem of industry and realize the necessity of cooperation.

Teachers must have leisure to prepare, to study, to journey in new fields, and to open new sources of knowledge and inspiration and experience for themselves. You cannot impart what you have not made your own. You cannot engender enthusiasm if you have lost it. Teaching is dead when the subject does not inspire enthusiasm in the teacher. Then there must be leisure to cultivate your pupils. The best teaching is often done outside of the classroom.

It always interests me how many Harvard men will speak of Professor Copeland's "Readings." They seem to look back on them as something particularly hallowed, and it seems to me that they have furnished inspiration to countless men whose lives have followed a hundred different paths. One cannot get to know young people in a crowd. Youth is shy and a teacher gets his best results both in the classroom and out when barriers *are* down, and it requires wooing before the barriers come down. But what patience and time unselfishly given to the problems and interests of individuals this means, only a good teacher knows, and he rarely tells.

When I was fifteen I came in contact with a really remarkable teacher, a strong and vital personality. All my life I have been grateful for her influence. She has been dead for many years, but to this day her presence lives with me. It was not so much the actual class work, tho I can still remember the wave of hot shame creeping over me when I had handed in a piece of shoddy work. She had great charity for mistakes, for real limitations in knowledge or experience, but if you tried to "get by" with inadequate research and preparation, or smart phrases instead of thought, you felt her scorn because she believed in you and felt you could do better and you had fallen down.

I think few of us worked under her without acquiring a conception of intellectual integrity and obligation at all times to do our best. I still remember evenings when she read to us and by her comments opened up avenues of thought. If ever in small ways I may do any good work in the world the credit will not be mine, but in part at least it will belong to the most inspiring teacher I ever knew.

A friend of mine says that in her class in high school almost every individual went out with the determination to do something in the world and make every effort to self-development. She says it was due to the contact with a teacher who lent them her books and talked them over (giving them their first appreciation of good literature), who went on picnics with them, and opened their eyes to the beauty of nature by her own keen appreciation and enjoyment.

I believe that each one of us, if we delve in our memories, can find some similar experience which will uphold my contention that a great teacher is more important than the most gorgeous building. Where no such contacts have been experienced, the most ideal surroundings will not make our school-days anything but a succession of dull and meaningless tasks.

There are many inadequate teachers today. Perhaps our standards should be higher, but they cannot be until we learn to value and understand the function of the teacher in our midst. While we have put much money in buildings and laboratories and gymnasiums, we have forgotten that they are but the shell, and will never live and create a vital spark in the minds and hearts of our youth unless some teacher furnishes the inspiration. A child responds naturally to high ideals, and we are all of us creatures of habit.

Begin young to teach the standards that should prevail in public servants, in governmental administration, in national and international business and politics, and show by relating to daily life and known experience the advantages derived from a well-run government. It will then be a logical conclusion that the ends cannot be achieved without the cooperation of every citizen.

This will be readily grasped by the child because his daily experience in school illustrates the point.

The school alone cannot teach citizenship, however, any more than it can really educate a child. It can do much in directing thought and formulating standards, in creating habits of responsibility and courage and devotion. In the last analysis our home surroundings are the determining factor in development, and the example of those dear to us and constantly with us is what makes the warp and woof of our lives.

If the elders break the laws, do not bother to vote in elections or primaries, do not inform themselves and listen to the discussion of public questions, and do not take the trouble to make up their own minds after real consideration, the child will do likewise. If the elders look upon public questions from purely selfish angles, with a view as to how they will be affected personally, and not as to what are the needs of the country or of the world, then it is safe to predict that youth will do the same. This teaching of citizenship in the schools must be supplemented by teaching and example in the home.

I recognize of course that on our public schools devolves the teaching of by far the greatest number of our children and the added responsibility of taking great groups of new entrants into this country, and, either through adult classes or through their children, teaching them the ideals and standards of American citizenship; and I think we, who are already citizens, should realize how greatly our attitude influences newcomers. As a rule they have come to this country filled with dreams of the wonderful advantages and opportunities which await them.

Through their children and in their evening classes they hear our history and have explained to them great speeches of illustrious Americans of the past. And then too often they learn that the deeds in this new country fall short of its words, and they become the victims of poor citizenship as it is practised by some native Americans and by some who have lived here long enough to have absorbed true ideals and high standards if these were really an integral part of the people's lives. I think our private schools and our citizens who are able to support them should feel more keenly their connection with the public school system.

It may be easier to develop leaders in a private school because more attention is possible for individual pupils. Whether this is achieved or not, one thing must be done, namely, there must be developed men and women who shall take an interest in, and have an understanding of, every group of citizens and every phase of our national life, and this is more difficult to accomplish in private schools because the children are more sheltered.

As the great majority of our children are being educated in public schools, it is all-important that the standards of citizenship should be of the best. Whether we send our children to private school or public school we should take a constant interest in all educational institutions and remember that on the public school largely depends the success or the failure of our great experiment in government "by the people, for the people."

55

The Ideal Education

It seems rather foolish for someone who has been teaching school as short a time as I have, to presume to write on the subject of education, but there are certain things which both as a mother and as a teacher attract my attention, and I am rather glad of this opportunity to discuss them.

It is natural that many people should differ as to what they consider education. Their conceptions vary according to their background and their home, social and educational achievements, and their life opportunities. In a general way we may say that all people desire that type of education which will enable them not only to maintain, but improve their social, material and intellectual status.

In our public schools the range of occupations for which education is sought is broad. In our private schools there is very often no definite position for which a girl is educating herself. Therefore, it is far more difficult to achieve a satisfactory result because neither parents nor pupils have a definite object toward which they are working. In a vague way they wish their children to be educated in order that they may meet other people on an equal footing, but they haven't even a conception of the kind of definite aim held by the average parent of a child in public school.

In the public school the children's school life is considered as a preparation for later life. In character-building and in every outside activity the central thought of eventually being able to earn a living by achieving some form of marketable proficiency shapes the course of the child's life in general.

In the private school the parents too often do not consider that the children have begun a life of their own. Therefore no stress is laid upon their personal responsibility toward their school life. Otherwise, how can we explain the fathers and mothers who, because they prefer to make holiday in warm climes, pick up their children from their tasks, which are for the time being their life work, and gayly whisk them off for varying lengths of time to places where study and a regular life are at best difficult? And how can we explain, otherwise, the mother who, when she is looking for a school for her daughter, does not inquire how well that school stands scholastically, but only whether the children that her daughter will meet will benefit her when she is ready to enter into that strange thing called "society."

I often wonder how many mothers and fathers in our big cities, or in our small ones for the matter of that, have ever stopped to think what they mean by that magic word "society." There was a time in New York City when the city was comparatively small and much was heard of "the four hundred."

The Woman's Journal 15 (October 1930): 8–10, 36.

Perhaps there were really only four hundred who could afford the gaieties and elegant leisure of the society of that day, which was represented by an old lady in a magnificent house, who gave remarkable parties to a few people, many of whom, while they may have belonged to the society of the "four hundred," scarcely can have been said to have either ornamented or elevated its standing in the greater social organization we call civilization.

Today there is no such thing in this country, in the larger cities at least, as any one group which may be called "society."

There are too many people to be included in any one group and there are too many interests. The country has grown in size, in population and variety of occupations, and we have groups of different societies. Here and there certain individuals mix in many different groups according to their ability and interests, but there is no such thing possible in this country as an aristocracy of society based on birth. We set up a material basis as the final criterion of social eligibility, certainly in our larger cities. The smaller places may have time to delve into people's history to find out if their ancestors have lived exemplary lives and held positions of trust, and now and then there are men who rise to the heights in the political or financial world whose families are examined in order to find out if anything in them will help to account for their achievements; but quite frequently, these men who arrive at the top are found to have very simple backgrounds, and sad though it may be for some people, if they go back but three or four generations, even in those families which consider themselves to be the most ancient aristocracy, they will find that the beginnings in this country were very simple. They will probably find also many plain people in every generation.

So why this insistence, when we are looking for an education, on the school's providing also "society," which in the old sense does not exist at all; and in the new sense can only be entered through the acquiring by the individual of the qualities which make for success in the world at large.

I am hoping that as we grow a little older our schools and our parents will cooperate to impress on our youth that there are many types of success, that one may be lacking in many material things such as automobiles, radios, etc., and yet be an outstanding success because of some service to mankind. Madame Curie is fêted over here, she is received everywhere with respect and recognition for the services which she and her husband have through years of patient study rendered to mankind, but the material returns have been very, very small.

I would like to see our schools and our parents cooperate in teaching the younger generation that the world as it is today requires of them an analysis of what they want to achieve and that the point of real education is an ability to recognize the spirit that is in a real human being, even though it may be obscured for a time by lack of education or opportunity to observe certain social customs. Military service in Europe brings this about to a certain extent because men of all kinds of social background find themselves privates together, and class distinctions for a time are wiped out. Our public schools should bring it about in this country, but unfortunately many of our children are so closely confined amongst the little groups of people which form their immediate circle of friends, that they have very little opportunity to develop any knowledge or judgment of human beings as a whole.

It always seems to me it is a part of the education of every child to show it as many as possible of the various types of lives which make up the world around it. To bring children up with a conception that their own particular lives are typical of the whole world is to bring up extraordinarily narrow people and parents should demand of the school in which they place their children that, if possible, there be a wide range of types in order that the child may be given an opportunity to develop its knowledge of the world and its own powers of choosing desirable companions.

When we go back even forty years in educational requirement we are struck by how very simple "book learning" was even as short a time ago as that. Whereas today the number of subjects which are required as the basis for this never-ending thing called education is quite appalling to grown-ups and would be to children if they realized what lay before them in the few years that are dedicated to school life.

Of course, most of us know that education only ends with death, but in the school years the tools are forged which must serve these children through all their lives. If these are not thoroughly taught and learned, this will limit the children's achievements almost as much as their lack of natural ability.

We should strive always to impart to students two fundamental things—curiosity and vision! Any person who has acquired the ability to read and write and knows the fundamentals of arithmetic, if she has curiosity, will educate herself, no matter where she may be, granted the possibility of obtaining books.

Vision means imagination and is absolutely necessary to the fostering of curiosity. We could not possibly teach all the facts in any one subject in the years from six to twenty-two or twenty-four, and innumerable children have only the years from six to fourteen, or at the most eighteen. Therefore, I think it is well in teaching any subject for the teacher to develop in pupils, if possible, the ability to find out things for themselves and a curiosity to know more on whatever line they are studying.

Mr. Theodore Roosevelt used to say, "Never read a book which does not really interest you," but I feel quite certain that his extraordinary versatility and wide range and varied knowledge were due to the fact that he had so much curiosity that there were very few books which did not really interest him.

There is a children's story of Kipling's which you may remember in which he illustrates this point very effectively. The elephant acquired his trunk because of his " 'satiable curiosity." We are far too prone to do as the relations of the elephant's child—either refuse to answer or spank our offspring who show signs of being eternal question marks.

But if their curiosity can be so trained and if their tools can be given them in school, so that they may not only want information, but know where to go to find it, we have made strides toward real education which should be a satisfaction to any teacher or school.

The two other important factors which are looked upon as essential points of education today are character building and physical health. But these two things are not primarily the responsibility of the school. Physical health depends very largely on the rules laid down in the home for the child's life, and on the willingness of the home to cooperate with the school in any plans for physical development of the child. Character building also begins at home, in the cradle, but is again a field where the home and the school should cooperate in every possible way. I have often wondered why parents are willing to allow their children to ask for special privileges or exemptions from school rules. Life makes it possible for very few of us to do exactly what we want all the time, and it would seem to be wise to begin early to teach children that they must decide themselves to give up certain things which may be pleasures if they conflict with the duties of the work required for school.

This is a type of cooperation which leads to real character building, and I think makes it easier for mothers and fathers, as well as for teachers. It is hard to keep constantly saying "no" to requests for permission to do this or that, but it should not be necessary, as the child should be taught very early that there are some things one decides for oneself and should not ask permission to do.

School is the beginning of the child's life work. This should be respected by the parents, and the child should be made to feel that, like all life work, it must come ahead of anything else, even if it means foregoing some pleasure and some opportunities which may possibly seem profitable in the light of future social activities.

The young people of today do not probably respond as readily to precept as they did in the years gone by, but I have yet to find any young people growing up in an environment where duty and obligation to life jobs take first place in the lives of the parents, who will not eventually absorb from the atmosphere this same feeling of obligation.

There is one thing which I wish we could give to all young people, and that is a real joy in books. If they find some kind of reading in which they can lose themselves, it will help them through many difficult times in their future lives. The only way to do this is by acquiring a habit of reading when young and having the opportunity to know many different kinds of literature in order that they may have knowledge of the things which in the past have brought joy and consolation and delight to many other human beings.

In closing, let me say that though I believe much in the influence and advantage to be derived from the education which is being given in schools, I believe even more in the influence and education which come from the home. And, above everything else, do I believe that contact with big people and remarkable personalities, whether obtained only through books or through actual association, molds and influences young people far beyond any other factor.

56

The Power of Knowledge

Someone said to me not long ago, "You seem to be interested in education!"

Of course I am interested in education. Who is not at the present time? It is the one subject that we cannot afford to neglect no matter what happens to public and private finances. By that I do not mean that we are going to continue to spend money in exactly the same way as we have spent it up to now, but that we must spend money and spend it wisely on education is, I believe, an incontrovertible fact.

For the purpose of this article, I want to begin by stating that I am not unfamiliar with the attitude of certain citizens who claim that the education which they received was good enough for them and that therefore there should be no change and no increase in cost at the present time. But they do not realize that conditions have changed and that we are educating for new conditions and that the type of education needed requires more money spent on the preparation of teachers than ever before.

At the present time we are confronted with this picture: Everywhere our economic situation has been difficult. In some places it has meant that whole communities have needed help to achieve the bare necessities of life and therefore throughout the country we find unsatisfactory conditions in the schools.

According to the National Education Association and the office of the division of education in the Department of the Interior, there are a million more children in the schools of the United States today than there were in 1930. This is partly the normal increase and partly the result of the fact that with greater numbers of people out of work we are trying to keep children longer in school in order that they may not enter the competitive industrial world.

While the number of children in our schools has increased, there are twenty-five thousand fewer teachers employed today than there were in 1930; and more than one out of every four cities have shortened their school terms in the past year. The sale of textbooks has dropped over thirty percent and expenditures by cities for other school supplies have been reduced. Of course, where it is necessary for the children attending school to buy their own supplies, the tools with which the teacher has to work are pitifully inadequate. I have lived much of my life in New York State, where we pride ourselves upon expending more of our state income for education than for any other single activity of government. Yet in a rural school in northern New York I found that the children whose families were obliged to buy the schoolbooks were totally

Woman's Home Companion 61 (March 1934): 4.

unable to have any new books this year. It is easy to see what a handicap that situation would be to teacher and student alike.

In education the thing which counts above everything else is the preparation of the teachers. Here we have always been inadequate, lavish though we have often been in the past in spending too much money on the embellishment of our school buildings.

But granting that our teachers are prepared and have started on their teaching careers, if their salaries are pitifully inadequate and they have to scrimp and save, they cannot have the quiet mind which is a requisite for good teaching. Neither have they money enough to continue to improve themselves and this also is necessary to good teaching.

Many a time have I heard people say what an easy life a teacher has with her long vacations.

They little realize that money received for the teaching year usually must be made to cover those long vacations unless the teacher turns to other work during these periods. Nor do they realize that a teacher's work is not over when she leaves the classroom. A really good teacher devotes much time to the children outside the classroom and spends much of her leisure time in acquiring more knowledge and more background so that she will have more to give her pupils. I wonder if you think this can be done adequately by those teachers who are receiving less than seven hundred and fifty dollars a year? One out of every four teachers receives not more than this sum. Eighty-four thousand rural teachers this year are receiving less than four hundred and fifty dollars a year, and one out of every thirteen Negro teachers in the United States receives twenty-five dollars a month or less.

In at least eighteen states teachers are being paid in warrants cashable at a discount ranging from five percent up, and nearly forty million dollars in back pay is due to approximately forty thousand teachers. It speaks volumes for the ideals of this profession and the devotion to their work and to the welfare of the children that our public schools are functioning during this period as well as they are.

Schools are dependent upon taxes—in many places they have been supported by general property taxes. Now private incomes have gone down and of course the public income has gone down also. Therefore there hasn't been as much public money as usual to spend on education, but I have often wondered, if women throughout the country really made an analysis of the way the tax money is spent, whether they might not find certain things that they would eliminate. I for one would like to see the women of the world sit in at the disarmament conferences for I have a feeling they would reach an agreement—which our governments seem to find so hard to reach—and if we could reduce our armaments one big outgo for our federal tax money would be forthwith removed.

But this perhaps is a far-away vision. Nearer at home each of us has city and county and township and village governments where a large portion of all tax money is spent. Why do not the women's clubs throughout the country study the small expenditures of local government with an eye to reducing them in order that there may be more money in their communities for adequate education?

This is a time when not only that education which will enable us to earn our living is needed, but education which will enable us to use our leisure profitably is needed. I heard of a locality the other day where what one man called the frills of education had been cut off on the plea of economy—the frills were music, art, drama, recreation, health education, nature study—all the things which make an art out of living, and in our ever increasingly mechanized world we have got to make living an art.

Lack of education in leisure-time interests and occupations will most certainly mean more people in our jails, more people cared for in our insane asylums and more children who are defective or delinquent.

This subject is one which lies very close to my heart and I have always thought that James Madison had stated a truth which our nation could not afford to forget when he said:

> Knowledge will forever govern ignorance and the people who mean to be our governors must arm themselves with the power that knowledge gives.

57

Facing the Problems of Youth

Education today is not purely a question of the education of youth; it is a question of the education of parents, because so many parents, I find, have lost their hold on their children. One reason for this is that they insist on laying down the law without allowing a free intellectual interchange of ideas between themselves and the younger generation. I believe that as we grow older we gain some wisdom, but I do not believe that we can take it for granted that our wisdom will be accepted by the younger generation. We have to be prepared to put our thinking across to them. We cannot simply expect them to say, "Our older people have had experience and they have proved to themselves certain things, therefore they are right." That isn't the way the best kind of young people think. They want to experience for themselves. I find they are perfectly willing to talk to older people, but they don't want to talk to older people who are shocked by their ideas, nor do they want to talk to older people who are not realistic.

We might just as well accept things which are facts as facts and not try to imagine that the world is different, more like what we idealized in the past. I have a letter just the other day from a mother who told me that she had brought up several daughters, and that they never did certain things which are very common today among young people. She was sure that if we never countenanced or spoke of certain things in our homes our children would never do those things. Well, it just so happens that I have a number of boys and they happen to know the mother's girls. I have, therefore, seen a good deal of them, and they did every single thing that their mother told me they never did. I think it would have been far better if she had established a type of genuine relationship with her children which would have allowed them to be honest with her. Then she would have had an opportunity to put across her own ideas with some kind of hope that they would at least be considered.

But if the relationship is such that youth has no desire to talk to older people, then, I think, it is entirely impossible to help the youth of today—and they need help badly. I think they are very glad to have it, too, when it is given in a spirit of helpfulness, not self-righteousness. We don't need to idealize things that are past; they look glamorous, but perhaps they were not so glamorous when we really lived through them.

My own feeling would be that the most important education is the education which will enable us, both in our homes and in our schools, to understand the real problems that our children have to meet today. It is easy enough to impart book knowledge, but it is not so easy to build up the relationship

National Parent-Teacher Magazine 29 (February 1935): 30.

between youth and older people which is essential to the working out of their problems—very difficult problems on which young people need our leadership and our understanding.

We cannot pass over the fact that the world is a hard world for youth and that so far we have not really given their problems as much attention as we should. We smile—I smiled myself the other day when one young boy said that he hoped to go in and clean up politics. Politics need to be cleaned up, of course. Everything that is human needs that particular kind of enthusiasm. But we older people know that we don't always succeed as easily as these young ones think they can. Yet I doubt if we should smile. I think that we should welcome their help, and find places where this tremendous energy that is in youth—if it cannot be used immediately in making a living—may at least be used where it is so greatly needed today.

I should like to leave with you this one idea which I have been thinking about a great deal of late: the necessity for us as parents, as teachers, as older people, to put our minds on the problems of youth, to face realities, to face the world as it is and the lives that they have to live—not as we wish they were, but as they are—and, having done that, to give our sympathetic help in every way that we can.

58

What Libraries Mean to the Nation

It has been a great pleasure to be here this evening and to hear all the things that have been said about libraries in the district and in general, and the librarians, without whom the libraries would be of little use, I am afraid. But as I sat here I fear that I have thought a good deal about the fact that there are so many places in the United States that have no libraries and that have no way of getting books.

What the libraries mean to the nation is fairly obvious to all of us, especially to those who are here this evening. We know that without libraries, without education, which is based largely on libraries, we cannot have an educated people who will carry on successfully our form of government, and it seems to me that what we really are interested in is how we can make this country more conscious of what it has not got, because we do pat ourselves on the back for the things that we have and that we do. I was looking over some maps which were sent to me and I longed to have these maps very much enlarged and put up in many, many places throughout this country, because I do not think that many people know how many states do not spend more than ten cents per capita for library books a year, and how many states have large areas, particularly rural areas, where one cannot get books.

One of the things that I have been particularly grateful for in the years of the depression—and, of course, I think, sad as it has been, we have some things to be grateful for—is that we have discovered so many things that we had not known before. These facts have come to the knowledge of a great many people who had simply passed them by before, because they did not happen to think about them, and one of these things, that we used to be able to hide, is the areas of the country which are not served in any way by libraries. I have seen photographs, for instance, of girls going out on horseback with libraries strapped on behind them, taking books to children and grown people in places that have been without libraries. We know a good deal about Mrs. Breckinridge's nursing service in Kentucky, but we know very little about the libraries that go out in the same way that her nurses do, on horseback.

I have lived a great deal in the country, in a state which prides itself in spending much money on education, and I am quite sure that some people think there is no lack of education and no lack of library facilities, and sometimes I long to take people and let them see some of the back country districts that I know, in New York State. I know one place in the northern part of the

American Library Association Bulletin 30 (June 1936): 477–479. Address at the District of Columbia Library Association dinner, April 1, 1936.

state where I camped for a while in the summer, and I went to the school and talked to the teachers. They are using schoolbooks which have been passed from one child to another. They have practically no books outside of the textbooks. The children in the district are so poor and some of them so pathetic that I suppose the struggle to live has been so great you could not think much about what you fed the mind, but I came away feeling that right there, in one of the biggest and richest states in the country, we had a big area that needed books and needed libraries to help these schools in the education of the children, and, even more, to help the whole community to learn to live through their minds.

We are doing a tremendous amount through the home economics colleges to help people to learn how to live in their homes, to better their standards of material living. We have got to think in exactly the same way about helping them to live mentally and to attain better standards, and we can do it only through the children. We can do groundwork with the children; we must begin with them; but we have got to do a tremendous amount with the older people.

I had a letter the other day which was pathetic. It was from a man who said he was 74 years old. He wrote to ask me to see that the adult education classes in that particular community were not stopped, because it had meant so much to him to learn to read. He did not think that I could understand what it meant never to have been able to understand a word on the printed page. He said, "I am not the only one. My next door neighbor is 81 and he learned to read last winter, and it has just made life over for us." It gave you the feeling that there is a good deal of education that is not being done in this country, in spite of all that *is* done.

We have come a long way. We have done a great deal, but we still have a lot that can be done to improve our educational system, and we still have a tremendous amount to do with our libraries. We have got to make our libraries the center of a new life in the mind, because people are hungry to use their minds.

A New Era Ahead

We are facing a great change in civilization, and the responsibility, I think, for what we do with our leisure time is a very great responsibility for all of us who have intellectual interests. Somebody said to me, "I would not be so worried that I would not mind facing the fact that we are working fewer hours, if I only knew what people would do with their free time. I would not know what to do myself if I had only to work six hours a day."

This is a challenge. We, here in this country, ought to know what to do with our time, if we have it. I do not know whether we are going to have it, but if we are going to have more leisure time, it is the library, and the people who live in the libraries and work in libraries, who are going to lead the way, who are going to give other people the curiosity and the vision of useful things, and pleasant things, and amusing things which can be done in those hours in which we may not have to work in the ways in which we have worked before. It is a very great responsibility, but it is also a very great interest.

Now, I think here in the city of Washington, and in nearly all big cities, the problem is a different one from the one I know so well in the country districts. I think that perhaps there are more facilities and, for that reason, there are more stimulating people engaged in solving the different problems that affect education in cities. But there is a great need, a very great need, in rural America. There is a great need for imagination in the ways used to stir the interest of old and young to use what library facilities they have, and to insist that they shall have more and to make them willing to pay for more, because, in the end, they will get something that they want out of it.

The more I have thought about the problem, the more I have felt that we do not use all our opportunities to stimulate an interest in books. Everything today in which people are interested, the radio, the movies—all of these—should, if properly used, stimulate the use of books. For instance, if there is a remarkably good movie, like *The Life of Pasteur*, it seems to me that it should be used by people in our rural schools and rural libraries to create an interest in the life of Pasteur, the things that Pasteur did, the people around him, and all the discoveries that have come from that time on. I am sure that if we put our minds on it, there are a great many ways in which we can use the things which are coming constantly into the lives of people throughout the country to stimulate an interest in the oldest and most interesting recreation there is.

But you do have to learn to love books, you do have to learn how to read them, you do have to learn that a book is a companion, and this is done in a great many different ways. I think we can do a great deal by having more copies of the same books, perhaps less expensive books, in the libraries so that we can have a good many people reading the same books and coming together for discussion.

I know, for instance, that even in a small group, like a family, we all want to read one book at the same time, and we all want to tear each other's hair out when we can't get a copy. It seems to me that here is something we should be thinking about, to stimulate the reading of books in families and large groups of people. I think the CCC has made me realize this. One boy said to me, "Do you know about that book? I am so glad to be able to talk about it. You know, it takes such a long time to get a book around." Now, if there had been a dozen or more copies of that book, the group would have talked about the book and it would have been a valuable contribution. It would have stimulated their intellectual thought.

I feel that the care of libraries and the use of books, and the knowledge of books, is a tremendously vital thing, and that we who deal with books and who love books have a great opportunity to bring about something in this country which is more vital here than anywhere else, because we have the chance to make a democracy that will be a real democracy. It will take on our part imagination and patience and constant interest in awakening interest in other people. But, if we do, I think we shall find that our love of books will bring us a constantly widening audience and constantly more interesting contacts in whatever part of the country we may go.

59

On Teachers and Teaching

I am a little flattered to be asked to write an editorial for the *Harvard Educational Review*, and I also feel extremely diffident. My only claim to experience on any educational front is a few courses given in a private school for girls, and a wide range of contacts with young people of varying backgrounds throughout the United States. From both sources, however, I have formed a few rather definite ideas about education.

Some of these ideas were brought into being by contacts with Harvard students, some of them by contact with youngsters who could not go back to school because they had no clothes to wear and, when the clothes materialized, were too old for the classes in which they would have to resume their studies. Thus they appeared to be candidates for our unskilled, uneducated labor group, which is perhaps our greatest problem in unemployment.

To both of these groups teachers are all important. I believe that teachers are born. Training is helpful, but certain things must be a part of their character and personality, otherwise their teaching will never be really vital. It seems to me that some of our schools and colleges have laid too much stress of late on buildings and equipment and learned professors with degrees and above all books to their credit on special subjects which prove their scholarship.

All these things are good, but it does not follow that because one is learned and has written books, one is a great teacher, for frequently a great teacher may inspire and help to educate a scholar, a writer, an inventor, an expert in some particular line of research. And one of these specialists, however, in his own line might never be able to impart what he knows, or light the spark of curiosity which encourages the devotion to certain ideals which in turn creates the expert in any line.

I wish that as a nation we would think first of teachers in terms of character, personality, and the special gift of imparting enthusiasm for acquiring knowledge. The basis of good national education is good teachers, and they are worthy of adequate pay and security in their old age. If they can accumulate degrees and write books along any line, well and good, but the first requisite should be their ability to inspire youth.

I am not minimizing the value of an atmosphere of simplicity and beauty in the school building, nor of adequate equipment, but they are distinctly secondary from my point of view. To illustrate what I mean, I would like to point to a particular individual. I think there has been at Harvard University, in the field of literature, a man who stands out as a great teacher. When I was young and heard of his courses, it made me resentful that Harvard did not

Harvard Educational Review 8, no. 4 (October 1938): 423–424.

allow girls to share in them! The generation of boys who sat in his classes had a growing curiosity and an interest in literature. I do not know whether it was the courses he gave or Mr. Copeland's ability to read and to talk with his students. I never heard him, but there must have been something inspiring in his personality and methods. There are certainly a very few among the Harvard boys whom I meet today who have real enthusiasm for literature. This was not so in the years when Copeland and Lowell were a paramount influence. This is important, because it seems to me that one of the fundamentals of education is that you should know how to express yourself in your own language. How can you learn unless you read and know the people who have been the masters of the English language?

I do not want to return to the handicaps which our forefathers had to overcome to obtain an education, and I am no believer in the "little red schoolhouse." I want consolidated schools and I think children should be given an opportunity to start their education in nursery schools, but in our haste to subscribe to all that which is new, I do not want us to lose that which is good in the past.

Abraham Lincoln's Gettysburg speech grew out of his knowledge of the Bible and certain other essentials which reading had given him. They are essentials which I feel we may lose now that we realize and emphasize so much the material needs of education, and therefore I put in my word for greater emphasis and consideration of the teachers and greater stress on the study of our own language.

60

Attitudes of Youth and Morale

It seems to me that this is a pretty large subject, for the attitudes of youth are as varied as the number of young people; all young people have different attitudes, I think.

One day, while in the office of Civilian Defense, they brought in a number of manuals. I know nothing about manuals, nothing about the subject matter that goes into them, but the name of the top manual caught my eye—it said, "Overall Manual." I wondered, what is an Overall Manual? I promptly said that I would look at that manual and I gave a copy to someone else at the same time. I read it; and the other person read it—brought it back to me with the remark, "It seems to me there are a great many words, but they don't say anything." Well, I felt the same way. There were a great many words but they didn't say a thing.

That is like what a great many of us do when we talk about youth attitudes and morale, because, as a matter of fact, most all youth attitudes stem from the attitudes of older people; not always from parents, sometimes from their teachers, sometimes from older friends of the family. It is commonly said that a great many attitudes stem from their own friends. I am not so sure of that.

I think that older people have a great deal of influence on youth attitudes; but there are certain things we may find in many of the young people themselves. I might just touch on a few of those.

One could say that one very prevalent attitude in youth is the desire to do, to stop talking about things and thinking about things and actually to do something. I think that is really one of the reasons why you hear people are troubled by the morale of boys in camp. I have never been very much troubled about that because when young people actually have something to do, they stop fussing and that is what the great majority of the boys are doing. Since we've been in the war this is proved to be true, for morale is high everywhere.

I don't mean to say that there aren't some young people who have some real fundamental difficulties in their thinking, who show confusion, or antagonism to certain things that are happening.

I came up on the train with a few of them the other day. I sat at a table with three who had been in training some months; two were draftees, one was an enlisted boy. We talked together and their dissatisfaction soon expressed itself. One complaint was that they hadn't enough materials to feel that they were really learning a great deal; the other complaint was that they had had

From *The Family in a World at War*, edited by Sidonie M. Gruenberg (New York: Harper, 1942), pp. 230–236.

their lives interrupted and had to stop doing something. They found that now all they thought of was food and the date they would receive their pay. Nobody talked to them about what was happening in the world. They couldn't really see that they were doing much. I think that is the psychology of all young people not only over the past few months, but at all times. Now they know there is a job to do, they are happy.

Mr. Lindeman refers to the failure of democracies to teach youths a sense of responsibility. Perhaps this is really due to the fact that in our modern life there are a great many young people who can't actually see that they are getting anywhere. I don't know whether that is so or not, but I get that from young people now and then. They may be doing the kind of job that doesn't seem to them to be accomplishing anything. Nearly all youth desire to be doing something that they see is constructive, something that grows, that goes on and develops and is a pathway which they can follow, and which leads to widening horizons.

As we look back, I think we will realize that that was so for our young people in the past. I always liked the story of my husband's grandfather who, when he was seventeen, was driven up to Boston by his father and put in a countinghouse, and shortly afterwards became a supercargo on a ship that sailed around the world. At the age of eighteen he was in charge of the cargo: sold it and bought new cargo; and what happened to that trip was partly his responsibility. He could see something developing before him as he went and he saw new countries, new opportunities.

That illustrates what, I think, we have got to do for this younger generation of ours. We have got to think about their attitudes in the light of providing them with widening horizons because one thing I feel is sure: they will not have a satisfactory attitude toward life unless they feel they are growing, and through their own work, developing new things, developing things that lead to something which most of them term rather vaguely "a better world."

Almost any group of young people you talk to will say that they want to help build a better world. They couldn't chart for you that better world. It is a phrase that they have become attached to, nevertheless. It expresses the real thing they are seeking; it is the thing that really means the aspirations of youth today.

They have many attitudes beyond that which we could talk about, some that I think are very encouraging. I would far rather put a question of tolerance up to a group of young people than I would to a group of older people. I think there are very few young people who hold the attitude today of some of my older friends who, partly because they don't realize it, have become fixed in certain prejudices. These older people don't think about it very much, but it comes out sometimes in word and in deed, without any thought on their part at all. But such prejudices and intolerance offend youth. I think that is one of the very encouraging signs of the attitude of youth.

I am not a bit afraid about the morale of our young people. I am much more worried that we older people won't keep up our morale so that we can really supply the proper background for the growth of young people. We are the ones, probably, who are going to lack courage; and of course we are the ones who are responsible in many ways for not opening wider horizons for our young people.

I have always remembered a story which I think Dorothy Canfield Fisher wrote about a girl who went back, after she had been around the world, to the place where she used to go in the summer. The farmer's family asked her to stay because they thought they would find out some new things from her. She had traveled all over the world but she had learned nothing that she could impart to anyone else because she had always been turned inward, she had never been turned outward. In her background, no one had ever taught her to understand the things she saw. So she was able to travel in Europe and come back and give nothing to the young people in the family with whom she went to stay. She had a rude awakening when she overheard them talking about her and saying that they had only taken her in because they had hoped for new horizons and that she seemed not to know anything about anything that was important.

I have felt that way about a great many people. I have taken a good many people into different parts of this country to see different situations and found, rather to my surprise, that they could see a great deal—and understand nothing.

One day I was asked by a group of young people if I would tell them something, some human stories about actual people that I had happened to tell to one of them. I told them with considerable misgivings, thinking that in all probability the attitude of youth would be rather cynical. I feared youth would say, "Oh, why be concerned about that? That is just a local thing. They are not really people to bother about. They just weren't any good and that is why those things happen to them." Instead of which I heard that afterwards one of them had made a remark which I have never forgotten because I think all of us who are older were more or less under indictment. This boy said, "You know, I never had heard about any of those things until this afternoon. I didn't know they existed anywhere in my country. I wonder why my mother never told me about it before."

So you see that perhaps some of the attitudes of youth come from our own attitudes. Perhaps we are the ones who really bear the responsibility for teaching the things which will create a sense of responsibility in youth. We can't expect, of course, that youth will have gray hairs, or that youth will constantly think about the serious things in life. In fact, it would be rather sad if that were the case. But I think we can open doors to youth which will create the morale we worry about so much. For it will give them an understanding of the whole of life. It will give them a real sense that they are a part of that whole, that they are not confined to one particular little individual situation, that they are a part of this whole flow of life which is going to change, change for us, change for the rest of the world, and which is going to mean that our young people, willy-nilly, must carry a great burden of responsibility.

Since our country was attacked and we became involved in war, there has been, of course, a complete change in the morale of the men in camps and of the civilians at home. Boys and girls are clamoring now to do the thing which will make them most useful to their country. Many of the boys are enlisting in the military services because of the urge to do something. They do not stop to consider whether their ultimate value to the country would be enhanced by finishing their education first.

The country calls and a vast majority of youth answer; but the country calls for an intelligent answer. That does not mean giving up the courses of study already embarked upon, if the country will benefit by the intervening months of better preparation, or special training.

I think all young people must make an effort to take a very practical attitude concerning their desire to be of service. They should pick out carefully the place where their services will be most useful, and prepare themselves to give their best in whatever they decide to do.

It is our task to give the young people the background of courage, intelligent leadership, and confidence that they can carry the responsibilities and have the morale, no matter in what situations they are.

61

Education Is the Cornerstone on Which We Must Build Liberty

Education is undoubtedly one of the bulwarks on which democracy must be built.

It is generally accepted that we must have a sound enough economic basis to give people enough to eat, decent shelter, clothing, and medical care, before education can really achieve its maximum results.

A minimum, decent standard of living once achieved, education is the cornerstone on which we must build liberty which is not license and a democracy which truly belongs to the people.

Every Teacher Has Obligation to the Future

Organized education has charge of the child during the formative years and during the larger part of the working day, so it has a grave responsibility in helping to win the war by making every child realize what his obligation is to the Nation at the present time and as he comes of age. But, at the same time, every teacher has an obligation to the future which necessitates the best possible preparation, a willingness to face real problems courageously, themselves, and not only to lead their pupils but to be an influence in the community among the parents. Under their leadership the communities as a whole will face the realities and the necessities for change in the future world.

Tools to Make Wise Decisions Forged During School Years

It is important for all to realize that the tools with which to make wise decisions are forged during the school years.

History, geography, the social sciences, and above all the training of the mind make it possible for young people to take the facts of a situation, analyze them, and find solutions. The value of their minds depends largely on the quality of teaching and on the leadership in the realm of education.

Education for Victory 1, no. 3 (April 1, 1942): 1.

62

The Role of the Educator

We learned in the last war that many people in this country had not had opportunity for adequate education, hadn't been properly fed, hadn't had medical care. But when peace came, we forgot all about them, and very little came out of the lessons we learned.

Now we are learning many of them all over again. We have rejected many people for illiteracy in this war. It wasn't for lack of native intelligence; some are being taught in camps and are learning quickly. It was lack of opportunity. I hope this time we are not going to forget when the war ends.

If we don't think thru our own problems, we are not going to be very well prepared to lead in solving problems that will face the United Nations as a whole. And facing those problems, we see that education is basic to democracy. You can have a government where from above the life of the people is directed either well or badly, but you can't have a people that govern themselves with wisdom, intelligence, and consistent interest unless you have education.

In this nation today schools are closing. Teachers are going from teaching into other fields, largely because of the rise in the cost of living and the greater opportunity to make money in other professions. The whole situation is a difficult one. We have in cities classes so large that it is impossible for any teacher to give proper attention to each child. It is equally impossible for one teacher to teach not only the number but the various ages of pupils in some of our rural schools.

Basically, we have to change the whole viewpoint of the country on the importance of the teacher. We do not in our communities give to teachers the proper position, the proper return in the terms we have set up to gauge success. Our values—our measuring of success largely in material terms—may change in the future, but there is no question but what the teaching profession must have the highest standard of remuneration. We must see that the training of citizens in a democracy is the most important thing that we can trust to any group.

And then I think of the freedom that must go with being a teacher. Many teachers are afraid to set problems with all their different angles before young people because of feelings it would arouse in the community. When this happens, we are not getting freedom of minds to function, which is basic in a democracy.

We should make every effort to ascertain that it is actually facts we are putting forth. But having done that, we should allow children, and from then

The Journal of the National Education Association 33, no. 3 (March 1944): 59-60. Address presented to the NEA, January 21, 1944.

on up, full access to the whole of any situation and let them try to think things out. Otherwise I don't believe a democracy can function. If we restrict the flow of ideas and discussion, it isn't going to be possible to work out a better basis for understanding and peace.

Since we all continue our education thruout out lives, much responsibility has to be undertaken by teachers in the field of adult education. Our schoolhouses should be centers from which radiate the ideas which motivate the community.

So you see why I feel *the role of the educator is the most important thing before the country today.* We have to find a way of making it possible for the country as a whole to give equal opportunity to our youngsters.

I know how hard it is with the feeling in many places that education is a secondary interest. "Why should teachers be paid higher salaries? Why should they have so much preparation? Look what an easy life they have—so many months of holiday." It must be disheartening. It must make teachers feel that nobody recognizes how important is their role.

Yet almost everyone who looks back upon his school years as the opening of a world of interests will tell you that one or more teachers gave him inspiration, curiosity about the world, the tools and desire to be an influence in his community and to accomplish something worthwhile in his life. We are not going to hold or to get people into the profession who have these abilities and qualities unless the job they are doing is recognized in the communities as being the important thing it really is.

How we are going to get this across is something I often ponder on. It is not easy. But the time is crucial. Unless we attract to the teaching profession people with ability and ideals and courage and unless we begin in our communities to give them the opportunity and freedom and respect and position which they should have, our hope for a different kind of world is greatly lessened.

I believe *we have to have federal aid to education.* There are many arguments made against it, that this is no time to add to expenses of the government, that if you have federal aid you restrict rights of states. I don't think those arguments are valid. You don't need to restrict rights of states. Every community has to evolve itself. You can't impose on a community a type of education it isn't prepared to have. But you can gradually lead a community to see from one change to another that there is something a little better than they have envisioned before. But we have to work thru our local educational systems.

There are going to be great physical changes in the next few years. Speaking of my son's ranch in Texas, Madame Chiang Kai-shek said, "Texas sounds very like North China. I think it would be a good idea if your son and daughter-in-law had a ranch in China too." I said, "They couldn't run both," and she answered, "Oh, easily. They could come to China for a weekend every month." I hadn't thought of China as a weekend visit!

I was talking to four boys who had spent eight months in Russia. They said, "We don't think the Russians have anything in comparison with our standard of living, but they seem happy and sure they are on the way toward what they want. And they enjoy art and music and know more about them than we do." Those boys got an understanding of the people there and we are going to do that more and more. Once this war is over, this intercourse will be extremely easy. Time and expense will be much less a factor.

Can't you see how many changes we are going to face, how many different things we are going to have to think thru? And if we are going to be leaders and use the strength that we have and many other countries lack, we shall need to have as great convictions about our democracy and where we are going and how we are getting there as any other people in the world. And I think largely this question is back in the laps of the teachers of the country!

63

Educational Programs for Veterans

I am sure that most of you who have been dealing with veterans, or who have seen a great deal of them, have a feeling that what is done in the educational field is going to be very important; and I don't think that we are quite ready to decide all that needs to be done.

I went the other day to a meeting where the subject for discussion was, "The Future of Education in America." One of the speakers said that the G. I. Bill of Rights might have served a very useful purpose in American education if educators had had something to do with writing it. I asked why they didn't; and the gentleman replied, "Well, we have no way of getting together, so we don't feel that that was a satisfactory bill. We think it could have been made much more useful to education and to veterans seeking education if different provisions had been written into it."

I think it is a rather unfortunate admission that educators had nothing to do with formulating a bill which is going to touch quite as many young people, as does that part of the G. I. Bill of Rights which deals with education. It really has a great deal to do with the future of this country as a whole. A great many of these boys have seen opportunities for advancement which they perhaps had never even thought of before; and they will use these opportunities or not use them, according to the ease with which they are made available to them when their work in the Army or the Navy is over.

Real Information Must Come From Educators

I am interested to see that Senator Pepper's Committee is going to reconsider many of the needs of veterans, and I think there is a great deal of good that will come out of interest on the part of Congress. But unless the people who are going to do the job really know what they need for facilities for education, or what they want to do, very little that is helpful is going to come from the investigation of any committee—because the real information has to come from educators. You must know what you think ought to be done as a result of your study and deliberations and must be able to put it in terms that will mean something to Members of Congress.

Teachers Must Be Educated to Give Instruction to Adults

Now it seems to me, from the contact I have had with veterans, that naturally the people on the college level are better off and, perhaps, a little more has

Education for Victory 3, no. 20 (April 20, 1945): 1–3. Address to the Conference on Educational Programs for Veterans.

been done to prepare for them than has been done for the others. Even on the college level, one thing has been neglected—but it is the same thing that has been neglected all the way down the line—the fact that we are going to get back from the war mature people—mature in certain ways at least—who know how to carry responsibility. Some of them have had a considerable amount of authority, but the technical training they need may be sadly lacking for doing a civilian job. Sometimes they know what they need; sometimes they do not know. Too often, veterans have no idea what they need in additional education. We must recognize the fact that we can't put mature people back to studying things with groups of children. They do not fit in. They are uncomfortable, and they require a different type of education.

Veterans may need knowledge of the same things you are teaching a child in grade seven or eight, but they should have a different presentation in order to be satisfied. I think it is going to mean that teachers must be properly educated so as to give instruction *to adults*. The veterans want to go faster and they will be able to go faster, and they don't want to sit down in the same class with children. There may not be such a great span of difference in age, nevertheless there will be a great span of difference in experience.

Educators and Employers Need to Cooperate

Then, too, there is another thing we have not done, which seems to me vital. We have not brought together the people who are going to be the employers of these young people and the educators; and, unless they do come together and know how they are going to complement each other, there are going to be a lot of young people, after they go to school again, who will be frustrated because they don't meet the needs of the employer. Training will have to be initiated by the educators because the employers in general are not going to think in terms of education. Nevertheless, it is important that these youngsters receive the training which is most quickly going to place them in such a position that the employer is going to say, "Yes, he has acquired the training he needs for this job. I will take him."

When you move up into the college group, there is a more complicated situation because the group which comes into the college level is going to need, probably, some guidance on entering the business field and on how to move rather rapidly into executive positions. That will require a good deal of work between educators and businesspeople because there, in that group, you are going to find not the boys who need skills and a certain level of education to meet the use of the skill; but you are going to find people who have really carried great responsibility; who have had a great deal of authority and who should very quickly reach positions of responsibility if they are going to have satisfaction out of their work. If they do not have satisfaction of that kind, I am afraid we will have some badly frustrated young people.

For example, take the commander of a P. T. Squadron, who, before the war, went to college. From there he came right into the Navy. In answer to a question as to his reaction accepting responsibility, he replies, "The first time I found I had any responsibility I was scared to death. Now, of course, it is perfectly easy." I asked, "Do you ever wonder what you will do after you are out of the Navy?" The response was, "I know what I would like to do." "What?" "I would like to take some of my buddies and clean up the city government. I would just like to run for office and clean up the city government." That, without preparation of any kind, is a wonderful idea that a great many young people may have. But this young commander would soon find that he might be the tool of the machine before he could turn it around because he has no education in that field.

And then I happened to see a youth of 23, a lieutenant colonel in the Air Force, who had done 90 missions over Germany. He has not been to college but has completed high school and is intelligent. He has had authority and has accepted great responsibility. What will you do with that young man? When frustrated young people do not see a vision of how they may have a satisfying life, they are a very serious problem.

I think that we ought to face the fact that we have trained a great number of young people in ways that they have never been trained before—military ways; and military ways lead to the use of force, and it is not going to be a very satisfactory condition which we will have to face unless we channel these energies and abilities in the right direction.

So Much Depends Upon What Veterans Really Want and Become

The last war offers no comparison with this war because the numbers involved were so much smaller in the former. We know pretty well that the men who have made up the veterans' organizations since the last war have had a great deal of influence. Just compare that with the numbers you will have in this war, and you will see that you are going to depend very greatly for what happens in your country, on these veterans; and it is extremely important, I think, that they get the very best that education has to offer.

I even think you ought to go beyond thinking through supplying them with what they ask for; you ought to be thinking about making boys in the service *want* things that they don't, perhaps, realize they want—because so much depends on what these men really want and what they become. I see a number of them here in Washington—boys who are studying at George Washington University, the American University, and boys still in the hospitals.

Discussions of Contemporary Problems Valuable in Preparing for Civilian Life

I was very much interested out at Forest Glen, in one of their discussions the other morning, and the type of questions asked me. The discussions, or forums, out there are very good. I wish the Navy had those forums in Bethesda, and in their various hospitals, because there is a consideration of contemporary problems which is valuable in preparing young men for civilian life. I see one result of it very often in the boys from the hospitals—the Navy boys have far fewer questions to ask than the Army boys. That is because they are not accustomed to this experience. The Army boys are very free in asking questions. I think that that comes from the habit they have of meeting and discussing things; and I think that that is a good thing, but it is not enough. You will find even among those boys some placidly going to sleep in the middle of a talk or discussion; and you will know the person speaking didn't know how to hold their interest. That means that you must have a technique. You will have to work on the type of people who are going to teach these young people. You are going to get the veterans when they are still not very strong, not completely well; and, unless they are really interested, you are not going to get very much across to them.

What Happens to This Country Is of Vast Importance to World

I have a feeling that out of this conference may come something of vast importance—not just to the veterans themselves, but to the whole future of the country; and what happens to this country is going to be of vast importance to the world as a whole.

You people are really, it seems to me, doing something that has very great possibilities for the future. I am going to wish you good luck; I know that I probably have not told you anything that you did not already know. I would like to leave with you the feeling that we have a deep concern about the type of education that is offered and the fact that it shall meet the employers' need. The aim of all young people is to work at something they enjoy and that they find gives satisfaction and a happy life. You are the people who will help to bring that about, and we will watch with great interest what you recommend and what you start to do. We hope that you will awaken the interest of the people of the country, and that you will have great success in accomplishing whatever you decide needs to be done.

64

This I Believe About Public Schools:

An Interview with Eleanor Roosevelt

Charl Ormond Williams

Background in Teaching

What led you into teaching, Mrs. Roosevelt, and did you find it rewarding work?

I began to enjoy teaching when I was a little girl in Tivoli when my grandmother had me teach the children on the place their Sunday school lessons. The year I came home from abroad I went into the Junior League and had classes in Rivington Street Settlement. They were not formal academic classes but classes in rhythmic dancing and gymnastics. This gave me a chance to know the children and to take trips with them.

Later when my friend, Marion Dickerman, became the co-principal of a school in New York City, she asked me to teach American and English literature and, later, a course in American history and civics. I agreed to teach the older girls, and I enjoyed it very much and found that developing a real love of reading, rather than looking on it purely as an assignment, was a very rewarding experience.

Schools Serve All Ages

What is your point of view concerning the school as the education center of the community, serving the broad needs of all ages from nursery school youngsters to grandfathers?

The school should be the center of activity in far more communities. Many neighborhoods have no community house or community facilities. The schoolhouse is an expensive building. It would be far cheaper to run it on an all-time basis to serve the needs of the people. I should like to see nursery schools and kindergartens developed all over the country. And I should like to see schools used right through the day and into the evening for the convenience of every age group.

Preschool Privileges

For several decades organizations like the General Federation of Women's Clubs and the National Congress of Parents and Teachers have been deeply interested in providing educational facilities for children under 6 years of age, but the results so far

The Nation's Schools 45, no. 3 (March 1950): 31–36.

have not been highly successful. How do you think interested parents and other citizens can go about obtaining such privileges for all children?

Bring pressure on the state and city governments. Keep pointing out the advantages of freeing the mother from child care for certain hours of the day and the importance of getting a child started in good habits of learning to live with other people. Only in that way can we educate the community to a willingness to pay the necessary taxes.

Community Colleges

Do you think community colleges, giving 13th and 14th grade work, are a good idea?

It would depend on the area. You could *not* expect small communities to have their own colleges, but a number of communities could have a college together, very advantageously. Most parents, once they realized the value of education, would be willing to pay the additional taxes. It is wise to keep young people at home during these 13th and 14th school years.

Twelve-Month Program

To what extent would it be advisable to direct our planning toward the all-year secondary school, placing the professional staff on a 12-month basis, with ample provision for vacation periods during the year?

It is a very good idea. Long holidays are not necessary for health or recreation if provision can be made to have recreation and relaxation in connection with educational programs. Without such provisions long holidays are a waste of time.

Rural Education

You were responsible for making possible the first White House Conference on Rural Education ever held. What do you think are some significant outcomes of this conference, which rural educators believe has charted the course of rural education in this country for the next 50 years?

There were a number of worthwhile outcomes: the reawakening of public interest in rural education; the organization of similar conferences on the state level; nine regional conferences on rural life and education held annually under the auspices of the department of rural education of the N.E.A.; organization of the National Conference of County and Rural Area Superintendents of Schools; the rapid increase in the reorganization of rural school districts in the last five years, and many others of equal importance, it seems to me.

Conserving Natural Resources

What should rural and other schools be doing about conservation of our natural resources? The nation knows about your husband's absorbing interest in this area.

We could take a leaf out of the book of the European countries. There a child is taught in school how to behave in the country around the city where he lives. He is taught that it is valuable to reforest and that he must protect forests against fires because they not only keep up the water level in the area but provide a steady revenue.

Health of All Youth

What do you think should be done in this country to ensure healthy boys and girls and strong men and women in the years to come?

As far as public schools are concerned, the health program should be confined to the teaching of good health habits, instruction in home economics classes, a knowledge of proper diet, and proper physical care. There also should be good physical instruction.

However from my point of view, the remedying of defects found in the medical area should be taken out of the schools completely. Every child in our country should be required under the Public Health Service to attend a clinic where he would periodically receive a careful examination and where, if the family means were not sufficient, the necessary work, whether dental, eye care, or even an operation, would be at the disposal of that child, free of charge.

We have learned in two world wars that we have an increasing number of people who are not physically fit and that in most cases these individuals did not have the available medical advice and the means to obtain the necessary remedial care. This is a service that the nation must give its young people if it hopes to remain strong and healthy as a nation.

Counseling and Guidance

Do you think parents and the general public understand counseling and guidance service?

Parents really welcome guidance because they know they haven't had the training; also, they know children are likely to listen to guidance that comes from outside the family. Counseling service should be developed to a greater extent because young people very much need guidance.

Responsibilities of Youth

There are about a thousand student councils in high schools throughout the country. What can these students do to help improve conditions in their own local communities?

They can do a great deal. They can tell their elders what they really feel are the needs of high school students. In many communities little provision has been made for recreation of young people. You would not expect such a question to arise in country villages, but it has been mentioned in my own village of Hyde Park. There is no place but the corner drugstore for young people to meet. Either the family does not have a house large enough for a group, or, if the family gives the young people a room the family then has no place. Young people can explain that if needs for recreation are met some aspects of juvenile delinquency will be lessened.

The young men and women who visited you this weekend impressed me as being deeply devoted to the principles of democracy and to ideals of service to their nation. Don't you think so?

Decidedly. I think young people are more serious, particularly those who went through the war, and even those who saw their elder brothers and sisters go through the war, than most of the young people of my generation were.

Whose fault is it that so many adolescents are committing revolting crimes? What can schools do to assist in crime and delinquency prevention?

It is not the fault of individual parents but of society and of the economy we older people have built. Schools can do a great deal by bringing home to young people what the failures of society are, so that tomorrow's citizens will approach the future with a clearer picture of what needs to be changed.

How can schools operate so as to convince students that they have duties as well as rights as American citizens?

In the first place, by giving them responsibility in areas in which they can accept it. Then by helping the parents to see that this sense of responsibility must be developed in the child.

Teacher Recruitment

What can parents do within their own homes and communities to encourage our most talented young people to prepare themselves for teaching in the elementary schools?

First of all, they can pay the teachers sufficiently so that their work will be considered valuable, since pay is often the criterion of the value of one's service. The teacher's standard of living has to be raised to the level of a profession.

The parents can make the position of teacher socially important in the community so that teachers will feel they are making a real contribution.

Loyalty Oaths

Do you believe that a loyalty oath demanded of a professional group, such as teachers, is a tacit assumption that that particular group is disloyal? Would you regard it as discrimination if you were a teacher in a state requiring the oath?

It might be said, of course, that this is done because teachers compose such an important group, but in any case it gives them a feeling that they are singled out because of suspicion.

I do not think definite groups should be asked to take a loyalty oath. If we are going to require loyalty oaths, everyone should be required to take them. It might be done when we come of age.

It is much wiser to have anything as important as loyalty to one's country a *universal* obligation.

Citizens' Groups

How can such a group as the newly created National Citizens Commission for the Public Schools, headed by Roy E. Larsen of Time, contribute most effectively to the progress of education?

By creating public opinion and by making people understand the value of the public schools. The future of the country depends on these public schools because the vast majority of children attend them.

Several generations have grown up in this country with very little appreciation of the background of our pubic schools and the great struggle this nation has gone through to set them up. What would you think of a unit of study devoted to the history, aims and achievements of the public schools?

I think that it should not be a separate unit of study. It should be done in connection with the study of the history of our country—an essential part of history.

Federal Agency

Do you favor the present Federal Security Agency setup with the Office of Education on a bureau status?

I believe that we should have a cabinet post for the Department of Education and Fine Arts. It is important enough to the nation to warrant a separate department.

The National Congress of Parents and Teachers, now 52 years old, has 5,000,000 members. How do you account for this marvelous growth?

I account for it by a natural interest on the part of parents in their children. It is not an extraordinary growth, but normal and natural. Through the P.T.A., parents and other citizens may cooperate with the professional staff of the school system to determine the scope and character of the educational program.

Funds for Research

The giant industries of this country spend huge sums annually for research in their particular fields. Does it seem reasonable to expect public education to have some similar amount for studies of student behavior, instructional processes, schoolhouse planning, and educational procedures?

It seems to me not only reasonable but imperative, because the only way in which we make improvements is through research. If it is worthwhile to industry, it certainly is worthwhile to education.

Minority Groups

What do you think are the best ways, practically and politically, of improving the educational opportunities of the Negroes and other minorities?

As soon as possible, equal opportunities for education should be given to all of our children regardless of race, color or creed. They should have completely equal opportunities in school housing and in the quality of teachers. Any available advantages should be equal for all young people. Wherever it is possible, education should be given in nonsegregated schools.

Women and Public Life

In 1944, a White House conference considered how women could share in postwar policy-making in local, state and national governments. What do you think the schools can do to train women for these policy-making positions?

We should train all children for citizenship much more diligently than we have done in the past. They should really learn what democracy means and why they believe in it. The only special education that needs to be directed at women is to give them confidence that they are able to fill positions in government, whether these are local positions or larger ones.

Naturally, their families are of primary importance, but women have as much responsibility as have men for taking an interest in the environment in which the family grows. Women not only should take seriously their ordinary minimum duties of citizenship, such as studying the issues, going to hear the candidates speak, and actually taking part in the elections, but also should follow what is being done, join organizations that act collectively to improve social and economic conditions in the community and, when possible, assume public responsibility.

My husband, when he was President, appointed a number of women to posts of importance. The one I think of first, of course, is Frances Perkins as a member of the Cabinet. When she first went into the Labor Department she outlined what she wanted to accomplish; when she left she had accomplished everything she had outlined. She was often criticized, but when the history of her term of office is written, her record will compare favorably with any man's.

There have been a number of judges, like Judge Florence Allen, who have made excellent records. Judge Marion Harron of the tax court has had as few challenges to her court opinions as any man. I think, too, of Mrs. Ellen Woodward, who is still working with the Federal Security Agency; of Mrs. Florence Kerr, who was with the W.P.A., and Mrs. Mary McLeod Bethune, who was director of the Negro division of the N.Y.A. I could go on indefinitely naming women who did remarkably good jobs and many who are still doing them.

When it comes to the field of school administration, there is no reason why women should not serve.

We must stop talking about putting people in positions because they are either men or women. Let's prepare qualified people and choose them for positions because they can do a competent job.

Now and then the question arises concerning the wisdom and possibility of having a woman President of the United States. You yourself have been suggested as the person eminently qualified for that place, but you have consistently maintained that the time is not ripe for a woman to be President. How can education prepare us men and women to accept a women President of the U.S.?

By teaching us when we are young to look for the person with qualifications to do the job and not to discriminate as to whether it is a girl or a boy that is fitted to do it.

International Relations

Some of the countries our government is helping have an illiteracy rate as high as 85 percent. How great an effort should our government make to help those countries remove illiteracy and to develop the latent talent of their people?

In every program undertaken by our government there should be an evaluation of the amount of education that is essential so that the people can take full advantage of the program. When that is ascertained, there should be an allocation of funds to make that education possible.

In what ways can our government best help other countries to develop in their people a determination to seek liberty and freedom?

The advantages of liberty and freedom must be demonstrated to people who never have had them. If they become convinced that individuals who have liberty and freedom really have a *better* life than people without them, they will strive to attain those ends. We should make it possible for them to observe such privileges in a country like ours through movies, radio and approved teaching materials.

Do you know of anything that will raise the economic level of a country as rapidly as the education of its people?

No, of course not.

The World Organization of the Teaching Profession has been granted consultative status as a nongovernmental organization under Article 71 of the United Nations Charter. Have you any suggestions as to how the organization can help the work of the United Nations?

It should have a representative attend the committee meetings of the General Assembly when they deal with subjects of interest to teachers. It also should have a representative attend such other commission and council meetings as are of interest. It should discuss those questions at its own meetings and make recommendations to the proper agencies in the U.N. so that the teachers' point of view can be heard. At the same time it should, whenever possible, make its point of view known to its own governments. In our case, that will help in forming the position of the State Department.

Do you think federal funds should continue to be provided for an international exchange of teachers and students?
Yes, I do.

Do you think an international exchange of letters between schoolchildren of the various countries is desirable and worth developing on a large scale?
I have seen the value of that when I have been abroad.

Do you think public schools should teach a foreign language in the elementary grades? What languages?
We make a great mistake in planning our curriculums not to take into account the fact that little children learn more easily through memory and by ear. Reasoning powers do not develop until they are older. I would teach languages to the very young very gradually. It is a great advantage to any child to know one or two languages besides his own.

The teachers of the Soviet and satellite countries have not joined World Organization of the Teaching Profession. How do you think the organization can promote peace, even without the teachers in the countries of the Russian orbit?
They can, of course, learn to live together and improve the understanding among the countries that have joined. The organization always should be kept open to the U.S.S.R. and the satellite countries to join. It is only through working together and being in such an organization together that greater understanding is created. We must hope in the long run to create that understanding and to live side by side, even with different ideologies.

Are we assuming too much when we expect other nations or groups to interpret our motives as friendly?
We take too much for granted. We feel very self-righteous about our motives. We think everything we do is done because of the best possible motives whereas often we act because of self-interest. When we are accused by other nations we are deeply hurt; we say they are ungrateful and do not understand what generous people we are. The best we can do about it is to teach our children history honestly and factually. This means we should not lead them to believe that everything this country does is perfect and that everything anyone else does is wrong.

Do you think we can ever "win the peace"?

I am hopeful that we can. If we keep up our military and economic strength, time is on our side. But no point can be set at which we can win the peace. We need patience and persistence. We must teach our children and our children's children that to make democracy work requires character, courage and conviction.

The world acknowledges our economic leadership, but our nation is not a leader morally and spiritually. The U.S.S.R. is most alluring in its promises ("all races are equal," etc.), and it dramatizes our every failure.

The first step toward cooperation will come, I think, in the economic field. Trade will be resumed with the democracies. But each of us in our own lives must show that democracy is trying to live up to its ideals. Only in that way can we persuade the U.S.S.R. that it can live in peace with us.

Accepting Criticism

The "mortality" rate among administrators of city school systems is very high. Can you tell school superintendents who, like you, are frequently publicly criticized how to acquire the technic of the "soft but firm answer"? Do you have to go through a cooling-off period before you reply to hecklers and vicious critics? If not, how did you acquire the ability to take unfair criticism?

Those who are in public life have to acquire an ability to take criticism, whether fair or unfair, with calmness. If it is constructive criticism, they should be grateful and consider it carefully. If it is purely destructive criticism, they should learn to ignore it. They have to reach a point where criticism never angers them but where they can think of it in an objective way and, if possible, without any bitterness.

Naturally, if people they care about are doing the criticizing, school administrators will want to consider very carefully whether these people are right or wrong, but outside of that they should try to be completely objective, hard as it is. It is a rather grueling experience, but it is useful.

65

The Joy of Reading

I was a lonely child. If I had not had books, I don't think I would have known anything about the world. But books told of people, and everything I read became a real, living story. I was fortunate, for my grandfather had the kind of library I suppose many people of that generation had, including all the classics. Nobody ever told me *not* to read anything. I am quite sure the result with me was never harmful. If I asked embarrassing questions about a book, the book occasionally disappeared; but that was only because I became too embarrassing to my young aunts.

Otherwise there was only one restriction and, oh, how I hated it! My grandmother thought you should never do on Sundays the same thing you did on weekdays, so I had special books for Sundays. Just as I would be getting interested in a Sunday book the end of the day would come and the book was taken away to be kept until the next Sunday. That was really a trial. What a way to observe the Sabbath!

I wish I could say that today I read as much as I read up to the age of 15. But I never seem to find the time to read the way I did as a child—just for pleasure—climbing into the branch of a tree and reading a whole morning through, coming in only when the bell range authoritatively from the porch to say "you have to come to lunch."

I would like that time to come again. I would like to sit for four hours and just read a book I really wanted to read, not something I was asked to or had to read, but something I had chosen.

I have never lost the habit of reading. I think if you acquire that habit while young, you realize how important the written word is. Nowadays, children have so many distractions: television, the movies, the radio. In many ways children are better informed than we were, but I think all these things accentuate the need for the written word. In the last campaign, for example, after watching the TV debates between the two candidates, I found that I wanted the record in the newspaper the next morning to be sure I had understood every point.

I was interested when one of my boys said to me the other day: "I wish I could read faster." I agreed: "Goodness, so do I." He replied: "Oh, you read twice as fast as I do." Perhaps he hasn't read enough lately; otherwise I am sure he could read faster in a short time.

But that points up one reason why some youngsters don't read much: they can't read fast enough. I think that we should give them every opportunity to learn how to read and absorb more quickly what they read.

Coronet 50 (September 1961): 74–75, 80.

I believe, too, that we should cultivate in young people the understanding of how beautiful a book is, the feeling that this is a treasure to hold in your hand and look at and guard. Too few of us really tell our children about beautiful things we may have collected—the stories behind why we may have treasured them. No wonder young people don't have an appreciation of the beautiful things of the past around them, but instead seem to take them for granted. They just need to know more about their history.

I think if we would just take the trouble to bring to young people an appreciation of beauty in books, in the content, in everything that goes into the making of a very precious book, there would be many more avid readers.

The other day I had an opportunity to go through the Morgan Library in New York, which exhibits manuscripts and early printed books. I thought how wonderful it would be for a child to have facsimiles of these early manuscripts—to see how they were corrected, to see the drawings, to see everything about the manuscripts reproduced for them.

This would add enormously to the interest young people might have in building a library of their own, which is the best way to learn the value of reading. The older generation knew its value, but I think sometimes we older people do not give our young people a chance to learn through their elders that this can be a great enjoyment.

At one dinner party in the White House I remember my husband saying to me across a table of young people (most of them still in college, and one a Hollywood starlet whom the boys thought very glamorous): "Darling, I have a young lady here who has never heard of Kipling's *The Brushwood Boy*. I just told her I think it would be a lovely thing in the movies and she would be lovely in it, but she's never heard of it."

After a pause he added: "I would like to go around this table and ask every one of you if you have ever read *The Brushwood Boy*." Of course, the only two who had read it were our own sons! And one of them very shamefully admitted: "But we wouldn't have, you know, if Mother hadn't read it to us."

Well, perhaps if we could impart our love, our enthusiasm and our enjoyment of reading to the young, it would add a great deal to their lives. There has never been a time in history when we needed so much to broaden our thinking. We cannot any longer allow our young people to think narrowly. The world is too close to us, and it grows smaller as our ability to reach into space becomes greater.

We must think in terms that are stretched constantly to include greater and greater thoughts, all leading to the realization that nothing stands alone, that everything is tied to everything else. People are tied together today, for everything we once considered of purely domestic interest has to be considered today in the context of world interest. I think if we can make our young people stretch their horizons and show them that reading is one of the ways in which this can be done, it will prepare them for life in our changing world as nothing else will do.

66

Modern Children and Old-Fashioned Manners

Etiquette, from my point of view, is not just a matter of knowing how a lunch or dinner should be served, or what the "proper" behavior is in this or that situation. There are many correct ways of behaving in almost any situation, and many proper ways of doing those things for which there are precise rules in formal etiquette books. But the basis of all good human behavior is kindness. If you really act toward people with kindness, you will never go far wrong. Most of us understand the importance of this principle in our relationships with other adults, but we sometimes fail to see that it is equally important with children. We forget all too often that a child is a person. Perhaps this is a more common failing in parents than it is in others, for no child ever lived who was not at times annoying. Yet adults are annoying also, and the well-adjusted man or woman takes annoyance from them in stride and does not become ill-mannered.

Parents owe to their children at least as much in the way of courtesy as they do to their contemporaries. Unless this truth is realized and acted upon, the peace of the home is shattered, and children grow up ill equipped for the social adjustment they must make with the world.

"Please" and "thank you" should be as commonly used by parents when speaking to their children as with others. If a parent finds that he has wrongly accused his child, or otherwise been unjust to him, an apology should be given as naturally as to any adult.

One of the fiercest and most insistent needs of the child is for identification, to be known as himself, a being distinct from all others. In this connection I always think of a little boy who came to me at one of the picnics I give every summer for disadvantaged children at Hyde Park. He had been there before and I remembered his face, but when he asked me his name I could not recall it and told him so. After he had told me and run off to play, he came back three times during the afternoon to ask me his name. Each time I was able to tell him, and, finally satisfied, he said, "Now maybe you won't forget."

The story has a profound significance for all parents. Though they are unlikely to forget the names of their own children, they all too often forget to pay the little tributes to individuality that is the due of each—praising the drawing of the one who likes to draw pictures; paying attention to the song one has learned to sing at school and repeats gladly at home; listening with

Redbook 119 (October 1962): 47, 122, 124–125, 127–128.

attention and respect to the fantasies of the imaginative one; and never, never laughing in ridicule at a small son or daughter (or a large one, for that matter). Laughing with your children at a joke, even when it is on one of you, is one of the most wholesome experiences of life. But there is no wound deeper for a child than being laughed at, and no wall more impenetrable than that built by habitual ridicule.

Such rules of behavior as this you would follow as a matter of course with your adult friends. They are even more important in your contact with your children. Adults, when a relationship with one friend deteriorates, may find companionship elsewhere; the child who faces an opaque and impassable wall between his parents and himself is alone in a shattered world.

The relationship with a child is complicated, of course, by the parents' responsibility to correct, and sometimes to punish, the child. But this in no way negates the rule of courtesy. Correction, constructive criticism and even punishment may be administered without rudeness. The bent of the natural, healthy child who feels secure in the knowledge of his parents' love is toward the kind of behavior that will win praise and approval. When sheer animal spirits, the overwhelming temptation to fulfill a desire by breaking a rule, or simply a perverse mood such as every child and every adult sometimes knows, results in mistakes or outright naughtiness, the child knows that he deserves correction or punishment. He counts on his parents to help him back to the path of good behavior.

But if the correction or punishment is administered wisely, there will be no belittling of the child as a person, no insulting expressions, no threats that the parent will not love the child as long as he behaves this way. Neither will the punishment be excessive simply because the parent has to work off his own annoyance or anger by taking it out on the child. And when the episode is over, let it be over and forgotten for both of you, as you would a difference that had been resolved between you and an adult friend.

"In the disciplined home the children have no rights," says A. S. Neill, headmaster of the Summerhill School in England. "In the spoiled home they have all the rights. In the proper home children and adults have equal rights."

Among these equal rights is the right to meet life's normal challenges. If in a friend's house your host were attempting to fix an electric-light connection or a dripping faucet and you took the work out of his hands, saying, "Let me do it," he would quite rightly consider you rude. In the same way you are showing rudeness and a lack of wisdom in your relationship with your child if you overdo the matter of helping him solve his problems. Who has not heard the disgruntled child say, "I want to do it my own self," or seen a very little one angrily knock down the house a doting parent has built with his blocks? Wait until the child asks for help, or until he is facing a serious problem that he quite obviously cannot solve for himself.

Similarly, accept the fact that you cannot protect your child from every danger that he will encounter throughout life, and do not overdo the matter of keeping him from the small dangers that always surround him. To do so is to

338

weaken his own capacity for protecting himself and is likely to fill him with unwarranted fears that may hamper him through life.

I remember a day at the country home of a friend when the eight-year-old son of my host climbed to the top of a tall ash tree, and there, clinging to a small limb, shouted with delight as the tree swayed back and forth in a high wind.

"Aren't you afraid he will fall?" I asked the father.

"My heart is just back of my teeth." he said grimly. "It scares me to death every time he does a thing like that. But I try not to let him see it. The important thing is that he isn't scared.

"When I was a child my mother would almost faint when I got more than two feet above the ground. If I were to climb to the roof of the barn, or into a tree, and she saw me, she would go white and say, 'Come down very carefully and slowly,' and stand watching me until I was on the ground again. I have been no good on a ladder or anywhere that is more than eight or ten feet above the ground ever since. I can't even stand comfortably by the rail of an ocean liner. In a hotel room that is above the second floor I find it difficult to sleep if my bed is anywhere near a window.

"I hope that the boy never falls, of course, but if he does, the chances are that he will do no more than break an arm or leg. Either of those can be mended. I doubt if what was done to me by my mother's fear ever can."

He was a wise father.

Many lessons can similarly be taught without saying a word, or with as few words as possible. This is true when it comes to teaching your children manners. In this your *example* will be more effective than any number of precepts. If parents are always courteous to each other and to their children, the children will eventually absorb courtesy.

Absorbing good manners from example does not happen all at once, of course. Kindly, courteous instruction is also necessary, and, as in all things, extreme patience. It is unrealistic and futile to expect from a four- or five-year-old the kind of manners you would take for granted in a gracious adult. The child who suddenly becomes aggressive in a room full of guests and begins to show off with loud talking and other demands for attention is not being consciously rude. He is simply obeying the demands of an individual identity seeking recognition. The same child may be quiet and well behaved in the company of a single understanding friend or surrounded only by his family.

Under such circumstances the wise parent will not make a scene and humiliate the child by severe correction in front of guests. Rather he will separate the child from the guests, to the advantage of both. The child should never feel belittled when this is done, however, or that he is unfit to meet his parents' friends. Obviously he needs to become gradually accustomed to meeting adults.

One family that I know with a five-year-old daughter has solved the problem nicely. When guests are invited for the evening, the parents ask them to come in time to say good night to the daughter. After 15 minutes or so, which both the little girl and the guests enjoy, the child is trotted off to bed.

The theory that children should be seen and not heard has as little validity today as the belief that the earth is flat. How can a child learn to communicate under an imposition of silence, or how can a parent learn to know his child or be enriched by the innate beauty and originality which so often issue from the mind of childhood if the child is not encouraged to speak freely?

Within the family, if one child interrupts another or one of the parents, he may be told, "It's Jackie's turn now," or, "Father is talking." If the parents pay considerate attention to the children, the latter will learn that each member of the family is entitled to the same attention, and the sense of fair play that is deeply embedded in the normal, secure child will dictate proper behavior.

In some homes where the family is large, it is the custom for children to eat at a separate table as long as they are young. This is sometimes a good plan because it does not cut them off from the family completely; and if there are guests, it is sometimes especially difficult to have little children at the main table. Once they are old enough, I think, the more they can be at the table with their family the better it is—first, because they feel that they are part of the whole family; and next, because they absorb certain things from their elders without needing to be taught.

The best example of this I have ever seen was Princess Juliana (now Queen Juliana) and her children when the latter were quite small, say five or six years old. The children always had breakfast with the family. Even Queen Wilhelmina made it her habit to breakfast very often with her daughter and Prince Bernhard and the children. At the end of the meal the youngsters were never expected to stay once they had finished. The older one would slide down from her chair and stand by the young one, helping her untie her bib. Then they would come to my chair, when they were staying with me, and ask to be excused. When at home they would of course go around to their mother's chair and ask to be excused. They were permitted to come to the table when there were guests for lunch or dinner only when they were considerably older. I think that this was done largely out of consideration for the guests, but perhaps it was also an incentive to them to learn good manners quickly so that they would be taken into the family circle more and more often.

How does one teach a child table manners? First of all by example. The behavior of parents is the most effective instructor. Yet precept is necessary too, and the more gently and patiently these precepts are administered, the more successful they are likely to be. Every child likes to eat with his hands. In the early high-chair stage it is futile and likely to set up a long-lasting rebellion to attempt to make him use a spoon. Fingers were not only made before forks; they are also used before forks by every normal human being. Gently and gradually as the mother feeds the child (who has so much to learn about many things), preferably with his own baby spoon, and finally puts the small spoon into the child's own hands, he will learn—only to abandon his new-found learning again and again.

Why should bread be eaten with the fingers, as adults do, and not the fascinating mashed potatoes, which feel so soft and warm to the touch? Why must two different methods be used to bring a cookie and a piece of cake or pie to the mouth? What is an arm for if not to reach across the table and seize a bit of food to carry to a hungry mouth? If one has something to say, something pressing hard for expression, what is more natural than to shout it out whether someone else is speaking or not?

These and many other tendencies, which in the adult are rightly considered discourteous, must be corrected in the child. The correction must be accompanied by patience and gentleness, however, if it is to be successful. And it must be repeated over and over again! Reasons should be given for the corrections: "It is pleasanter not to get your fingers all messy and soil your dress and other things with them. Why not use the fork or spoon?" . . . "If you reach for food that way, you are likely to upset your glass of milk. Ask your father and he will pass it to you."

But do not expect too much too soon. And do not commit a greater rudeness than his, both to the child and to the others at the table, by shouting angrily at him when he has committed some understandable infringement of good table manners. Above all, teach your children that while the home is a place for relaxed informality in many things, table manners should be essentially the same there as in the most august assemblage at a restaurant or at a dinner party.

Among the rules that have fluctuated in different times and places are those connected with eating what is put on the plate. In many homes in the past it has been (and doubtless still is in some) a rule that a child must eat everything that has been served him. At the same time many have been taught that when they are guests they must always leave a little on their plates so that they may not seem to be greedy. Both rules carried out to a literal extreme are silly.

No child should be allowed to be too choosy about his food. The habit is as often as not a method of gaining attention, and will be less likely to become established if his parents in all things give him the normal attention that is every child's due. But if he is allowed to demand special foods habitually at home and reject others, he will probably become one of those young nuisances who, as guests, look with disgust at their plates and, if they do not say loudly, "I don't like broccoli," shove it disdainfully aside.

Sometimes a child's fussiness about what he eats is soundly based. Perhaps he has a genuine dislike for a certain food. If you demand that he "choke it down," he may do just that, with a physical nausea and emotional resentment which are not only bad for his young digestion but which may well establish an unconquerable revulsion toward this food for the rest of his life.

A friend of mine as a child was forced every Sunday to eat a large helping of steamed pudding smothered in marmalade. He still dislikes marmalade so much that he cannot bear it even on a piece of toast for breakfast.

If instead of insisting that a child eat food he doesn't like you try fixing it differently and giving him a little of it without direct comment to him, you may solve the problem smoothly.

Sometimes, perhaps because of a mild stomach upset, the child simply isn't hungry. In such cases do not force food on him, any more than you would on an adult guest. Quietly remove it, consider the meal over and let that be the end of the matter. Hunger will return and the child will eat normally again.

No child of tender age should be expected to sit through protracted conversation among adults after a meal is over. But he should also be taught the graciousness of asking to be excused. If the family is alone, he should ask one or both of his parents, saying simply, "Will you please excuse me?" or, "May I be excused?" If there are adult guests, he should ask both parents and guests.

The matter of children's overhearing adult conversations presents some special problems. If a child happens to come into the room just as his parents are discussing something it is best for him not to hear, the wise parent will make no special circumstance of the matter but simply drop the subject—in the middle of a sentence, if necessary. If the child becomes curious and insists on knowing what the conversation was about, the parent may say simply, "It is something we were talking over in confidence, dear," explaining in the first instance what "confidence" is. Every child must be taught to respect the confidences of his friends and those that others hold, and there is no age too young at which to begin this instruction. Secrets are a child's delight, and an adult confidence is, after all, a secret. But in order to make the instruction meaningful, a parent must respect the child's confidences and not pry into the "secrets" he shares with his contemporaries.

Conversations should never be carried on before children by spelling out words in order to make them unintelligible. Every child instinctively resents it, for it is as discourteous as is speaking in a foreign language before an adult in order to conceal what you say.

Another bad habit many parents fall into is that of constantly using the first person plural "we" instead of the second person singular "you." "Are we feeling well this morning?" "Are we going to eat all of our oatmeal?" It would be a very stupid child who would not soon notice that this was a form of address quite different from that used by adults to one another, and thus feel somehow belittled by it. Also it is not good training in the use of the English language. When you mean "you," say "you." When you mean "we," say "we."

And the more you can legitimately use the latter, thus including the child in the planning and decisions made by the family, the better. "Shall we all go to the country this weekend?" is a better question than "Shall Mommy and Daddy take you to the country this weekend?" When it is possible and wise to ask the child to participate in the business of making decisions that affect the entire family, it is fine to do so. It increases his wholesome sense of importance and speeds the process of growing up. It is also a lesson in courtesy. But save the use of "we" for occasions when you mean "we."

Every child should be taught respect for his elders, not in such a way as to make him hypocritically unable to see anything wrong in those older than himself, but simply as one of the graces of life, a courtesy that youth in the abstract pays to age. He should learn to say not simply "yes" and "no," but to add "Mother," "Father," "Mr. Smith" or "sir" to the monosyllable. He should learn, if seated, to rise when older persons enter the room, and not to sit down again until they are seated.

Today it is almost a forgotten thing for youngsters to stand in school when their teacher enters the room, and yet, if this were done automatically, it might strengthen the unconscious respect of the students in a way that could be important for many other situations that arise.

A male child should be taught quite early to render to his small sister or girl playmate traditional little courtesies—seeing that she is seated before him, allowing her to precede him through doors, picking up things she has dropped—the kind of behavior he will be expected to show ladies when he is an adult. Here, as in all matters of training children in gracious behavior, the most effective element will be the example the father sets in his treatment of the mother.

Children must, of course, be taught respect for the property of others. And here again, the soundest base for this instruction is the respect parents show for the children's property. The father or mother who gives a child's dog away, or sends one of his most treasured, though possibly shabby, toys off as a contribution to some charity drive—or to the garbage can—without first consulting the child about it, ought not to be surprised to find a son or daughter treating the property of others in the same fashion.

Accepting individual property ownership is difficult for most children, and patience is needed to make them understand it. All living creatures are acquisitive. Dogs will fight over a bone; birds will try to push one another away from a choice worm or the rim of a bird feeder. The individual's instinct to gratify his own desire or satisfy his own need is a strong one. When a child first begins to understand that ownership is possible, the concept applies only to himself. He thinks of *his* toy, *his* food, *his* piece of candy. It is a very gratifying realization, and it is only natural that he should try to increase it by adding other objects to his possessions.

Here, where bad manners, if not corrected, may become something more serious, he must be educated to understand that everyone feels about his own property as the child himself does. Here too the examples set by his parents, both in regard to things that belong to him and those that belong to each other, are the most influential teachers. For if these examples are not good, a verbal lesson is very likely to misfire.

A child must also be taught to respect privacy, to knock on closed doors before entering, not to stand about listening to his parents' or brothers' or sisters' phone calls, not to read other people's letters, not to peek through keyholes. But instruction in these matter will fall on deaf ears if the respect you ask him to accord to others is not accorded to him.

Children should, by all means, be taught habits of neatness and cleanliness, and be made to realize that it is rude to leave toys and clothing scattered about the home the whole family shares, or to come to the table with dirty hands and face or uncombed hair. Yet it is almost as easy to overdo this as it is to neglect it. Parents who insist that a child keep spotless at play have short memories for the joys of mud pies, sandboxes, tree climbing and the healthy games children enjoy even though (and perhaps a little because) they become somewhat messy.

Every home in which there is a televisions set, or even a radio, and one or more children has a combination that presents a classic contemporary problem in behavior.

Training a child to proper use, and not abuse, of the television or radio is not an easy task. There the instrument stands. It is so simple to turn it on and forget the chores or studying one should be doing. Yet if you can help him to see that he will enjoy it only if he regards its use as a privilege to be enjoyed under proper conditions, you will have done him a service that should stand him in good stead in many other aspects of his life—with other human beings, with his obligations and with that self within the self that is the constant companion and judge of each of us.

When he is permitted to watch television, he must learn to keep the sound turned down to the lowest volume at which he can hear it, so that it will not disturb others in the house or in the neighborhood.

He should be taught to turn it off when his parents have guests and when he is reading or studying, rather than keep it going as background noise from which he derives no real entertainment.

The television set also should be regarded as something for the whole family to enjoy. No one member should be permitted to monopolize it for his favorite programs. If the child finishes his homework and finds that his parents—or, for that matter, one of his brothers or sisters—is watching a program other than the one he wants to see, he must be taught to wait until it is finished, and not interrupt it with a demand to have his own program. If he misses his program entirely as a result of his courteous behavior, he should learn to take the disappointment graciously.

If he has a guest and they decide to spend some of their time together watching television, his guest's choice, rather than his, should determine what program they will watch.

If he has brothers or sisters and their favorite programs vary, he must learn to work out with them a schedule by which all may see some of their favorite without interfering with too many favorites of the others. The principle of adjustment, of give-and-take, of sharing fairly with others, is one of the most important of all rules of community living, and if the child learns to follow it in his earliest years partly through his television habits, it will serve him well in many contacts throughout his life.

The child who habitually evades his responsibility to studies, or such duties as he has in his own home, in order to watch television is forming habits which will make it easier for him to evade his obligations to others, including those of courtesy.

There is a word which, in the past, was often (perhaps too often) used in training children and which, for many, has seemed to slip out of the English language. But I know of no real substitute for it. It is a little word of four letters with a profound significance. It is still a good word, a useful word, that should be made familiar to every child—somehow in such a way that it will retain its freshness and excitement, rather than become the label for a boring concept the child rejects impatiently: Duty. Fulfilled, it gives a child a sense of accomplishment, increases his self-respect, sets his mind at rest and frees him for fun uncomplicated by a nagging sense of guilt. These, the rewarding after-maths, and the avoidance of unpleasant self-censure are the elements that should be stressed in teaching a child the importance of duty, or, if you dislike the word as much as many people do, of being a responsible human being.

Among the strongest influences toward family solidarity and understanding are games the whole family, children and adults, can play together, thus enabling them to enjoy that kind of all-embracing family humor which is genuine, wholesome and never vindictive. Games, played in a happy atmosphere, often furnish opportunities for parents to further the training of the children in social behavior. A wise parent may frequently find it possible to solve a temporary problem in behavior with a child by seeing an element of humor in the situation and gently, without ridicule, making the child see it too. And sometimes even a very young child will be able to turn a situation which is marked by excessive annoyance or anger on the part of the parent back into normal, pleasant channels by the same method.

I remember once seeing an overwrought mother suddenly flare up in anger at her three-year-old son; the boy listened calmly for a moment to her tirade, and then as she paused to catch her breath, quietly and with twinkling eyes he misquoted an admonition she had often delivered to him. "Don't lose your temperature, Mommy," he said. The tension of the moment was released in laughter, the two were united in the affectionate companionship that was basic to their relationship and both mother and child had received a lesson in behavior—in this case from the child himself.

There are many games that are grand fun for both adults and children of every age. Further, they provide one of the best of all opportunities for lessons in fair play, courtesy and give-and-take. Many an adult's happiest memories of childhood center about the fun he and the rest of his family had together.

I still remember how, in my grandmother's home at Tivoli, Columbia County, New York, I played such games as tag and I spy with my aunts and their friends—running around the old porch where you could look through the windows and catch a glimpse of someone on the other side. There were any number of games a lonely girl (as I was) would never have played if the adults had not been willing to join in. As I grew older we played many of the word games, and even charades, which were hilarious at times, and brought joy to a child's heart, especially if she was allowed to dress up.

One of the things I remember most vividly is that on Sunday evenings we all gathered around the piano and sang hymns. That is a tradition I wish (if I had been a good enough musician) I could have preserved in my own family, for I remember it as something I enjoyed deeply as a little girl.

The wise parent can often adapt a game to the understanding and abilities of the younger children. I remember an occasion on which this was done skillfully by an English mother. She, her ten-year-old son and I were playing I spy.

In case you don't know how to play it, it goes like this: Each player in turn says, "I spy with my little eye something that begins with—" and mentions a letter of the alphabet which is the first letter of the word spelling the object. Then the other players guess in turn what it is. When it has been guessed, the play passes to the one who has successfully identified it.

We were going along at a great rate, all three of us having a wonderful time, when the three-year-old daughter entered the room. Her mother at once asked the little girl to join us, but since the child had not learned to spell, changed the game to one in which the object was identified by color instead of by name. The key statement then became, "I spy with my little eye, something that is blue," or "red," or "white," or "has no color at all," and the game went merrily on.

But several important things had been accomplished besides having fun. The family had remained a unit, with no member of it feeling left out; a child had been spared the pain of feeling inferior; and a ten-year-old child had been given an excellent lesson in adjusting his activities to the ability of one who had not yet attained the same stage of development as he had—a situation he would meet again and again, in one form or another, throughout his life and must, if he was to conduct his social relations graciously, learn to manage with courtesy and consideration. This, of course, is the heart of good manners.

Part F
Political and Policy Analysis

67

Why Democrats Favor Smith:
As a Practical Idealist

I am for Governor Smith, because of his astonishing knowledge of government, his power of clear, straight thinking, his intolerance of trickery and chicanery, his courage and unswerving honesty, but above all because he has a human heart and does not consider that success in the life of individual or nation can be measured by a bank balance or treasury credit.

The big question before our people today is whether we are to be more material in our thinking, judging administrative success by its economic results entirely and leaving out all other achievements. History shows that a nation interested primarily in material things invariably is on the downward path. Great wealth has ruined every nation since the day that Cheops laid the cornerstone of the Great Pyramid, not because of any inherent wrong in wealth, but because it became the ideal and the idol of the people. Phoenicia, Carthage, Greece, Rome, Spain, all bear witness to this truth, which is far more fundamental and vital to us than Prohibition, high or low Tariff, Catholic or Protestant Presidents. Somehow or other during the next decade we will find a way to have practical temperance. We will not always have an ineffectual, politically minded, partisan Tariff Commission. Religious intolerance is already dying out. But if we do not stem the tide of crass materialism, we are headed for a really dangerous and critical situation.

We have had in our last three Presidents three distinct types: Wilson, the Idealist, with no knowledge of practical politics, and therefore without the ability to translate his dreams into facts; Coolidge, who apparently has no dreams, who glories in shrewd politics and firmly believes that economy is the first of the Ten Commandments, and that prosperity is in some way a kind of spiritual triumph. Between these two we had a President who unfortunately lacked the courage to denounce his friends when they proved corrupt and untrustworthy. The ideals of President Wilson failed to be established as the ideals of our Republic, because he lacked tact and understanding of men and measures; they were lost in the mire of corruption which marked Harding's Administration, and they have been completely forgotten under the dollar and cents regime of President Coolidge and his advisers. What we need, and it is a crying need, is a President who will combine Wilson's ideals with Coolidge's practical knowledge of how to achieve political results, who will not spare his dearest friend if he fails to measure up to his conception of the high honesty and responsibility required of every public servant. I believe Governor Smith is such a man.

North American Review 224 (November 1927): 472–475.

His courage has been shown in this State in many political battles; for instance, in his steady and unswerving refusal to bow to the influence and power of a great newspaperman who had used his power for personal ends and earned the opprobrium of many good citizens; also, in his long fight for the people to control their water power, as against control by the big utility interests.

He is of the people and understands and respects them, but also realizes that they must be led.

He is a leader because his whole political life shows that he has a wonderful power of convincing people regardless of their usual political affiliations that he is right; a power due, I think, to the fact that he believes himself to be right with all his heart and soul, and never goes ahead until he is himself convinced. It is fortunate that a man of this rare ability has also the keen power of analysis and clear thinking which make his conclusions in the great majority of instances the right answers to the problems of the hour. Compared to these qualities his personal attitude on Prohibition is of minor importance, especially in view of the fact that, in my opinion, this is not a question between parties, but within the parties, between individuals who wish their party to be either completely wet or completely dry. So far no group has won out in either party, and as a President, with all his influence, cannot vote on any law, this question remains one to be settled in Congressional Districts, regardless of whether the President wishes the Volstead Act modified or not. When we elect enough Congressmen who are convinced that their constituents want the Volstead Law or any other law strictly enforced, we will have it done and not before.

As to the religious question, Governor Smith has made his own answer and the country seems as a whole to approve. If a few captious souls still fear the influence of Rome, it is because they must find something to fear and this is nearest at hand.

One often hears it said: "Yes, Smith has been a wonderful Governor; but will he grasp National and International questions? Have his education and opportunities been sufficient to make this possible?" My answer is that you judge a man by his record and character. His record as an executive is unimpeachable, and no one has ever dared claim the authorship of any Smith policy. He has been constructively minded in the State. Why should he not be in the Nation? All will agree that his appointments have been made with merit as the first consideration; he believes in Civil Service and supports it and refuses to use Government employees primarily as factors in a political machine.

As Governor of New York State he has had to show executive and administrative ability, he has had to choose men to head departments which required technical ability, integrity and a general grasp of varied conditions, he has had agricultural and urban problems, questions of water power development, of waterways and highways, of labor conditions, of education, of public buildings and institutions, of taxation and finance; and in his handling and solution of these questions a vast majority of the citizens of New York State have repeatedly declared their confidence in his judgment, ability and character. The field is more restricted in area, but the problems are strikingly similar to National problems, and we can say at least that no man has been to a better school in preparation for added and broader responsibilities.

Can he grasp International situations? No one can tell until the need arises, but a clear thinking man is a great asset in any situation, whether it be abroad or at home. He has grown up in a party which believes in the people knowing what the Government is doing, and that the Government should be responsible to the will of the people. This principle applied to foreign affairs means open, straightforward diplomacy. The tradition established by the last Democratic President, Woodrow Wilson, added to this principle a spirit of friendliness. Under him we created the impression abroad that we were not looking at International questions in a purely selfish spirit, but that we were willing to take into consideration the other fellow's point of view, and above all that we wanted to find a way by which International differences could be settled by justice and not by might. It would seem safe to assume that this spirit would still exist in the heart of any leader of Democratic men and women, at least to a greater extent than it has been exhibited in the diplomacy and International relations of the last two Administrations under our political opponents. Governor Smith stated in his answer to Mr. Marshall, in speaking of Mexico: "I believe in peace on earth, good will to men, and that no country has the right to interfere in the internal affairs of any other country." Furthermore, a man who knows the value of experts in dealing with questions at home and has shown good judgment in picking his advisers, we may confidently hope will exercise this same ability when it comes to dealing with International affairs.

These are my reasons for considering Governor Smith the logical Democratic candidate for President in 1928.

68

Jeffersonian Principles
the Issue in 1928

The outstanding issue today is much as it was in Jefferson's day—trust in the people or fear of the people. He said "call them, therefore, liberals, serviles, Jacobins and ultras, Whigs and Tories, Republicans and Federalists, aristocrats and Democrats, or by whatever name you please, they are the same parties still and pursue the same object. The last appellation of aristocrats and Democrats is the true one expressing the essence of all."

The Democrats today trust in the people, the plain, ordinary, everyday citizen, neither superlatively rich nor distressingly poor, not one of the "best minds" but the average mind. The Socialists believe in making the Government the people's master; the Republicans believe that the moneyed "aristocracy," the few great financial minds, should rule the Government; the Democrats believe that the whole people should govern. They have no quarrel with big business; they know we need business, big and little, for prosperity, but they do not believe the Government should be in control of any business group. The old dictum, "Equal rights for all, special privileges for none," still is the old democratic principle accepted by all. The country has been since 1920 under Republican rule, and our particular difficulties of the moment have developed logically from the Republican theories of government.

The Republicans fear their own people; therefore they distrust other people, and, instead of trying to eradicate an evil when it appears, they cover it up, until those who are interested enough to think about the men in power today in Washington are more worried by their willingness to keep silence in the face of appalling disclosures of graft than they are really troubled about the comparatively few men who have actually committed the crimes.

Shall Aristocrats Rule?

Therefore, it looks to me as if the fundamental issue between Republicans and Democrats must be fought out again: Is the Government to be in the hands of the aristocrats, some of whom may have been corrupt but who will, on the whole, give as they say an "able" administration with great material prosperity for a few perhaps and a fair amount of it for many, or shall it again be in the hands of the people who may make more mistakes but who will be free, responsible citizens again?

Current History 28, no. 3 (June 1928): 354–357.

Let us examine the results of the first theory as evidenced by the record of the last eight years.

First, we have had great scandals among men in high places; even some members of the Republican Party seem to concede this as a paramount issue.

Second, we have an agricultural problem on our hands which has been evaded so long that no one seems to have the courage to face it squarely and think it through. One section of our people, the farmers, are in a very bad way; they are gradually struggling out of their depression, but they are still "sick." They buy in a protected market and sell in an unprotected one; by this I mean that our high tariff, passed since the Republicans took office in 1920, makes it possible for manufactured goods to be sold here at so a high price that there can be no outside competition. Very little that the farmer sells is protected; so he has to meet competition and often gets very little return for his work, while he pays high for all the necessary things which he must buy and receives low compensation for what he must sell. The result is bankruptcy for him and for many banks and stores in small towns. It is quite natural that these conditions have not seemed of major importance to the men in power at present. Most of them see the problems of big business and industry, not the individual on his farm or in his corner store, and they are able and anxious to have the Government favor exclusively their interests. This is foreign to the Democratic idea of fair dealing to all. The Democrats want no restraint on legitimate business enterprise, but they do not want one group to prosper as the result of Government favor while another languishes as the result of Government neglect.

The Cause of Unemployment

Third, wages are high; they must be to meet the cost of living, but have we had a March or April in many years when unemployment has been so great as today? And why? Because the cost of everything is turning many small employers back into the class of employees; they are not able to carry the burden of creating more work and must go back to selling their own labor in competition with their fellows. In spite of all our vaunted prosperity, mills and shops are closing in many parts of our country.

Fourth, we are disputing over the length and breadth of our land whether our great water supply shall be harnessed and used to create power for our people's use either by giant companies or by the State. The claim is made that the big companies can do it more efficiently and economically and that it will mean political jobs and waste if left in the hands of the State. Yet private companies have to borrow capital at the prevailing rate of interest, and the Government can borrow it more cheaply. Little by little statesmen and politicians are learning that the kind of politics which manufactures unnecessary jobs does not pay anymore. The people are waking up and turning out of office men who use their Government positions to build up political machines; they demand the same efficiency as in private undertakings, and it is coming about.

We have seen it in New York State, and I feel sure, if the Democratic plan for water-power development goes through, we shall see it in many States.

Fifth, flood control bids fair to be a real issue for the lives and welfare of those living in a vast area who are being threatened by the long delay in any constructive policy for their relief. The bill in Congress seems to be a political football. Though temporary relief may have been given, if nothing more permanent is done in the near future, the people living in those States can scarcely feel satisfied, and the Democratic Party, which originally urged the President to call a special session of Congress to consider permanent measures of relief, can hardly be expected to be satisfied either.

Democrats' Foreign Policy

Sixth, eight years ago we were highly respected and liked in almost every foreign country. Today we are not so popular. This is partly perhaps unavoidable. We have become a creditor instead of a debtor nation, but our high tariff has prevented other nations from paying their debts in goods, which is probably the only way in which they could pay. We handled out debt agreements in none too conciliatory a spirit and with a finality which in some cases means that the grandchildren of this generation will still be paying us a good part of all they earn. All this is not pleasant for our debtors to contemplate.

We suggested a League of Nations and a World Court, and in the case of the World Court, when our first reservations were not at once accepted with joy by all the countries, we were unwilling to consider their questions or continue further negotiations.

On this side of the Atlantic we have in prospect a Pan-American Congress brought about by the Havana conference which may help greatly, but our past record is not so good that Mr. Hughes had an easy task in Havana. Our Nicaraguan policy does seem to some of our neighbors on this side of the ocean apparently open to criticism, and it took all Mr. Hughes's great ability to carry the conference to a close without some outburst against us.

We held a Naval Disarmament Conference some years ago and have since patted ourselves on the back for what we accomplished, but this year we are spending more than ever on naval armament.

I think perhaps Jefferson's foreign policy, "Peace, commerce and honest friendship with all nations, entangling alliances with none," well expresses the desire of the Democrats today, and it may help us to regain some of our lost good-will.

The Prohibition Issue

Prohibition I have left to the last. While I consider it an issue in the country today, it does not seem to be an issue between the two major parties. In both parties there are Wets and Drys, and neither party can say that it is either for complete enforcement or repeal or modification. Even if individual leaders come out with general statements, they cannot go into details and explain how they will enforce the law or how they will modify it. Therefore, I see no hope of any decisive action for some time, but look forward to an active campaign of education for some years and a final decision in the future by the people as a whole as to what course they wish to pursue.

In summing up, I feel that to a Democrat the Government today seems to have become a vast, well-oiled machine, too closely allied with special interests. Our desire is to see the conception of government return to something with a little more human outlook and understanding, not controlled by any interests, but concerned primarily with fostering the interests of all the people, thinking first of the average man's happiness, his health, his education, his labor conditions, his opportunities for joyous living. This is simply Jeffersonian Democracy—the same today as it was in 1792.

69
Old Age Pensions

I do not feel that I have to discuss the merits of old age pensions with my audience. We have come beyond that because it is many years now since we have accepted the fact, I think, pretty well throughout the country, that it is the right of old people when they have worked hard all their lives, and, through no fault of theirs, have not been able to provide for their old age, to be cared for in the last years of their life. We did it at first in what I consider a terrible way—through poorhouses—but now we have become more humane and more enlightened, and little by little we are passing old age pension laws in the various states.

District Law Should Be a Model

The state that I am most familiar with is New York. A pension law was passed there during my husband's administration. I would like tonight—because there is a law here under consideration for the District of Columbia, and because *I feel that the law should be as nearly a model law as possible because the eyes of the nation will be focused on it*—to discuss a few of the things that have come up in the administration of our law there.

No fixed sum is specified either in New York or in Massachusetts. I think that is a very good thing because it allows the investigation of every individual case by trained workers. It saves money, I believe, to the taxpayers and yet allows the needs of each case to be met. But it requires a good administration and it means that you are more dependent on having really good trained case workers; otherwise you will have unequal administration and unfairness in many ways, and, of course, the minute you have that, you have unfairness on the part of the people who are benefiting.

Seventy-Year Age Limit "A Bad Feature"

But we have an age limit: the age limit is 70 in New York State and I think that is a bad feature. I have found that in many cases where people have appealed to me much suffering might have been saved if it had been possible to have more elasticity. There are people at 70 who are better able to get along than some people at 65 or even 60, and it seems to me that in considering

Social Security 8 (February 1934): 3–4. Address to the District of Columbia branch of the American Association for Social Security, the Council of Social Agencies, and the Monday Evening Club, January 5, 1934.

a law there should be some arrangement made for flexibility as to age and some other consideration besides age alone.

I also think that our law has another disadvantage: it is dependent on yearly appropriations. The expense is met half by the locality and half by the state. I believe that we should depend, when this becomes universal, on some method of insurance—some fund which is paid into over a whole period of a person's life, or earning life at least.

First Lady's Personal Experience

The reason that I am not discussing the necessity for this law is that I feel that most of us have had personal experiences which have brought that necessity home to us. But I will tell you what first made me feel what it would mean if old people could have enough money to stay on in their own homes: There was an old family—two old sisters and two old brothers—who had lived on a farm not far from us in the country just as long as I could remember. I was away a great deal and I didn't see them often, but on Election Day either my husband or I usually drove them to the polls, and we always talked about farm conditions and whatever the happenings in their lives had been during the year. Well, I did not see them for two or three years. Then, one Election Day, I went to get them and I found one old lady in tears because that day one surviving brother had been taken to the insane asylum because the worry of how they were going to get enough to eat and enough to pay their taxes had finally driven him insane, and she was waiting to go to the poorhouse. The other old sister had already gone, and the other brother had died.

The Community Is to Blame

Well, I can hardly tell you how I felt. In the first place, I felt I had been such a bad neighbor that I did not know just what to do. I felt so guilty, and then it seemed to me as though the whole community was to blame. They had lived there all their lives; they had done their duty as citizens; they had been kind to the people about them; they had paid their taxes; they had given to the church and to the charities. All their lives they had done what good citizens should do and they simply had never been able to save. There always had been someone in the family who needed help; some young person to start; somebody who had gone to the city and who needed his rent paid. Somehow or other there was always some demand and no money was saved. And if I had needed any argument to settle the question for me—that the community owes to its old people their own home as long as they possibly can live at home—these old neighbors would have supplied it. And I think it costs us less in the end. We may, of course, run our poorhouses very inexpensively; we may find that institutional care is inexpensive, but I think our old people will live at home as cheaply as they possibly can.

We can hardly be happy knowing that throughout this country so many fine citizens who have done all that they could for their young people must end their days divided—for they usually are divided in the poorhouse. Old people love their own things even more than young people do. It means so much to sit in the same old chair you sat in for a great many years, to see the same picture that you always looked at!

Pensions Would End Bitter Situation

And that is what an old age security law will do. It will allow the old people to end their days in happiness, and it will take the burden from the younger people who often have all the struggle that they can stand. It will end a bitter situation—bitter for the old people because they hate to be a burden on the young, and bitter for the young because they would like to give gladly but find themselves giving grudgingly and bitterly because it is taking away from what they need for the youth that is coming and is looking to them for support. *For that reason I believe that this bill will be a model bill and pass without any opposition this year.*

70

Subsistence Farmsteads

It was a bright and sunny day in a mining camp in West Virginia, and a relief worker was walking down between two rows of houses, talking to a stranger as she went.

"In this house here, where we are going now," she said, "lives a young couple with two children. They have done remarkably well with the garden they started. He was a farmer before he came to the mines, and she is a very energetic young woman. She has canned dozens and dozens of things and sold all she is able in a nearby town. But their neighbors are not so fortunate. Right next door there is a family where the children undoubtedly have tuberculosis."

By this time we had reached the steps. We found the interior of the house clean, although the young woman who let us in apologized for the fact that her children were rather dirty, and her kitchen full of the mess which canning creates. It was easy to see that here was a young woman who was trying hard to bring up a healthy family and who had the standards of good and well-planned farm living in her mind. Before we had talked ten minutes, she asked the relief worker eagerly, "Is there any chance that we can get some land?" She knew that an effort was being made to persuade either the state or the mining companies to divide some land amongst the unemployed miners and she was most anxious to remove her children from the danger of tuberculosis and the family across the way, where the men spent a good deal of time drinking.

The case worker answered, "Yes, we hope that something will be done." As she emerged, she sighed a little and said, "I wonder when it will be done or if it will be done in time to serve any of these people." They had never heard of "Subsistence Farms" but they were the kind of people ideally suited to go and live on one.

II

The objective of subsistence farming is not to compete with regular farming or add to the burden of agricultural overproduction. The idea is that families engaged in subsistence farming consume their own garden products locally instead of sending them to distant markets. They are not expected to support themselves entirely by raising food, like the successful commercial farmers of the country. The plan is that they shall be situated near enough to an industry for one member of the family to be employed in a factory a sufficient number of days in the year to bring in the amount of money needed to pay for the

Forum 91 (April 1934): 199–201.

things which the families must have and cannot produce for themselves. In this way farming will be helped by industry, and industry will be helped by farming. There will be no competition with agriculture nor with industry. Industry must be centralized in order to clear up the congested slum areas of our big cities. Subsistence farms will make possible shorter hours of work in the factories as well as the decentralization of crowded populations.

This new self-supporting manner of American living is being projected under the direction of the Division of Subsistence Homesteads of the Department of the Interior. Last spring $25,000,000 was appropriated for study and practical illustration of this idea of new social and economic units. We have several models to build upon in this country, and there is always the example of the self-sufficiency of village life in France. Round about the country various model projects are being planned. In Monmouth County, New Jersey, a community is being projected for two hundred families of Jewish needle workers from nearby crowded manufacturing cities. A factory is to be built for their use; the best soil is to be set aside for homesteads; and the less fertile land is to be devoted to cooperative agriculture to serve solely the consumption of this community.

III

Recently I have observed at first hand the subsistence-farming project near Reedsville, West Virginia. In that state a great many mines have closed down; some will probably never reopen; some may reopen for a certain number of days a week during part of every year. It is being urged upon the owners of these mines that they use the land which they own above the ground for this new type of subsistence farm. The miners can still work in the mines even though their jobs may not be steady day in and day out.

The government experiment near Reedsville is designed to provide for one hundred twenty-five families especially chosen from those miners who are permanently out of work. The West Virginia College of Agriculture had made a study of unemployed miners' families and found that many of them had come to the mines only within the last few years and because they were attracted by the very high wages paid. The high wages, alas, lasted in some cases not even long enough to pay for the cheap car bought on the installment plan, and these homes are devoid of all improvements. Living conditions in the mining villages are so bad that many of the families who have come from farms long to get back again. There is good land available for the Reedsville project, with watershed hills and a certain amount of valley bottom, typical of much of the West Virginia farming land. A factory will supply the industry, and every homestead will have five acres. There will be some land suitable for pasture only, which will be owned by the community and operated on model cooperative principles. The houses, while very simple, are being planned to meet the needs and aspirations of comfort of the people who are going to live in them. They want certain very definite things, among these a chance to be clean, a shower or a bathtub in every house, a suitable tub in which to wash clothes, enough room so that each member of the family can have a bed of his own. These desires suggest some of the things which the miners lack in their present houses.

Some of the men who have been building the foundations for the first fifty houses, which are now nearing completion, will probably occupy them. You hear one builder saying, "I want to live on a hill," while another man declares emphatically, "I don't like hills." Each farm family will plan for crops suited to its own land: the man who chooses to live down in the valley will grow one thing, and the man on the hillside another. Both men will have, during the first year, the advantage of expert advice and direction from the State College of Agriculture.

These new farming families will all remain on public relief until the factory is opened and the first crops are harvested; but when a family makes its first payment the title to the land will pass to the individual homesteader. In twenty or thirty years the individual will own it free and clear of debt. This plan varies in different projects.

Plowing was going on near Reedsville all through last autumn. Now roads are being built. The question of the type of government which the community wishes to set up is a difficult one, but it is hoped that some way will be found to organize a town-meeting type which may be changed easily to fit into the state government at the end of the first year.

There are in the vicinity a number of high schools which can accommodate the children who will be sent to them. An old barn is to be converted into a local grammar school and made attractive under the direction of the Department of Education. In this building a number of experiments will be tried: for instance, it may be possible to give more vocational guidance and more handicraft work than is usually done in schools. It may also be feasible to have a nursery school to which the mothers themselves may come for a couple of hours at definite times during the week to cooperate with the teachers and learn how best to feed and discipline their children.

All these things are being discussed, and some will be actually tried out. There is the possibility that one hundred twenty-five families will be too few for this community of graduate miners, and that the population will have to be enlarged. Eventually there may be two or three factories instead of one, but in any case the farms will be kept out of competition with those farms which are run for profit.

IV

If the West Virginia experiment succeeds it may be the model for many other similar plans throughout the United States. It is easy to see in advance, however, that the people living on these subsistence farms will be far more secure than the unemployed people living today in towns, whether small or large. It is possible, too, that on these farmsteads home crafts of different kinds may be started which will furnish added income. The Editor has asked me not to fail to mention in passing the modest village furniture industry of which I have for several years been chairman in Dutchess County, New York.

If directed from some central point where good designs and color schemes may be furnished by really good artists, and the products marketed in some co-operative way, a limited but still a good and remunerative occupation may be furnished to those who stay at home on the farms and yet can find spare time to do hand work.

We shall know more about subsistence farming when the first new projects have been working for a number of years. Already there is hope that this program will solve the difficulties of a good many people throughout our country who are now suffering from unemployment or the inability to better the poor standards of living imposed on them by slums and congested areas.

71

The New Governmental Interest
in the Arts

I think that we all of us now are conscious of the fact that the appreciation of beauty is something which is of vital importance to us, but we are also conscious of the fact that we are a young country, and we are a country that has not had assurance always in its own taste. It seems to me, however, that we are now developing an interest and an ability to really say when we like a thing—which is a great encouragement to those of us who think that we want to develop in a democracy a real feeling that each can have a love of art, and appreciate that which appeals to him as an individual, and that he need not be afraid of saying when he doesn't know a great deal: "Well, I like that, I may be able to develop greater appreciation as I know more, but at least I have reached a point where I know that I like this." I have been tremendously impressed by the interest which has developed since art and the Government are beginning to play with each other. I have been interested in seeing the Government begin to take the attitude that they had responsibility toward art, and toward artists. I have also been interested in the reaction of the artists to an opportunity to work for the Government. I have had a number of letters, saying, "I have been working on a Government project. It is the first time that I ever felt that I, as an artist, had any part in the Government." I think it is a wonderful thing for the Government, and I think it is a wonderful thing for the people—for the people of the country in general—because through many of these projects I think there are more people today throughout the country conscious of the fact that expression—artistic expression—is something which is of concern to every community.

Just a few days ago in talking with a rather varied group of women, I found that those who came from other and older countries had all been to the Corcoran Art Gallery to see the exhibition there. Two of the Americans had been—but two had not been, and one of them said she hadn't even heard there was such a thing. Finally, they said that they would make an effort to go, and one of the women who came from a country across the ocean replied, "But you must not miss it. It is the most significant thing in Washington." I was very much interested that that should come to a group of American women from a foreigner. From my point of view, it is absolutely true, for in a way that exhibition expresses what many of us have felt in the last few years but could not possibly have either told or shown to anybody else. That is the great power

American Magazine of Art 27 (September 1934): 47. Address to the Twenty-fifth Annual Convention of the American Federation of Arts, Washington, D.C., May 1934.

of the artist, the power to make people hear and understand, through music and literature, or to paint something which we ordinary people feel but cannot reveal. That great gift is something which, if it is recognized, if it is given the support and the help and the recognition from people as a whole throughout this country, is going to mean an enormous amount in our development as a people. So I feel that if we gain nothing else from these years of hard times, if we really have gained the acceptance of the fact that the Government has an interest in the development of artistic expression, no matter how that expression comes, and if we have been able to widen—even make a beginning in widening—the interest of the people as a whole in art, we have reaped a really golden harvest out of what many of us feel have been barren years. I hope that as we come out of the barren years, those of us who can will give all the impetus possible to keeping up this interest of the Government, and of the people in art as a whole.

I hope that in all of our communities, as we go back to them, we will try to keep before the people the fact that it is money well spent to beautify one's city, to really have a beautiful public building. I could not help this afternoon, when my husband was giving a medal of the American Institute of Architects to a Swedish architect, thinking of the story which has been told by the Government that he must finish this beautiful building in three years. When the three years were up he told them he couldn't finish it, that he must go on and take the time to really make it his ideal, the thing he had seen in his dreams—he did not like what he had done. And it was not the Government officials who said, "Go ahead and make this thing as beautiful as you can make it"—it was the people of the country who insisted that if he wanted ten years, he should have ten years—and he should make of this thing something that really was the expression of a "love"—a piece of work that was done because he loved to do it.

That is something I hope someday we shall see over here, and that is what this Federation is fostering, I know. I hope that in every community throughout this country, that spirit can be fostered which makes a piece of work worthwhile because you love to do it, regardless of the time you put into it, and because it is worth everything that you can put into it to give to the world a really perfect thing. All that I can do tonight is to wish you all great success in the work that you are doing, and hope that those of us who are only learning and who need much teaching, will sometime be able to help you. Thank you.

72

The Unemployed Are Not
a Strange Race

The work that you women have done and the understanding you have shown is very gratifying to everyone who knows what you are doing. Let us try, if we can, to bring to people who are not in this group that we call the unemployed and who have no knowledge of our successful efforts the story of what is really happening. We must encourage visitors to come to our centers of work where they will be certain to be impressed with our sincerity and efficiency.

Another task for us to undertake and a very important one, is to convince many unthinking people that the unemployed are not a strange race. They are like we would be if we had not had a fortunate chance at life. Some of us regard the unemployed remotely, as if they were thousands of miles away, and had no personal call on anyone's sympathy. It isn't the intention to be cruel and indifferent. It's just that it is very hard for people who do not come face to face with suffering to realize how hard life can be.

I have a feeling that in the next few years in addition to helping themselves, we in this group must take on the task of educating the fortunate people into an understanding of the lives of the unfortunate.

If the fine characters can be developed against such odds as we see about us, we surely can and must solve these problems that make it difficult for the great majority of our people to live decent lives.

We simply cannot sit back and say, "all people cannot live decent lives." We've got to try to make this goal our particular responsibility. I'm not a very wise person but I do know that this cannot be accomplished unless people who have much get to know about people who have little.

We must all see how well worthwhile it is to help those who are struggling heroically, for if once we have this kind of understanding, good will and brains and enthusiasm will put over a magnificent job.

Democratic Digest 13 (June 1936): 19. Address to the Washington Conference of the Women's Professional Project of the WPA, Washington, D.C., May 4, 1936.

73

Helping Them to Help Themselves

Some of us who have been going around America are impressed with the fact that one type of organization might possibly be a real help in carrying people through hard times without needing so much Government assistance. It requires, however, a consciousness on the part of the whole community that there are difficulties to be solved and a willingness to set its shoulders to the wheel and help to solve them. The particular activity I have in mind is the self-help cooperative. To many people that is just a name and means very little, but to some people it means the preservation of self-respect, the development of a new skill or the practice of an old one, and a chance to start out again with a background of security.

The first self-help cooperative that I remember hearing much about was the one established in Richmond, Virginia. The principle of the self-help cooperative is that anyone, old or young, if he has need to do so, may come in and work, and that his work hours will be exchanged for scrip which can, in turn, be exchanged for commodities and services performed by others, also members of the cooperative. In 1938 in the Richmond Citizen's Service Exchange, 211,300 hours were worked by the members. For this work, scrip was issued to the workers and they exchanged it for food, clothing, shoes, bedding, and fuel wood.

In some places even shelter may be provided in this way, and frequently beauty-parlor work and barbering are done. In order to do this, all these activities must be carried on in the exchange, which means, for instance, that if you have a man who is capable of being a baker, you must give him a bake oven and the material for making bread. So the community must be conscious enough of the need to furnish the bake oven and the materials for bread. The baker, in return for his hours of labor, may want to buy a suit. Some other person who gets his bread in exchange will have spent his hours of labor in repairing, cleaning, and pressing a suit which somebody in the community has not needed and has therefore turned in to the self-help cooperative to be renovated for someone who does need it. You see, you cannot start a self-help cooperative with nothing.

The more things the people who come in are able to do, the more things you have to get from the community in order to enable them to go to work. For example, if you have good laundry workers, somebody has to donate laundry machinery; if you have people who know how to make and upholster furniture, somebody has to donate the necessary machinery. But in the end

The Rotarian 56 (April 1940): 8–11.

369

these people who work in the exchange do not suffer from the stigma of being unemployed and on relief.

Of course, on the Works Projects Administration (WPA) there should be no sense of stigma, because one gives work in return for what he gets, but I am sorry to say that in many places I have found deep resentment at the attitude of those who interview WPA workers. On the other side of the picture, there is a resentment on the part of many people toward the WPA worker which prevents him from getting a job on the outside, which he could frequently fill and would give a great deal to obtain.

In the self-help cooperative these feelings are not present. What is furnished by the community is usually material which would otherwise be wasted, and, except in the case of money granted by the Government or by some other source to pay for trained supervision or for certain definite expenses which cannot be eliminated, there is very little direct tax in the way of cash taken from the taxpayer.

The Richmond Citizens' Service Exchange served as a model for the establishment in Washington, D.C., of a self-help exchange, though it has developed differently to fit the needs of a different community. In 1939 this exchange gave work to between 600 and 680 people a month. In 1939, 422,554 hours of work were provided. It is interesting to see the ways in which those workers spent the scrip earned: 181,524 pieces were spent for meals and bread; 103,553 pieces for clothing and such household supplies as sheets, towels, and table linen; 27,354 for furniture and furniture repair; 15,884 for fuel; 13,023 for shoe repair; 10,547 for barbering and beauty-shop services.

In that list of scrip spent, which represents hours of labor, is the tale of the possibility of getting a new job. If you can get something to eat, even if it is not entirely adequate; if you can get new clothes and have your shoes repaired, and go to a barber or a hairdresser, you can start again on the job-hunting business in the frame of mind which gets a job.

Self-help, like WPA, is something to tide us over until the nations of this world solve their economic problems and recognize the fact that no civilization can possibly survive which does not furnish every individual who wishes to work a job at wages on which he can live decently.

I grew up in an era when I remember hearing many people say with some contempt that this or that individual felt the world owed him a living. The idea was that the individual in question was unwilling to work and that, therefore, society had no obligations toward him. I am inclined to agree with the idea, but we are up against a different problem now.

Most of the people who are out of work are ready and willing to work. You and I can pick out, of course, individuals who like to live on other people's labor and who perhaps have to be forced to work. The great majority of people who are not ill or too old are ready and anxious to work, however, and in this curiously complicated civilization which we have created through the centuries, there is no work for them to do. We ought to change that old saying and say that a civilization and an economic system which does not recognize its responsibility to answer this question of how work at a living wage can be furnished every individual, should be held in as great contempt as we used to hold the individual who had the attitude that he could go through life effortlessly and expect the world to look after him.

The self-help cooperative has no use for anyone who is not willing to do a good day's work, but the cooperative has this advantage—every age is served alike. In different parts of the United States self-help has been a spontaneous response of workers to prolonged unemployment. Both in Richmond and in Washington, D.C., it was initiated by people who saw that it might solve certain difficulties and wished to make a demonstration of what could be done; so that in these two instances it has not sprung up so clearly from the people themselves. I have seen it, however, with curious vitality, spring up in places where you would expect to find utter discouragement and loss of all initiative. Such things as this have happened: unemployed workers have borrowed idle tractors and asked nearby farmers if they would take their labor for unsold potatoes. It is just going back to the early days of America and using mother wit and neighborliness to keep alive.

During the last seven years, for the first time, these sporadic efforts of idle workers have been systematized and certain precise economic aims and definite techniques of operation have been worked out, and in certain of these the Government has supplied funds with which to buy necessary tools.

Self-help cooperatives should be looked upon as a protection for industrial workers who are subject to the present extremes which require in many industries at times a maximum of employment and at other times throwing great numbers of people back on their own resources. In another field, the Farm Security Administration, an effort has been made to help the small farmer provide himself with a broad base of real income by expanding his productive activities so as to supplement his cash income in good years and in bad years to make him more self-sustaining.

The last Government grants to these self-help cooperatives were made in 1936, and 125 exchanges are still in existence and going strong. The essential activities are always the production of food, the cutting of fuel wood, and the making of clothing, but many other things have been done in different parts of the country, such as dairying, poultry raising, fishing, plumbing, carpentry, baking, operating cafeterias and beauty shops, and repairing automobiles, radios, and shoes.

The Barter Theater in Abingdon, Virginia, was based on much the same barter idea which furnished the springboard for nearly all self-help cooperatives, and I have never forgotten a delightful story I heard told at a luncheon a year ago by Robert Porterfield. He told of looking out of the window and seeing a man and his wife and a cow standing outside the theater. Shortly the man came in and inquired how much milk would be needed for a ticket to the show. He was told and went out and brought the milk in. Mr. Porterfield asked if the farmer's wife was not to attend also, and he answered: "Sure, but I ain't doing her milking for her."

So you see, everybody must do his own work, but the cooperative spirit which underlies the whole movement is valuable education for a democracy. Every day you work you realize that you cannot work for yourself alone, but all the other workers must be producing too in order that you may barter for what you wish and need. The more you help the others, the more you really gain yourself. Good doctrine to inculcate in the citizens of a great democracy!

It seems foolish to have to repeat that the cooperative does not compete with factory production, but it is necessary to say so over and over again apparently. Industry has at times been fearful lest these self-help groups might become a menace, but after all, they need these workers at times and they need workers who have skills and who are accustomed to work with good equipment.

In a way, the running of a self-help exchange is insurance for industry that its workers will not come back rusty and have to be reeducated in their work when they are needed. What they produce in the exchange is for consumption among themselves. With no income they could not buy from outside. If they were not working in the exchange, they would be a complete charge upon the community. This would not perhaps be serious if it meant that you could take care of them through relief in the cheapest way possible for the short time and that then they would return at the call of industry to their usual jobs, but that is not what happens as a rule. If they are idle, they are underfed, their families lack food, a decent home, and a chance for recreation, and so disintegration begins. A young criminal may develop in a family which has never had that kind of a blot before; some of the children may develop tuberculosis. When a worker is called back, his background, his own condition, unfits him to be of any value.

This is the thing which too few people think about when they count the cost of giving men and women work in self-help exchanges or even on the WPA or any place which is not the usual form of employment in either urban or rural localities.

I do not see how it is possible to study the results of the self-help exchanges without being anxious to see this work supported and extended. True, there have been some failures, frequently because of lack of leadership or lack of knowledge on the part of the community or group working out their particular community problem. We need to give more study and thought to helping people to help themselves, and that is why I hope that communities all over the United States will take an interest in self-help cooperatives.

74

Address to 1940 Democratic Convention

Delegates to the convention, visitors, friends: It is a great pleasure for me to be here and to have an opportunity to say a word to you.

First of all, I think I want to say a word to our National Chairman, James A. Farley. For many years I have worked under Jim Farley and with Jim Farley, and I think nobody could appreciate more what he has done for the party, what he has given in work and loyalty. And I want to give him here my thanks and devotion.

And now, I think that I should say to you that I cannot possibly bring you a message from the President because he will give you his own message. But, as I am here, I want you to know that no one could not be conscious of the confidence which you have expressed in him.

I know and you know that any man who is in an office of great responsibility today faces a heavier responsibility, perhaps, than any man has ever faced before in this country. Therefore, to be a candidate of either great political party is a very serious and a very solemn thing.

You cannot treat it as you would treat an ordinary nomination in an ordinary time. We people in the United States have got to realize today that we face now a grave and serious situation.

Therefore, this year the candidate who is the President of the United States cannot make a campaign in the usual sense of the word. He must be on his job.

So each and every one of you who give him this responsibility, in giving it to him assume for yourselves a very grave responsibility because you will make the campaign. You will have to rise above considerations which are narrow and partisan.

You must know that this is the time when all good men and women give every bit of service and strength to their country that they have to give. This is the time when it is the United States that we fight for, the domestic policies that we have established as a party that we must believe in, that we must carry forward, and in the world we have a position of great responsibility.

We cannot tell from day to day what may come. This is no ordinary time. No time for weighing anything except what we can best do for the country as a whole, and that responsibility rests on each and every one of us as individuals.

No man who is a candidate or who is President can carry this situation alone. This is only carried by a united people who love their country and who will live for it to the fullest of their ability, with the highest ideals, with a

The New York Times, July 19, 1940, p. 5.

determination that their party shall be absolutely devoted to the good of the nation as a whole and to doing what this country can to bring the world to a safer and happier condition.

75

Why I Still Believe in the Youth Congress

When you and I were young, there was no need for a youth congress. We sat and listened to our elders. We went out, when the time came to earn a living, and we found jobs—at low wages, to be sure, and with pretty hard working conditions; but that was what we expected to find. We did the jobs, and a surprising number of us managed to find new avenues opening up, new opportunities, new worlds to conquer. The rest of us lived and died in drab and difficult surroundings, with our enjoyments frequently curtailed to some rather elemental things.

I once asked a woman who held a baby in her arms, and was surrounded by half a dozen other children of varying ages, why, in her community, all the men and some of the women got drunk on paydays. Her answer was: "There are only two pleasures we can have. One is drink and the other is sex." Hence the preponderance of drunks in the old days in what was known as the "lower classes" and the numberless children of the poor.

Enough people went out and found new opportunities for us to forget those who did not.

The need for a government program to help unemployed people; the need for a government program to help youth get more training for a job; and the need for various groups to get together to discuss their own difficult situations, is why we have forums, workers' alliances, and a youth congress. That is why people do not see in a name just a happy group of youngsters, and why some people are afraid of them. In reality, it is not the youngsters, nor even what they do or what they say or think, but it is the circumstances which have led to these groups getting together which inspire people with fear. So far, these groups are not very strong, but nobody knows when they may be. That is why we find the comfortable people of the world looking at them warily. Between four and five million unemployed young people is the estimate made by the American Youth Commission. That means that there are more people unemployed today below the age of twenty-five than over. A serious problem for youth.

Let us stop for a minute to consider just what our attitude as older, responsible citizens in a democracy should be. We cannot deny that we have a certain responsibility, because the world as it is today was made by us. If we have wars in Europe and the Far East, it is not the young people of twenty or thirty who carry any of the responsibility. It is we who saw war, the last war of

Liberty 17 (April 1940): 30–32.

twenty years ago, who have been directing public affairs, either actively or indifferently, ever since, who must now wake up in the night and wonder just what kind of world we have built for the youth of today.

Oh, we can hide behind such remarks as: "Life is no more difficult today than it was forty years ago." . . . "Those who want to work really can get ahead." . . . "Youth has gone soft. We have done too much for them." All these things are probably true in isolated instances. But the big thing is that we made the world such as it is today, and we had better face the fact that at least youth has a right to ask from us an honest acceptance of our responsibility, a study of their problems, cooperation with them in their efforts to find a solution, and patience in trying to understand their point of view and in stating our own.

Like so many other countries in the world, we are seizing upon the fear of Communism as a good excuse for attacking anything we do not like. Of course we have Communists in this country, and of course they appeal to the youth. The Communist Party leaders are giving youth training; they will help them to live while they volunteer as workers in something which they believe is going to help other young people. They are giving them a feeling that they are important in the world, a wide brotherhood working to improve the conditions of their fellow human beings. We who believe in democracy could do just the same for youth if we would take the trouble; but we have either failed in intelligent understanding of youth, or we have been apathetic ourselves, and believed that the apathy which is the attitude of the greater part of youth even today would continue and make unimportant the activity of any small number of people.

Even when a reputable journalist like Mr. Fulton Lewis, Jr., starts out to give a report on a meeting of a youth group, he does not take the trouble to get the details of the picture accurately—and that is one of the things which make youth resentful. For instance, he says that "the Dies Committee subpoenaed the head of the Youth Congress, Joseph Cadden." If he would look back in the records, he would find that the Dies Committee subpoenaed no one before making a statement to Congress about the Communist control of the Youth Congress; that committee was then requested to allow some of the Youth Congress leaders a hearing, and did nothing about it until November, after the report had been made to Congress in the previous January. Then, not Mr. Cadden, who had been secretary for two years, but Mr. William Hinckley, who had been chairman two years before, was subpoenaed. Mr. Hinckley was notified that the hearings were postponed, and then one afternoon a telegram arrived at the office of the American Youth Congress asking Mr. Hinckley to appear before the committee in Washington the following morning.

At this hearing a request was made that Mr. Cadden and Mr. Jack McMichael, the present chairman of the Youth Congress, should testify with Mr. Hinckley because the latter was not familiar with many of the activities of the Youth Congress during the past two years. This was allowed. Mr. Lewis proceeds to say that I was at Mr. Cadden's elbow and helped him and his companions to plan their testimony, and that I suggested the tactics, and at midday recess and in the evenings dined them at the White House. That last statement is the only statement which is true. I went to the hearings, but I was not at Mr. Cadden's elbow, nor did I plan the testimony nor the tactics.

Then you come to the description of what Mr. Lewis called "the Youth Congress Institute of Citizenship." And again the statement is inaccurate; because the Youth Congress sponsored and arranged the Citizenship Institute, but the people who attended were not of necessity affiliated with the Youth Congress. It has been said that they were not a cross section of the youth of America, and we will have to accept that as true; because a cross section, to be truly representative, would have to have in it a great many young people who would never leave home to go to any institute of any kind.

These youngsters came from all over the United States, however, and from every type of background; and it was quite reasonable to suppose that among such a big group here would be at least an organized representation of the Communist group, and that, having been trained while many of the others had not, they could make themselves felt. There is nothing very surprising about that.

Now let us come down to the actual meeting. Mr. Lewis says that Mr. Cadden told him that about 1,900 of the 5,130 young people who registered came from New York City, and that other officials said that close to 4,500 of this group were from New York City. I am sure Mr. Cadden was speaking from his knowledge of the registration, but I have asked for the final check, and find that 2,212 young people came from New York City. I also found that thirty-eight states and the District of Columbia had representatives at this Institute.

As to the difficulties which my young cousin, Archie Roosevelt, and his friends had in being heard, I can only say that I think they showed very little intelligence if they really were interested in getting over their point of view and not merely interested in making a disturbance. My experience is that if you want to get over a point of view, you find out the correct way of being heard. These two young men attempted to present a resolution during a meeting which was scheduled for speeches only, and no discussion. When informed that it was not the time to present a resolution and that the Institute could pass no resolutions, Mr. McArthur or Peter Tropea threw a book of rules governing the Senate and the House at the chairman of the meeting, and were then hustled out by those who felt that the meeting should proceed as scheduled. The next morning, before the opening meeting, the rules governing the procedure were adopted. Everyone wishing to speak could send up his or her name and, in the order in which the slips were received, would be allowed to come to the platform and speak for two minutes. You can say a good deal in two minutes if you are willing to be concise and clear. Here was the chance for these two young men to put over their point of view; but they did not take advantage of the opportunity.

At the last session, young Archie Roosevelt sent up a question to me in the proper manner, and I answered it—in fact, picked it out to answer first, so as to be sure that it would not be overlooked.

I have attended a great many meetings in the course of a long life, and I have seen steamroller tactics used by adults, and I have yet to see those methods used in the American Youth Congress meetings.

It is true that only every fourth person from New York City asking to speak was given a hearing, but that was done to get a greater variety of speakers before the group.

This was a serious crowd of young people. Most of them had barely enough money to come to Washington for the three days. They sat up all night in buses and in cars. The fact that 20 percent of those present were Negro youth simply means that Negro youth has many problems.

It did not mean that these youngsters were out on a spree, whether white or colored.

Now to the question of the meeting on the White House lawn. Many young people started to parade after spending the night in buses with very little sleep. It was raining and it was cold. The young people to be addressed stood without any protection. There was nothing in the weather to encourage enthusiasm or to inspire a mood in which reproof could be accepted without rancor. The President tried to be ingratiating and he certainly had a kindly feeling toward his audience. It is true the young people showed bad manners, but how many older people would have gone through that ordeal and have accepted criticism gracefully? I do not condone bad manners, nor do I condone disrespect for a high office; but only a fraction of those present showed such disrespect. I think all of us in public life understand the type of audience we are addressing, and we do not expect, under certain conditions, the kind of self-discipline and self-restraint which might be expected from older people or even from young people with different backgrounds. I wonder if older people would always be able to rise above the feeling of being baffled by their problems when those to whom they look for leadership and reassurance seem to fail them?

No, I do not condone bad manners, but I am experienced enough to understand them sometimes in both old and young. Youth should not be pampered, but they should be treated fairly and sympathetically. They must learn by their own mistakes, but we must not make them feel that their mistakes are irretrievable.

Now as to the hisses which greeted some of my statements. Why should anyone who goes before a group of people to express points of view which conflict with those held by some of the audience expect not to be hissed?

The Columbia University students mentioned in Mr. Lewis' article were quite right when they said: "Do we have to pay for her help by subscribing to what she says?" I never for a minute would expect such a thing. I hold no office which requires respect. The President does. That is why bad manners on the lawn of the White House was worse than bad manners in the auditorium. I did not go to answer questions for the Citizenship Institute as the President's wife. I went as Eleanor Roosevelt, to answer, as honestly as I could, questions that were going to be put to me as an individual. I had the obligation not to place the President or the administration in any difficulties through my answers. Outside of that, I had an obligation to be truthful and give whatever information I could. The young people had an obligation to listen to me because they had asked me to come, but no obligation whatsoever to agree, nor to suppress their feelings, whatever they might be.

The disturbance in the gallery of the Congress was, of course, unfortunate. Had these youngsters been older, they would have realized that it was very foolish and that it would bring them discredit. In addition, it would tend to create antagonism to the bill in which they were interested.

Mr. Lewis quotes Mr. Ernest Lindley as writing: "They [the American Youth Congress] have washed themselves out. It is doubtful whether even Mrs. Roosevelt could obtain a hearing of their case [in public opinion] after their performance here." This is perfectly true as far as newspapers and certain sections of public opinion are concerned, but they haven't washed themselves out with the young people. Whatever else the Institute did, it awakened in a great many young people a realization that there are others who are struggling with the same questions that they are struggling with. A boy earning two dollars a week told me that the main thing he got out of the meeting was the feeling that he had a lot of friends all of whom had similar problems to his own. It gave the young people a sense of fellowship.

All the attacks made upon the congress have only consolidated the feeling of "youth against the world." That is a danger, I think; because what we want to do is to have all ages work together to solve the problems of today. We have gone about obtaining this cooperation most stupidly. Whether we can retrieve what we have lost, and make these youngsters feel that the attacks that have been made upon them in the press do not represent the attitude of thinking and sympathetic older people, I do not know. If we cannot, then I think we have done a dangerous thing; because, whatever else this meeting did, it awakened a great many more young people to the fact that they were being attacked as young people, and that is not a good spirit to foster.

There are many young people who attended the Institute who differ with many things which were said, and who do not hold many of the beliefs expressed even by some of the American Youth Congress leaders. Young people are no more apt to think alike on every subject than are older people. The fact remains, however, that a big group of young people who have taken very little interest in their government, or in the attitude of their elders, or even in the troubles of other young people, are beginning to stir.

The American Youth Congress may lose some of the groups which were affiliated with them, but they will be sorry if they lose any members, because I think it is important to join together in work on the main issues—namely, (1) to try to help young people to get jobs; (2) to try to advance the cause of civil liberties in this country; (3) to try really to study what will bring us more permanent peace in the future.

So much for the Institute!

The American Youth Congress itself, because of the action of its New York City Council, was condemned for withholding approval from Finland and tacitly approving the Russian invasion. At the last meeting, the cabinet which is the governing board of the American Youth Congress voted to "dissociate itself from the statement on loans to Finland made at the pre-Institute meeting in New York," and pointed out that this New York City meeting was not empowered to act for either the American Youth Congress or the New York City Council of the Congress.

I wish we could look at this whole question of the activities of youth-led organizations from the point of view of the wisest way for older people to help youth. We certainly cannot help by attacking them, or by refusing to cooperate when we are asked for financial assistance or for speakers to attend their meetings. Making inaccurate statements about them is not helpful. We must go and deal with them as equals, and we must have both courage and integrity if we expect respect and cooperation on the part of youth.

76
A Spanking

I think I remember reading once upon a time that the most unpardonable sin was stupidity. I am not sure, however, that imputing stupidity to others is not even less easily forgiven.

There appeared some weeks ago an article in this magazine, the opening paragraphs of which were addressed to me by the authors, Archie Roosevelt and Murray Plavner.

One of the authors of this article had sent me word that he would like to see me during the Citizenship Institute in Washington, D.C., last February. I responded that I should be delighted to have him dine with me, but that he would find some members of the American Youth Congress present, two members of the New York Junior League, besides my own son and a friend of his from the University of Virginia. I thought it would be a good opportunity for these young people to meet and have a general clearing up on certain points in fair and open discussion. Archie's answer was that he had to go back to New York City and would see me another time. I have had no further direct word from him.

I wonder if only with age do we acquire certain values. I was busy too at that time, and yet I felt that it was important to talk things out in order to find a basis for unity instead of dissension among the young people.

Our young authors tell us about the preparation of their two resolutions and their efforts to introduce them. They acknowledge that they knew they would not be allowed to introduce them but they were trying to show publicly that the A.Y.C. leaders are Red. I wonder if these young people realize that because of their stupidity they have quite legitimately awakened among a great many young people the idea that they are not so much interested in the problems with which American youth is primarily concerned as they are in destroying the A.Y.C. Of course this is hard to believe, and yet this is the impression they have managed to create in the minds of a number of young people.

I am sure if these two young men had come to the Institute with constructive resolutions, and suggestions as to how to go to work to help young people find jobs, or as to how to obtain better preparation, or how to organize young people to protect their civil liberties, or how young people can help promote peace in the world, they would have found no difficulties in the way of presenting their resolutions and suggestions.

It was not the correct time to introduce resolutions, in the middle of a speech, and at a session where no discussion was scheduled, and among a

Liberty 17 (June 22, 1940): 6–8.

group of young people who had no power to pass resolutions for the A.Y.C. No one can prevent any people gathered together from passing resolutions, but these young people could do nothing which would in any way affect the A.Y.C. This Citizenship Institute was sponsored by the A.Y.C., but many of the people attending had no affiliation with the Congress. On the last morning, the Assembly of the A.Y.C. had a small meeting, but even the Assembly cannot make new policies for the whole American Youth Congress. They must recommend to the national convention, which will meet next July.

I could not help thinking, when I saw the young men get up and try to offer their resolutions, of how stupid were their tactics. Had they waited until the next day and sent up their names, they would have been allowed to make a two-minute speech on anything they wanted, and even if they could not pass resolutions they could have got their ideas across for the consideration of the group. That made me suspect that they were not really interested in getting the group to consider the ideas which they were interested in, but that they might be more anxious to create a disturbance and force the group to put them out in order to create a disagreeable situation.

Stupid tactics are not the kind to endear one to the youth of America. I have always found our youth responded to honesty and fair play. They may disagree, they may fight you, but they will respect you unless you are not honest or lack courage.

Appended to their article is a most interesting document which I suppose they prepared, though it comes at the end of their article and is entitled: How Some Youth Congress Utterances Compare with Avowedly Red Ones. In parallel columns are placed: Excerpts from the Declaration of Rights of American Youth, promulgated by the A.Y.C., and excerpts from the extreme leftist pamphlet, In a Soviet America—Happy Days for American Youth.

Obviously this is an attempt to show that the A.Y.C. patterned its declaration on the declarations in the Communist pamphlet. Of course, as one reads through these similar utterances, there is very little in either one that, as good American citizens, we might not advocate. The point which is left out is that the Communist pamphlet was published in August, 1935. The A.Y.C. Declaration was drawn up at the Detroit meeting in July, 1935, a month before this pamphlet was published. This would lead one to suppose the young Communists had taken from the A.Y.C. such poetic and patriotic utterances as they could readily agree with.

Imitation is the sincerest form of flattery, so instead of the A.Y.C. being influenced by the Communists, it seems to be the other way round, and one should rejoice.

I think it would have been interesting if either the editor of this magazine or the authors of this article had searched through some of the Republican and Democratic Party platforms, and appended to this document some similar sentiments which I am quite sure they could have found. I vaguely remember both platforms saying something about being interested in American youth, in education, and usually somewhere there is mention of labor's rights to organize and bargain collectively. In both platforms there is mention of flood control, mention of farm life and what should be done to help the farmer.

The things which these young men do not point out are the divergences between the Communist pamphlet and the A.Y.C. Declaration. The essence of the Communist pamphlet is that this potentially splendid country can only be restored to its people by the establishment of a "Soviet Socialist America" through a "working-class revolution." "Laws protect bosses," says the Communist pamphlet. "If, therefore, the workers continually violate the law when they fight for their rights, it must be because the law not only does not defend their interests, but contradicts them. It can only be because the laws are enacted to protect and defend the capitalists. . . . In order to change the conditions under which we live, completely, it is necessary to abolish the rule of the capitalists completely."

The Youth Congress in no way advocates the overthrow of capitalism, and the essence of its position is that we must work within the existing framework of legality and constitutionality for the improvement of the conditions of youth and the strengthening of the American system of government.

The importance of these two documents lies in their difference, and not in their similarities; but I suppose when one desires to prove something it is hard to recognize even something as essential as this.

Now to their questions (addressed to me):

"1. The credo of the American Youth Congress, which she so graciously endorsed, was simply a rewrite of Communistic doctrines."

I suppose by the credo they mean the creed which was read to the Dies Committee. It is quite true that the young Communists subscribed to it, but I think it is no less good on that account. Incidentally, the members of the Dies Committee seemed to think well of it.

If you read this creed—and I print it at the end of this article—I think you will agree that it is in essence the expression of democracy and American feeling.

"2. Under Communist influence, the boys and girls of the Youth Congress adopted a platform that could hardly have been Redder."

I cannot tell what platform is referred to, but I have read most of the resolutions, the constitution, and bylaws of the A.Y.C., and while I do not always agree with the details of their thinking, I have yet to find anything "Red" in their pronouncements.

"3. Certain of these young people have two names, one for the Congress and the other the real name."

I do not happen to know of any of the young people who have two names. However, I have known other people, adults, to use two names. Some rather well known authors do that, and a number of women use one name for business and another for personal life. Unless this changing of names is done for sinister reasons, there is nothing very terrifying about it, and if they are doing it for sinister purposes, then you may be sure that sooner or later these people will be suspect because of some destructive action. Then the arm of the law will reach out and examine into their comings and goings. If the legally constituted authorities find something wrong in their actions, they will be called to account.

Perhaps, if these young authors had asked me, I would have told them that in the course of a long life I have probably read much more Communist literature than they have, and, I am sure, more A.Y.C. literature.

The description given in the article of the meeting on the White House lawn is fairly accurate, but they seem to suggest in one paragraph that the President knew that their little group of four was offering certain resolutions. Of course the President was as ignorant of their existence and of anything they intended to do as was any other official of the government, because only the people who really take the trouble to follow very closely meetings of this kind would have known anything about such unimportant occurrences.

I am glad that the young men think that the President would make an effort to take me "off the spot." That would be a chivalrous thing to do, but I am afraid that the President would hardly think it necessary. He accepted many years ago the fact that I was prepared to fight my own battles.

These young men speak as though the entire 5,130 delegates, except for their own four, all thought alike on every question. As a matter of fact, there was probably as much divergence of opinion as there would be in a group of that size composed of adults, or of labor, or of farmers.

If these young men could have access to my mail they would soon discover what a variety of interests those young people had and in what a variety of ways they thought about matters which came up at the Institute. This was no regimented group. The A.Y.C. is a loosely held together group of varied organizations, but the Citizenship Institute was not even an organized group. They were a number of individuals come together with the impelling desire to get in touch with their government and impress them that they wanted a chance to get a job, and to get started in life, as well as a chance to preserve their civil liberties, and peace for the world—all burning questions to them.

The leaders of the A.Y.C. may hold views on the role of youth, and on the effect which war may have, which might not agree with mine; but I would be perfectly certain that, whatever their views, they would be honest views arrived at after real thought and consideration. They would not try to hide them, nor would they be afraid to defend this country and our democratic form of government at any time. They are willing to work to achieve for youth the things which they believe will make our form of government safer and this country a happier place in which to live.

I would far rather back them than I would young people who are concerned in the tearing down of an organization but not especially concerned with helping solve the problems for which that organization has been established.

The other day I was asked by what rule I would try to discover young Communists if they did not honestly answer my question when I asked them.

Of course I would hope that no young people would be afraid to tell me and trust me; but if such an unfortunate feeling were to develop, I think that I would work with them until I found that their methods were destructive. If this continued for any length of time, I should of course become suspicious, and finally become convinced that if they could not work constructively for the things which were obviously for the good of our democracy, they must be interested either in Fascism and Communism and therefore of no value in the efforts which I was making.

Now as to the last paragraph in our young friends' article: "Yes, we're sorry to have caused embarrassment; but . . . we've torn the mask off the A.Y.C." My dear young things, of course you caused embarrassment, but to no one but yourselves, and you unmasked no one but yourselves. You would "like to destroy the Red influence in the youth movement" and you want to "build a real American youth organization"; but I am afraid you cannot do that, for you haven't shown that you cared about the problems facing American youth.

In closing I should like to suggest that it might be worthwhile seeing something of the young people who think themselves Communists. If they get jobs their ideas may eventually change, but one thing is absolutely certain, namely that the surest way to create and confirm young people in being Communists is to leave them friendless. You can always find people to uphold you if you do not disagree with them. Young people with ideas of their own are apt to be more valuable, in the end, than are those who simply agree with their elders and accept whatever is handed to them. Therefore, even if I thought that amongst this group of young people there was a larger number than I now believe who considered themselves Communists or Fascists, I would still not be afraid to associate with them and would still have hopes for them in the future.

The Creed of the American Youth Congress

I dedicate myself to the service of my country and mankind.

I will uphold the American ideal, which is the democratic way of life. I will help assure its bounty to all races, creeds and colors.

I will maintain my country, founded by men and women who sought a land where they could worship God in their own way, as a haven of a free conscience and the free religious spirit.

I will safeguard the heritage of industrial development, technical skill, natural resources and culture which has made my country the inspiration for the youth of all lands, and I will use whatever talents I have to add to that heritage.

I will be a social pioneer helping to forge new tools for an era in which education, the chance to make a decent living, the opportunity for health, recreation and culture will assure the fullest development to all.

I will respect and defend the Constitution, keystone of American liberties, which includes the Bill of Rights granting freedom of religion and press, of speech and assemblage. I will seek progress only within the framework of the American system of government which is founded on the principle that all political power is vested in the people, and I will oppose all undemocratic tendencies and all forms of dictatorship.

I will help make the United States a force for peace and pledge that my patriotism will not be at the expense of other peoples and nations, but one that will contribute to the brotherhood of man.

I will not permit race prejudice, religious intolerance, or class hatred to divide me from other young people. I will work for the unity of my generation and place that united strength at the service of my country, which I will defend against all enemies.

I pledge allegiance to the Flag of the United States of American and to the Republic for which it stands, one Nation, indivisible with liberty and justice for all.

77

Workers Should Join Trade Unions

I have always been interested in organizations for labor. I have always felt that it was important that everyone who was a worker join a labor organization, because the ideals of the organized labor movement are high ideals.

They mean that we are not selfish in our desires, that we stand for the good of the group as a whole, and that is something which we in the United States are learning every day must be the attitude of every citizen.

We must all of us come to look upon our citizenship as a trusteeship, something that we exercise in the interests of the whole people.

Only if we cooperate in the battle to make this country a real democracy where the interests of all people are considered, only when each one of us does this will genuine democracy be achieved.

We hope to make the great battle which is before us today a battle of democracy versus a dictatorship.

I could not help thinking as we sang "God Bless America" that you who have seen hardship for so many weeks in your fight to better conditions for everyone involved must sometimes think that things are not as they should be in this country. I am afraid that I agree with you.

I know many parts of the country and there are many conditions that I would like to see changed, and I hope eventually they will be changed.

But in spite of that I hope that we all feel that the mere fact that we can meet together and talk about organization for the worker and democracy in this country is in itself something for which we ought to be extremely thankful.

There are many places where there can be no longer any participation or decision on the part of the people as to what they will or will not do. And so, in spite of everything, we can still sing "God Bless America" and really feel that we are moving forward slowly, sometimes haltingly, but always in the hope and in the interest of the people in the whole country.

I just want to say that my education in the labor movement has come largely through Rose Schneiderman. I happened to join the Women's Trade Union League years ago and she has taught me many things I wouldn't have known otherwise.

I worked with Hilda Smith on her programs of workers' education throughout the country. I always ask everybody what they are doing in the work project. I get funny answers. They say that they thought it was a dangerous

American Federationist 48 (March 1941): 14–15. Address to Local 3 of the International Brotherhood of Electrical Workers at Leviton Manufacturing Company strike headquarters.

subject. I said it doesn't seem that way to me. We must have education and the ability of the people to understand the whole problem.

We should have projects to study the employees' problems and I wish we had employers' educational projects, too.

The important thing is to try to learn what conditions are throughout the country as a whole, and what the people are really thinking and what they are striving for.

As I look over the past few years, the thing that gives me the most hope for the future is the fact that, on the whole, people are standing together, people are working for the good of a group, not just for themselves. When we learn that I think we are going to find that we can move forward faster and faster.

I wish those of us who are employers would learn that it is through cooperation that we achieve more—that through stating our problems and asking people to work with us to solve them that we really get somewhere.

But that requires constant education for all of us, and I think we ought to bring all we can into really understanding the problems that are before the nation as a whole and as they affect our own particular situation.

We ought to try to solve the problems in our situation so that we can be more helpful in the solution of the problems that face the nation.

We find ourselves at a serious moment in the history of the world. We face problems not only as citizens of the United States; we face them as part of the entire world.

The greatest thing we can get out of the present crisis is to develop the habit of working together and realizing that whatever happens is going to affect us all.

I want to leave you this morning and express my gratitude to you for having stood together to gain those things, materially and spiritually, that will make life for your group richer and more productive.

I hope the day will come when all the people of this country will understand that cooperation will bring us greater happiness, and will bring us in the end a better life for the whole country and enable us to exert a greater influence on the world as a whole.

78

Social Gains & Defense

The preservation of any gains at any time in a democracy depends primarily on the will of each individual to do his share toward that preservation. We are gradually waking up to the fact that living in a democracy is not an easy thing. We have taken a great deal for granted in the past. I think that many of us have felt that always, no matter what we did, some inherent rights were ours which would affect our way of life.

Well, we're waking up to the fact that a form of government which is called a democracy requires everybody to work every day and to live for that way of life and develop it through his efforts. We can't take anything for granted and we can't sit back and think it's somebody else's responsibility. And perhaps when we talk about whether we can keep certain social gains while the defense program is being developed and is going on, we'd better accept that basic fact first of all.

It depends on us as individuals. We can have what we want. But we'll have to pay for it in self-discipline, in sacrifice, in work, in determination to preserve certain things. I sometimes hear people make remarks which would indicate that they think one achieves things in this world without any effort. Of course we are going to pay for everything we get. It all depends upon whether we care enough to pay the price.

One way to preserve the gains we've made is to have mediums for discussion in which we can say frankly what we feel, what we think, and *Common Sense* is one of those mediums. It is essential, I think, to all social gains, that we realize that we can't simply maintain a status; we have to go on. If we stand still we slide back. And we must always examine everything at every step of the way. It's well to be critical of ourselves, of the things we do, but always to be critical with the objective of finding something better—not just to tear down but to suggest and to experiment with doing something better.

I feel very strongly that no one today, looking at our own country and really knowing it, can be satisfied. If you ask me if I want to merely "maintain" under the defense program, gains we have made in various lines of social service to the country in the last few years—or of social justice—I will say that I will not be satisfied just to maintain those gains. I feel that we still have many things to do before we can even begin to feel that we are really a democracy.

I do not see why, under the defense program, we cannot move forward. It seems to me that in housing alone there is a great opportunity for experiment in the next few years. There is an awareness, I think, of the things we may attempt to do. I don't think we can expect that every attempt will be

Common Sense 10 (March 1941): 71–72.

successful, but we really have an opportunity to find out, under the defense program, what things must be done in the field of housing in a variety of situations. One thing which I am very much interested in at the moment is not merely whether we shall provide shelter but whether the government hasn't an obligation—when it draws people together in a community either temporarily or with the idea of permanency—to sit down with the state and local governments and work out opportunities for good living in that community. For instance, at this very moment, in Bremerton, Washington, there are something like twenty-five hundred children with no school available. That is not exactly a satisfactory way to plan a life for people who are doing a very essential work for the defense program.

"Great Opportunities"

There are places where there is no medical care whatsoever. And we are going to find that just as in the line of housing which we are bound to face, we are going to meet all kinds of new problems and decide just where the responsibility lies and find out how we are going to work it out. In this direction lie great opportunities for education for life in a democracy and its responsibilities.

Under the defense program we are, of course, confronted with the need for emphasizing certain kinds of production, and to certain people that production is a paramount obligation. We all acknowledge that that must be achieved. But I think it will be better achieved if at the same time we achieve for human beings a constantly increasing satisfaction in their way of life. If we establish that, I think we will find that a desire to produce for defense along the entire front will outstrip even the hopes of our most ardent planners. I think that people who feel that they are constantly moving forward in a way of life which they can see is better for them and for their families—a way which promises more opportunities for education, for recreation, for health, can have no hesitation then in deciding that what they have is worth defending.

Understands Letter

I am entirely frank in saying that I can understand the point of view of many people in this country today who are not sure whether what they have is worth defending. Of course, you and I can look across the water and say that no matter what our conditions are they are worth defending in comparison with what we see in other lands. And I think that's true, if one can look at life from a standpoint of historical knowledge or from the vantage point of comparative ease. But I have great sympathy with a woman who wrote me a most vituperative letter the other day. (I grieve to say that she did not sign her name. If she had I might have done something about her situation.) What made her write the letter was the significant thing. She said, "I am starving and my children are starving. What do I care—if Hitler will give me any kind of a living and promise it to me steadily—what do *I* care who is in power and who wins the war! I don't want my son to be killed when it doesn't seem to me to matter what happens."

There is a case for that woman, just as there was for a youngster who said to me once that it was all very well for those young people who had jobs and who had educations they hadn't had to work very hard to get, and who always had plenty to eat, to say that they were willing to defend the country. For his part, he had spent six years wandering over the country and he had never been able to find a job, except now and then for a day or so, and the country had not given him much of a home or much of a job or much of an education. And he did not see that it was best for him to defend a way of life that for him was not very good. Well, we don't agree; we say that even as it is it is better than domination by one man, or by a few men. We must understand their point of view, however, because only by understanding it, only by knowing what brings it about, are we going to move forward in our social gains. Only by knowing that we have to move forward, will we be prepared to broaden the base. And only when the base is broadened can all the people be certain that a way of life beneficial to them is a stake, and that therefore they have an individual responsibility to render service in the pattern of democracy. Then will they have something for which they are willing to work. Then will they have something for which they are willing to sacrifice.

"A Better Future"

Only with equal justice, equal opportunity, and equal participation in the government can we expect to be a united country—a country that is prepared to win out in any battle, the battle of economic production and of solving of our social questions, or the battle of ideas which is perhaps today the most important of all, for ideas know no barriers. It is only the knowledge that you are fighting for a better future which makes life worth living.

79

Harold J. Laski's *The American Presidency, An Interpretation*

It is interesting to read the impressions of one deeply concerned with democracy, and familiar with the British parliamentary system, of the part in our system played by its highest officer. Anyone who has watched closely the progress of government in this country will readily recognize that Mr. Laski has put his finger on one of the difficult situations in our present-day government, when he comments on the essential antagonism between the Presidency and Congress.

It is understandable that the framers of the Constitution should try to prevent the concentration of power in the hands of one man, but they could not foresee what future conditions would be. Today, as Mr. Laski so clearly points out, a different situation exists, a situation which requires a much more thoughtful and active electorate and a stronger leader. I think his concluding observations as to the position of the President in our government are most important, particularly his feeling that we must have stronger Presidents in order that they may unify Congress. This can be done only if they can also lead a majority of the people, because they must be trusted with power. This power will be dangerous unless, at the same time, the people can be trusted to think.

The whole analysis of this extremely difficult and responsible office of the President of the United States is interesting and valuable. I think it may be helpful to many a future President, for no one in that position has time to sit and think where and how he needs help. A President may be conscious of what he lacks, every now and then, in the assistance which he is receiving, but he is so busy trying to meet specific situations as they come up, that he has few opportunities to think about his needs in a comprehensive manner. As you read this book, you get a better picture of what kind of a set-up might really give a President more constant touch with the nation, better contacts with Congress and more expert information.

One sentence in the book sticks in my mind: "Thinking government always provokes a maximum resentment against itself, since the first thing upon which man economizes is thought." We have reached a point in history when in meeting our own problems and those of the world we have to think, and we can no longer "economize" in thought if we wish to keep our democracy alive.

Harvard Law Review 54 (June 1941): 1413–1414.

In studying a great office, this book brings out, I think, the fact that we require a great people back of the office to bring about any kind of coordination and real functioning of our government. Under a Constitution which was drafted at a time when most people felt that a government should carry comparatively little responsibility, and that it should therefore be so weak as to be safe at all times, the people and their President today must be strong. We cannot afford any longer to be too weak because our government has to assure not only political democracy to its people, but economic democracy as well. This additional task requires a stronger and more centralized government, controlled, however, by a thinking people exercising their democratic rights.

I hope that this book will be very widely read, not just because of the understanding which it gives of the importance of the office of President, but because of the understanding it should convey to every citizen of his individual responsibility.

80

What's Wrong with the Draft

Everyone has a pet idea about what changes should be made in the draft. The changes I am going to suggest are not all my own. They are the result of questions I have been asking all kinds of people about the Selective Service Act and how they would like to see it improved.

Out of the mass of suggestions two things emerge which I think may be helpful.

First, the local draft boards should take the public into their confidence. A great many persons feel that this should be done to give the people the feeling that the draft boards' decisions are in the interest of everyone.

Boards should publish in the press not only names of all men drafted but the classification of all men in the draft, and the reasons for their classifications. There seems to be cropping out in various places the same old feeling which existed in World War I, that favoritism is shown—that important people running industries, and in rural districts the farmers, will ask deferment for men who really should not be deferred and would not themselves ask for it.

Publication of each draft board's decisions and the bases for them would add enormously to confidence in the local draft boards. Many newspaper reporters now feel that they are not welcome when they try to get facts. This makes them suspicious, and they get across in their stories that something is being withheld.

Second, the age limit should be lowered. In the Army and in the Central Draft Board, there seems to be a strong feeling that drawing from the 21-to-25-year age group is very advisable. When men are older they are apt to have skills and therefore to be needed in some kind of defense industry. It is also very probable that there will be a greater burden of dependency on them, and the dislocation of family and community life will be greater after 25.

One fact, I think, is little known and should be given publicity: namely, that the volunteers who have entered the services in this period of emergency are largely between the ages of 18 and 21. I gather that in the services—except the training service for pilots, where two years of college are generally required—there is no objection to such youth, from either the physical or mental standpoint. In addition to the demand for the two major changes in the draft law which I have mentioned, there is also a great deal of feeling that certain rules should be laid down for the guidance of local draft boards so there will be more uniformity in practice.

Look 5 (July 15, 1941): 23–25.

For instance, in some places all married men are deferred. In other places, if a wife or even a wife and child are not dependent, the man is considered as though he were single.

Tuberculosis Tests Needed

Another thing brought to my attention is that doctors feel strongly that every boy should be given a psychiatric test and also that X-ray tests for T.B. should be made in each case.

In New York, for instance, T.B. tests are being tried, and they have been given in other places. An alarming number of cases of incipient T.B. have been discovered which, if they had been allowed to go undetected, would not only have been bad for the boys themselves but would have resulted in danger of contagion for other boys.

Some College Boys Won't Be Deferred

In the case of college groups, the Association of College Presidents, which has just met, has promised to give the fullest cooperation under the Selective Service Act to the local draft boards by making careful recommendations on students. If the colleges do not feel that a student should be deferred, they will honestly say so, even if his line of study might make him eligible ordinarily for a deferred classification.

To illustrate: A chemist or an engineer might be considered more valuable to the country after his college education was completed. But, if a boy's record is such that the college officials feel deferment is not justified in his case, they will honestly say so. If, in their opinion, the contrary is indicated, they will be just as honest.

There is a great desire not to create any special groups which are automatically deferred but to consider each case individually and to defer only those who unquestionably can be more useful after finishing their education than by taking training in the military service before completing their college studies.

What Civilians Can—and Should—Do

There is a feeling prevalent everywhere that the public needs to take a greater interest in the workings of the draft boards. They need to demand publicity and they need to take an interest in the boys beyond the period of classification. If a boy goes to camp, he should still be able to feel that the people in his home community are interested in him, that they want him to have recreation, good care and a feeling that home is still there backing him up in his effort to serve his country. And not only should the people of our communities take this interest in their own boys who may be sent to some distant point. They should, if they happen to be near a camp, do something to make the boy in that camp feel at home in his new environment.

Home Cooking Builds an Army

I was much interested by a story told me the other day. An appeal had been made to all the people in a certain area near a rapidly expanding camp to invite the boys to their homes for a home-cooked meal. The result was immediately evident. The boys did better work in camp; they behaved better when they were in the nearby villages and towns, because they felt they were part of the life of the community instead of being shut out, lonely and homesick.

There is one more thing which, while it has nothing to do with any changes in the Selective Service Act, I should like to mention here because the draft has created an obligation on all of us to change an attitude which never was a good one.

There has been a feeling in many places that soldiers and sailors on leave must be rowdy, nosy and misbehaved. Therefore, restaurants, hotels and places of amusement have frequently turned them away from the door.

Today the boy in a "gob" uniform or the boy in khaki without any stripes may be your boy or mine. We should always have felt this way and applied to these boys the same rules of conduct we apply to anyone else. In a public place all of us are expected to behave with regard for the pleasure and comfort of those around us. If we don't, we may be asked to leave; but, when we do, all of us should be welcome.

I think this reform would safeguard the boys against misbehavior and be an improvement in the attitude of a democracy toward the men of its armed service.

I have tried to pass along to you some of the suggestions which have been made to me, of which the two most important are: (1) that all local draft decisions be made public; (2) that the draft age be lowered.

Objection to this second proposal comes largely from mothers. One cannot blame them. With the likelihood of war before us, it is natural for mothers to want to keep this possibility out of their children's lives as long as possible. On the other hand, it may be some comfort to remember that the volunteers, of whom we have so many between 18 and 21, seem to survive training, at least, without showing undue strain.

How You Can Change the Draft Law

Any changes in Selective Service must be made by Congress. Many people are thinking and talking about ways to improve the Act. It is the duty of us all to think about these questions, and there is an obligation on us to make our judgments known to our representatives, who must eventually decide what changes to make.

81

What Does Pan-American Friendship Mean?

It seems to me that Pan-American relationships divide themselves broadly along three lines.

First there are the political relationships which represent the policies conceived and carried out by the various governments. Here we have an impressive record.

The hemisphere began to work for Pan-Americanism in 1836, when the great Liberator, Simon Bolivar, called the first meeting of American States. It was the birth of one of the greatest experiments in international relationships that the world has seen. In its 115 years of life it has progressed from a dream to a reality.

The First International Conference of American States was held at Washington for promotion of inter-American trade and furtherance of peace through arbitration.

In 1890, the basis for the Pan-American Union was provided for in the "Commercial Bureau of the American Republics." The Union was formally christened and its building dedicated in 1910.

In 1901–02, the Second Conference of American Republics was held in Mexico City. The main topic of discussion was the peaceful settlement of international disputes, in line with which was the adherence given by the delegations to the Hague Convention.

In 1906 the Third International Conference met at Rio de Janeiro, which again dealt with the problems of international arbitration and the matter of collection of public debts by force. This was a delicate matter which we had not in the past handled wisely or tactfully. Our attitude of taking responsibility alone has now changed, and we now propose to share it with our neighbors. This meant great reassurance to such nations as had doubted motives and feared aggression on our part as a threat to their independence.

Between 1910 and 1928, the Fourth, Fifth, and Sixth International Conferences took place, and were concerned primarily with economic and cultural matters; and finally, in 1928–29, the Pan-American Conference on Conciliation and Arbitration met at Washington. It adopted a convention providing for conciliation of disputes and a General Treaty of Inter-American Arbitration, which was another real step forward in gaining mutual confidence.

In 1933, President Roosevelt conceived and enunciated the Good Neighbor policy, and the Seventh International Conference was held at Montevideo.

Liberty 18 (October 4, 1941): 10–11, 35.

A nonintervention resolution which was embodied in the Convention was ratified by the United States Senate, June 14, 1934.

In 1936, the Inter-American Conference for the Maintenance of Peace was held at Buenos Aires. Provisions were made for settlement of disputes by consultation, arbitration, etc., and for Pan-American consultation "in the event of an international war outside of America."

In 1938, the Eighth International Conference was held at Lima. The Declaration of Lima provided machinery for consultation in the event of a threat from outside the hemisphere.

In 1939, the Conference of Ministers of Foreign Affairs met at Panama to agree on common measures with regard to defense of their neutrality, in accordance with the Declaration of Lima; and in 1940, the Conference of the Ministers of Foreign Affairs met at Havana to deal with special problems after the fall of the Low Countries and France.

The Havana Declaration, forbidding transfer of European colonies to non-American Powers, provided for an "Inter-American Commission of Territorial Administrations," in case the occupation of any colonies became necessary. This collaboration is the final step in real inter-American confidence.

During the past few years our government has, I think, been making great efforts to understand some of the political problems of the other nations in our hemisphere, and at the same time tried to make it possible for the people in Central and South America to better understand the problems of the United States.

A second division takes in all the economic interests of our various countries and here we have a wide field in which there are many problems today. While these problems existed in the past, they were never brought into such focus as now, because of the war situation in Europe and in the Far East.

The third division is the division of cultural relations. This, I think, in a broad way can be described as the knowledge and understanding which people acquire and develop about each other. Language and literature and the arts are all involved in a real knowledge and appreciation of groups of people for each other. In the long run this is, perhaps, the most important point in the intercourse and development of our relationships, because both political and economic matters will follow the trend of cultural understanding between the people themselves.

It is all very well for our government to enunciate the Good Neighbor policy, which is an excellent framework within which the people of our nation as a whole may think out the methods by which they are going to find a sympathetic basis for work and play. They must have, however, a reciprocal appreciation of each other's qualities as human beings if a real understanding is to exist among nations. Unless the people take hold, the good-will policy of our government will die. The government may undertake to formulate reciprocal trade agreements, it may try to find avenues through which trade can flow back and forth among our nations, but unless the people decide that these agreements shall be made mutually helpful, there is little chance that they will ever be tried out honestly.

The government may start students, professors, and books going from one country to another, but unless the people read the books and unless they get to know the professors and the students, little will be gained by all the expenditure of money and effort.

No one will deny that to completely change the pattern of trade relations between certain groups of nations is a difficult thing to do. For a long while, many of the things produced in Central and South America have found their readiest market in European and Asiatic ports. Now this interchange is impossible and we find that, to take one example, coffee alone causes a tremendous change in the economic pattern in many of our sister republics. Fourteen of the twenty Latin American nations produce coffee, and ten of the fourteen coffee-producing nations have this commodity as one of their chief exports. Colombia, El Salvador, Nicaragua, Haiti, Brazil, Costa Rica, Cuba, Venezuela, Mexico, all have coffee as one of their chief exports. European markets, for the time being, are out of the question. Therefore, as a temporary expedient, our government has lent many of those Central and South American governments some money to tide them over the emergency. But that is not a long-term solution. The greater purchase of coffee in this country has been one of the things advocated, and a working agreement has been reached.

In 1940 the United States increased its purchases from South and Central America by $170,000,000, compared with 1938, and during the first five months in 1941 we purchased $434,500,00 worth of goods, which is almost as much as we bought in the whole year of 1938.

Efforts are being made to locate new sources of goods in Central and South America which previously the United States purchased in Europe, and our government departments are cooperating with those of the other republics in searching for complementary products that will not compete with our own, and which, therefore, can be successfully marketed in the United States. As evidence of this, there is a very interesting exhibit being prepared for next winter in New York City in one of the large department stores under a very able fashion adviser which will show to our people some of the possibilities for the purchase and use of Central and South American products.

This effort is an effort to become traders, not merely sellers. We must never forget that in buying we are sure also to increase our sales, and that the trade situation is enormously dependent upon the general situation of the people as a whole in every country involved.

Our government will cooperate in the problem of the great staples— coffee, corn, cocoa, wheat, and sugar. We have paved the way already by the agreements on coffee which we may well feel may lead the way to further agreements.

But after consideration of each of these fields, we come back to the third field, which I think is the basis of all real understanding and mutual prosperity. Some of the things which I feel any individual interested in hemispheric solidarity can do are:

Study Spanish and Portuguese.

Read books on Latin American history, culture, economics, etc. Get the local library to maintain a good Latin American bookshelf.

Investigate local stores for Latin American products, foodstuffs, wines, fruit, cheese, furs, ceramics, glassware, hand-decorated metal, leather goods, etc., to see if they stock these products.

Constitute one-man hospitality committees for any visitor from any other American republic who comes to town.

The above points are stressed by the group under our government which is working to develop better relationships among us all; but I should like to add one more, namely, that the effort to do all of these things will be of value only if we make of ourselves a humbler people than we have been on many occasions. We must come to realize that other cultures and other races have things to offer us, and that we must be willing to accept benefits from them in the same manner that we hope they will accept something from our economic and cultural life which may prove of benefit to them.

There are great differences among us which will require patience to understand. In some ways we seem uncouth to our neighbors who have been trained in other manners and customs. In some ways they seem to us not to have advanced, from the point of view of the whole population, to a standard of living which we have come to look upon as necessary for all of our citizens.

These are superficial differences, and if we really make an effort to understand them, they can be solved easily, but this will require a real effort on the part of every one of us.

For instance, a friend of mine who has recently returned from Peru insists that the rural tenant in Peru has a far more satisfying and dignified life than have our sharecroppers because of certain traditions and customs which surround their existence. In studying situations in other countries and comparing them with our own, we should always be looking for the things we may learn from those countries which may point to new values that we haven't recognized in daily living.

It is not enough to learn a language, if in that language you do not express your thoughts with sympathy and understanding.

It is not enough to read books, if they do not illuminate for you, through your power of imagination and vision, the people who lie behind them.

It is not enough to find things which you can buy and sell between nations, if back of the trade there does not lie a real desire for mutual benefit.

It is not enough to receive and entertain guests from other countries, if they do not feel that there is a genuine kindness back of the hospitality which is tendered them.

It is not enough to persuade other nations that their self-interest must lead them to stand with us in military defense. They must know that in peace, as well as in war, their interests will receive consideration from us which will make it of mutual advantage to stand together at all times.

82

What Must We Do to Improve the Health and Well-Being of the American People?

I seems to me that the Government can do a great deal for the health of the nation at the present time which it might not have been able to do except in a period of emergency. I think we should face our health problems just now, first on the level of defense, and then on a level of long-range problems and plans.

In the category of defense efforts, I think we should immediately set about rehabilitating every man who has been rejected under the Selective Service Act because of correctable or remedial physical defects. The highest percentage of men rejected was for defective teeth. There has been suggested a plan for dental clinics by a very able doctor which I hope is now being given very careful consideration by the Surgeon Generals of the Army and Navy, as well as by the Surgeon General of the United States Public Health Service.

It has always seemed to me that we neglect this important phase of health where schoolchildren are concerned. I question very much whether we can leave this question of the young people's health entirely to the individual parents. I think we must begin to consider the health of the children of every community as a community responsibility. It is important to every citizen that the generation that is growing up shall do so with an opportunity for adequate medical care, in order to prevent serious defects in later life.

I am sure that all of us are concerned to learn that fifty-seven thousand of the first million men examined for the army were rejected because of vene-real disease, but it is a relief to know that all these men can be made fit for service in a short time.

General Hershey estimates that malnutrition is responsible for about one-third of all rejections made on physical grounds. Here again, I think we are at fault as citizens in that we do not see that every child in school receives one balanced meal a day. The Oslo Breakfast, which was carried on in Norway by prominent nutritionists, and which has been adopted in many other coun-tries, is used either as a breakfast when children first come to school, or as a luncheon at noon, and it should be duplicated in every school in our country. It would be a good investment if it prevented the waste of human beings through tuberculosis and other ailments that have their roots in malnutrition.

We are now reconditioning boys for the army in camps run by the National Youth Administration. With good food—which, incidentally, many of them have to be taught to eat—and with exercise to correct bad posture and to promote coordination, rest, and regular hours, most of them will be able to

Town Meeting 7, no. 8 (December 8, 1941): 13–5.

go into the Service. A certain amount of health work has been carried on in the National Youth Administration and in the Civilian Conservation Corps, and if these agencies are now coordinated under one head, it is hoped that this health work will become an integral part of the whole plan, because so far it has only been incidental.

Many of the countries already at war show a rise in the rate of tuberculosis. This is probably due to fatigue, increase in strain due to increased employment in industry, and poorer nutrition in the face of the rise in the cost of food and the necessity for rationing. While we are not in as serious a position as they are, there undoubtedly will be a percentage of increase here, and we should be preparing for it now by getting extra hospital beds for the care of tubercular patients, and by trying both in government and in industry to make up for it through extra care—to make up for the added strain under which people are working.

The clinics we now have for the treatment of venereal diseases are not sufficient and should be extended. The community should now begin to think about the prevention of infection as well as the treatment of infected persons, and if communities cannot achieve the necessary care themselves, they should obtain assistance from the Federal Government.

The Public Health Service and the Children's Bureau should work closely with the state and local health agencies. Programs should be developed for the care of the mother and the child in every community.

We should try to look ahead to the problems which greater employment in factories for women will necessitate. The establishment of day nurseries and the organization of nursery schools and kindergartens in order to provide adequate care for children is now a necessity. We should do all we can to encourage the entry of qualified young women into the nursing service, and the Government should take steps immediately to stop the rise in the cost of living which will eventually increase malnutrition among the children of this generation.

One section which I notice in a report from Surgeon General Parran is entitled: "Health as a Part of Health Education." He says:

> There is too much emphasis on a winning football or track team; there is too little physical education of all pupils.
>
> There are too many superficial physical examinations; there are too little corrective medical and dental care.
>
> Courses in physiology are too theoretical, emphasizing the mechanics and chemistry of the body; they emphasize too little practice in healthful living.

I think it is the duty of the Government to bring before the people their responsibility to see as far as possible that the community provides the services needed and acquaints the people in every locality with the existence of such services. We must reach the goal of a healthy nation, sound in mind and in body.

83

Henry A. Wallace's *Democracy Reborn*

Democracy Reborn is a collection of the speeches and writings of Henry Wallace, some of which go back to 1932 and 1933, when he became Secretary of Agriculture. This is a valuable collection; first, because it is a contribution to the understanding of a human being who has become a statesman; and second, because it drives into the minds of the American people certain truths which Mr. Wallace makes clear as no other statesman in this period has done.

The introduction written by the editor, Russell Lord, is an essential part of the book. Mr. Lord reveals the background and hereditary influence which illumines the personality of the Vice President. Some of his ideas are better understood today because of the knowledge of what his grandfather was, and Mr. Wallace's extensive training in journalism and in the technique of scientific experiment help one to understand the patience which he showed as Secretary of Agriculture. Mr. Wallace never was a politician and is not a very good one now, but he has long been a thinker and writer. That is why his speeches, until very recently, read much better than they sound. He has had to become a speaker.

If one were to pick out the one outstanding and continuing theme of all that Wallace says, it is his belief that whatever is done, must be done for the general welfare of the majority of the people. This belief colors his attitude on domestic as well as international problems.

You will hear people say that they are afraid of Henry Wallace because he is a dreamer, an impractical person, a mystic. No one who reads these speeches attentively would be afraid on any of these counts. They would recognize instead a man of curiosity, of deep religious feeling, not bound by any particular doctrine. They would know that he had to be practical because his scientific training was too intense to allow loose thinking. They would know that out of his background, nothing which was not truly American could possibly grow. He has traditional American attitudes on so many things that this fear of him which has been implanted in some people's minds, will seem strange to anyone who reads him carefully.

He is a realist. In 1933 he recognized the he could not embark on the realization of his own theory of abundance until he had cleared away the wreckage left by the past, and changed the political and economic philosophy which had preceded him. That is the attitude of a practical, straight thinking person.

There is a unity of thought in what he writes about the hopes the American people have for the future. It runs through every year of his life. Back in 1933 we find him saying:

The New Republic 3 (August 7, 1944): 165–166.

In brief, then, we wish a wider and better controlled use of engineering and science to the end that man may have a much higher percentage of his energy left over to enjoy the things which are non-material and non-economic, and I would include in this not only music, painting, literature and sport for sport's sake, but I would particularly include the idle curiosity of the scientist himself. Even the most enthusiastic engineers and scientists should be heartily desirous of bending their talents to serve these higher human ends. If the social will does not recognize these ends, at this particular stage in history, there is grave danger that Spengler may be proved right after all, and a thousand years hence a new civilization will be budding forth after this one has long lain fallow in a relative Middle Ages.

And in 1944 we find the following:

Big business must not have such control of Congress and the executive branch of government as to make it easy for them to write the rules of the postwar game in a way which will shut out the men who have made such a magnificent contribution to the productive power of America during the war. We need them to furnish the jobs which are so important both to labor and to agriculture.

The big three—Big Business, Big Labor and Big Agriculture—if they struggle to grab federal power for monopolistic purposes, are certain to come into serious conflict unless they recognize the superior claims of the general welfare of the common man. Such recognition of the general welfare must be genuine, must be more than polite mouthing of the high-sounding phrases. Each . . . has unprecedented power at the present time. Each is faced with serious postwar worries. Each will be tempted to try to profit at the expense of the other two when the postwar boom breaks. Each can save itself only if it learns to work with the other two and with government in terms of the general welfare. To work together without slipping into an American fascism will be the central problem of postwar democracy.

The most revealing speech from the point of view of the man himself, his tenderness and sensitivity, is the one made at the commencement exercises of the Connecticut College for Women. His mind was wholly engrossed with the death of the son of his good friend, Milo Perkins, a boy whom he had known and loved. This boy had pointed out that though young men fight wars, it is fifteen or twenty years before they come to the position where they really control the postwar activity, or the political climate in which the results of the war are really accomplished. The boy wondered and doubted whether the older men in power would make the kind of a peace he was willing to fight for. Henry Wallace points out the responsibility of the older generation and then appeals to the youth coming out of college, urging them to grasp their responsibilities and carry out the duties which a people assume when they govern themselves.

In 1942 Mr. Wallace cited the four duties of the American people as he saw them. We were in the war and this was the people's pact:

The duty to produce to the limit.

The duty to transport these products as rapidly as possible to the field of battle.

The duty to fight with all that is in us.

The duty to build a peace—just, charitable and enduring.

In 1943 he defined the responsibilities of the peace. He lists for us the six assets which will be ours when the war comes to an end:

Manpower by the million: skilled workers from war industries, military manpower and young people coming of working age.

The largest industrial plant capacity in the world.

The greatest resources, both natural and artificial, to make peacetime products—and thousands of new inventions waiting to be converted to peacetime use.

The largest scientific farm plant in the world.

The biggest backlog of requirements for housing, transportation, communications and living comforts.

The greatest reserve of accumulated savings by individuals that any nation has ever known.

Vice President Wallace found Mr. David Lilienthal's book on the TVA one of the most exciting books he had read in the past year. That in itself is another key to the personality of Henry Wallace. He warns us of the possible danger of American fascism. He knows our weaknesses, he knows our temptations, but he has a deep-seated faith in the common sense, idealism and purpose which our people have. As far back as 1940 he said, "There has continually flamed in the hearts of Americans the belief that this continent is different. On this new soil, we have thought, mankind would escape from the compulsions, the suspicions and the greeds of the Old World."

But Mr. Wallace knows that we have to grow with the times and he is trying to point out the way we must travel. I hope many people will read his collection of speeches, for I doubt that it would be possible in any other way to get the full impact of his belief that successful democracy must have an underpinning of religious belief, and that the future, which may be a glorious one, depends on what we in America think and feel and determine to do. He believes in individual responsibility, but he knows that unless we work for the good of the common man there is no future for any of us.

You Can't Pauperize Children

You have been reading of Mrs. Smith and the marvels she has accomplished on her allowance in California. California is a fairly liberal state, but even in California there are strange rules that are difficult to understand. Mrs. Smith cannot take on any extra work at home and add to the opportunities of her children or to the comforts of her home, because if she does she forfeits from her allowance the amount that she makes. Unless the job pays her more than her total allowance and is completely secure, she is not going to risk being without any income at a given point, because the procedure to get back on to the state welfare will probably leave her without resources for a period of time.

It might be possible in some cases for a child to earn a little money here and there, but if he is enterprising enough to do so that also, according to the story of Mrs. Smith which you have been reading, is deducted from the allowance, so we discourage initiative and a desire to become better off.

It seems to be fairly evident that no child under sixteen or eighteen, attending school, could possibly earn such large sums of money that they would be defrauding the state. A mother might be allowed only certain kinds of homework, since we do not want to return to the old sweatshop-labor conditions in any home. Certain services could be rendered by a woman at home, however, and she could add something perhaps to her meager allowance.

What can a child do when it is deprived of its mother's care by death or illness, and the father has to go to work? What can a child do if the father is removed from the family circle for any one of a number of good reasons? The mother may go to work, you say, but in many cases that is impossible, because it means no care at home for the child.

Every now and then I hear murmurs against certain programs developed in the interests of giving people, young and old, a greater sense of security in their daily lives. I have had people tell me that this stepping in of government with unemployment insurance, old-age compensation, and so on, "was really a very dangerous and pauperizing program, since people should be thrifty and lay up money themselves for bad times, emergencies, old age, and not count on government to look after them."

During the depression I think that it was pretty well proved that there are many cases in which it is practically impossible for people to lay up anything in the way of savings to make a family secure for any length of time.

Many of us may differ as to the value of much assistance which is given to older people in the community. But no matter how much we argue, where young children are concerned there can be very little difference of opinion,

Ladies' Home Journal 62 (September 1945): 128–129.

since obviously they have had no opportunity for saving money themselves and are helpless to do anything for themselves during their early years.

Children, rich and poor, are the wealth of a nation. Their hands and their heads are going to determine what happens in every country in the world, as they grow to maturity. So I think we look with great interest on what is being done to make it possible for children to grow up under healthy conditions even when adversity of various kinds comes their way.

Assistance to dependent children, which is a program carried on under the Federal Security Agency, has been, of course, a very great help, but it seems to me that we should constantly be scrutinizing our program for aid to children to see how we can make an improvement in it.

First let us review the past. Before the Social Security Act was passed, most of the states had what was called Mothers' Aid laws or Widows' Pensions. The effect of the Social Security Act was that the legislatures revised and broadened their laws because they had to comply with the more liberal provisions of the Social Security Act.

The difference between the old laws for assistance to dependent children and the Social Security law is that in order to get the money, the assistance must be made statewide. In the past, the assistance was not statewide, and one city or county would give assistance here and there.

Many of the laws were permissible rather than mandatory. Some left the entire administration of the program to local units with no state supervision provided. Even now, in general, the payments made under Aid to Dependent Children are lower than those made under Old Age Assistance and Aid to the Blind.

In April, 1945, the average aid to a family was $46.83 per month, the family consisting of a mother or a relative and two and a half children as a unit of survey. The lowest average was $20.79 in one state and the highest was $87.24, and five states averaged payments less than $25.00 a month.

Also, under the old laws, a child had to live with a mother. Under the Social Security Act the child can live with any relative. Even after the Social Security Act went into effect, some states did not provide the money to carry out the program.

All states now, except Nevada, have broadened their laws to comply with the Aid to Dependent Children provision of the Social Security Act. Nevada still has a mothers' aid program, but it is not statewide and not so broad as the Social Security Aid to Dependent Children.

In a survey which was carried on by sixteen states on a voluntary basis, it was found that while the Federal definition of a dependent child is fairly liberal, states are often very rigid. The Federal Government defines a dependent child as one under sixteen or under the age of eighteen if still attending school, who, because of death, continued absence from home or mental or physical incapacity, is deprived of parental care. The child, to obtain assistance, must be living with a parent or other specified relative. Many of the states, however, have rules and regulations which prevent the giving of aid for a variety of technicalities. In some cases, the child or its parents must have lived for a year within the state; in others, if they become dependent children, it has to be proved that the parent has been absent for a year and that legal steps have been taken against the parent to make him contribute support. Otherwise the state will not allow them to receive aid.

These are just examples of the kind of differences that make the dependent child's life precarious.

Most of us know there are two things all children need above all others—one is love, and the other is a sense of security. No matter how much the mother and father may love a child, if there is no assurance that there will be shelter and food and clothing for that child, and at least a minimum standard of living in the home, the child's sense of security is endangered.

The laws in the various states are so very different that it is not possible to say what the general program for the care of dependent children really is throughout the country. We can only say that we have succeeded in creating an awareness of the need and in meeting it better since the Social Security Agency came into being than when society depended entirely on private charity to meet its obligations.

We cannot say that every child in this country is getting an opportunity to grow up under favorable conditions. That would not be true. We can be grateful, however, that families like the Smith family—though the conditions under which they live may not be ideal, and all women may not be as capable and intelligent as Mrs. Smith—still have the advantages of medical care, for instance. This means a great deal to the mother with a growing family, even if the allowance for food in some states seems absurdly small even with the most careful budgeting.

A widow whose case was brought to my attention a few days ago could not give her children adequate meals, and yet the welfare department insisted that they were extremely careful to have a dietitian go over the allowance. In this particular case, there were two young children in the family, and the allowance for milk alone would have left for the other food requirements six cents per meal per day.

On the other hand, I remember a case in West Virginia where the man was killed in a mine accident, leaving a large family of children. In that case, in the past, there would have been a purse made up, to which the owners and the managers of the mine would have made substantial contributions, but much of the money would have been paid out for funeral expenses and before long the family would have been destitute. When that time arrived, everyone would have forgotten about the man's death. The result would have been grudging charity or inadequate state-welfare assistance. The children might have been sent to homes away from their mother and the woman might have gone to work when undoubtedly she was far better fitted to look after her family at home than to do an outside job. In the case to which I refer, what the woman and her children received under Social Security kept the home together and made for a greater sense of security than would have been possible otherwise.

Even when we know of these good results, however, we must not complacently sit back and think, "Now the job for widows and children is done, the children are cared for in their homes, widows and widowers do not need to be separated from their children, our obligation as citizens is finished." In our own interest we must strive as citizens to improve the conditions of children throughout the country, because every child who grows up a good citizen, self-respecting and self-supporting, adds to the wealth of the country. Every child who grows up physically and mentally unstable, morally insecure, may cost us, as citizens, far more when they grow older than it could cost us for good care at home throughout their childhood.

85

Plain Talk About Wallace

So Henry Wallace is really going to head a third party and run for President in 1948! What strange things the desire to be President makes men do! He has probably forgotten, but I remember his coming to see me in the summer of 1945 in Washington. At that time, I felt very strongly that it would be good for the country if Henry Wallace, whom we all believed in and admired, would leave active politics and become the leader of the independents of the country. Their vote had increased greatly in the years between 1929 and 1945, but they needed leadership and organization.

They were neither Republicans nor Democrats. They were primarily interested in getting the kind of leadership which would keep them free of economic depressions. And they wanted to continue what had been a peaceful but steady revolutionary movement which had given us, over the years, a greater number of people in the middle-income brackets and fewer people in the millionaire group or in the substandard-income groups. . . .

At that time, Henry Wallace told me he believed it was his duty to stay and work in the Democratic Party. I knew then, as I know now, that he was doing what he thought was right. But he never has been a good politician, he never has been able to gauge public opinion, and he never has picked his advisers wisely.

All of these things might have been less important if he had been a disinterested, nonpolitical leader of liberal thought, but as a leader of a third party he will accomplish nothing. He will merely destroy the very things he wishes to achieve. . . .

I read with great care Henry A. Wallace's speech in Chicago Monday. Affirmatively, he stands for "a positive peace program of abundance and security, not scarcity and war. We can prevent depression and war if we only organize for peace in the same comprehensive way we organize for war."

There is no country in the world where the people would not agree they wished to organize for peace and abundance and security. But in this speech Mr. Wallace oversimplified the problems that face us today. . . .

To begin with, let us take the political situation which a third party faces. No one in this country wants a third party as much as the Communists do. All over the world they are working for confusion because that is the way to create economic chaos and political weakness, and this is their one hope of defeating democracy in the world and proving that communism is the only thing people can turn to.

The Democratic Digest 25 (April 1948): 2.

The American Communists will be the nucleus of Mr. Wallace's third party. I know all the old arguments in favor of working with people who want the same objectives as you do. But I have worked rather more steadily and closely with the representatives of the USSR than has Mr. Wallace. I like all those I know and I hope that we can get on with them in a peaceful world, but I know that our only approach is an economic approach . . . they understand strength, not weakness. . . .

When Mr. Wallace assumes that by changing certain of our policies until we resemble Mr. Chamberlain, hat in hand, approaching Hitler, we will have the results which he calls "peace and abundance," I am afraid he is doing more wishful thinking than realistic facing of facts.

A totalitarian government, whether it is Fascist or Communist, has certain earmarks. Secret police rule is one of them. Another is benefits to the people but no freedom. We live, in fact, in a much more complicated world than Mr. Wallace seems to understand. . . .

Henry Wallace says he is in favor of helping Greece and he believes in the humanitarian side of the Marshall Plan, but that he would turn the aid program over to the United Nations and that aid should be given without consideration of political beliefs, on a basis of need, with the only strings attached being that nothing be used for preparation for war.

Let's look at that program. Most of the aid for Europe has to come from us or through arrangements which we make with other nations. We have no means for inspection. How would we know that none of the aid we sent was used for war preparation?

We have offered a perfectly fair system for control of atomic energy by the UN and for inspection of all the nations under that plan. The people who have stymied it right along are the Russians. . . .

Neither Great Britain nor the U.S. has such great military power in Greece that the Greeks are under any compulsion to have a government of which they do not approve. The "government" established recently by the guerrillas is led by a known Communist. Certainly the Greeks have a right to ask for help in remaining a democratic state; and certainly the steady progress of the USSR's political influence over every state which they have taken over shows that they have every intention of spreading communism wherever they can. . . .

Oh, Mr. Wallace, if you were President you would not have such pat sentences to offer us! You would find it far harder to act constructively than you suggest in your speeches!

86

Liberals in This Year of Decision

The role of the liberal today is a very difficult role, particularly in this country. We acquired through the fortunes of war the position of being the leading democracy in the world. We didn't like it very much; we have no particular desire to be responsible for what happens in the rest of the world. But because we were left in an economic position which no other country in the world could approximate, because we did not have to rebuild our cities, and our factories; because our civilians, at least, did not suffer as civilians suffered in most of the other countries where war had come to them, we find ourselves as the great democracy on which all other eyes are turned, and it has brought us a searching which I think probably we would far prefer to escape.

But whether we like it or not, that is the position we find ourselves in, and those of us who are liberals find that we are put in the position very often in international meetings of explaining the weaknesses of our democracy. Now you can explain them and excuse them, but you just can't say those weaknesses don't exist, because they do. It is a little trying, because we need very badly a unified country, and at the moment our country is very far from unified. We need that unity because of the position of leadership in which we find ourselves.

We are in a world where force still is the ultimate way of deciding questions. It should be law, but it still isn't law; it still is force. And yet we personally are very adverse to acknowledging that force is still such an important factor. Being less touched than other countries by the war, we wanted as quickly as possible to forget about it and get back to normal. So we reduced our forces; we did away with as many of the restrictions as possible; and we tried to feel that the rest of the world would get back to normal as easily as we would get back to normal.

I think that it has been rather a shock to all of us to find that you cannot fight a war of complete destruction in part of the world for four years, and then settle down as though nothing had happened. Now we have to face the facts, and because we have these conditions and these facts to face, the role of the liberal is twice as difficult.

We feel strongly the desire to think the best of other people—by thinking the best, to draw out the best. It doesn't always work that way. We find that in our own country fears have grown. If they have grown here they probably have grown in other countries just as much, probably more; and we keep wondering what happens from fear and what happens from real

The Christian Register 127 (June 1948): 26–28, 33. Address to the Middle Atlantic Laymen's League Conference.

malevolence. We watch our own country and we find things happening that we would like to denounce, and, yet, we don't know quite how far to go in denouncing those things.

I'll give you an example. As a liberal, I don't like loyalty tests at all. I have a feeling that it's much more important for us to find out why we believe in democracy and really to know why we believe in it, and to put as much into it as the USSR puts into its Communism, because I have always found that you get a great deal more out of the things you can be positive about. I don't think we should have in the government people whose loyalty we really question handling documents which should be secret documents. I think that would be terrible. But, on the other hand, it doesn't seem to me quite democratic to brand people as disloyal before you give them a chance to bring witnesses and answer their accusers. And so with all the feeling I have that we must not have disloyalty, I am also torn as to whether we really are building up our democracy and doing the positive things that we ought to be doing, or whether we're just tearing our democracy down.

The role of the liberal is hard and decisions are terribly difficult in these days. In the world picture there is no question but that the discrimination in this country hurts our position. It has been up to this time a domestic question. I felt that we could take time about it—time for white people to adjust; time for colored people to become educated, or, referring to other types of racial and religious discrimination, I felt that there was time, and that we needn't move too fast, that we could do it step by step, and gradually. I don't know whether we can now. Never, since I started to work in the United Nations, has there been a meeting where the question of our discrimination has not been brought up, and where we haven't had to answer for our country. It comes up on all kinds of things—it comes up on the question of freedom of information.

I was making what I thought was a perfectly safe speech, explaining why I thought freedom of information was valuable, and why I thought it was far better to have all kinds of opinions printed in the press and have an educated people that would make their decisions on what they read, than it was to have censorship, particularly government censorship. A gentleman whose country does have government censorship, said, "Madam, do you mean that in countries where there is a so-called free press there is no discrimination?" I had to say "touché." Nevertheless, I still believe in a free press because it does allow those of us who would like to fight discrimination to know where it exists, and we can get at the facts.

The very fact that we have discrimination and that we are the leading democracy, brings the whole of democracy into question. It is brought up against us in practically every meeting. I have come to feel that, as a liberal, wanting to defend democracy, we can no longer think of this question purely as a domestic question. We have to think of it in the implication of what it means to our world leadership, and that is very difficult to do at the present time.

I think, too, that probably one of the most difficult things we face is wanting peace, as undoubtedly all the people of the world want it. We still find ourselves in the position where, having set up machinery in the United Nations to create an atmosphere in which peace can grow, the will of the peoples for peace seems to be lacking. We find ourselves increasingly having decisions to make between the USSR and ourselves.

At home, we have certain people who say "we are the only true liberals in the country" and "we will not say that communism is bad. We will work with communism when it agrees with us." That sounds like a good, liberal way to feel. But then your actual experience makes you doubt whether that really is the way that you can feel. I've had quite a long experience with American Communism, because I began with youth groups in '34, and it has been very interesting. My first real disillusionment came when I found they wouldn't tell me the truth, and then, later, when the youth groups, led by the communist element, were picketing the White House. Then suddenly, when Russia was invaded, they had another meeting, and they sent me a telegram saying, "Now we can work together because now we are for preparedness for war," and I had to send the word back to them, "I am sorry but you lied to me and I can't work with anyone who lies." It was one of the most useful things that I ever did, because I learned all the communist tactics.

Many times in our United Nations meetings I have found that if there is a subject up that the USSR wants to get a certain vote on, you won't be able to get a vote easily, and you wonder why the delay. You go on and on until everybody is very tired and they drift out as groups do in these meetings, and if you don't watch, the move will be made for a vote and they will have won the vote while everyone was drifting out. I learned that a long while ago in one of our meetings. Everyone went scurrying to get the people back because the vote was going to be taken and we would have lost.

You learn that dealing with the Russians is not at all a question of "sweetness and light and sense." It is a question of strength. I don't happen to believe that it is a question only of economic and military strength, though I have come to believe that those two are controlling factors. But it's also a question of the strength of individuals and their convictions. You've got to believe in what you stand for just as strongly as they do. Otherwise you're going to be defeated. And that's one of the places where we're not quite as strong as we should be. In a democracy, we allow such latitude for argument on slight differences of opinion, that to get a feeling of a unified backing for certain big things is quite a problem. The lack of such latitude is, of course, the strength of a totalitarian dictatorship.

There isn't a single representative on any of the committees from the USSR, or from any of the satellite states who doesn't know how he's going to vote right straight down the line when he comes into that meeting. Everyone is going to vote just exactly as he was told to vote. He is going to attack just as he was told to attack—and nothing you say is going to make any dent, then. Six months from now, after it has gone back to the Kremlin, to the Politburo, and attitude may be changed. But it's awfully trying, and annoying, and enraging to find yourself answering first, the USSR. Then perhaps the Byelorussians say something and make the same attack and you have to answer them, too. During this last Assembly at one of the committees, I didn't answer the second time. I thought, "Well, I answered it once; I don't have to answer it each time," and the next day the delegate from the USSR got up and said, "Mrs. Roosevelt didn't answer this yesterday, so of course of must have been true!" so I discovered that each time I would have to get up. We had four attacks, exactly the same, and every time I had to say the same thing all over again. That's very enraging, and you wonder why grown people should want to do anything as time-consuming and as stupid. But that's the way it is and you just have to learn.

And, for the liberal, who wants to believe that people are all more or less the same, that they have the same motivations, and that they respond to fair and decent treatment, it is really a very disillusioning thing to work in that fashion with the USSR because you are tempted to come to the conclusion that it isn't important to do what you feel is right. You may have been brought up to believe that if you say you are going to do something, it's important that you do it for your own self-satisfaction. But you wake up to find that you are going to get cooperation only because you are stronger than they are. Now that's a rather awful thing for a liberal to have to face in this world of today, and I think a good many people probably now feel that I am not a liberal in my attitude towards the USSR.

I believe very strongly that while we have to be strong, we also have to be friendly; and that's one of the most difficult things in the world because they are so irritating. However, if you can remember the fact that they are not acting as individuals; that they are acting as government representatives, and they talk as government representatives, then you cannot dislike them as individuals. You keep your sense of liking them as people, even if you dislike their attitude and dislike what they stand for.

I think we might do some things that we haven't done so far. I think our attitude at times has been highly stupid. We do not recognize very often the fact of how sensitive they are because of insecurity. Many times and in many little ways we do not realize their insecurity and we do things that bring about bitterness, very often in little ways that are not important but have important results.

I have discovered often in working with them on committees that they respect the fact that you are not tired, that you can stand up to them, that you will put them through what you had intended to have them do. The Russians respect this. We as liberals need to make our country understand clearly that we feel our sense of security, that we are sure our democracy can be what we want it to be, and that we are going to work to make it what we want it to be. I think that is as important as the economic and military strength.

There is no doubt that we have to have the economic strength. The economic strength is the point from which we should work with Russia because it is the point where she has a tremendous respect for us. But to get that respect depends upon the liberals in this country, those among us whose convictions can make them believe that democracy is going to bring to the greatest number of people the greatest possible opportunity—those who really know that we want justice and opportunity for all the peoples. I think the liberals must accept the fact that force is still here in the world, and yet be strong enough to watch their own country so that force doesn't go to its head, which is always a danger. At the same time we must work to improve what we have and feel about it as the Communists do. They really have a crusading spirit. They really feel. And when you talk to them you understand why they feel the way they do.

In twenty-five years they have taken a people that was ninety percent illiterate and made it ninety percent literate. They haven't been able to become experts in a lot of things, and that is the cause of one of their greatest feelings of inferiority. They have been unable to join a lot of the organizations like UNESCO, for instance. They say that they won't join UNESCO because it is too expensive to join all those specialized agencies. But the truth is they haven't got the people to put there. Moreover, they always have two representatives instead of one, because no USSR representative goes alone. And, of course, when you have to have two, always, instead of one, that doubles your expense. You very soon know when you are working with people that are not at all qualified in many fields—they are not prepared for the work they have to do. In twenty-five years you don't create experts in every field. In making their nation literate they have accomplished a lot.

They are still 200 years behind us in many things. But they are a strong and a very young nation. They haven't much more than they ever had before, and when you compare it with what we have, they are awfully afraid of the comparison. I think they were terribly worried about their soldiers who had to go into decadent democracies and see that life was so much easier than they had it at home. I think that worried them very much. On the other hand, they feel they have gained a great deal and in some ways the government has given them a great deal. Far more people, for instance, go to the opera in Russia, probably, than ever go here. Certainly more people go to plays and sit through Shakespeare from beginning to end, uncut. The government has done that with the idea of taking them out of the misery in which most of them still lived. Nonetheless we are dealing with people who are ruthless at times, and we are dealing with people who are hard and who do believe in force—and, yet, who have given their people a sense of crusading. With all our years of civilization in back of us, I think we have got to face the situation as it is and we've got to know that this requires moral and spiritual leadership. It requires a friendly spirit. But it also requires the facing of realities and the knowledge that anything which can be used against us will be used against us. They believe in their way of life and if we believe in ours we've got to fight for it. We've taken it pretty much for granted up to this time.

We liberals, being liberals, are divided. We all like to go off on our own little tangents and just work on the things we are particularly interested in. There is no question in my mind but the things we do at home in a year which is a decisive year are probably very decisive in the international picture, too. There isn't anyone, I think, today—particularly among the young people, who is not really worried whether we are going to be at war in a short time or not. There is no question but what we have people in the government, and certain people outside, who feel that it would probably be much simpler to drop a few bombs on Russia right now than to wait until she is stronger. I have a lot of people say to me, "Really and honestly, now, don't you think it would be a lot better if we wiped up Russia right now?" The trouble with that, from my point of view, is that we would not really settle anything. We could destroy her cities—but she is a whale of a country. And, having once used atom bombs none of us would sleep very peacefully from then on, because somebody some-day is going to have atom bombs just as we have them, and if we get into the habit of using them sooner or later we are going to be destroyed. Nobody wins a modern war.

I think that it is the major job of a liberal, if he can get together suffi-ciently with other liberals to do a job, really to see to it that his community does think through problems, knows what they really are, has a plan and elects people in Congress and then keeps in touch with them. Of course, that is a difficult thing to do. We've taken our rights too loosely, and we haven't thought so much about the fact that we have to preserve them, and now we are facing the need to preserve them. They are at stake. I am much more interested in seeing the liberals achieve a positive program than seeing them just on the defensive. Just being on the defensive is not going to win a peace; I think the other people of the world must feel very strongly about this, too. It's a ques-tion of letting government get out of hand.

Now it's very true that the Russians can't control their government, but if we don't control ours it will be because those of us who are liberals don't do the job. Yes, the role of the liberal in this decisive year is a hard one. We've got to do our job at home as we've never done it before in many long years. And we've got to be willing to subordinate these differences among us in order to be able to do it. We've got to be willing to sacrifice. And probably the only thanks we will get is that many people will say that we are not doing the right thing, that we are making many mistakes. They can say so many things. But I think perhaps we had better forget about what people are going to say and try as hard as we are able in the way we think is right to keep the world at peace, to keep ourselves strong in every possible way, and not to be fooled. That is as important as anything else. We can be fooled. I think Henry Wallace is being fooled. I have always been very fond of Henry Wallace, but he never has had to work with the Russians, and I have. And I don't feel that just "sweetness and light" by itself is going to win a just peace. I think we need clear facing of facts and holding on to our own ideals, and trying to bring the world to a sense of our strength in all ways. Without it I don't see any reason why we should win against the other great power that stands out against us today.

87

Address to Americans for Democratic Action

Mr. Chairman, ladies and gentlemen, it's a very inspiring thing these days to come to a meeting such as this and find so many people coming together to discuss and make plans for an organization devoted to obtaining in our country as good a government as we can have. This organization is made up of both Democrats and Republicans.

I was amused the other night to have a young boy at a meeting where we were discussing good government say, "Mrs. Roosevelt, you've talked about the liberals, but if you really have conservative convictions, what should you do?" I think the thing that makes one happy about ADA is that it really has convictions. And the people who belong, belong because they want to find a way to put those convictions to work. They recognize—everyone in this room at this meeting knows—that our democracy is not perfect. But they also know that it's working to improve democracy. That is the important thing. Those who are satisfied—those who feel that there is nothing they can do—they are the people who will do harm to the Government and the citizenship in the United States.

We live in a time when every single one of us must realize that what actually is important in a democracy is that sense of individual responsibility. And there are certain things here in our country that I think we must watch very carefully. It is true, as has been said, that there is a sense of insecurity—I might almost say a sense of fear—among many people in this country of ours. With some people it's a fear of the possibility of war; with others it's a fear of what the new weapons of war may mean if we should come to war; with others it's a fear of what may happen to them personally if by chance they offend in any way. That is the fear that bothers me most—the fear of people who are afraid to be themselves, to hold convictions, to stand up for them—because that fear, I think, is the fear which can really hurt our democracy more than any other.

This is a time when it takes courage to live. It takes the kind of courage that it took in the earliest days of our history. I'm quite sure that George Washington and his men must have had moments when they wondered how on earth the United States was ever going to exist. And I'm sure that there have been other times in our history which have looked black indeed to the citizens of the country and its leaders. But at present we need all the courage

April 1, 1950. Entered into the *Congressional Record* by Senator Herbert H. Lehman, April 19.

that our forefathers had and perhaps a little more, because we have a job to do at home and a job to do in the world.

The job at home has to be done, and has to be done first. We have to be unafraid. And we have to realize that here is where we as individuals have to fulfill our belief in democracy. If we cannot prove here that we believe in freedom, in the ability of people to govern themselves, if we cannot have confidence in each other, if we cannot feel that fundamentally we are all trying to retain the best in our democracy and improve it, if we cannot find some basic unity even in peace, then we are never going to be able to lead the world. This is the problem that is before us today. If we do not lead the world, who is going to lead it? We have to accept the fact that it's what we do here that makes us fit to lead the world. So every day in our daily lives as citizens we are building our world leadership.

Our great struggle today is to prove to the world that democracy has more to offer than communism. You can't just say that anyone who understands communism must be against it. You have to face the fact that this is a struggle, and a very great struggle. If we want to win the cold war, if we want to reach a greater security—I think it's going to take us a long time, and I think we have to develop a courage and a staunchness that perhaps we have never had. If we want to achieve it, then we must prove to the world what we can offer. That means we have to take certain definite steps. We have, for instance, to make sure that we have civil rights in this country. There was a time when we could look on that question as a purely domestic one—that we could take all the time we wanted to educate ourselves to solve the problem. It isn't any longer a domestic question—it's an international question. It is perhaps the question which may decide whether democracy or communism wins out in the world.

I sit in the United Nations; have sat in the General Assembly since 1946, and I sit in the Human Rights Commission. Over and over again the failures of democracy are pointed out to me in terms of specific instances of things that have happened in our country. I don't try to say they didn't happen, because usually I know that they did. All I can say is that we know about them, and those of us who really care, work to improve our democracy. Therefore, we must actually look at ourselves with more critical eyes than we have in the past.

Where do we fail, and how hard do we try to live up to the things we've given lip service to? It's not a domestic question; it's a question that perhaps is one of the most important factors in the winning of the struggle. Of course, economic questions enter into this struggle, too. We cannot be complacent about the unemployment in our country—about injustices. Not long ago I remember hearing in a certain city that the papers actually printed what certain rather well-paid officials would have as pensions in an industry, and yet when it came to the point of pensions to the workers, that was too heavy a burden for the industry. Well now, I'm not a Socialist. I'm a very practical capitalist, I'm sure. But if we want to keep capitalism, we in this country have got to learn that there must be a real sharing, a real understanding, between management and labor. They must plan together because their interests are really identical. But both sides must realize it.

Now, the answer to unemployment. I didn't get an answer when I asked some of our Democratic Senators the other day, "What is the answer to unemployment?" I doubt if many people know. I think it's one of the things that perhaps we need to experiment, and perhaps it may be tied up, too, with some of our decisions in the realm of foreign affairs. Perhaps backing the United Nations with our own four-points program, seeing what can be done through them, to work with other nations in the world, that may have some tie with unemployment. There may be other things that I know nothing about, but I never like to feel that we don't face problems and that we don't set people to work on finding the answers. There's no reason why we shouldn't say we don't know the answer now; there's every reason why we shouldn't say we're not trying to find out. It is essential, I think, to our winning this struggle that we actually find answers, because in this economic area communism has a program. And democracy has to have a better one. If it doesn't, we're being judged before the bar of the world, and we have to win. We have to win because we have a conviction that democracy does offer people something that no other form of government and no other way of life can offer.

There's one thing that always strikes me, and that is that the Communist representatives in the United Nations never talk about liberty; they never mention it. On one occasion when Mr. Vishinsky was forced to do so, he said that was a foolish thing to talk about because no one could have liberty. Well, you and I know quite well that everyone's liberty is conditioned by the rights of other people. But we must think about liberty, because that is really one of the basic reasons why we prefer democracy to communism. And somehow we must keep ourselves free from fear and suspicion of each other. I sit with people who are representatives of Communist countries, and to sit with them is a lesson in what fear can do. Fear can take away from you all the courage to be an individual. You become a mouthpiece for the ideas which you have been told you must give forth. I have no feeling of real antagonism toward these representatives because, poor things, they can do no other. They must do that; their lives depend on it.

Now, it seems to me that the ADA is an organization that has thinking people in it, and we must preserve the right to think and to differ in the United States. We must be able to disagree with people, and to consider new ideas, and not to be afraid. The day that I am afraid to sit down in a room with people that I do not know because perhaps 5 years from now, someone will say, "You sat in the room and five people were Communists, and so you are a Communist," that day will be a bad day for democracy. We must be sure enough of ourselves, of our own convictions, to sit down with anyone and not be afraid of listening to what they have to say, and not be afraid of contamination by association. It's true that the company you keep may say something about what you are. But to be able to meet with people and argue your own point of view, and to meet with people whom you do not have to screen beforehand to be sure they are safe to meet with—that must be a part of the freedom of every citizen in the United States.

So I'm grateful that ADA prods us to think that it has an opportunity to bring before us the ideas that seem important, that it also has the opportunity of backing people in elections who promise to be good public servants. I'm grateful that it is representative of people in both political parties, and I'm grateful for the numbers that have come today. I think it shows that we as a Nation are waking up to the need to preserve our basic ideas in our Republic, that we are waking up to the fact that we have to live those ideals, and that we have to improve our democracy by the way we live. To do that we must come together, and consult together, and get other people to help us where we need help. There must be no one who fights the battle of good government, of freedom of thought, of real democracy, with a sense of doing it alone. That is the value of ADA—you do not have to be alone.

I was speaking to a little group of college students the other day who had started an organization where they tried to live the ideals of democracy, and one of them said to me, "I graduate this year. What do I do when I go home?" And I said, "You find people who feel as you do." He said, "I don't know any, where I live." Now, that shouldn't happen to any young person, because they should be sure that if they were really trying to live their convictions they would find support in their community. That's why I stress that it is in our own communities that we must fight this struggle, not only the struggle against communism but the struggle for peace.

We will have on a worldwide scale, a human rights convention, probably before the General Assembly next autumn at the United Nations, and then before our Senate, a ratification. That's part of our struggle. If we don't ratify, who else will ratify in the world? And yet human rights are basic to establishing peace. A common understanding throughout the world of human rights—of the value of human personality and freedom—that understanding, spread throughout the world, is one of the cornerstones on which we must build for peace.

88

If I Were a Republican Today

If I were a Republican today, I think I would ask my party to take a clearcut stand. At present, it is *not* clearcut. They say, for instance, they're *against* the present Administration's health bill because it is "socialized medicine," but they acknowledge that we *need* more medical care throughout the country, and so they are vaguely for better medical care without specifying exactly how it is to be accomplished. They are for freedom as against socialism, but no one in the Democratic Administration is a Socialist.

The Republicans believe in a bipartisan foreign policy. They complain that the Administration has of late laid down the policy and consulted the Republicans after the policy was made and not before. They *could*, however, suggest machinery by which they could take part in all this policy-making either by returning to the former practice of legislative representation in the delegation for the United Nations General Assembly, or by some type of close coordination between the State Department and the foreign relations committees in both the Houses of Congress.

If I were a Republican, I would want my party to formulate exactly *what* it stood for in foreign affairs and state *why* it was for certain policies and against others, so that it would not be *quite* so difficult for the public to understand just what the Republican stand on foreign policy actually is. Their program as recently stated is curiously evasive. I would want my party to state what kind of peace policies it would pursue in *contrast* to those of the present administration. I would want a clearcut statement on the defense of my country, which is closely tied to the policy of peace. The present statement is in very general terms, and it does not face the realities of the situation.

In the last campaign for the presidency, the Republican candidate came out *against* certain types of farm aid. If I were a Republican, I would want my party's stand on price support and handling of surplus crops, etc., very *clearly* stated. I would also want to know in unmistakable terms my party's stand on conservation and development of natural resources, because in the place where we are today, the development of water power, the control of floods, and soil and forest conservation are of primary importance to the future of the people of the country.

Both parties state we must have civil rights for all regardless "of race, religion, color, or country of origin." When it comes to making these words effective in *law*, both parties are divided and a coalition of Democrats and Republicans prevents any legislation from becoming law.

Cosmopolitan 128 (June 1950): 29, 172.

It used to be said of the two political parties that the Republican Party believed in looking after the interests of the people at the top. If they prospered, the prosperity would carry on down to all the people; on the other hand, that the Democratic Party believed that they had to look after the well-being of the people at the bottom, and that if they prospered and had a satisfactory life, the people at the top would also prosper.

These are two basically different theories, but today you can find people in both parties who believe in either one or the other theory. If I were a Republican, I think I would consider it *important to have that point cleared up* so that one could choose the philosophy one felt was the most sound. If we have reached a point in our economic development where it is clear to all of us that the interests of the top and the bottom are so closely tied that they must be mutually developed, then I think it would be well for either party, or both parties, to state that as a new policy.

As I read over the Republican pontifical bible as it has just been issued, it seems to me that they have gone over the things that they think elected President Truman, and they have accepted them all, saying: "Gentlemen, we will do all of these things and more, and we will reduce your taxes, which will give you more money to spend as you wish." This *may* fool the voters but I do not *think* it will, and I, for one, would like both parties to be clear and explicit in the philosophy that underlies whatever they do. Then we would not get out the confused vote, and we would have the kind of participation by the voters one saw in the last election in Great Britain. We never get as big a percentage of the vote out as they did, and that is largely, *I think, because the policies of the two major parties are at present so lacking in clarity* that the people wait and make their final decision on the candidates and what each says in the campaign. Many people do not vote because they honestly do not understand what the policies back of the oratory are, and they decide that it will not matter much *which* party wins, and therefore they stay away from the polls.

In this country we believe in a two-party system, but in the past few years it has sometimes, it seems to me, been difficult to form a clearcut idea of what the two political parties actually represent. I believe it is important always to have a strong opposition party no matter *which* party is in power, and that is why the issues should be clear.

As a Democrat, I would say that the majority of the Democratic Party is more liberal and progressive than the majority of the Republican Party, but the Dixiecrats, for instance, line themselves up with the most reactionary element in the Republican Party, and it must be difficult for some of the Republican liberals when they see their proposals more frequently urged by the Democratic Party than by the Republican majority.

A short time ago, on my television program, Senator Wiley of Wisconsin read me the new Republican Party platform, and I could not help thinking that it has some curiously reminiscent planks that might almost have made their first appearance in the New Deal. The Republicans say they are for a reduction in taxes but are not for a reduction in any of the services rendered the people!

The services are all to be met by more economical administration of government! That, of course, is always the slogan of the party out of power because it is not in the position of administering these agencies of government, and when you are not actually doing the job it is always easier to say it could be done more economically. But the history of the Republican Party is not the history of retrenchment in government personnel or expenditure.

It is true that services to the people usually have been started in Democratic Administrations and then adopted and continued in Republican platforms.

It is true that the cost of government goes up with these services. However, I do not think it will be proved by close scrutiny of our past history that the Republicans employ any fewer Republicans than the Democrats employ Democrats in political places.

89

Why Are We Cooperating with Tito?

In charting our diplomatic and military defensive against Soviet communism, we in the United States have, officially, embraced a Communist state and a dictator who looks upon communism as a particularly endowed means of governing. The state is Yugoslavia. The man is Marshal Tito.

Perhaps there is no more contradictory situation in our postwar diplomacy. Certainly, in my travels around the United States, there is no question on international affairs which I am asked more often than: "Why are we doing business with Tito?"

In practical terms, of course, there is no real question on why we support President Josip Broz (Tito) today. He and his regime are against the Soviets, and, in the temper of these times, this puts Tito and Yugoslavia on the same defensive footing as we of the Western world are. In simple realism, more people in the United States are more afraid of the Soviets than are afraid of Yugoslavia.

Yugoslavia, for its own part, has aligned itself more closely with the West through a pact with Greece and Turkey. These three nations have pledged to defend themselves together against attack from without. This has drawn them more closely to the Atlantic Pact defense system, and to the West as a political unit, than ever before.

With the very forthright idea that whoever is against the Soviets is our friend, many people in this country have accepted Yugoslavia as an ally. This large group of Americans thus agrees to support Tito with military and economic aid, but still has reservations on whether this democratic nation should be doing business with a one-man regime. The problem is that most of us in this country do not understand how Tito's communism differs from the Russian variety.

As the guest of Tito and his wife at their summer villa on the island of Brioni in the Adriatic, I devoted several long conversations to trying to place this man, his ideas and his system of government into perspective.

I entered the long reception room the morning he first received me, and I could not help thinking that it required only a great desk at the far end of the room to resemble the places where Mussolini and Stalin greeted their guests—making the visitor walk the entire length of the room to be received. But Tito arose and came forward quickly. He seemed friendly, and appeared genuinely kind and warm.

We sat down to talk, and I studied his face. His chin is firmly molded, he looks at you without evasion, and the lines in his face attest experience a

Look 18 (October 5, 1954): 80, 82–83.

younger man could not have had. He is not tall, but his is a commanding figure. When he speaks to give an order, there is no question that he knows what he wants and that he does not expect to be misunderstood or misinterpreted.

Our discussions turned almost at once to the relationships between his country and Russia, as to forms of government, as to viewpoint, as to aims. He talked first of Russia, cautioning against the West's overestimating the occasional apparent signs of weakness in the Soviet Union. He kept reminding me that there was a great army in Russia. He pictured the Soviets as always pretending to the role of protectors of weaker nations, so as to keep their influence in the satellites intact. He emphasized that any apparent threat against Russia itself would serve only to unite the Russian people.

I probed particularly for his real thoughts on communism as it is practiced in Yugoslavia. His reply was quick, and to the effect that communism existed nowhere, least of all in the Soviet Union, which he called an imperialist state with state capitalism. He pictured communism as an ideal which could only be reached when people ceased to be selfish and greedy and when everyone would be willing to see each individual receive according to his needs from communal production. But that condition, he told me, was a long way off.

Once I asked him to classify himself in governmental philosophy. Tito smilingly said he supposed he might call himself a social democrat. The Marshal explained that practically everything in Yugoslavia was nationalized, but he did not believe that everyone liked that. He said all the people lived on the salaries they earned, but there was a belief in private property—as in a house or a small farm not exceeding 20 acres.

Tito dislikes what is evolving in Yugoslavia being called communism. He also objects to calling it Titoism or Yugoslavianism. His theory is that every country should develop according to its own needs, and he does not want his methods held up as an example for another country where they might not work at all.

He Says He's Not a Dictator

Eventually, we turned to his own role and I found him adamantly opposed to being called, or thought of, as a dictator. He told me of his colleagues, a group of World War II partisans like himself, who worked together to develop each phase in the reshaping of Yugoslavia. He proudly told me how they would draft a new law and have it printed in the press, and how the government would hold up applying the law until reaction had been measured. Individual letters concerning the new law would be analyzed, and the proposal then would be redrafted and resubmitted for comment. This process of steady and continuing referendum he took as proof that he was not running a one-man show.

I was moved to the conclusion that Tito conceives of his as popular government, not too far removed in his mind from that of our country. Of course, the basic difference is that it is government from the top down rather than from the bottom up—and that's the difference between day and night. In speaking of these processes of referendum, he was quite expansive—almost as a father toward a favorite child. I realized that he felt this was a government of transition—a step toward a more elaborate system to meet the needs of people coming out of a monarchy until they should become more educated to the methods of self-government.

We got around to talking about his concept of internal communism. I asked him about the one-party system, and was told that more than one candidate for an office always was put up—so the people had a choice (as in a primary). Then he added with a smile: "There is no great difference between your system and ours. We have one party and you have only two—just one more!"

There are sharp differences, I think, between the peoples of Yugoslavia and Russia. The Russian peasants for years were unprotesting slaves, and when they were driven to seek any measure of improvement, these revolts were led by the intellectuals. On the other hand, the Yugoslav groups have been constantly in revolt, constantly fighting for freedom. This has produced in them a character far different from that of the Russians. I think that it must be conceded that Tito himself has this basic difference in quality, and that he recognizes it in his people—which may be the great reason for the split between Yugoslavia and the Cominform.

As we chatted about Yugoslavia's break with the Cominform, I pressed the Marshal for an answer to one question which lurked in my mind. Although he had rebelled at Russian efforts to impose the Kremlin's will in Yugoslavia's internal affairs, he had never repudiated, to my knowledge, the concept that the Cominform was designed to spread world communism.

Tito thought there was a trend in the world toward socialism, but he insisted that nations must develop in their own way, without others trying to impose plans and methods upon them.

This led to a sore point. I gathered at once that he felt quite strongly that the great powers in the West should no more interfere in the way other nations wished to carry on their affairs than should other nations interfere in the affairs of the Western nations. I explained to Tito that many Americans understood that his country needed economic aid and that I had been impressed by the gratitude shown for that aid. But I told him flatly that I felt that such gratitude did not prove that, when the aid was no longer needed, his government might not return to Stalinist methods.

The Marshal was shocked—as much apparently by the implication that there were many other Americans with such reservations as by the fact that I told him this. He emphatically assured me that the break with the Cominform had brought an end, for good and all, to Stalinist methods in Yugoslavia. He repeated an earlier assurance to our then Ambassador, Mr. George Allen, that regardless of whether we extended aid or not, the attitude of Yugoslavia toward the Cominform and the Soviet Union would not change.

From Tito on down, nowhere in Yugoslavia did I find any evidence of any intention to rejoin the forces of world communism. From the Ministry of the Interior, I inquired about the secret police and about the rumors one hears of political prisoners and various other types of prisoners. There I was told that the secret police make arrests every month, but that the search is for Soviet infiltration and Soviet agents who are attempting to win over the Yugoslav people to collaboration with Russia. This sort of infiltration just is not allowed in Yugoslavia, any more than it is allowed in the United States.

Tito and the people I met and talked with in Yugoslavia seemed to have the warmest feelings toward the United States. That doesn't mean that we always will agree on methods, since Yugoslavia is a socialist state, at the present time extremely concerned with its own internal economic and social affairs, and ours is a representative republic with a capitalist economy.

Tito's Yugoslavia, despite its break with the Soviets, remains part of the Communist world. Let us not fool ourselves that it has any sympathy for, or understanding of, our free-enterprise system. But also, let us not become so obsessed with the words that we disregard Yugoslavia's importance to us as a powerful enemy of the Soviet imperialism which is the greatest menace to our free world.

90

Address to 1956 Democratic National Convention

Twice before I have spoken to a National Democratic Convention; once I came when you had nominated my husband to be your standard bearer and spoke with a message from him, and once I came at the invitation of President Truman to speak to you about the United Nations and what it meant to all of us.

Tonight I come at the invitation of the National Chairman of the Democratic Party to speak to you as a fellow Democrat.

I cannot talk to you about my choice as your standard bearer, but I do want to talk to you about our Party and our duty. You here have a heavier responsibility than even I have, because you are delegates. You are going back into your communities all over the country, and you will tell your friends, your neighbors what you believe a Democratic victory should mean. I do not believe that victory in itself is enough. I want victory, and I believe we will have it in November—but I want even more, that each and every one of you, as you go back into your communities, take the message of what you want that victory to mean. We must be a united Party.

It is true we have differences, but everywhere in our country we know that today our differences must somehow be resolved, because we stand before the world on trial, really, to show what democracy means, and that is a heavy responsibility, because the world today is deciding between democracy and Communism, and one means freedom and one means slavery.

You have seen a film tonight, which I think must have moved you, as it moved me, to pride in our record, to a recognition of what our Party has meant to our country and to the world.

Great leaders we have had, but we could not have had great leaders unless they had had a great people to follow. You cannot be a great leader unless the people are great. That is what I want to remind every one of you tonight. You must be a great people with great objectives.

I remember very well the first crisis that we met in '32, and I remember that we won out, because the people were ready to carry their share of the burden, and follow and carry through the words, "All you have to fear, the only thing you have to fear, is fear itself."

You must have the action of the people or your leadership will not be true leadership.

Conrad Hilton Hotel, Chicago, August 13, 1956.

433

Now the world looks at us again, and what we do at home is going to be watched in the world. I have been around the world a number of times of late, and I know that much of the good will that was a reservoir for us in the world came from the fact that here at home we had decided that government had a real responsibility to make the pursuit of happiness an objective of government, and caring for the individual was a responsibility of government. That meant that we try to help all of our people to a better life, and it meant to the peoples of the world hope for the same kind of thing to happen to them as well.

Now they look to us again for the meaning of democracy, and we must think of that very seriously. There are new problems. They must be met in new ways. We have heard a great deal, and we were fired with enthusiasm by the tradition of our Party. Thus, the new problems we face cannot be met by traditions only, but they must be met by imagination. They must be met by understanding and the feel of the people, and not only the people at home, but the people of the world. And it is a foolish thing to say that you pledge yourself to live up to the traditions of the New Deal and Fair Deal—of course, you are proud of those traditions; of course, you are proud to have the advice of the elders in our Party, but our Party is young and vigorous. Our Party may be the oldest Democratic Party, but our Party must live as a young Party, and it must have young leadership. It must have young people, and they must be allowed to lead. They must not lean on their tradition. They must be proud of it. They must take into account the advice of the elders, but they must have the courage to look ahead, to face new problems with new solutions, and in so doing, we will not only meet our own difficulties at home and find ways to solve them, but we will also meet some of the difficulties that in that great speech that you heard from Governor Clement, are those pointed out as being the issues between ourselves as the Democratic Party, and the Republican Party.

We have great issues. I believe that it is absolutely imperative that the Democratic Party come back to power, but they must come back with the right leader. They must come back with your considered and careful choice, and you must feel a very great individual responsibility when you choose your leader, when you have chosen your leaders, then to back them, then to go in and work.

It isn't just fight. It is work, and some of it is dull work, but you must be ready to go in and work because that is the way that parties win victories at election time.

The things that are done by each one of you and through you by each person in your community, that is what will win for you a victory on Election Day, and I personally hope that you will remember the things which have been said tonight, even those for which we prayed in the invocation for guidance and inspiration and courage. It will take all those things for us to remember the objectives for which we want a victory, for us to resolve difficult questions which will be hard for many of us to face.

It will take understanding and sympathy to think of the problems of the world and to realize that today the world has narrowed, and that we feel very quickly the sufferings of other areas of the world, and they add to our sufferings.

We might just have a vision, and I would like to give you the idea: You will remember that my husband said in one of his speeches that our job was not finished, because we still had a third of our people who were ill-housed, ill-clothed, ill-fed. Twenty percent today is the figure they give us.

We have lessened that group in our country that are ill-housed, ill-clothed, ill-fed, but we still have a job to do.

Could we have the vision of doing away in this great country with poverty? It would be a marvelous achievement, and I think it might be done if you and I, each of us, as individuals, would really pledge ourselves and our Party to think imaginatively of what can be done at home, what can make us not only the nation that has some of the richest people in the world, but the nation where there are no people that have to live at a substandard level. That would be one of the very best arguments against Communism, that we could possibly have.

And if we do it at home, it will spread through the world, and we will have again that surge of hope from the other peoples, that surge which brought us before good will and trust and confidence, and which will do it again, but it requires from every one of you the imagination and willingness to make a great leader and to do the work to put your leaders across in November.

91

Campaign Address, Charleston, West Virginia

I want to tell you why I came back into active political work. I worked for the United Nations for six years and in doing that I tried to act as a representative of the American people not as a Democrat or a Republican, but for all the people of the country. I went to the first meeting in London to organize the UN and that is where I first really came to know Adlai Stevenson. I had met him before, but never really knew him as a person. I think because I have become conscious that we were losing, not gaining friends in the last four years that I began to think who was the best candidate to bring us back to world thinking, and to realize that now practically all domestic problems tied into the problems of the world. At that first meeting Adlai Stevenson did all the preparatory work since the meeting in San Francisco up to the London meeting. Every country had a group of people working in the Preparation Committee, he headed ours and did wonderful work. He knew all the other people and told us when we came who they were and what they did. I was worried as I was the only woman and felt I was looked on not as "one of the crowd." Mr. Dulles and Mr. Vandenberg were not happy that I was along, so I worked with great care and read all the time on the steamer about the State Department position papers. They were quite hard to understand for the State Department has a language all its own devised to keep others from understanding it, and I had to learn this new language. There were briefings every day for all delegates and for the press, and other than that I spent all my spare time reading these papers. One day I met Mr. Vandenberg in the corridor and he said "we decided to ask you to serve on Committee 3." This made me feel that they were all meting without me, and I had no idea what Committee 3 was, but I said I would be delighted to serve, and then went on to find out what work Committee 3 did.

Adlai Stevenson told us about the people in the other delegations. He really made a study of the people we would deal with, and what the setup would be and much background information. This made all the difference in our ability to work with the others. I watched Adlai Stevenson from then on, and he worked on several of the Committees. Some people gain respect and others lose respect when you are working with them. Adlai Stevenson gained. All the trips taken by the Secretary of State have not gained friends for us—we have had four years of dealing with crises. We have no one who has looked at the whole world and tried to map out what we are going to do. It is not

October 1, 1956.

necessary to reach a crisis if you prevent them from happening. We must have a clearcut policy and we need to state it. Otherwise we must just drift along and hope trouble will disappear, but it doesn't. Little things are often important in relation to other countries—using the wrong word—handling people without understanding of background—lead to real trouble when we are trying to make them see things from our point of view. On my trips around the world I have been confronted in country after country with stories of little things. The story of Dulles going to Egypt's ruler just when Great Britain had finally negotiated to leave, and presented him with two pistols. Of course Great Britain was angry. It is an amusing thing to tell, but it didn't make friends for us! And when the Secretary of State was in Israel and was presented with a remarkable Bible, beautifully bound—he said "of course this includes the New Testament?" Ben-Gurion got red up the back of his neck. These things are not really funny, as they are the things that lose friends for us in the world.

I remember after the 1952 elections Adlai Stevenson went on a trip around the world. I followed him in most places and particularly in Asia. Always I was told "We like your Mr. Stevenson—he listened to what we had to say." This taught me a lesson. If you want to learn it is a good idea to listen. I discovered that we Americans have a reputation for doing all the talking. If you don't know much about the people and their background doing all the talking and not finding out their ideas, is not a wise thing to do. One difficulty of course, is that we have become the leaders of the free world and possibly this came without our wanting it and without much preparation, so we need to learn. Adlai Stevenson took his trip to Africa because he had not seen this Continent which he realized was one area where our problems would lie in the next few years, and he felt obliged to learn about these people. A person must take the trouble to learn what he needs to know if new problems are to be solved in new ways.

How about things happening here at home? There is hardly a domestic problem that doesn't touch on international problems. Civil Rights is an example. We must use patience. We can't do everything at once, nor as quickly in every place, but we must move and we must show that we really intend that every citizen shall have equality of opportunity, recognition as a citizen and live without feeling that he is not an equal of every other citizen in our democracy. If this doesn't happen and we show that we are not in earnest, it will hurt in our world leadership. We must bear in mind that 2/3rds of the world's population is colored, and we are the minority race. We have often exploited the people of other races, but this is not wise. Today they long for freedom in all areas of the world. We are the people who lead in the struggle for freedom and we can't afford to let people see any exploitation here at home. That is not the example of a nation that says everyone is created free and equal!

I am deeply concerned about education, and if you have been listening to Adlai Stevenson you will know that he too is deeply concerned in giving young people a better life. We may think this is just a domestic problem and that it doesn't tie up with the struggle between Communism and Democracy and in the defense of our country. We may think it is just a difficulty in our own community to get good teachers and more classrooms. I think we had better face the fact that if we go on not meeting the crisis in education we are losing out on the biggest challenge that Communism has put before us. Why? Because today in the Soviet Union 90% of the people can read and write. Any young person who shows an ability to use higher education can achieve it. Not only an education, but a subsidy grant while he is getting his education. Of course it is a type of education you would not like. We don't want to be regulated and indoctrinated, but it is a tremendous challenge to our system. We should know it and face it. Last year the Soviets trained 1,200,000 young engineers and physicists for export to be sent in their program of Technical Assistance to countries to whom they promised help. We trained 900,000 and our own industries took them all. Last year the *Herald Tribune* Forum had the Deputy Commissioner of Education from the Soviet Union here for a visit. She was a woman, and from peasant stock. Our State Department did nothing to plan this woman's trip, for she was not here on official business. One day I was called in New York and told about this woman and asked if I would not like to have her come for tea. I said I would be delighted, and I am glad that I did. I learned much about the Soviet teaching program. If a student is going to be sent to Brazil they are told to learn Portuguese. If they are going to Burma they are taught the Burmese dialects. Then when they go to a country they can not only offer their skills, but they have a common language so that it is much easier to import their thoughts. It means a great deal to people if you have taken the time to learn their language. You have gained much confidence for your efforts. I believe our young people should know as firmly why they believe in Democracy as the young Soviets know why they believe in Communism. We do our jobs because we understand—we believe in our democracy—we believe that individual personality is endowed by God with certain inherent freedoms and therefore we have something as individuals which we can delegate to our government which gives us a stronger basis than the Communist people. As I told the Deputy Commissioner we can demonstrate this—we are not ordered as you are, we do what we do because we want to. If we go outside of our own country to work we do so because we want to—not because our government says we must. There are large areas of the world that have never known freedom and don't know what it is, so to many it seems freedom to be allowed to have an education. When you speak of freedom you mean something your government has given you, we mean something inherent in us as a gift of God. So, this women told me her story. She is a peasant woman and did not have much opportunity and had no chance for education. She said that she had worked hard for what she had, but her government gave her every opportunity. She said "I am here because of my government. How can I separate my rights and the rights of my government?"

So, we can no longer put questions in one package and say we are just interested in more classrooms or more teachers or more schools. We must know what the challenge is, and then have a plan for meeting it.

92

Campaign Address, Detroit, Michigan

I am going to begin by speaking of the two things which President Eisenhower has said were most important—peace and prosperity. There is no question but we have prosperity, but it is spotty. You don't find it everywhere. There is no question but we have peace, but it hangs by a slender thread in areas of the world. The Suez is one. At least it has been brought to the UN, but we would have had perhaps a better opportunity for calmer solution of the question if at a very early stage when we found it difficult to come to an agreement we had decided to come to the UN before all nations had a crystallized point of view. In addition we should have protested when Egypt denied passage to the two ships. Instead we temporized and did nothing and now we have a weaker case in consequence. I don't feel that we can say today that we have a successful foreign policy. The Soviet Union has succeeded in extending influence in the Near East, something they have wanted for a long time and it will give them easier access to the Continent of Africa. It was done without our having an idea of the object of Soviet aid to Egypt. We have been losing friends in the world. People are less trusting of the United States, more questioning of our motives and understanding than they were four years ago. This is one of my main reasons for coming back into active political life. I had been in the UN where I felt I must represent the American people not as a Democrat or a Republican, but as an American. But, I felt we needed the best possible candidate to head the Democratic ticket we could get. I feel that Adlai Stevenson and Estes Kefauver are a very good team and I think you realize as I do that we must give our team support. We must have Congressmen, Senators and Governors, and Democratic machinery all down the line working to make this country an example of what freedom an democracy mean for the whole world.

Civil Rights is one of the important issues in this campaign even though President Eisenhower didn't happen to mention it. It is not a domestic issue only, it is an international issue because we are the leaders of the free world. Two-thirds of the peoples of the world are colored, the white race is a minority race. Many of the colored peoples have been exploited, by white people and they are suspicious of us now and watch all we do and when we deny to any of our citizens equal rights it is proof to them that freedom is no more real in the United States than it is in the Soviet Union. It is natural that our citizens should want to have full equal rights and I don't wonder at all that there is impatience among the negroes. We must face the facts. I have heard that some negroes are saying that perhaps the Republicans will do more than the Democrats. Except for the Supreme Court decision the Republicans have done

Masonic Temple, October 3, 1956.

nothing, and even that couldn't have been except for gains made during years of the Democratic Administration. I want to point out one thing about platforms—I'm practical—one thing must happen before we have much legislation in the way of Civil Rights. There must be a change of rules of the Senate to make possible, after presentation of views, at a given point a vote. I made a careful check in 1952 and again this year. The Democratic platform includes a plank for changing that rule. This is not in the Republican platform. Of course it is not important if the President doesn't intend to make any effort along this line. We must get the man elected who wants to live up to the Constitution, and that man is Adlai Stevenson.

The civil rights plank is not very strong in either platform. I was willing to compromise for I felt we should stay united within the party. We could do more together than if there was a separation. I may be wrong in this but, the best words are not important unless you had elected someone with courage to say that once elected he had to uphold the Constitution and the law of the land. I want to add one more word—I don't think this can happen as quickly in one place as in others. In the North there is one step—before integrating our schools we must get rid of segregated housing, and that is not easy. We can do it but it will take determined and continued pressing forward. We should move as quickly as possible to set an example at home and abroad of what can be done.

In the South the first problem is the right to vote. Until we have that we cannot do anything. This is a Federal right and the Federal government can do something about it. We must realize that all of this will be slow, but we must move. To keep our prestige in the world it is important that we do not stand still. In the movie we saw it stressed the pursuit of happiness. I hope you realize that Adlai Stevenson has set a tone in campaigning which stresses this and he is covering the needs we have for happiness. If we are successful at home in giving our people greater happiness we will give hope all over the world. To people who have disease, poverty, poor land, just to know that there is a place in the world where the government cares about individuals and their happiness—well, perhaps someday we can succeed too. Hope is what many people live on in the world. We must continue to give that hope. We must see to it that all of our friends and neighbors and coworkers are registered. Remember if you don't register you can't vote. Then on November 6th, elect Adlai Stevenson and Estes Kefauver, and elect Democratic Congressmen, Senators and Governors to help them lead us.

93

Why I Am Opposed to "Right to Work" Laws

I am frequently asked why I oppose laws which certain groups are trying to enact in our states under such slogans as "right to work," "voluntary unionism" and the like.

I am glad to give my views because much confusion as to the wisdom of this legislation has resulted from misrepresentations by its sponsors.

I feel that if I can help clear away the fog, I will have performed a useful service to my fellow Americans.

If our nation is to meet the needs of today and continue to go forward, all of us must be able to distinguish that which is good for the general welfare from that which is bad. I consider "right to work" laws to be bad for the individual states and bad for the nation.

They are bad not just for working people but for employers as well, many of whom shortsightedly support this legislation.

Such laws would impose grave injustices on all working people. But employers would suffer, too, for the end result would be not only lower wages but a shrinking national economy and a drying up of purchasing power for America's mass production economy.

This would mean that our farmers also would be hurt. Everybody would be harmed in one way or another.

Most people realize we are a nation of workers and that whatever is harmful to the majority of our citizens is hurtful to the whole nation. It follows, then, that every man and woman who is dependent upon a job for his livelihood should understand the time bomb that is concealed in these laws under plausible-sounding but untruthful slogans and labels.

The labels "right to work," "voluntary unionism," "voluntary union membership" and the like are misnomers, of course.

They are the sugar coating to make palatable the bitter pill of the real intent of the laws which, I am afraid, most people do not take the time to read.

The "right to work" label is an implied promise that the legislation does not carry out. Such laws do not guarantee anyone a job or even the right to have a job.

The "voluntary union membership" slogan is another deceptive distortion to divert attention from the fact that this legislation makes legal a compulsory open shop, destroying the right of employers and employees to agree mutually on a union shop at the collective bargaining table.

AFL-CIO Federationist 66 (February 1959): 5–7.

This right is, of course, a key provision of the federal Taft-Hartley Act. Therefore, the agitation to enact state "right to work" laws is a highly suspect maneuver to override and nullify federal law.

As simply as I can say it, I am opposed to "right to work" legislation because it does nothing for working people, but instead gives employers the right to exploit labor.

Not only does it do nothing for working people, but it robs them of the gains they have made over more than a half century of bitter struggle for betterment.

These rights to a fair return for their labor and skills, to decent working hours and reasonable job security were first recognized nationally, and became federal labor policy, in the presidential administration of my late husband.

I believe the Wagner Labor Act of 1936 was, in its way, as important a contribution to human progress as the Magna Carta and our own Bill of Rights were to our forebears.

I cannot bring myself to believe that anyone in his right mind would seriously advocate abolition of the freedoms brought into being by those documents.

Nor can I believe that the majority of our people will permit a backward step through "right to work" laws toward the grinding toil and impoverishment that were the workers' lot in the past century.

I am glad that my faith in the wisdom of our people was borne out in the November election. As we all know, five out of six states where "right to work" was an issue voted overwhelmingly against it.

I thought Senator Lyndon Johnson expressed it very well when he said the election outcome showed Americans "will not veto the Twentieth Century."

The election result has taught the "right to work" sponsors at least one lesson. In New Mexico, since the election, they have changed their name from "Citizens' Right to Work Committee" to "Educational Committee for Voluntary Union Membership." But I do not believe this new slogan will deceive our citizens any more than did the "right to work" label.

As I have said, our federal laws clearly state workers have a right to a voice in determining what shall be fair pay for their labor and skills. These laws provide that a majority of workers in a plant may select a trade union of their choice to represent them in collective bargaining with management.

This certainly seems a fair arrangement to me. The workers gain strength by sticking together which they otherwise would not have. The union provides them with a voice through which to present their side.

But suppose workers had no unions to represent them. Each employee would have to make his own arrangement with his employer. What chance would one worker have in an argument with management over a pay raise or better working conditions?

And if the employer decided he could hire two young workers for the wage he was paying an older, more experienced hand, what could the older worker do about it without the collective strength of a union to protect his rights?

The federal labor-management act also provides for reasonable union security. If a majority of workers decide there should be a union security clause, and this is agreed to by management, then it becomes a part of the contract and a "condition of employment."

A worker does not have to be a member of the union to get a job. But he is expected to become a member of the union after a period of thirty to sixty days.

This gives the union fair and reasonable security to carry out its responsibilities with the employer which arise because under the Taft-Hartley Act the union must by law represent all employees in the plant.

It would not be fair to the majority of workers, who have chosen a union to represent them and pay dues to support the continuing costs of union organization, to have to pay for obtaining a wage increase, or to prevent a wage cut, for a few workers who might try to get these benefits free.

A union requires membership of all in the plant, too, to prevent watering down of its strength through normal turnover or employment expansion and to combat establishment of company-dominated union or non-union shop.

Here, again, the principle of union security is not only recognized by federal law but is in keeping with the American system of democratic government, which says that the will of the majority shall prevail.

It is this union security clause which gives workers a fair balance with management at the collective bargaining table. Without it, the strength of the workers' union can be whittled down to the point where an employer can pay the lowest possible wages.

It is at this keystone of strength that the "right to work" sponsors have aimed their laws. When this is understood I feel sure all will agree that it shows the true purpose of these laws as seeking first to weaken and in the end to destroy all unions, and with them the whole structure of collective bargaining between labor and management.

To make this part of the American democratic system appear odious and suspect, the "right to work" sponsors use another slogan. They call the union shop clause "compulsory unionism," which, as I have explained, is not true. This is simply a demagogic maneuver by employers to play on man's natural feeling that no one should be forced to do what he does not want to do.

It is a "nice" way of putting controlling power back into the hands of employers.

The extent to which "right to work" sponsors go to try to make us believe they are something they are not would be ludicrous were the aim of their deceptions not so dangerous to the nation's welfare.

Someone sent me a copy of a recent leaflet put out over the name of a so-called "National Right to Work Committee." It has on its cover the figure of a man, obviously representing "management," shaking hands with another, obviously a worker. The caption reads: "A coalition of employers and employees united in a common cause."

The inference, of course, is that employers are sponsoring "right to work" laws to help the workers, and that workers are behind them, when nearly everyone knows this is just the opposite of fact and truth.

By now it is certainly well known that sponsorship of "right to work" laws stems from the National Association of Manufacturers, the U.S. Chamber of Commerce and the American Farm Bureau Federation which they control, and that the large amounts of money spent in various states in an attempt to force passage of the laws comes mainly from some of our large corporations.

Perhaps it is not as widely known that the National Association of Manufacturers launched its first campaign to "break" trade unions at its national convention in 1903—more than a half century ago—and has been hard at it ever since.

As to the question of whether workers look to employers or trade unions to protect their interests, we have the answer in U.S. government records.

Between 1947 and 1951 the federal government conducted 46,119 secret ballot elections on the question of whether workers want the union shop. In 97 percent of the elections the workers voted for the union shop.

I think it is not unreasonable to question the motives of the "right to work" sponsors in view of these facts.

I can best sum up my opposition to "right to work" laws in these words:

I am opposed to this legislation because it is narrow in concept, punitive and discriminatory against wage-earners, and is designed solely to benefit employers.

I am opposed to it because its real aim is to destroy American labor.

I am opposed to it because the campaign to enact "right to work" laws is based on dishonesty and deception.

I am opposed because it would upset the present balance between labor and management that has become a basic guarantee of a prosperous national economy.

I am opposed to "right to work" laws because they promote industrial strife instead of industrial peace.

It is true that unions have become powerful over the years. But we should not forget that the power of the unions is puny compared to the power that goes with the enormous wealth of Big Business. And business had power first.

Whether unions have grown and with this growth have become powerful is not the problem today.

The problem, rather, is to make both labor and business feel the responsibility that goes with power, and to use this power mutually for the benefit of all.

94

"Meet the Press" Interview

Panel: Marquis Childs, *St. Louis Post-Dispatch*
        Richard Clurman, *Newsday*
        May Craig, *Portland* (Me.) *Press Herald*
        John Oakes, *The New York Times*

Moderator: Ned Brooks

ANNOUNCER: Ladies and gentlemen, "Meet the Press," the prize-winning program produced by Lawrence E. Spivak. Ready for this spontaneous, unrehearsed conference are four of America's top reporters. Please remember their questions do not necessarily reflect their point of view; it's their way of getting a story to you. Here is the Moderator of "Meet the Press," Mr. Ned Brooks.

MR. BROOKS: And welcome once again to "Meet the Press." Our guest is Mrs. Franklin D. Roosevelt, whose world travels recently took her to Russia. Her visit came at a time when world attention more than ever before is fastened on the Soviet Union. Russia has captured the spotlight by her launching of the earth satellite, by her boast of having perfected new and fearsome weapons and by her latest moves to gain a foothold in the Middle East. The free world is left to guess what lies behind Russia's tough talk, whether she is plunging toward a war of annihilation or is engaging in a gigantic campaign of bluff and propaganda. Mrs. Roosevelt spent 27 days in the Soviet Union. In the course of her visit she was granted a privilege seldom given to foreign visitors, a three-hour interview with Communist leader Nikita Khrushchev. Mrs. Roosevelt went to Russia as a reporter. For many years she has had a keen interest in foreign affairs. She served for six years as a delegate to the United Nations. Her observations and impressions are now being brought to the American people through her newspaper column and a series of lectures.

MR. CHILDS: Mrs. Roosevelt, you reported your interview with Khrushchev at great length. I want to ask you whether you think all these interviews give Khrushchev a propaganda forum he wouldn't otherwise have, and whether it does more harm than good for the free world?

MRS. ROOSEVELT: It seems to me that it is good. It may give him a forum where he can say things which he really means or does not really mean, but I think that it is a good thing to have people on record. I asked him if he would

October 20, 1957.

mind being recorded, and Dr. Gurewitsch recorded what he said and listened to the interpreter, so that he knew when the interpreter was not giving a full report, because he knew Russian. He also made no objections to having photographs taken, and I think that some of Dr. Gurewitsch's photographs are as revealing as anything that I have seen.

MR. CHILDS: I notice he said at the beginning of your interview that politicians never cast aside political obligations. Now was this an obligation to you because you were Mrs. Roosevelt, or was that an obligation to his ideology, to spread that ideology?

MRS. ROOSEVELT: I think it was like so many things, a mixture. Wherever we went, always, they did not forget that my husband was someone that helped them in the war, and they always spoke of it. Of course, we helped them in the war for selfish reasons, because if any of us failed, we all failed. It is no extraordinary thing that that is remembered; it was, of course, vital to all of us, but I think it was only partly that. I think that also he was curious to see what I would ask. He asked to have the questions ahead of time, but he also agreed that we would talk afterwards and that I could use the talk, but of course, I said that I would not directly quote, except what I recorded.

MR. CHILDS: I noticed you've sized him up as a pretty ruthless and power-loving figure. Do you think he's likely to make a move that will start another war?

MRS. ROOSEVELT: No. I said I think that we all of us know that he is ruthless, because he wouldn't be where he was if he wasn't ruthless. But I think he is honest when he says that war is unthinkable. Now, that is not because he just can't bear that human beings should suffer. That is because he and other leaders have made up their minds in the Soviet Union that they can win what they want without a war, because they now know that new weapons mean destruction to such an extent that they would actually win a world in ruins, and that they don't want.

MR. OAKES: You referred to the Soviet Union as a government that understands the value of research. Were you implying in that remark that you felt that the United States government didn't fully understand the value of research?

MRS. ROOSEVELT: Yes, because you will recognize if you go back a little that it's only a very few years ago that we induced Congress to give us a small amount of government money—we've done a great deal with private money—for cancer research and research in heart trouble. It's very much more difficult in a democracy to educate the people and for them to educate their representatives to needs. In a government like the Soviet Union where all it requires is for a certain group of people to recognize the value, it's very, very easy and they are carrying on an enormous amount of research. They're putting a great deal of money into it. They're putting as many men as are needed, and women, and it is done on a colossal scale.

MR. OAKES: Do you suggest that our failure adequately to appreciate the values of research is the reason that the Russians put the satellite up first?

MRS. ROOSEVELT: I think that's partly the reason, and then, also, you have to remember that scientists are as free as long as they are just scientists and working as scientists as any people in the Soviet Union. A writer, a painter, may be reprimanded by Mr. Khrushchev because what he has done does not serve the Soviet Communist idea or Socialist idea, whichever word they choose to use, but as scientist, everything that he discovers serves that purpose. If you ask him a political question he says to you at once, "Oh, I'm no politician; I don't know anything about politics." As long as he sticks to what he is doing in his science, he's free, and that, of course is a great advantage.

MR. OAKES: Mrs. Roosevelt, It's very difficult to think of anything about you as elderly, but I think one can refer to you as an elder stateswoman of the Democratic Party?

MRS. ROOSEVELT: Oh, I'm not an elder stateswoman.

MR. OAKES: May I ask if you feel this question of the satellite and the Russian success with the Sputnik is a proper subject of political argument between the Democrats and the Republicans?

MRS. ROOSEVELT: I'd say first of all it was important scientifically. I'm no scientist; I don't know how much value it has from a military standpoint; but, scientifically, it has value, and psychologically because, of course, neutral countries are always watching both sides. This has a psychological effect. You can't brush that aside.

MR. OAKES: But a proper subject of argument, I mean, between Democrats and Republicans from a political point of view?

MRS. ROOSEVELT: Anything which bears on the scene is a proper question for argument; oh yes, anything is when it bears on our safety.

MRS. CRAIG: You have been quoted as describing Khrushchev as being cordial, simple, outspoken. How can you think that any Communist, particularly a top official, can be simple?

MRS. ROOSEVELT: I meant when I said that, of course, that in his manner and in the way of receiving you he was simple. I don't mean he's simple-minded, if that's what you think. I simply mean that he received me with only one person,

449

the person who was going to take notes. He was walking up and down outside his house. I saw him under probably the best auspices. Most of the people who see him see him at big parties where much drinking is going on. I had been told beforehand that he's an impossible person, vulgar, drinking, disagreeable. He was none of those things. It was ten o'clock in the morning, and he greeted me as any quiet, ordinary person would.

MRS. CRAIG: You also are quoted as saying you found him very likeable though you disagreed with his views. How could you like anybody who has done what he did in supporting murder?

MRS. ROOSEVELT: I did not mean that I found him likeable. I said he was the type of person, at least I meant to say, that could be likeable. Lots of people can be likeable whom fundamentally you don't like. I simply meant that, as far as his appearance was that morning, he made no trouble about the interview, once I got it. I had a great deal of trouble before, but he made no trouble about being recorded. He made no trouble about being photographed. He was a perfectly pleasant, agreeable person. We differ on so many things that at one point I thought he was ready to throw me out, but he was right in being irritated because I almost did not say the truth, and he heard me begin, and he immediately said, "We are going to have a frank discussion." I knew what he meant was we'd have none if I wasn't frank.

MRS. CRAIG: Did you think he was putting it on, or is it because he's that kind of person who appears likeable that he has succeeded?

MRS. ROOSEVELT: He is a peasant stock. He's like peasants, if you know the peasant type in eastern Europe; he's peasant stock. His fingers, his hands, his whole build is that of a peasant. He has the peasant canniness and cautiousness, but he is, on the other hand, extremely articulate. He asked me to submit questions, but I never saw a sign that he had them before him or that anything was in the back of his mind. He had simply asked for them, and whether he looked at them or not, I don't know; he answered perfectly without hesitation. I would say that it was as good an interview as you could have. Whether he absolutely was being truthful in everything he said, I would highly doubt. On the other hand, there were certain things that I felt he really believed, and I think it's a good thing to know what your, let's say rival, actually seems to believe.

MR. CLURMAN: May we get some of your general conclusions as a result of being to Russia and having talked to Khrushchev? I wonder, for example, what is your feeling about the possibility of peaceful coexistence with the Soviet Union? Can America and Russia peacefully coexist?

MRS. ROOSEVELT: At the present moment, I think it will take some time. We're living in a time when everything is changing. I think that we have to consider that there may be changes there, and there may be some changes here. I would not say that as they are today there would be any basis for co-existence. We can live in the same world, of course, but cooperatively, it would be difficult. We can live apart. I think, however, there may be changes. I consider that what I saw was a challenge, that we should know about it. There's no use in belittling your rival. There's no use in putting your head in the sand and saying I don't want to know. It's much better to know because what we have to prove to the neutral world, or the world that is judging between us all the time, is that with freedom we can actually do more for the lives of people than they can do with their system; and that's the important challenge; that's what we have to meet. It can't be met just with guns.

MR. CLURMAN: What specifically more should we be doing? For example, in such a complicated area as the Middle East, what should we now be doing in our struggle with the Russians that we're not doing?

MRS. ROOSEVELT: We should have begun a long while ago. We never should have allowed the Suez crisis to happen. We could have done much better right there, and we should recognize right now that arms to the Middle East is so much down the drain, because they could no more actually stand up against the Red Army without an atom war than they could fly.

MR. CLURMAN: But are you optimistic in general about our winning this competitive coexistence with the Russians? What is going to happen? People are very concerned about it.

MRS. ROOSEVELT: If we have good leadership, and if the people of the United States actually know what it is they have to do, I haven't any question but what we can win out, and we can find a way to bring about changes.

MR. CLURMAN: Is it your feeling that we don't now have good leadership?

MRS. ROOSEVELT: I can't tell. That's for the people of the United States to tell.

MR. CLURMAN: I mean your personal feeling? You, after all, are an eminent and representative person in America. Is it your feeling, your personal feeling, we don't have good leadership?

MRS. ROOSEVELT: I would say that we as a people have not been curious enough to bring about the right kind of leadership in the past few years.

MR. BROOKS: Mrs. Roosevelt, you were mentioning a moment ago some of these decisions in the past. I'm wondering if you think, in the light of what has happened, that it was a mistake for our country to recognize Russia when we did?

MRS. ROOSEVELT: No, I don't think we could have gone on without recognizing a country as great as the Soviet Union and its people. What good would it do us to know that all this was happening and that we had no way of even having a contact? It's far better to have a contact than to have none.

MR. BROOKS: Then would you apply that same principle to the recognition of Communist China?

MRS. ROOSEVELT: At present Communist China can't qualify for membership in the UN because you have to strive for world peace. You have to be trying. She'd have to withdraw her troops from North Vietnam and North Korea. If she does, and can honestly say, yes, we're trying to be a peace-loving nation, I think we have to begin and find out how we can work that question out, a complicated question.

MR. BROOKS: I was speaking not of the membership in the UN but rather recognition by this government.

MRS. ROOSEVELT: I would like to see us at least have some communication. I think it's just nonsense that the press can't tell us something about what goes on inside of Communist China, and I would like to see us by stages find out, because if we could get the press honestly reporting to us, then we'd know whether we should or shouldn't. I think it's necessary to know.

MR. CHILDS: I'd like to come back a moment, to this matter of leadership. You said the other day in an interview in St. Louis, in the *Post-Dispatch:* "You want to know what you really believe, what you're fighting for." You were speaking about our knowledge of Russia, but I'd like to ask you if you think we really in this country know what we are fighting for in this cold war?

MRS. ROOSEVELT: I think that's one of our troubles. We've had democracy a long while; we've had freedom; and we have grown passive about it. We take it for granted, and we don't even formulate what are the things that we believe in and that we are ready to die for, or to live for, which is more important just at present.

MR. CHILDS: Many people have said that this is partly the fault of President Eisenhower, that he doesn't supply the leadership. Would you agree with that?

MRS. ROOSEVELT: I'm not here to criticize anyone in the government, either the President or anyone else. I would much prefer to say that in a democracy the main burden is the burden of the people, and the people must, if they choose to be free, insist on certain kinds of leadership.

MR. CHILDS: I'd like to ask you something that maybe is not exactly in line, but still I'm sure you won't mind. You were often accused in the past of being soft on Communism. Do you think that a great many of us woke up too late, and is that one of the reasons why we don't know what we're fighting for or where we are going?

MRS. ROOSEVELT: No, I think we have been led by certain people in the last few years to be afraid of Communism, and we have not been led to the realization that the way you win is to be for something passionately. Now we are waking up to the fact that there are people in the world who are dedicated to their system and that we have to be dedicated to ours.

MR. OAKES: You are aware, I suppose, that the Democratic Advisory Council this morning in a published statement said that the Eisenhower Administration "placed fiscal objectives and domestic political consideration ahead of the nation's security." That's pretty strong language. I wonder what comment you would care to make on that?

MRS. ROOSEVELT: All I could say would have to be said as a Democrat. I would have to say that I felt this had been a businessmen's Administration, and that probably, if you really analyzed Mr. Humphrey's leadership, and some of the other leadership, you would find that not adding to taxes, reducing taxes, there had been more concern about financial questions. But I am neither a financier nor am I a member of the Advisory Committee.

MR. OAKES: But you're a good Democrat, and the Democratic Party, of course, controlled the last Congress. Can you point to any serious effort on the part of the Democratic leadership in the Congress—

MRS. ROOSEVELT: I cannot, and I think our leadership has been poor.

MR. OAKES: In other words, you would say that the Democratic Party as a Congressional control—

MRS. ROOSEVELT: I said our leadership.

MR. OAKES: —has been poor?

MRS. CRAIG: Mrs. Roosevelt, do you think we should ask Marshal Zhukov to come, and how could we take the hand of the general who slaughtered the Hungarians?

MRS. ROOSEVELT: In the first place, you would have to realize that in the Soviet Union at the present time the people there are being told that we are responsible, because it was our radio and our propaganda that incited a small group in Hungary to revolt and that the Soviets had to go in because they had to uphold the will of the majority for a Socialist country. To you and to me that's perfect nonsense, but a lot of people all over the Soviet Union have been fed that and believe it, and you would almost say when you talk to the leaders—I mean the heads of the Cabinet—that they all believed it, and so you have to reckon with that as being fed even to Mr. Zhukov probably.

MRS. CRAIG: But should we ask him? Should we invite him here?

MRS. ROOSEVELT: I don't know. That is a decision for the President to make. If there is something to be gained that is of value to us, I would have Marshal Zhukov here. If there is nothing to be gained that is of value to us, I would not have him, but I would certainly have him if by seeing him we can gain something of value to us.

MR. CLURMAN: You said rather emphatically that the leadership of the Democratic Party in the Congress had been very poor. Do I take that to mean you think that Lyndon Johnson's leadership has been very poor?

MRS. ROOSEVELT: I think Mr. Johnson is one of the ablest people at maneuvering that we have in the party. He has maneuvered very well, but I have seen no real decisions as to what the Democratic Party stood for, as to where it was actually heading, and that is what I think the Democratic Party has to decide.

MR. CLURMAN: I'm going to ask you a question now that almost every Democrat has asked, and we very seldom get an answer to. I think it's a question that a great many people really want the answer to, so that they can determine in what direction the Democratic Party might be going, that is, who do you think in the Democratic Party now in 1960 could be a possible Presidential candidate?

MRS. ROOSEVELT: It's much too early to decide. No one can be a prophet. Who can decide now who will turn out in 1960?

MR. CLURMAN: But are there men in the Democratic Party now whose leadership—

MRS. ROOSEVELT: Oh, there are plenty of young men coming along, and I'm not a bit afraid of lack of material, but I don't think you ought to decide now in 1960.

MR. CHILDS: On this program last week you were suggested as a possible candidate for President yourself.

MRS. ROOSEVELT: For what?

MR. CHILDS: For President, for the nomination.

MRS. ROOSEVELT: I am 73 years old, wake up.

MR. CHILDS: I didn't make the nomination. Do you think we shall ever have a woman President?

MRS. ROOSEVELT: Yes, of course, we will.

MR. CHILDS: How soon?

MRS. ROOSEVELT: Oh, I don't know how soon. That depends on how many women do well in offices, and how many women win offices and are appointed. You can't tell, but someday it will happen when you get to the point where you look at people in politics and in positions of political importance as people and not as either women or men.

MR. CHILDS: Are there women today who could be President of the United States?

MRS. ROOSEVELT: I've never given it much thought, but I'm sure there probably are.

MR. OAKES: One political question again on the Democrats: Do you share the opinion of many northern Democrats that the party would be better off if it could divest itself of the southern wing?

MRS. ROOSEVELT: I am not active, and I do not think that I should make the statements which should come from the Democratic Advisory Committee. I do think that as a party in Congress—and it's very difficult; I recognize all the difficulties—we have not had a clear political stand on things that are very important, and that will be important in the coming years, to the country more than to the party even.

MR. OAKES: You wouldn't be quite prepared to say that the party would be stronger if it did not have the southern civil rights problem hanging around its neck?

MRS. ROOSEVELT: You can't remove the civil rights problem. It's with us, and not only the Democrats have it, but the Republicans have it. That is something that will be with both of our parties.

95

Mike Wallace Interview

WALLACE: Good Evening. Tonight my guest is a woman who has been called the "First Lady of the World." She is Mrs. Eleanor Roosevelt. I shall ask Mrs. Roosevelt to talk about Dwight Eisenhower, Nikita Khrushchev, Westbrook Pegler, and garlic pills. What you're about to see is unrehearsed, uncensored, my name is Mike Wallace. And now to our story. At the age of seventy-four Eleanor Roosevelt has seen a lot of the world and the world has seen a lot of her. Tonight I shall ask Mrs. Roosevelt about some of the most pressing world issues, about America's leadership or lack of it, about the Soviet menace and indications that we may be losing our strength as a nation to resist it. Later in the program we'll talk with Mrs. Roosevelt about her code of values and her family life. Mrs. Roosevelt, first of all let me ask you this: You've seen great leaders like Winston Churchill, Mahatma Gandhi, your own husband. I wonder if in a capsule fashion you can tell me what qualities enabled these men to shape the course of history as they did, what did they have that made them the leaders they were?

ROOSEVELT: I never met Mahatma Gandhi, but, I think everyone felt they knew him even if they hadn't met him. I think one thing they had in common, all these men, was great courage, both spiritual, mental and physical courage. Mahatma Gandhi I would say had perhaps a greater spiritual quality whereas Winston Churchill has besides the courage, ability and above everything else, the ability to put into words what his people felt so that he could always lead them. And my own husband I think had great patience, which you need in a democracy because you have to come to do fundamental things, you have to have the patience to have people educated; and then I think he had a deep interest in human beings as human beings.

WALLACE: What about intellectual capacity and physical vigor? How important do you think those two qualities were in these people?

ROOSEVELT: I think it's important to have both. Of course Mahatma Gandhi you might say did not have so much physical vigor but he certainly seemed to have extraordinary resistance which perhaps is rather different from physical vigor.

WALLACE: Yes . . . And intellectual capacity?

ROOSEVELT: Oh, I think they all had intellectual capacity. All of them, perhaps in different ways but they all had intellectual capacity.

November 23, 1957.

WALLACE: Well now quite candidly from all of the things that you've talked about now, how do you think that Dwight Eisenhower measures up?

ROOSEVELT: Well, that's of course a very difficult thing to say because I barely know the President. I've seen him as a General when he was in Germany, I've seen him in London as a General. I would say that he was a diplomat. I would say that he was very good at carrying out things that had been planned and probably a fine General, though he was of course in the field under General Marshall's general direction. From the standpoint of intellectual capacity, I am no judge except that I would say that he probably had less what I would call intellectual interest in a great variety of subjects than either, again I can't say about Mahatma Gandhi, but that either Winston Churchill or my husband had.

WALLACE: I ask you this—what I'm trying to do now is to find out about our present leadership. President Eisenhower in two or three years now will no longer be our President. Can you name for me, Mrs. Roosevelt, any leading Democrats or Republicans who are in the same league with a Churchill or a Gandhi or a Roosevelt, who have the stature to lead our free world against the threat of Communism?

ROOSEVELT: Well, at the present time I don't think it would be fair to name any particular people because . . . it is very often the opportunity which brings out the qualities of a man and most of the leaders on the Democratic side have not had the opportunity to meet the responsibilities and to show us whether they have the leadership qualities that are needed at the present time. Many of them have shown ability and certain different qualities but we have not yet seen, I don't think, any in a position to show whether they had the full leadership quality that the present day seems to require. Now on the Republican side of course the only one who stands out is Mr. Nixon, and he has made no mistakes of late. He's been extremely careful. I would say he had ability, how much conviction is another question.

WALLACE: Well, you mentioned Mr. Nixon in your column in *McCalls* magazine in January of nineteen fifty-six. You wrote about Republican leaders and about Mr. Nixon you said the following: "Richard Nixon would be the least attractive. I know that given great responsibility, men sometimes change"—which in a sense is what you're just saying. You say, "I know that given great responsibility men sometimes change, but Mr. Nixon's Presidency would worry me," you said. Why do you reserve this special criticism for Mr. Nixon?

ROOSEVELT: Because I think that in great crises you need to have deep rooted convictions and I have a feeling from the kind of campaigns that I have watched Mr. Nixon in in the past that his convictions are not very strong.

WALLACE: But you do admit that over the past year in particular Mr. Nixon seems to have changed, possibly to have grown with the times?

ROOSEVELT: I . . . have no idea whether he has grown. I would say that he was a very intelligent person and that he had a very clear idea of what he wanted and had conducted himself wisely to achieve the ends he desires.

WALLACE: By the same token would you have said that Harry Truman had shown great conviction prior to his being thrown into the Presidency?

ROOSEVELT: No, I would not have. Again I did not know him very well before. I would say of Mr. Truman that he rose to the responsibilities thrust upon him in a manner which was very remarkable, really, and that his big decisions very likely are going to mean that he will go down in history as one of our very good Presidents.

WALLACE: With really insufficient background to expect that he would have acted that way?

ROOSEVELT: Yes, quite certainly.

WALLACE: Well, now I'm not obviously asking you to endorse any politician here and now but the fact is that within the next ten years or so the fate of the free world may very well be decided and the President of the United States may play a major role. As a Democrat then, I put this to you, do you see even the beginnings of the makings of a Washington or a Lincoln or a Wilson or a Roosevelt in Jack Kennedy or Stuart Symington or Robert Meyner or Soapy Williams, who are the four men most talked about as potential Democratic Presidents?

ROOSEVELT: I cannot tell you what will happen in the next two years. At the moment the only person I see those beginnings in is Adlai Stevenson who has twice run for the Presidency and who has said he would not run again.

WALLACE: What lack was there in Mr. Stevenson that caused the American people to reject him not once but twice and reject him more severely, if you will, the second time than they did the first?

ROOSEVELT: Well, I think partly it is not so much a lack in him as it was a hero worship of the President, and perhaps a little bit the McCarthy Period that we were still close to, but also in him a—perhaps an inability to quite put the things he believes in in the language or in the emotional way that will come home to the average human being.

WALLACE: I think possibly that you'd go along with me when I say that it will be difficult should Mr. Stevenson decide to run again . . .

ROOSEVELT: Yes . . .

WALLACE: . . . to sell the Democratic Party on nominating him once again . . .

ROOSEVELT: Yes.

WALLACE: In view of this, let me read to you from something written by the *New York Post* Columnist William Shannon on November eleventh. Writing of two of the so-called glamor boys of the Democratic Party, he said as follows: He said about Jack Kennedy's qualifications as a Presidential hopeful, quote "Kennedy at forty is utterly without executive experience. He's never bossed any operation bigger than his own Congressional office" and of New Jersey's Governor Bob Meyner, Shannon wrote: "Meyner at forty-nine is debarred not by the thinness of his experience but by its provincial character. Trenton, New Jersey cannot by itself be a training ground for a world statesman." And yet we have to agree in all conscience that these are the men that the Democrats are talking about right now, Mrs. Roosevelt—men who would have to sit down opposite Nikita Khrushchev.

ROOSEVELT: I don't know but I think we can among them find one that can sit opposite Nikita Khrushchev. But I think the thing we must look for actually is a growth in our people and in whoever comes in a quality of courage to tell our people just what world conditions are.

WALLACE: Let me ask you a bold question. Do you think Walter Reuther would make a good President of the United States?

ROOSEVELT: I have never thought of it but I have a high regard for Walter Reuther's intelligence, and given the opportunity and the responsibility he might because he has a knowledge of the world's peoples; he's been around the whole world as a worker and has worked in almost every country of the world, and that is a good background for knowing about people and countries. I have never really given this much thought before, but I think he might be a person able to grow, and whoever takes it has got to be able to grow.

WALLACE: You talk about the necessity for the American people to grow. Now what seem to be, if we are to believe a good deal of what we read, what seem to be the main preoccupations of the American people today? Bigger and better tail fins on automobiles; westerns on television? Sex-drenched movies? Fur coats; push buttons; alcoholism continues to increase; our mental institutions are full. Perhaps it's a too grim picture, but nonetheless a reasonably accurate picture. When we talked with architect Frank Lloyd Wright a few weeks back he told us that because of all this the United States is in grave danger of declining as a world power, as a civilization, and he underlines that in his current book, *Testament.* Do you think that Mr. Wright is completely wrong, Mrs. Roosevelt?

ROOSEVELT: I think that estimate of the American people is completely wrong. I feel quite sure that what the American people lack is knowledge. I feel quite sure that the American people if they have knowledge and leadership, can meet any crisis just as well as they met it over and over again in the past. I can remember the cries of horror, when my husband said we had to have fifty thousand airplanes in a given period, but we had them and the difference was that the people were told what the reason was and why and I have complete faith in the American people's ability if they know and if they have leadership. No one can move without some leadership.

WALLACE: And for the time being you feel that we are bereft of leadership?

ROOSEVELT: Yes.

WALLACE: During the Depression your husband said "The only thing we have to fear is fear itself." Do you think that it's that simple today? Do we have anything concrete to fear from the Russians?

ROOSEVELT: Oh, yes, we have to fear the fact that they have a definite objective, around which they've built their whole policy. We have met crises as we came to them, but I would find it hard to answer the question of what our future objective was for the world and how we were building our policy to achieve it and that's what I think we need in order to meet the Communist objective. I think that is something we have to fear. They have a distinct objective and they have patience in planning and they plan a long time ahead, and also they are dealing with a situation where everything that comes to a people is better than it was before, so that they have a constant feeling that they are moving forward.

WALLACE: Is it possible, Mrs. Roosevelt, that Communism, State Socialism any way is the wave of the future and that Capitalism is on its way out?

ROOSEVELT: Well, that is what Mr. Khrushchev says. I don't know much about Capitalism, but I do know about Democracy and freedom, and if Capitalism may change in many, many ways, I'm not really very much interested in Capitalism. I'm enormously interested in freedom and retaining the right to have whatever economy we want and to shape it as we want and having sufficient Democracy so that the people actually hold their Government in their own hands.

WALLACE: Then you do not think if we wanted it that it would be a catastrophe if Socialism came peacefully to the United States as it has come to other nations in the world?

ROOSEVELT: To a certain extent I don't see any real need for socialism in the United States immediately, but things change and it may be that there will come a need for partial changes in our economy. I don't know. I'm not an economist and I'm not a financier. But I'm not worried by that side of it. I'm intensely anxious to preserve the freedom that gives you the right to think and to act and to talk as you please. That I think is essential to happiness and the life of the people.

WALLACE: Mrs. Roosevelt, I'd like to get your reaction to the charges made by perhaps your most severe critic, Westbrook Pegler. He once wrote this about you, he said, "this woman is a political force of enormous ambitions. I believe she is a menace, unscrupulous as to truth, vain and cynical—all with a pretense of exaggerated kindness and human feeling which deceives millions of gullible persons." I would like to get your opinion of Mr. Pegler, your reaction to that charge.

ROOSEVELT: Well, it seems to me a little exaggerated let us say, no one could be quite as bad as all that, and as far as political ambition goes I think that's rather answered itself because I've never run for office and I've never asked for an office of any kind. So I can't have very much political ambition, but I can see that Mr. Pegler probably believes all these things and I suppose one does things unconsciously that makes you seem like that, and perhaps I do seem like that to him, and I think it must be terrible to hate as many things as Mr. Pegler hates, and I would be unhappy, I think and therefore I am afraid that he's unhappy, and I'm sorry for him, because, after all, we all grow older and we all have to live with ourselves, and I think that must sometimes be difficult for Mr. Pegler.

WALLACE: Mrs. Roosevelt, I am sure that you understand the sense in which I put this question to you, but I think that you will agree that a good many people hated your husband, they even hated you.

ROOSEVELT: Oh yes, a great many do still.

WALLACE: WHY? Why?

ROOSEVELT: Well, if you take stands in any way and people feel that you have any success in a following, why those who disagree with you are going to feel very strongly about it.

WALLACE: But there is more than just disagreement involved. There are people who disagree with Mr. Eisenhower, and yet they do not hate him. I lived in the middle west for a good many years while your husband was President, and there was a real core of more than just disagreements there.

ROOSEVELT: No, there was a real core of hatred, the people who would call him "that man" and the people who would—gladly—I remember one man who rejoiced actually, when he died. But I suppose that is just a feeling that certain people had, that he was destroying the thing that they held dear and felt touched them, and naturally you react to that with hatred, and I suppose that's what brought it about, they still fight him. I mean I sometimes think that campaigns are largely fought on my husband rather than on the actual person who's running and as far as I was concerned, I think mine was largely again for that same reason—I was touching something which to some people seemed a sacred thing they had to keep hold of and a major part of my criticism has been on the negro question, of course, and I've had many others, but that is the major part. And I think that that is quite natural, because for some people that seems to be destroying something that to them is very dear.

WALLACE: One of the things the press leaped on last year was the fact that your son, Franklin, acted as legal representative in the United States for the Dominican Dictator Trujillo. As a crusader for Democracy and for freedom yourself, how did you feel about your son's working for Trujillo?

ROOSEVELT: Well, I asked my son about what he was doing, and he told me he was representing the Government, not Mr. Trujillo personally; that he felt that it was a legitimate thing for him to do as a lawyer and that he was not doing it for any political reasons but for pure business reasons as a lawyer. I do not, as a rule, interfere, and I did not feel that I was entitled to interfere in this case with my children. I leave them to do, after they are grown, what they think right, as I think all young people have a right to do.

WALLACE: Do I detect then, that you would have been just as happy had he not represented Trujillo?

ROOSEVELT: As it turned out, I think it might have been wiser, yes, but I do not hold my judgment above his, he was doing what he felt was legitimate to do and I think he had a right to make his own mind up on that subject.

WALLACE: And now the final question, the one that I promised at the beginning that I was going to ask, and that is about garlic pills.

ROOSEVELT: (LAUGHS)

WALLACE: I understand, that you—I don't know if you do still, but at one time in the not too distant past you ate garlic pills and I'd like to know why and how they worked out.

ROOSEVELT: My doctor told me to take them to help my memory. It doesn't help my memory much, but nevertheless that is what I was given them for.

WALLACE: And do you still?

ROOSEVELT: Oh, yes.

WALLACE: In spite of the fact that it hasn't helped your memory?

ROOSEVELT: Well, that's of course age. You gave me one more year and at my age, you don't like to add to your years, because they come too quickly away.

WALLACE: It's only 73?

ROOSEVELT: I'm really only 73.

WALLACE: Only 73? I beg your pardon.

ROOSEVELT: But, that doesn't matter in many ways, only that they go so fast when you get to be my age and I suppose that it's that that gives poor memory, not the garlic pills.

WALLACE: Mrs. Roosevelt, I thank you for taking the time and for coming and talking with us this evening.

ROOSEVELT: Thank you.

WALLACE: Because she will fight courageously for what she believes, Eleanor Roosevelt has had to pay a certain price, bitter criticism, a lack of privacy, the infighting of partisan politics, but Eleanor Roosevelt has also reaped what must be the most satisfying of all rewards, the respect and with it the affection of hundreds of millions of persons around the world.

96

Statement on Behalf of
the National Consumers League

I am very happy to have the opportunity to talk to you gentlemen this morning, because the bill before you (S. 1046) is one about which I have very strong feelings and convictions. I was eighteen years old when I first went for the Consumers League into sweatshops in New York City. (By the way, I am speaking to you today for the National Consumers League of which for many, many years I have been a vice-president.) For the first time in my life I saw conditions I would not have believed existed—women and children working in dark, crowded, dirty quarters, toiling, I was told, all day long and way into the night, to earn a few pennies, carding safety pins or making little things of feathers.

Those conditions I can never forget. So when some twenty years ago the Congress passed and my husband signed the Fair Labor Standards Act, I rejoiced. At last we had tackled on a national scale the basic problem of poverty—the non-living wage. The minimum wages established in 1938 were low, 25 cents to begin with, later increased to 30 cents and then to 40 cents an hour. But low as they were, they provided a floor below which in those depression days no worker, covered by the Act, could legally be paid. That was a tremendous step forward and a firm foundation on which to build.

I am glad to say in the past 20 years we have made some progress. We have gone from 40 cents an hour to 75 cents, and today our minimum wage is $1.00 an hour. But the cost of living has risen too. I am sure that none of us here believes that a workman who is paid $1.00 a hour today is four times better off than he was in 1938 when his wage was 25 cents an hour. Nor do we believe it was the intent of the Congress, which passed the Fair Labor Standards Act, that the standard of living of workers at the minimum level should remain static—that the minimum wage should increase only as much as the cost of living rises. I am sure it was the hope of Congress that as we worked out of the depression into better times, the lowest as well as the highest paid workers should share in the growing national prosperity, and that as the economy can afford it the minimum wage should be increased. Certainly the present proposed increase of 25 cents an hour is modest indeed. I read only recently that a workman would have to earn $2.25 an hour in order to provide a family of four with the food, clothing, shelter and other necessities contained in a "modest but adequate" budget prepared a few years ago for a working

Before the Subcommittee on Labor of the Committee on Labor and Public Welfare, United States Senate, May 14, 1959.

man's family by the Department of Labor. And yet I understand that the wages of millions of workers would be increased by the adoption of the $1.25 rate.

My friends have been telling me of a recent attempt in Texas to establish a legal minimum wage in that state of 50 cents an hour. Studies showed that departments stores were paying wages of $18 to $25 a week; laundries from $12.50 to $35; restaurants were paying kitchen help as little as $15 a week. The arguments raised against establishing any legal minimum wage were the same as those which have been used by employers over the past 50 years. The proposed 50-cent minimum wage would be a "socialistic toehold" toward a higher minimum. It would ruin many small businesses. The state would be taking over and ruining free private enterprise.

I have always believed that in a democracy it is the obligation of the government to give to its citizens the protection and care they need for the benefit of the individual, the family and the nation as a whole. Comparatively few workers earning less than $1.25 an hour today belong to labor unions. Therefore, they are in a very poor position to bargain individually with their employers for higher wages. For them the state and the federal governments have an obligation to set a floor below which no employer may go in setting wages. I believe a minimum wage law is a protection for decent businessmen as well, men who recognize the need and wisdom of paying adequate living wages, but who must meet the competition of less conscientious employers who use wage cutting as a means of gain. Moreover, our entire economy would benefit if millions of workers at the minimum level were enabled by a 25 cent increase in the hourly minimum wage to buy more food, clothing and medical care they so badly need.

I understand the bill Mr. Kennedy and Mr. Morse are sponsoring would not only raise the minimum wage but would bring minimum wage protection to 7 or 8 million more workers than are now covered by the Fair Labor Standards Act. This I think is very important. There is no moral or economic justification which I can see for protecting the families of one group of American workmen against want and not protecting the others. I realize the federal government has the constitutional authority to legislate only for those industries engaged in or affecting interstate commerce. But I see no legal excuse for the Congress exempting any workers who have the constitutional right to be covered from the provisions of the Fair Labor Standards Act.

I want to say an urgent word for a group of workers which is always left out when social legislation is written. They are the expendables. The ones who are bargained out of a piece of social legislation as the price for getting something else in. I am speaking of farm laborers, including the migratory agricultural workers and their families. Today they compare economically to the workers in the industrial sweatshops of the early 1900's.

I know that the bill to amend the Fair Labor Standards Act which you are considering today does not provide protection for agricultural workers. But I understand that Mr. McNamara and Mr. Clark are sponsoring a bill in the Senate which would provide for legal minimum wages for farm laborers. I presume you will be holding hearings on Senators McNamara's and Clark's bill later on in the session. But as it may be impossible for me to appear at that time, I want to take this opportunity to tell you how exceedingly important I think it is that immediate action be taken to relieve the plight of these unfortunate citizens.

I am a member of the National Advisory Committee on Farm Labor, and have had ample opportunity to know of the misery and destitution of farm workers and their families. Poor housing, low wages, child labor, all the privations and sufferings that go with poverty. I always like to quote from government bulletins when citing figures, because I believe they seldom exaggerate a situation. So let me tell you the annual earnings reported by the Department of Agriculture last September for hired farm workers in the United States for 1958. Migratory farm workers earned on the average $745 for the year from agricultural employment. Nonmigratory farm workers earned $737. The migrants increased their earnings to $859 by working an average of 16 additional days at non-farm labor; and the nonmigrant workers by working an average of 20 days off the farm added $161 to their average annual earnings, bringing the total to $895.

These figures speak for themselves. That no family could more than subsist on such earnings is obvious. To relieve their suffering they must depend on charity in times of sickness, unemployment and other emergencies. Secretary Mitchell said at a recent meeting on the problems of farm labor:

> It is intolerable and indecent for a society to produce by overworking and underpaying human beings. Even if the product may cost more, we, in this country, usually accept the difference in cost because it is the man— that counts—not the thing. . . . It is my conviction that the migrant farm worker will never take his place as a fully useful citizen, and never be able to successfully resist exploitation, until, first, federal legislation guarantees him a decent minimum wage upon which he can build a decent and independent life.

Much needs to be done for these people. They should be covered by unemployment and workmen's compensation laws. The application of the Social Security Act to farm workers should be improved. Better housing, medical care, education for their children should be provided. But the most immediate need is a minimum wage law that will assure decent wages to these hardworking, neglected American citizens.

Hand-in-hand with a minimum wage law should go a measure to prohibit the employment of little children in commercialized agriculture. Thousands of children, 8, 9, 10 years of age and even younger work in the fields beside their parents day after day. One understands why such conditions seem necessary when one knows what the parents earn. Every additional penny earned relieves a bit the desperate family need. But doctors, educators, social workers all know that growing children suffer more from fatigue than do adults. The American Medical Association has recommended for the protection of children's health "a general 14-year minimum age requirement for the employment of children."

You know, of course, that the Fair Labor Standards Act prohibits the employment of children under 16 years of age during school hours in industry. Outside of school hours the employment of youngsters under 14 years is illegal. To me the importance of extending these same regulations to the employment of children in agriculture cannot be too strongly emphasized. I am not proposing that parents living on small family farms should not be allowed to use their own children to help with the family chores. I am speaking only of children employed on commercial farms as hired labor.

I thank you, gentlemen, for this opportunity to talk to you about these serious matters which are before you, and to congratulate you on your efforts to find effective ways of reducing the extent of our social and economic problems.

97

Are Political Conventions Obsolete?

Countless observers of the two recent political conventions were left with an acute feeling of dismay. It seemed to them that the choice of a presidential candidate—the fundamental, basic, right of every American citizen—was no longer a result of public thinking or an expression of the wishes of the majority of the people of the country; that, instead, it represented the decision of party bosses.

This kind of thinking, of course, should not be allowed to go on. The American people can bring about a reform if they insist upon having it.

Our political conventions, as they now function, are outmoded machinery. In the early days, when travel and communications were difficult, it was essential to establish this cumbersome system. But the need for it has gone. Our present need is to evolve a new method by which the voice of the people is heard and they again arrive at their own choice of the candidates who are to lead them and carry out their wishes in government. Under the democratic way of life, this is of paramount importance.

At the present time, the result of this obsolete system of choosing candidates has been the development of highly efficient, smoothly oiled machines by which political bosses and not the voters of the country dictate who the nominees are to be.

The working of smooth political machines, such as we observed in the two recent conventions, is not new. It is only an intensification of a process that has been going on for many years. Inevitably, as time goes on, such a situation deteriorates. The mere fact that people become accustomed to it leads to a fading of protest, until the flagrant abuse of the two conventions comes as so great a shock that the citizens awaken to what is happening and declare, "This is intolerable. We cannot permit it to go on."

In order to function at all democracy depends upon the participation of the people in their government. It cannot survive by boss rule.

I do not believe that the people of this country would submit passively to boss rule, and meekly abdicate their own rights and privileges, if they were clearly aware of the situation and understood the working of the machinery which makes boss rule possible. Certainly, the first step is to start not at the top but at the bottom of the pyramid and curb the power of the local city and state leaders of the political machine who, unchallenged, become the party bosses and, in a very real sense, our bosses.

The core of boss rule, naturally, is patronage. That is why, by the very nature of things, the chief interest of the boss lies in building his local power.

Unpublished article, 1960.

For instance, the political boss of New York City would rather carry a majority for the city than for the Presidency, because national patronage is never very large but there is a great deal in the city. That is why one often sees that a political organization will work hard for the election of its mayor and lose the national ticket. It has still achieved the victory which was most important to it.

There are too many Americans who have little idea of how the machinery of politics is handled. They have too little sense of responsibility in regard to its functioning. And yet boss rule can exist only where there is widespread indifference.

"But what can we do about it?" people ask me. "I know it is disgraceful but we're helpless to do anything."

The answer to that, of course, is that we are not in the least helpless. We can always do something if we care enough. It was in protest against the bosses of the Republican machine—Hanna and Platt—that Theodore Roosevelt started his Bull Moose party.

Several years ago, at Buffalo, both the governor and the mayor of New York said they preferred a certain candidate for the Senate. Carmine De Sapio, the boss of the democratic machinery in New York, calmly turned them down and took it upon himself to name his own candidate. The result was that he defeated the party's chance of victory by forcing upon the voting public an unacceptable candidate.

Because of this high-handed action, in March, 1959, Senator Herbert Lehman, Thomas Finletter and I signed a statement, backing reform groups in New York City. We declared that the people were weary of bossism.

The response of the people was swift. They set up a clamor to be heard as citizens with a right to a voice in their own government. Once started, the revolt began to grow and it is still growing and gaining strength. The result was that the regular party organization discovered they would go down in defeat unless the reform groups threw in their support and worked with them. But the reform groups made clear that, unless they were free of all control from the local organization, it would not have that support. The only way to get rid of one's chains is not to complain or to call for help. It is to knock them off.

What is the effect of local organizations on the choice of a presidential candidate? Unless checked by the people, it is a stranglehold. It works like this. The delegates to a convention are appointed by the state machinery. Generally a caucus is held of the delegates of each state and they are told that the leaders have decided they are to support a certain candidate. And why do the delegates supinely do as they are told? Because most of them hold some kind of public office or have relatives who do. They do not want to risk their positions.

It is the rare delegate who, like Senator Lehman, can say: "I will not serve unless I am given complete freedom to vote as my conscience dictates." A delegate can do this only if he wants nothing for himself. There are, unhappily, few people who want nothing but to perform a public service to the best of their ability.

Having been committed to the machine, the delegate can only carry out his instructions. He remains deaf to the voice of his constituents. He may receive thousands of telegrams favoring another candidate but he disregards them. It is not the voice of the people but the voice of the machine boss which he heeds.

On one occasion, at the 1960 Democratic Convention in Los Angeles, a large box of telegrams was handed to Mr. Prendergast. He opened one or two, saw they were in favor of Adlai Stevenson, and threw the box away.

What emerges most clearly from all this is that such men should not have in their hands the power to control the votes of the delegates. Such action abrogates, makes a mockery of, a system in which the men and women of America presumably have the choice of their own leaders in their own hands.

What can be done about it? Well, it seems to me that the delegates should be chosen, not by a State Committee or by the appointment of city leaders, but by the direct vote of the people of the districts. Of course, this is a matter that requires some elasticity because the methods differ from state to state.

In New York, the state I know best, Senator Lehman was not to be appointed a delegate to the 1960 Democratic convention because the leaders were indignant over his sponsoring of the reform movement in New York City. What they overlooked was the reaction of the people. This was so immediate and so strong that it could not be ignored. When the people insist upon being heard, the bosses must listen. In this particular case, they found it needful to ask the Senator to serve as a delegate and the State Chairman, who had insisted on ignoring him, resigned to give his own place to the Senator.

This was a flagrant—but unhappily, typical—example of an attempt at boss rule, an attempt to force the selection of the delegates, ignoring the wishes of the people. But instead of meek acceptance there was a powerful protest. The people insisted on being heard. Too often, even when people are aware of this abuse of power, their reaction is too weak, too disorganized, to have any effect. In that case, the local leaders are able to go on doing whatever they have decided to do.

It must be obvious to anyone who attended or watched the recent conventions that if the delegates chosen cannot represent what they consider to be the majority opinion of the people in their district they might as well stay at home. The convention could, as efficiently, be attended solely by the two or three high-ranking bosses from each state.

All that would be lacking would be the demonstrations, which are, as a rule, artificial displays of enthusiasm arranged by the machines or the candidates themselves. These demonstrations are largely controlled, in their extent, noise and length of time, by the National Committee which allots to each candidate the number of tickets to which they feel he is entitled, according to his apparent strength. This choice rests upon the decision of a single man.

It was rumored at the 1960 Democratic convention that Mr. Kennedy's group, which was undoubtedly the strongest, received a far greater number of passes than those assigned to Mr. Stevenson's headquarters.

This situation was greatly simplified in the 1960 Republican Convention at Chicago, for there the people were offered no choice of candidates for the presidency.

The restriction of tickets for the Stevenson group was overcome, to some extent, by a trick. Those who went in on the original passes sent out one man with all of them. These he passed to a second group. This maneuver was repeated until a sufficient number of people had been admitted to put on as good a demonstration as anyone else. It was also, as I believe everyone felt, a more spontaneous demonstration, fired by emotional feeling and sparked by the youth and fervor of the supporters who had paid their own way and slept on cots in a kind of barracks to make the trip to Los Angeles possible.

It has been a great many years since, in Baltimore, I attended my first political convention for the nomination of a President. At that time I felt, and I feel still, that to select the standard bearer of a party in an atmosphere of noise, bands and balloons, to the accompaniment of the manufactured and synthetic excitement of parades, is to strip one of the most important features of our system of its dignity and meaning. The circus has almost overshadowed the serious purpose and far-reaching effect of these deliberations. One can imagine, in horror, the effect of accompanying debates in the Senate or in the House by interpolations of noise and music from the partisans of either side of the question.

Today, with many people in the country still profoundly shocked by the feeling that the two national conventions were conducted without regard for their wishes or their welfare, with their voices and demands stifled, the time has come to restore the choice of a presidential candidate to the people themselves.

How can this be done? One possibility has occurred to me. Instead of continuing to leave the selection of the men who, in turn, select the candidate, in the hands of the city and state committees, we should elect the delegates ourselves. The simplest and most direct procedure would be, at the primary nearest the convention, to have the names of all the presidential aspirants listed on the ballot. Each voter could check the name of the candidate of his choice. The delegates to the convention would be required to vote for the candidate with the majority vote in that primary.

Of course, beyond the first ballot, it might not be practicable to hold the delegate to the original choice. An occasion might arise in which there would be a deadlock and it would be impossible to come to any definite conclusion.

The answer to this seems to me to lie in the caucus held by each state delegation. In the past, this, too often, has resulted in the issuing of definite instructions from the boss, instructions, which, as a rule, the delegate has not dared to ignore.

If the law required a secret ballot, so that the delegates could be free to vote, as all Americans are presumed free to vote, according to their consciences and the will of their constituents, it would be possible to achieve a system that would come much closer to reflecting the wishes of the people of the United States than we now have.

This, of course, is only a suggestion, though I do believe that the idea of a secret ballot is of primary importance. No doubt, sound suggestions will be made by others.

The important thing is that the whole concept of the rules governing a convention should come before the American people to be reassessed and discussed. While many points can be brought up in opposition to my own suggestions, some kind of change must be made. With the exception of the political bosses themselves, I have heard nobody claim to be satisfied that the system, as it has recently been revealed, is a good way of choosing candidates, or that it represents the thinking of the people, or even, indeed, that it represents the deliberations of the delegates. This is a serious matter, striking at the very roots of our system of government, and it is a challenge to us all, a challenge which we must meet.

Another outmoded piece of machinery in the selection of the president seems to me to be the presidential primary as it now functions. The chief trouble here, I think, is that the candidates spend their time running down their rivals in the same party. The net result is to furnish a large amount of ammunition to the opposition party in the campaign. An example is the Republican use, in campaign propaganda, of everything Senator Johnson said about Senator Kennedy in the preconvention days.

I have been talking from the point of view of a Democrat because I am more familiar with their tactics. But it appears to an observer that the same tactics exist in both parties. In both cases, one had the feeling that the convention did not greatly matter. The votes had been sewed up beforehand. Nothing the people themselves had to say would have any effect upon the delegates. They were committed not to the constituents but to the party leaders.

You will say, perhaps, that once Wendel Willkie stampeded a convention in Philadelphia and got the nomination over the opposition of the party leaders. But the circumstances were, I think, unusual. Mr. Willkie's strength at the convention grew out of the weakness in the leadership. There was little party unity, and deep, almost unbridgeable differences of opinion between various factions of the party. The leaders were, too, much swayed by the awareness of the type of opposition which they felt they had to meet during the campaign. But such a situation rarely occurs.

We have four years before we again choose a presidential nominee. In the next election it will be possible for whoever is president to be renominated but, under the law passed by the Republicans, no president can now retain office more than eight years.

So eight years from now there will again be a convention in which no presidential incumbent can be a candidate. Eight years in which to re-examine our machinery for making one of the most vital and far-reaching choices that fall to the lot of an American citizen. There is time ahead to re-examine our party machinery on a city and state, as well as national, level, to see how it functions, to learn whether we are abrogating our rights as citizens, to find a method to insure that each of us can make our voices heard as independent and responsible voters. We can do it if we want to.

As Adlai Stevenson said, during the hush that followed the realization of his defeat at the last democratic convention, "Cheer up—all is not lost."

Part G
This Troubled World

98

This Troubled World

The Case as It Stands

The newspapers these days are becoming more and more painful. I was reading my morning papers on the train not so long ago, and looked up with a feeling of desperation. Up and down the car people were reading, yet no one seemed excited.

To me the whole situation seems intolerable. We face today a world filled with suspicion and hatred. We look at Europe and see a civil war going on, with other nations participating not only as individual volunteers, but obviously with the help and approval of their governments. We look at the Far East and see two nations, technically not at war, killing each other in great numbers.

Every nation is watching the others on its borders, analyzing its own needs and striving to attain its ends with little consideration for the needs of its neighbors. Few people are sitting down dispassionately to go over the whole situation in an attempt to determine what present conditions are, or how they should be met.

We know, for instance, that certain nations today need to expand because their populations have increased. Certain people will tell you that the solution of this whole question lies in the acceptance or rejection of birth control. That may be the solution for the future, but we can do nothing in that way about the populations that now exist. They are on this earth, and modern science has left us only a few places where famine or flood or disease can wipe out large numbers of superfluous people in one fell swoop. For this reason certain nations need additional territory to which part of their present populations may be moved; other nations need more land on which to grow necessary raw materials; or perhaps they may need mineral deposits which are not to be found in their own country. You will say that these can be had by trade. Yes, but the nations possessing them will frequently make the cost too high to the nations which need them.

It is not a question today of the "free" interchange of goods. If standards of living were approximately the same, throughout the world, competition would be on an equal basis and then there might be no need for tariffs. However, standards of living vary. The nations with higher standards have set up protective barriers which served them well when they were self-contained, but not so well when they reached a point where they either wished to import or export.

New York: H. C. Kinsey & Company, Inc., 1938.

When you take all these things into consideration, the size of this problem is apt to make you feel that even an attempt to solve it in the future by education is futile. Faint heart, however, ne'er won fair lady, nor did it ever solve world problems!

Peace plan after peace plan has been presented to me; most of them, I find, are impractical, or not very carefully thought out. In nearly all of them someone can find a flaw. I have come to look at them now without the slightest hope of finding one full-fledged plan, but I keep on looking in the hope of finding here and there some small suggestion that may be acceptable to enough people to insure an honest effort being made to study it and evaluate its possible benefits.

For instance, one lady of my acquaintance brought me a plan this past spring which sounded extremely plausible. Her premises are: We never again wish to send our men overseas; we wish to have adequate defense; we do not need a navy if we do not intend to go beyond our own shores, with guns along our coasts as an added protection. Therefore, we do not need an army, for our men are going to stay at home. With our coast defenses strong, nobody will land here, so why go the expense of an army? We do not need battleships or, in fact, any navy beyond submarines because we do not intend to own any outlying possessions.

In this way, said the lady, we will save vast sums of money which can be applied to all the social needs of the day—better housing, better schools, old age pensions, workmen's compensation, care of the blind and crippled and other dependents. There is no limit to what we might do with this money which we now spend on preparation for destruction.

It is a very attractive picture and I wish it were all as simple as that, but it seems to be fairly well proved that guns along our coasts are practically useless. No one, as far as I know, has ever devised an adequate defense by submarines and airplanes, or calculated whether the cost of the development of these two forces would really be any less than what we spend at present on our army and navy.

The greatest defense value of the navy is that its cruising radius is great enough to allow it to contact an attacking force long before that force reaches our shores. If we trusted solely to submarines and airplanes we would have to have them in sufficient number really to cover all our borders, and this type of defense would seem to be almost prohibitive in cost for a nation with a great many miles of border to defend.

Has anyone sounded out the people of this country as to their willingness to wait until an attacking enemy comes within the cruising radius of our planes and submarines? Have we faced the fact that this would mean allowing an attacking enemy to come unmolested fairly near to our shores and would make it entirely possible for them to land in a nearby country which might be friendly to them, without any interference on our part? Have our citizens been asked if they are willing to take the risk of doing without trained men? We have always had a small trained army forming the first line of defense in case somebody does land on our borders, or attempts to approach us by land through a neighboring country. Our army has not been thought of as an attacking force; do we want to do away with it?

Are all the people in this country willing also to give up the outlying islands which have come into our possession? Some of them cost us more than they bring in, but others bring certain of our citizens a fair revenue. Can we count on those citizens to accept the loss of these revenues in the interests of future peace?

Perhaps this is part of what we will have to make up our minds to pay someday as the price of peace; but has any one as yet put it into concrete form to the American people and asked their opinion about it?

One of the things that is most frequently harped upon is the vast sums of money spent for war preparation in this country. Very frequently the statements are somewhat misleading. It is true that in the past few years we have spent more than we have for a number of preceding years because we had fallen behind in our treaty strength but, in a world which is arming all around us, it is necessary to keep a certain parity and these expenditures should be analyzed with a little more care than is usual.

For instance, few people realize that in the army appropriation is included all the work done under the army engineers on rivers and harbors, on flood control, etc. One other consideration which is frequently overlooked is that, because of the higher wages paid for labor in this country, whatever we build costs us more than it does in the other nations. One significant fact is that we only spend twelve percent of our national income on our army and navy, as against anywhere from thirty-five to fifty-five percent of the national income spent by nations in the rest of the world. It is well for us to realize these facts and not to feel that our government is doing something that will push us into a position which is incompatible with a desire for peace. We are the most peaceloving nation in the world and we are not doing anything at present which would change that situation.

One very intelligent friend of mine developed an idea the other day which seems to me common sense for the present time, at least. "Why do we talk," she asked, "about peace? Why don't we recognize the fact that it is normal and natural for differences to exist? Almost every family, no matter how close its members may be, is quarrelsome at times." Quarrelsome may be too strong a word, so we might better say that differences of opinion arise in the family as to conduct or as to likes and dislikes. Why should we expect therefore, that nations will not have these same differences and quarrels? Why do we concentrate on urging them not to have any differences? Why don't we simply accept the fact that differences always come up and concentrate on evolving some kind of machinery by which the differences may be recognized and some plan of compromise be worked out to satisfy, at least in part, all those concerned? Compromises, of course, have to be made; they are made in every family. There are usually some members of a family, who, by common consent, are the arbitrators of questions that arise, and who hold the family together, or bring them together if relationships become strained.

The League of Nations was an effort to find for the nations of the world, a method by which differences between nations would automatically be brought before the court of public opinion. Some kind of compromise would be made and those involved would feel that substantial justice had been done, even though they might not at any one time achieve all of their desires.

Many of us have become convinced that the League of Nations as it stands today cannot serve this purpose. The reason for this is unimportant. The important thing now is that we should concentrate on finding some new machinery or revamping what already exists so that everyone will function within it and have confidence in its honesty.

The people of the United States have congratulated themselves on the fact that they have made a beginning towards the development of this machinery in their conferences with the representatives of the other American governments.

Perhaps we have a right to feel a sense of satisfaction for as a nation we have made a small beginning. We were cordially disliked throughout South America for years because we were the strongest nation on this continent. We took the attitude of the big brother for a long time and constituted ourselves the defender of all the other nations. We were not only the defender, however, we also considered it our duty to set ourselves up as the judge, and the only judge, of what should happen in the internal as well as the external affairs of our various neighbors.

To them it seemed a bullying, patronizing attitude. As they grew stronger, they resented it, but we went right on regardless of their feelings. During the past few years we have put ourselves imaginatively into their situation. The final result is that we have reached an amicable understanding and actually are in a fair way to get together and discuss subjects of mutual interest with little or no sense of suspicion and fear being involved in the discussion. This can, of course, be spoiled at any time by the selfishness of individual citizens who may decide that, as individuals, they can exploit some other nation on the North or South American continents. The restraint of these individuals will not be a question of government action, but of the force of public opinion which, it is to be hoped, will be able to control and exert a potent influence because of the sense of responsibility acquired by our citizens.

This is satisfactory, but there is still much to be done before we can feel that even here in the Americas we have a thoroughly sound working basis for solving all misunderstandings. We cannot be entirely satisfied with anything, however, which does not include the world as a whole, for we are all so closely interdependent today that we can only operate successfully when we all cooperate.

We have had the experience and can profit by the mistakes and the difficulties through which the League of Nations has passed. Every nation in the world still uses policemen to control its unruly element. It may be that any machinery set up today to deal with international difficulties may require policemen in order to function successfully, but even a police force should not be called upon until every other method of procedure has been tried and proved unsuccessful.

We have some economic weapons which can be used first and which may prove themselves very efficient as the guardians of peace.

Ultimate Objectives

What are our ultimate objectives and how shall we achieve them? First, the most important thing is that any difficulties arising should automatically go before some body which will publish the facts to the world at large and give public opinion an opportunity to make a decision. Then, a group of world representatives will have to decide with whom the fault lies. If their decision is not accepted by the nations involved and either nation attempts to use force in coercing the other nation, or nations—in opposition to what is clearly the majority opinion of the world—then and then only, it seems to me, the decision will be made that the nation using force is an aggressor nation. Being an aggressor, the majority of nations in opposition would be obliged to resort to some method designed to make that nation realize that they could not with impunity flout the public opinion of the majority.

We need to define what an aggressor nation is. We need to have a tribunal where the facts in any case may be discussed, and the decision made before the world, as to whether a nation is an aggressor or not. Then the steps decided upon could be taken in conjunction with other nations.

First of all, trade should be withdrawn from that nation and they could be barred as traders in the countries disagreeing with them. It would not seem probable that more than this economic weapon would have to be used but, if necessary in the end, the police force could be called upon.

In the case of a clearly defined issue where the majority of nations agreed, the police force would simply try to prevent bloodshed and aggression, and it would be in a very different position from an army which was attempting to attack a country and subjugate it. Even the use of a police force, which so many think of as tantamount to war, would really be very different and there would be no idea of marching into a country or making the people suffer or taking anything from them. It would simply be a group of armed men preventing either of the parties to a quarrel from entering into a real war.

Of course, I can imagine cases in which the police force might find itself in an unenviable position, with two countries engaged in a heated quarrel trying to do away with the police so they could get at each other!

All we can hope is that this situation will not arise and that the non-aggressor party to the quarrel, at least, may be willing to sit peacefully by and see the police force repulse the enemy without wishing to turn into aggressors themselves.

With all our agitation about peace, we lose sight of the fact that with the proper machinery it is easier to keep out of situations which lead to war than it is to bring about peace once war is actually going on.

I doubt very much whether peace is coming to us either through plans, even my own as I have outlined it, or through any of the theories or hopes we now hold. What I have outlined is not real peace, just a method of trying to deal with our difficulties a little better than we have in the past, in the world as it is today. We may, of course, be wiped off the face of the earth before we do even this. Our real ultimate objective must be a change in human nature for I have, as I said, yet to see a peace plan which is really practical and which has been thought through in every detail. Therefore, I am inclined to believe that there is no perfect and complete program for bringing about peace in the world at the present moment.

I often wonder as I look around the world whether any of us, even we women, really want peace. Women should realize better than anyone else, that the spirit of peace has to begin in the relationship between two individuals. They know that a child alone may be unhappy because he is alone, but there will be no quarreling until another child appears on the scene, and then the fur will fly, if each of them desires the same thing at the same time.

Women have watched this for generations and must know, if peace is going to come about in the world, the way to start is by getting a better under- standing between individuals. From this germ a better understanding between groups of people will grow.

In spite of this knowledge, I am sure that women themselves are among the worst offenders when it comes to petty quarrels. Mrs. J— will refuse to speak to Mrs. C— because Mrs. C—'s dog came through the hedge and mussed up Mrs. J—'s flower bed. No one will deny that occurrences of this kind are irritating in the extreme, but is it worth a feud between two neigh- bors, perhaps old friends or even acquaintances who must live next door to each other and see each other almost every day?

At the moment we, as a nation, are looking across the Atlantic and the Pacific, patting ourselves on the back and saying how fortunate we are to be away from all their excitements. We feel a little self-righteous, and forget that we ourselves have been engaged in a war on the average of every forty years since our nation was founded. We even fought a civil war, complicated by the alignment of other nations with one side or the other, though no foreign soldiers actually came to fight on either side.

The people who settled in New England came here for religious freedom, but religious freedom to them meant freedom only for their kind of religion. They were not going to be any more liberal to others who differed with them in this new country, than others had been with them in the countries from which they came. This attitude seems to be our attitude in many situations today.

Very few people in any nation today are inclined to be really liberal in allowing real freedom to other individuals. Like our forebears we want free- dom for ourselves, but not for those who differ from us. To think and act as we please within limits, of course, caused by the necessity for respecting the equal rights which must belong to our neighbors, would seem to be almost a platitu- dinous doctrine, yet we would frequently like to overlook these limits and permit no freedom to our neighbors. If this is our personal attitude, it is not strange that our national attitude is similar. We are chiefly concerned with the rights and privileges of our own people and we show little consideration for the rights and privileges of others. In this we are not very different from other nations both in the past and in the present.

I can almost count on the fingers of one hand the people whom I think are real pacifists. By that I mean, the people who are really making an effort in their personal lives to bring about an atmosphere which will be conducive to a solution of all our difficulties in a peaceful manner.

The first step towards achieving this end is self-discipline and self-control. The second is a certain amount of imagination which will enable us to understand situations in which other people find themselves. We may learn to be less indignant at any slight or seeming slight, and we may try to find some way by which to remove the cause of the troubles which arise between individuals, if we become disciplined and cultivate our imaginative facilities. Once we achieve a technique by which we control our own emotions, we certainly will be better able to teach young people how to get on together. They may then find some saner way of settling questions under dispute than by merely punching each other's noses!

When we once control ourselves and submit personal differences to constituted authorities for settlement, we can say that we have a will to peace between individuals. Before we come to the question of what may be the technique between nations, however, we must go a step farther and set our national house in order. On every hand we see today miniature wars going on between conflicting interests. As the example most constantly before us, take capital and labor. If their difficulties are settled by arbitration and no blood is shed, we can feel we have made real strides towards approaching our international problems. We are not prepared to do this, however, when two factions in a group having the same basic interests cannot come to an agreement between themselves. Their ability to obtain what they desire is greatly weakened until they can reach an understanding and work as a unit. The basis of this understanding should not be hard to reach if the different personalities involved could forget themselves as individuals and think only of the objectives in view, and of the best way to obtain them.

Granted that they are able to do this, then we can approach our second problem with the knowledge that more deeply conflicting interests are at stake but that those with common interests can state their case so the public may form their opinion. Here again, if you could take it for granted that on both sides a real desire existed amongst those representing divergent interests to consider unselfishly ultimate goals and benefits for the majority, rather than any individual gain or loss, it would undoubtedly be possible to reach a peaceful agreement.

Human beings, however, do not stride from peak to peak, they climb laboriously up the side of the mountain. The public will have to understand each case as it comes up and force divergent interests to find a solution. The real mountain climber never gives up until he has reached the highest peak and the lure of the climb to this peak is always before him to draw him on.

That should be the way in human progress—a peaceful, quiet progress. We cannot follow this way, however, until human nature becomes less interested in self, acquires some of the vision and persistence of the mountain climber, and realizes that physical forces must be harnessed and controlled by disciplined mental and spiritual forces.

When we have achieved a nation where the majority of the people is of this type, then we can hope for some measure of success in changing our procedure when international difficulties arise.

What we have said really means that we believe in one actual way to peace—making a fundamental change in human nature. Over and over again people will tell you that that is impossible. I cannot see why it should be impossible when the record of history shows so many changes already gone through.

Only the other day I heard it stated that there are only two real divisions which can be made between people—the people who have good intentions, and the people who have evil intentions. The same man who made this distinction between people, made the suggestion that eventually there should be in the government, a department where business—the business that wishes to be fair and square—could lay its plans before a chosen group of men representing business, the public and the government. They could ask for advice as to whether the plans proposed were according to the best business interests of the country and the majority of the people and receive in return a disinterested, honest opinion. Immediately the remonstrance was made that this would be impossible because it would be difficult for an advisory group to know if the plans laid before them were honestly stated, and people of evil intentions could use such a group to promote plans for selfish interests rather than for the general welfare. This is undoubtedly true, and we are up against exactly the same situation in trying to obtain peace between groups within nations as we are on the international fronts.

Human beings either must recognize the fact that what serves the people as a whole serves them best as individuals and, through selfish or unselfish interests, they become people of good intentions and honesty. If not we will be unable to move forward except as we have moved in the past with recourse to force, and constant, suspicious watchfulness on the part of individuals and groups towards each other. The preservation of our civilization seems to demand a permanent change of attitude and therefore every effort should be bent towards bringing about this change in human nature through education. This is a slow way and, in the meantime, we need not sit with folded hands and feel that no steps can be taken to ward off the dangers which constantly beset us.

Immediate Steps

We can begin, and begin at once, to set up some machinery. Our international difficulties will then automatically be taken up before they reach the danger point. One of our great troubles is that it is nobody's business to try to strengthen out difficulties between nations in the early stages. If they are allowed to continue too long, they grow more and more bitter and little things, which might at first have been easily explained or settled, take on the proportions of a bitter and important quarrel.

We do not scrap our whole judicial machinery just because we are not sure that the people who appear before the bar are telling the truth. We go ahead and do our best to ascertain the truth in any given case, and substantial justice seems to be done in a majority of situations. This same thing would have to satisfy us for a time at least in the results achieved by whatever machinery we set up to solve our international difficulties.

I am not advocating any particular machinery. The need seems fairly obvious. To say that we cannot find a way is tantamount to acknowledging that we are going to watch our civilization wipe itself off the face of the earth.

For those of us who remember the World War, there is little need to paint a picture of war conditions, but the generation that participated in that war is growing older. To the younger group what they have not seen and experienced themselves actually means little.

I heard a gentleman who loves adventure say the other day that he could recruit an army of young people at any time to go to war in any part of the world. They would believe that the danger was slight, and the fun and comradeship and adventure would be attractive. I protested violently that youth today was not so gullible, but down in the bottom of my heart I am a little apprehensive. Therefore, it seems to me that one of our first duties is constantly to paint for young people a realistic picture of war. You cannot gainsay the assertion that war brings out certain fine qualities in human nature. People will make sacrifices which they would not make in the ordinary course of existence. War will give opportunities for heroism which do not arise in everyday living, but that is not all that war will do.

It will place men for weeks under conditions which are physically so bad that years later they may still be suffering from the effects of the "period of adventure" even though they may not have been injured by shot or shell during this time of service. Upon many people it will have mental or psychological effects which will take them years to overcome. In many countries of the world there are people to attest to the changed human beings who have returned to them after the World War. Men who could no longer settle down to their old work, men who had seen such horrors that they could no longer sleep quietly at night, men who do not wish to speak of their experiences. It is a rather exceptional person who goes through a war and comes out unscathed physically, mentally or morally.

Secondly, it is one's duty to youth to point out that there are ways of living heroically during peacetimes. I do not imagine that Monsieur and Madame Curie ever felt the lack of adventure in their lives, for there is nothing more adventurous than experimentation with an unknown element. Their purpose was to find something of benefit to the human race. They jeopardized no lives but their own.

I doubt if Father Damien ever felt that his life lacked adventure; and I can think of a hundred places in our own country today where men or women might lead their lives unknown or unsung beyond the borders of their own communities and yet never lack for adventure and interest. Those who set themselves the task of making their communities into places in which the average human being may obtain a share, not only of greater physical well-being, but of wider mental and spiritual existence, will lead an active and adventurous life to reach their goal.

This will need energy, patience and understanding beyond the average, qualities of leadership to win other men to their point of view, unselfishness and heroism, for they may be asked to make great sacrifices. To reach their objectives they may have to hand over their leadership to other men, their characters may be maligned, their motives impugned, but they must remain completely indifferent if only in the end they achieve their objectives. Moral courage of a rare kind will be required of them.

In the wars of the past, deeds of valor and heroism have won decorations from governments and the applause of comrades in arms, but the men who lead in civic campaigns may hope for none of these recognitions. The best that can happen to them is that they may live to see a part of their dreams come true, they may keep a few friends who believe in them and their own consciences may bring them inner satisfactions.

Making our everyday living an adventure is probably our best safeguard against war. But there are other steps which we might well take.

Let us examine again, for example, the ever-recurring question of the need for armaments as a means of defense and protection and see if something cannot be done immediately. Many people feel the building of great military machines leads us directly into war for when you acquire something it is always a temptation to use it.

It is perfectly obvious, however, that no nation can cut down its army and navy and armaments in general when the rest of the world is not doing the same thing.

We ourselves have a long unfortified border on the north which has remained undefended for more than a hundred years, a shining example of what peace and understanding between two nations can accomplish. But we also have two long coastlines to defend and the Panama Canal, which in case of war must be kept open, therefore it behooves us to have adequate naval defense. Just what we mean by adequate defense is a point on which a great many people differ.

Innumerable civilians have ideas as to what constitutes adequate military preparedness and the people most concerned, our military forces, have even more definite ideas. Many people in the United States feel that we are still rendered practically safe by the expanse of water on our east and west coasts. Some people even feel, like Mr. William Jennings Bryan, that if our nation needed to be defended a million men would spring to arms overnight. They forget that a million untrained, unarmed men would be a poor defense. We must concede that our military establishments have probably made a more careful, practical study of the situation than anyone else, for they know they would have to be ready for action at once.

Whether we accept the civil or the military point of view on preparedness, we can still move forward. We can continue to try to come to an understanding with other nations on some of the points which lead to bad feeling. We can begin, first, perhaps, with the Central and South American nations and continue later with other nations, to enter into agreements which may lead to the gradual reduction of armaments. If we only agree on one thing at a time, every little step is something to the good. Simply because we have so far not been able to arrive at any agreement is no reason for giving up the attempt to agree. No one has as yet discovered a way to make any of the methods of transportation by which we all travel around the world, absolutely safe, but nobody suggests that we should do away with ships and railroads and airplanes. I feel that the people of various nations can greatly influence their governments and representatives and encourage action along the lines of reduction in arms and munitions.

Every international group that meets must bear in mind that they have an opportunity to create better feeling, but to move forward along this particular front also requires the backing of public opinion at home. This opinion may be formed in many little groups all over the world and may be felt in an ever widening circle of nations until it becomes a formidable force in the world as a whole.

Then there is the matter of private interests involved in the manufacture of arms and munitions. I know there are many arguments advanced against government ownership of the factories making arms and munitions. When you know the story of the part played by certain families in Europe whose business it has been to manufacture arms and munitions, however, you wonder if the arguments advanced against this step are not inspired in large part by those whose interests lie in this particular business?

It is true that a government can lose its perspective for a number of reasons. The need for employment may push them to overproduction, as well as fear of their neighbors, and they may manufacture so much that the temptation to use it may be great. Some governments today manufacture practically all they need for peacetime purposes and this is a safeguard, but for wartime use, all governments would have to fall back on private manufacturers who could convert their plants easily for the manufacturing of war materials. Some governments today encourage private manufacturers to produce arms and munitions needed in peacetime by buying from them, but the great danger lies in the uncontrolled private production which is used for export. The element of private profit is a great incentive towards the increase of this business just as it is in any other business. Governments are not tempted in the same way, for they do not manufacture for export or for profit.

It seems to me that we must trust someone and I think perhaps it is wiser to trust a government than the more vulnerable and easily tempted individual. Besides which, a democracy has it within its power to control any government business and, therefore, the idea that our government should control the manufacture of arms and munitions fills me with no great trepidation.

This control of the manufacture of arms and munitions is a measure which could be undertaken by one government alone. It does not have to wait for all the other governments to concur, and so I believe either in complete government ownership or in the strictest kind of government supervision, allowing such manufacture as will supply our own country but which will not create a surplus for exportation, thus removing the incentive for constantly seeking and creating new markets.

The next step will be the mutual curtailment, very gradually I am sure, of the amount of armaments the world over. This is a difficult step, because it requires not only an agreement on the part of all the nations, but sufficient confidence in each other to believe that, having given their word, they will live up to the spirit of the agreement as well as to the letter of it, and not try cleverly to hide whatever they have done from possible inspectors.

They will not, for instance, destroy a battleship and add a half dozen airplanes, telling the other members to the agreement that they have carried out the promised reduction, but forgetting to mention the additions to some other arm of their military service.

This lack of integrity, or perhaps we should call it more politely the desire to be a little more clever than one's neighbor, is what promotes a constant attitude of suspicion amongst nations. This will exist until we have accomplished a change in human nature and that is why for the present it seems to me necessary to have inspection and policing as well as an agreement.

The objection will be made that in the nations which are not democracies a government might build up a great secret arsenal; but in those countries this could be done today for most of them control the press and all outgoing information with an iron hand.

Outside of the democracies, government ownership is a much more serious danger on this account. If all nations were obliged to report their military strength to some central body, and this body was allowed to inspect and vouch for the truth of their statements, then all governments could feel secure against that hidden danger which is now part of the incentive for a constant increase in the defense machinery of every nation.

Here again we are confronted with the need of some machinery to work for peace. I have already stated that I doubt if the present League of Nations could ever be made to serve the purpose for which it was originally intended. This does not mean that I do not believe that we could get together. We might even begin by setting up regional groups in different parts of the world which might eventually amalgamate into a central body. It seems to me almost a necessity that we have some central body as a means of settling our difficulties, with an international police force to enforce its decisions, as long as we have not yet reached the point everywhere of setting force aside.

Joint economic action on the part of a group of nations will undoubtedly be very effective, but it will take time to educate people to a point where they are willing to sacrifice, even temporarily, material gains in the interests of peace, so I doubt whether we can count at once on complete cooperation in the use of an economic boycott. To be a real weapon against any nation wishing to carry on war, it must be well carried out by a great number of nations.

Another small and perhaps seemingly unimportant thing might be done immediately. It might be understood that in wartime everyone should become a part of the military service and no one should be allowed to make any profit either in increased wages or in increased interest on their capital investment. This might bring about a little more universal interest in peace, and more active interest in the efforts to prevent war whether a man were going to the front or staying at home.

Of course, when we talk of "the front" in connection with future wars, we are taking it for granted that future wars will be much like those of the past, whereas most people believe that future wars will have no fronts. What we hear of Spain and China makes this seem very probable. Gases and airplanes will not be directed only against armed forces, or military centers, they may be used for the breaking of morale in the opposing nation. That will mean shelling of unfortified cities, towns and villages, and the killing of women and children. In fact this means the participation in war of entire populations.

One other element must be considered, namely, the creating of public opinion today. Wars have frequently been declared in the past with the backing of the nations involved because public opinion had been influenced through the press and through other mediums, either by the governments themselves or by certain powerful interests which desired war. Could that be done again today in our own country or have we become suspicious of the written word and the inspired message? I think that as a people we look for motives more carefully than we did in the past but whether issues could be clouded for us is one of the questions that no one can answer until the test comes.

I am inclined to think that if a question as serious as going to war were presented to our nation we would demand facts unvarnished by interpretation. Whether we even in our free democracy could obtain them is another question. Who controls the dissemination of news? Is the process totally, uncompromisingly devoted to the unbiased presentation of all news insofar as possible? Is it possible for groups with special interests to put pressure on the press and on our other means of disseminating information, such as the radio and the screen, and to what extent?

This is an interesting study in every country where people are really interested in good will and peace. If these sources of information are not really free should not the people insist that this be one of our first reforms? Without it we can have no sound basis on which to form our opinions.

These are things we can work for immediately, but some of my friends consider that one point transcends all others and epitomizes the way to "peace."

Summary

We can establish no real trust between nations until we acknowledge the power of love above all other power. We cannot cast out fear and therefore we cannot build up trust. Perfectly obvious and perfectly true, but we are back again to our fundamental difficulty—the education of the individual human being, and that takes time.

We cannot sit around a table and discuss our difficulties until we are able to state them frankly. We must feel that those who listen wish to get at the truth and desire to do what is best for all. We must reach a point where we can recognize the rights and needs of others, as well as our own rights and needs.

I have a group of religious friends who claim that the answer to all the difficulties is a great religious revival. They may be right, but great religious revivals which are not simply short emotional upheavals lifting people to the heights and dropping them down again below the place from which they rose, mean a fundamental change in human nature. That change will come to some people through religion, but it will not come to all that way, for I have known many people, very fine people, who had no formal religion. So the change must come to some, perhaps, through a new code of ethics, or an awakening sense of responsibility for their brothers, or a discovery that whether they believe in a future life or not, there are now greater enjoyments and rewards in this world than those which they have envisioned in the past.

I would have people begin at home to discover for themselves the meaning of brotherly love. A friend of mine wrote me the other day that she wondered what would happen if occasionally a member of Congress got up and mentioned in the House the existence of brotherly love. You laugh, it seems fantastic, but this subject will, I am sure, have to be discussed throughout the world for many years before it becomes an accepted rule. We will have to want peace, want it enough to pay for it, pay for it in our own behavior and in material ways. We will have to want it enough to overcome our lethargy and go out and find all those in other countries who want it as much as we do.

Sometime we must begin, for where there is no beginning there is no end, and if we hope to see the preservation of our civilization, if we believe that there is anything worthy of perpetuation in what we have built thus far, then our people must turn to brotherly love, not as a doctrine but as a way of living. If this becomes our accepted way of life, this life may be so well worth living that we will look into the future with a desire to perpetuate a peaceful world for our children. With this desire will come a realization that only if others feel as we do, can we obtain the objectives of peace on earth, good will to men.

Part H
Issues of War and Peace

99

Because the War Idea Is Obsolete

My first wish is to see this plague of mankind [war] banished from the earth.
George Washington

Is the war idea obsolete?

I have asked many, many people if they thought that war itself was actually obsolete, and a great many have agreed that war should be obsolete, but invariably they insist that, for one reason or another, the continuation of war in the world is probably inevitable.

What I want to prove to you is that the war idea is obsolete, but that we haven't as yet recognized it. The day that the majority of people throughout the world recognize this truth, that day war itself will be obsolete.

We had a period in our own history which illustrates what I mean when I say that an idea may be obsolete, but that until the fact that it is obsolete is recognized it continues to be a menace. I am thinking of the time in our early history when the witch idea ruled the minds of the American people. From the beginning there were groups who fought it, saw it as an obsolete superstition and made a concerted effort to educate the people against it. But in spite of all they could do, the idea that human beings were witches held its ground for a time. Then suddenly the belief disappeared from the pages of our history. Almost overnight it was gone. What had happened was that the knowledge of science had grown so rapidly that people could no longer be fooled by the witch idea. It had become recognized as an obsolete idea. That does not mean that there are not instances, up to the very present, of people who are still ridden by a belief in witches. In New Mexico, not so many years ago, a young girl fell ill. She did not recover and her fiancé and a comrade set forth to wreak vengeance on an old woman who, the fiancé was convinced, had bewitched her. They tied a rope to each of the old woman's wrists, one young man took one rope, one took the other, both put their horses to a run, and they dragged the old woman over the rough road until they killed her. In Pennsylvania quite recently, a young man became so wrought up by his conviction that a witch had put a curse on him that he shot the supposed witch to death. If examples of this kind show how tenacious the witch idea is, they also show how obsolete it is. When people revert to it, as in the cases quoted, we now say they are crazy.

There was another time in our history when many of our best minds subscribed to the almost universal custom of settling personal disputes by force. Duels were fought to settle points of honor between individuals. There

From *Why Wars Must Cease*, edited by Rose Young (New York: Macmillan, 1935), pp. 20–29.

was a time, too, when police forces were not only less adequate than now, but in many parts of the country there were none at all, so an individual had frequently to protect his own life and property by the use of force.

But times have changed. We no longer fight duels. No city today is without its police force and nearly all rural districts are protected by some kind of peace officers. Though there are still crimes of violence, it is only in sporadic instances that the individual feels it is his responsibility to do his own protecting of himself and his property by reverting to force. In the affairs of our daily lives we are gradually learning to cooperate for peaceful existence and the old law of the jungle is becoming obsolete in the relations between individuals. We can say that, by and large, it has been accepted amongst private individuals that the war idea, or the use of force as the one means of settling a dispute, is obsolete insofar as private affairs are concerned.

But in the case of the affairs of nations the war idea, like the witch idea in the individual case, hangs on and is still put into practice with outmoded and long-drawn-out cruelty. We still have wars because the majority of people, considered as national groups, do not yet recognize that the war idea is obsolete. Wars, as we very well know from many an example in the past, often give us instances of the danger of not recognizing crucial things, by dragging on over a long period beyond their finish simply because it is not recognized that the war has come to an end. Historians tell us that the Civil War actually was ended at Gettysburg and yet the fighting went on for more than a year after that bloody battle was fought and many more lives were sacrificed. They now tell us that in the World War the Allies had really won at the Marne, that from that date forward the end was sure, and yet the war continued four long years and every nation sacrificed hundreds of thousands of lives. It is even more terrible to contemplate the fact that on Armistice Day itself everybody in the high command knew that an armistice would be declared during the morning, and yet the firing went on till eleven o'clock and during those morning hours many lives were lost. History records many bloody battles which were fought for no better reason than that it was impossible to communicate with the combatants and tell them the war was over.

Let me define now what I conceive to be the meaning of the phrase "the war idea is obsolete" when applied to the affairs of nations and their inter-relations. An idea, or ideal, is obsolete if, when applied, it does not work. Going back into our own history again, we could not say that the war idea was obsolete at the time of our War of the Revolution, because we desired separation from England and we achieved it. There were two objectives for which the Civil War was fought. One was the question of the right of any one of our states, or a group of states, to secede and become a separate country—in other words, the question of the unity of this country. The other was slavery and its continued existence in this country. The Civil War freed the slaves and imposed upon those states which fought to secede the obligation to remain a part of the United States and preserve this country as a unified nation. The underlying cause of the Civil War, of course, was the quarrel between the agrarians and the industrialists, the agrarians being more numerous in the South and considering that slaves were necessary for their well-being, whereas the industrialists were more numerous in the North where slavery seemed unnecessary. This broader point, however, was probably not realized by the people who actually fought the war, though it stands out clearly to those who look back upon that war. On both points, however, we have to concede that the war idea was not obsolete at that time because, while we may think that both questions might have been settled more easily and efficaciously by joint agreement, still this war did accomplish what it set out to do, even though in a wasteful and costly manner.

The world conflagration which began in 1914 and ended in 1918, in which the great nations of Europe as well as the United States and Japan were involved, proved for the first time in our history that the war idea is obsolete as far as settling difficulties between nations is concerned. It did not achieve its objectives. We were told the World War was fought, at least by our own country, to preserve democracy, to prevent the people of Europe from coming under the control of a despotic government which had no regard for treaties or the rights of neutral nations, and, above all, to end all future wars. Judged by the actual accomplishment of objectives, these four years were absolutely wasted. Far from preventing future wars, the settlements arrived at have simply fostered hostilities. There is more talk of war today, not to mention wars actually going on the Far East and in South America, than has been the case in many long years. The world over, countries are armed camps and many peacetime industries have taken on potential value primarily as a preparation for war. How far forward the preparations for war are projected is shown by the fact that across the water a great leader tells his people that boys must be trained for war from the age of eight. Some time ago I drove over the French battlefields. The fields were covered with green but there were curious hollows where before the war the ground had been flat. The hollows were the remains of shell holes. The woods we passed through looked green, too, for Mother Nature rapidly covers up the ravages of man's stupidity, but the new growth was small and the old trees which once upon a time had been the giants of the forest were now gaunt, bare stumps. Out of the fields at evening came old men and boys. Apparently two generations were missing in these French villages where placid rural life was again being carried on. One generation lay under the sod in the acres and acres of cemeteries that fill the French countryside. The next generation was in military training, getting ready to take the places of those who had already died for their country. War maneuvers were in progress and the young men who had grown up since the World War were learning to use bayonets and charge across the fields where their fathers had died.

The same handing on of the war idea, the war tradition, is as apparent in one great European nation as another. We are in danger of actual war today simply because we cannot convince enough people that the war idea is obsolete.

We are perhaps in this country the very best example of the fact that the war idea is obsolete and no longer accomplishes even part of what it sets out to do in practice. Though the underlying cause of the Civil War has not been even yet settled, though there still is a constant friction between agrarian and industrial states because their interests still conflict, we do not tolerate the suggestion that we should go to war about it. We acknowledge the fact that California has certain interests which we in the East do not share, but we know that, though probably no one will be completely happy, some sort of compromise will have to be reached. We do not intend that any state from Maine to Arizona shall drag us into civil war on local differences of opinion.

People are prone to say that history repeats itself and that today in the United States they can see the period of Roman decadence, if not actually repeating itself, at least drawing nearer and nearer. They are prone to say, too, that Greece and Rome were conquered by barbarians because they ceased to be able to fight. I doubt if these countries were conquered simply because they ceased to be as warlike as the barbarians. I think they were conquered because they ceased to be a forward-moving civilization. They had the opportunity and they failed. They came to a point where they declined physically, mentally and morally. It was not only that they could not fight from a physical standpoint, they were worthless and gradually decaying from every point of view.

If we do not find another way to settle our disputes and solve the problems of our generation, we will probably find our civilization disappearing also, but that will not happen because we are unable to fight, but because we do not find a substitute for war. There is no further use for war in business, or war between labor and capital, or war between the rich and the poor. The time for unbridled competition, or war, is at an end. We must cooperate for our mutual good.

It is high time to look realistically at this war idea. Many people in the past have felt that war brought a nation not only material gain when it was victorious, but certain moral gain. I have heard people of my generation say that war developed certain qualities of comradeship and loyalty and courage which nothing else could do so well, but we seldom hear the equally true statement that war also gave the opportunity for the development of greed and cupidity to an extent scarcely possible under any other conditions. There has never been a war where private profit has not been made out of the dead bodies of men. The more we see of the munitions business, of the use of chemicals, of the traffic in other goods which are needed to carry on a war, the more we realize that human cupidity is as universal as human heroism. If we are to do away with the war idea, one of the first steps will be to do away with all possibility of private profit.

It does not matter very much which side you fight on in any war. The effects are just the same whether you win or whether you lose. We suffered less here in America in the World War than did the people of European countries, but at least some of our families can share the feelings of those across the sea whose sons did not come back, and today as a country we are realizing that economic waste in one part of the world will have an economic effect in other parts of the world. We profited for a time commercially, but as the rest of the world suffers, so eventually do we.

496

The easy answer to it all is that human nature is such that we cannot do away with war. That seems to me like saying that human nature is so made that we must destroy ourselves. After all, human nature has some intelligence and the world's experience has already proved that there are ways in which disputes can be settled if people have intelligence and show good will toward one another. To do this on a national scale, as it is done on the individual, people must first be convinced that the war idea is obsolete. When people become convinced of this they will convince their governments and the governments will find the way to stop war.

100
Fear Is the Enemy

When fear enters in to the hearts of people they are apt to be moved to hasty action. Here in this country today we find people who have never sufficiently cherished their democracy to understand fully their obligation as citizens; yet now they are taking fright because ideas which have obtained a hold in other countries have crossed the water and are appearing in certain groups in the United States. These ideas can only appeal to those who do not really understand what democracy means, or who for one reason or another have had their faith shaken in the efficiency of democracy.

We who believe in democracy should not be so much concerned with stamping out the activities of these few groups or individuals as with developing among the people in this country a greater sense of personal responsibility toward a democratic way of life. It is our job to know what democracy means, and to try to attain real democracy. We do not move forward by curtailing people's liberty because we are afraid of what they may do or say. We move forward by assuring to all people protection in the basic liberties under a democratic form of government, and then making sure that our government serves the real needs of the people.

In a recent article by Dr. Eduard Lindeman I read his definition of democracy and it ran something like this—democracy is the acceptance by the people of the belief that the greatest possible benefits shall be shared by all the people. In other words, our government, our basic liberties, our way of life must be constantly looking toward an ideal whereby the mass of the people shall be benefited. Let us beware of unreasoning fear which will make us curtail these liberties and prevent a free expression of new ideas. Where the majority rules, there is little danger of moving too fast. When the power becomes concentrated in the hands of a few, there is great danger that the majority will not be able to move at all.

The Nation 150 (February 10, 1940): 173.

101
Defense and Girls

"Dear Mrs. Roosevelt: What can I do? I feel that the women and girls of this country ought to be doing something just as well as the young men, but I don't know just what to do. I am nineteen and my young man has just gone to camp, and it doesn't seem right for me to sit at home and go around doing the same things I have always done."

Granted that a year of service for boys is finally satisfactorily adjusted, I personally hope that a year of compulsory service will also be considered for girls. I do not, of course, think of girls as taking the same training, or doing the same kind of work that the boys will probably do, nor do I think of them serving in camps. However, just as there are boys whose interests and capacities vary, so have girls varied interests and capacities. I think the opportunity should be offered to girls to work and train themselves along many different lines.

To be specific, I think of girls doing their year of service, in large part, in their own communities. For instance, they could obtain training in a local hospital during part of the year. In this way not one, but two things might be achieved. The girl would be getting something which would be valuable in her own life in the community later on. The hospital would be better able to meet the needs of the community because of the service which she could give. I have seen many a woman facing an illness of a husband or a child with trepidation because she did not even know how to take a temperature or what an ear syringe looked like. A little early training in sanitation, home nursing and diet would make a great difference in the health of the nation as a whole.

I should like to see set up, in the schools, highly efficient courses in home economics. The schools could be used as laboratories by providing free hot lunches for every child, or the girls could run school cafeterias by way of practice in properly feeding groups of people. This again would achieve a double end by improving the health of the children of the community, and by giving the girls the knowledge and experience which would help them to raise the standards of their own future homes.

I know of a community in which cooking for the nursery school was the first time that some of the mothers had any intimation that such things as cold coffee and pancakes were not desirable diets for one- and two-year-old children.

This course should teach buying and cooking for large numbers. Such preparation might be valuable in cases of evacuation of people, either because of fire or flood or disaster of any kind, even including war.

In order to vary the training, some girls could work out budgets for different income levels and run an ordinary sized family on such budgets as part of their training. Of course, you may say that for some girls, who are

Ladies' Home Journal 58 (May 1941): 25, 54.

never actually going to cook the meals for their families later on, this kind of training would not be useful. I insist that it is useful training for any girl, even if she never cooks another meal in her whole life. It gives a girl a sense of self-confidence. Further, it makes her better able to judge other people's work when and if she is later an employer. If a girl is going into business or one of the professions, it trains her in the planning of her time and in the handling of people. Both these things are important, no matter what she does during the rest of her life.

In rural areas, farm-management courses in schools would be valuable. I believe that a sense of the value of cooperation could be learned through such courses. For example, gardens could be grown cooperatively for the hot school lunches. Every person in the community could feel that she was contributing in this way toward the better health of the children in her community. I have seen projects of this kind used to increase the practical knowledge of the use of cooperatives. I think this would be of value to people in urban as well as rural areas.

I can imagine that some girls might want mechanical training of some kind, which might be better acquired in resident centers such as the National Youth Administration has already set up. That would, of course, be optional; but if a girl wished to go there, she could obtain training for a job, in case of an emergency, ordinarily filled by a man. And there is mechanical work suited to a woman's ability in many peacetime industries.

As a matter of fact, I saw ten girls on an NYA project of Boston, Massachusetts, who were learning to make some parts for trucks for the use of the city government. I was told that a larger project was being set up where girls would be taught how to assemble these machines before they went to work on them. There was certainly nothing beyond the physical ability of any girl in this work; and with the opportunities opening up in the future, an increase in mechanical skill seems to me wise for girls if they are interested in this type of training. Many a housewife would find it extremely valuable and economical if she could make small repairs in her own home. And I have seen women who were handier with tools than some men!

I can hear some of my young friends, particularly those so influenced by certain political beliefs, bringing up the question as to why this year's service should be compulsory. They would claim that this is a Fascist or Nazi scheme leading us straight to the system of German work camps. I feel that these young people, and even some of the other people who think the same way, are ignorant of the principles of democracy.

Thomas Jefferson himself believed in a compulsory school law. We have accepted that compulsion as an ideal ever since the public-school system was originally established. In fact, the idea that education belonged solely to the privileged class is one of the beliefs which democracy has attempted to destroy. If we compel our children, for their own good, to go to school, I see nothing undemocratic in giving the people of the country an opportunity to decide at the polls whether they believe a year's service at a given age for the boys and girls of the nation would be of value to them as individuals and to the nation as a whole.

I believe that girls, if it is decided to require of them a year of service, should be placed on exactly the same footing as men, and they should be given the same subsistence and the same wage.

Of course, if a girl lives at home, what is allowed the boys as subsistence in camps should be allowed to the home for the girl's subsistence, and she should receive the same cash remuneration which the boys receive. The difference in the type of service rendered makes no real difference, and they are entitled to remuneration on the same basis as the young men.

This year of service should give us an opportunity to check on the health of our girls also, and we should be able to remedy defects which might have been overlooked in the preceding years.

It should also give girls a good opportunity for understanding what democracy really means. Girls are the potential mothers of the future generation, and with a full realization of what democracy means, what its obligations and responsibilities are, they can teach the children at home to supplement what is taught, or what we hope will be taught, in our schools.

This year of service should give our girls new friends and a wider knowledge of the people who make up this country. They will learn to cooperate in work and in play.

All of this could be accomplished on a voluntary basis, but it would not be. My main reason for believing that it is important to have this year of service compulsory is that I believe so much in the value of knowing many sides of our national life. While I know quite well that there are a good many of our young people who would gladly volunteer for this year of service, I also know that there are a considerable number who would not volunteer. They constitute the very group who force the majority of the nation to make the opportunity for training and education compulsory.

Another important reason why girls should give a year of service to our country is that through so many years we have been constantly increasing our placid acceptance of what the men in our country provided, and that frequently includes their participation in government and their defense of us in wars. Wars today are back where they used to be, and women stand side by side with the men.

Our forefathers fought a daily fight for the preservation of their hard-won liberty. The women of the pioneer days stood side by side with their husbands, shared every hardship, and were often left to fight the battle of life all alone.

We accepted our freedom as a gift from the pioneers and from heaven, and yet it is more than evident today that there are constant assaults on our liberty, perhaps not the least of which is our own apathy. If we wish democracy to survive we must be constantly alive to the many-sided battle we wage.

Take the question of freedom of religion. That was established in our Constitution. It made our country a haven for persecuted people, but feeling runs high today—against Roman Catholics in certain sections, and against Jews in other places. We are a nation of many races and yet there is feeling against the Negroes. I have heard different derogatory names applied to various other racial groups, and this scorn of different races is tied up closely with religious intolerance. All intolerance is based on fear, and fear is usually a lack of understanding. The elimination of these threats to our freedom requires a continuous battle on our part for the principles of democracy.

I feel, therefore, that young people who have worked and played and lived together in groups in communities or in camps for the period of a year will understand one another better throughout their lives.

There would be no strikes, for instance, in which the public would not know on which side it stood, and would not speedily force a conclusion through the weight of public opinion. The fear which now seems part of the psychology of the young people, as well as of the older generation, would speedily depart from their consciousness. They would realize how little real security there is in the world unless we create it, and that that security is bound up with the better cooperation which must exist between all individuals in the community, in the state and in the nation.

In the case of a real emergency such as we are facing at present, of course, older people and even young people below draft age should be willing to render whatever services they are qualified to give, but today I am not discussing what I consider home defense for an emergency period. I am writing of what I consider participation in home defense should be as we look at the future. It should include training for our girls, and a thorough understanding on their part of democracy as a way of life. This will lead to the determination to hand on this democracy to their children, not as a permanent, static thing, but as an ideal to grow as future generations grow, and they will continue to strive for something better for all of us.

102

What We Are Fighting For

A young officer said to me the other day, "If I asked my men why they are fighting, the answer probably would be, 'Because those are our orders.'"

A great many people think in much the same terms—in fact, the great mass of people in our country, if asked why they are fighting, would answer, "Because we have to."

No great conviction seems to have come as yet to the people of the nation to make them feel that they fight for something so precious that any price is worth paying.

To me, it seems we fight for two things. First, for freedom. Under that we list:

> Freedom to live under the government of our choice.
> Freedom from economic want.
> Freedom from racial and religious discrimination.

Second, for a permanent basis for peace in the world. Under this we list:

> A world economy guaranteeing to all people free trade and access to raw materials.
> A recognition of the rights and the dignity of the individual.
> Machinery through which international difficulties may be settled without recourse to war. This necessitates international machinery as well as an international police force.

Gradually our people have accepted the fact that we are fighting for freedom, but I am constantly told that they are not really conscious of what freedom has been lost or endangered. They still feel safe. War is still remote, save for the families who have men in the Armed Forces. The individual civilian's place in this war is still not well defined.

Groups of people, especially young people, talk a great deal about post-war aims. They say the war is worth fighting only if, by fighting it, we are going to create a brave new world. But what kind of a new world?

We'd better be fairly sure of the kind of new world we want. When we look over the past few years, we discover that the war, as we know it now, is only a phase of something which has been going on ever since the last war—a kind of world revolution. It is a worldwide uprising by the people which manifested itself first in those countries where the pressure was greatest. It is a determination to accept whatever offered the promise of giving them and their families, their parents and their children, a better way of life.

The American Magazine 134 (July 1942): 16–17, 60–62.

Russia, Germany, and Italy had felt the pinch of material hardship. In addition, Germany felt spiritual humiliation because of the conditions laid down in the Versailles Treaty. This alone might not have been enough to galvanize the German people into action, but a strong personality appeared who offered them the type of organization they could understand. He promised them a life that provided them with the necessities of daily living in return for hard work. At the same time, he offered them an ideal which proclaimed them the super race of the world. He assured the German people they would dominate the world. This dream of power restored a lost self-respect and gave them a hope of eventually removing all the material difficulties under which they labored.

In Russia, in addition to material desires, the revolution was furthered by the ideal of a people's government. These revolutionary movements, of course, could have developed in one of two ways—the democratic way or the totalitarian way. They began in the totalitarian way but came at a time when the same type of revolution was brewing in many other countries—democratic countries. I think the Russian results have sometimes been very different from those originally envisioned. Russia hoped for a world revolution. Hitler, on the other hand, thought of revolution perhaps for his own people, but he did not realize that this was a world revolution. Nor did he see that in this world upheaval there would be only one point at issue—whether it would be carried out his way or the democratic way represented by the United States of America.

Once we recognize this basic issue between the two opposed types of revolutions, all the other things going on in the world are easier to understand. We know the conquered countries have never been really conquered. Czechoslovakia, Norway, Greece, the Balkan countries, the Free French, all are still fighting the totalitarian way of revolution in spite of persecution, hunger, and hardship. No one of them is resigned to accept the revolution on the basis of Hitler's totalitarianism.

Some people have questioned the wisdom of this. They ask, "What is the use of fighting against Germany? We might better accept the philosophy of Fascism."

We fight Germany simply because there are two methods of winning the revolution, and Hitler's way is not our way. His is a method by which you obtain certain material things, but by which you do not obtain the spiritual things. You accept bondage even though your masters may give you material things, such as better housing, a little more to eat and drink. The State will be paramount—the individual a controlled cog in the wheel. Our way permits the freedom of the individual.

Today we in the United States find ourselves a nation involved in this revolution, and the war is only its outward and visible sign. We are a part, our people are a part, of a worldwide desire for something better than has been had heretofore.

The same seeds have been germinating here that germinated and burst through the ground in Russia, Germany, Italy, Spain, and France. That they were still only germinating in Great Britain and in the United States when the war began is because we have been a little better off and have had people among us with sufficient wisdom to recognize some of the aspirations of human beings and to try to meet them. However, neither in Great Britain nor in the United States were they really being fully met.

Time and again I have heard the claim: "But what we have had has been good. Oh, to be sure, during the depression some of our people were hungry, some of our people went without shelter and clothing, but look at what we did for them! Our government began to feed them. We provided them with work which, though not very remunerative, kept them alive. Then they always had the hope that things would be better. We might get back to those good old days of the 20s, when all but some five million people actually had jobs, and some people really had more material things than they knew what to do with." But we were not getting back to "those good old days" as quickly as some people hoped. The five million had been added to, and there was a question in a great many people's minds whether the good old days were good enough for the vast majority of people.

I think most of us will agree that we cannot and do not want to go back to the economy of chance—the inequalities of the 20s. At the end of that period we entered an era of social and economic readjustment. The change in our society came about through the needs and the will of society. Democracy, in its truest sense, began to be fulfilled. We are fighting today to continue this democratic process. Before the war came, all the peoples of the world were striving for the same thing, in one way or another. Only if we recognize this general rising of the peoples of the world can we understand the real reason why we are in the war into which we were precipitated by the Japanese attack. Only if we realize that we in the United States are part of the world struggle of ordinary people for a better way of life can we understand the basic errors in the thinking of the America First people.

A few short months ago the America First people were saying that they would defend their own country, but that there was no menace to this country in the war going on in Europe and Asia. Why could we not stay within our own borders and leave the rest of the world to fight out its difficulties and reap the benefit ourselves of being strong from the material standpoint when others were exhausted? We would make money out of other nations. We would lose nothing, we would only gain materially, and we would be safe. Why stick our necks out? This sounded like an attractive picture to many people, but unfortunately it wasn't a true one.

One phase of the world revolt from which we could not escape concerns something which people do not like to talk about very much—namely, our attitude toward other races of the world. Perhaps one of the things we cannot have any longer is what Kipling called "The White Man's Burden." The other races of the world may be becoming conscious of the fact that they wish to carry their own burdens. The job which the white race may have had to carry alone in the past, may become a cooperative job.

One of the major results of this revolution may be a general acceptance of the fact that all people, regardless of race, creed, or color, rate as individual human beings. They have a right to develop, to carry the burdens which they are capable of carrying, and to enjoy such economic, spiritual, and mental growth as they can achieve.

In this connection, a problem which we Americans face now at home is the activity of the Japanese and Germans in sowing seeds of dissension among the ten percent of our population comprising the Negro race. The Negroes have been loyal Americans ever since they were brought here as slaves. They have worked here and they have fought for our country, and our country fought a bloody war to make them citizens and to insist that we remain a united nation.

They have really had equality only in name, however. Therefore, they are fertile ground for the seeds of dissension. They want a better life, an equality of opportunity, a chance to be treated like the rest of us before the law. They want a chance to hold jobs according to their ability, and not to be paid less because their skins are black. They want an equal break with the men and women whose skins happen to be white.

They must have a sense of economic equality, because without it their children cannot profit by equal education. Moreover, how can they have equal education if they haven't enough to eat, or if their home surroundings are such that they automatically sink to the level of the beasts? They must have, too, a sense that in living in a Democracy, they have the same opportunity to express themselves through their government and the same opportunity as other citizens for representation. They aspire to the same things as the yellow and brown races of the world. They want recognition of themselves as human beings, equal to the other human beings of the world.

Of course, they are a part of this revolution—a very active part because they have so much to gain and so little to lose. Their aspirations, like those of other races seeking recognition and rights as human beings, are among the things we are fighting for. This revolution will, I think, establish that the human beings of the world, regardless of race or creed or color, are to be looked upon with respect and treated as equals. We may prefer our white brothers, but we will not look down on yellow, black, or brown people.

Another of our aims undoubtedly is to assure that among our natural resources manpower is recognized as our real wealth. No future economic system will be satisfactory which does not give every man and woman who desires to work, an opportunity to work. Our people want to be able to earn, according to their abilities, not only what this generation considers the decencies of life, but whatever else they can gain by their labors. Standards of living may vary with the years, but we must see to it that all our men and women have the opportunity to meet them. The world we live in will not be the same after this war is over, but no one who travels through the length and breadth of the country will believe we need accept a low standard of living. We are still an undeveloped country. We still have untold natural resources. All we have to do is to face the fact that real wealth lies in the resources of a country and in the ability of its people to work. You may lose everything you have put away in the safe-deposit box, but if you can work and produce with your hands or with your head, you will have wealth. For the wealth of a people lies in the land and in its people and not in the gold buried somewhere in vaults!

The economists can work out the details of our adjustments, but, in a broad way, this war will establish certain economic procedures. We will no longer cling to any type of economic system which leaves any human beings who are willing to work, without food and shelter and an opportunity for development. The people themselves are going to run their own affairs; they are not going to delegate them to a few people and become slaves to those few. Having established that, we will still be carrying out the revolution, the revolution of people all over the world.

Lastly, we are fighting, along with many other people, in other countries, for a method of world cooperation which will not force us to kill each other whenever we face new situations. From time to time we may have other world revolutions, but it is stupid that they should bring about wars in which our populations will increasingly be destroyed. If we destroy human beings fast enough, we destroy civilization. For many years after the war we will be finding ways to accomplish things which the people want to accomplish without destroying human beings in battle. We must set up some machinery, a police force, even an international court, but there must be a way by which nations can work out their difficulties peacefully.

The totalitarian way of revolution being abhorrent to us, we, in the United States, are dedicating all we have to the revolution which will make it possible for us to go forward in the ways of freedom. We cannot stand still for the pleasure of a few of our citizens who may grow weary of the forward march. We accept the will of the majority of our citizens. We fight this war in about the same spirit in which our first Revolution was carried on. We will have to part with many things we enjoy, but if we determine to preserve real values, the essentials of decent living for the people as a whole, and give up trying to keep them in the hands of a few, we will win the war in the democratic way. The ways of Fascism and Nazism will be defeated and the way of democracy will triumph.

Most of our present-day ideals were present in the last war twenty-five years ago. President Wilson's Fourteen Points really dealt with these same questions. The men who fought the war to end war—the war to establish democracy—were not as realistic as we are today, however. They had not been tried as we have been tried in the past few years. They had never been obliged to define the specific things for which they fought. Most of us today who have a clear picture of what we think is happening in the world are sure of the objectives for which we are going to sacrifice, but we are not willing to sacrifice for anything less than the attainment of these objectives.

Once the people as a whole understand that these are the objectives of the leaders of the United Nations, there will be sorrow at the young lives that are being sacrificed, but not bitterness. All will be willing to accept civilian hardships and sacrifice, for there will be full understanding that failure to win the revolution in the way of democracy would bring only unbearable disaster.

The war is but a step in the revolution. After the war we must come to the realization of the things for which we have fought—the dream of a new world.

103

Must We Hate to Fight?

Can we kill other human beings if we do not hate them? I suppose the answer must come from those in our fighting forces. Some young people will tell you that unless you hate the people of Germany and Japan, you cannot possibly win. On the other hand, many a young soldier going into the war, will assure you that he cannot hate the individuals of any race. He can only hate the system which has made those individuals his enemies. If he must kill them in order to do away with the system, he will do so, but not because he hates them as individuals. If those who say that to win the war we must hate, are really expressing the beliefs of the majority of our people, I am afraid we have already lost the peace, because our main objective is to make a world in which all the people of the world may live with respect and good will for each other in peace.

If we allow the hate of other men as individuals to possess us, we cannot discard hate the day we have won and suddenly become understanding and cooperative neighbors.

There will be no victory if out of this war we simply develop armed camps again throughout the world. We may in the interests of self-preservation cut down the actual race to obtain guns, planes, and battleships because no people will survive if it goes on, nor will those who survive have the wherewithal for the decencies of life. Even if we cut out all weapons of force, there can exist armed camps in the minds of people, which express themselves through the economic systems which we set up and through all the barriers which we set up between peoples to keep them from real understanding. If we really do not mean that after this war we intend to see that people the world over, have an opportunity to obtain a satisfactory life, then all we are doing is to prepare for a new war. There is no excuse for the bloodshed, the sacrifices, and the tears which the world as a whole is now enduring, unless we build a new worthwhile world.

The saving grace for most of us is that hope does spring eternal in the human breast. We do believe that just around the corner is that solution to our problems which we have long been looking for and that human beings will never give up till they find the answers.

I believe that the solution will be easier to find when we work together, and when all the plans, all the abilities of people the world over, are concentrated on finding positive solutions, but if we hate each other then I despair of achieving any ultimate good results.

The Saturday Review 25 (July 4, 1942): 13.

I will acknowledge that it is easier to urge upon our people that they hate those whom we now must fight as individuals, because it is always easier to build up contempt and dislike for that which is making us suffer than it is to force ourselves to analyze the reasons which have brought about these conditions and try to eliminate them.

In small ways we see over and over again that the child who is badgered and punished in youth, grows up to treat anyone weaker than himself in much the same way. That is probably what we will do to the people of our nation as a whole when we tell them that in fighting to stamp out cruelty and hate, dominated by force, they must hate. Somehow as a whole the thousands in our fighting forces must preserve a belief and a respect for the individual and a hate only of the system, or else we will go down ourselves, victims of the very system which today we are striving to conquer.

104
The Issue Is Freedom

"Is Democracy right or wrong? If it is right then let us dare to make it true." With those words Pearl Buck ended a letter to *The New York Times* and that letter, together with other articles and speeches of hers, are gathered together in a little book called *American Unity and Asia*.

I think this is a very important book because Pearl Buck has lived so much of her life in the Orient that she really knows what it is that we white people must do in order to allay the distrust which our attitude in the past toward the people of Asia, has brought about.

Miss Buck has the courage to tell us what she sees as the only way open to us to lay the foundation of peace for the future. On our West Coast we have had to face the fact that there has been justified fear that our standard of living would be undermined if we permitted free immigration from Oriental countries. Yet I think we must face, in the future, the fact that we cannot treat these countries differently from other countries, and that they have a right to the same consideration which we accord to other nations. If we allow nationals of other countries to become citizens of the United States of America, the Oriental races must have that right also. We can cut down on immigration, but we must do it for all alike. In other words, we must build up in human beings throughout the world a sense that we really believe in democracy, and that we intend to meet the problems which it brings, whether at home or abroad, with the faith that they can be solved in a democratic way.

We seem to have made great strides in our own education in the Philippines, and perhaps that will help us in our contacts with the other people of the Pacific.

When it comes to our problems here at home, which of course is bound up with the whole racial problem, we have something even more delicate and difficult to handle. It is always hard to build something that is good on a bad foundation, and in our relationship with the Negro people in this country we have been struggling to undo the harm brought about by the importation and use of slaves.

Perhaps the most striking bit in this little volume is the letter to Colored Americans. I should like to see one part of it read and reread by every person in this country:

> If democracy did not win, the white people would have to make themselves
> into a great standing army, highly trained, constantly prepared to keep the
> colored peoples subdued, and there could be no greater slavery than that

The New Republic 107 (August 3, 1942): 147–148.

necessity. It is possible, in this grave moment, that in such a place as Australia there might be white people made slaves by their conquerors, just as white people are now slaves in certain countries and no less slaves because their rulers are other white men. The issue today is not one of race, colored or white. It is freedom.

Pearl Buck is right—the issue is freedom, and at the present time there are people in our country without freedom, and one of the main destroyers of freedom is our attitude toward the Negro race.

I am quite sure that Pearl Buck is right that all the Axis people believe that if they are defeated, freedom will never again exist for any of them—German, Italian, Japanese—and that they probably will fight more desperately because of this conviction. Perhaps one of the most important things that we can do is to persuade the peoples of the world that freedom is inherent in successful democracies. They may thereby gain enough confidence to overthrow their present form of government and try to live in peace with the rest of the world. We, however, must recognize that the cruelty and the horrors of this war will have brought about a certain personal vindictiveness which will mean policing for a long time to prevent personal revenge. In addition to that, the very thoroughness with which the children in the Axis countries have been indoctrinated to the use of force will require a certain amount of control until a change can be brought about in the mental and spiritual outlook of the people.

Pearl Buck's chapter on "What Are We Fighting For?" brings out many interesting points, but there is one aspiration which she attributes to some of the Chinese that I think may be found in some people in every free nation:

> For such Chinese it is not enough merely to win a military victory. They want to establish freedom as a human principle in the world. . . . I have been humbled and amazed when I have talked with Chinese, many of them, after all these years of their bitter war with an invader, to discover that they have no hate for the Japanese people. They have a fierce hatred for the sort of man and mind which will invade another people. They will fight forever against the aggressive, military, warlike mind in the world which is responsible for injustice and suffering.
>
> The real passion that I have discerned in the Chinese has been to have a world in which there can be peace and human cooperation. This to the Chinese is a war aim strong enough to have nerved them to a bravery, a courage, an endurance which none of us has equaled. They have fought without hatred toward Japanese militarists who have made the war. Their aim is to do away with such men, driving them first from their soil and then from the world.

These aims are not universal always, but I think in every one of the United Nations we will find a number of people who are fighting for just such aims, and Pearl Buck gives us a real challenge when she says:

> Is the white man strong enough to sound a real battle cry to which all can unite to win the war? It is freedom for all, freedom and human equality. We

had better proclaim it while there is yet time, while we ourselves are yet free people.

We have needed this book and I hope it will find its way into the hands of the great masses of people in our nation who are the backbone of our democracy—the people who will win and hold freedom for us, and for the world. I, for one, am grateful to Pearl Buck for her courage, grateful for her understanding and grateful for the ability which is hers to say things in a way which makes them hard to forget.

105

A Challenge to American Sportsmanship

I can well understand the bitterness of people who have lost loved ones at the hands of the Japanese military authorities, and we know that the totalitarian philosophy, whether it is in Nazi Germany or in Japan, is one of cruelty and brutality. It is not hard to understand why people living here in hourly anxiety for those they love have difficulty in viewing our Japanese problem objectively, but for the honor of our country, the rest of us must do so.

A decision has been reached to divide the disloyal and disturbing Japanese from the others in the War Relocation centers. One center will be established for the disloyal and will be more heavily guarded and more restricted than those in which these Japanese have been in the past. This separation is taking place now.

All the Japanese in the War Relocation centers have been carefully checked by the personnel in charge of the camps, not only on the basis of their own information but also on the basis of the information supplied by the Federal Bureau of Investigation, by G-2 for the Army, and by the Office of Naval Intelligence for the Navy. We can be assured, therefore, that they are now moving into this segregation center in northern California the people who are loyal to Japan.

Japanese-Americans who are proved completely loyal to the United States will, of course, gradually be absorbed. The others will be sent to Japan after the war.

At present, things are very peaceful in most of the Japanese Relocation centers. The strike that received so much attention in the newspapers last November in Poston, Arizona, and the riot at Manzanar, California, in December were settled effectively, and nothing resembling them has occurred since. It is not difficult to understand that uprooting thousands of people brought on emotional upsets that take time and adjustment to overcome.

Neither all the government people, naturally, nor all of the Japanese were perfect, and many changes in personnel had to be made. It was an entirely new undertaking for us, it had to be done in a hurry, and, considering the number of people involved, I think the whole job of handling our Japanese has, on the whole, been done well.

Influx from the Orient

A good deal has already been written about the problem. One phase of it, however, I do not think has as yet been adequately stressed. To cover it, we must get our whole background straight.

Collier's 112 (October 16, 1943): 21, 71.

We have in all 127,000 Japanese or Japanese-Americans in the United States. Of these, 112,000 lived on the West Coast. Originally, they were much needed on ranches and on large truck and fruit farms, but, as they came in greater numbers, people began to discover that they were competitors in the labor field.

The people of California began to be afraid of Japanese importation, so the Exclusion Act was passed in 1924. No people of the Oriental race could become citizens of the United States by naturalization, and no quota was given to the Oriental nations in the Pacific.

This happened because, in one part of our country, they were feared as competitors, and the rest of our country knew them so little and cared so little about them that they did not even think about the principle that we in this country believe in: that of equal rights for all human beings.

We granted no citizenship to Orientals, so now we have a group of people (some of whom have been here as long as fifty years) who have not been able to become citizens under our laws. Long before the war, an old Japanese man told me that he had great-grandchildren born in this country and that he had never been back to Japan; all that he cared about was here on the soil of the United States, and yet he could not become a citizen.

The children of these Japanese, born in this country, are citizens, however, and now we have about 47,000 aliens, born in Japan, who are known as Issei, and about 80,000 American-born citizens, known as Nisei. Most of these Japanese-Americans have gone to our American schools and colleges, and have never known any other country or any other life than the life here in the United States.

The large group of Japanese on the West Coast preserved their national traditions, in part because they were discriminated against. Japanese were not always welcome buyers of real estate. They were not always welcome neighbors or participators in community undertakings. As always happens with groups that are discriminated against, they gather together and live as racial groups. The younger ones made friends in school and college, and became part of the community life, and prejudices lessened against them. Their elders were not always sympathetic to the changes thus brought about in manners and customs.

There is a group among the American-born Japanese called the Kibei. These are American citizens who have gone to Japan and returned to the United States. Figures compiled by the War Relocation Authority show that 72 percent of the American citizens have never been to Japan. Technically, the remainder, approximately 28 percent, are Kibei, but they include many young people who made only short visits, perhaps as children with their parents. Usually the term Kibei is used to refer to those who have received a considerable portion of their education in Japan.

While many of the Kibei are loyal to Japan, some of them were revolted by what they learned of Japanese militarism and are loyal to the land of their birth, America.

Enough for the background. Now we come to Pearl Harbor, December 7, 1941. There was no time to investigate families or to adhere strictly to the American rule that a man is innocent until he is proved guilty. These people were not convicted of any crime, but emotions ran too high. Too many people wanted to wreak vengeance on Oriental-looking people. Even the Chinese, our allies, were not always safe from insult on the streets. The Japanese had long been watched by the F.B.I., as were other aliens, and several hundred were apprehended at once on the outbreak of war and sent to detention camps.

Approximately three months after Pearl Harbor, the Western Defense Command ordered all persons of Japanese ancestry excluded from the coastal area, including approximately half of Washington, Oregon and California, and the southern portion of Arizona. Later, the entire state of California was added to the zone from which Japanese were barred.

Problems in Relocation

At first, the evacuation was placed on a voluntary basis; the people were free to go wherever they liked in the interior of the country. But the evacuation on this basis moved very slowly, and furthermore, those who did leave encountered a great deal of difficulty in finding new places to settle. In order to avoid serious incidents, on March 29, 1942, the evacuation was placed on an orderly basis, and was carried out by the Army.

A civilian agency, the War Relocation Authority, was set up to work with the military in the relocation of the people. Because there was so much indication of danger to the Japanese unless they were protected, relocation centers were established where they might live until those whose loyalty could be established could be gradually reabsorbed into the normal life of the nation.

To many young people this must have seemed strange treatment of American citizens, and one cannot be surprised at the reaction that manifested itself not only in young Japanese-Americans, but in others who had known them well and had been educated with them, and who asked bitterly, "What price American citizenship?"

Nevertheless, most of them realized that this was a safety measure. The Army carried out its evacuation, on the whole, with remarkable skill and kindness. The early situation in the centers was difficult. Many of them were not ready for occupation. The setting up of large communities meant an amount of organization which takes time, but the Japanese, for the most part, proved to be patient, adaptable and courageous.

There were unexpected problems and, one by one, these were discovered and an effort was made to deal with them fairly. For instance, these people had property and they had to dispose of it; often at a loss. Sometimes they could not dispose of it, and it remained unprotected, deteriorating in value as the months went by. Business had to be handled through agents, since the Japanese could not leave the camps.

An Emotional Situation

Understandable bitterness against the Japanese is aggravated by the old-time economic fear on the West Coast and the unreasoning racial feeling which certain people, through ignorance, have always had wherever they came in contact with people who were different from themselves.

This is one reason why many people believe that we should have directed our original immigration more intelligently. We needed people to develop our country, but we should never have allowed any groups to settle as groups where they created little German or Japanese or Scandinavian "islands" and did not melt into our general community pattern. Some of the South American countries have learned from our mistakes and are now planning to scatter their needed immigration.

Gradually, as the opportunities for outside jobs are offered to them, loyal citizens and law-abiding aliens are going out of the relocation centers to start independent and productive lives again. Those not considered reliable, of course, are not permitted to leave. As a taxpayer, regardless of where you live, it is to your advantage, if you find one or two Japanese-American families settled in your neighborhood, to try to regard them as individuals and not to condemn them before they are given a fair chance to prove themselves in the community.

"A Japanese is always a Japanese" is an easily accepted phrase and it has taken hold quite naturally on the West Coast because of some reasonable or unreasonable fear back of it, but it leads nowhere and solves nothing. Japanese-Americans may be no more Japanese than a German-American is German, or an Italian-American is Italian. All of these people, including the Japanese-Americans, have men who are fighting today for the preservation of the democratic way of life and the ideas around which our nation was built.

We have no common race in this country, but we have an ideal to which all of us are loyal. It is our ideal which we want to have live. It is an ideal which can grow with our people, but we cannot progress if we look down upon any group of people among us because of race or religion. Every citizen in this country has a right to our basic freedoms, to justice and to equality of opportunity, and we retain the right to lead our individual lives as we please, but we can only do so if we grant to others the freedoms that we wish for ourselves.

106

What I Saw in the South Seas

Human beings seem to me to have a tendency to meet the demands which circumstances make upon them, but very few among us go beyond the requirements of necessity. Some of the old proverbs tend to prove that this is a trend in human nature which has long been recognized.

Our men in the Southwest Pacific have been doing a magnificent job. Many of them, under ordinary conditions, would not have developed the ingenuity or the determination which has made of them inventors, builders, good fighters in entirely new environments. If this is so of men, it is apt to be doubly true of the women.

I have come back from my trip to the Southwest Pacific with a deeper sense of the obligation which we owe to this generation today than I had in the past, if that is possible. I have a deeper admiration for them, and a surer faith that they can do the job, no matter how hard it is, if we give them the tools and the backing which they need in their tremendous task.

It is quite true that there may be in our Army one third of the boys to whom the standards of cleanliness and personal hygiene, of good food, of some kind of shelter, probably mean a better standard of living than they have known in the past. To the others, however, the lack of privacy, eating from mess kits or tin trays and washing them off outside the mess hall, in clean garbage cans with a fire under them so the water is kept boiling hot, sleeping on Army cots—frequently with only a blanket on it—eating food which, though healthful and plentiful, is rarely appetizing, is a hard and unattractive life. Because of their hard work, the food does taste good; and getting medical and dental care, because they must be in fighting shape, is a great advantage, for they know quite well that their enemy is not only the wily Jap but the ever-present mosquito, and good physical condition is a help against the latter. On the whole, a great many boys are enduring a harder life than they have ever experienced before, and yet they adjust to all of this; they adapt themselves because they must.

In Great Britain the whole population faced a Dunkirk before they woke up to the realization that the situation required of them the mobilization of their entire energies. Out of sheer necessity the men and women in Great Britain, overnight, poured their whole strength into the defense of their country. They went into factories, if that was what was needed. They went into the military services, doing a surprising variety of work. They met home restrictions and home requirements in a truly gallant manner and they stood up under weeks of bombings, of horror and bloodshed, of sorrow, of loss, and

Ladies' Home Journal 61 (February 1944): 26–27, 88–90.

never even complained, because they knew it had to be endured to preserve their country and their freedom.

Australia and New Zealand have known the fear of invasion. Owing to a Jap submarine in an Australian harbor, and a Jap air raid which did considerable damage to an Australian city, the war for a time seemed very close to every Australian home. Both of these countries saw their men go off to fight in North Africa and in the Near East when they were far from certain that their own shores would not be attacked. Australian and New Zealand women who were needed, therefore, went to work and continue at work.

Where absolute necessity is proved, all women do just as the British women have done and accomplish unbelievable things to meet a crisis. In New Zealand they told me that where the men who owned farms had gone to the war, the women were running the farms. Being a dairy country as well as a sheep country, the women now often go back to heavy work with a baby scarcely a week old. It is heavy work to milk a whole herd of cows, and to help in the lambing season. I saw the little wobbly lambs standing by their mothers in the fields, and thought that there must have been some pretty wobbly human mothers to look after them.

In Australia, also, where the big sheep and cattle farms are called "stations," they told me that women, when their men went off to the wars, stuck to the job of running the stations miles away from a city or town, often in a lonely place, doing work which was heavy and unaccustomed, but never shirking, because it had to be done.

In the military services in Australia and New Zealand they do not use women for so great a variety of activities as they do in Great Britain, but neither have we made full use of our women in the military services, and the reason in all three countries is the same: we do not really have to do it. We still have men enough to make the repairs on our PT boats; we still have plenty of men to train for every type of air force work. Rather grudgingly we allow women to fly the ferry planes within the United States, but they are still on a civilian basis. We do not allow our Waves to go outside the United States, and even our Wacs haven't undertaken to drive as many varieties of vehicles as do the young women in the ATS in Great Britain. There are other differences, of course, but these will serve as examples.

The young women who are in our military services, as well as those in Australia and New Zealand, are doing a good job. Their training is good, they take it seriously, they are smart, well drilled and competent, but they can go only as far as necessity requires.

New Zealand and Australia, up to the present time, have been almost entirely agricultural countries, except for a few rather unimportant industries that derived their being from the processing of what they could raise from the land. In Australia, exports were almost entirely wool, mutton and beef; in New Zealand, dairy products, wool and mutton. Now both countries are producing vegetables, and both countries have established a large number of second-line industries; and since these industries are new and there is a labor shortage, they are taking women in as they open up new occupations. For instance, in one factory which I saw, making high explosives, there were over 80 percent women workers. In a large canning factory, which before the war had produced almost entirely for the British trade, I found a great increase in the number of women employed; and to my amusement, also, I found them coping with certain American tastes: For the first time they were making corned-beef hash with onions and potatoes for the United States Army. They looked upon it as something peculiar, but they showed it to me with considerable pride!

All the women of New Zealand and Australia do a great deal of voluntary work. Much of it is for the Red Cross in their hospitals and canteens as well as in ours. Some of their soldiers have now come home, though many are still fighting in the Solomons and the Middle East. Among the returned men they have many wounded.

The memory and traditions of the last war have not yet faded out, and in both of these countries there has been no need to pass new legislation for the benefit of war veterans. These laws have been on the statute books since the last war. I think there was some realization in both New Zealand and Australia of how many handicapped men were coming back to them from the present war, but there are more than even they had expected.

We find ourselves, in this country, facing a more serious situation. No basic legislation has as yet been passed for servicemen. We have the means established for the care of disabled servicemen, but no overall plan for the demobilization of servicemen or our war-industry workers.

Because in the last war our handicapped men were few, comparatively speaking, we, as a country, have never known what it was to try to help men to pick up the threads of their lives again and to feel able to cope with life in spite of serious handicaps. There is a very important psychological factor involved. A well man must feel, on his return from the war, that he is really needed. His wife may have been successful in holding the family together while he was gone, but in some way she must make him realize that he was the missing center around which the world would have revolved, and would have revolved to far greater purpose, had he been home. His arrival is a signal for renewed activity. A sick man has greater need to be made to feel he is important to those around him, and that they depend on him, and that his work is still there to be done and will not be done by anyone else. We must be sympathetic to suffering, and yet not so much shocked by deformity or physical scars that we cannot hide our feelings and behave as though the man in our midst was as normal in every way as before he left us. This is a difficult thing to do, and it is the next test which women will meet in Great Britain, in Australia, in New Zealand and here at home.

Our women have met the needs of the Red Cross, of OCD, the Women's Voluntary Services, the church organizations, the school organizations and civic and patriotic groups. They have given unstintingly of their time, both in the hospitals and in places of recreation. The women of Australia and New

Zealand have done all these things, too, and because they are younger countries with smaller organizations, they have done more in a personal way than most of us here have had a chance to do.

If soldiers from New Zealand and Australia pass through our big cities they are well entertained, but we have taken rather few into our homes. The following letters, given me by our hospital Red Cross people in New Zealand, will show how very personal has been the hospitality given our boys:

> My friend, Mrs. Scholefield, has told me that you sometimes know of American convalescents who would like to spend a quiet holiday in the country.
>
> My father, R. L. Gibson, and I live between four and five miles out of Marton on a sheep farm and would be very pleased to have two boys to stay with us at any time, but please tell them that we live very quietly.
>
> My husband, who was killed in Libya, always longed for some private home to go to, to get away from Army life for a few days, while he was overseas. For his sake, I'd like to be able to give some boys the pleasure he did not get.

> I thought I would write to you and let you know how very much we enjoyed having the two American boys with us, also to thank you for their extension of leave, which was much appreciated by the boys and ourselves.
>
> We also wish you to know that we are still willing to billet two more at a date for you to fix.
>
> If at any time the two who have just gone back have leave at a future date, they will be more than welcome.

> . . . He is having a pleasant holiday and has given the people in Waverly a very good impression of what the majority of the American lads are like. They have made him feel very much as one of themselves, and my sister has asked me to see if there is another lad who would care to spend his leave with them.
>
> I like in my small way to do for your boys what the people of Britain did for my son before he was killed—to feel that they are welcome in a home.

> My husband and I were very thrilled indeed on receiving your card. It has given us both great pleasure and happiness, having your servicemen with us; we feel now we have done a little good by having them. I must say they were very fine fellows. Being a mother with four of the family in the services, I know what all this war business means. One son has been in the Middle East three years now, one in the Pacific, one in the Air Force in New Zealand, and our daughter also in the Air Force. We are very proud of our family and, like thousands of other people, are looking for the day when this business is all over. I hope in the not too far distant future we may have the pleasure of having more of your servicemen to stay with us.

> I would like to take this opportunity of sincerely thanking you for your kindness regarding our little patient.
>
> This lad, as I told you, had become part of our family and he seemed to cling to me for moral support. He was in a highly nervous state of mind and I

know that my bullying and frequent visits did him a world of good, and it was only your kindness and co-operation that made this possible.

He has left for home now, and it is a good feeling to know that we have both done all that is possible to help at least one of those poor sick lads—they have sacrificed so much for us.

I thank you for your kindly letter of the fifth instant which reached me on the fifteenth. It is very gratifying to learn that your troops enjoyed their holiday in Hamilton. I can assure you that the hostesses equally enjoyed having them and that their conduct and deportment were beyond reproach.

It was indeed a pleasure to entertain such a group of splendid ambassadors of your country.

Out there artists from every entertainment field have willingly gone into danger to bring entertainment to the men serving in distant fields, just as our artists and craftsmen are doing. I have found artists in both Australia and New Zealand who gave one day a week to come into Red Cross clubs and make drawings of the boys which they could send home to their families. One very satisfactory thing about this war work is the fact that so many people with skills of various kinds have been able to feel that they had a contribution to make. Sometimes I think that people believe everyone should make the same contribution in wartime. These people forget that each individual has certain special gifts, and the only way he can make the greatest contribution is to give in the way that is suited to his particular ability.

In Australia and New Zealand, women on the whole have met less difficulty so far in running their homes and in everyday restrictions than we have here in this country. To be sure, our armies in the Southwest Pacific have taken away from them a considerable amount of food, and at one time eggs in New Zealand went as high as $1.75 a dozen. There simply was no butter to be bought. In Australia they have been providing our men with meat, and the Australians have been somewhat short of milk, because, particularly in our hospitals and in our Red Cross rest homes, milk has been given unstintingly and our boys seem to be able to drink unlimited quantities. They told me that it was nothing at all unusual for a boy to drink from four to eight glasses at a meal when he first returned from the fighting fronts and had been more or less starved for some time.

But on the whole, I do not think there has ever been the same pinch in any of our three countries, nor the same real fear of starvation which faced Great Britain. We have grumbled considerably at our rationing and shortages, but we have always known that we would have enough to eat, even if it were not just what we were accustomed to or wanted to eat. Starvation has never stalked this country. This is also so of Australia and New Zealand.

They have resorted to one method of making women enter different types of employment which we have not as yet found necessary. In Australia they have a law which forbids the housewife to employ more than one maid except in cases of illness or when the care of children or old people is involved. Government houses, where admittedly more hospitality must be extended and

525

a certain formality must be observed, are allowed employees who are too old for other work or have some particular handicap which makes other employment inadvisable, but no one else is exempt from the law.

Taking all these things into consideration, I would say the women of New Zealand and Australia are carrying on the same work which they did before the war and have increased the field work, military service, factory work, office and shop work, besides much augmented Red Cross and service-club work. They have met the needs as they arose; they have entered the field of industry and gone into the military services and have so far met the requirements for personnel in each of these categories. Their outstanding achievement seems to me in the traditional field of agriculture, where they have really carried much heavier work than many of them were accustomed to doing before.

In New Zealand the Maoris and in Australia the aborigines have furnished women to all the branches of work, and especially to the agricultural field. Here they have been extremely helpful, and in some cases stronger than some of the men who have given up these agricultural pursuits for more lucrative labor in the towns, if they are not in the army.

I have come home with great admiration for the work which the women are doing in both of these countries, but also with a great admiration for the work which our American women are doing at home and abroad. The nurses and Red Cross workers whom I saw while on this trip are meeting the needs which they know cannot be shirked, and I only pray that they will have the strength to go on as long as they are needed.

The women of Great Britain have stood up under the strain of war for over four years, but they looked tired a year ago as they stood at their machines—and to be accurate, the mothers of families looked desperately tired a year ago. Today our women are just getting to the apex of our industrial power. They are not so tired, because we have been in the war as a whole nation only since December, 1941; and I feel sure that as long as the women of the United States are needed they will stick to whatever work they have undertaken, and that same feeling is strong within me as regards the women of Australia and New Zealand.

As long as the soldiers are backed by families at home who believe that victory is theirs, and who are fighting at home to the best of their abilities, so as to give the soldiers a better chance to fight in the field, I believe we will really see a continuous march to victory.

107

Women at the Peace Conference

No peace conferences seems to be confronting us at the moment, but when and if there is one, I am confident that we will see women not only in the United States delegation but also from other countries. The interests of women who are fighting this war alongside the men cannot be ignored in any decisions for the future.

Through the years men have made the wars; it is only fair to suggest that women can help to make a lasting peace. Women are, because of their natural functions, the great conservers of life; men spend it. Men are now giving up, though rather reluctantly, their ancient prerogatives of deciding, without feminine assistance, the great questions of public policy.

Queen Elizabeth, Mrs. Winston Churchill, Lady Reading and many other British women stand out today as having prepared themselves during the war to face the problems of the postwar world. Certainly Queen Wilhelmina and Princess Juliana have been doing the same. From Madame Molotoff down, every woman in Russia has been taking her part in assisting the armed services. Madam Chiang Kai-shek is never far away from her husband's side. In every country there are women ready to think in terms of postwar developments on a world scale.

As each future conference of the nations meets, women should be among the delegates, no matter what the subject under discussion. This is not only a question of the recognition of women, it is a question of education for citizenship.

If women do not sit side by side with men and hear the arguments as they develop, decisions will be made without the proper basis of knowledge, decisions which cannot be carried out unless the majority of the women in every country cooperate in making them successful. News travels fast through women's clubs; such organizations would help greatly in spreading information if some of their members sat in important councils with men.

I was proud that our nation had women present at the Food Conference, and was glad that on our delegation at the United Nations Relief and Rehabilitation Conference we had not only women delegates but several women as observers. The observers were women with interests in special fields; they brought up points that otherwise would not have been given adequate consideration. I hope that, as more conferences are called, we will see an increasing number of women take their places with the men.

All nations are ruled primarily by self-interest, and women are not going to be different from men in that respect. But the men often think that our self-

Reader's Digest 44 (April 1944): 48–49.

interest lies in reaching out for more power through force or through trade. Isn't it conceivable that women may think our self-interest lies in giving all the world a chance to envision something a little better than has been known before? That conception does not exist because women are more unselfish; it is because women value the conservation of human life more highly than the acquisition of power. Women will try to find ways to cooperate where men think only of dominating.

You will say that my thesis cannot be proved—and I will agree with you. Yet in the past, whenever women have shared in the councils of the mighty, there have been shining examples among them: Queen Elizabeth and Queen Victoria gave their country good leadership. Queen Wilhelmina is doing so today.

I can remember when women first began to be a factor in politics in this country, when it was generally said that "politics is no place for women." Men took off their coats and smoked big black cigars and put their feet on the tables and drank liquor and insisted that their political gatherings would offend the ladies. (The ladies seem to be surviving, however!)

Perhaps women haven't accomplished all they might have in politics, but there is a good deal more social legislation than there ever was before women had the vote. When a question comes up which really arouses the women of this country, believe me, the men know that women are now a real factor in politics.

My plea is not for women at a peace conference only. It is for women in every meeting which deals with postwar problems; more women among our state legislators, in our city governments; more women in Congress; more women in high appointive positions of responsibility. They will not be there to oppose men, but to work with men, to have a share in shaping the new world which, whether we want it or not, is going to confront us someday. Men and women will have to live in this new world together. They should begin now to build it together.

Part I
The United Nations and Human Rights

108

Universal Declaration of Human Rights

Preamble

Whereas recognition of the inherent dignity and of the equal and inalienable rights of all members of the human family is the foundation of freedom, justice and peace in the world,

Whereas disregard and contempt for human rights have resulted in barbarous acts which have outraged the conscience of mankind, and the advent of a world in which human beings shall enjoy freedom of speech and belief and freedom from fear and want has been proclaimed as the highest aspiration of the common people,

Whereas it is essential, if man is not to be compelled to have recourse, as a last resort, to rebellion against tyranny and oppression, that human rights should be protected by the rule of law,

Whereas it is essential to promote the development of friendly relations between nations,

Whereas the peoples of the United Nations have in the Charter reaffirmed their faith in fundamental human rights, in the dignity and worth of the human person and in the equal rights of men and women and have determined to promote social progress and better standards of life in larger freedom,

Whereas Member States have pledged themselves to achieve, in cooperation with the United Nations, the promotion of universal respect for and observance of human rights and fundamental freedoms,

Whereas a common understanding of these rights and freedoms is of the greatest importance for the full realization of this pledge,

Now, Therefore,

The General Assembly

proclaims

This Universal Declaration of Human Rights

as a common standard of achievement for all peoples and all nations, to the end that every individual and every organ of society, keeping this Declaration

---

As the United States representative to the Social, Humanitarian and Cultural Committee, Eleanor Roosevelt guided the drafting and adoption of the Universal Declaration. More than any other document in this volume, it reflects her vision of the world. It is a fitting summation of "what she hoped to leave behind." The documents which follow both elaborate on ER's beliefs about the United Nations and human rights and document the drafting of the Universal Declaration.

constantly in mind, shall strive by teaching and education to promote respect for these rights and freedoms and by progressive measures, national and international, to secure their universal and effective recognition and observance, both among the peoples of Member States themselves and among the peoples of territories under their jurisdiction.

Article 1

All human beings are born free and equal in dignity and rights. They are endowed with reason and conscience and should act towards one another in a spirit of brotherhood.

Article 2

Everyone is entitled to all the rights and freedoms set forth in this Declaration, without distinction of any kind, such as race, colour, sex, language, religion, political or other opinion, national or social origin, property, birth or other status.

Furthermore, no distinction shall be made on the basis of the political, jurisdictional or international status of the country or territory to which a person belongs, whether it be independent, trust, non-selfgoverning or under any other limitation of sovereignty.

Article 3

Everyone has the right to life, liberty and security of person.

Article 4

No one shall be held in slavery or servitude; slavery and the slave trade shall be prohibited in all their forms.

Article 5

No one shall be subjected to torture or to cruel, inhuman or degrading treatment or punishment.

Article 6

Everyone has the right to recognition everywhere as a person before the law.

Article 7

All are equal before the law and are entitled without any discrimination to equal protection of the law. All are entitled to equal protection against any discrimination in violation of this Declaration and against any incitement to such discrimination.

Article 8

Everyone has the right to an effective remedy by the competent national tribunals for acts violating the fundamental rights granted him by the constitution or by law.

Article 9

No one shall be subjected to arbitrary arrest, detention or exile.

Article 10

Everyone is entitled in full equality to a fair and public hearing by an independent and impartial tribunal, in the determination of his rights and obligations and of any criminal charge against him.

Article 11

(1) Everyone charged with a penal offence has the right to be presumed innocent until proved guilty according to law in a public trial at which he has had all the guarantees necessary for his defence.

(2) No one shall be held guilty of any penal offence on account of any act or omission which did not constitute a penal offence, under national or international law, at the time when it was committed. Nor shall a heavier penalty be imposed than the one that was applicable at the time the penal offence was committed.

Article 12

No one shall be subjected to arbitrary interference with his privacy, family, home or correspondence, nor to attacks upon his honour and reputation. Everyone has the right to the protection of the law against such interference or attacks.

Article 13

(1) Everyone has the right to freedom of movement and residence within the borders of each State.

(2) Everyone has the right to leave any country, including his own, and to return to his country.

Article 14

(1) Everyone has the right to seek and to enjoy in other countries asylum from persecution.

(2) This right may not be invoked in the case of prosecutions genuinely arising from non-political crimes or from acts contrary to the purposes and principles of the United Nations.

Article 15

(1) Everyone has the right to a nationality.

(2) No one shall be arbitrarily deprived of his nationality nor denied the right to change his nationality.

Article 16

(1) Men and women of full age, without any limitation due to race, nationality or religion, have the right to marry and to found a family. They are entitled to equal rights as to marriage, during marriage and at its dissolution.

(2) Marriage shall be entered into only with the free and full consent of the intending spouses.

(3) The family is the natural and fundamental group unit of society and is entitled to protection by society and the State.

Article 17

(1) Everyone has the right to own property alone as well as in association with others.

(2) No one shall be arbitrarily deprived of his property.

Article 18

Everyone has the right to freedom of thought, conscience and religion; this right includes freedom to change his religion or belief and freedom, either alone or in community with others and in public or private, to manifest his religion or belief in teaching, practice, worship and observance.

Article 19

Everyone has the right to freedom of opinion and expression; this right includes freedom to hold opinions without interference and to seek, receive and impart information and ideas through any media and regardless of frontiers.

Article 20

(1) Everyone has the right to freedom of peaceful assembly and association.

(2) No one may be compelled to belong to an association.

Article 21

(1) Everyone has the right to take part in the government of his country, directly or through freely chosen representatives.

(2) Everyone has the right of equal access to public service in his country.

(3) The will of the people shall be the basis of the authority of government; this will shall be expressed in periodic and genuine elections which shall be by universal and equal suffrage and shall be held by secret vote or by equivalent free voting procedures.

Article 22

Everyone, as a member of society, has the right to social security and is entitled to realization through national effort and international co-operation and in accordance with the organization and resources of each State of the economic, social and cultural rights indispensable for his dignity and the free development of his personality.

Article 23

(1) Everyone has the right to work, to free choice of employment, to just and favourable conditions of work and to protection against unemployment.

(2) Everyone, without any discrimination, has the right to equal pay for equal work.

(3) Everyone who works has the right to just and favourable remuneration ensuring for himself and his family an existence worthy of human dignity and supplemented, if necessary, by other means of social protection.

(4) Everyone has the right to form and to join trade unions for the protection of his interests.

Article 24

Everyone has the right to rest and leisure, including reasonable limitation of working hours and periodic holidays with pay.

Article 25

(1) Everyone has the right to a standard of living adequate for the health and well-being of himself and of his family, including food, clothing, housing

and medical care and necessary social services, and the right to security in the event of unemployment, sickness, disability, widowhood, old age or other lack of livelihood in circumstances beyond his control.

(2) Motherhood and childhood are entitled to special care and assistance. All children, whether born in or out of wedlock, shall enjoy the same social protection.

Article 26

(1) Everyone has the right to education. Education shall be free, at least in the elementary and fundamental stages. Elementary education shall be compulsory. Technical and professional education shall be made generally available and higher education shall be equally accessible to all on the basis of merit.

(2) Education shall be directed to the full development of the human personality and to the strengthening of respect for human rights and fundamental freedoms. It shall promote understanding, tolerance and friendship among all nations, racial or religious groups, and shall further the activities of the United Nations for the maintenance of peace.

(3) Parents have a prior right to choose the kind of education that shall be given to their children.

Article 27

(1) Everyone has the right freely to participate in the cultural life of the community, to enjoy the arts and to share in scientific advancement and its benefits.

(2) Everyone has the right to the protection of the moral and material interests resulting from any scientific, literary or artistic production of which he is the author.

Article 28

Everyone is entitled to a social and international order in which the rights and freedoms set forth in this Declaration can be fully realized.

Article 29

(1) Everyone has duties to the community in which alone the free and full development of his personality is possible.

(2) In the exercise of his rights and freedoms, everyone shall be subject only to such limitations as are determined by law solely for the purpose of securing due recognition and respect for the rights and freedoms of others and of meeting the just requirements of morality, public order and the general welfare in a democratic society.

(3) These rights and freedoms may in no case be exercised contrary to the purposes and principles of the United Nations.

Article 30

Nothing in this Declaration may be interpreted as implying for any State, group or person any right to engage in any activity or to perform any act aimed at the destruction of any of the rights and freedoms set forth herein.

[Adopted by the General Assembly of the United Nations on April 10, 1948.]

The United Nations and You

I was to talk to you about what you could do for the United Nations. One thing I feel very strongly. You've just heard about the crisis at present in college education. Well, you know that crisis points up a great deal that we are constantly hearing about. We're always meeting crises because nobody has enough imagination to look a little bit ahead and realize that we're going to have these crises, that they're coming inevitably.

Now young people could develop imagination, and while you are in high school is a very good time to develop it, and while this happens to be a very small crisis from my point of view, nevertheless, it points to the fact that you need to have imagination in every field, and you need to have it in the future of the world. Now I heard the end of a speech which was very interesting to me, because it pointed up something that I wanted to say to you in your relation to the United Nations. What you do in your own communities and in your own lives is vital, because the United Nations are fifty-one nations, and they have to be brought together and understand each other and work together, and each one has to recognize the good things about the other and the things that they don't understand they must try to gain an understanding of, and that's going to require imagination.

And it's going to require, for the future, a vision and a vision above everything else, of our responsibility as individuals, to accept the fact that what we do at home, in our community, builds the kind of a nation we have and the kind of influence that nation is going to have in this group of fifty-one nations now, but which will later be even greater.

Now one thing I kept thinking about in London was the fact that always we compared other people to ourselves, as we were now. We seemed to have so little perspective on the growth of nations and the development of nations, and we seemed to forget what we ourselves had been in our own development.

Now you are learning history. Now don't just learn history as a question of dates and wars. Try to make this history that you learn come alive. Think of it in terms of people, of different stages, and when you meet people from other nations think of your contact as historic contacts, contacts in which you are making history for the future.

Now, sometimes, I think that one of the things that excite us most today is how are we going to get on with the countries in Europe and in Asia that we don't know much about and that are handling their problems in a different way from the way we handle ours today.

Vital Speeches of the Day 12 (May 1, 1946): 444–445. Address to the New York Herald Tribune High School Forum, New York, April 13, 1946.

Remember Our Own Past

Well, if we will remember the way we handled problems a hundred years ago it'll help us a great deal. And that's one of the things that I think while you are in high school you can do. Another thing is that we are in the United States have always looked down, really, upon people from other parts of the world. We haven't wanted to learn their languages. Now I happen to believe that the best thing we could do for peace is to find a language—and I know all the political difficulties attached to choosing a language—but if we could overcome them through the United Nations and find a language which all over the world all of us will learn, besides our own, it would mean a great deal for better understanding in the future. That language barrier was one of the things that struck me over and over again.

I wanted to talk to a woman from Byelorussia. Well, first of all, I had to find out what part of Russia was Byelorussia, which shows how bad my own geography was. When she told me Minsk was the capital, why then I knew, because I remembered watching what happened around Minsk. But I knew very little about Byelorussia.

We could get along all right with an interpreter when we were just talking to each other, but when it came to a discussion, she was way behind, because no interpreter can interpret fast enough to tell you what a lot of people are talking about all around.

So, you young people, talk to other young people whenever you get a chance, from other countries, and try to not look down on foreign languages, and try to come to some agreement that all of you everywhere will gradually be learning one language which you can talk to each other without interpreters. That's one of the greatest barriers.

The woman from Byelorussia had a lot to tell me that I really needed to know, and a lot that made it clearer why certain things were felt in certain parts of the world, but it took a long while for me to find out. It would have been much easier if I had been able to really talk.

And I think one little story which will amuse you, but which illustrates this language trouble, will help to clarify it for you.

I served on a committee which discussed the rights of individuals to self-determination, and in the course of it a subcommittee was appointed because our Russian representative felt sure we would come to some better agreement than we had reached in the whole committee. And we'd argue for days on a phrase. And finally, one day, my adviser handed me a phrase he thought might do—it was just a couple of sentences—and I read it out to the committee. Before I had finished reading it the British representative, who was typically British Foreign Service-trained, with generations behind him of training, spoke. We used to be worried by that kind of British diplomat—we always felt we were inferior. Nowadays we don't feel that anymore because we're grown up. But he was on his feet immediately.

He said: "Mrs. Roosevelt, in the interest of good English, I think we should say that thus and so," and he put in about a hundred words for my twenty. I was quite willing to accept it, but before he had finished the Russian delegate was on his feet. He was Dr. Arutiunian, professor of economics in Moscow, and he said, "I have been caught by Sir George's good good English before." Sir George promptly came back with "I have been caught by Dr. Arutiunian's tricks before," and I promptly said, "Gentlemen, it means the same thing. Mine's good American, his is good English." And Dr. Arutiunian said, "I like good American. I can understand it."

You see, all agreements, and all peace are built on confidence. You cannot have peace and you cannot get on with other people in the world unless you have confidence in them. You know that just as well as I do. Now, what we are building in the United Nations—what we're trying to build—is confidence. Now, if they look at us in our communities in this country—and remember that all races and all religions are represented—if they look at us and find us prejudiced, doing things without regard to our Constitution and our Bill of Rights, they wonder whether what we say about democracy is what we really mean or whether it's just a kind of lip service. One of the things I noticed was the fact that so many of our young people in the Army were not always able to say really what they believed democracy meant in action. They'd heard a good many things in schools, but they had never translated it into the way you live, day in and day out. And, after all your government is the expression of the way you live and believe.

Now sometimes it's awfully hard to live up to the beliefs and the things that you have read about and accepted, just taken for granted. But when you come to actually live up to them, those things sometimes lead you into difficult situations.

The best thing, I think, that you young people can do is to face up to your difficult situations at home. You will be much better prepared to support the United Nations and face up to the difficult situations that arise between nations. There are always going to be difficulties among human beings. Now, young people have a great advantage. They've had no disappointments to speak of about human nature. As you grow older you have more disappointments. But when you're young you have more courage, more confidence, because you haven't had so many disappointments, and that is a very good thing, because very often people live up to what is expected of them, and if you expect a great deal, people will often live up to it. So the approach of youth is a valuable approach, both in international relations and in our own domestic relations, and you want to feel that you have a real job to do, a job which you can do day by day.

You can be preparing yourself with what you learn through your understanding for the responsibilities which will fall upon you as you grow older. But in everything you do, day by day, you're getting ready for those responsibilities and you are helping to create public opinion.

What you feel and how you do things will have an effect even on your elders. So you have a responsibility already in the community as a whole. Be courageous in approaching responsibility. Have imagination about it. Have vision. People will tell you that you dream dreams. Well, remember that every step forward is the result of somebody who dreamed dreams. Never be afraid of wanting to go forward too fast. You'll be slowed up by circumstances anyway. Have your beliefs clearly in mind and have the courage to live up to them. Have heroes and follow them and you'll find that they will be stronger and better because of your trust.

Good luck to you and God bless you.

110

Human Rights and Human Freedom:

An American View

I realize that the other delegates speak from different points of view and I understand why to them this seems different from what it does to me.

I cannot remember a political or a religious refugee being sent out of my country since the Civil War. At that time I do remember that one of my own relatives, because he came to this country and built a ship that ran contraband to the South, was not included in the amnesty. But since then this has not been a question that has entered into my thinking.

Europe has had a succession of wars and changes in population, as well as changes in ownership of land; and therefore it is natural that we approach the question from a different point of view; but we here in the United Nations are trying to frame things which will be broader in outlook, which will consider first the rights of man, which will consider what makes man more free: not governments but man.

I happen to come from the United States. I used in the committee an example: I am going to use it again; it is purely hypothetical. We happen to have an island in the Caribbean called Puerto Rico. Now in Puerto Rico there are several factions. One faction would like to become another State. Another faction would like to be entirely free. Another faction would like to stay just the way they are in their relation to the United States.

Suppose, just for the sake of supposing, that we had a refugee camp. We belong to the United Nations, but are we going to say that the Puerto Ricans, who happen to want to be free from the United States, shall receive no letters from home, none of their home papers, no letters perhaps from people who have gone to live in other places or information from other places? I think that we can stand up under having them free to get whatever information comes their way and make up their own minds. They are free human beings.

What is propaganda? Are we so weak in the United Nations, are we as individual nations so weak that we are going to forbid human beings to say what they think and fear whatever their friends and their particular type of mind happens to believe in? Surely we can tell them, their own Governments can tell them, all we want to tell them. We are not preventing them from hearing what each country wants them to hear, but we are saying, for instance, that in the United States we have people who have come there from war-torn Europe. They are in two different camps. They will write their relatives as

The New York Times Magazine, March 24, 1946, p. 21. From a debate between Eleanor Roosevelt and Soviet delegate Andrei Y. Vishinsky, at the UNO General Assembly.

they hear they are in different camps in Europe and they may not always say things that are exactly polite or in agreement with the United Nations. They may even say things against the United States, but I still think it is their right to say them and it is the right of men in refugee camps and women to hear them and to make their own decisions.

I object to "no propaganda against the United Nations or any member of the United Nations." It is like saying you are always sure you are going to be right. I am not always sure my Government or my nation will be right. I hope it will be and I shall do my best to keep it as right as I can keep it, and so, I am sure, will every other nation. But there are people who are going to disagree and I think we aim to reach a point where we on whole are so right that the majority of our people will be with us and we can always stand having among us the people who do not agree, because we are sure that the right is so carefully guarded among us and the freedom of people is so carefully guarded that we will always have the majority with us.

For that reason I oppose including in a report which we have to accept this amendment, which I consider restrictive of human rights and human freedom.

Clare Boothe Luce addressing a dinner in ER's honor at the Waldorf Astoria Hotel on May 21, 1950. She described ER as "the best loved women in the world" and concluded ". . . No woman has ever so comforted the distressed or distressed the comfortable." [*The Bettmann Archive*]

Pictured with ER in an informal chat before the opening of the Seventh United Nations General Assembly are Secretary of State Dean Acheson and Edith S. Sampson, the first African American to be a member of the American delegation. (10/14/52) [*The Bettmann Archive*]

Hubert Humphrey, ER and Adlai Stevenson caucus at the Americans for Democratic Action annual banquet. A founding member of ADA, ER became its honorary chair when McCarthy threatened to investigate it. [*Library of Congress*]

ER strongly supported the Montgomery Bus Boycott and urged speedy compliance with the Brown decision. She joined Martin Luther King, Jr. and Autherine Lucy at a Madison Square Garden fundraiser in May of 1956, where she praised Lucy, who tried to integrate the University of Alabama, for her courage, dignity, and determination. [*The Bettmann Archive*]

ER, broadcasting to the Soviet Union in June of 1957 via Radio Liberation declared that "We, as a people, want peace and have more control over our Government than there is probably in any other nation in the world at present." She was responding to charges published in a New York newspaper by a Soviet housewife, Mme. N.A. Kopytskaya, of Leningrad, that the United States sought an atomic war with the Soviet Union. [*The Bettmann Archive*]

Three Democratic Party stalwarts are shown at the 1958 campaign conference of Democratic women in Washington: (left to right) Adlai Stevenson, Averell Harriman (then governor of New York), and ER. [*The Bettmann Archive*]

ER escorts Soviet Premier Nikita Khrushchev (right), Mrs. Khrushchev (left) and Soviet Foreign Minister Andrei Gromyko (left rear, with hat) to FDR's grave. (9/18/59) She has visited Khrushchev two years earlier in the Soviet Union. [*The Bettmann Archive*]

ER and David Ben-Gurion confer during the Israeli Prime Minister's visit to New York in March of 1960. ER had just returned from a trip to Jerusalem where part of the University of Jerusalem was dedicated in her honor. Despite years of political battles, the two remained committed to a Arab-Israeli peace. [*The Bettmann Archive*]

ER had questioned JFK's fitness for the presidency and endorsed him only after he spoke out on civil rights in early October. Ten days later, the day after her 76th birthday, the two Democrats strike a friendly pose for the press. ER would later chair JFK's Presidential Commission on the Status of Women. (10/12/60) [*The Bettmann Archive*]

Dorothy Height and ER shared both a deep devotion to Mary McLeod Bethune and a long commitment to civil rights, dating from their efforts to integrate southern restaurants in the early 1950s. Here Height, Bethune's successor as president of the National Council of Negro Women, presents ER with the Mary McLeod Bethune Human Rights Award. (11/12/60) [*The Bettmann Archive*]

Golda Meir, Foreign Minister of Israel, embraces ER at a 1960 Israeli reception for United Nations delegates. In 1969, Meir would become Prime Minister and refer to ER in many of her addresses. [*The Bettmann Archive*]

ER entered the 1960 Democratic convention determined to secure the nomination for Adlai Stevenson. Despite the deep divisions among the delegates, when she reached the podium to place Stevenson's name in nomination, a 16 minute spontaneous demonstration in her honor prevented her from speaking. Here she thanks the delegates and tries to begin her address. [*The Bettmann Archive*]

Eleanor Roosevelt possessed a rare combination of determination, political shrewdness and compassion. Philippe Halsman understood this and masterfully captured her spirit in this portrait.

111

The Importance of Background Knowledge in Building for the Future

I think background knowledge, when we really want to build wisely for the future, is very important. I know that you have heard from people who are really experts on the I.L.O. and on the League of Nations and the interim period. Mr. Sweetser could tell you much more than I about the United Nations. I had so little knowledge when I was named a delegate—not having been at San Francisco and not having been at Dumbarton Oaks—that I had to take every opportunity the State Department advisers would give us on the steamer to learn something about the work that formed the background of knowledge for what we were going to do in London.

I used to feel very inadequate when those very intelligent young people would refer to the Charter by chapter and section and I would have to look it up. I couldn't possibly remember what it was. Nevertheless, there were some things that old age—just old age and opportunity—did provide, and I think that they were things which perhaps in building for the future we should have in mind.

One thing struck me particularly, and that was, that if you had had an opportunity to know people in many places for a long time, you found it a little bit easier to understand the feelings that people might have under certain circumstances—the motives that might underlie certain actions. I think if we are really determined that we want a United Nations and we want it to live and help us build a peaceful world, then we should look into the past.

A Glimpse at Europe

Take Europe for instance. Remember what Europe was like physically and what its people were like before either of the two World Wars. You may think that it doesn't make much difference what they were like or what Europe was like. The difference is that I think it will make us realize what great strides have been made in the possibilities of physical destruction over a comparatively short period of time. I can remember, because forty-five years ago, I lived with various families as a student in a number of the European countries. It was then I saw the front—the front that we had fought over in France—within six weeks of the Armistice of the first World War. After the

The Annals of the American Academy of Political and Social Science 246 (July 1946): 9–12.

second World War, I spent two and a half days, when I had finished in London, in our zone in Germany. Now, our soldiers coming home can tell us more vividly than anybody else what destruction we have accomplished in the present war—and, without the atomic bomb. But they, being young for the most part, will have very little power of comparing what we have accomplished by way of ability to destroy between the last war and this one. They will have even less ability to gauge what has happened to the people through the type of modern warfare that they experienced twice in one generation—the latter time extending over a longer period and causing far greater destruction.

I don't know how many of you have been on the continent of Europe lately. In Great Britain, I had a feeling that people were desperately tired, but I had a feeling that there still was a solid basis in the ability of the British people to pull themselves together and make a new effort. But on the Continent—it is foolish to say that in two and a half days you really observe anything; however, you can get a kind of feeling and impression—I went to four displaced persons camps. I talked to two German women whom I had known forty-five years ago. One of them went to school with me. I had a feeling that the peoples, particularly the peoples in the occupied countries of Europe, have very little power of recuperation left within themselves. I think there is a sense of a crumbling civilization which is going to require a great deal of assistance, both materially and spiritually, in order that it can come back and rebuild itself. I think that, in doing this, a background knowledge is extremely important.

I have heard so many of our soldiers coming back from France say, "Oh, the French aren't any good. Why, they don't even try to do anything to rebuild their country. Why, we do a lot more than they do. They just aren't making any effort, so why should we bother about them?" I have heard a lot of our young soldiers in Red Cross clubs and various places in Berlin and Frankfurt say, "We don't know why we fought the Germans. They are really very nice people. They are much more like us. They have plumbing. They tell us that Hitler gave them pretty good housing. We go out into the countryside where things have not been destroyed and the houses are pretty good, and they are much more like those we have at home. They have radios and they have little cars, little three-wheeled cars that are half-truck and half-car, that were designed by Hitler for people of medium incomes and are now reappearing from hiding. We just don't understand why we fought these people. They are nice people." Well, that is because, of course, we sent our boys out with no background knowledge at all, so they fell an easy prey to something that those of us who remember the last war can see being repeated, because our soldiers at the end of the last war said exactly the same thing. They found, when they were billeted on the Rhine, that they were among more familiar surroundings. And, we are repeating our same mistakes—largely, because we did not think it important to have, as a nation, much background knowledge.

Facing the Issue

I think it very important for the future that our young people remember that twice in twenty-five years the Germans started world wars. I think it very important that they know what lies back of the starting of these wars. But above everything else, I think it important that they have the background knowledge which clearly shows that we arrive at catastrophe by failing to meet situations—by falling to act where we should act. Our consciences are not tender enough. We can always find good excuses why the present moment is not the moment in which to take a stand. Background knowledge would make us review every step—and, the many steps where we really knew that things were happening that we didn't approve of, but we first didn't say so because we could always make ourselves believe that something worse might happen if we took a stand. If we did anything, if we said anything, something worse might happen! We might have a war! And we ended by having the war because we did nothing. I think this is the most important thing that we should learn from background knowledge—that one should not hesitate to stand for the right as one sees it because if one does not, the opportunity passes and the next situation always is more difficult than the last one.

I hope very much that out of the background which some people have acquired and out of the knowledge of what this war has brought to people in Asia and in Europe we are going to get the necessary purpose to make us work hard in the days to come for an organization, a really functioning organization, of United Nations. The idea that we can do as we did with the League and take a distant interest only is, I think, part of our background knowledge. We know it doesn't work. So I hope we have learned that we really have to work if we want the United Nations to achieve anything.

I have tried this out on a good many audiences but I am not going to try it on you because I know that you know too much! To a good many people, however, I point to something that I used to wonder about years ago. We once had a delegate, a very fine man, a very valuable public servant, who used to go to the disarmament conferences in Geneva, and I used to wonder why no one took any interest in his going or the slightest interest when he returned. We didn't seem to care what he did or what happened. The result was that I don't think we accomplished very much even though we did destroy some armaments at one time. And because of that I came to the conclusion that one very clear lesson that you learn from background knowledge is that just having a few people in the government take an interest in trying to achieve peace is never going to achieve peace, that it has to be done by the interest of the people, and unless all the people—the men who work on the farms, the men who work in the factories, the scientists and teachers, and all the people who make up a nation—take an interest, we will fail. Young people have to care and older people have to contribute what they know because this is something that has to be worked on day in and day out. It is a long-term job. It isn't something that you can sign a piece of paper and achieve. It has to come very slowly. And I think probably the only way it will come is by our actually working together and always keeping in mind the background knowledge that we learn as we work.

A Comparison

To take just one example—I think we would get on a great deal better with Russia if we would remember our own background. I think it would explain to us many things about the Russians. They have been closed off from the rest of the world. They know that their economic and political theories are opposed to those of the rest of the world. They feel a certain antagonism. If we would think back to our early days, I wonder if we wouldn't remember that we were closed off by natural barriers which then existed but which exist no more. I wonder if we wouldn't remember the time when we thought a good many people in the world disapproved of the experiment that we were trying and when we were somewhat suspicious and antagonistic and had a chip-on-our-shoulder feeling.

Only last night I was asked a question which I hadn't been asked in a long time and which I thought had receded far into the background of our thinking. Someone got up in an audience and said, "Mrs. Roosevelt, do you think that our people who deal with foreign diplomats are still at a great disadvantage because we always have felt that our people couldn't deal with the trained diplomats of Europe?" Well, I thought we had lost that fear. That used to be said frequently, but lately I have had the feeling that we have gained so much confidence that we almost look down our noses at people rather than fear that they will look down their noses at us. But here it came again. Now, as a matter of fact, I think we are quite able and have been for a long time to deal with any statesmen or diplomat anywhere in the world. But where the British are concerned, they have had generations of people in families that have gone into government service or into the Parliament, or into the diplomatic field, and they sometimes have a manner which, while it doesn't bother us anymore, does bother the Russians. If we would think back and use our own background, we would understand certain things.

I will tell you of one incident in a committee in which I was working. We had worked about two weeks on wording and certain fundamental differences that we knew we never could agree on. But finally the very able State Department adviser with me handed me a sentence, and I read it through. It seemed all right to me, and I read it to the committee. My British co-member on the committee, who is a very nice person—just as nice as he can be, but very learned—got up and said, "Well, Mrs. Roosevelt, in the interests of good English I think we should say it this way"— and he proceeded to give me about 100 words for the 10 or 15 that I had handed him. Well, I was willing to accept it, but my Russian colleague was on his feet in a minute. He was a Professor of Economics in Moscow, and he said, "I have been caught by Sir George's good English before." Sir George said, "And I have been caught by your tricks before." Well, I thought it was getting a little touchy, so I said, "Look, gentlemen, it means the same thing. It is better English. Mine was just good American." My Russian friend got up and said, "I like good American. I can understand it." Now, that is a good story, but there is something to remember in that. We were different in Daniel Boone's day, when we were younger and a little afraid of what was going to happen to us. Now I don't mean that we should ever be weak. I think one of the essential things that we must do is to know what we mean when we say we believe in democracy and know it clearly and stand up for our beliefs and show by our acts that we mean to live our beliefs as well as to give them lip service. I don't think that that is anything we should ever be backward about doing, and when a principle is involved and other people can't understand the principle, I think the sooner we show that we can stick to it as long as anyone else, that we can't be worn down and we can't be tired out, the better we will get on with everyone, including our Russian friends.

I think we also should learn from our background that we have acquired new attitudes from the past, that we have gained and changed our standards, and in turn our actions have been changed by our new standards, and that those things have taken us time and perhaps they will take others time. Perhaps we, as a strong nation whose land has not been invaded, should remember that Russia was invaded on a very large scale. Therefore, she is, also, one of the countries of Europe that has to rehabilitate a great part of her land. We have no invaded land to rebuild; we have no factories and no homes that have been destroyed by bombs or enemy action. I think we have the strength, therefore, to give a little more understanding and study to our relations with others and use our background knowledge for that purpose. I think we may be the instrument, if we do this, through which a peaceful future may be built.

112

The Russians Are Tough

I was leaving in the early morning by Army plane for Berlin. The argument on displaced persons had dragged itself out until a very late hour. When the vote was finally taken and adjournment was finally announced, I made my way over to my opponent, Mr. Vishinsky, the delegate from the U.S.S.R. I did not want to leave with bad feeling between us. I said, "I hope the day will come, sir, when you and I are on the same side of a dispute, for I admire your fighting qualities." His answer shot back: "And I, yours."

That was February, 1946. When I saw Mr. Vishinsky again, it was October, 1946. He came to join his delegation at the second session of the United Nations General Assembly in Flushing, New York. I realized that we might again have some acrimonious discussions. But I had no personal bitterness. I have never had any personal bitterness against any of the people in any of the Eastern European group. I have had, nevertheless, to argue at some length with them because we could not agree on fundamental problems.

I have found that it takes patience and equal firmness and equal conviction to work with the Russians. One must be alert since if they cannot win success for their point of view in one way, they are still going to try to win in any other way that seems to them possible.

For example, the Eastern European group has but one interest in the International Refugee Organization set up to deal with displaced persons in Europe: the repatriation of as many of their nationals as possible. We, on the other hand, while agreeing that repatriation is desirable, feel there will be people who do not wish to return to their home countries. And our belief in the fundamental right of human being to decide what they want to do must impel us to try to prevent any use of force against displaced persons. We must find the opportunity, if we possibly can, for people to carry out new plans for resettlement somewhere in the world.

I have worked over this and similar questions with the Russians at two meetings of the General Assembly of the United Nations. They are a disciplined group. They take orders and they carry them out. When they have no orders they delay—and they are masterful in finding reasons for delay. They are resourceful and I think they really have an oriental streak—which one finds in many people—which comes to the fore in their enjoyment of bargaining day after day.

When they find themselves outside their own country in international meetings or even in individual relationships, they realize they have been cut off from other nations. They are not familiar with the customs and the thinking

Look 11 (February 18, 1947): 65–69.

of other peoples. This makes them somewhat insecure and, I think, leads them at times to take an exaggerated, self-assertive stand which other people may think somewhat rude. I think it is only an attempt to make the rest of the world see that they are proud of their own ways of doing things.

I always remember that my husband, after one effort to make me useful since I knew a little Italian, relegated me to sightseeing while he did the buying in old bookshops in Italy. He said I had no gift for bargaining! Perhaps that is one of my weaknesses. I am impatient when, once I think the intention of a thing is clear, the details take a long time to work out. Gradually, however, I am coming to realize that the details of words and expressions are important in public documents.

I admire the Russians' tenacity, though it is slightly annoying to start at the very beginning each time you meet and cover the same ground all over again. I have come to accept this as inevitable. It means one hasn't convinced one's opponent that the argument presented was valid. It is perhaps only fair, therefore, that they should go on until they either decide it is useless to continue or one is able to convince them that the opposing stand has truth in it.

I can point to a resolution which was presented after we had finished our discussion on the International Refugee Organization charter and the vote had been taken. Some seventy-odd amendments had been presented and considered. Apparently, it was all over. Then our Yugoslav colleague presented a resolution.

In many ways that resolution tried to do the things which the Eastern European group felt essential regarding displaced persons. Its passage would have nullified many of the things accepted. Our committee voted down the first parts of the resolution, but the third paragraph had in its first line the word "screening," which represented something everybody could agree on.

I think most of our colleagues did not want to show prejudice against the Yugoslav representative. So without reading beyond the first line, they voted "yes" on this paragraph. The last few lines, however, referred back to the former paragraph which we had voted down. It was not until the vote came to the Netherlands that a "no" was heard. He gave no explanation and the "yes" continued to be voted until it came to me. I voted "no" saying, "voting 'yes' on this paragraph makes no sense." I was greeted with laughter. But when they came to read the paragraph, it could only make sense if the preceding paragraph was attached. This paragraph, however, we had voted down!

It was a triumph for our Yugoslav colleague. I hope he realized that the committee desired to show some personal friendliness to him as an individual.

There are many factors which make working with representatives of the U.S.S.R. difficult. Their background and their recent experiences force upon them fears which we do not understand. They are enormously proud to be Russians and are also proud of the advance of their country over the past 25 years.

They also labor under one great disadvantage. Communism started out as a world revolution and undoubtedly supported groups in the other nations of the world which were trying to instill communist beliefs. Leaders of communism today in Russia may or may not believe the whole world should hold the same political and economic ideas. They do realize that for the time being, they have all that they can well do in their own areas. Though they wish to influence the governments of neighboring states to insure safety from aggression, they no longer think it possible to convert the world to communism at present.

It is unlikely that the Russian leaders today would actively encourage groups to work within other non-communist nations. In fact I think they find it embarrassing to have these groups active. It not only creates in the democracies an active desire to fight back, but extends very often to a general feeling against the U.S.S.R.

I feel sure that the representatives of the U.S.S.R. in this country have little desire to be associated with the American communist groups. One of the difficulties arising here is that among our own citizens we have disagreements about situations in their native lands. For instance, we have Poles who support the present government which is friendly to the U.S.S.R. We have Poles who oppose the Russians and probably would support the old regime in Poland.

There are Russians here who left Russia after the first revolution. There are some who left more recently from Ukraine or from the Baltic states. They all form groups here supporting different groups in Europe.

This makes for us a complex situation. It must make it difficult for representatives of existing governments when they come here.

These differences will eventually be resolved. It is fairly obvious that if existing governments continue to be supported by their people, the rest of the world will have to accept what those people have accepted and learn to work with those governments.

In working with the U.S.S.R., we will have to divorce our fear and dislike of the American communists, as far as possible, from our attitude as regards the representatives of the Soviet government. We will have to insist that the Soviet government give no help or comfort to a communist group within our country. I think when this is clearly established, we can work with Russia as we have with the socialist government in Great Britain. Both differ from our political and economic views, but these views are not static anywhere.

Words alone will never convince the Soviet leaders that democracy is not only as strong, but stronger than communism. I believe, however, that if we maintain as firm an attitude on our convictions as the Russians maintain on theirs, and can prove that democracy can serve the best interests of the people as a whole, we will be giving an effective demonstration to every Soviet representative coming to this country.

We know that democracy in our own country is not perfect. The Russians know that while communism has given them much more than they had under the Czar, it's sill not perfect.

The question is, which group will fight more earnestly and successfully for its beliefs? We must come in contact with each other. Therefore, the battle is an individual battle to be fought by every citizen in our respective countries. The language barrier is, of course, one of the things which makes it difficult to work with the Russians. More and more they speak English. I wish I could say that more and more we speak Russian! I have always heard that because the Russian language is so difficult, the Russians learn foreign languages more easily than we do. Perhaps we ought to acknowledge that we are lazier and rely on other people learning the English language.

Talking through an interpreter never encourages friendly relations. I think we feel that it is more difficult to know the representatives of the U.S.S.R. and of the Eastern European group than it is to know someone, for instance, from France, Great Britain, Italy, or any of the South American countries.

It is true, I believe, that official representatives of the U.S.S.R. know that they cannot commit their country without agreement with the Kremlin on some special program of action. It makes them extremely careful in private conversation. We who feel we can express our opinions on every subject find a Soviet representative unsatisfactory on a personal basis. This might not be the case if we met just plain, unofficial Russians who felt they had no responsibility and could converse freely on any subject with a plain American citizen!

We undoubtedly consider the individual more important than the Russians do. Individual liberty seems to us one of the essentials of life in peacetime. We must bear this in mind when we work with the Russians; we cannot accept their proposals without careful scrutiny. We know the fundamental differences which exist between us. But I am hoping that as time goes on, the differences will be less important, that we will find more points of agreement and so think less about our points of disagreement.

On the higher levels, where questions of expansion of territory, trade and influence have to be settled, I think we have to remember our own young days as a new Republic, and that Russia is a young, virile nation. She has to be reminded that world cooperation, international ownership and activity seem more important than any one country's interests. Not an easy lesson for any of us to learn, but one that is essential to the preservation of peace.

113

The Promise of Human Rights

The real importance of the Human Rights Commission which was created by the Economic and Social Council lies in the fact that throughout the world there are many people who do not enjoy the basic rights which have come to be accepted in many other parts of the world as inherent rights of all individuals, without which no one can live in dignity and freedom.

At the first meeting of the Economic and Social Council in London, early in 1946, a Nuclear Commission was named to recommend a permanent setup for the full Commission of Human Rights, and to consider the work which it should first undertake. These first members of the Nuclear Commission were not chosen as representatives of governments, but as individuals. Naturally, however, each government was asked to concur in the nomination from that country. There were nine members nominated, but two of them were not able to come; and one or two nations insisted on nominating their own representatives. I was one of the members of the original Nuclear Commission, and when we met at Hunter College, I was elected chairman. The other members were: Mr. Fernanda de Husse, Belgium; Mr. K. C. Neogi, India; Professor René Cassin, France; Dr. C. L. Haai, China; Mr. Dusan Brkish, Jugoslavia; Mr. Borisov, U.S.S.R.

The representative from the U.S.S.R. was at first a young secretary from the Soviet Embassy. The other members of the Nuclear Commission did not realize that he was not the regular representative and was not empowered to vote. It was not until three days before the end of the meeting that the regular member, Mr. Borisov, arrived; and then we discovered that the representative of the U.S.S.R. who had been attending the meetings actually had no right to vote, and such votes had to be removed from the record. The Commission was a little disturbed because a number of concessions had been made in order to obtain unanimity. Also, this change made it impossible for any decision to be unanimous, since the Soviet representative had been told that he could not commit his government by a vote on any subject and therefore registered no vote on the first recommendations for the Commission's organization and program of work.

The Commission made a number of recommendations. For instance, we agreed that persons should be chosen as individuals and not merely as representatives of governments. We agreed that there should be 18 members of the full Commission—an example of a minor point on which we had made concessions to the representative of the U.S.S.R., because originally the various members of the group had differed as to what the proper size of the Commission

Foreign Affairs 26 (April 1948): 470–477.

should be. I had been told that it made very little difference to the United States whether the Commission numbered 12 or 25, but it was felt the number should not be less than 12 because unavoidable absences might cut it down to too small a group; and it was felt also that the number should not be more than 25, for fear a large group might make our work very difficult to accomplish.

When I found out how many varieties of opinion there were, I made the suggestion as chairman that we might make the number 21, since we were apt to discuss some rather controversial subjects, and if there was a tie the chairman could cast the deciding vote. Most of the members agreed with this until we came to the representative of the U.S.S.R. He insisted that we should be 18, because our parent body, the Economic and Social Council, was made up of 18 members. As we did not feel that the size of the Commission was vitally important, and as he could not be induced to change, we agreed to recommend that the Commission consist of 18 members.

Among a number of other recommendations in our report we suggested that the first work to be undertaken was the writing of a Bill of Human Rights. Many of us thought that lack of standards for human rights the world over was one of the greatest causes of friction among the nations, and that recognition of human rights might become one of the cornerstones of which peace could eventually be based.

At its next meeting, the Economic and Social Council received our report, which I presented, and it was then studied in detail and a number of changes were made. The members of the Commission were made government representatives, chosen by their governments. The 18 governments to be represented on the Commission were chosen by the Economic and Social Council. The United States was given a four-year appointment and my government nominated me as a member. At present the following are represented on the commission: Australia, Belgium, Byelorussia, China, Chile, Egypt, France, India, Lebanon, Panama, the Philippines, Ukraine, the U.S.S.R., Jugoslavia, Uruguay, the United Kingdom and the United States.

The first session of the full Commission was called in January 1947. The officers chosen at that time, in addition to myself as permanent chairman, were Dr. Chang of China as vice-chairman and Dr. Charles Malik of Lebanon as rapporteur. In that first meeting we requested that the Division of Human Rights in the Secretariat get out a yearbook on human rights, and receive all petitions and acknowledge them. Since we were not a court, we could do nothing actually to solve the problems that the petitions presented, but we could tell the petitioners that once the Bill of Human Rights was written, they might find that their particular problems came under one of its provisions.

We considered some of the main points which should go into the drafting of the Bill of Human Rights, and we named a drafting committee which should present the first draft to the next meeting of the full Commission. This work was entrusted to the officers of the Commission, all of whom were available in or near Lake Success, and to Dr. John Humphrey, as head of the Division of Human Rights in the Secretariat. But when the Economic and Social Council received the report of this procedure considerable opposition to the appointment of so small a committee was expressed. As it had been under-stood in our meeting that the chairman of the committee was to call upon other members of the Commission for advice and assistance, I at once urged that the drafting committee be increased to eight members. This was done.

The drafting committee then met in June 1947. The delegate from the U.S.S.R., Mr. Koretsky, and the delegate from Byelorussia, neither of whom was authorized to vote on an unfinished document and both of whom lacked instructions from their governments, participated very little in the general discussion of the drafting committee, though they did agree to the principles that all men are equal and that men and women should have equal rights. The second meeting of the full Commission was called in Geneva, Switzerland, because some members felt strongly that the Human Rights Commission should hold a session in Europe. We were scheduled to meet on December 1, 1947, but as many of the members were delayed in arriving we actually met on December 2.

We mapped out our work very carefully. The position of the United States had been that it would be impossible in these initial meetings to do more than write a Declaration. If the Declaration were accepted by the General Assembly the next autumn, it would carry moral weight, but it would not carry any legal weight. Many of the smaller nations were strongly of the opinion that the oppressed peoples of the world and the minority groups would feel that they had been cruelly deceived if we did not write a Convention which would be presented for ratification, nation by nation, and which when accepted would be incorporated into law in the same way that treaties among nations are accepted and implemented. The Government of the United States had never, of course, been opposed to writing a Convention; it simply felt that the attempt would not be practical in these early stages. When it was found that feeling ran high on this subject, we immediately cooperated.

The Commission divided itself into three groups. The group to work on the Declaration consisted of the representatives of Byelorussia, France, Panama, the Philippines, the U.S.S.R. and the United States. The group to work on the Convention was made up of the representatives of Chile, China, Egypt, Lebanon, the United Kingdom and Jugoslavia. The third group, to work on methods of implementation, which would later, of course, be included in the Convention, consisted of the representatives of Australia, India, Iran, Ukraine and Uruguay.

At the first meeting of the Commission, the representative from Australia made the suggestion that a Court of Human Rights be created. There had been a good deal of discussion of this idea in previous meetings. The general feeling was, however, that this action could not be taken under the Charter as it now stands and would raise the problem of revision of the Charter.

At the start, the United Kingdom had brought to the drafting committee a Declaration and a Convention which included suggestions for implementation. The U.S.S.R., while still not committing itself to any vote, as the Soviet Government still insisted that until a finished document was prepared they could not vote on it, nevertheless was willing to participate in the discussions which concerned the writing of a Declaration. Their representative took an active part, particularly in the discussion and formulation of the social and economic rights of the individual which are considered in some detail in the Declaration.

This was a hard-working committee, and I was extremely gratified both at the willingness of the members to put in long hours and at the general spirit of cooperation. In spite of the fact that a good many of the members must frequently have been very weary, there was always an atmosphere of good feeling and consideration for others, even when questions arose which called forth strong differences of opinion

We finished our work at 11:30 P.M. on the night of December 17, and I think the documents which have now gone to all of the member governments in the United Nations are very creditable. A Declaration and a Convention were written. The group working on implementation made suggestions which, of course, must be more carefully considered before they are fully incorporated in the Convention. We now await the comments. These were requested in early April, so that the Human Rights Division of the Secretariat could go over them carefully and put them in shape for the drafting committee which will meet again at Lake Success on May 3, 1948.

The full Commission will meet at Lake Success on May 17, to give final consideration to this Bill of Human Rights, or Pact, as our Government prefers to have it called. The Economic and Social Council received the report of the documents written in Geneva, and sent them to the governments in January. They will now make their comments and suggestions. The final opportunity for consideration by the Economic and Social Council will come at its meeting next July, and the pact or charter which is finally adopted at that meeting will be presented to the General Assembly in the autumn of 1948.

II

Three Articles in the Declaration seem to me to be of vital importance. Article 15 provides that everyone has the right to a nationality; that is, all persons are entitled to the protection of some government, and those who are without it shall be protected by the United Nations. Article 16 says that individual freedom of thought and conscience, to hold and change beliefs, is an absolute and sacred right. Included in this Article is a declaration of the right to manifest these beliefs, in the form of worship, observance, teaching and practice. Article 21 declares that everyone, without discrimination, has the right to take an effective part in the government of his country. This aims to give assurance that governments of states will bend and change according to the will of the people as shown in elections, which shall be periodic, free, fair and by secret ballot.

Some of the other important Articles are broad in scope. For instance, Article 23 says that everyone has the right to work, and that the state has a duty to take steps within its power to ensure its residents an opportunity for useful work. Article 24 says that everyone has a right to receive pay commensurate with his ability and skill and may join trade unions to protect his interests.

Other Articles in the Declaration set forth rights such as the right to the preservation of health, which would give the state responsibility for health and safety measures; the right to social security, which makes it the duty of the state to provide measures for the security of the individual against the consequences of unemployment, disability, old age and other loss of livelihood beyond his control; the right to education, which should be free and compulsory, and the provision that higher education should be available to all without distinction as to race, sex, language, religion, social standing, financial means or political affiliation; the right to rest and leisure—that is, a limitation on hours of work and provisions of vacations with pay; the right to participate in the cultural life of the community, enjoy its arts and share in the benefits of science. Another Article asserts that education will be directed to the full physical, intellectual, moral and spiritual development of the human personality and to combatting hatred against other nations or racial or religious groups.

If the Declaration is accepted by the Assembly, it will mean that all the nations accepting it hope that the day will come when these rights are considered inherent rights belonging to every human being, but it will not mean that they have to change their laws immediately to make these rights possible.

On the other hand, as the Convention is ratified by one nation after another it will require that each ratifying nation change its laws where necessary, to make possible that every human being within its borders shall enjoy the rights set forth. The Convention, of course, covers primarily the civil liberties which many of the nations of the world have accepted as inherent rights of human beings, and it reaffirms a clause in the Charter of the United Nations which says that there shall be no discrimination among any human beings because of race, creed or color.

The most important articles of the Convention are subjects with which every American high school student is familiar. Article 5 makes it unlawful to deprive a person of life except as punishment for a crime provided by law. Article 6 outlaws physical mutilation. Article 7 forbids torture and cruel or inhuman punishment. Article 8 prohibits slavery and compulsory labor, with exceptions permitted as to the latter in the case of military service and emergency service in time of disaster such as flood or earthquake.

A provision which is new in an international constitutional sense, though not new in practice to Americans, is Article 11, which guarantees liberty of movement and a free choice of residence within a state, and a general freedom to every person in the world to leave any country, including his own. Article 20 makes all sections of the Convention applicable without distinction as to race, sex, language, religion, political or other opinion, property status, or national or social origin; and Article 21 requires the states to forbid by law the advocacy of national, racial or religious hostility that constitutes incitement to violence. In general, every nation ratifying the Convention will have to make sure that within its jurisdiction these promised rights become realities, so it is the Convention which is of the greatest importance to the peoples throughout the world.

A possible stumbling block to general ratification of the Convention is the fact that some federal states, like the United States, operate constitutional systems in which the primary laws affecting individuals are adopted by the constituent states and are beyond the constitutional power of the federal government. The Convention provides, in Article 24, that in such cases these federal governments shall call to the attention of their constituent states, with a favorable recommendation, those Articles considered appropriate for action by them.

One of the questions that will come before the Human Rights Commission in May is whether all the Articles included in the Convention shall be submitted to the various nations for ratification in a single document, to be taken all in one gulp, so to speak, or shall be divided into separate conventions, in the thought that this procedure would avoid the rejection of the entire document because of objection to one or two articles, as might happen in many cases. Of course, it is quite evident that in the future there will have to be many conventions on special subjects, and that the work of the Human Rights Commission should be directed for years to come on those subjects as they arise. A convention on the subject of nationality and stateless persons seems to be knocking at our doors for consideration almost immediately.

III

As I look back at the work thus far of our Human Rights Commission I realize that its importance is twofold.

In the first place, we have put into words some inherent rights. Beyond that, we have found that the conditions of our contemporary world require the enumeration of certain protections which the individual must have if he is to acquire a sense of security and dignity in his own person. The effect of this is frankly educational. Indeed, I like to think that the Declaration will help forward very largely the education of the peoples of the world.

It seems to me most important that the Declaration be accepted by all member nations, not because they will immediately live up to all of its provisions, but because they ought to support the standards toward which the nations must henceforward aim. Since the objectives have been clearly stated, men of good will everywhere will strive to attain them with more energy and, I trust, with better hope of success.

As the Convention is adhered to by one country after another, it will actually bring into being rights which are tangible and can be invoked before the law of the ratifying countries. Everywhere many people will feel more secure. And as the Great Powers tie themselves down by their ratifications, the smaller nations which fear that the great may abuse their strength will acquire a sense of greater assurance.

The work of the Commission has been of outstanding value in setting before men's eyes the ideals which they must strive to reach. Men cannot live by bread alone.

114
Making Human Rights Come Alive

We worked as eighteen representatives of Government on the Human Rights Commission. We are very happy to know that UNESCO accepted the first fruits of our labor and adopted the Universal Declaration of Human Rights. You know what it will mean if all the various Commissions of UNESCO really help to tell the people of the various countries about this document. It is an educational document because it is simply a declaration that sets standards and puts down things for which we want to strive. It has no legal binding value, but it is a preparation for the coming bill of rights. When the Covenant is written, then we will have to be prepared to ask our various nations to ratify that covenant and to accept the fact that the Covenant has legal binding value.

Now, of course, the first Covenant will probably be a very simple document. It will probably not contain all the things that are in the Declaration, because in the Declaration we could write some aspirations, but nevertheless we know quite well that we will go on. Perhaps the first Covenant will not cover all the things that we will want to have covered in the future. We will keep our minds open and we will be prepared to meet new needs and new circumstances as they arise, but we have to make a beginning, and the beginning can only be made if we really make the Declaration a living document, something that is not just words on paper but something which we really strive to bring to the lives of all people, all people everywhere in the world.

Study the Document

Now to do that we, all of us, will have to study this document. We will have to understand how it came to be written, why certain things are in it. I think perhaps the best way to explain to you how difficult a universal document is to put down on paper, the best way to explain that to you is to tell you a little about what happened in Committee III of the General Assembly in Paris, when we presented as a result of the Human Rights Commission's work over a period of two and a half years that document that we thought was quite a good piece of work, over which we thought possibly there might be some discussion but not too much, and we were to find that there was going to be a great deal of discussion, so much discussion that at one point I thought perhaps we would never get agreement.

Phi Delta Kappan 31 (September 1949): 23–33. Speech to the Second National Conference on UNESCO, Cleveland, Ohio, April 1, 1949.

M. Laugier, out of his wisdom, said, "This is very valuable. People who discuss as much as this over ideas are going home to talk about them afterwards." I hope that he was right, because that is the way this document will come to mean something in the lives of people all over the world.

I will take the first three Articles and tell you a little about them. In Committee III there are quite a number of women who sit as delegates. I imagine that you know that that is a good committee on which to put women! In the first place, they are naturally interested in humanitarian questions, but in addition, I think some of the members of our delegations believe, we might not do so well if we were put in the political committees or legal committees. We really might get into trouble, so Committee III has quite a number of women.

Right away they saw something in our document that we brought to them which we had not given much thought to. As we presented the document, it was perhaps a little too Anglo-Saxon, a little too much like the American Declaration. It said "all *men*" in the beginning of a great many paragraphs; the final Article reads, "All *human beings* are born free and equal in dignity and rights. They are endowed with reason and conscience and should act towards one another in a spirit of brotherhood."

After I got home I received a letter from a gentleman who said, "How could you as the United States Delegate vote for Article I of the Universal Declaration when it is not like our Declaration?"

Now I will tell you how I could. The women on Committee III—and remember there were 58 representatives of governments in Committee III, not 18—58—and the women said " 'All men,' oh, no. In this document we are not going to say 'all men' because in some of our countries we are just struggling to recognition and equality. Some of us have come up to the top but others have very little equality and recognition and freedom. If we say 'all men,' when we get home it will be 'all men.' " So you will find in this Declaration that it starts with "all human beings" in Article I, and in all the other Articles is says "everyone," "no one." In the body of the Article it occasionally says "his," because to say "his or hers" each time was a little awkward, but it is very clearly understood that this applies to all human beings.

I want to tell you that to pass the first three Articles in Committee III took four weeks and a great deal of argument, a great deal of real feeling was expressed.

Words in Different Languages

Perhaps one of the things that some of us learned was that in an international document you must try to find words that can be accepted by the greatest number of people. Not the words you would choose as the perfect words, but the words that most people can say and that will accomplish the ends you desire, and will be acceptable to practically everyone sitting round the table, no matter what their background, no matter what their beliefs may be. So that's what happened to us.

In the next few words of Article I you will notice that instead of saying: "All men are created equal," it says: "All human beings are born free and equal in dignity and rights."

Now, I happen to believe that we are born free and equal in dignity and rights because there is a divine Creator, and there is a divine spark in men. But, there were other people around the table who wanted it expressed in such a way that they could think in their particular way about this question, and finally, these words were agreed upon because they stated the fact that all men were born free and equal, but they left it to each of us to put in our own reason, as we say, for that end.

There is one other word that I want to tell you about because it cost us a great deal of time, and it illustrates one of the difficulties of writing a document of this kind. It is in Article II which reads:

> Everyone is entitled to all the rights and freedoms set forth in this Declaration, without distinction of any kind, such as race, colour, sex, language, religion, political or other opinion, national or social origin, property, birth or other status.
>
> Furthermore, no distinction shall be made on the basis of the political, jurisdictional or international status of the country or territory to which a person belongs, whether it be independent, trust, non-selfgoverning, or under any other limitation of sovereignty.

Now, the word we had so much difficulty about was the word "birth" in the first paragraph. Our Russian colleague was making a speech, stating something he wished to have included in the Article, but he and the translator had a different opinion as to the way his idea was translated, and he stopped and said "That translation is wrong. It does not say what I mean." So he was finally asked if he would explain what he wanted to express. And he said that he wanted to say in French the word "état"; in English the word "estate." There is no distinction of any kind such as "état." Well, Professor Cassin, who is the Delegate of France and a very distinguished and interested delegate on the Human Rights Commission, said: "I am afraid that wouldn't mean a great deal today. There was a time when it might have meant something in France. It was 'état,' but today I don't think it would be very meaningful to people in my country." I said: "Well, I don't think the word 'estate' would mean a great deal to people in the English-speaking countries."

So, our Russian colleague said he would accept the word "class," and that I didn't like very much. I said: "I think in many countries we're getting away from the use of that word, and it would be a mistake to write it in a universal document." So, finally, after long discussion we settled on the word "birth" as a translation that our Russian colleague would accept and I thought that was all settled. But then our China colleague, who, perhaps, is more interested in the English language even than we who call it our mother tongue, Dr. P. C. Chang of China, decided that since we were going to put the word "birth" it should come after the word "race" and should read: "without distinction of any kind such as race, birth, colour, sex," etc.

Our Russian colleague would have none of it; that was not the right place. We argued for a long while, and finally it was put after "property." Then for a reason that I have never been able to understand, our Russian colleague sat back apparently feeling that he had gained a complete victory—that it now meant something that it had not meant before, and was perfectly satisfied and voted for that Article. Of course, in the end he abstained on the whole Declaration.

That is a very good illustration of one of the difficulties of translation; one of the difficulties of really understanding what is going on in the minds of other people; because to this day I don't really know why that was a victory. Perhaps you do, M. Laugier, but I never have understood. Someday I hope to understand, but I never have.

And so I think these three things all give you an idea of some of the difficulties of writing documents which is to mean something to a great many different peoples at different points of development, with different religious beliefs, and different legal systems, and with habits and customs that vary very greatly.

UNESCO Will Help Us Gain Peace

Now, UNESCO is going to help us all to understand each other better. It is going to do the work that I feel really needs to be done to teach us more about what makes man the kind of animal he is. Man has learned to use nature very well, to control it very well. He has learned a number of secrets which are nature's secrets. But he hasn't learned a great deal about himself, and that is probably what UNESCO is going to help us all to achieve; and, perhaps, one of the best ways will be in really making people understand why human rights and freedoms are one of the foundations on which we hope to build peace. Peace isn't going to just drop on us all of a sudden. We have machinery in the United Nations which we can use, if we will, to help us create an atmosphere in which peace may grow, but we will have to work to keep that machinery doing its job. And the study of human rights, the acceptance of human rights and freedoms, may be one of the foundation stones in giving us an atmosphere in which we can all grow together towards a more peaceful world.

Precedents in Laws

I remember very well when Professor René Cassin in the early days of our discussion in the Human Rights Commission, suggested an article. It is not now in the words that he used in first suggesting it, though the idea is in that direction. I have often thought of it because it not only illustrated the difficulties of different legal systems, but it also illustrated the belief which many of the representatives in our Commission had, that certain things must never happen again because they had been one of the causes that brought on World

War II. I will tell you about it because I think it is interesting. His suggestion was that we have an article that would read in French, "Personne ne doit être privé de sa personalité juridique," and I, without any legal knowledge, translated it into English as "No one shall be deprived of their juridical personality."

Well, I didn't know what I had started. Behind my back, where lawyers sit from the departments in Washington, there was a storm. They all said, "There is no such expression as 'juridical personality' in English or American law." And all the United Kingdom gentlemen who were lawyers put their heads together and said "No" very firmly at me. So I knew that I hadn't gotten the right word. Behind my back they kept arguing, saying what it means is "without due process of law," but how do you say it? Well, it took a long while to argue that out and finally one day one of my Department of Justice youngish lawyers handed me a piece of paper and said, "You can accept the translation 'juridical personality,' it was once used in American law."

And when do you think it was used? It was used in the Dred Scott case when Justice Taney said "a slave has no juridical personality." So I accepted it.

There was no trouble at all with any of the Latin American countries, all of which accepted the French idea quite happily because they had the same system of law. The trouble lay with the Anglo-Saxon people, and finally our United Kingdom delegate said that it didn't mean anything in English law, but he couldn't think of any better expression, so for the time being, he would accept it. Professor Cassin himself finally thought of something better in the way of wording and the idea is in the document, though the words are changed. But I always felt that it was a very good illustration of some of the difficulties that came up on the legal side.

There Are No Guarantees

We had a very good illustration of our difficulties from a different point of view between the U.S.S.R. and ourselves. Their chief amendments were two: one was to come at the end of many articles and say "these rights" whatever they might be, "are guaranteed by the state." That was a kind of national implementation which many of us thought very unwise and so it was not accepted, but it gave the U.S.S.R. a reason for abstaining in the end because they said there was no way for any of the things that were written here to be guaranteed, which is completely true. There is no way. It is an educational declaration and the only way we can guarantee that these rights will be observed is by doing a good job educationally. People really strive to have their governments and their people understand that these are the kind of rights that give dignity to man, and, therefore, they insist that they be observed.

Now, we have great belief, I think, in the force of documents which do express ideals. We think that, in themselves, they carry weight. But they carry no weight unless the people know them, unless the people understand them, unless the people demand that they be lived. And perhaps Article 2 is one of the articles that we, in this country, and in most of the democracies, should think about, but perhaps it is more important for us in the United States because we have to recognize that there are two ideas that must live side by side in the world.

Well, the only way that they can live in the same world is for the recognition of their equal strength to come about. At present, the U.S.S.R. is quite convinced that their idea is stronger than the democratic idea.

They feel quite sure that what they have to offer in their attitude of equality of all races, of a kind of economy which they consider gives greater equality than other types of economy in the world, of a kind of political government which they say is government by workers for workers—they are quite sure that if they make those promises there are masses of people in the world who will feel that they are better promises than we of the democracies can make, and that is why they single out over and over again the United States and the United Kingdom for attack—the United Kingdom on colonial policies, the United States on racial policies, the way we treat minorities—because there is no better forum for propaganda than the United Nations.

The United Nations Is a Forum

You are talking in every committee to the representatives, in the last meeting of 58 nations, in the next I think of 60 nations. That is quite a forum! There are quite a number of people that can hear what you are saying and you cannot blame the U.S.S.R. for feeling that they are offering what they feel will appeal to the people throughout the world who have perhaps not felt that they were on a basis of equality, who have perhaps felt that their economic security was a little insecure. There are a good many peoples of the world who have often been not only one day away from starvation but actually have starvation among them, and yet they have seen a few people who still have a good deal.

So this offering—it is only promises, of course—and that is another thing we must remember. The U.S.S.R. can make promises because very few people get in to verify what they promise, but the United States, the United Kingdom, the other democracies, they are all open to inspection, so it is very easy to find out what actually goes on, and that is one of the reasons why it is so important that we in the democracies make human rights and freedom a reality. It is true that these very words that are in Article 2 have been in our own Bill of Rights, but we felt it was a domestic question. We had plenty of time. We could set our house in order when we felt the time had arrived. We could have a little more time for education. We could let people gradually grow out of their prejudices. Now it is a part of the great question of whether democracy or communism really offers most to the people of the world. It is no longer a domestic question. It is an international question, and for that reason you can't wait any longer. You are open for inspection.

We Are Inspected

Nothing ever happens in any part of the United States that, if we are in session, whether it is the Human Rights Commission or the General Assembly, that wherever I am sitting the U.S.S.R. delegate doesn't manage somehow to tell the story of what has happened, and then he will turn to me and say, "Is that what you consider democracy, Mrs. Roosevelt?" And I am sorry to say that quite often I have to say, "No, that isn't what I consider democracy. That's a failure of democracy, but there is one thing in my country: we can know about our failures and those of us who care can work to improve our democracy!"

You see, there is one very interesting thing. Communism is perfect! I have never heard one of the U.S.S.R. delegates say that there was anything that could be improved! Now that is interesting about something which still remains human, because human things are rarely perfect, but I have never heard one U.S.S.R. delegate acknowledge that you could improve something in communism.

Another thing which is interesting is that all through the Declaration the value of economic and social rights is emphasized. The U.S.S.R. delegates fought for those and many of their suggestions are included in those articles, but they still abstain on the whole from the Declaration. They fought for those economic and social rights because to them those are the really important things. They never offer anybody freedom and I have often wondered whether those who listened to their promises ever noticed that freedom was left out.

Conceptions of Freedom

The interesting thing is that they are quite safe in doing so because many of the peoples to whom they talk don't know the meaning of freedom as we know it. In Japan, for instance, freedom only means license. There was no character in the Japanese language which meant freedom as we understand it, so that when we tried to explain what freedom meant, they had to evolve a new character, because when they speak of a child who acted with complete irresponsibility and complete license, they said he was acting with freedom.

That is something we must remember, because when you argue with Mr. Vishinsky, he will say there is no such thing as absolute freedom, and of course you and I know that is true. All freedom is conditioned by the freedom of other people, but nevertheless there is for human beings something very precious, which we know as freedom, the freedom to help govern ourselves, the freedom to help develop the future. These are very important things for us, more important perhaps than the actual assurance by the state of certain economic and social rights.

Now I am going to read you just one Article, because it will explain to you why it was impossible for the U.S.S.R. to vote in favor of this document, and it will show you the cleavage in thought which somehow, some day, we have to bridge. We are not going to bridge it right away. It is going to take time, but the understanding of it is necessary before we can begin to decide how we can work.

The Article is one of freedom of movement. It reads:

> Everyone has the right to freedom of movement and residence within the borders of each State. Everyone has the right to leave any country, including his own, and return to his country.

The amendment they wanted to that was:

> Everyone has the right to leave any country, including his own, and to return to his country according to the laws of his country.

That would have meant that the law said you couldn't leave your country without permission of the government.

Naturally, in discussion it was brought out that many countries have regulations. I have to pay my income tax; I have to take the little piece of paper from my doctor saying when I was vaccinated. I must have been vaccinated within the last three years or I can't come back. But when that is done, I can leave and come back, and I can move anywhere within my own country and I can do it when I wish, and I can settle where I wish.

After defeat of the amendment, I went over to talk to Mr. Pavlov, and I said: "Mr. Pavlov," (I should say that he speaks French very well) "do you see no difference between the regulations which my country puts on freedom of movement, and the regulations of the U.S.S.R. which forbid a citizen to leave without permission from his government, and to give no permission?" He looked at me and he said: "All regulations are the same." Now that is a very interesting thing because that is a good illustration of where we think differently.

Now, I don't expect that gulf to be bridged for a long while. But I do feel that we can reach the point where we can live in the same world, but I think the only way we will reach it is if we show in the democracies that our beliefs are as strong; that we intend to crusade just as much as they do, and that we are as determined that all human beings shall eventually have the rights and freedoms set forth in this document, and that we are not going to be intimidated; neither are we going to be despondent.

I think they count on wearing out our patience, on making us feel that it is hopeless, on getting us discouraged to the point where we will give up and decide that there is no way to live in the same world. The day we do that we have lost, and I hope, therefore, that we will concentrate on making our own selves, our own communities, our own country, the real democracy that we have given lip service to for so many years. And in doing that, that we will be the spearhead and the spiritual and moral leader of all the other democracies that really want to see human rights and human freedoms made the foundation of a just and peaceful world.

For Better World Understanding*

In the United Nations we are trying to work for better world understanding. You would feel, I am sure, that we in the United Nations ought to find the answers. I agree that we ought to, since we have delegates from so many nations. There were fifty-eight delegates at the last meeting in Paris, and there are going to be sixty at the next meeting. That makes a good many delegates in the General Assembly, for each delegation is composed of five delegates, five alternates, and quite a number of advisers. You get to know and to talk to many people from different countries. And this, perhaps, ought to give us the answers on how to promote world understanding. But I confess that at each meeting I learn something new. Surprising facts are thrust upon me that I had never thought of before. So I have come to feel that one of our troubles is lack of awareness of the differences between peoples.

I will illustrate for you by something that happened to me in Paris. I have always been assigned to Committee III. That is the committee that deals with education, cultural, and humanitarian subjects. When I was first put on this Committee, I felt quite sure that one reason for the assignment was that our delegation was worried about having a woman as one of the delegates. They said, "Committee III—that's safe. She can't do anything there." Sometimes I think it has not been quite as safe as they thought it would be at the beginning. But I want to get back to my story, because it illustrates the points of our difficulty in understanding. The Committee was discussing, at the last meeting in Paris, the Declaration of Human Rights. On my right, since we sit alphabetically, was the delegate from Uruguay, and he was making many objections and giving many legal arguments. I thought, in order to save time, the delegate from Chile, who sat in the Commission on Human Rights, might explain some things to him, so I asked Mr. S. if he would have a talk with the delegate from Uruguay and explain certain things to him. He looked at me and said,

"I have been on the Human Rights Committee for quite some time and have become accustomed to this document, and you must let him become accustomed to it because it is an Anglo-Saxon document."

"But," I protested, "It is the result of eighteen nations and they were not all Anglo-Saxon nations."

He insisted, "It still is an Anglo-Saxon document. In time, the delegate from Uruguay will grow accustomed to it, but just now he is very much shocked, just as I was when I first read it."

I had been thinking that it was a joint document which we had produced and I was sure there were a great many things in it that were not the result of Anglo-Saxon thinking. You see how unaware we are of the fact that other

*The following is from a speech by Eleanor Roosevelt to Pi Lambda Theta at Columbia University, New York, March 30, 1949. The complete speech is published under the title "For Better World Understanding" in the *Pi Lambda Theta Journal* 22 (May 1949): 196–203. *Phi Delta Kappan* has excerpted sections of this presentation which supplement the preceding speech.

nations think of things that come up in terms of not representing their thinking, or their type of law, or their type of religious feeling, and, as my Chilean colleague said, it had taken him time to grow accustomed to it but finally he began to agree with the strange ideas that were Anglo-Saxon. I don't know whether it should always be just that way, for certainly sometimes we should become accustomed to thinking in their terms, as well as having them thinking in our terms. That flow backwards and forwards of ideas and understanding is one of the great contributions of the United Nations, but it isn't the only thing that must take place before we get to the bottom of what it is that divides people. The increase of intellectual understanding, the exchange of ideas, and the gradual coming to see what affects other people on the intellectual levels is very important, but there are other things, too.

I have thought a great deal, of course, about our first and most important difficulty, which is the U.S.S.R. I suppose you read what their delegates say to us. They say: "Perhaps in the military and economic sense you have the upper hand." (They never say, *"We have . . ."* they say *"perhaps."*) "But time is on our side. We can afford to wait, because our ideas are much stronger than yours; our ideas, our belief in communism, are going to gain the world. It makes a great appeal because we believe in basic human rights. We believe that all races, all people are equal; we believe that men and women are equal."

The Committee gets long dissertations about that equality and occasionally it will cause a funny incident to occur. One day we had listened for one hour to a gentleman talk on the equality of men and women in the U.S.S.R. A little later, he happened to accept an invitation to lunch with us that day. The Russians will seldom accept an invitation without another member of their delegation going along, but he came alone. At the table some remark was made and he turned to me and said, "That is just women's gossip," and I said, "Oh, no, if men and women are completely equal then there is no more 'women's gossip!' If you really believe they are equal in the U.S.S.R., then you must not say it is women's gossip; it is men and women's gossip."

He looked at me and said not another word.

When they state what they believe, they are very sure of their philosophy of equality, and they state it so simply that they are certain that the downtrodden people of the world will accept it much more easily than they will accept our democratic theories. They say, "Our government is a government of workers, for workers. Our economy is perhaps having a little hard time at present, but basically, as commodities increase, everybody will share alike. There will be none of this having a great deal for certain groups as you have in your decadent democracy; we will all share alike." That sounds simple, doesn't it? And, of course, there is something in what they say when one considers that they are offering these ideas to people who are perhaps, not more than a day away from famine. Nearly all of these people have seen small groups in their midst having a great deal and the masses having little, and to them these promises are very alluring. The question is whether people who are better off are willing to accept such promises with no proof. We Americans surely have difficulty making our promises sound as simple as theirs.

It is quite possible to know what goes wrong anywhere in our country, and those of us who really care can work to make our democracy better. Of course we cannot get in to see what happens in the U.S.S.R. and therefore it isn't profitable to make statements that can't be proved. I have had in my briefcase for two sessions a report from our embassy in the U.S.S.R. telling me a great many things which are probably true but are difficult to prove for no one has actually seen them. They are only hearsay. It is not our fault that we have not seen these things. We have not been allowed to see them. But I have never used that document.

In the last session of the 3rd Committee we had as a delegate, for a short time, from the United Kingdom, a young member of Parliament. This British delegate had sat through some pretty stiff attacks on the United Kingdom's colonial policy. There is never a time when we touch on the problems of a colonial country, that the U.S.S.R. goes not give us at least an hour of attack on the United Kingdom. I realized that our job was to get the Declaration of Human Rights accepted, and I knew that the U.S.S.R. would like very much to delay it so that we wouldn't have time to vote on it. Up to the time of the last meeting, they always abstained from voting, saying that they could not commit their government to an unfinished document, but at Paris it was a finished document, and it would be difficult to go home and say that they had abstained on a declaration of human rights. That was not going to be easy, so the delaying tactics were used to confuse us so that we would take longer. I am sorry to say that, unwittingly, a number of our other colleagues helped the delay. They were really interested in certain points and wanted to have a chance to talk them over. These colleagues were from the South American countries and they had a document on human rights in which they took great pride. They had the Declaration of Bogota and some of them were anxious, for reasons of pride, to have the same wording used in the universal declaration. Every time one of them would make a very long speech concerning this, it was amusing to watch one of the delegates from the U.S.S.R. or a satellite country go to him and say, "That was a most enlightening speech—wonderful—I hope tomorrow you will make another speech on some other point. We need enlightening." And it always meant tomorrow they made the other speech.

Also, the delegate from England couldn't take the constant attack on his country for all its colonial policies. The next day he spent one and a quarter hours answering the Russians, which of course he had to do. For if one fails to answer an accusation they were sure to say, "Oh, Mrs. Roosevelt did not answer yesterday, so of course what we said must be true." The United Kingdom delegate gave his rebuttal, which was fine, but he then proceeded to launch forth on an attack of the Russians which lasted well over an hour. If it had ended there, we could have spared the time, but instead we have two solid days, four full sessions, in which every member of the satellite states, as well as the U.S.S.R., answered the speech of the United Kingdom's delegate, and the U.S.S.R. could deny everything in it because it was hearsay; there was no complete proof. You can say that people who have come out of Russia have said certain things, but the U.S.S.R. can say that these people lie. Shortly after this incident, England sent a new delegate to serve on Committee III. This delegate was Mrs. Corbett Ashby. I immediately said to her, "Look, we have a declaration to get through. We have spent two days listening to attacks and the answers. Do you think it is more important to get the declaration through or to attack the U.S.S.R.?" While it is true that the Russians must be answered, Mrs. Ashby agreed that is was more important to get the Declaration of Human Rights through. By bringing the Declaration up for a vote, we would obligate the Russians to say why they had to abstain. This was more revealing for the rest of the world, and perhaps in the long run more revealing to them, than all the attacks we could have made. It certainly leaves less bitterness. I believe we must never compromise a principle. We must be very persistent, very patient, because we have a long way to go in understanding.

I was talking the other day to a very learned gentleman on how we could ever understand the U.S.S.R. He said, "Read Didemus," and I thought, "Oh, when will I get time to read Didemus, and why?" So I thought I had better ask honestly why I should read Didemus. He said, "Because all the rest of Europe received its civilization from Rome, but the Russians, from their first beginnings, drew their civilization from the Byzantines. You will find more explanation for Russia by going back to Byzantine thought than you will in trying to think of Russia as a part of the European scene." But I haven't had time to read Didemus. I am going to try, for I do know that there is a great deal for us to learn.

One thing that makes it hard to learn, is that we are never talking to people. You are always talking to government representatives who are saying what they were told to say. You never know what they think as individuals. Our delegation says what it thinks in the hope that it may be taken back to their country, for they have very extraordinary powers of memory and concentration, and I think they report very clearly.

You who are teachers probably understand some things that I am still groping about. I would like to know how it is possible for the Russian delegation to work in the way it does. There is no other delegation whose leader always takes part in the final argument in the General Assembly. But their leader never fails to argue, not only the things that were argued in committee, but every single point that has been worked over in every committee. He displays a complete grasp of every detail and every single thing that has happened during the work of that committee. With us, the United Kingdom, and nearly all the other delegations, the delegates who clear the work in the committees are the ones who argue the points in the final General Assembly. But Mr. Vishinsky has argued for the U.S.S.R. every time. . . .

The Declaration of Human Rights was looked upon as so important because many people believed it to be one of the things on which we might build understanding in the future, if enough nations could agree on what the basic rights and freedoms were. Even though the Declaration has no legal binding value, it is a document to be used for education in preparation for a Covenant. The Covenant won't cover many things, but the Declaration includes the aspirations that we hope, in time, to achieve. It was written with the aim in view that all the countries that accepted it would make a study of its ideas.

We have even included a resolution asking the governments to see that schools and colleges become sufficiently familiar with the document to quote from it and to discuss it intelligently. It is quite true that it has no legal binding value and that is why some people say, "It is just words—more words— and we have plenty of words—why do we bother with more words?" Well, the Declaration is only half of the Bill of Rights. The second part of the Covenant, if accepted, must be ratified by each nation and that will have legal binding value as a treaty. . . .

A criticism that is often made about this Declaration is that rights alone are set forth, but that with every right there goes a responsibility, and that those responsibilities are not set forth with each article. That was discussed for a very long time, and it was decided that, if you tried to set forth with each article all the responsibilities, it would make a very long and detailed document that would not have the same impact on people as a declaration that was shorter and more concise. After all, this is the Declaration of rights and freedoms, and so it was decided to have one article as a general over-all limitation and that reads—

> Everyone has duties to the community in which alone the free and full development of his personality is possible. In the exercise of his rights and freedoms, everyone is subject only to such limitations as are determined by law solely for the purpose of securing due recognition and respect for the rights and freedoms of others and of meeting the just requirements of morality, public order and the general welfare in a democratic society. These rights and freedoms may in no case be exercised contrary to the purposes and principles of the United Nations.

The feeling was that this article covered in a general way and would not detract from the really important thing which was to get down on paper, for people all over the world, with different backgrounds, customs, and stages of development, the basic idea that every individual had certain rights and freedoms that could not be taken away from him. It gave respect and importance to the individual, which is, of course, a basic tenet of democracy.

Now, I think, perhaps, you would be interested in the article on religion. We thought we had consulted most of the interested people who were represented by consultants in the Human Rights Commission. We found that one group had had no representation. They had never asked for it. But when it came to the final decision, that group differed among themselves as to the interpretation they could put on certain things in their own religious law, and they nearly voted against the whole Declaration because they did not think they could accept just one thing in this article. The article reads:

> Everyone has the right to freedom of thought, conscience and religion; this right includes freedom to change his religion or belief, and freedom,

either alone or in community with others and in public or private, to manifest his religion or belief in teaching, practice, worship and observance.

And the group that had not asked for representation and with whom we had not consulted beforehand was the large group of Mohammedans, and they said, through their representatives in Committee III. "We can't accept that because in our religion you may not change your belief." Saudi Arabia stuck to that until the end. And Saudi Arabia abstained from voting. Pakistan changed. And the statement of the head of their whole delegation before the Assembly was as follows: "I think our delegate misinterpreted the Koran. The Koran says that 'he who will shall believe; he who cannot believe shall disbelieve.' The only unforgivable sin is to be a hypocrite!" I repeat this statement at every opportunity, for I think it is something all of us would do well to remember. He voted for the Declaration.

Education

You might be interested in the article on education. There is one point in it that I regret very much and voted against, but it was included and I will tell you why when I have read it.

> 1. Everyone has the right to education. Education shall be free, at least in the elementary and fundamental stages. Elementary education shall be compulsory. Technical and professional education shall be made generally available and higher education shall be equally accessible to all on the basis of merit.
> 2. Education shall be directed to the full development of the human personality and to the strengthening of respect for human rights and fundamental freedoms. It shall promote understanding, tolerance and friendship among all nations, racial or religious groups, and shall further the activities of the United Nations for the maintenance of peace.
> 3. Parents have a prior right to choose the kind of education that shall be given to their children.

That number three was put in by the Catholic nations. They were very insistent on the right of the family and the right of parents. We realized that they said this because they aimed to prevent a repetition of Hitler's training of youth, and of course of the Communistic training of youth. On the other hand, this statement caused other difficulties to arise. For instance, I know families in my own country-area with whom one really had to fight to get them to allow their children to have more education than they themselves had had; I am not quite sure that always the parents' rights rather than the rights of children should be the permanent, final decision. I think the parents naturally have great rights. You couldn't educate children against the will of their parents along certain lines, but the children have a right to certain opportunities for education and should be allowed to take advantage of them. It was very difficult for me to accept paragraph 3, but I was outvoted. We had a full and complete argument, and it was easy to understand why anyone familiar with

Hitler's youth training, and Communistic training today, should want to safeguard their children against it. You do have to adjust to different countries at different times and anything that is completely rigid will put us in a straight-jacket. This, after all, is just a statement of standards and aspirations and a very good document for us to become educated upon—but when you come to the Covenant it is going to be extremely difficult and extremely necessary for us to watch every single thing that we agree to.

I can't tell you much more, but I hope that I have given you some idea of some of the problems that come in writing international documents and some of the problems that exist when you start out to really achieve world understanding. I have a feeling that in practice this document will do a great deal for even those countries where it will not be published. It will not be published in any of the satellite countries, but, curiously enough, knowledge seems to seep through even Iron Curtains. And I can't help but believe that working together on some of these things and writing them down may be a good basis for beginning a little more understanding and confidence. Much of our difficulty today lies in our fears. We fear the Russians; they fear us. How you get away from fear, I don't know yet. I am hoping that if we can stay together, and work together, each year that we live we perhaps will build a little more confidence and destroy a little of the fear. All of you who are going to teach the next generation—the generation that is going to live with this when we are dead—can perhaps teach them the willingness to be patient, to experiment, to believe in human beings even when they seem so contrary and so difficult. I get so angry sometimes with my U.S.S.R. colleagues. Then each time that I do, I say to myself, "Remember that you really like these people as people. If you could meet them as people you would like them. So try to begin again with good will, with a sense of objectivity, of understanding why it is so hard for them. They couldn't possibly accept this document because freedom of movement is one of the articles. They don't allow any freedom of movement. There are lots of things that they can't accept, and it will take them a long time. Children growing up today are going to live in a world that is a very adventurous world and not a very secure one. After all, many generations have lived that kind of life. It takes more character, more calm, but perhaps the challenge of today is the ability to stay in the United Nations and watch ourselves as the leading democratic nation of the world, a nation which all the world watches. If they can see that our beliefs are as strong as theirs and that we are not going backward, they might begin to live in the same world with us and make some compromises. That is almost as important as to have more military power and more economic power. We have a difficult job because all of our failures are seen. At the same time, our successes are seen and, for that reason, I hope we are going to be strong enough, and imaginative enough, and take the future with enough spirit of adventure so that we will live it with joy and never grow hopeless. Never get a feeling that we cannot succeed, because I think with the help of all of you, and the help of many other people in our country, we can succeed. All we can do is pray that we will grow more tomorrow and that others will grow with us, and together we will be able to win a peaceful world."

115

What I Think of the United Nations

I know that a great many people in the United States and other nations today wonder what is the use of having a United Nations. "It is just a debating society. It doesn't do anything." Those are criticisms one can hear almost anywhere, though to my mind they are quite unjustified.

I would like to ask everyone who has made or been tempted to make some such criticism of the United Nations to remember just one fact: When the United Nations was set up in the spring of '45 we thought that as soon as the war came to an end we would make the peace. And the organization that was set up was to function in a peaceful world, maintaining the new peace and creating an atmosphere in which lasting peace could grow and develop. But peace has never been made, and because of that there is dumped in the lap of the United Nations a large number of political questions it was never expected or designed to deal with.

In addition, in this period in which no peace has been made, a rift has developed and widened between the world's two great nations. As long as they cannot come to an agreement on certain questions, the complete organization of the UN is impossible.

For example, they cannot agree on what shall happen in the realm of atomic energy. Therefore, there can be no agreement on what kind of force there should be at the disposal of the United Nations, and until the world has force within the United Nations it is obliged to have force somewhere else. That is one reason you hear such constant complaints as, "Why do we have to pour money into Greece?—And why must we build up the armies of the Atlantic Pact nations? Why must we do this and why that? If the United Nations were really doing its job, there would be no need of our doing it."

But the United Nations cannot use force, or even the threat of force to maintain peace until its member nations are able to complete their organization, establishing collective force. And there cannot be collective force until there is some kind of agreement as to how communism and democracy are to live in the world together.

All this means, of course, that we must look at the United Nations from a different point of view, emphasizing what it *has* been *permitted* to accomplish rather than what it *had* been *expected* to do.

The Security Council, for example, was intended to take care of problems that were a threat to world peace. It was expected to use force if necessary. It can render decisions, and has done so, stopping or localizing warfare in a number of areas and eliminating other threats to the peace. But it has no

United Nations World 3 (August 1949): 39–41, 48.

collective force to put behind its decisions. And while moral force has value—as events in Palestine, Kashmir, Indonesia and elsewhere have proved—moral force has not the same value as the ability to say to an aggressor, "You must stop or be stopped." When you put moral force behind something, you have to persuade—you cannot order—and persuasion takes far longer and requires far greater understanding.

Important as the Security Council is, however, I prefer to focus attention on those other parts of the organization which the Charter set up to encourage in the world an atmosphere in which peace might grow.

The people who wrote the Charter did not assume that peace was going to drop down on us like a beneficent blanket from heaven and be with us forever. They were quite realistic about it. They knew that, even though we made a peace, we would have to work year in and year out, day in and day out, to keep that peace, and to see that the atmosphere of the world was conducive to its growth. They knew that throughout the world there were tremendous difficulties, that it would take a long while, for instance, to make it possible for the people of our country to understand what was happening to someone in South Africa, or in India, or in Siam.

They set up, therefore, some specialized agencies, such as the Food and Agriculture Organization, to begin to do things in the world that would increase understanding and, being done on a world scale, would help bring about world understanding of special problems.

I can recall very well the days when we thought that our Great Plains were doomed to be largely desert. But we started then something which was called a "shelter belt" area. Many thought that it was the greatest nonsense in the world. At the time some of the foresters came to me and said: "The President is crazy. It just can't be." But about eight years later I saw people in the "shelter belt" region, who had not believed in it, but who suddenly found that their fields were holding soil again. And they were growing crops where they had not been able to grow them before.

That special problem of wind erosion of farmland is one a limited number of Americans now know how to meet. It is one of the multitude of agricultural problems that need to be tackled on a world scale, and for the first time it is being done. For the first time a group of nations is meeting together to find ways of holding and restoring the world's topsoil. It is really exciting because it is a fundamental thing. The nations in FAO are trying to prevent, by providing more food, the wars which have resulted when hunger forces peoples to move out of devastated areas.

Another important specialized agency is the World Health Organization. To be sure all the nations aren't in it yet, but it is functioning—and very effectively. This year it is attacking a problem that a citizen of the United States may not think important because we have faced and met it pretty well. Tuberculosis isn't a terrifying disease to us. But when I was in Paris at the United Nations Assembly last autumn, I met with a good many students. One night a group came in to see me. They wanted to get in touch with young people of similar interests in this country.

In the course of conversation an older woman who was in charge said their major needs were clothes and food. I asked if they had a good deal of illness. She said, "Oh, yes, Madame. Fifty percent of our students are either tubercular or on the border."

What would you think if 50 percent of the students in an American university were either tubercular or on the border?

When I was in Holland a year ago last spring I went with Queen Juliana to see the first and only—and small—hospital where they were caring for young tuberculous students who couldn't keep up with their university studies. Queen Juliana told me that they didn't know yet the percentage of tuberculosis among their children. She guessed that of the resistance movement youngsters who would soon attain university age there were probably between 40 and 50 percent who had the disease.

Conditions similar to those in Holland can be found in other countries, and it is vital that tuberculosis be attacked on a world scale. This would be true even if we Americans were the only ones concerned. Our children are going to have to run the world with these Dutch and French and other children and, unless physical and mental and spiritual help comes to the youngsters of all the countries in the world, our children are going to have a hard time—a harder time than we had. No matter how healthy and fortunate otherwise they may be, the world isn't going to be a normal place to live in if the peoples of other nations are warped by disease and hunger and frustration.

FAO and WHO, and 11 other specialized agencies, are connected with the United Nations through the Economic and Social Council. Under the Council also, set up almost immediately after its organization, is the Human Rights Commission. I want to cite a few of the difficulties confronting this organization which should make you more tolerant of its operation and help you realize how trying it is to work in an international group.

Many persons feel the Human Rights Commission can be important because it has written the Universal Declaration of Human Rights which was adopted by the General Assembly in Paris and which may become one of the pillars of world peace in the future.

After I came home from Paris I had a letter from a gentleman who asked: "How could you as the United States delegate accept Article I of the Universal Declaration of Human Rights when our declaration [in the US Bill of Rights] is different?"

The reason, of course, is that there were 58 nations sitting around the table in Committee Three, which brought the draft to the Assembly, and there were 58 nations in the General Assembly and of these 48 nations approved it. Committee Three spent four weeks on the first three articles and we made three changes. In Article I we changed the familiar, "All men are created equal," to, "All human beings are born free and equal in dignity and rights."

Why say all human beings? Because in Committee Three, which deals with humanitarian, social and cultural matters, there are a number of women. They are the ones who changed "all men" to "all human beings." Many of them come from countries where the great mass of women have no equality and no recognition, and they are very conscious of that situation. That's the first change, and it illustrates that conditions in different parts of the world have great effect on an international document and on an international situation.

The differences in languages are another source of problems. We have five official languages—English, French, Russian, Chinese and Spanish—into which all statements are translated. It frequently happens that there is a disagreement between the man who speaks and his interpreter. The speaker will stop the translator—we listen with earphones to whichever of the five languages we wish—and say he isn't getting the meaning, and sometimes the speaker will take over the translating for a sentence or two himself. When the Russian delegate did just this at one of our meetings, I told him his insistence on making the English translation, "no discrimination because of estate," would mean very little to us. So he changed it to, "no discrimination because of class." I said: "We think we are getting away from classes that divide human beings, so let's not say 'class.' " He finally settled on "birth" as translating his idea. And then the Chinese delegate, who is much more of a stickler for proper English than most of us who speak it, said he would accept "birth" but that it must be preceded by the words, "race or—." This did not please the USSR delegate and it took us some time not only to get the right word but to put it in the place which was satisfactory.

Religion is another subject that creates problems for us. In our article on religion we thought we had satisfied everyone, but we found we had overlooked a final consultation with the Mohammedans. As a consequence they had very nearly decided to abstain from voting or vote against the article because of an apparently minor clause that said any person had a right to change his or her belief. But some feel the Koran does not allow a Mohammedan to change his religious belief. In the end, however, Pakistan, Lebanon and some of the other Arab states decided that the Koran permitted a change in belief. Saudi Arabia held to the last that a change was not permissible, and it cast one of the abstaining votes.

These international differences and intricacies are all so interesting, though often discouraging, because one is constantly learning new things about other peoples—learning to understand them and cooperate with them. But the problems are so many and we need to know so much that, when an agreement is finally reached, one often wonders how it ever was achieved.

The agreements are coming, however. As the delegates learn to appreciate and sympathize with each other's points of view, one can see the growth of a new spirit of trust—of willingness to talk frankly in an earnest search for compromise. I have not yet found this to be true with the Soviet delegates—I wish I had—perhaps because they are always conscious of being government representatives, and do not permit themselves to be themselves. They are tied by the line they have to follow. But with the other delegates there is a growing urgency to find areas of understanding and agreement.

It is going to take a great deal of time to find and develop such areas with the Eastern European nations. But we have to recognize that they must be found, and that we must do much of the searching.

We know that the USSR and the communist parties are making promises for communism that sound very attractive to the downtrodden peoples of the world. We know that we should recognize that the fight today is in Asia, in Africa and in the islands of the Pacific among the peoples who have felt that they are looked down on by the white race. One cannot observe the United Nations in action—one cannot look around that great table at which now sit the representatives of 59 nations without realizing that the white race is a minority race in the world, and that there are more peoples believing in other religions than there are Christians.

Our first task in finding ways to get along with the Communists is to find ways to make democracy mean what we say it does. And we have to make democracy work in our own country where other peoples can see it function. They can't see inside Russia, but here they can see everything that happens, and can see that freedom of information is in itself one of our first advantages.

This country can, and must, show that democracy isn't just a word, but that it means regards for the rights of human beings; that it means that every human being, regardless of race or creed or color, has equal dignity and equal rights; that it means that we care about the kind of freedom which allows people to grow, and allows them to develop their own potentialities and their own interests; that we recognize that democracy, as a basis for government, has to assume certain obligations to its citizens.

It will not be enough to establish as fact that we have military superiority. It will not be enough to prove our economic superiority. We are going to have to persuade the Russians and their friends that compromise is not only desirable but quite possible, and that it has to be reached. We must somehow convince them—and the most stubborn on our own side—that their ideology and ours can live in the world together without open conflict.

Finally, if democracy—and the blessings of it both as a way of government and a way of life—are going to win this contest for the support of the peoples of the world, we must have moral conviction and spiritual leadership. That is the challenge to America today. That is the challenge that we face in strengthening and making the United Nations work as a whole. Those are the standards that we set ourselves and, in the interest of the future, those are the standards by which we must live.

116

A Front on Which We May Serve

It was once widely believed that such diseases as cancer, poliomyelitis and heart disease attack only the comparatively well-fed and long-lived peoples. The Africans, Asiatics and the Indians of the Americas were regarded as impervious to these scourges. As time has passed, we have learned that our ignorance of the world facts makes almost any conclusion virtually useless at this time.

Certainly diagnosis of poliomyelitis has greatly improved in the US. This may largely account for the rise of diagnosed cases from around 7,000 a year in the 1930s to around 10,000 today. In the underdeveloped areas of the world, doctors have only recently begun to look for these "civilized" diseases. And this must certainly be the explanation for such apparently shocking rises as Algeria's of 400% since the 1930s, of Angola from one case to 15, of Panama from two cases to 33 in 1947, of Yugoslavia from 46 to 171 in 1949. Even healthy Uruguay's polio increased from five cases a year to 128 in 1947.

It can hardly be supposed that the totals of actual cases have multiplied in any such ratio in any of these countries. It seems probable that the cases were always there, though scientists have kept an open mind to the possibility that polio is actually on the increase everywhere. All we actually know is that diagnosis has somewhat improved all over the world, that the doctors are finding cases where they had not previously looked for them, and that we are constantly being shown an enlarging problem of world health.

This universal condition of ignorance came to light in a most touching episode in 1946. An American boy named Jeffrey Kroll was touring Mexico City with a group of 65 schoolmates, when he contracted polio. The Mexican doctors were able to diagnose the disease correctly but that was all they could do. There were no artificial respirators or "iron lungs" in Mexico. This sad news stirred the boy's parents and young friends and his uncle, Brooks Mendell, the well-known US Air Force officer-teacher in self-protection, health education and rehabilitation. Mr. Mendell flew a portable respirator to Mexico but then it was too late. The boy was dead.

Mr. Mendell, whose favorite nephew Jeffrey Kroll had been, thereupon undertook one of those personal crusades which are sometimes so much more effective than formal official programs. He had discovered that Mexico's doctors had a very limited familiarity with polio and no specialists in the treatment of the disease. "The people," he has said, "thought it a disgrace to admit to polio. Any one who had been crippled by the disease was likely to explain that he had simply fallen off a horse."

United Nations World 4 (June 1950): 50–51.

A similar shame might be felt and a similar explanation given in North Africa, in India or Iran or China.

However, Mr. Mendell made Mexico his personal responsibility. The first thing to be done, which he could do, was to get some respirators to Mexico. The Jeffrey Kroll Foundation was formed; a fund was collected from the boy's family and friends; and finally Mr. Mendell bought and delivered two iron lungs to Mexico City in a plane personally provided by Mexico's President Manuel Aleman. Later he followed this up with the gift to Mexico of a library dealing with the history, cause, prevention and treatment of the disease, and the rehabilitation of its victims.

Something about Mr. Mendell's one-handed efforts for the welfare of the country where his nephew had died unnecessarily, caught the imagination first of the Mexican press and then of the Mexican people.

He had persuaded the National Foundation for Infantile Paralysis in the US to set up fellowships for other countries' scientists and doctors in US universities, hospitals and laboratories. He was empowered to offer several of these to the Mexican Government. Mexico declined the fellowships with thanks, preferring to stand on its own feet. It sent seven scientists to the US to study polio in the country where most of the existing knowledge is concentrated.

Now seriously mobilized, Mexico's statesmen began to conceive that, while the larger nations were preoccupied with the problems of peace, such small countries as Mexico might worthily take upon themselves the cause of the improvement of man's health everywhere. Mexico established a subsidized research institute and took the lead in the United Nations to prosecute a truly global health program, which is under way today. Mexico enlarged its own program to embrace the whole field of virus study, including plant and animal diseases.

Virus research is on the agenda of the World Health Organization of the United Nations. WHO's publications have described the worldwide appearance of polio as "the most ominous of unsolved mysteries which the last half-century has posed to epidemiologists."

As if to corroborate this, India last year broke out with its first recognized epidemic of polio, centered in Delhi and Bombay. Like Mexico, India found itself tragically short of iron lungs. Its government promptly cabled WHO a request for iron lungs, rush.

Unharassed by the difficulties that had hampered Mr. Mendell as a private citizen, WHO was able to round up 16 iron lungs in a few days and load them on planes bound for India. There is no doubt that an appreciable number of lives were saved. In at least this one instance, the whole world had put up a united defense to the enemy which attacks simultaneously at a thousand points.

WHO later sent a team of polio specialists to examine the situation in India. It found every indication that India has had polio for at least the past fifty years, that last year's epidemic was by no means an unprecedented phenomenon. It further reported that India has far too few orthopedic surgeons and that physical therapy does not exist in India. Following the example set by the "March of Dimes" in the US to stimulate public attention and fund-raising, India now has its own "March of Annas" (an anna equals a little over a penny).

WHO has asked its member nations whether they would join in an international pool of iron lungs from which any country might draw at the moment it found itself in the grip of an epidemic. The proposal has the heartwarming quality to be found among the neighbors in any village when sickness strikes in a single home and would tend to create one world on the level of the deepest emotion, of help in time of trouble.

Such neighborliness is, furthermore, far from being entirely unselfish. It was shown very clearly in 1946 and 1947 that a polio epidemic cannot be confined within any given national boundaries. In the former year polio took on epidemic proportions in the US, but at the same time it was also raging in such far-spread places as Argentina (525 cases), Puerto Rico (292), Dutch East Indies (198), Iceland (471), Norway (860) and Switzerland (932). The following year it was extended to the UK (8,000 cases), Austria (3,900), Hungary (1,000) and Madagascar (242). But on the island of Car Nicobar, the rate of cases reached the unbelievable high of 8,000 per 100,000 people.

In 1949, the epidemic swept the US total to 42,382 cases. In the same period, Iceland's cases had risen to 579, which is a rate of 494 per 100,000 people, Sweden's to 2,584 and Japan's to 3,133. In the faraway Congo there were 207 cases and on Mauritius 362.

This is a war that is never cold. The governments and the United Nations are best equipped to prosecute the main defense for mankind. But there are certainly many hard-pressed sectors where individuals, like Mr. Mendell, have an opportunity to fight a local action and prepare the way for the main forces. It is fervently to be hoped that we will all dedicate ourselves to searching out a front where we may serve.

117

Statement on Draft Covenant on Human Rights

I am pleased that we are now undertaking to consider the substantive questions relating to the Draft Covenant on Human Rights in this Committee. It is particularly important at this time that the Assembly give adequate consideration to human rights.

Three years ago, when the General Assembly met in Paris, the chairman of the United States delegation, Secretary Marshall, said that the "systematic and deliberate denials of basic human rights lie at the root of most of our troubles and threaten the work of the United Nations. . . ." In this Assembly, Secretary Acheson made clear that these words are even more pertinent today than they were in 1948.

It is a tragic commentary on the status of civilization in the middle of the twentieth century that the systematic and deliberate denials of human rights by some governments are so widespread in certain areas of the world that they are almost taken for granted. The kind of callous brutality which would have shocked the conscience of mankind a century ago is now unfortunately a commonplace occurrence in those areas.

All members of the United Nations have a responsibility, individually and collectively, to see that the lights of freedom are not further extinguished throughout the world.

Every member has a responsibility to see that the rights of men are safeguarded, for no country is perfect in protecting the individual rights of its citizens.

Three years ago in this same city the General Assembly proclaimed the Universal Declaration of Human Rights. That Declaration has already become the yardstick by which all can measure the conduct of governments. The language of that Declaration has been written into the constitution of a number of states. The United Nations must now move ahead to develop new methods for advancing human liberty and for translating human rights and fundamental freedoms into action. One of these methods is the Draft International Covenant on Human Rights.

The task of drafting the Covenant, of putting human rights into treaty form, is not an easy one. We have been working in the United Nations on this draft Covenant since 1947.

I would like in particular to discuss the matter of economic, social, and cultural rights.

Department of State Bulletin, December 31, 1951, pp. 1059, 1064–1066.

When the General Assembly last year called on the Commission on Human Rights to include economic, social, and cultural provisions in the Covenant on Human Rights, the United States fully cooperated in the 5-weeks' session of the Commission this spring in Geneva in drafting these provisions. The United States delegation voted last year in the General Assembly against the inclusion of economic, social, and cultural rights in the same Covenant with civil and political rights. At no time, however, did my delegation to the Commission on Human Rights question the responsibility of the Commission to prepare a draft with these provisions for the consideration of the General Assembly. The United States delegation to the Commission felt that, as a member of a technical commission, we should cooperate in doing that which the General Assembly had asked us to do at that time.

We did vote at the end of the Commission session for a resolution introduced by the delegate of India requesting a reconsideration by the General Assembly of the question of including economic, social, and cultural rights in the same Covenant with civil and political rights. This resolution did not, however, interrupt the technical work of the Commission. This Indian resolution pointed out that economic, social, and cultural rights, though equally fundamental and therefore important, formed a separate category of rights from that of the civil and political rights in that they were not justiciable rights and their method of implementation was different.

At this session of the General Assembly we have before us a resolution of the Economic and Social Council inviting the General Assembly to reconsider its decision of last year. It is entirely appropriate for us in the General Assembly this year to reconsider this matter. In view of the importance of the Covenant on Human Rights, we must be willing to study and restudy the basic problems involved in the drafting of this document. There may be differences of opinion in this Committee on the question of whether there should be one covenant or two covenants, but at no time should anyone argue that this Committee should avoid a further consideration of this very important question.

Principal Provisions of the ECOSOC Resolution

The resolution of the Economic and Social Council points out that there are certain differences between the provisions on civil and political rights and the provisions on economic, social, and cultural rights and that these differences warrant a consideration of two covenants rather than a single covenant. The Council resolution also refers to the difficulties which may flow from embodying in one covenant two different kinds of rights and obligations.

Let us examine these differences which have been recognized by the Commission in a number of ways in drafting the provisions of the Covenant.

In the first place, article 19 of the draft Covenant recognizes that the economic, social, and cultural provisions are objectives to be achieved "progressively." This obligation is to be distinguished from the obligation applicable to the civil and political rights in the Covenant. In the case of civil and political rights, states ratifying the Covenant will be under an obligation to take necessary steps fairly quickly to give effect to these rights. A much longer period of time is clearly contemplated under the Covenant for the achievement of the economic, social, and cultural provisions. This is obvious and is, of course, to be expected.

For example, in the field of health, it would be necessary to undertake training programs for doctors and nurses, to establish experimental stations, build hospitals, obtain hospital beds, medical supplies, etc. Similarly, in the field of education, it will take a considerable period of time to train teachers, write school texts, obtain necessary supplies, build schools, et cetera. In these fields, it will take years to reach the objectives set forth in the Covenant. As you well know, my delegation fully supports the attainment of these objectives. I am simply stressing the longer period of time it will of course take and the long-range planning that will be necessary to achieve the objectives of the economic, social, and cultural provisions of the Covenant.

It has taken years to achieve progress in the United States in these fields, as it will no doubt take years to achieve further progress in these fields in my country as well as in other countries.

For example, with respect to education in the United States, which under our federal system is essentially a matter within the jurisdiction of our states, in 1900, in one-third of the United States, there was no compulsory-school-attendance law and in only a few sections of the country was there legislation requiring compulsory school attendance until the age of 16. Fifty years later, all sections of the United States require school attendance for all boys and girls at least until the age of 16, and in some areas school attendance is required until the age of 17 or 18. Since 1910 we have increased our expenditures per student in our schools 300 percent.

In the field of health in the United States, it has taken us 30 years to reduce infant mortality by more than two-thirds. Pneumonia and tuberculosis, which were the two leading causes of death in the United States in 1900, now are in sixth and seventh places as causes of death.

I mention these instances, not to claim we have achieved our goals in these fields but simply to indicate that it takes a long time to move toward these economic, social, and cultural objectives. In contrast, in the case of civil and political rights, it is anticipated that these rights will be effectuated promptly. It is this time difference between these two types of rights that I am stressing.

A second difference between the civil and political provisions and the economic, social, and cultural provisions is the manner in which the obligation is expected to be performed. In the case of the civil and political rights, they can in general be achieved by the enactment of appropriate legislation, enforced under effective administrative machinery. On the other hand, it is recognized that economic, social, and cultural progress and development cannot be achieved simply by the enactment of legislation and its enforcement. Private as well as public action is necessary. The Commission on Human Rights repeatedly rejected the proposal by two members of the Commission to limit the achievement of economic, social, and cultural rights solely through state action. The Commission fully recognized the importance of private as well as governmental action for the achievement of these rights.

A third difference between the civil and political provisions and the economic, social, and cultural provisions relates to the difference in the implementation contemplated. Initially the Commission on Human Rights drafted provisions for the establishment of a Human Rights Committee to which complaints by one state against another state may be filed. The Commission did not then have time at its session this spring to decide whether this machinery should also be applicable to the economic, social, and cultural provisions, but there actually was general sentiment in the Commission that this complaint machinery should be limited to the civil and political provisions of the Covenant. It was felt by those with whom I discussed this matter in the Commission that this machinery is not appropriate for the economic, social, and cultural provisions of the Covenant, since these rights are to be achieved progressively and since the obligations of states with respect to these rights were not as precise as those with respect to the civil and political rights. These members of the Commission thought that it would be preferable, with respect to the economic, social, and cultural rights, to stress the importance of assisting states to achieve economic, social, and cultural progress rather than to stress the filing of complaints against states in this field.

Instead of a complaint procedure, a reporting procedure was devised by the Commission with respect to the progress made in the observance of the economic, social, and cultural provisions of the Covenant.

A fourth difference between the civil and political rights and the economic, social, and cultural rights relates to the drafting of these rights. The economic, social, and cultural provisions were necessarily drafted in broad language as contrasted to the civil and political provisions. For example, article 22 simply provides that "The States Parties to the Covenant recognize the right of everyone to social security." It was thought in the Commission that since economic, social, and cultural provisions were being stated in terms of broad objectives, general language would be adequate.

It seems to my delegation that these four basic differences between the civil and political rights and the economic, social, and cultural rights warrant the separation of the present provisions of the Covenant into two covenants, one covenant on civil and political rights and another covenant on economic, social, and cultural rights. By a separation of these rights into two separate covenants we would avoid a great deal of confusion that is naturally inherent in a combination of all these different provisions in one covenant.

Equality of Importance in the Two Groups of Rights

Of course, I realize that some members of this Committee argue for a single covenant to include all the provisions now before us. The principal argument urged by those pressing this view is that there should be no differentiations in importance between civil and political rights and economic, social, and cultural rights. In the proposal that I wish to make to the Committee there is no question raised with respect to the importance of one group of rights as against another group of rights. I consider each group of rights of equal importance. My proposal would maintain this equality of importance.

My delegation proposes that two covenants of equal importance be completed in the United Nations simultaneously and be opened for signature and ratification at the same time. Neither one nor the other covenant would be called the first or the second covenant. Each of the two covenants would be on human rights, one setting forth the civil and political rights, and the other setting forth the economic, social, and cultural rights. We would request the Commission on Human Rights to prepare both of these covenants for the consideration of the General Assembly next year.

If members of the Committee will look at the present text of the Covenant, they will observe how naturally its parts may be divided into two covenants. The provisions on civil and political rights are in parts I, II, and IV. These parts can constitute one covenant. The economic, social, and cultural provisions are in parts III and V. These parts can constitute another covenant. Part VI contains general provisions which should accordingly be repeated in both covenants.

The basic differences between civil and political rights and economic, social, and cultural rights warrant this division into two covenants. The option will, of course, remain open for countries wishing to ratify both covenants at once to do so. To insist on the inclusion of all the provisions in one covenant will delay the coming into force of any covenant on human rights. A separation of these provisions into two covenants would accelerate their ratification by many states.

I hope that this proposal that I have made will be supported and will facilitate reaching agreement in the Committee on the question of economic, social, and cultural rights. The situation this year is very different from the situation last year in the General Assembly. At that time we were considering the drafting of a first covenant on human rights, containing only civil and political rights. A covenant on economic, social, and cultural rights was proposed to be drafted at a later date. Now that the Commission on Human Rights has drafted provisions on economic, social, and cultural rights, we are in a position to visualize two covenants, simultaneously completed, one on civil and political rights and the other on economic, social, and cultural rights. This changed situation warrants a decision by the General Assembly calling for two covenants rather than one covenant.

I will not at this time discuss other aspects of the covenant. I may comment on these other matters later. I have devoted my attention in these remarks to the importance of drafting two covenants, one on civil and political rights, and the other on economic, social, and cultural rights, because I feel this to be the most important question facing us.

118

Reply to Attacks on U.S. Attitude Toward Human Rights Covenant

This statement is a reply to the views expressed by Byelorussia, Czechoslovakia, Poland, the Ukraine, and the U.S.S.R. concerning the United States in this Committee. My observations in this statement accordingly relate to these five countries.

I am interested that these five countries place so much stress on the unity of the provisions of the Universal Declaration of Human Rights in our debates here. In 1948 those five countries did not vote for the Declaration. At that time they were critical of it. Now they cite it for their own purposes. They seem to praise the Declaration one time and minimize its importance another time, so that I must question the sincerity of their reliance on the Declaration at this point.

The delegates of a number of the countries expressed concern that an "illusory" Covenant on Human Rights might be drafted in the United Nations. The term "illusory" is descriptive of the type of covenant which the delegates of these countries are seeking to have drafted in the United Nations. For example, the Soviet Union has repeatedly taken the initiative in the General Assembly and in the Commission on Human Rights for the elimination of any provision in the Covenant on implementation. In the General Assembly last year, the Soviet Union proposed that these articles be deleted on the ground that "their inclusion would constitute an attempt at intervention in the domestic affairs of states and would encroach on their States sovereignty." This proposal was rejected in the Third Committee last year in a roll-call vote. Only the five members of this Committee now attacking the United States voted for this proposal. A similar proposal was rejected by the Commission on Human Rights at its 1951 session.

These countries protest that the implementation of the provisions of the Covenant would be "shameful." What nonsense is this? A Covenant on Human Rights would indeed be illusory if the proposal of the U.S.S.R. were accepted to delete all implementation provisions from it. It seems to me that freedom must be preserved primarily as we were reminded yesterday. The right to think and freedom to speak freely are among the most important rights, and some of you may realize that these are rights that have become rather illusory in some countries.

Even Mr. Vishinksy himself acknowledges the lack of freedom in his country when he observes in the book he edited on *The Law of the Soviet State*

Department of State Bulletin, January 14, 1952, pp. 59–61.

that in his state "there is and can be no place for freedom of speech, press, and so on, for the foes of socialism." Thus he proclaims a so-called freedom for only those supporting the dictates of the state. Freedom is not really freedom unless you can differ in thought and in expression of your thought.

The speakers from these five countries insist over and over again a condition of perfection exists in their countries. It always seems to me that when things are so absolutely perfect that it would almost shine out and you would not have to express it so frequently. I can only say that I wish it were possible for all of us to be allowed to go to the Soviet Union, for example, to see for ourselves the actual conditions which exist there. It would be very helpful if even some impartial observers were allowed to report to us on the actual conditions existing there.

Now let me turn to the charge made by some of the delegates of these five countries that the United States is disregarding the interests of the Negroes in our country. Unfortunately there are instances of American Negroes being victims of unreasoning racial prejudice in my country. However, we do not condone these acts in the United States. We do everything possible to overcome and eliminate such discrimination and racial prejudice as may still exist. Racial discrimination in my country is irreconcilable with the fundamental principles of humanity and justice which are embodied in our Bill of Rights.

The Negro in the U.S.

Affirmative steps are continually being taken to combat racial discrimination. Recently the President of the United States issued an Executive Order to insure protection against racial discrimination in employment under Government contracts.

The President has on several occasions established advisory commissions to provide evaluations of the progress being made in the United States. The recommendations of these commissions have served to spur further action to obtain the equality we are seeking in my country. Channing Tobias, now on the United States delegation to the United Nations, was one of the Negroes who served on some of these commissions. Some of the recommendations and reports of those commissions were quoted here which show that we do not hide anything that is wrong.

Acts of prejudice and discrimination by private individuals or groups in my country are more than merely deplored by the Government and by the vast majority of the people of the United States. Not only through laws but also by the process of education and in many other ways, efforts are constantly being made to eliminate racial discrimination. It is the official policy of the U.S. Government, as expressed on many occasions by President Truman, that the remaining imperfections in our practice of democracy, which result from the conduct of small groups of our people, must be corrected as soon as possible.

Increased activity in the political life of our country has been characteristic of Negro Americans. They have become a vital factor in the life of our local, State, and National Government. A reflection of this is seen in the number of Negroes holding Government Civil Service appointments. In 1938 there were 80,000 Negroes holding such appointments; this number has increased to 270,000. Not only has there been an increase in the number of such appointments, but also they are constantly assuming more and more responsible positions in the Government.

Negroes in the United States are voting in increasing numbers in all sections of our country.

It was suggested here that in certain places they were still having difficulty under the poll-tax laws. Those laws are rapidly being changed and in many parts of the country where it was not possible it is now possible for Negro citizens to vote.

In addition, the years from 1940 to the present have seen the election of Negro citizens to a number of important local, state, and national offices.

At the same time I wish to point out we do not claim to have reached perfection. We feel that our recognition of how much more yet remains to be done is a source of strength to us because it serves as a stimulant to press ahead with our task in this respect.

It so happens that the very countries which are criticizing the United States in this Committee are not themselves progressing in the fields of human rights and fundamental freedoms in their own countries. That may be only because of the difficulty of communication, but it seems to us that there is a great silence among the people of those countries. It is the silence of a people shut up behind an Iron Curtain where human rights and life are being stifled.

I will not take the time of the Committee to list all the many economic and social advances taking place in my country. They are well-known to all of you even though the five countries to whom I am addressing my remarks repeatedly disclaim knowledge of these facts. Many of you have traveled in the United States. I will simply mention, however, one point—the number of hours per week that the working man is now working in my country. The Federal Fair Labor Standards Act has established a standard workweek of 40 hours by requiring penalty payments for overtime labor. The average of hours worked in all manufacturing industries has now declined to 40½ hours a week. In the railroad transportation industry, the average is 40½ hours a week. In power laundries 42 hours a week is the average. In textile mills, production workers average 41 hours a week. In printing and publishing, workers average slightly less than 40 hours a week.

The charge has also been made that the United States favors two covenants on human rights instead a of a single covenant because the United States does not favor economic and social progress in other countries. This is obviously a ridiculous and false argument. It perhaps is unnecessary to answer this argument, since its falsity is so obvious; yet, I should stop for a few minutes to answer it frankly, since from time to time by the repetition of a particular argument, its falsity may soon be forgotten and the fact that it has been repeated so many times without answer tends to lull some into thinking that there perhaps is some merit to the assertion.

What does the record show?

U.S. Aid to Other Countries

The United States Government, in the course of the past 6 years, has made available over 30 billion dollars in the form of loans and grants to various countries. Of this amount, a total of over 5½ billion dollars had been made available to countries in underdeveloped areas. This financial assistance by the U.S. Government does not include our subscription of 635 million dollars to the International Bank. Nor does it include contributions which we have made to U.N. programs such as the International Children's Emergency Fund, the International Refugee Organization, Relief and Rehabilitation for Refugees of Palestine, and the U.N. expanded Technical Assistance Program, contributions which have in large part been used to assist in the improvement of economic and social conditions in underdeveloped areas.

During the fiscal year 1951 alone, the U.S. Government made available on a grant basis over a quarter of a billion dollars for programs of technical and economic assistance of underdeveloped areas.

As is well-known in this Committee, of the total financial contributions to UNICEF—some 155 million dollars—the United States has contributed about 100 million dollars.

Of the 5½ billion dollars made available to underdeveloped areas during the past 6 years by the United States, almost 1½ billion dollars was made available by the U.S. Export-Import Bank. This assistance has been in the form of loans for economic-development purposes to Latin America, the Near East, Africa, and Asia. During a recent period of 1 year, the Bank loaned over 395 million dollars. Of this amount over 96 percent went to underdeveloped areas.

Meeting the needs of underdeveloped areas for basic facilities in such fields as transportation, power, communications, and public health serves as a springboard for attaining higher standards of living for the people in these areas.

I have cited these figures of capital made available for economic development from the United States not for the figures themselves, nor for self-praise. I have cited them only as concrete evidence that the Government and people of the United States are very much interested in the economic development of other countries—and in more than an academic way.

The Congress of the United States this year decided to increase the lending authority of the Export-Import Bank an additional 1 billion dollars. This brings the basic lending capacity of the bank up to 4½ billion dollars at the present time.

In addition, Congress recently appropriated over 400 million dollars to support a widespread program of economic and technical assistance to agriculture and industry in the Near East, Africa, Latin America, and Asia. These funds are to be made available almost entirely on a grant basis.

The U.S. Technical Cooperation Administration, established about a year ago, has been constantly gaining momentum. During the first year of its expanded program, almost 500 requests for technical assistance were approved.

By August of this year, programs were underway in 36 countries in every part of the world.

In addition, Congress has provided that up to 13 million dollars may be available as the United States contribution to the United Nations expanded Technical Assistance Program for the next fiscal period.

I might also mention that the United States share of the 1950 gross assessment budget of the many specialized agencies, including the International Labor Organization, the International Children's Emergency Fund, and the Palestine Refugee Organization, is always a good and fair share. I would like to point out that no contributions to these organizations have been made by the nations attacking the United States.

We understand the difficulties faced by the Soviet Union in rebuilding her economy after the war. We also understand that she is expending funds to assist the countries along her borders whose economy she is now dominating. But if the Soviet Union would cut down the large expenditures she has continued to make since the end of the war for her large armed forces, she would have more funds and resources with which to build a peaceful economy and to assist other countries.

I am not suggesting that the Soviet Union undertake to assist the economic development of other countries as much as the United States is doing—that would not be possible since our economy is so much stronger than that of the Soviet Union—but I am suggesting that the Soviet Union should make some contribution to the many economic and social programs of the United Nations and the specialized agencies, to show in practice as well as in their speeches that it has a real interest in the economic and social progress of other nations, particularly and underdeveloped countries.

I hope, Madame Chairman, that I have made it amply clear that the support of my delegation for two covenants on human rights does not stem from any lack of interest in the economic and social progress of people in our own country or any disinterest in the economic and social progress of other countries.

The United States supports two covenants because we believe that two covenants would constitute a practical approach to the question before us. We do not believe it advisable as proposed by some delegations that everything go into one covenant. For all the reasons I have previously stated in this Committee, we would make much greater progress in the achievement of human rights and freedoms in the world by the simultaneous completion of two documents—one on civil and political rights and the other on economic, social, and cultural rights, and the attacks of the countries which I have been answering have not changed my point of view on this subject.

119
First Need:
Resettlement

The subject of the evening is one in which I am very much interested because I have just been briefly in three Arab states and in Israel. I could not possibly know a great deal after the short time that I was there, but I have had considerable contact with people from those countries in the United Nations and through that contact I have learned some things.

Reason no longer really operates when you arrive at a point of emotion such as has been reached between the Arab States and Israel. Israel, strangely, is more objective—though perhaps it is not really so strange, because it is always easier for persons to remain objective when they have the edge in their favor. And I think that, in the war between the Arabs and Israel, probably Israel had the edge in its favor.

I sit in a United Nations committee, the Humanitarian, Educational and Cultural Committee, where, I think, we should behave as charitably as possible and at least preserve the amenities. The U.S.S.R. and the U.S.A. representatives manage to say good morning to each other, even though as a rule between times, we attack each other quite vigorously. The Israeli delegate sits between two Arab delegates and I have never known the Arab representatives to say good morning, or apparently to recognize that the Israeli delegate exists. That is not exactly conducive to the best sort of cooperation.

But once you have been in the Near Eastern countries, the impression you come away with is that if the United Nations succeeds in resettling those poor, wretched Arab refugees, who are in worse camps than almost any I have ever seen, then there would be a chance of getting somewhere. And there is nothing to be done *but* to resettle them. They have been trained both by Communists who have come in and by the Arab leaders to get hold of you wherever you meet them and to tell you: "We want to go home." You know it is a slogan, because they say it in unison. Most of them do not talk English, but you walk into a schoolroom and all the little boys get up together and say, "We want to go home." And you know quite well there is no home for them to go to in most cases.

If finally they are resettled, I think the logic of the situation will gradually bring about Arab-Israel cooperation. And nothing is more desirable, because

The Nation 174 (June 7, 1952): 556–557. Address to The Nation Associates Conference, New York, May 25, 1952. The topic of the Conference was Arab-Israel Peace—Key to Middle East Stability.

Israel has a great deal of administrative and organizing ability, and would be in a position to help.

In the Arab states there is a stirring. Here are countries that have just recently become free; they are very nationalistic because their freedom is a new thing. The leaders have not had much training as yet in administration and organization. Their people as a whole want not just to exist any longer; they want to live. Their governments know that, but they do not quite know how to meet these desires for an improved standard of living. I think if one could just transfer a little of the ability to administer and organize into the Arab governments, their business circles, their agriculture, one would find the problems of the Arab countries solving themselves very rapidly.

Israel at present probably has the greatest capacity in the area for using any aid that comes to it, and if the Israelis could help in the development of other countries, I think it would be the way to remove the fear that the Arabs have. The Arabs are not very logical because in one breath they tell you, "We are impressed by the fact that Israel is receiving all this immigration. Israel is a very small country and some fine day they are going to be crowded and they are going to take us over." Then in the next breath they, "Ah, but the Arabs have long memories and someday we will drive the Israeli people into the sea." Well, the two just do not go together. It is not logical.

So you are left with the feeling that you have to live through the present period, you have to put everything you can into trying to clear up the refugee situation, and then, perhaps, with help from the rest of the world, you may get the cooperation which will make of the Near East a stabilizing element which is badly needed in this area. Once you have cooperation, I believe Israel can make its best contribution and the Arab States can develop and be a real factor for peace in the world.

120

UN: Good U.S. Investment

So much has been said lately about the failures of the United Nations that some people in the United States have begun to feel the UN is only a burden to them, a cost in taxes for which they receive nothing in return.

Because of this I think that, particularly during UN week, October 19 to October 25, we should look first at what the UN really is, what it has done and what our share in this undertaking has brought us.

What is the United Nations? It is an organization of 60 sovereign nations which have agreed to abide by the articles of the UN Charter in an effort to live in a more peaceful world atmosphere among the peoples of the world. Each nation retains its sovereignty. It can withdraw from the society of nations at any time. The effort is made to conduct the business of the UN in as democratic a fashion as possible, and the will of the majority is respected, but none of the members can force any nation to do anything it does not wish to do. The best illustration of this is that the United States has just announced that henceforth it will not pay as high a percentage of UN expenses as it had agreed to pay in the past, and will start the reduced scale in 1952, although American representatives had previously accepted this obligation on the assumption that our Congress, which has the final word in matters of finance, would agree to pay on the old scale for another year. No matter what this may mean in curtailing the work of the UN, if the United States sticks to its decision there is no way of coercing us and there would be no way to coerce any other nation.

Russia, as we all know, decided that the North Koreans were not behaving in an aggressive manner when they crossed the 38th Parallel in Korea and tried to take over South Korea, and the UN has not been able to force Russia to change its position.

So the UN remains a voluntary aggregation of nations, primarily affected by the climate of world opinion.

It is the desire of our nations themselves to increase good will in the world. This perhaps seems a weak reed to lean on, but so far I think the acceptance of decisions made by the UN shows we can count on the fact that world opinion will carry weight, and for the greater part we can count on good will among the nations.

The specialized agencies of the UN were set up as independent agencies reporting back to the UN Economic and Social Council so that it would be possible for them to have either more or less members than the UN and to

Foreign Policy Bulletin 32, no. 2 (October 1, 1952): 1–2.

function independently. The specialized agencies have done more than any other organs of the UN to promote better understanding and good will.

For example, through the work of the World Health Organization we are gradually learning a great deal more about the needs of our fellow human beings around the world whose populations are not properly fed and not protected against diseases which are now well enough understood to be prevented. The WHO is putting on a campaign on a world scale against malaria and tuberculosis. This is important, because until people have enough health and energy to work they cannot accomplish any of the things that are essential to raising their standard of living and improving their material condition to the point where they may consume such things as are manufactured by the more highly developed peoples.

Another specialized agency, the Food and Agriculture Organization (FAO), is gradually putting together for us a picture of the world food situation and promoting greater knowledge of agriculture.

None of these agencies alone could meet any of the world problems, but joined together and working in cooperation they will succeed in doing a tremendous job that will not only benefit the underdeveloped nations but also the developed nations which need markets for their goods. Their cooperation will lead to the purchase of raw materials by the developed nations, which can then sell the finished goods to the less industrialized countries.

Attacks on UNESCO

The specialized agency known as UNESCO—the educational, scientific and cultural organization—has perhaps been more violently attacked than any other for the reason that its task was less easy to perform.

Education is essential to both health and the improvement of the world food supply. Controversies can develop, however, as to the methods which shall be employed to give that education. Any organization which really sets out to do something in the intellectual field where it not only touches governments but directly affects the peoples of the world is bound to have a controversial task. In any country differences of opinion as to what are the aims of education and how they shall be achieved are constantly discussed, but when an organization tries to find answers and work on a world scale it is dealing with a very difficult problem. To awaken interest in the interchange of thought and intellectual knowledge must be a concern of UNESCO, and some nations will resent and resist these efforts.

I am sure in the long run we are going to discover that we would never have reached a level of better understanding without the aid of UNESCO, but we must be patient and wait for results, for this work, like all other international work, is experimental.

I wish that everyone in the United States would take the trouble to write to the UN and get its booklets telling of the work of the specialized agencies and, where possible, get its film strips, because everyone can understand pictures and it is thus easier to see what is really being accomplished.

Some people are disappointed because peace hasn't fallen upon us like manna from heaven. There is still fear and misunderstanding in the world, and I am afraid we must all make up our minds that peace will require as much hard work as winning a war and that we must use the UN and back it up loyally and enthusiastically, or else its efforts for gradual improvement in understanding will fail. It is the only machinery we have through which we can acquire greater knowledge of other peoples and they can acquire knowledge and understanding of us.

The return for our investment is that communism has been prevented from overrunning the world. We have allies and friends and a place where we can work together and grow to better understanding. Many misunderstandings have been cleared up short of war, and where there is war we do not stand alone. From my point of view our membership in the United Nations is a good investment.

121

The Universal Validity of Man's Right to Self-Determination

Before giving the views of my delegation on the question of the self-determination of peoples, I should like to reserve my delegation's right to reply at a later stage to the misstatements and distortions of fact about the United States, particularly with reference to territories under U.S. administration, contained in the statements of the representatives of Byelorussia and Poland, as well as to any other such misstatements that may be made in the course of this debate.

The desire of every people to determine its own destiny, free from dictation or control by others, is one of the most deep-seated of all human feelings. Throughout history groups of individuals having common bonds of language, religion, and culture have developed a sense of solidarity as a people and have tended to resent any effort of the outsider, the foreigner, to interfere with them. So strong is this feeling that men of many peoples have at various times been willing to lay down their lives to be free from domination by others.

The fact that wars have sometimes resulted from the failure of one people to respect the wishes of another led us all as members of the United Nations to agree that one of our major purposes is "to develop friendly relations among nations based on respect for the principle of equal rights and self-determination of peoples." In our present discussion we find ourselves faced with the problem not only of giving greater moral weight to this principle but at the same time giving it clearer definition so that it may have universal validity in the complex world of today.

While the underlying concept of self-determination is, I suppose, as old as human society, the term "self-determination" is relatively new. It appears to have been used first with regard to the nineteenth-century struggle of certain European peoples for a separate national existence. It occurs in the writings of the radical German philosophers of 1848 as *Selbstbestimmungsrecht*, which was translated into English as "the right of self-determination of nations" in a resolution adopted by a Conference of European Socialists in 1915. As a number of speakers, including the representatives of Egypt and the United Kingdom have pointed out, this phrase was given wide currency as a principle of international diplomacy by an American President, Woodrow Wilson. However, as several speakers have also reminded us, Woodrow Wilson from the beginning recognized that the principle of self-determination has its limitations. Because I think it important that we keep President Wilson's thought in this matter

Department of State Bulletin 27, no. 702 (December 8, 1952): 917–919.

clearly in mind, I should like to quote again the statement he made in setting forth his "four principles" before the U.S. Congress on February 11, 1918. He asserted

> that all well defined national aspirations shall be accorded the utmost satisfaction that can be afforded them without introducing new, or perpetuating old, elements of discord and antagonism that would be likely in time to break the peace of Europe and consequently the world.

Today we discuss the question of self-determination in quite a different and much more complex setting. The stage is no longer Europe alone; it is worldwide. In a single resolution of a few paragraphs, we are setting forth certain guidelines for the respect of a principle, not only in Europe but in Asia, Africa, and the Americas as well. Consider for a moment the wide variety of cultures of the peoples with whose self-determination we are concerned—the culture of the spear and the earthen hut, the culture of vast rural peasantries, the complex culture of industrial cities, and confused combinations of culture. The complexity would seem to me enough to make us cautious lest we be too precise, narrow, or rigid in drawing up rules for promoting respect for the principle of self-determination.

In this debate, as with any resolution we adopt, we are molding for generations to come a principle of international conduct. If self-determination is a right which belongs to all people, it is inappropriate for us to express ourselves here in a general resolution with respect only to certain people. Our words and phrases must be made to apply as much to those who once exercised the right and had it snatched from them as to those who have never possessed it.

Emergence of New and Larger "Peoples"

We, like others before us, would ask ourselves, therefore, what may constitute a "people" to whom the principle of self-determination shall be applied. What are their characteristics? What are their cultural or political or geographical boundaries?

In our search for an answer we find the very concept of a "people" undergoing rapid evolution. Possibly the very first group of human beings seeking to maintain itself as an entity free from the control of others was the family or kinship group. The trend of history, in varying degrees and with numerous setbacks, seems to have been that larger and larger groups of once separate peoples have been formed and have come to think of themselves as a single people. Almost every nation represented at this table is composed of disparate elements of population that have been combined in one way or another into a unified or federated political system.

Here differences among formerly separate peoples either have been or are being submerged and new and larger peoples are emerging. This process of evolution and merger is still going on. It is a trend which diminishes the possibilities of conflict. Must we not exercise the greatest care lest anything we do here tend to freeze the pattern of peoples along present lines and thus instead of promoting the unity of mankind, emphasize certain obstacles to such unity?

We in the United States have gained the conviction from our own experience that the combination of peoples is a process of enrichment. Right here in New York City the number of persons of Irish descent total nearly 550,000, more than in the city of Dublin; the Italian population, similarly defined, is well over 1,000,000 and exceeds the population of Naples. New York has more people of Jewish origin than all Israel. Our 12,000 Arabic-speaking people are the equivalent of a small Middle Eastern city. Yet, as I am sure you have seen demonstrated many times, their children are not Irishmen, Italians, Jews or Arabs. They are Americans.

We do not claim for one moment that the process of creating a new people is easy or that we have fully succeeded in doing so for all elements of the population, but we know it can be done and we are convinced that this process is to be preferred to clinging overzealously to the separateness of peoples.

At the same time we believe it is possible and desirable to retain a good deal of diversity within large political entities. Through our federated system of government, each state and each community preserves for its people the maximum voice in their own affairs. Louisiana has continued its legal system adopted from France, passed on from the earliest settlers of the region. Arizona and New Mexico have Spanish as one of the official languages of their legislatures. Throughout the country, people worship in Norwegian and Russian, publish newspapers in German and Greek, broadcast over the radio in a variety of tongues. In every state, county, and town the people decide for themselves who shall teach in their schools and what shall be taught. Their policemen come from their own communities and are subject to their control.

This is self-determination exercised to a high degree, yet without sacrificing cooperation in the larger fields of common interest. Each element of the national community contributes to the national government, takes part in it, and helps to shape the decisions which lead to a national destiny. Yet it must be equally clear that to grant the automatic exercise of the absolute right of political self-determination to every distinct section of our population would be detrimental to the interests of the population as a whole. And such considerations would apply to the territories whose future rises or falls with ours.

In this context we might ask ourselves: Does self-determination mean the right of secession? Does self-determination constitute a right of fragmentation or a justification for the fragmentation of nations? Does self-determination mean the right of people to sever association with another power regardless of the economic effect upon both parties, regardless of the effect upon their internal stability and their external security, regardless of the effect upon their neighbors or the international community? Obviously not.

As I have suggested, the concept of self-determination of peoples is a valid and vital principle, but like most other principles it cannot be applied in absolute or rigid terms. Surely it is not consonant with realities to suggest that there are only two alternatives—independence or slavery. Just as the concept of individual human liberty carried to its logical extreme would mean anarchy, so the principle of self-determination of peoples given unrestricted application could result in chaos. Is either principle thereby invalidated? Certainly not! On the contrary, we feel sure that human freedoms can find their fullest expression only in the context of responsibility.

The resolution before us, in at least one other respect, raises the question of absolutes. It speaks of granting the right of self-determination, upon a "demand for self-government," by ascertaining the wishes of the people through a plebiscite.

We are compelled to ask, is this not an extremely limited concept of self-determination? Is the demand for self-government the only question on which the people should be consulted? Is the plebiscite the only method of consultation?

The Essence of Self-Determination

Were self-determination synonymous with self-government, we would find these questions easier to answer. But self-determination, as applied to non-self-governing territories, whose peoples have not had the opportunity to attain their full political growth, is a much more complicated matter. It has application at all stages along the road to self-government.

Self-determination is a process. It is in essence the process of democracy as contrasted with the process of dictation in any society developed or under-developed. It is, as has been said by other speakers, a process which involves responsibilities as well as rights. It is the process by which people develop their own laws and provide their own justice. This means not merely the right to compose a code of law, nor even the actual writing of a code; it also means general agreement to abide by the laws in the interests of society as a whole, even though one's individual or group freedoms are thereby limited. Self-determination is the process by which people agree to finance their own affairs, spread their burdens among themselves, and see that individual contributions to the common good are made. Self-determination is the building of roads and schools; not just deciding to build them, but finding the engineers, the money, the workmen, the teachers, and seeing the job through.

These matters are the essence of self-determination. If self-determination can be increasingly developed in all phases of the life of a people, their self-governing or independent institutions, when achieved, will be strong and lasting. If we conceive of self-determination as synonymous with self-government, we ignore the nature of the process by which true self-government is attained. Mistaking the form for the substance, we might in fact jeopardize the very rights we seek to promote.

There are not only many aspects of the life of any people to which the principle of self-determination can be applied; there are also many ways of learning the wishes of the people, and they must be appropriate to the question involved, as well as to the literacy and understanding of the citizens.

606

Furthermore, as I indicated a moment ago, it would be unfortunate if we limited our concept of self-determination to the non-self-governing world. We have seen in our own time flagrant examples of peoples and nations, vigorous and proud and independent, which have been overrun by a conqueror and subjected to his dictatorial control. These peoples and nations are entitled to the restoration of their independence.

At a time in history when the freedoms of so many individuals and peoples have been destroyed or are seriously threatened, it is, in the view of my delegation, important that the United Nations reaffirm the principle of self-determination and promote international respect for it. It is important that it do so for *all* peoples, and not solely for peoples in some form of colonial status. In considering the recommendations to this end drafted by the Commission on Human Rights, my delegation would strongly urge that we consider them within the framework of universality and of responsibility lest we frustrate the very purpose for which the principle of self-determination was set forth in the Charter—that is, "to develop friendly relations among nations."

122

Communist Charges Against U.S. Territorial Policies

I should like to express the appreciation of my delegation for the serious and responsible way in which most of the members of this Committee have conducted this debate on the self-determination of peoples—a matter on which practically all of us have very strong feelings. We are also appreciative of the interest and understanding which our amendments to resolution A have so generally received.

Unfortunately, during the course of this debate an effort has been made by certain delegations to distort and discredit not only our motives in this debate but also U.S. policies, particularly with regard to the territories under our administration. So familiar and so stereotyped have such attacks become that we who have heard them over and over again are inclined to react to them much as we do to a bit of disagreeable weather. However, so that the principal misstatements may not remain unchallenged in the records, and so that those who are not familiar with these misstatements may not be misled, I should like to introduce a few facts to set the record straight.

Puerto Rico Cited as an Example

The distinguished representative of the Byelorussian Soviet Socialist Republic at our meeting of November 13 spoke at some length on what he called the "deplorable conditions" in Puerto Rico. Among other things, he alleged that the national culture had been annihilated. This is indeed a strange charge when one considers that after 54 years of U.S. administration, less than 25 percent of the people know English well. While English is taught in the schools, Spanish is the predominant language. The preamble to the 1952 Constitution of the Commonwealth of Puerto Rico, written by the Puerto Rican people and ratified by them in a popular referendum, "recognizes as one of the determining factors in their life the coexistence in Puerto Rico of the two great cultures of the American hemisphere." This duality of culture, with full freedom of choice, is expressly recognized in Puerto Rican political life. Fore example, there is a qualification that a member of the legislative assembly must be able to read and write either the Spanish or the English language.

The distinguished representative of Byelorussia alleged that the economy of Puerto Rico was adapted solely to the needs of the United States. It is hard to reconcile such a statement with the fact that the Puerto Ricans have freely

Department of State Bulletin, December 29, 1952, pp. 1032–1033.

chosen to retain the same tariff and trade protections as enjoyed by States of the United States and that under their own economic development program they have experienced over the past 10 years a notable expansion of local industry and enterprise. He charged that large numbers of Puerto Ricans had been deprived of their lands. Not only is this a gross distortion of the facts but he said nothing of the agrarian reform introduced in 1941. This was undertaken through the establishment of the Land Authority to enforce the law prohibiting corporate ownership of over 500 acres of land and to aid *agregados*, or landless peasants, to acquire land on which to build homes.

He referred to certain statistics on the extent of unemployment. Unemployment in Puerto Rico is admittedly a serious problem, but he failed to point out that it is, in fact, a result of improved conditions and consequent population growth and that the Puerto Ricans are, with our help, overcoming the problem. This is illustrated by the fact that the number of persons employed in 1951 increased by 20,000 over the previous year.

The representative of Byelorussia also made some charges concerning the average annual wage in Puerto Rico. If he had based himself on the official information supplied to the United Nations by my Government instead of on a magazine article, he would have given quite a different impression. For example, on page 45 of our latest report on Puerto Rico it is stated that the average wage rate in all industries in Puerto Rico in 1950 (the most recent year for which statistics have been supplied) was 44 cents an hour. While this is not a high rate when compared with wages in the United States, it is much higher than the figure quoted by the representative of Byelorussia, and it compares favorably with wage rates in the region. Furthermore, as the report also shows, wage rates in Puerto Rico have in almost all cases been steadily rising from year to year, while between 1948 and 1950 the consumer's price index rose only about 1 percent, a situation which many of us might envy.

Similarly, in the fields of health and education, where the Puerto Rican and U.S. Governments made no effort to hide the difficult problems that exist, the representative of Byelorussia, by ignoring the substantial progress made in overcoming these problems, left no doubt that the purpose of his comments was to mislead and confuse.

Ignorance of Democratic Processes

As for his reference to the new Puerto Rican Constitution, it may be that his failure to understand the free democratic processes by which it was drawn up by elected representatives of the Puerto Rican people and ratified in a popular referendum by an overwhelming majority is due to a lack of personal familiarity with such democratic processes.

With regard to the Trust Territory of the Pacific Islands administered by the United States under a trusteeship agreement with the United Nations, it is scarcely necessary to deal here with the wholesale charges made the by distinguished representatives of Byelorussia and the Ukraine. These charges have been made before by Soviet representatives in the Trusteeship Council and have been answered fully and frankly by U.S. representatives. It is perhaps sufficient to point out that after examining the most recent report on the Pacific Islands, the Trusteeship Council, with the sole exception of the Soviet representative, "noted with approval the progress made in the political, economic, social, and educational fields during the period under review."

In closing, I cannot help commenting on the bitter irony in hearing certain representatives among us support the self-determination of peoples, when we are convinced that the system they represent is devoted to the systematic denial of that principle. One of the ideas expressed by Secretary Acheson in his opening statement to this Assembly is highly pertinent to this aspect of our present discussion. I refer to that passage in which he said:

> The unfortunate fact is that we cannot approach this problem, or indeed any other problem before this Assembly, without being mindful of the events that are taking place in another part of the world. There, whole nations have been swallowed up and submerged by a new colonialism. Others have been reduced to a state of servile dependence. The tragic events behind this dark boundary not only are in stark contrast with the evolutionary process toward self-government [in non-self-governing territories] . . . but they are so fraught with danger to all of us that we can never afford to forget them.

Thus, in our present discussion of the self-determination of peoples we must not forget the vast populations who have been deprived of their self-determination. I am sure none of us will be deceived for a moment by the pretended support of this principle by the representatives of a movement which purges all those who seek any form of self-determination which differs from that dictated by their leaders.

123

Soviet Attacks on Social Conditions in U.S.

After the speakers' list was closed, the Committee heard the distinguished delegates of the Ukraine, Soviet Union, Poland, and Byelorussia talk at great length about social conditions in the United States. These four speakers, like another speaker earlier in the debate, made many allegations about declining standards of living in this country, about our inadequate facilities for housing, education, health, and social welfare, about racial discrimination, and about the high cost of living in the United States. These speakers all asserted that the defects in American life are due primarily to the preparations of our Government for war.

This is the seventh year in which I have heard these same old, stale charges hurled against the United States. On several previous occasions I have replied to these charges, point by pint, with the true facts. But, after all, no one ever expects replies to Soviet slanders to have any effect whatsoever on their representatives. Each year I present the facts about the situation in the United States; and then the next year these representatives offer up the same old distortions of fact.

The Committee is so far behind in its schedule that I will not delay it today with any detailed rebuttal. I should like merely to summarize what I have said on six previous occasions, knowing full well it will not prevent this group of representatives from saying the same thing all over again next year.

First, the U.S. Government and the American people do not want another world war; they are not preparing for another world war; they are doing, and will do, everything in their power to maintain international peace and security and to resist aggression.

Second, social conditions in the United States are not perfect and the standard of living of large numbers of the American people is far from satisfactory. It does not require this annual shower of crocodile tears by this group of representatives to make me aware of the defects in American life. I am fully aware of these defects, for I have spent the better part of my life fighting to help correct them.

Third, despite the fact that the standards of health, education, social welfare, housing, and race relations are not as high in the United States as we Americans would desire, they are much higher than the distinguished delegate of the Soviet Union and her colleagues would lead the Committee to believe.

Department of State Bulletin, January 19, 1953, pp. 116–117.

Every year, the distinguished delegate of the Soviet Union and her colleagues quote a long list of figures to show what a small part of the *Federal* budget of the United States is devoted to education, health, social insurance, and similar activities. Every year I have to remind these delegates that the major expenditures in our country for education, health, social insurance, and similar activities comes not out of the Federal budget, but from the States, the counties, the cities, and the towns, and from private sources of many kinds. Let me cite just one figure, for probably the seventh time, to show the utter falseness of all these charges. The distinguished delegate of the Soviet Union stated that less than 1 percent of the budget of the Federal Government in the United States is devoted to education. That is a correct statistic because education is not the primary responsibility of the Federal Government, but that statement gives a completely false impression. The States, local communities, and private institutions are primarily responsible for education in the United States. In the fiscal year 1950-51 our State and local governments spent a total of $7,500,000,000 on education, or 34.1 percent of their total expenditures; and our private institutions in addition spent many millions of dollars on education.

Fourth, despite all the imperfections in our American society and despite all I have heard about the perfect paradise that exists in the Soviet Union, Poland, Byelorussia, and in certain other countries—I am sure every person with decent instincts still prefers to live in imperfect freedom than in a propaganda paradise without freedom. For the last 20 years in this country, the Republican Party, a majority of our newspapers, and millions of our citizens have been criticizing and denouncing the Government; and for the next 4 years, the Democratic Party, many of our newspapers, and millions of our citizens will be criticizing and denouncing the new Administration. Yet not one Republican politician or diplomat has been imprisoned or hanged for his opposition to the Government in power. Not one newspaper has been suppressed. Not one citizen has been shipped off to a slave-labor camp. Nor will anything of this kind happen in the next 4 years to any American who happens to disagree with the Republican Administration.

In conclusion, Mr. Chairman, we in the United States know better than these critics the many things that are lacking in our country. We have done much in the past, and we are doing much today, to correct these injustices and these low standards. We would be doing even more today if we were not compelled by the aggression in Korea and by the threat of aggression elsewhere to help strengthen the free world and to preserve the peace.

124

U.N. Deliberations on Draft Convention on the Political Rights of Women

Statement of December 12

As most of you know, the subject of this convention—equal suffrage for women—is very close to my heart. I believe in active citizenship, for men and women equally, as a simple matter of right and justice. I believe we will have better government in all of our countries when men and women discuss public issues together and make their decisions on the basis of their differing areas of experience and their common concern for the welfare of their families and their world.

In the United States, and in most countries today, women have equal suffrage. Some may feel that for that reason this convention is of little importance to them. I do not agree with this view. It is true, of course, that the first objective of this convention is to encourage equal political rights for women in all countries. But its significance reaches far deeper into the real issue of whether in fact women are recognized fully in setting the policies of our governments.

While it is true that women in 45 of our 60 member nations vote on the same terms as men, and in 7 more already have partial voting rights, too often the great decisions are originated and given form in bodies made up wholly of men, or so completely dominated by them that whatever of special value women have to offer is shunted aside without expression. Even in countries where for many years women have voted and been eligible for public office, there are still too few women serving in positions of real leadership. I am not talking now in terms of paper parliaments and honorary appointments. Neither am I talking about any such artificial balance as would be implied in a 50-50, or a 40-60 division of public offices. What I am talking about is whether women are sharing in the direction of the policy making in their countries; whether they have opportunities to serve as chairmen of important committees and as cabinet ministers and delegates to the United Nations.

We are moving forward in my country in this regard, for we have had women in all these posts, but not enough of them, and they do not always have a full voice in consultation. I do not expect that there will ever be as many women political leaders as men, for most women are needed in their homes while their children are small and have fewer years in which to gain public recognition. But, if we are honest with ourselves, we know that all countries

Department of State Bulletin, January 5, 1953, pp. 29–32.

have a long way to go on these matters. I believe it is this situation, far more than the continued denial of equal suffrage in a few countries, which has spurred interest in this convention and brought it before our Committee to-day. This situation cannot be changed entirely by law, but it can be changed by determination and conviction. I hope we will use this discussion to deepen these convictions in ourselves and in our governments.

This convention is the result of work in the Commission on the Status of Women. The United States is proud of the contribution it has been able to make to this Commission through the participation of our representatives, Judge Dorothy Kenyon and Mrs. Olive Goldman.

The terms of the draft convention before us are simple. Articles 1 and 2 provide for the right to vote and to be elected to publicly elected bodies, such as parliaments, established by national law. These are the basic rights which all people must have to express their interest and protect themselves against discrimination or deprivation of liberty. The Charter of the United Nations reaffirms in its preamble the principles of equal rights for men and women. The first General Assembly endorsed these rights when it unanimously adopted the resolution recommending that all member states, which had not already done so, adopt measures necessary to fulfill the purposes and aims of the Charter in this respect by granting to women the same political rights as men. This convention spells out this recommendation in clear and practical terms, on which all parties in a country can unite.

I think I am correct in saying that 24 countries have taken action to extend suffrage rights for women since the Charter was signed in 1945. The most recent of these changes have been in Lebanon and Bolivia. Important gains have been made within the past few years in a number of other countries—Greece, for instance, and in Haiti.

Article 3 of this convention goes beyond the basic rights in articles 1 and 2 into the matter of public office. It provides that women shall be entitled to hold public office established by national law on the same terms as men, and to exercise all public functions in the same way. The object of this article—to encourage opportunities for women in government service—has my hearty endorsement, and that of my Government. Women today hold many important Government posts and an increasing number are in executive positions and in Foreign Service. The wording of article 3 presents certain problems that I believe we should discuss, and in a moment I will go into them in more detail. In principle, however, I am sure we are all in agreement with article 3.

We are also asked to consider formal clauses to complete the convention, on the basis of texts proposed by the Secretary-General. The United States is in general agreement also with these proposals. This is a very simple convention, and it would seem to us that the formal clauses should be limited to the fewest necessary to make the convention effective. These would presumably be those providing for ratification or accession, entry into force, settlement of disputes, notification, and deposit. The Secretariat has proposed certain other clauses which, of course, can be included if the Committee desires, but they do not seem to me to be essential. The simpler and shorter we can keep this convention, the more readily people will understand it and the more effective it will be.

There are other questions we will no doubt want to debate in regard to this convention. I hope, however, that in our debates we will never lose sight of the significance and importance of our objectives.

Now I want to go back to article 3. This is a very interesting article, for the right to "hold public office" includes both elective and appointive office. The right to be *elected* to public office has usually been recognized along with the right to vote. For instance, the Inter-American Convention on the Granting of Political rights to Women, formulated at Bogotá in 1948, includes the right to vote and to be elected to national office. Article 2 of this convention covers a part of this right, the right to be elected to such bodies as parliaments. However, the right to be *appointed* to public office has not previously been included in an international convention, so that we are now considering its expression in treaty terms for the first time.

In relation to appointive office, the language in article 3 is very broad.

The term "public office" is taken to include appointments to posts in the (1) civil service, (2) foreign (diplomatic) service, and (3) judiciary, as well as (4) posts primarily political in nature, such as cabinet ministers or secretaries. The number of appointive offices established by national law is usually large, far larger than the number of offices filled by election, and the tasks to be performed by appointive officers are likely to vary widely in substance and in level of responsibility.

Article 3 specifies offices are to be held "on equal terms with men." This is also an inclusive phrase, covering such matters as recruitment, exemptions, pay, old age and retirement benefits, opportunities for promotion, employment of married women. All these are important matters on which women have sought equality for many years.

As I said before, in the United States women have the rights specified in this convention, including the rights we believe article 3 is intended to cover, and we have long urged that women in all countries have similar opportunities. A question does arise, however, as to whether the term "public office" is intended to include military service. My delegation believes it is not so intended. Almost all countries make some distinctions in the kinds of military duty they regard as suitable for women. The most usual distinction, and a natural and proper one, is that women are not used as combat troops and are not appointed to certain posts which might involve the direction of combat operations. Our attitude toward article 3 is, therefore, based on the understanding that it does not include military service.

The United States also has some difficulty with the phrase "public functions," which occurs in the second part of article 3. The U.S. law "Public Office" covers all public posts and this may be true in other countries. The term "public functions" accordingly does not seem to add anything to the text. The phrase might be clarified, however, if the words "related thereto" were inserted after "public functions." This would make it quite clear that no traditional or legal limitation on women in any country, such as restrictions on a woman's right to serve in certain professions or to bring suits at law would interfere with her capacity to serve in public office.

If the phrase is retained in its present form, the view of the United States would be that the public functions referred to in this convention are coterminous with public office.

This convention on political rights of women is not in itself an answer to the problems of modern government. But it points up, I believe in useful ways, how governments can expand their resources by taking full advantage of the energy and experience of their women citizens. Women's organizations throughout the United States have stated their belief in its principles and its value. The convention is a symbol of the progress women have made in the past 100 years, and a challenge to them to claim and make full use of the political rights they achieve. It is for these reasons that the United States hopes that this Committee may agree on a text to which we can give unanimous endorsement.

Statement of December 15

I want first to say just a little about the statements which the distinguished delegate of the Soviet Union and several of her colleagues have made on the situation of women in the United States. These delegates seem concerned, for instance, that in most of our States women share the domicile of their husbands and vote from it as their legal residence. Of course, this is true also of the men; their legal residence is the family domicile shared by their wives. In the United States we assume that husbands and wives wish to live together, and we protect their right to do so, and to share in the management of family affairs and the guardianship of their children. If the woman desires to be separated from her husband, she can set up a separate domicile. The courts also decide how best to protect the welfare of children of separated couples, and unless there is good reason to the contrary, the mother is almost always preferred to take care of young children.

A great many of the other comments which have been made seem to spring from the same source—a difference of opinion, really, as to the importance of the family in all our relationships, including our responsibilities as individuals toward our governments. We were struck, for instance, with the distinction the distinguished delegate of Byelorussia made Saturday afternoon. She said, I believe, that one of the great values in the provision of crèches and nursery schools in the Soviet Union was that it permitted a woman to fulfill her role as mother and at the same time share in the public life of her country. We do not think of the "role of mother" in our country as separating women or denying women a full share in our public life. We feel rather that it is the family which is the center for men and women alike, and for their children, and we try to make it possible for the father of the family to earn enough so that the woman can stay home and care for their children if she wishes. At the same time, as you all know, American women participate fully in all professions and public activities, and more than half our employed women are married women.

Our family relationships result in a number of legal and judicial distinctions which limit the husband as well as the wife. Our laws are changed if these distinctions become unjust to either party, and changing conditions, particularly in modern business, have led to various changes. But the family is still the center of American living.

I am puzzled by certain other comments that have been made because, so far as I can see, what my Soviet colleagues wish us to do is to discriminate against men.

For instance, people in the United States speak many languages. Here in New York you will hear many different languages in the streets and restaurants. In some of our states, however, one seldom hears any language but English. In those States, voters are usually required to be literate in English. But in others—for instance, our Southwestern States, where Spanish is frequently spoken—voters may qualify in either language. In our courts, interpreters are always provided for those who cannot speak or understand English. In no case is there discrimination against women as such.

The distinguished representatives of Czechoslovakia and the Soviet countries have spoken also of the situation of Negro voters in the United States. As you know, great progress has been made in recent years in assuring Negro voters full security in casting their votes. Many more Negroes voted in this past election than ever before in our Southern States as well as Northern. The figures these delegations quoted seemed to be somewhat out of date in this regard. It was implied that the difficulty Negro women have experienced in regard to suffrage is connected with the existence of a poll tax in some of our Southern States. The poll tax is a per capita tax, once usual in many countries, but it is now being replaced almost everywhere by other forms of taxation. It now exists in only five of our States. It applies equally to all people, whites as well as Negroes. However, since it applies equally to men and women, I do not see how any provision on the poll tax could be included in this convention without its resulting in discrimination against men.

I have been glad to hear that Soviet women hold many public offices and participate widely in public life. I have been glad to note this year that the Soviet Union, the Ukraine, and Byelorussia have included women on their delegations to the General Assembly. There have been very few women on these delegations in the past—in fact, I do not recall any since the first General Assembly in 1946. I hope that this convention may lead to greater participation by women in the true organs of power in the Soviet Union, such as the Presidium and the Secretariat of the Central Committee of the Communist Party, in which I understand no women are now included. The experience women have achieved in the more formal and subsidiary bodies throughout the Soviet Union should entitle them to recognition also in bodies which determine the major policies of their Government.

The Soviet Union has brought in a number of amendments, and I want also to discuss these briefly. I understand those on the first three articles of the convention are similar to those presented in sessions of the Commission on the Status of Women and in the Economic Council. Both the Commission and the Council rejected the changes and additions in these proposals on the ground that they are unnecessary in so simple a convention as this one. I would like to point out, however, that the language proposed by the Soviet Union, presumably to assure application of this convention "without discrimination," is in fact very discriminatory, because it enumerates only a few grounds and omits others. The most notable omission is in regard to political opinion. The Soviet amendment also omits the phrase "without discrimination of any kind," which might otherwise cover "political opinion." It seems to me that in a convention on political rights, if you are going to provide any guaranties against discrimination, the most important one would be freedom for all types of political opinion. But, as I said before, the intent of this convention to apply to all women is entirely clear, and we believe any such additional clause would be confusing and might in fact have the result—as the Soviet proposal does—of limiting its effect.

The proposal to expand article 2 by enumerating certain other bodies also seems unnecessary, since all those mentioned in the Soviet draft are included within the phrase "publicly elected bodies" already in article 2. Neither does it seem necessary to add their proposed article 4, calling for implementing legislation. In so simple an agreement as this, the convention itself is sufficient.

Another proposal has to do with the proposed clause on settlement of disputes and provides for arbitration rather than a reference to the International Court of Justice. The United States regards this proposal as a departure from the procedures already approved as part of our U.N. structure and will oppose it accordingly.

Several countries have proposed that the convention include a clause on the extension of the convention to non-self-governing and trust territories. Women in all territories under the administration of the United States have the rights in this convention, and we believe all women everywhere should have them. As I said earlier, this is a very simple convention, and the simpler and briefer we can keep the formal clauses, the easier it will be for people to understand it and the more effective it will be. However, the United States has no objection to the addition of such a clause, if the majority desire it.

We have been listening with great care to the statements on this convention, because, you remember, the United States indicated in its statement that we do not believe the convention applies to military service, and asked whether that was the general opinion among the delegates. We, therefore, appreciated greatly the strong expression of agreement with our position by the distinguished delegate of France, and also various other statements which supported this view. I believe no contrary view has been expressed and take it there is general agreement that the present convention does not include military service. As I said earlier, the United States regards the obligation it would under-take under this convention with regard to "public functions" as coterminous with "public office."

I have not answered certain charges against the United States as to the economic situation of women—Negro women especially—because this is a convention on political rights, and I have not wanted to take the time of this Committee for irrelevant matters.

125

The U.N. and the Welfare of the World

I am very happy to come before you today because I believe that the parent-teacher organization is one of the most influential organizations in America. You are made up of two very important groups of people—parents and teachers—and on those two groups depends what may happen to our country in the near and far-off future. I think it is quite fitting, therefore, that I speak to you about the United Nations—what it is, what it does, and what it may do in years to come.

Since I left the United Nations last January, I have been working with the American Association for the United Nations, which has as its primary purpose that of reaching the people of this country with information. I thought this was important because there are groups of people—some of them patriotic, honest groups—who are troubled about the United Nations. And there are other organized groups that are attacking it. They have done the same thing before, only they are not using the same points of attack that they used previously. That is why it seemed to me that the people as a whole should know as much as they could about the United Nations.

Our nation has always been a great nation. We have always had so much territory that for years we had to concentrate on our own development. We did not turn to the rest of the world as much as we would have done if we had been a small nation and more evidently dependent on other countries to meet many of our needs. But now we've found ourselves in a situation where we must know about all the other peoples of the world. We must know about the way they live, what they are like, what their beliefs are, what their aspirations are. Why? Because suddenly we are the leading nation in the democratic, free world.

That has been quite a transition for us—to be responsible not for what we have done in developing our own country but for what we have stood for as a democracy. It is a little hard to realize, but it is true that what happens in every one of our own communities is painting the story of what democracy actually is. If you serve in the United Nations you become very conscious of how carefully we are watched by the rest of the world.

The Will to Learn

You have heard, as many of us have heard, the current saying, "What good has come from the United Nations? Hasn't the United Nations failed? It was set

National Parent-Teacher 47 (June 1953): 14–16, 35. Address to Illinois Congress of Parents and Teachers.

up to bring us peace, and we don't have peace." But that is really a most unfortunate misconception. The object that the sovereign states hoped for when they wrote the Charter in San Francisco was that we could use this machinery as united nations to achieve a peaceful world. But it's only machinery, and machinery doesn't work by itself. It's the people that make it work.

We have also heard it said that the United Nations is just a debating society, that it never accomplishes anything. Yet we have found over the years that it requires a good deal of talk for people to learn to understand one another. Even in the Congress of the United States we don't always find an immediate meeting of minds. Well, you take sixty sovereign nations, all representing peoples with different customs and habits, frequently different religions, frequently different legal systems. How can you expect them immediately—within six or seven years, that is—to arrive at a meeting of minds? True, the breach has widened between us and the Soviets, but that breach might have broadened into a war if there hadn't been a place where we *had* to meet and where we were able to talk.

And if the United Nations is a debating society, do you feel that you have learned all you should about what conditions are all over the world—for instance, in India? I am sure that many of you have no conception of what it is to live in a country where there is always a famine somewhere. I know it wasn't until I went to India and saw the famine districts that I realized what it would be like if some part of my own country was always living under famine conditions. I know of no way in which we can learn these things as quickly as we are learning them from the information that comes to us through channels provided by the United Nations.

I get a lot of letters from people who say, "How can you expect the United Nations to succeed when you do not recognize God in the United Nations?" We have in the U.N. building a little room known as a prayer room to serve all devout people. From those who live according to their own religious standards I have learned a tremendous amount. I have learned to respect them, for I sometimes think that the same spirit pervades the good people in all religions. If you want others to respect your beliefs, you must in return give respect for theirs.

These are some of the things that you learn as you find yourself in close association with people from different parts of the world. It is because they are things that we all need to learn that I believe parents and teachers today have such a tremendous responsibility. They have to prepare our children for living as leaders in a world that will follow their leadership—if the world can respect it. And that will require of our children a greater knowledge of the rest of the world than any of us have ever had before. They are going to be leaders in a world where not only are there different religions and habits and customs but different races—and two thirds of that world is made up of peoples of different color.

At a press conference in the Near East last year the very first question the newspaper people asked me was, "How do you treat your minorities in the United States?" That is always the first question we are asked in other countries. It is less difficult to answer in India because there the people understand. They have the problem of the untouchables. They know that it takes time, sometimes a long time, to change the hearts of men. They know that although all caste in India has been outlawed, some of the old feelings still exist. Law makes a good background for change, but law of itself doesn't change the feelings of human beings.

I think the problem of minorities in India has probably been worse in some ways because all human life is so cheap in that land of three hundred and fifty million people. One little thing made me realize this feeling about human life—seeing the sweepers in the streets. They are usually old people of the lowest caste. To sweep the streets they use little bundles of sticks tied together. My first natural question was, "Why don't they put handles on those brooms so the people don't have to bend down?" I was looked at with surprise. "Oh, but handles would cost money. They would be expensive." So handles cost more than human beings. You see people bent double all their lives, sweeping the streets, because no one will pay for the handle of a broom.

It is hard for us to realize too that great masses of human beings go hungry all their lives—for generations. But these are all things we have to learn, things parents and teachers should know. And the only machinery we have that is working to increase our knowledge is the United Nations.

The Hope to Teach

A great many people feel it would be much better if the Soviets and their satellites were not a part of the United Nations. I don't feel that way because I think education is slow. To me the fact that there is contact, a bridge on which we can meet and talk, has value. I am not afraid of the contact because I believe that we have more strength, spiritually and morally, than the Soviets have, and therefore we are able to stand up against them.

It's a good thing, too, for another reason. I do not believe that a Soviet representative dares tell his government the truth about what he sees in a country like ours. But there is one thing that never can be falsified, and that is the way the delegates vote in the United Nations. Over and over again it is five votes against all the rest of the world, and that report goes straight from the Secretary General to every nation. The government in Moscow knows by that vote what the opinion of the rest of the world is. I think very likely this is one of the strongest factors that have deterred the Soviets from doing things that would certainly be unwise—things they might easily do if they thought all the information they received was correct.

When all is said and done, then, what we need is to know more about the United Nations and its action groups—the specialized agencies—if only because this is machinery that we people of the different nations must use. For if we do not know about it and if we do not back it up, it isn't going to be used as well as it might be. Furthermore, I feel very strongly that with more knowledge, many of the fears we have had about the United Nations will be dispelled.

Remember, this cooperation is so new, so new in every field, that it's very hard for any of us to work together even on what we think are simple things. So we shouldn't be discouraged when we do not achieve peace all at once. Peace is not going to drop on us from heaven. It is going to have to be worked for, with the hearts and minds and wills of human beings. I believe it can be achieved, but we are going to have to work much harder. We must know about the machinery that we can use, then try to use that machinery to strengthen it, at the same time learning about the rest of the world.

The Courage to Lead

This is why parents and teachers today must have courage enough to stand up against waves of public opinion. At present we are going through a period of what I call unreasonable fears, fears that cause great suspicion among us. Many people are afraid to say what they think because it might by chance be something that somebody else might think subversive. Yet our nation has been built on differences of opinion, stated openly. Throughout our history we have had quite a number of people who stood for almost revolutionary ideas. But we have weathered the years, and we have come to be the leading nation of the world. And now it is a question of how well we prepare the next generation to take the burden from their elders. These young people have to know much more than we knew. *We* had to know about our own country; *they* have to know about the world. They have to feel and understand things that we didn't have to feel and understand at all.

You are the people who are preparing the next generation for leadership. And, believe me, it can't be done with fear. Men can never lead if they are afraid, for the leader who is afraid will never be followed.

I've always remembered a story one of my sons told me. He had been in the Marine Corps and in the first Makin Island raid. Some years later he went back with a new group to Makin Island, but this time he went as an observer. All the observers were told they should follow, not lead. And they did this until they realized that the younger men ahead of them had no leaders because quite naturally they were frightened. Everybody is frightened at first. And my son said to me, "You see, after you've done it enough times, Mother, you get the feeling that if a bullet has your number, it has your number. But until your number is up, you're okay." So, he said, suddenly the observers, who were without fear, found that they were going ahead, and then everybody followed.

We must all have that feeling of confidence if we are to be leaders of the world, the free world. It's a very sobering thought, but it's the thought that we have to bear in mind. We have to have unity; we have to believe in each other. We cannot be suspicious of everybody. Surely there are people among us who perhaps do not believe in the things that we think essential, but I think the vast majority of us are well rooted in the beliefs of freedom.

I think we can stand up against any infiltration or propaganda, but first we must have a feeling of confidence. We must really care about bringing to the people of the world a leadership that is good, a leadership that is strong. I do not mean strong just in a military and economic way but in a spiritual and moral way. If we do have that feeling and can impart it to our young people, I believe we can do this job, the biggest job any nation has ever had. We are at the crossroads. It is up to us whether we move forward—slowly, to be sure, but step by step—to a better world or whether we fail.

What is going to happen? I do not know. If we succeed, it will be because you and I, as individuals, believe in ourselves and in the need to work with our neighbors throughout the world. I think we will hand on to our children a struggle, but a struggle that will give our nation the capacity to lead the world toward peace and righteousness and freedom.

126

Is a UN Charter Review Conference Advisable Now?

I am a member now of the American Association of the United Nations, and have been working for them for the past 2 years, organizing throughout the country, so that we might have more information about the United Nations. At the same time, in having more information, I hope that people may become more interested in doing things which would strengthen the United Nations.

I have felt that there were different ways of strengthening the charter. There are, of course, chances that, given the world situation at present, if one held a full revision conference with the intention of changing the charter, that instead of strengthening it and getting a better charter, we might find it harmful to the charter.

I have felt that there is still in our country a great lack of detailed knowledge about the work of the United Nations. There is, however, in almost every citizen, a feeling that this machinery which has been set up under the United Nations Charter is all we have to help us in our great desire to maintain peace in the world. It is the best machinery we have in the world to work toward those aims.

Many people have been disappointed because they felt that simply ratifying a charter meant that we would have peace. People have turned to force for a very long while and it will take time, I think, for us to find the ways to greater understanding, through appreciation of each other, of our cultures, of our religions, of our legal systems, of all the things that make nations different, but that nevertheless when understood, we find that basically we have many points where we can meet and work together.

I have felt that the people of the United States basically believe in the United Nations, and in our strengthening and using the United Nations.

Now, the reason I say that I doubt if at present we could improve the charter by a full-dress revision conference is because the world as a whole is still a very troubled state. I doubt if we would have calm and objective deliberations.

I think it might be for educational purposes a good thing to call a committee together, and have them study for the future. I think we also have to see that certain changes have come about since the charter was originally written. The difficulties that have come up have had to be met. For instance, the veto which has been wrongly used by the Russians made it imperative in questions which dealt with situations where we might be brought to war to find a way, if

Congressional Digest 34 (November 1955): 275, 277.

the Security Council could not act, for the General Assembly to act. And the Uniting for Peace Resolution was simply a method to meet that situation. Now, it has been met. Once a subject is no longer before the Security Council—and that happens as soon as the veto is cast—then it may be brought up, if it affects the peace, by call for a General Assembly meeting, which can be done in 24 hours. And the question can then be decided by a two-thirds vote of the General Assembly, if it is a very important question, or a majority vote, otherwise.

I think that the question which disturbs most of us, of course, is the question of using the veto against new memberships. So far, we have not found a solution. The General Assembly cannot act, except on recommendation of the Security Council. I feel that that, too, may be met, and we may be able to find some solution.

My own feeling is that, for educational purposes, it may be very well to have a committee to study possible revisions. But the countries of the world are not yet, I think, fully prepared in their knowledge of the United Nations, and of the ways in which it works, to actually revise the charter and do something better than what we have. We can strengthen the United Nations by the member states loyally living up to their undertakings when they ratified the charter.

I think we must remember that the charter is really a declaration of basic principles of how member states—sovereign states—can work together.

While the charter is a treaty, the setting up of machinery under the charter, of course, makes it possible to change the machinery, from time to time, and that has been done. People are apt to talk about the United Nations as though it was some concrete thing that acted by itself. Of course that is not true. It is the machinery and it is the member states that make it work. Those states are all of them sovereign states. So far, I think that we must not forget that in any treaties entered into through the United Nations, they have to be ratified by the Senate, and I have always felt that that should be emphasized, because the Senate does not, as a rule, ratify treaties without due consideration and deliberation and I am not really afraid that we will wildly go into unwise treaties. I am quite willing to leave the safety of our rights and the consideration of the well-being of the United States to a two-thirds vote of the Senate. I think we will be well guarded.

For that reason, I have felt that our actual undertakings under the charter were important for us to live up to. It is difficult for a great nation, accustomed as we have always been—all great nations—to act alone; to come to the habit of actually working in an international group. But the values that can be attained through working together, I think, are very great, and I think if we look over these 10 years—the 10th birthday of the United Nations will be next October 24—I think we would feel that without the United Nations we might easily have had world war III. Without it, we could have now international chaos, because we would not have a place where world opinion could come together and where it could be formed. That does not say that world opinion will always be right. We believe in majority rule in this country, but sometimes we think majority rule is not always right—it has to change and grow, and so internationally we have much education that has to be done.

I noticed that President Hoover has said that he felt it was wise for the Soviet Union to be a member of the United Nations. I was interested in that because I have always believed that it was wise for the Soviet Union, and in time, I hope, every nation will be brought in as a member of the United Nations. But the reason that I have felt it was important for the Soviet Union to be a member is perhaps a little different from the one I have usually heard given. Of course, it is valuable for the education to go on that must go on, whenever a nation is a member of the United Nations, but the Soviet Union is a government by fear and therefore I have never felt that either its delegates to the United Nations, or its spies, could be trusted to report truthfully to their government. The minute there is a government of fear, you report what you think will be acceptable and you do not so carefully report the truth. I can just imagine what would happen to a delegate from the Soviet Union who went home and said, "On the whole, the United States seems to me to be in pretty good condition." I don't think he would be very acceptable in the Kremlin.

Therefore, I have always felt that the fact that the Soviet Union was a member, and that all the votes that were taken in the United Nations are reported directly from the Secretary General back to the governments of the various nations, was probably a tremendous safeguard because, at times, if you have the biggest army in the world, it must have been a temptation to think, "Well, why don't we roll across Europe and isolate the United States?"

For that reason, I had felt we had a very special reason for keeping the Soviet Union in the United Nations. From my point of view, the sooner we have a universal membership, it will be better from the educational point of view, it will be better from the point of view that we will grow in understanding. But this particular thing is also important, wherever there are governments which are governments by fear.

We are a representative form of government, but it is our peoples who speak through our representatives, and therefore I think it is quite safe to say that the United Nations represents the people of the world, their aspirations, their desires, and I think for that reason that we have come a long way in these 10 years under the charter as it is. I think it can be improved, I think it can be developed, but I am not sure that we have reached a point at which these revisions should be made. Therefore, I would submit that our position, if possible, should be one of acceptance of a committee for study, but not of insisting that we have revision at the present time.

Eleanor Roosevelt

A Bibliographical Essay

The papers of Anna Eleanor Roosevelt are housed in the Franklin D. Roosevelt Library in Hyde Park, New York. The papers are voluminous and are divided into two sections: 1884–1945 and 1945–1962. Those interested in investigating ER's life should also consult the following collections, which are also housed at the FDR Library: Franklin D. Roosevelt papers, Lorena Hickok papers, Molly Dewson papers, Henry Morgenthau papers, the Eleanor Roosevelt Oral History Project, Anna Roosevelt Halstead papers, Franklin D. Roosevelt Jr. papers, Joseph P. Lash papers, and the Democratic Women's Committee papers.

Material relating to ER that is housed outside the FDR Library may be found in the following collections in the Library of Congress: NAACP papers, CORE papers, Edith Helm papers, Agnes E. Meyer papers, and the Democratic Study Group papers. There is also a substantial collection of information related to ER in the Adlai E. Stevenson papers housed in the Princeton University Library. Joseph Lash has published two collections of ER's correspondence, *Love, Eleanor* (New York, 1982) and *World of Love, Eleanor* (New York, 1984), which reflect her political and personal opinions.

Eleanor Roosevelt was a prolific writer. She wrote four autobiographies, *This Is My Story*, *This I Remember*, *On My Own*, and *The Autobiography of Eleanor Roosevelt*, as well as several monographs, the most important of which are *It's Up to the Women*, *This Troubled World*, *The Moral Basis of Democracy*, and *Tomorrow is Now*. Her column "My Day" was published six times a week from 1936 until 1962 and is a wonderful source for her daily activities and political positions. She also wrote a series of monthly columns: "Mrs. Roosevelt's Page" for the *Democratic Digest* (December 1937 until January 1941), "If You Ask Me," for *Ladies' Home Journal* (May 1941–1949), and *McCall's* (1949 through 1962). John A. Edens's *Eleanor Roosevelt: A Comprehensive Bibliography* (Westport, Conn., 1994) provides the most extensive and thoroughly annotated compilation of ER's articles to date.

Maurine Beasely has edited all the extant transcripts from ER's press conferences, *The White House Press Conferences of Eleanor Roosevelt* (New York, 1983), and assesses ER's career as a journalist in *Eleanor Roosevelt and the Media* (Urbana, 1987). Susan Ware's *Beyond Suffrage: Women in the New Deal* (Cambridge, 1981) clearly illustrates ER's influence within the administration and reform circles.

There have been dozens of works published about ER. Of those contemporaries close to ER who wrote biographies of her, the best are Lorena Hickok, *Eleanor Roosevelt: Reluctant First Lady* (New York, 1962) and Ruby Black, *Eleanor*

Roosevelt (New York, 1940). For children, Russell Freedman's Newbery Award-winning *Eleanor Roosevelt: A Life of Discovery* (New York, 1993) is a wonderful overview of ER's life and accomplishments.

Although many have tried, most biographers create a superficial, one-dimensional portrait of ER. Blanche Wiesen Cook's *Eleanor Roosevelt, Volume One* (New York, 1992) is a thorough and thoughtful reconstruction of her life before the White House. Joseph P. Lash's *Eleanor and Franklin* (New York, 1970) is the most comprehensive study of ER's White House years published to date, despite its protective slant. Joan Hoff Wilson and Marjorie Lightman's anthology *Without Precedent: The Life and Career of Eleanor Roosevelt* (Indianapolis, 1984) offers a scholastic assessment of ER's political education and political performance before and during her tenure as First Lady.

Unfortunately, ER's post–White House career has not yet received equal treatment. The only serious study of ER's contribution to diplomacy is Jason Berger's *A New Deal for the World* (New York, 1981). My book, *Casting Her Own Shadow: Eleanor Roosevelt and the Shaping of Postwar Liberalism* (New York, 1995), documents and analyzes ER's evolving commitment to civil rights, civil liberties, and Democratic Party reform.

Allida M. Black

A Bibliography of the Articles of Eleanor Roosevelt

The following is a comprehensive listing of the published articles of Eleanor Roosevelt, excluding her "My Day" columns.

1921

"Common Sense Versus Party Regularity." *News Bulletin* (League of Women Voters of New York State) (16 Sept. 1921).

1922

"The Fall Election." *L.W.V. Weekly News* (New York League of Women Voters) (1922).

"Organizing County Women for a Political Party." *L.W.V. Weekly News* (New York League of Women Voters) (1922).

1923

"American Peace Award." *Ladies' Home Journal* 40 (Oct. 1923): 54.

Untitled. *L.W.V. Weekly News* (12 Oct. 1923).

"Why I Am a Democrat." *Junior League Bulletin* 10 (Nov. 1923): 18–19.

"I Am a Democrat." *Women's Democratic Campaign Manual, 1924*. Washington: Democratic Party, National Committee 1924–1928, 1924. 85

1924

"How to Interest Women in Voting." *Women's Democratic Campaign Manual, 1924*. Washington: Democratic Party, National Committee 1924–1928, 1924. 102–3.

"M'Adoo [*sic*] Mobilizes His Forces Here." *New York Times*, 8 June 1924: 5.

"Statement of Policy Committee." *The Winning Plan Selected by the Jury of the American Peace Award*. New York: n.p., 1924. 4–6.

"What Has Politics Gained by the Women's Vote?" *National Democratic Magazine* 1 (Apr. 1924): 21.

1925

"New York Rebuilt." *Women's City Club Bulletin* (June 1925): 5–6.

Women's Democratic News. Ed. Eleanor Roosevelt.

1926

"The Democratic Platform." *Women's City Club of New York* (Oct. 1926): 14–15.

1927

"As a Practical Idealist." *North American Review* 224 (Nov. 1927): 472–75.

Congressional Record (6 Jan. 1927): 1154.

L.W.V. Weekly News (New York League of Women Voters) (Dec. 1927).

"On Albany Hill." *Quarterly* (Women's City Club of New York) (June 1927).

"What I Want Most Out of Life." *Success Magazine* 11 (May 1927): 16–17, 70.

"What Is Being Done in Albany." *Quarterly* (Women's City Club of New York) (Mar. 1927): 10–11.

1928

"Committee on Legislation." *Quarterly* (Women's City Club of New York) (June 1928): 28–29.

"Governor Smith." *Junior League Magazine* 15 (Nov. 1928): 23, 110.

"Governor Smith and Our Foreign Policy." *Woman's Journal* n.s. 13 (Oct. 1928): 21.

"Jeffersonian Principles the Issue in 1928." *Current History* 28 (June 1928): 354–57.

"News of Democrats and Their Activities." *Bulletin* (Women's National Democratic Club) 3 (Dec. 1928): 18–19.

"Women Must Learn to Play the Game as Men Do." *Red Book Magazine* 50 (Apr. 1928): 78–79, 141–42.

"The Women's City Club at Albany." *Quarterly* (Women's City Club of New York) (Mar. 1928): 16–17.

1929

"Education for Girls." *Independent Education* 3 (Dec. 1929): 7–8.

1930

"Building Character." *Childhood and Character* 7 (May 1930): 6–7.

"Good Citizenship: The Purpose of Education." *Pictorial Review* 31 (Apr. 1930): 4, 94, 97.

"The Ideal Education." *Woman's Journal* n.s. 15 (Oct. 1930): 8–10, 36.

Introduction. *Margaret Fuller*. By Margaret Bell. New York: Boni, 1930. 13–14.

"Mrs. Franklin D. Roosevelt Looks at this Modern Housekeeping." *Modern Priscilla* 44 (Apr. 1930): 13, 64.

"Servants." *Forum* 83 (Jan. 1930): 24–28.

"A Summer Trip Abroad." *Women's Democratic News* 5 (Apr. 1930): 2, 12, 16; 6 (May 1930): 6, 13; 6 (June 1930): 16; 6 (Aug. 1930): 6, 16; 6 (Oct. 1930): 14, 24; 6 (Dec. 1930): 16; 6 (Feb. 1931): 14; 6 (Apr. 1931): 7, 16; 7 (May 1931): 16; 7 (July 1931): 2.

"What Is a Wife's Job Today?" *Good Housekeeping* (August 1930): 34–35, 166, 169–73.

"Women in Politics." *Women's City Club of New York Quarterly* (Jan. 1930): 5–7.

1931

"Building Character: An Editorial." *Parents' Magazine* 6 (June 1931): 17.

"How I Make My Husband Happy: An Interview." *Babylon (N.Y.) Leader* (November 30, 1931).

"Let Every Child Have His Own Library." *Wings* (Literary Guild of America) 5 (Jan. 1931): 16–17.

"Mrs. Franklin D. Roosevelt Tells the Story in a Nutshell: A Word to the Woman in the Home and to the Woman in Business by the First Lady of New York." *Baltimore and Ohio Magazine* 19 (May 1931): 21.

"Ten Rules for Success in Marriage." *Pictorial Review* 33 (Dec. 1931): 4, 36.

"This Question of Jobs." *Junior League Magazine* 17 (Jan. 1931): 14.

"Travels of a Democrat." *Women's Democratic News* (February, March, and April 1931).

1932

Introduction. *Alice's Adventures in Wonderland, Through the Looking-Glass, and The Hunting of the Shark*. By Lewis Carroll. Washington: National Home Library Foundation, 1932. [2].

Babies—Just Babies. Ed. Eleanor Roosevelt. 1–2 (Oct. 1932–June 1933).

"Be Curious—and Educated!" *Liberty* 9 (2 July 1932): 30–31.

"Children of School Age." *School Life* 18 (March 1933): 121–122.

"Christmas." *New York American* 24 Dec. 1932.

"Economic Readjustment Necessary." *Democratic Bulletin* (August 1932): 14, 27.

"Grandmothers Can Still Be Young." *Liberty* 9 (20 Feb. 1932): 38–40.

"Grow Old Gracefully." *Reader's Digest* 21 (Sept. 1932): recto and verso of back cover.

"How to Choose a Candidate." *Liberty* 9 (5 Nov. 1932): 16–17.

Introduction. *John Martin's Book: Tell Me a Story*. Jacket Library, 1932.

"Make Them Believe in You: An Editorial." *Babies—Just Babies* 1 (Nov. 1932): 3.

"Merry Christmas! An Editorial." *Babies—Just Babies* 1 (Dec. 1932): 3.

"Preparing the Child for Citizenship." *New York Times*, 24 Apr. 1932, sect. 3: 7.

"Presenting 'Babies—Just Babies.' " *Babies—Just Babies* 1 (Oct. 1932): 5–6.

"Today's Girl and Tomorrow's Job." *Woman's Home Companion* 59 (June 1932): 11–12.

"What Are the Movies Doing to Us?" *Modern Screen* 4 (Nov. 1932): 26–27, 102.

"What Religion Means to Me." *Forum* 88 (Dec. 1932): 322–24.

"What Ten Million Women Want." *Home Magazine* 5 (Mar. 1932): 19–21, 86.

"Wives of Great Men." *Liberty* 9 (1 Oct. 1932): 12–16.

"Women's Political Responsibility." *Democratic Bulletin* 7 (Jan. 1932): 12.

1933

"The Camp for Unemployed Women: A Novel American Experiment Under the Relief Administration." *World Today: Encyclopedia Britannica* 1 (Oct. 1933): 1.

"A Child Belongs in the Country: An Editorial." *Babies—Just Babies* 1 (Apr. 1933): 3.

"Consider the Babies: An Editorial." *Babies—Just Babies* 2 (May 1933): 3.

"A Happy New Year: An Editorial." *Babies—Just Babies* 1 (Jan. 1933): 3.

"Has Life Been Too Easy for Us?" *Liberty* 10 (4 Feb. 1933): 4–7.

"I Answer Two Questions." *Woman's Home Companion* (Dec. 1933): 24.

"I Want You to Write to Me." *Woman's Home Companion* (August 1933): 4.

"In Appreciation of Anne Alive!" [Foreword] *Anne Alive! A Year in the Life of a Girl of New York State*. By Margaret Doane Fayerweather. New York: Junior Literary Guild & McBridge. 1933. vii–ix.

"Lives of Great Men: An Editorial." *Babies—Just Babies* 1 (Feb. 1933): 3.

"The Married Woman in Business." *Woman's Home Companion* (Nov. 1933): 4.

"Mobilization for Human Needs." *Democratic Digest* 8 (Nov. 1933): 3.

"Mrs. Roosevelt Replies to the Letter of an Unknown Woman." *McCall's* 60 (Mar. 1933): 4.

"Mrs. Roosevelt Urges Women to Have Courage of Convictions and to Stand on Own Feet." *Clubwoman GFWC (General Federation of Women's Clubs)* 13 (Feb. 1933): 10.

"On Girls Learning to Drink." *Literary Digest* (January 1933): 3.

"Passing Thoughts of Mrs. Franklin D. Roosevelt." *Women's Democratic News* 8 (February 1933): 6.

"Passing Thoughts of Mrs. Franklin D. Roosevelt." *Women's Democratic News* 9 (June 1933): 6–7.

"Ratify the Child Labor Amendment." *Woman's Home Companion* (September 1933): 4.

"Recreation as a Preparation for Life." *Recreation* 27 (Nov. 1933): 374, 394.

"Setting Our House in Order." *Woman's Home Companion* (October 1933): 4.

"Should a Wife Support Herself?" *Every Woman* 1 (July 1933): 9.

"The State's Responsibility for Fair Working Conditions." *Scribner's Magazine* 93 (Mar. 1933): 140.

"What I Hope to Leave Behind." *Pictorial Review* 34 (Apr. 1933): 4, 45.

"When Nature Smiles: An Editorial." *Babies—Just Babies* 2 (June 1993): 3.

"White House to Mrs. Roosevelt." *New York Times*, 2 Apr. 1933, sect. 2: 1–2.

1934

"Adventures with Early American Furniture." *House & Garden* 65 (Feb. 1934): 21–23.

"Appreciations." *Miss Wylie of Vassar*. Ed. Elisabeth Woodbridge Morris. New Haven: Yale University Press for the Laura J. Wylie Memorial Associates. 149–55.

"By Car and Tent." *Woman's Home Companion* (Aug. 1934): 4.

"Exposition Farms: A New Idea in Experimental Farming." *Consumers' Guide* 1 (13 Aug. 1934): 3–4.

"First Lady Pleads for Old Age Pensions." *Social Security* 8 (Feb. 1934): 3–4.

Foreword. *Getting Acquainted with Your Children*. By James W. Howard. New York: Leisure League of America, 1934. 5–6.

"I Have Confidence in Our Common Sense." *Woman's Home Companion* (June 1934): 4.

"Learning to Teach." *Virginia Teacher* 15 (May 1934): 100–101.

"Let Us Be Thankful." *Woman's Home Companion* (Nov. 1934): 4.

"Living and Preparation for Life Through Recreation. *Recreation* 28 (Nov. 1934): 366–369.

"A Message to Parents and Teachers." *Progressive Education* 11 (Jan. 1934): 38–39.

"The National Conference on the Education of Negroes." *The Journal of Negro Education* 3 (Oct. 1934): 575–575.

"The New Governmental Interest in the Arts." *American Magazine of Art* 27 (Sept. 1934): 47.

"On Education." *School Life* 19 (Jan. 1934): 102–3.

"Our Island Possessions." *Woman's Home Companion* (Oct. 1934): 4.

"The Power of Knowledge." *Woman's Home Companion* 3 (Mar. 1934): 5.

"Recreation." *Woman's Home Companion* (Jan. 1934): 4.

"The Right to Give." *Woman's Home Companion* (Dec. 1934): 21.

"Subsistence Farmsteads." *Forum* 91 (Apr. 1934): 199–201.

"Too Old for the Job." *Woman's Home Companion* (Feb. 1934): 4.

"Traditional Holidays." *Woman's Home Companion* (Sept. 1934): 4.

"Youth Facing the Future." *Woman's Home Companion* (May 1934): 4.

"What Does the Public Expect from Nursing?" *American Journal of Nursing* 34 (July 1934): 637–640.

"The Woman's Crusade." *Daughters of the American Revolution Magazine* 68 (Jan. 1934): 8–10.

"The Women Go After the Facts about Milk Consumption." *Consumers' Guide* 1(28 May 1934): 3–5.

1935

"Because the War Idea Is Obsolete." *Why Wars Must Cease.* Ed. Rose Young. New York: Macmillan, 1935. 20–29.

"Building for the Future." *Woman's Home Companion* (Feb. 1935): 4.

"Can a Woman Ever Be President of the United States?" *Cosmopolitan* (Oct. 1935): 22–23, 120–21.

"Children." *Hearst's International Cosmopolitan* (Jan. 1935): 24–27.

"Facing Forward." *Woman's Home Companion* (Jan. 1935): 4.

"Facing the Problems of Youth." *National Parent-Teacher* 29 (Feb. 1935): 30.

"Facing the Problems of Youth." *Journal of Social Hygiene* 21 (Oct. 1935): 393–94.

"Five Years: What Have They Done To Us?" *Hearst's International Cosmopolitan* (Jan. 1935): 24–27, 146–147.

"Gardens." *Woman's Home Companion* (March 1935): 4.

"In Defense of Curiosity." *Saturday Evening Post* 208 (24 Aug. 1935): 8–9, 64–66.

"In Everlasting Remembrance." *Woman's Home Companion* (May 1935): 4.

"Jane Addams." *Democratic Digest* 12 (June 1935): 3.

"Maternal Mortality." *Woman's Home Companion.* (July 1935): 4.

"Mountains of Courage." *This Week* (4 Nov. 1935): 7, 25.

"Mrs. Roosevelt Believes in Paroles and Providing Jobs for Released Men." *Periscope* (U.S.N.E.P. Lewisburg, Pa.) 3 (Oct. 1935): 5–6.

"The Place of Women in the Community." *National Education Association Proceedings.* 1935: 313–316.

"Traveling Thoughts of Mrs. Franklin D. Roosevelt." *Women's Democratic News* 11 (Oct. 1935): 6–7.

"Tree Worship." *Woman's Home Companion* (July 1935): 4.

"We Can't Wait for the Millennium." *Liberty* (1935): 18–20.

"We Need Private Charity." *Current Controversy* (Nov. 1935): 6, 47.

"Woman's Work Is Never Done." *Woman's Home Companion* (April 1935): 4.

1936

"About State Institutions." *Caswell News* (Caswell Training School, Kinston, N.C.) 1 (May 1936): 3, 8.

"Are We Overlooking the Pursuit of Happiness?" *Parents' Magazine* 11 (Sept. 1936): 21, 67.

Bulletin (National Committee on Household Employment) 4 (Jan. 1936).

"A Fortnight in the White House." *Women's Democratic News* (New York State Section of the *Democratic Digest*) (Feb. 1936): 3–4.

"Goal Kicks for '36." *School Life* 21 (Jan. 1936): 105.

"The Homesteads Are Making Good." *Democratic Digest* 13 (Mar. 1936): 10.

"A Month at the White House." *Women's Democratic News* (New York State Section of the *Democratic Digest*) (June 1936): 3.

"The Negro and Social Change." *Opportunity* (Jan. 1936): 22–23.

"Persistence Wins." *School Press Review* (Oct. 1936): 1–2.

"Safeguard the Children." *American Child* 18 (Jan. 1936): 1.

"The Unemployed Are Not a Strange Race." *Democratic Digest* (June 1936): 19.

"What Libraries Mean to the Nation." *American Library Association Bulletin* (June 1936): 477–79.

"The White House and Here and There." *Women's Democratic News* (New York State Section of the *Democratic Digest*) (July 1937): 2.

1937

"A Busy Month in and out of the White House." *Women's Democratic News* (New York State Section of the *Democratic Digest*) (July 1937): 2.

"A Christmas Letter." *Post-Intelligencer* [Seattle, Wash.], 25 Nov. 1937.

"A Christmas-Spirited Housecleaning." *Reader's Digest* 31 (31 Dec. 1937): verso of front cover, recto and verso of back cover.

"Highlights of a Busy Month." *Women's Democratic News* (New York State Section of the *Democratic Digest*) (May 1937): 2.

"Highlights of a Month at the White House." *Women's Democratic News* (New York State Section of the *Democratic Digest*) (Aug. 1937): 2, 4.

"Highlights of the Past Few Months." *Women's Democratic News* (New York State Section of the *Democratic Digest*) (Mar. 1937): 2.

"In Praise of Molly Dewson." *Democratic Digest* 14 (Nov. 1937): 15.

"A Month in the White House." *Women's Democratic News* (New York State Section of the *Democratic Digest*) (Apr. 1937): 2, 4.

"My Month." *Women's Democratic News* (New York State Section of the *Democratic Digest*) (Dec. 1937): 3.

"A Peaceful Month in the Country." *Women's Democratic News* (New York State Section of the *Democratic Digest*) (Oct. 1937): 2, 4.

"Questions." *Progressive Education* 14 (Oct. 1937): 407.

"Should Wives Work?" *Good Housekeeping* 105 (Dec. 1937): 28–29, 211–12.

"South by Motor and West by Plane." *Women's Democratic News* (New York State Section of the *Democratic Digest*) (July 1937): 2.

"This Is My Story." *Ladies' Home Journal* 54 (Apr. 1937): 11–13, 48, 50, 53, 55; 54 (May 1937): 14–15, 47–48, 50, 52–53; 54 (June 1937): 14–15, 100, 102–4, 106–7; 54 (July 1937): 22, 76–80; 54 (Aug. 1937): 29, 68–70, 72; 54 (Sept. 1937): 30, 52–53, 55–56; 54 (Oct. 1937): 18, 88, 90, 93, 95; 54 (Nov. 1937): 19, 55–56, 58–60, 63; 54 (Dec. 1937): 29, 49, 51–52, 54–55; 55 (Jan. 1938): 23, 55–57.

"A Vacation Month Spent in Guest House at the Val-Kill Cottages." *Women's Democratic News* (New York State Section of the *Democratic Digest*) (Sept. 1937): 2, 4.

Foreword. *The White House: An Informal History of Its Architecture, Interiors and Gardens.* By Ethel Lewis. New York: Dodd, Mead, 1937, v–vi.

"When the First Lady of the Land Entertains: An Interview." *Democratic Digest* 14 (Sept. 1937): 16–17.

1938

"Americans I Admire." *Woman's Day* 1 (Sept. 1938): 4–5, 43–44; 2 (Nov. 1938): 8–9, 42; 2 (Jan. 1939): 8–9, 43; 2 (Mar. 1939): 16, 49.

"Cherry Blossom Time in Washington." *Reader's Digest* 32 (Apr. 1938): 57–58.

"Cherry-Blossom Time." *Reader's Digest* 82 (Apr. 1963): 228c.

"A Christmas Letter." *Post-Intelligencer* [Seattle, Wash.], 24 Nov. 1938.

"Divorce." *Ladies' Home Journal* 55 (Apr. 1938): 16.

"Education, a Child's Life." *Progressive Education* 15 (Oct. 1938): 451.

"Henry Street's Pioneer." Rev. of *Lillian Wald: Neighbor and Crusader* by R. L. Duffus. *Survey Graphic* 27 (Dec. 1938): 616.

"Lady Bountiful Rolls up Her Sleeves." *Reader's Digest* 32 (Mar. 1938): 53–55.

"Mrs. Roosevelt Answers Mr. Wells on 'The Future of the Jews.' " *Liberty* 15 (31 Dec. 1938): 4–5.

"My Children." *McCall's* (Apr. 1938): 4, 75.

"My Day." *Consumers' Cooperative* 24 (Feb. 1938): 19.

"My Days." *Quote* 1 (Nov. 1938): 36–37.

"My Home." *McCall's* (Feb. 1938): 4, 46, 132.

"My Job." *McCall's* (Mar. 1938): 4, 68.

"My Month." *Women's Democratic News* (New York State Section of the *Democratic Digest*) (Feb. 1938): 2, 4.

"On Teachers and Teaching." *Harvard Educational Review* 8 (Oct. 1938): 423–24.

"Resolutions I Wish Consumers Would Make for 1938: A Dozen Targets for Consumers Who Want to Make Their Buying Power Count Toward a Better New Year." *Consumers' Guide* 4 (3 Jan. 1938): 3–8.

"Seeking a Place in Community." *Southern Workman* 67 (June 1938): 165–171.

"Should Married Women Work? A Californian Asks Mrs. Roosevelt to Explain Her Statement in the Democratic Digest." *Democratic Digest* 15 (May 1938): 24.

"Success Formula for Public-Spirited Women." *Democratic Digest* 15 (Aug. 1938): 39.

"Trialog on Office Holders." *Independent Woman* (Jan. 1938): 17–18.

"Two Paths to Peace." *Democratic Digest* (Aug. 1938): 19.

"Youth." *Hearst's International Cosmopolitan* (Feb. 1938): 26–27, 134–36.

1939

"Adventures with Early American Furniture." *House and Garden* (Feb. 1939): 21–23.

"American Democracy and Youth." *New University* (Mar. 1939): 7–8.

"Challenge." *The Guardian* (Dec. 1939): 1–2.

Common Sense Neutrality. Ed. Paul Comly French. New York: Hastings, 1939. 182–97.

"Conquer Fear and You Will Enjoy Living." *Look* 3 (23 May 1939): 6–11.

"Current Quotations." *Education Digest* 4 (May 1939): 7.

"Do Our Young People Need Religion?" *Liberty* 16 (17 June 1939): 12–13.

"Eleanor Roosevelt Says." *Educational Music Magazine* 18 (Jan./Feb. 1939): 6–7.

"Flying Is Fun." *Collier's* 103 (22 Apr. 1939): 15, 88–89.

"Food in America." *Woman's Day* (Oct. 1939): 27–29, 33.

"Good Manners." *Ladies' Home Journal* 56 (June 1939): 21, 116–17.

"Government Becomes Alive." *Daily Times* [Chicago, Ill.], 6 Sept. 1939: 55.

"Keepers of Democracy." *Virginia Quarterly Review* 15 (Jan. 1939): 1–5.

"Mrs. Roosevelt Awards Medal." *Crisis* (Sept. 1939): 265, 285.

"Mrs. Roosevelt Counsels Women." *Democratic Digest* 16 (Jan. 1939): 11.

"Mrs. Roosevelt on Democratic Women's Day." *Democratic Digest* 16 (Dec. 1939): 29.

"Our American Homes." *Child Study* 16 (May 1939): 182.

"Security Begins Beyond the City Limits." *Hearst's International Cosmopolitan* 106 (May 1939): 38–39, 90–91.

"Security for Youth and Age." *Time* (March 6, 1939): 11.

"Talk to Birds." *Good Housekeeping* 109 (Dec. 1939): 27–29.

To Enrich Young Life: Ten Years with the Junior Literary Guild in the Schools of Our Country. Garden City: Junior Literary Guild, 1939. [24].

"A Vision for Today." *New York Times Magazine*, 24 Dec. 1939: 4.

"War! What the Women of America Can Do to Prevent It." *Woman's Day* 2 (Apr. 1939): 4–5, 46–47.

Introduction. *Washington, Nerve Center. The Face of America*. By Edwin Rosskam; Ruby A. Black, co-editor. New York: Alliance, 1939. 5–6.

"Why I Am Against the People's Vote on War." *Liberty* 16 (8 Apr. 1939): 7–8.

"Why I Am a Democrat." *Junior League* (Sept. 1939): 29, 60.

"Women in Politics." *Democratic Digest* 16 (July 1939): 13–14.

"The Women of America Must Fight." *This Week Magazine* 16 (2 July 1939): 7.

"You Can Prevent Crime." *Woman* (Nov. 1939): 36–37.

1940

"The American Home and Present Day Conditions." *What's New in Home Economics* 4 (April 1940): 1, 11.

"Art and Our Warring World." *Round Table* (November 24, 1940).

Foreword. *American Youth: An Enforced Reconnaissance*. Ed. Thacher Winslow and Frank P. Davidson. Cambridge: Harvard University Press, 1940. ix–xi.

Foreword. *American Youth Today*. By Leslie A. Gould. New York: Random House, 1940. vii–viii.

"Christmas 1940: A Short Story." *Liberty* (28 Dec. 1940): 10–13.

"Christmas—A Story." *Eleanor Roosevelt's Christmas Book.* New York: Dodd, Mead. 1963. 3–5.

"Civil Liberties, the Individual and the Crisis." *Reference Shelf* 14 (1940): 173–182.

"Eleanor Roosevelt on Recreation." *Recreation* 34 (Dec. 1940): 570.

"Farm Youth of Today." *American Farm Youth* 6 (Nov. 1940): 3.

"Fear Is the Enemy." *Nation* 150 (10 Feb. 1940): 173.

"A Guest Editorial." *Opportunity* 18 (Mar. 1940): 66.

Foreword. *Happy Times in Czechoslovakia.* By Libushka Bartusek. New York: Knopf, 1940. [iii].

"Helping Them to Help Themselves." *Rotarian* 56 (Apr. 1940): 8–11.

"Helping People to Help Themselves." *Ladies' Home Journal* 57 (Aug. 1940): 12.

"Homes for Americans: An Editorial." *Woman's Day* 3 (Apr. 1940): 3.

"In Appreciation." *Synagogue Light* 8 (Oct. 1940): 4.

"Insuring Democracy." *Collier's* 105 (15 June 1940): 87–88.

"Intolerance." *Cosmopolitan* (Feb. 1940): 24–25, 102–3.

"The Man from Jail." *World Digest* 12 (June 1940): 61–62.

"Men Have to Be Humored." *Woman's Day* 3 (Aug. 1940): 12–13, 58.

"Mrs. Roosevelt's Advice on Public Speaking." *Democratic Digest* 17 (Feb. 1940): 3.

"Mrs. Roosevelt Speaks." *Democratic Digest* 17 (Aug. 1940): 16.

"My Advice to American Youth." *Look* 4 (27 Aug. 1940): 56–58.

"Read the Bill of Rights." *Democratic Digest* 17 (Jan. 1940): 12.

"Shall We Enroll Aliens? No." *Liberty* 17 (3 Feb. 1940): 13.

"Sixty Years Consecutive ORT Work." *ORT Economic Bulletin* 1 (Nov. 40): 1–2.

"A Spanking." *Liberty* 17 (22 June 1949): 6–8.

"Twenty-four Hours." *Ladies' Home Journal* 57 (Oct. 1940): 20, 58, 60.

"What Can We Do for Youth?" *Occupations* 19 (Oct. 1940): 9–10.

"What Value Has the Ballot for Women?" *Democratic Digest* 17 (June/July 1940): 25.

"The White House Speaks." *Ladies' Home Journal* 57 (June 1940): 21, 121–24.

"Why I Still Believe in the Youth Congress." *Liberty* 17 (20 Apr. 1940): 30–32.

"Women in Politics." *Good Housekeeping* 110 (Jan. 1940): 8–19, 150; 110 (Mar. 1940): 45, 68; 110 (Apr. 1940): 45, 201–3.

"Women in Politics." *Woman's Press* (Y.W.C.A.) (Apr. 1940): 165.

Foreword. *Youth—Millions Too Many? A Search for Youth's Place in America.* By Bruce L. Melvin. New York: Association Press, 1940. 5–6.

1941

[Review]. *The American Presidency: An Interpretation.* By Harold J. Laski. *Harvard Law Review* 54 (June 1941): 1413–14.

"Appreciating the Great Outdoors." *Student Life* 7 (May 1941): 2.

"Defense and Girls." *Ladies' Home Journal* 58 (May 1941): 25, 54.

"Girls and National Defense." *Women in America: Half of History.* Ed. Mary Kay Tetreault. Chicago: Rand McNally, 1978. 60–64.

"First Lady Addresses Workers' Wives." *Trade Union Courier* 6 (1 Sept. 1941): 6.

"First Lady in Her Own Right." *Echo*. (March 1941): 3–5.

"If I Were a Freshman . . ." *Threshold* 1 (Oct. 1941): 5–6.

"Important as Ever." *Our Bill of Rights: What It Means to Me, a National Symposium.* By James Waterman Wise. New York: Bill of Rights Sesqui-centennial, 1941. 116.

"An Inspiration to All." *Opinion* 12 (Nov. 1941): 12.

"Know What We Defend." *Democratic Digest* 18 (May 3, 1941): 12–13.

"Larder for the Democracies." *Democratic Digest* 18 (Oct. 1941): 7.

"My Week." *Our Country* 1 (May 1941): 16.

Foreword. *The New Program of the United States Committee of International Student Service.* New York: The Committee, 1941. 4–5.

"Our Widening Horizon." *Democratic Digest* 18 (Feb. 1941): 9.

"Shall We Draft American Women?" *Liberty* 18 (13 Sept. 1941): 10–11.

"Social Gains and Defense." *Common Sense* 10 (March 1941): 71–77.

"Speech Training for Youth." *Quarterly Journal of Speech* 27 (Oct. 1941): 369–71.

"Tower Club." *The Tower: Yearbook of the Tower Club, Ohio State University, 1941.* 2.

"Weaving: An Old American Handicraft." *Woman's Day* (Feb. 1941): 27–28.

"What Does Pan-American Friendship Mean?" *Liberty* 18 (4 Oct. 1941): 10–11 and *Congressional Record Appendix* (22 Oct. 1941): A4784–85.

"What Is the Matter with Women?" *Liberty* 18 (3 May 1941): 12–13.

"What Must We Do to Improve the Health and Well-Being of the American People?" *Town Meeting* (December 8, 1941): 13–22.

"What's Wrong with the Draft." *Look* 5 (15 July 1941): 23–25.

"Women in Defense: A Script by Mrs. Roosevelt." *New York Times Magazine*, 7 Dec. 1941: 6–7.

1942

"Attitudes of Youth and Morale." *The Family in a World at War* edited by D. M. Gruenberg. Harper and Brothers, 1942.

Foreword. "Born in the USA." *Baby Talk* 7 (July 1942): 11.

"The Community and Morale." *Educational Record* 23 (Jan. 1942): 63–68.

"The Democratic Effort." *Common Ground* 2 (Spring 1942): 9–10.

"Education Is the Cornerstone on Which We Must Build Liberty." *Education for Victory* 1 (1 Apr. 1942): 1.

"For American Unity." *American Unity* 1 (Oct. 1942): 3.

"How about Your Vacation?" *Cosmopolitan* (Apr. 1942): 28–29.

"The Issue Is Freedom." Rev. of *American Unity and Asia*. by Pearl Buck. *New Republic* 107 (3 Aug. 1942): 147–48.

"Let Us Earn a True Peace." *Country Gentleman* 112 (Dec. 1942): 9, 52–53.

"Let Us Have Faith in Democracy." *Land Policy Review* 5 (Jan. 1942): 20–22.

"Marching . . . with Eleanor Roosevelt: This Month Your Government Asks That You . . ." *McCall's* 69 (Mar. 1942): 57.

"Messages." *Free World* 4 (Oct. 1942): 7–18.

"Mobilizing Human Skills." *Common Sense* 11 (July 1942): 240–42.

"Mrs. Roosevelt Sends Columbus Day Message to Jewish People Through Jewish Mirror." *Jewish Mirror* 1 (Oct. 1942): 3.

"Must We Hate to Fight? No." *Saturday Review of Literature* 25 (4 July 1942): 13.

"My Day." *Democratic Digest* 19 (Sept. 1942): 14.

"My Day—The Polish Day." *Pulaski Foundation Bulletin* 1 (Dec. 1942): 3.

"Race, Religion and Prejudice." *New Republic* 106 (11 May 1942): 630.

Preface. *Refugees at Work*. Comp. Sophia M. Robinson. New York: King's Crown, 1942. [v]–vi.

Special Issue on Morale. Ed. Eleanor Roosevelt. *Saturday Review of Literature* 25 (4 July 1942).

"To Care for Him Who Shall Have Borne the Battle." *Collier's* 110 (28 Nov. 1942): 20.

"War Work Is Not Enough." *Democratic Digest* 19 (Oct. 1942): cover, 10, 14.

"What Is Morale." *Saturday Review of Literature* 25 (4 July 1942): 12.

"What We Are Fighting For." *American Magazine* 134 (July 1942): 16–17, 60–62.

1943

"Abolish Jim Crow!" *New Threshold* 1 (Aug. 1943): 4, 34.

"The Four Equalities." *Negro Digest* 1 (Sept. 1943): 81–83.

"The Case Against the Negro Press. Con." *Negro Digest* 1 (Feb. 1943): 53.

"A Challenge to American Sportsmanship." *Collier's* 112 (16 Oct. 1943): 21, 71.

"Eleanor Roosevelt Visits the South Pacific: As the First Lady Views It." *Democratic Digest* 20 (Sept. 1943): 8–9.

"First Lady on Home Safety." *Home Safety Review* 1 (May/June 1943): 10, 15.

"Freedom: Promise or Fact." *Negro Digest* 1 (Oct. 1943): 8–9.

"How Britain Is Treating Our Soldier Boys and Girls." *Ladies' Home Journal* 60 (Feb. 1943): 24–25, 125–26.

"It's a Ladies' Fight." *Kelly Magazine* (San Antonio Air Service Command) 1 (Christmas 1943): 7.

"It's Patriotic to Teach." *Educational Leadership* 1 (Oct. 1943): 3 and *Teacher's Digest* 4 (Feb. 1944): 56.

"A Message to the Mountain Folk." *Arcadian Life Magazine* 2 (Spring/Summer 1943): 5.

"Monthly Posters Are Vital in War Bond Sale." *Minute Man* 2 (15 May 1943): 5.

"Noted Women Write on World We Want—First Article by Mrs. Roosevelt." *Christian Science Monitor* 5 Jan. 1943, Atlantic ed.: 8.

"The World We Want." *Letter from America* 13 (22 Jan. 1943): 1.

"The Red Cross in the South Seas." *Ladies' Home Journal* 60 (Dec. 1943): 30, 158–60.

"Studying Spanish." *Saturday Review of Literature* 26 (10 Apr. 1943): 10.

"They Talk Our Language Differently." *Collier's* 111 (27 Feb. 1943): 18, 20, 22.

"Trained Minds and Trained Hearts." *Smith Alumnae Quarterly* 34 (May 1943): 125.

"Women at War in Great Britain." *Ladies' Home Journal* 60 (Apr. 1943): 22–25, 70, 72.

"Women Students—the Men Are Counting on You!" *Intercollegian* 61 (Dec. 1943): 7.

"Your New World." *Life Story* 7 (Feb. 1943): 33.

1944

"American Red Cross 'Down Under.' " *American Lawn Tennis* 37 (Apr. 1944): 16–17.

"The American Spirit." *Congressional Weekly* 11 (June 9, 1944): 10–11.

"American Women in the War." *Reader's Digest* 44 (Jan. 1944): 42–44.

"As Johnny Thinks of Home: He Idealizes What He Left Behind." *Social Action* 10 (15 Mar. 1944): 5–7.

"Eleanor Roosevelt Says." *Ammunition* (UAW-CIO) 2 (Aug. 1944): 1.

"Equality Is Labor's Cause." *Workmen's Circle Call* 12 (July 1944): 10.

"Henry Wallace's Democracy." Rev. of *Democracy Reborn* by Henry Wallace. *New Republic* 111 (7 Aug. 1944): 165–66.

"How to Take Criticism." *Ladies' Home Journal* 61 (Nov. 1944): 155, 171.

"If You Ask Me." *Reader's Digest* 45 (Sept. 1944): 100–101.

"In Unity There Is Strength." *Workmen's Circle Call* 12 (July 1944): 10.

"Is the Human Race Worth Saving?" *Liberty* 21 (23 Dec. 1944): 15, 54.

"It's Patriotic to Teach." *Teacher's Digest* 4 (Feb. 1944): 56.

"New Stepping Stones in the Pacific." *Survey Graphic* 33 (Jan. 1944): 5.

"Our Homes in the Post-War World." *National Parent-Teacher* 38 (June 1944): 22–23.

"The South in Postwar America." *Southern Patriot* 2 (June 1944): 1–2.

"To the Women of the B & O Family." *Baltimore and Ohio Magazine* 30 (June 1944): 3.

"We Must Have Compulsory Service." *Parents' Magazine* 19 (Nov. 1944): 16–18.

"Should the U.S. Adopt Peacetime Compulsory Military Training? Pro." *Congressional Digest* 24 (Jan. 1945): 16.

"What I Saw in the South Seas." *Ladies' Home Journal* 61 (Feb. 1944): 26–27, 88–90.

"What Kind of World Are We Fighting For?" *Canadian Home Journal* (Jan. 1944): 12–13.

"What Will Happen to Women War Workers in Post-War America." *Southern Patriot* 2 (Apr. 1944): 1–2.

"What Will Victory Bring?" *Argosy* 318 (Apr. 1944): 16–17.

"Woman's Place After the War." *Click* 7 (Aug. 1944): 17–19.

"Women at the Peace Conference." *Reader's Digest* 44 (Apr. 1944): 48–49.

Foreword. "Women in the Postwar World." *Journal of Educational Sociology* 17 (Apr. 1944): 449–50.

"Young Men Must Look Forward." *Future* 6 (June 1944): 9.

1945

"Address to Conference on Educational Programs for Veterans." *Education for Victory* 3 (April 1945): 1–3.

"From the Melting Pot—An American Race." *Liberty* 22 (14 July 1945): 17, 89.

"If You Ask Me." *Negro Digest* 3 (Feb. 1945): 9–10.

"Milestone in Human Relations." *Council Women (National Council of Jewish Women)* 7 (May/June 1945): 4–5, 16.

"One of Many." *Reader's Digest* 46 (June 1945): 26.

"Personal Sorrow Lost in Humanity's Sadness." *Democratic Digest* 22 (June 1945): 9.

"Mrs. Roosevelt Says." *Bayonet* 1 (Jan. 1945): 16.

"Music in the White House." *Your Music* (Nov. 1945).

"Now for the World We Are Fighting For." *Modern Mystic and Monthly Science Review* 5 (July 1945): 124–25.

"Tolerance Is an Ugly Word." *Coronet* 18 (July 1945): 118 and *Negro Digest* 3 (Oct. 1945): 7–8.

Introduction. *The White House Conference on Rural Education, October 3, 4, and 5, 1944.* Washington: National Education Association of the U.S., n.d. 11–13.

"You Can't Pauperize Children." *Ladies' Home Journal* 62 (Sept. 1945): 128–29.

1946

"American Women in the War." *Reader's Digest* (Jan. 1946): 42–44.

"Can America Be Prosperous in a Sea of Misery?" *Ladies' Home Journal* (May 1946), 35, 131–132, 134.

Foreword. *As He Saw It.* By Elliott Roosevelt. New York: Duell, Sloan and Pearce, 1946. vii–ix.

Congressional Record (18 July 1946): 9401.

"Eleanor Roosevelt to the German American." *German American* 5 (15 Oct. 1946): 3.

"For an International Bill of Rights." *Democratic Digest* 23 (July 1946): 4–5.

"Human Rights and Human Freedom." *New York Times Magazine*, 26 March 1946: 21.

"If You Ask Mrs. Roosevelt." *Practical English* 2 (17 Mar. 1947): 7.

"Importance of Background Knowledge in Building for the Future." *Annals of the American Academy of Political and Social Science* 246 (July 1946): 9–12.

Preface. *The Jew in American Life.* By James Waterman Wise. New York: Messner, 1946. 5–6.

"A Message to American Girls." *American Girl* 29 (Feb. 1946): 4.

"The Minorities Question." *Toward a Better World.* Ed. William Scarlett. Philadelphia: Winston, 1946. 35–39 and in *Christianity Takes a Stand: An Approach to the Issues of Today, a Symposium.* Penguin, 612. Ed. William Scarlett. New York: Penguin, 1946. 72–76.

"The Refugees Place in American Life." *Talks (CBS)* IV (January 1946): 28–29.

"Mrs. Roosevelt Speaks." *Summary* (Elmira, N.Y. Reformatory) 64 (29 Mar. 1946): 2.

"My Father and I." *New York Times Magazine*, 16 June 1946: 28.

"The People Interview Mrs. Roosevelt." *Saturday Review of Literature* 29 (23 Mar. 1946): 24.

"The United Nations and You. *Vital Speeches of the Day* 112 (May 1, 1946): 444–45.

"U.S. Position on International Refugee Organizations." *Department of State Bulletin* 15 (Nov. 24, 1946): 935–38.

"Why I Do Not Choose to Run." *Look* 10 (9 July 1946): 25–26.

"Why I Travel." *Holiday* (Apr. 1946): 24–26.

1947

Foreword. *F.D.R. Columnist: The Uncollected Columns of Franklin D. Roosevelt.* Ed. Donald Scott Carmichael. Chicago: Pellegrini & Cudahy, 1947. [ii–iii].

Foreword. *F.D.R.: His Personal Letters, Early Years.* Ed. Elliott Roosevelt. New York: Duell, Sloan and Pearce, 1947. xv–xvi.

"Getting Over Having a Baby." *Babies Keep Coming: An Anthology*. Ed. Rebecca Reyher. New York: Whittlesey House-McGraw-Hill, 1947. 400–1.

"I Tell My Life Story in Pictures." *Look* 11 (16 Sept. 1947): 26–33.

"If I Had It All to Do Over Again." *Babies Keep Coming: An Anthology*. Ed. Rebecca Reyher. New York: Whittlesey House-McGraw-Hill, 1947. 321–23.

"In Pursuit of Happiness." *Woman's Journal* 11 (Aug. 1947): 20.

"International Bill of Human Rights." *Methodist Woman* 8 (Nov. 1947): 14.

"Message from Mrs. Franklin D. Roosevelt, Chairman, Commission on Human Rights." *United Nations Weekly Bulletin* 2 (25 Feb. 1947): 170.

"Roosevelt Christening Charm." *Babies Keep Coming: An Anthology*. Ed. Rebecca Reyher. New York: Whittlesey House-McGraw-Hill, 1947. 123–24.

"The Russians Are Tough." *Look* 11 (18 Feb. 1947): 65–69.

"Should a Negro Boy Ask a White Girl to Dance?" *Negro Digest* 6 (Dec. 1947): 41–42.

"Women and the United Nations." *General Federation Clubwomen* 27 (Sept. 1947):17–18.

1948

"Acceptance Address." *Bryn Mawr Alumnae Bulletin* 28 (April 1948).

"A Comment by the Commission Chairman: Mrs. Franklin D. Roosevelt." *United Nations Bulletin* 5 (1 July 1948): 521.

"A Decade of Democratic Women's Days." *Democratic Digest* 25 (Aug. 1948): 16.

Foreword. *F.D.R.: His Personal Letters, 1905–1928*. Ed. Elliott Roosevelt and James N. Rosenau. New York: Duell, Sloan and Pearce, 1948. xvii–xix.

"He Learned to Bear It." *The Roosevelt Treasury*. Ed. James N. Rosenau. Garden City: Doubleday, 1951. 74–75.

"Letters from Our Honeymoon." *Ladies' Home Journal* 65 (Dec. 1948): 42–43, 95–97, 99, 102, 104–105.

"Liberals in This Year of Decision." *The Christian Register* 127 (June 1948): 26–28, 33.

"Plain Talk about Wallace." *Democratic Digest* 25 (Apr. 1948): 2.

"The Promise of Human Rights." *Foreign Affairs* 26 (Apr. 1948): 470–77.

"Toward Human Rights Throughout the World." *Democratic Digest* 25 (Feb. 1948): 14–15.

1949

Editorial. *ADA World* 3 (20 Apr. 1949): 2.

Introduction. *Freedom's Charter: The Universal Declaration of Human Rights*. Headline Series, 76. By O. Frederick Nolde. New York: Foreign Policy Association, 1949. 3–4 and Headline Series, 76. By O. Frederick Nolde. Millwood: Kraus Reprint, 1973. 3–4.

"Human Rights." *Peace on Earth*. New York: Hermitage House, 1949. 65–71.

"If You Ask Me." *Negro Digest* 7 (July 1949): 20–23.

"Importance of the Covenant." *United Nations Bulletin* 7 (1 July 1949): 3 and *The Covenant on Human Rights*. By Charles Malik and Mrs. Franklin D. Roosevelt. New York: International Documents Service, 1949. 4–5.

Foreword. *Mark Twain and Franklin D. Roosevelt*. By Cyril Clemens. Webster Groves: International Mark Twain Society, 1949. [11].

"International Children's Emergency Fund." *Relief for Children* Department of State Publication 3415, International Organization and Conference Series III, 24. (Feb. 1949): 1–8.

"Making Human Rights Come Alive." *Phi Delta Kappan* 31 (Sept. 1949): 23–28.

"A Message to College Men." *Prologue* (Bowdoin College) 2 (May 1949): 7.

"Messages on Human Rights." *United Nations Bulletin* 7 (15 Dec. 1949): 743–45, 747–49.

"The Rights of Assembly." *United Nations Bulletin* 6 (Jan. 1, 1949): 5.

"This I Remember." *McCall's* 76 (June 1949): 11–15, 116–28, 138–39, 141–42, 144–49, 156, 159, 163–64; 76 (July 1949): 16–19, 95–98, 101–2, 109–12, 120, 123–24, 127–28; 76 (Aug. 1949): 14–15, 99–102, 109–13, 116, 119–20, 123–24, 127–28; 76 (Sept. 1949): 16–17, 111–16, 128, 130, 132–39, 143–45, 148; 77 (Oct. 1949): 18–19, 33–34, 36–38, 40–42, 44, 46, 59–60, 62, 66–70, 80; 77 (Nov. 1949): 20–21, 112–26, 136; 77 (Dec. 1949): 20–23, 80, 82, 84, 86, 88–89, 91.

"Universal Declaration of Human Rights." *School Life* 31 (Mar. 1949): 8–10.

"What I Think of the United Nations." *United Nations World* 3 (Aug. 1949): 39–41, 48.

"Eleanor Roosevelt: The United Nations." *Annals of America.* Vol. 16. Chicago: Encyclopedia Britannica, 1968. 613–17.

1950

"A Brief History of the Drafting of the Universal Declaration of Human Rights and of the Draft Covenant on Human Rights." *Negro History Bulletin* 14 (Nov. 1950). 29–30, 46.

"Continue the Fight for Better Schools." *School Life* 33 (Dec. 1950): 33–34.

Foreword. *F.D.R.: His Personal Letters, 1928–1945.* Ed. Elliott Roosevelt and Joseph P. Lash. New York: Duell, Sloan and Pearce, 1950. xvii.

"A Front on Which We May Serve." *United Nations World* 4 (June 1950): 50–51.

"If I Were a Republican Today." *Cosmopolitan* 128 (June 1950): 29, 172.

"A Message to Boys' Village . . . and You!" *Southwest Louisiana Boys' Village News* 3 (Aug. 1950): cover.

"Mrs. Roosevelt Discusses Human Rights." *United Nations Reporter* 3 (Apr. 1950): 3.

Foreword. *Pandit Nehru's Discovery of America.* By Philip Pothens. Madras: Indian Press, 1950). 9.

"The Real Perle Mesta." *Flair* 1 (Oct. 1950): 31, 110.

"Reason . . . Must . . . Dominate . . ." *United Nations Bulletin* 8 (1 Apr. 1950): 327.

"This I Believe about Public Schools." *The Nation's Schools* 45 (March 1950): 31–36.

"This I Remember." *Omnibook* 12 (May 1950): 1–45.

"United Nations: All of Us Can Help." *Book of Knowledge 1950 Annual.* New York: Grolier Society, 1950. 161–62.

"What Liberty Means to Me." *Liberty* (1950) and *The Liberty Years, 1924–1940.* Ed. Allen Churchill. Englewood Cliffs: Prentice-Hall, 1969. 426–27.

"Women Have Come a Long Way." *Harper's* 201 (Oct. 1950): 74–76.

Introduction. *The World We Saw.* By Mary Bell Decker. New York: R. Smith, 1950. 3.

1951

"A Collector's Characteristics." *The Roosevelt Treasury.* Ed. James N. Rosenau. Garden City: Doubleday, 1951. 199–201.

"The Elementary Teacher as a Champion of Human Rights." *Instructor* 61 (Sept. 1951): 7.

"The Faces of the People." *The Roosevelt Treasury*. Ed. James N. Rosenau. Garden City: Doubleday, 1951. 445–49.

"Franklin Was a Practical Politician." *The Roosevelt Treasury*. Ed. James N. Rosenau. Garden City: Doubleday, 1951. 380–81.

"He Disliked Being Disagreeable." *The Roosevelt Treasury*. Ed. James N. Rosenau. Garden City: Doubleday, 1951. 155–57.

"The Home: A Citadel of Freedom." *Jewish Parents Magazine* (Apr. 1951): 4–5.

Introduction. *No Time for Tears*. By Charles H. Andrews. Garden City: Doubleday, 1951. 7–8.

"Redrafting the Human Rights Covenant." *United Nations Bulletin* 10 (15 Apr. 1951): 386.

"Report on the Covenant." *United Nations World* 5 (Aug. 1951): 17–18.

"A Report on the Covenant of Human Rights." *Delhi Mirror* 1 (24 Feb. 1952): 4, 13.

"The Role of the Elder Statesman Appealed to Him." *The Roosevelt Treasury*. Ed. James N. Rosenau. Garden City: Doubleday, 1951. 190–92.

"The Seven People Who Shaped My Life." *Look* 15 (19 June 1951): 54–56, 58.

"Statement on Draft Covenant on Human Rights." *Department of State Bulletin* 25 (13 Dec. 1951): 1059, 1064–66.

Foreword. *The Story of My Life*. By Helen Keller. 1951 and New York: Dell, 1961. 7–8 and 1972. 7–8.

"That Was Characteristic of Franklin." *The Roosevelt Treasury*. Ed. James N. Rosenau. Garden City: Doubleday, 1951. 116–17.

"To My Complete Surprise." *The Roosevelt Treasury*. Ed. James N. Rosenau. Garden City: Doubleday, 1951. 186–87.

"A World for Peace." *International Home Quarterly* 15 (Summer 1951): 136–40.

1952

Foreword. *Beauty Behind Barbed Wire: The Arts of the Japanese in Our War Relocation Camps*. By Allen H. Eaton. New York: Harper, 1952. xi–xii.

"Communist Charges vs. US Territorial Plans." *Department of State Bulletin* 27 (27 Dec. 1952): 1032–37.

"Convention Headlines." *Democratic Digest* 29 (Aug. 9, 1952): 10.

Introduction. *The Diary of a Young Girl*. By Anne Frank. Garden City: Doubleday, 1952. 7–8.

Foreword. *A Fair World for All: The Meaning of the Declaration of Human Rights*. By Dorothy Canfield Fisher. New York: Whittlesey House, 1952. 5–6.

"Restlessness of Youth: An Asset to Free Societies." *Department of State Bulletin* 26 (21 Jan. 1952): 94–97.

"Growth That Starts from Thinking." *This I Believe [1]: The Living Philosophies of One Hundred Thoughtful Men and Women in All Walks of Life*. Ed. Edward P. Morgan. New York: Simon & Schuster, 1952. 155–56.

Foreword. *To Win These Rights: A Personal Story of the CIO in the South*. By Lucy Randolph Mason. New York: Harper, 1952. [ix] and Westport: Greenwood, 1970. [ix].

"UN: Good U.S. Investment." *Foreign Policy Bulletin* 32 (1 Oct. 1952): 1–2.

"The United Nations and You." *See* 11 (Nov. 1952): 10–13.

1953

"The Education of an American." *House & Garden* 104 (Aug. 1953): 60–61.

"The Japan I Saw." *Minneapolis Sunday Tribune Picture Roto Magazine*, 11 Oct. 1953: 4–5.

"The Need for Intellectual Freedom." *Say* 5 (Spring 1954): 4.

Foreword. *Peace Through Strength: Bernard Baruch and a Blueprint for Security*. By Morris V. Rosenbloom. Washington: American Survey Association—Farrar, Straus and Young. 1953. 23–26.

Foreword. *Roosevelt and the Warm Springs Story*. By Turnley Walker. New York: Wyn, 1953. [v].

"Should UN Remain a Major Plank in U.S. Policy?" *Foreign Policy Bulletin* 33 (15 Oct. 1953): 4–5.

"Some of My Best Friends Are Negro." *Ebony* 9 (Feb. 1953): 16–20, 22, 24–26 and *White on Black: The Views of Twenty-one White Americans on the Negro*. Ed. Era Bell Thompson and Herbert Nipson. Chicago: Johnson, 1963. 3–17.

"Speaking of Teaching." *National Parent-Teacher* 48 (Nov. 1953): 20.

"To Answer Their Needs . . ." *United Nations Bulletin* 14 (15 Jan. 1953): 92.

"U.N. and the Welfare of the World." *National Parent-Teacher*. 47 (June 1953): 14–16.

1954

Foreword. *The Captains and the Kings*. By Edith Benham Helm. New York: Putnam's, 1954. v–vii.

"Churchill as a Guest." *Churchill by His Contemporaries*. Ed. Charles Eade. New York: Simon and Schuster, 1954. 186–92.

Foreword. *G. P. A. Healy, American Artist: An Intimate Chronicle of the Nineteenth Century*. By Marie De Mare. New York: McKay, 1954. xv–xvi.

Foreword. *The Man Behind Roosevelt: The Story of Louis McHenry Howe*. By Lela Stiles. Cleveland: World, 1954. [vii].

"Memo to the Field." *AAUN News* 26 (Nov. 1954): 7.

"Mrs. Roosevelt and Mr. Dies Debate." *US News and World Report* 37 (27 Aug. 1954): 94–95.

"The Need for Intellectual Freedom." *Say: The Alumni Magazine of Roosevelt College* 5 (Spring 1954): 4.

"Negotiate with Russia: Never Use the H-Bomb." *Time* 64 (30 Aug. 1954): 16.

"Patience, Persistence, Vision and Work." *The Christian Register* 134 (July 1955): 17–18.

"Roosevelt Day Greetings." *ADA World* 9 (Feb. 1954): 2M.

"Should You Help Your Children?" *Lifetime Living* 3 (Dec. 1954): 26.

"The U.S. and the U.N." *Guide to Politics, 1954*. Ed. Quincy Howe and Arthur M. Schlesinger, Jr. New York: Dial, 1954. 60–64.

"Why Are We Co-operating with Tito?" *Look* 18 (5 Oct. 1954): 80, 82–83.

1955

"Children of Israel." *Midstream* 1 (Autumn 1955): 110–11.

"In the Service of Truth." *Nation* 181 (July 9, 1955): 37.

"Is a UN Charter Review Conference Advisable Now?" *Congressional Digest* 34 (Nov. 1935): 275–277.

"Memo from the Field." *AAUN News* 27 (Mar. 1955): 7.

"Memo from the Field." *AAUN News* 27 (May 1955): 7.

"Memo from the Field." *AAUN News* 27 (June 1955): 7.

"Memo from the Field." *AAUN News* 27 (Sept. 1955): 7.

"Memo from the Field." *AAUN News* 27 (Oct. 1955): 7.

"Memo from the Field." *AAUN News* 27 (Feb. 1955): 7.

"Obligation of Leadership." *Childhood Education* 32 (Sept. 1955): 2–3.

"Report to the Membership." *AAUN News* 27 (Dec. 1955/Jan. 1956): 1.

"Social Responsibility for Individual Welfare." *National Policies for Education, Health and Social Services*. Ed. James Earl Russell. Columbia University Bicentennial Conference Series. Garden City: Doubleday, 1955. xxxv–xxxvii.

"Your United Nations." *Bulletin of the American Library Association* 49 (Oct. 1955): 491.

1956

"Age, Health and Politics: An Interview." *Journal of Lifetime Living* 21 (April 1956): 24–27.

"Attorney General's List and Civil Liberties: Replies to an Anvil Questionnaire." *Anvil and Student Partisan* 7 (Spring/Summer 1956): 17.

"Do the Kind Thing." *Every Week* 23 (15–19 Oct. 1956): 48.

"If You Ask Me." *Ladies' Home Journal Treasury*. New York: Simon & Schuster, 1956. 314–16.

"Memo from the Field." *AAUN News* 28 (Mar. 1956): 7.

"Memories of F.D.R." *Look* 20 (17 Apr. 1956): 101.

"Mrs. Roosevelt Applauds Labor's Strength and Unity." *Railway Clerk* 55 (Jan. 1, 1956): 3.

"Prayer for a Better World." *Parents' Magazine* 31 (June 1956): 76.

"The Right to Vote." *Voting Guide, 1956: How to Make Your Vote Count*. Washington: Americans for Democratic Action, 1956. 4–5.

"Roosevelt Day Greetings." *ADA World* 11 (Feb. 1956): 2M.

"Salute to Montgomery." *Liberation* 1 (Dec. 1956): 4–5.

"This Is My Story." *Ladies' Home Journal Treasury*. New York: Simon & Schuster, 1956. 262–67.

1957

"F.D.R. as Seen by Eleanor Roosevelt." *Wisdom* 2 (July 1957): 30.

"From the Wisdom of Eleanor Roosevelt." *Wisdom* 2 (July 1957): 31.

Introduction. *Letters from Jerusalem*. By Mary Clawson. London, New York: Abelard-Schuman, 1957. [xiii].

"Roosevelt Day Greetings." *ADA World* 12 (Feb. 1957): 2M.

"Schoolday Tips from Mrs. Roosevelt." *Sunday Star Magazine* [Washington], 25 Aug. 1957: 28–29.

Foreword. *300,000 New Americans: The Epic of a Modern Immigrant-Aid Service.* By Lyman Cromwell White. New York: Harper, 1957, ix.

Introduction. *Youth Aliyah: Past, Present and Future.* By Moshe Kol. F.I.C.E. Documents 1, Israel. Jerusalem: International Federation of Children's Communities, 1957. 7–8.

1958

"Among My Favorites: A Massachusetts Coast Scene by Ludwig Bemelmans." *Art in America* 46 (Spring 1958): 39.

"A Brief Message to Japanese Women." *Today's Japan* 3 (Sept. 1958): 16.

"How to Get the Most Out of Life." *Star Weekly Magazine* [Toronto], 30 Aug. 1958: 3–4.

"Mrs Roosevelt: An Interview." *Equity* 43 (Oct. 1958): 10–14.

"On My Own." *Saturday Evening Post* 230 (8 Feb. 1958): 19–21, 66, 68–70; (15 Feb. 1958): 32–33, 106–8; (22 Feb. 1958): 30–31, 56–57, 60–62; (1 Mar. 1958): 30, 95–96, 98; (8 Mar. 1958): 32–33, 72–74.

[Foreword]. *The Shook-up Generation.* By Harrison E. Salisbury. New York: Harper & Row: 1958. [5].

Foreword. *Talks with Teachers.* By Alice Keliher. Darien: Educational Publishing, 1958. 3–4.

"The Value of Human Personality." *Intercollegian* (YMCA) 76 (Sept. 1958): 4.

"Values to Live By." *Jewish Heritage* 1 (Spring 1958): 44–45, 54.

"We Can Meet the Soviet Challenge." *New Lincoln School Conference News* (Spring 1958): 3.

Foreword. *World Youth and the Communists: The Facts about Communist Penetration of WFDY and IUS.* By Nils M. Apeland. London: Phoenix House, 1958. [7–8].

1959

"A Dessert Mother's Helper Can Prepare." *Kids' Stuff* (Fall 1959): 11.

Preface. *From the Morgenthau Diaries, Years of Crisis, 1928–1938.* By John Morton Blum. Boston: Houghton Mifflin, 1959. [v].

Introduction. *Give Us the Tools.* By Henry Viscardi. New York: Eriksson, 1959. xvii–xix.

"Is America Facing World Leadership?" *Journal of the American Association of University Women* 53 (Oct. 1959): 7–11.

"The Meaning of Freedom." *This Week Magazine* (3 May 1959): 2.

"Mrs. Roosevelt Reports on Her Trip to Russia." *Equity* 44 (May 1959): 3.

"On Reaching Her 75th Birthday Eleanor Roosevelt Praises Television's Contribution to the Senior Citizen." *TV Guide* 7 (17 Oct. 1959): 6–8.

"Segregation." *Educational Forum* 24 (Nov. 1959): 5–6.

"What Are We Here For?" By Eleanor Roosevelt and Huston Smith. *The Search for America.* Ed. Huston Smith. Englewood Cliffs: Prentice-Hall, 1959. 3–12.

"Where I Get My Energy." *Harper's* 218 (Jan. 1959): 45–47.

"Why I Am Opposed to 'Right to Work' Laws." *American Federationist* 66 (Feb. 1959): 5–7.

1960

"Education Is Essential." *Bryn Mawr Alumnae Bulletin* 40 (Winter 1960): 7.

[Foreword]. *FDR Speaks.* Ed. Henry Steele Commager. Washington: Washington Records, 1960. 3.

"Mrs. Roosevelt's Page." *Woman* 47 (26 Nov. 1960): 17; 47 (3 Dec. 1960): 21; 47 (10 Dec. 1960): 25; 47 (17 Dec. 1960): 21; 47 (24 Dec. 1960): 47 (31 Dec. 1960): 23; 48 (7 Jan. 1961): 23; 48 (14 Jan. 1961): 16; 48 (21 Jan. 1961): 18.

"My Advice to the Next First Lady." *Redbook* 116 (Nov. 1960): 18–21, 95–96.

"You Learn by Living." *True Story* 83 (Oct. 1960): 37, 112–16; 83 (Nov. 1960): 56–59, 98.

1961

[Review]. *Dag Hammarskjold: Custodian of a Brushfire Peace.* By Joseph P. Lash. Garden City: Doubleday, 1961. On dust jacket.

"The Joy of Reading." *Coronet* 50 (Sept. 1961): 74–75, 80.

"A Policy Toward Castro's Cuba." *Current* 14 (June 1961): 19.

"A President's Planning." *Saturday Review* 44 (8 July 1961): 10.

"Social Responsibility for Individual Welfare." *National Policies for Education, Health and Social Sciences.* Russell and Russell: 1961.

"What Has Happened to the American Dream?" *Atlantic* 207 (Apr. 1961): 46–50.

1962

Introduction. *The Adventure of America.* By John Tobias and Savin Hoffecker. New York: Geis, 1962. vii.

Foreword. *Brutal Mandate: A Journey to South West Africa.* By Allard K. Lowenstein. New York: Macmillan, 1962. [v]–vi.

Foreword. *From the Eagle's Wing: A Biography of John Muir.* By Hildegarde Hoyt Swift. New York: Morrow, 1962. 7–8.

Foreword. *The Long Shadow of Little Rock: A Memoir.* By Daisy Bates. New York: D. McKay, 1962. xiii–xv.

"Modern Children and Old-Fashioned Manners." *Redbook* 119 (Oct. 1962): 47, 122, 124–25, 127–28.

Foreword. *The Road to the White House. F.D.R.: The Pre-Presidential Years.* By Lorena A. Hickok. Philadelphia: Chilton, 1962. vii–viii.

"Statement of Mrs. Eleanor Roosevelt, Chairman of the President's Commission on the Status of Women." *Congressional Record* (15 Feb. 1962): 2281.

"The Teaching Challenge of the Future." *Graduate Comment* (Wayne State University) 6 (October 1962): 12–15, 23.

Foreword. *This Is Our Strength: Selected Papers of Golda Meir.* Ed. Henry M. Christman. New York: Macmillan, 1962. ix–xiv.

"To All AAUN Members West of the Mississippi." *AAUN News* 34 (Mar. 1962): 6.

"A Woman for the Times." *Boston Sunday Globe Magazine*, 27 May 1962: 3.

"What Can I Do about Peace and People?" *Bookshelf* (National Board of the YWCA) 45 (Summer 1962): 1, 10.

Introduction. *You're the Boss: The Practice of American Politics.* By Edward J. Flynn. New York: Collier, 1962. 7–9.

1963

"Eleanor Roosevelt from This Is My Story." *A Reader for Parents: A Selection of Creative Literature About Childhood.* New York: Norton, 1963. 61–69.

"I Remember Hyde Park: A Final Reminiscence." *McCall's* 90 (Feb. 1963): 71–73, 162–63.

"Israel Will Become a Great Nation.: *The Mission of Israel.* Ed. Jacob Baal-Teshuva. New York: Speller, 1963. 32.

Introduction. *My Darling Clementine: The Story of Lady Churchill.* By Jack Fishman. New York: McKay, 1963. 1–5.

Foreword. *Planning Community Services for Children in Trouble.* By Alfred J. Kahn. New York: Columbia University Press, 1963. vii–viii.

"Tomorrow Is Now." *Ladies' Home Journal* 80 (Sept. 1963): 39–45.

"A Visit to Campobello." *Ford Times* 56 (Apr. 1963): 2–6.

Index